Beginning JavaScript®

Beginning JavaScript®

Fourth Edition

Beginning JavaScript®

Fourth Edition

Paul Wilton
Jeremy McPeak

WILEY
Wiley Publishing, Inc.

Beginning JavaScript® Fourth Edition

Published by
Wiley Publishing, Inc.
10475 Crosspoint Boulevard
Indianapolis, IN 46256

www.wiley.com

Copyright © 2010 by Wiley Publishing, Inc., Indianapolis, Indiana

Published simultaneously in Canada

ISBN: 978-0-470-52593-7

Manufactured in the United States of America

10 9 8 7 6 5 4 3 2

For general information on our other products and services please contact our Customer Care Department within the United States at (877) 762-2974, outside the United States at (317) 572-3993 or fax (317) 572-4002.

Library of Congress Control Number: 2009933758

In memory of my mum, June Wilton, who in 2006 lost her brave battle against cancer.
She was always very proud of me and my books and showed my books
to anyone and everyone she happened to meet however briefly and whether they
wanted to see them or not! She's very much missed.
— Paul Wilton

To my family: Starla, Hayden, and Evan (whom we haven't yet met in person).
To my parents: Jerry and Judy.
Thank you all for your love and support.
— Jeremy McPeak

About the Authors

Paul Wilton started as a Visual Basic applications programmer at the Ministry of Defense in the UK and then found himself pulled into the Net. Having joined an Internet development company, he spent three years helping create Internet solutions. He's now running his own successful and rapidly growing company developing online holiday property reservation systems.

Jeremy McPeak is a self-taught programmer who began his career by tinkering with web sites in 1998. He is the co-author of *Professional Ajax, 2nd Edition* (Wiley 2007) and several online articles covering topics such as XSLT, ASP.NET WebForms, and C#. He is currently employed in an energy-based company building in-house conventional and web applications.

Jeremy can be reached through his web site www.wdonline.com.

Credits

Acquisitions Editor
Scott Meyers

Project Editor
Maureen Spears

Technical Editor
David M. Karr

Production Editor
Rebecca Anderson

Copy Editor
C.M. Jones

Editorial Director
Robyn B. Siesky

Editorial Manager
Mary Beth Wakefield

Marketing Manager
David Mayhew

Production Manager
Tim Tate

Vice President and Executive Group Publisher
Richard Swadley

Vice President and Executive Publisher
Barry Pruett

Associate Publisher
Jim Minatel

Project Coordinator, Cover
Lindsay Stanford

Compositor
Craig Johnson, Happenstance Type-O-Rama

Proofreader
Kathryn Duggan

Indexer
J & J Indexing

Cover Image
© Photographer's Choice/Punchstock

Acknowledgments

First, a big thank you to my partner Beci, who, now that the book's finished, will get to see me for more than 10 minutes a week.

I'd also like to say a very big thank you to Maureen Spears, who has worked very efficiently on getting this book into print.

Thanks also to Jim Minatel for making this book happen.

Many thanks to everyone who's supported and encouraged me over my many years of writing books. Your help will always be remembered.

Finally, pats and treats to my German Shepherd Dog, Katie, who does an excellent job of warding off disturbances from door-to-door salespeople.

— *Paul Wilton*

First and foremost, a huge thank you to my wife for putting up with my late nights.

Just as huge thanks go to the people at Wiley Publishing: Jim Minatel and Scott Meyers for making this happen; Maureen Spears who was absolutely wonderful to work with in getting this book into its final, printed form; and David M. Karr for keeping me honest.

Lastly, thank you Nicholas C. Zakas, author of *Professional JavaScript, 2nd Edition* (Wiley 2009) and co-author of *Professional Ajax, 2nd Edition* (Wiley 2007), for getting me into this business.

— *Jeremy McPeak*

Contents

Contents

Contents

Contents

Contents

Contents

Contents

Contents

Contents

Introduction

JavaScript is a scripting language that enables you to enhance static web applications by providing dynamic, personalized, and interactive content. This improves the experience of visitors to your site and makes it more likely that they will visit again. You must have seen the flashy drop-down menus, moving text, and changing content that are now widespread on web sites — they are enabled through JavaScript. Supported by all the major browsers, JavaScript is the language of choice on the Web. It can even be used outside web applications — to automate administrative tasks, for example.

This book aims to teach you all you need to know to start experimenting with JavaScript: what it is, how it works, and what you can do with it. Starting from the basic syntax, you'll move on to learn how to create powerful web applications. Don't worry if you've never programmed before — this book will teach you all you need to know, step by step. You'll find that JavaScript can be a great introduction to the world of programming: with the knowledge and understanding that you'll gain from this book, you'll be able to move on to learn newer and more advanced technologies in the world of computing.

Whom This Book Is For

To get the most out of this book, you'll need to have an understanding of HTML and how to create a static web page. You don't need to have any programming experience.

This book will also suit you if you have some programming experience already and would like to turn your hand to web programming. You will know a fair amount about computing concepts, but maybe not as much about web technologies.

Alternatively, you may have a design background and know relatively little about the web and computing concepts. For you, JavaScript will be a cheap and relatively easy introduction to the world of programming and web application development.

Whoever you are, we hope that this book lives up to your expectations.

What This Book Covers

You'll begin by looking at exactly what JavaScript is, and taking your first steps with the underlying language and syntax. You'll learn all the fundamental programming concepts, including data and data types, and structuring your code to make decisions in your programs or to loop over the same piece of code many times.

Once you're comfortable with the basics, you'll move on to one of the key ideas in JavaScript — the object. You'll learn how to take advantage of the objects that are native to the JavaScript language, such as dates and strings, and find out how these objects enable you to manage complex data and simplify your programs. Next, you'll see how you can use JavaScript to manipulate objects made available to you in the browser, such as forms, windows, and other controls. Using this knowledge, you can start to create truly professional-looking applications that enable you to interact with the user.

Long pieces of code are very hard to get right every time — even for the experienced programmer — and JavaScript code is no exception. You look at common syntax and logical errors, how you can spot them, and how to use the JavaScript debuggers for Firefox, Internet Explorer, Safari/Chrome, and Opera to aid you with this task. Also, you need to examine how to handle the errors that slip through the net, and ensure that these do not detract from the experience of the end user of your application.

From here, you'll move on to more advanced topics, such as using cookies and jazzing up your web pages with dynamic HTML and XML. Finally, you'll be looking at a relatively new and exciting technology: Ajax. This allows your JavaScript in a HTML page to communicate directly with a server, and useful for, say, looking up information on a database sitting on your server. If you have the Google toolbar you'll have seen something like this in action already. When you type a search word in the Google toolbar, it comes up with suggestions, which it gets via the Google search database.

Finally, you'll explore some of the time saving JavaScript frameworks such as jQuery, Prototype, and MooTools and seeing how they work and how they can help you create sophisticated JavaScript powered applications.

All the new concepts introduced in this book will be illustrated with practical examples, which enable you to experiment with JavaScript and build on the theory that you have just learned.

You'll find four appendixes at the end of the book. Appendix A provides solutions to the exercises included at the end of most chapters throughout the book. The remaining appendixes contain the reference material that your authors hope you find useful and informational. Appendix B contains the JavaScript language's core reference. Appendix C contains a complete W3C DOM Core reference — as well as information on the HTML DOM and DOM Level 2 Event model. Appendix D contains the decimal and hexadecimal character codes for the Latin-1 character set.

What You Need to Use This Book

Because JavaScript is a text-based technology, all you really need to create documents containing JavaScript is Notepad (or your equivalent text editor).

Also, in order to try out the code in this book, you will need a web browser that supports a modern version of JavaScript. Ideally, this means Internet Explorer 8 or later and Firefox 3 or later. The book has been extensively tested with these two browsers. However, the code should work in most modern web browsers, although some of the code in later chapters, where you examine dynamic HTML and scripting the DOM, is specific to particular browsers; but the majority of the code presented is cross-browser. Where there are exceptions, they will be clearly noted.

Conventions

To help you get the most from the text and keep track of what's happening, we've used a number of conventions throughout the book.

Try It Out

The *Try It Out* is an exercise you should work through, following the text in the book.

1. It usually consists of a set of steps.

2. Each step has a number.

3. Follow the steps with your copy of the database.

As you work through each *Try It Out*, the code you've typed will be explained in detail.

> **Boxes like this one hold important, not-to-be forgotten information that is directly relevant to the surrounding text.**

Tips, hints, tricks, and asides to the current discussion are offset and placed in italics like this.

As for styles in the text:

❑ We *highlight in italic type* new terms and important words when we introduce them.

❑ We show keyboard strokes like this: Ctrl+A.

❑ We show file names, URLs, and code within the text like so: `persistence.properties`.

❑ We present code in two different ways:

```
Important code in code examples is highlighted with a gray background.
The gray highlighting is not used for code that's less important in the present
context, or that has been shown before.
```

Source Code

As you work through the examples in this book, you may choose either to type in all the code manually or to use the source-code files that accompany the book. All of the source code used in this book is available for download at `www.wrox.com`. Once at the site, simply locate the book's title (either by using the Search box or by using one of the title lists) and click the Download Code link on the book's detail page to obtain all the source code for the book.

Because many books have similar titles, you may find it easiest to search by ISBN; this book's ISBN is 978-0-470-52593-7.

Once you download the code, just decompress it with your favorite compression tool. Alternately, you can go to the main Wrox code download page at `www.wrox.com/dynamic/books/download.aspx` to see the code available for this book and all other Wrox books.

Errata

We make every effort to ensure that there are no errors in the text or in the code. However, no one is perfect, and mistakes do occur. If you find an error in one of our books, like a spelling mistake or faulty piece of code, we would be very grateful for your feedback. By sending in errata, you may save another reader hours of frustration, and at the same time you will be helping us provide even higher-quality information.

To find the errata page for this book, go to www.wrox.com and locate the title using the Search box or one of the title lists. Then, on the book details page, click the Book Errata link. On this page you can view all errata that have been submitted for this book and posted by Wrox editors. A complete book list, including links to each book's errata, is also available at www.wrox.com/misc-pages/booklist.shtml.

If you don't spot "your" error on the Book Errata page, go to www.wrox.com/contact/techsupport.shtml and complete the form there to send us the error you have found. We'll check the information and, if appropriate, post a message to the book's errata page and fix the problem in subsequent editions of the book.

p2p.wrox.com

For author and peer discussion, join the P2P forums at p2p.wrox.com. The forums are a web-based system on which you can post messages relating to Wrox books and related technologies and interact with other readers and technology users. The forums offer a subscription feature to e-mail you topics of interest of your choosing when new posts are made to the forums. Wrox authors, editors, other industry experts, and your fellow readers are present on these forums.

At http://p2p.wrox.com you will find a number of different forums that will help you not only as you read this book, but also as you develop your own applications. To join the forums, just follow these steps:

1. Go to p2p.wrox.com and click the Register link.
2. Read the terms of use and click Agree.
3. Complete the required information to join as well as any optional information you wish to provide, and click Submit.
4. You will receive an e-mail with information describing how to verify your account and complete the joining process.

   You can read messages in the forums without joining P2P, but in order to post your own messages, you must join.

Once you join, you can post new messages and respond to messages other users post. You can read messages at any time on the Web. If you would like to have new messages from a particular forum e-mailed to you, click the Subscribe to this Forum icon by the forum name in the forum listing.

For more information about how to use the Wrox P2P, be sure to read the P2P FAQs for answers to questions about how the forum software works, as well as many common questions specific to P2P and Wrox books. To read the FAQs, click the FAQ link on any P2P page.

Beginning JavaScript®

Fourth Edition

Introduction to JavaScript and the Web

In this introductory chapter, you look at what JavaScript is, what it can do for you, and what you need in order to use it. With these foundations in place, you will see throughout the rest of the book how JavaScript can help you to create powerful web applications for your web site.

The easiest way to learn something is by actually doing it, so throughout the book you'll create a number of useful example programs using JavaScript. This process starts in this chapter, by the end of which you will have created your first piece of JavaScript code.

Introduction to JavaScript

In this section you take a brief look at what JavaScript is, where it came from, how it works, and what sorts of useful things you can do with it.

What Is JavaScript?

Having bought this book, you are probably already well aware that JavaScript is some sort of *computer language*, but what is a computer language? Put simply, a computer language is a series of instructions that tell the computer to do something. That something can be one of a wide variety of things, including displaying text, moving an image, or asking the user for information. Normally, the instructions, or what is termed *code*, are *processed* from the top line downward. This simply means that the computer looks at the code you've written, works out what action you want taken, and then takes that action. The act of processing the code is called *running* or *executing* it.

In natural English, here are instructions, or code, you might write to make a cup of instant coffee:

1. Put coffee crystals in cup.
2. Fill kettle with water.

3. Put kettle on to boil.

4. Has the kettle boiled? If so, then pour water into cup; otherwise, continue to wait.

5. Drink coffee.

You'd start running this code from the first line (instruction 1), and then continue to the next (instruction 2), then the next, and so on until you came to the end. This is pretty much how most computer languages work, JavaScript included. However, there are occasions when you might change the flow of execution or even skip over some code, but you'll see more of this in Chapter 3.

JavaScript is an interpreted language rather than a compiled language. What is meant by the terms *interpreted* and *compiled*?

Well, to let you in on a secret, your computer doesn't really understand JavaScript at all. It needs something to interpret the JavaScript code and convert it into something that it understands; hence it is an *interpreted language*. Computers understand only *machine code*, which is essentially a string of binary numbers (that is, a string of zeros and ones). As the browser goes through the JavaScript, it passes it to a special program called an *interpreter*, which converts the JavaScript to the machine code your computer understands. It's a bit like having a translator translate English to Spanish, for example. The important point to note is that the conversion of the JavaScript happens at the time the code is run; it has to be repeated every time this happens. JavaScript is not the only interpreted language; there are others, including VBScript.

The alternative *compiled language* is one in which the program code is converted to machine code before it's actually run, and this conversion has to be done only once. The programmer uses a compiler to convert the code that he wrote to machine code, and this machine code is run by the program's user. Compiled languages include Visual Basic and C++. Using a real-world analogy, it's a bit like having a Spanish translator verbally tell you in English what a Spanish document says. Unless you change the document, you can use it without retranslation as much as you like.

Perhaps this is a good point to dispel a widespread myth: JavaScript is not the script version of the Java language. In fact, although they share the same name, that's virtually all they do share. Particularly good news is that JavaScript is much, much easier to learn and use than Java. In fact, languages like JavaScript are the easiest of all languages to learn, but they are still surprisingly powerful.

JavaScript and the Web

For most of this book you'll look at JavaScript code that runs inside a web page loaded into a browser. All you need in order to create these web pages is a text editor — for example, Windows Notepad — and a web browser, such as Firefox or Internet Explorer, with which you can view your pages. These browsers come equipped with JavaScript interpreters.

In fact, the JavaScript language first became available in the web browser Netscape Navigator 2. Initially, it was called LiveScript. However, because Java was the hot technology of the time, Netscape decided that JavaScript sounded more exciting. When JavaScript really took off, Microsoft decided to add its own brand of JavaScript, called JScript, to Internet Explorer. Since then, Netscape, Microsoft, and others have released improved versions and included them in their latest browsers. Although these different brands and versions of JavaScript have much in common, there are enough differences to cause problems if you're not careful. Initially you'll be creating code that'll work with most browsers, whether

Firefox, Internet Explorer, or Safari. Later chapters look at features available only to current browsers like Firefox 3 or later and Internet Explorer 7 and 8. You'll look into the problems with different browsers and versions of JavaScript later in this chapter and see how to deal with them.

You'll sometimes hear JavaScript referred to as ECMAScript. The ECMA (European Computer Manufacturers Association) is a private organization that develops standards in information and communication systems. One of the standards they control is for JavaScript, which they call ECMAScript. Their standard controls various aspects of the language and helps ensure that different versions of JavaScript are compatible. However, while the ECMA sets standards for the actual language, they don't specify how it's used in particular hosts. By *host*, we mean hosting environment; in this book, that will be the web browser. Other hosting environments include PDF files, web servers, Macromedia Flash applications, and many, many other places. In this book, we discuss only its use within the web browser. The organization that sets the standards for web pages is the World Wide Web Consortium (W3C). They not only set standards for HTML, XHTML, and XML, but also for how JavaScript interacts with web pages inside a web browser. You'll learn much more about this in later chapters of the book. Initially, you'll look at the essentials of JavaScript before the more advanced stuff. In the appendices of this book, you'll find useful guides to the JavaScript language and how it interacts with the web browser.

The majority of the web pages containing JavaScript that you create in this book can be stored on your hard drive and loaded directly into your browser from the hard drive itself, just as you'd load any normal file (such as a text file). However, this is not how web pages are loaded when you browse web sites on the Internet. The Internet is really just one great big network connecting computers. Access to web sites is a special service provided by particular computers on the Internet; the computers providing this service are known as *web servers*.

Basically, the job of a web server is to hold lots of web pages on its hard drive. When a browser, usually on a different computer, requests a web page contained on that web server, the web server loads it from its own hard drive and then passes the page back to the requesting computer via a special communications protocol called *Hypertext Transfer Protocol (HTTP)*. The computer running the web browser that makes the request is known as the *client*. Think of the client/server relationship as a bit like a customer/shopkeeper relationship. The customer goes into a shop and says, "Give me one of those." The shopkeeper serves the customer by reaching for the item requested and passing it back to the customer. In a web situation, the client machine running the web browser is like the customer, and the web server providing the page requested is like the shopkeeper.

When you type an address into the web browser, how does it know which web server to get the page from? Well, just as shops have addresses, say, 45 Central Avenue, Sometownsville, so do web servers. Web servers don't have street names; instead, they have *Internet protocol (IP) addresses*, which uniquely identify them on the Internet. These consist of four sets of numbers, separated by dots (for example, `127.0.0.1`).

If you've ever surfed the net, you're probably wondering what on earth I'm talking about. Surely web servers have nice `www.somewebsite.com` names, not IP addresses? In fact, the `www.somewebsite.com` name is the "friendly" name for the actual IP address; it's a whole lot easier for us humans to remember. On the Internet, the friendly name is converted to the actual IP address by computers called *domain name servers*, which your Internet service provider will have set up for you.

One last thing: Throughout this book, we'll be referring to the Internet Explorer browser as IE.

Why Choose JavaScript?

JavaScript is not the only scripting language; there are others such as VBScript and Perl. So why choose JavaScript over the others?

The main reason for choosing JavaScript is its widespread use and availability. Both of the most commonly used browsers, IE and Firefox, support JavaScript, as do almost all of the less commonly used browsers. So you can assume that most people browsing your web site will have a version of JavaScript installed, though it is possible to use a browser's options to disable it.

Of the other scripting languages already mentioned, VBScript, which can be used for the same purposes as JavaScript, is supported only by Internet Explorer running on the Windows operating system, and Perl is not used at all in web browsers.

JavaScript is also very versatile and not just limited to use within a web page. For example, it can be used in Windows to automate computer-administration tasks and inside Adobe Acrobat PDF files to control the display of the page just as in web pages, although Acrobat uses a more limited version of JavaScript. However, the question of which scripting language is more powerful and useful has no real answer. Pretty much everything that can be done in JavaScript can be done in VBScript, and vice versa.

What Can JavaScript Do for Me?

The most common uses of JavaScript are interacting with users, getting information from them, and validating their actions. For example, say you want to put a drop-down menu on the page so that users can choose where they want to go to on your web site. The drop-down menu might be plain old HTML, but it needs JavaScript behind it to actually do something with the user's input. Other examples of using JavaScript for interactions are given by forms, which are used for getting information from the user. Again, these may be plain HTML, but you might want to check the validity of the information that the user is entering. For example, if you had a form taking a user's credit card details in preparation for the online purchase of goods, you'd want to make sure he had actually filled in those details before you sent the goods. You might also want to check that the data being entered are of the correct type, such as a number for his age rather than text.

JavaScript can also be used for various tricks. One example is switching an image in a page for a different one when the user rolls her mouse over it, something often seen in web page menus. Also, if you've ever seen scrolling messages in the browser's status bar (usually at the bottom of the browser window) or inside the page itself and wondered how that works, this is another JavaScript trick that you'll learn about later in the book. You'll also see how to create expanding menus that display a list of choices when a user rolls his or her mouse over them, another commonly seen JavaScript-driven trick.

Advances in browser sophistication and JavaScript mean that modern JavaScript is used for much more than a few clever tricks. In fact, quite advanced applications can be created. Examples of such applications include Google Maps, Google Calendar, and even a full-fledged word processor, Google Docs. These applications provide a real service. With a little inventiveness, you'll be amazed at what can be achieved. Of course, while JavaScript powers the user interface, the actual data processing is done in the background on powerful servers. JavaScript is powerful but still has limits.

Tools Needed to Create JavaScript Web Applications

The great news is that getting started learning JavaScript requires no expensive software purchases; you can learn JavaScript for free on any PC or Mac. You'll learn in this section what tools are available and how to obtain them.

Development Tools

All that you need to get started creating JavaScript code for web applications is a simple text editor, such as Windows Notepad, or one of the many slightly more advanced text editors that provide line numbering, search and replace, and so on. An alternative is a proper HTML editor; you'll need one that enables you to edit the HTML source code, because that's where you need to add your JavaScript. A number of very good tools specifically aimed at developing web-based applications, such as the excellent Dreamweaver from Adobe, are also available. However, this book concentrates on JavaScript rather than any specific development tool. When it comes to learning the basics, it's often best to write the code by hand rather than rely on a tool to do it for you. This helps you understand the fundamentals of the language before you attempt the more advanced logic that is beyond a tool's capability. When you have a good understanding of the basics, you can use tools as timesavers so that you can spend more time on the more advanced and more interesting coding.

Once you become more proficient, you may find that a web page editor makes life easier by inclusion of features such as checking the validity of your code, color-coding important JavaScript words, and making it easier to view your pages before loading them into a web browser. One example of free web development software is Microsoft's Visual Web Developer 2008 Express Edition, which you can download at `http://www.microsoft.com/express/vwd/`.

There are many other, equally good, free web page editors. A Google search on web editing software will bring back a long list of software you can use. Perhaps the most famous paid-for software is Adobe Dreamweaver.

As you write web applications of increasing complexity, you'll find useful tools that help you spot and solve errors. Errors in code are what programmers call bugs, though when our programs go wrong, we prefer to call them "unexpected additional features." Very useful in solving bugs are development tools called debuggers. Debuggers let you monitor what is happening in your code as it's running. In Chapter 4, you take an in-depth look at bugs and debugger development tools.

Web Browsers

In addition to software that lets you edit web pages, you'll also need a browser to view your web pages. It's best to develop your JavaScript code on the sort of browsers you expect visitors to use to access your web site. You'll see later in the chapter that although browsers are much more standards based, there are differences in how they view web pages and treat JavaScript code. All the examples provided in this book have been tested on Firefox version 3+ and IE versions 7 and 8. Wherever a piece of code does not work on any of these browsers, a note to this effect has been made in the text.

If you're running Windows, you'll almost certainly have IE installed. If not, a trip to `http://www.microsoft.com/windows/internet-explorer/default.aspx` will get you the latest version.

Firefox can be found at `www.mozilla.com/firefox/all.html`.

By default, most browsers have JavaScript support enabled. However, it is possible to disable this functionality in the browser. So before you start on your first JavaScript examples in the next section, you should check to make sure JavaScript is enabled in your browser.

To do this in Firefox, choose Tools ➪ Options on the browser. In the window that appears, click the Content tab. From this tab, make sure the Enable JavaScript check box is selected, as shown in Figure 1-1.

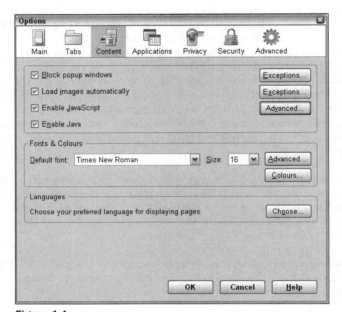

Figure 1-1

It is harder to turn off scripting in Internet Explorer. Choose Tools ➪ Internet Options on the browser, click the Security tab, and check whether the Internet or Local intranet options have custom security settings. If either of them does, click the Custom Level button and scroll down to the Scripting section. Check that Active Scripting is set to Enable.

A final point to note is how to open the code examples in your browser. For this book, you simply need to open the file on your hard drive in which an example is stored. You can do this in a number of ways. One way in IE6 is to choose File ➪ Open and click the Browse button to browse to where you stored the code. Similarly, in Firefox, choose File ➪ Open File, browse to the file you want, and click the Choose File button.

IE7 and IE8, however, have a new menu structure, and this doesn't include an Open File option. You can get around this by typing the drive letter of your hard drive followed by a colon in the address bar (for example, C: for your C drive). In Microsoft Windows, you can press Ctrl+O for the Open file menu to appear. Alternatively, you can switch back to the Classic menu of earlier versions of IE. To do this, you can click Tools ➪ Toolbars, and ensure the Menu Bar option is selected (see Figure 1-2).

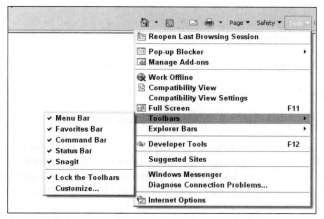

Figure 1-2

Where Do My Scripts Go?

Enough talk about the subject of JavaScript; it's time to look at how to put it into your web page. In this section, you'll find out how you add JavaScript code to your web page.

Including the `type` attribute is good practice, but within a web page it can be left off. Browsers such as IE and Firefox use JavaScript as their default script language. This means that if the browser encounters a `<script>` tag with no `type` attribute set, it assumes that the script block is written in JavaScript. However, use of the `type` attribute is specified as mandatory by W3C (the World Wide Web Consortium), which sets the standards for HTML.

Linking to an External JavaScript File

The `<script>` tag has another arrow in its quiver: the ability to specify that the JavaScript code is not inside the web page but inside a separate file. Any external files should be given the file extension .js. Though it's not compulsory, it does make it easier for you to work out what is contained in each of your files.

To link to an external JavaScript file, you need to create a `<script>` tag as described earlier and use its `src` attribute to specify the location of the external file. For example, imagine you've created a file called MyCommonFunctions.js that you wish to link to, and the file is in the same directory as your web page. The `<script>` tag would look like this:

```
<script type="text/javascript" src="MyCommonFunctions.js"></script>
```

The web browser will read this code and include the file contents as part of your web page. When linking to external files, you must not put any code within the `<script>` tags; for example, the following would be invalid:

```
<script type="text/javascript" src="MyCommonFunctions.js">
var myVariable;
```

```
if ( myVariable == 1 )
{
        // do something
}
</script>
```

If your web page is an XHTML document, you can omit the closing `</script>` tag and instead write this:

```
<script type="text/javascript" src="MyCommonFunctions.js" />
```

Generally, you use the `<script>` tag to load local files (those on the same computer as the web page itself). However, you can load external files from a web server by specifying the web address of the file. For example, if your file was called MyCommonFunctions.js and was loaded on a web server with the domain name `www.mysite.com`, the `<script>` tag would look like this:

```
<script type="text/javascript" src="http://www.mysite.com/MyCommonFunctions.js">
</script>
```

However, beware of linking to external files if they are controlled by other people. It would give those people the ability to control and change your web page, so you need to be very sure you trust them!

Advantages of Using an External File

The biggest advantage of external files is code reuse. Say you write a complex bit of JavaScript that performs a general function you might need in lots of pages. If you include the code inline (within the web page rather than via an external file), you need to cut and paste the code into each of your web pages that use it. This is fine as long as you never need to change the code, but the reality is you probably will need to change or improve the code at some point. If you've cut and pasted the code to 30 different web pages, you'll need to update it in 30 different places. Quite a headache! By using one external file and including it in all the pages that need it, you only need to update the code once and instantly all the 30 pages are updated. So much easier!

Another advantage of using external files is the browser will cache them, much as it does with images shared between pages. If your files are large, this could save download time and also reduce bandwidth usage.

Your First Simple JavaScript Programs

Enough talk about the subject of JavaScript; it's time to look at how to put it into your web page. In this section, you write your first piece of JavaScript code.

Inserting JavaScript into a web page is much like inserting any other HTML content; you use tags to mark the start and end of your script code. The tag used to do this is `<script>`. This tells the browser that the following chunk of text, bounded by the closing `</script>` tag, is not HTML to be displayed but rather script code to be processed. The chunk of code surrounded by the `<script>` and `</script>` tags is called a *script block*.

Basically, when the browser spots `<script>` tags, instead of trying to display the contained text to the user, it uses the browser's built-in JavaScript interpreter to run the code's instructions. Of course, the code might give instructions about changes to the way the page is displayed or what is shown in the page, but the text of the code itself is never shown to the user.

You can put the `<script>` tags inside the header (between the `<head>` and `</head>` tags) or inside the body (between the `<body>` and `</body>` tags) of the HTML page. However, although you can put them outside these areas — for example, before the `<html>` tag or after the `</html>` tag — this is not permitted in the web standards and so is considered bad practice.

The `<script>` tag has a number of attributes, but the most important one is `type`. As you saw earlier, JavaScript is not the only scripting language available, and different scripting languages need to be processed in different ways. You need to tell the browser which scripting language to expect so that it knows how to process that language. Your opening script tag will look like this:

```
<script type="text/javascript">
```

Including the `type` attribute is good practice, but within a web page it can be left off. Browsers such as IE and Firefox use JavaScript as their default script language. This means that if the browser encounters a `<script>` tag with no `type` attribute set, it assumes that the script block is written in JavaScript. However, use of the `type` attribute is specified as mandatory by W3C, which sets the standards for HTML.

Okay, let's take a look at the first page containing JavaScript code.

Try It Out   Painting the Page Red

This is a simple example of using JavaScript to change the background color of the browser. In your text editor (we're using Windows Notepad), type the following:

```
<html>
<body bgcolor="WHITE">
<p>Paragraph 1</p>
<script type="text/javascript">
    document.bgColor = "RED";
</script>
</body>
</html>
```

Save the page as `ch1_examp1.htm` to a convenient place on your hard drive. Now load it into your web browser. You should see a red web page with the text Paragraph 1 in the top-left corner. But wait — don't you set the `<body>` tag's BGCOLOR attribute to white? Okay, let's look at what's going on here.

The page is contained within `<html>` and `</html>` tags. This block contains a `<body>` element. When you define the opening `<body>` tag, you use HTML to set the page's background color to white.

```
<body bgcolor="WHITE">
```

Then you let the browser know that your next lines of code are JavaScript code by using the `<script>` start tag.

```
<script type="text/javascript">
```

Everything from here until the close tag, `</script>`, is JavaScript and is treated as such by the browser. Within this script block, you use JavaScript to set the document's background color to red.

```
document.bgColor = "RED";
```

What you might call the *page* is known as the *document* for the purpose of scripting in a web page. The document has lots of properties, including its background color, `bgColor`. You can reference properties of the `document` by writing `document`, followed by a dot, followed by the property name. Don't worry about the use of `document` at the moment; you look at it in greater depth later in the book.

Note that the preceding line of code is an example of a JavaScript *statement*. Every line of code between the `<script>` and `</script>` tags is called a statement, although some statements may run on to more than one line.

You'll also see that there's a semicolon (;) at the end of the line. You use a semicolon in JavaScript to indicate the end of a statement. In practice, JavaScript is very relaxed about the need for semicolons, and when you start a new line, JavaScript will usually be able to work out whether you mean to start a new line of code. However, for good coding practice, you should use a semicolon at the end of statements of code, and a single JavaScript statement should fit onto one line rather than continue on to two or more lines. Moreover, you'll find there are times when you must include a semicolon, which you'll come to later in the book.

Finally, to tell the browser to stop interpreting your text as JavaScript and start interpreting it as HTML, you use the script close tag:

```
</script>
```

You've now looked at how the code works, but you haven't looked at the order in which it works. When the browser loads in the web page, the browser goes through it, rendering it tag by tag from top to bottom of the page. This process is called *parsing*. The web browser starts at the top of the page and works its way down to the bottom of the page. The browser comes to the `<body>` tag first and sets the document's background to white. Then it continues parsing the page. When it comes to the JavaScript code, it is instructed to change the document's background to red.

Try It Out   The Way Things Flow

Let's extend the previous example to demonstrate the parsing of a web page in action. Type the following into your text editor:

```
<html>
<body bgcolor="WHITE">
<p>Paragraph 1</p>
<script type="text/javascript">
   // Script block 1
   alert("First Script Block");
</script>
<p>Paragraph 2</p>
<script type="text/javascript">
   // Script block 2
   document.bgColor = "RED";
   alert("Second Script Block");
```

```
</script>
<p>Paragraph 3</p>
</body>
</html>
```

Save the file to your hard drive as ch1_examp2.htm and then load it into your browser. When you load the page, you should see the first paragraph, Paragraph 1, followed by a message box displayed by the first script block. The browser halts its parsing until you click the OK button. As you see in Figure 1-3, the page background is white, as set in the <body> tag, and only the first paragraph is displayed.

Figure 1-3

Click the OK button, and the parsing continues. The browser displays the second paragraph, and the second script block is reached, which changes the background color to red. Another message box is displayed by the second script block, as shown in Figure 1-4.

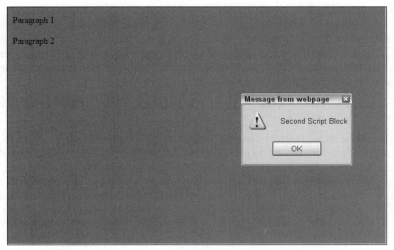

Figure 1-4

Click OK, and again the parsing continues, with the third paragraph, Paragraph 3, being displayed. The web page is complete, as shown in Figure 1-5.

Figure 1-5

The first part of the page is the same as in our earlier example. The background color for the page is set to white in the definition of the <body> tag, and then a paragraph is written to the page.

```
<html>
<body bgcolor="WHITE">
<p>Paragraph 1</p>
```

The first new section is contained in the first script block.

```
<script type="text/javascript">
    // Script block 1
    alert("First Script Block");
</script>
```

This script block contains two lines, both of which are new to you. The first line —

```
    // Script block 1
```

is just a *comment*, solely for your benefit. The browser recognizes anything on a line after a double forward slash (//) to be a comment and does not do anything with it. It is useful for you as a programmer because you can add explanations to your code that make it easier to remember what you were doing when you come back to your code later.

The alert() function in the second line of code is also new to you. Before learning what it does, you need to know what a *function* is.

Functions are defined more fully in Chapter 3, but for now you need only think of them as pieces of JavaScript code that you can use to do certain tasks. If you have a background in math, you may already have some idea of what a function is: A *function* takes some information, processes it, and gives you a result. A function makes life easier for you as a programmer because you don't have to think about how the function does the task — you can just concentrate on when you want the task done.

12

In particular, the `alert()` function enables you to alert or inform the user about something by displaying a message box. The message to be given in the message box is specified inside the parentheses of the `alert()` function and is known as the function's *parameter*.

The message box displayed by the `alert()` function is *modal*. This is an important concept, which you'll come across again. It simply means that the message box won't go away until the user closes it by clicking the OK button. In fact, parsing of the page stops at the line where the `alert()` function is used and doesn't restart until the user closes the message box. This is quite useful for this example, because it enables you to demonstrate the results of what has been parsed so far: The page color has been set to white, and the first paragraph has been displayed.

When you click OK, the browser carries on parsing down the page through the following lines:

```
<p>Paragraph 2</p>
<script type="text/javascript">
    // Script block 2
    document.bgColor = "RED";
    alert("Second Script Block");
</script>
```

The second paragraph is displayed, and the second block of JavaScript is run. The first line of the script block code is another comment, so the browser ignores this. You saw the second line of the script code in the previous example — it changes the background color of the page to red. The third line of code is the `alert()` function, which displays the second message box. Parsing is brought to a halt until you close the message box by clicking OK.

When you close the message box, the browser moves on to the next lines of code in the page, displaying the third paragraph and finally ending the web page.

```
<p>Paragraph 3</p>
</body>
</html>
```

Another important point raised by this example is the difference between setting properties of the page, such as background color, via HTML and doing the same thing using JavaScript. The method of setting properties using HTML is *static*: A value can be set only once and never changed again by means of HTML. Setting properties using JavaScript enables you to dynamically change their values. The term *dynamic* refers to something that can be changed and whose value or appearance is not set in stone.

This example is just that, an example. In practice, if you want the page's background to be red, you can set the `<body>` tag's BGCOLOR attribute to "RED" and not use JavaScript at all. Where you want to use JavaScript is where you want to add some sort of intelligence or logic to the page. For example, if the user's screen resolution is particularly low, you might want to change what's displayed on the page; with JavaScript, you can do this. Another reason for using JavaScript to change properties might be for special effects — for example, making a page fade in from white to its final color.

Displaying Results in a Web Page

In this final example, you'll discover how to write information directly to a web page using JavaScript. This proves more useful when you're writing the results of a calculation or text you've created using JavaScript, as you'll see in the next chapter. For now, you'll just write "Hello World!" to a blank page using JavaScript:

```
<!DOCTYPE html PUBLIC "-//W3C//DTD XHTML 1.0 Transitional//EN"
"http://www.w3.org/TR/xhtml1/DTD/xhtml1-transitional.dtd">
<html xmlns="http://www.w3.org/1999/xhtml">
<body >


<p id="ResultsP"></p>

<script type="text/javascript">
   // Script block 1
   document.getElementById('ResultsP').innerHTML = 'Hello World!';
</script>

</body>
</html>
```

Save the page as ch1_examp3.htm to a convenient place on your hard drive. Now load it into your web browser and you'll see Hello World! in the page. Although it would be easier to use HTML to do the same thing, this technique will prove useful in later chapters.

The first part of the page is the same as in our earlier examples, except the following line has been added:

```
<!DOCTYPE html PUBLIC "-//W3C//DTD XHTML 1.0 Transitional//EN"
"http://www.w3.org/TR/xhtml1/DTD/xhtml1-transitional.dtd">
<html xmlns="http://www.w3.org/1999/xhtml">
```

This lets the web browser know that you're using XHTML, the standard used throughout this book. It doesn't actually make any difference to the code; it would work just fine without the extra lines.

Consider this line:

```
<p id="ResultsP"></p>
```

You'll notice the <p> tag has been given an id using the id attribute. This id must be unique in the web page, because it is used by the JavaScript to identify the specific HTML element in the following line:

```
document.getElementById('ResultsP').innerHTML = 'Hello World!';
```

Don't worry if this seems complex at the moment; you'll learn more about how this works in later chapters, especially Chapters 6 and 12. Basically, the code is saying, "Get me the document element with id ResultsP and set the HTML inside that element to Hello World!"

It's important in your example that the code accessing the paragraph is after the paragraph. Otherwise, the code would be attempting to access a paragraph before it existed in the page and would throw an error.

A Brief Look at Browsers and Compatibility Problems

You've seen in the preceding example that by using JavaScript you can change a web page's document background color using the bgColor property of the document. The example worked whether you used a Netscape or Microsoft browser, because both types of browsers support a document with a bgColor property. You can say that the example is *cross-browser compatible*. However, it's not always the case that the property or language feature available in one browser will be available in another browser. This is even sometimes the case between versions of the same browser.

> *The version numbers for Internet Explorer and Firefox browsers are usually written as a decimal number; for example, Firefox has a version 1.5. This book uses the following terminology to refer to these versions: By* version 1.x *we mean all versions starting with the number 1; by* version 1.0+ *we mean all versions with a number greater than or equal to 1.*

One of the main headaches involved in creating web-based JavaScript is the differences between different web browsers, the level of HTML they support, and the functionality their JavaScript interpreters can handle. You'll find that in one browser you can move an image using just a couple of lines of code but that in another it'll take a whole page of code or even prove impossible. One version of JavaScript will contain a method to change text to uppercase, and another won't. Each new release of IE or Firefox browsers sees new and exciting features added to its HTML and JavaScript support. The good news is that to a much greater extent than ever before, browser creators are complying with standards set by organizations such as the W3C. Also, with a little ingenuity, you can write JavaScript that will work with both IE and Firefox browsers.

Which browsers you want to support really comes down to the browsers you think the majority of your web site's visitors, that is, your *user base,* will be using. This book is aimed at both IE7 and later and Firefox 2 and later.

If you want your web site to be professional, you need to somehow deal with older browsers. You could make sure your code is backward compatible — that is, it only uses features available in older browsers. However, you may decide that it's simply not worth limiting yourself to the features of older browsers. In this case you need to make sure your pages degrade gracefully. In other words, make sure that although your pages won't work in older browsers, they will fail in a way that means the user is either never aware of the failure or is alerted to the fact that certain features on the web site are not compatible with his or her browser. The alternative to degrading gracefully is for your code to raise lots of error messages, cause strange results to be displayed on the page, and generally make you look like an idiot who doesn't know what you're doing!

So how do you make your web pages degrade gracefully? You can do this by using JavaScript to determine which browser the web page is running in after it has been partially or completely loaded. You can use this information to determine what scripts to run or even to redirect the user to another page written to make best use of her particular browser. In later chapters, you see how to find out what features the browser supports and take appropriate action so that your pages work acceptably on as many browsers as possible.

Summary

At this point, you should have a feel for what JavaScript is and what it can do. In particular, this brief introduction covered the following:

❑   You looked into the process the browser follows when interpreting your web page. It goes through the page element by element (parsing) and acts upon your HTML tags and JavaScript code as it comes to them.

❑   Unlike many programming languages, JavaScript requires just a text editor to start creating code. Something like Windows Notepad is fine for getting started, though more extensive tools will prove valuable once you get more experience.

❑   JavaScript code is embedded into the web page itself, along with the HTML. Its existence is marked out by the use of <script> tags. As with HTML, script executes from the top of the page and works down to the bottom, interpreting and executing the code statement by statement.

Data Types and Variables

One of the main uses of computers is to process and display information. By processing, we mean the information is modified, interpreted, or filtered in some way by the computer. For example, on an online banking web site, a customer may request details of all moneys paid out from his account in the last month. Here the computer would retrieve the information, filter out any information not related to payments made in the last month, and then display what's left in a web page. In some situations, information is processed without being displayed, and at other times, information is obtained directly without being processed. For example, in a banking environment, regular payments may be processed and transferred electronically without any human interaction or display.

In computing, information is referred to as *data*. Data come in all sorts of forms, such as numbers, text, dates, and times, to mention just a few. In this chapter, you look specifically at how JavaScript handles data such as numbers and text. An understanding of how data are handled is fundamental to any programming language.

The chapter starts by looking at the various types of data JavaScript can process. Then you look at how you can store these data in the computer's memory so you can use them again and again in the code. Finally, you see how to use JavaScript to manipulate and process the data.

Types of Data in JavaScript

Data can come in many different forms, or *types*. You'll recognize some of the data types that JavaScript handles from the world outside programming — for example, numbers and text. Other data types are a little more abstract and are used to make programming easier; one example is the object data type, which you won't see in detail until Chapter 4.

Some programming languages are strongly typed. In these languages, whenever you use a piece of data, you need to explicitly state what sort of data you are dealing with, and use of those data must follow strict rules applicable to its type. For example, you can't add a number and a word together.

JavaScript, on the other hand, is a weakly typed language and a lot more forgiving about how you use different types of data. When you deal with data, you often don't need to specify type; JavaScript will work that out for itself. Furthermore, when you are using different types of data at the same time, JavaScript will work out behind the scenes what it is you're trying to do.

Given how easygoing JavaScript is about data, why talk about data types at all? Why not just cut to the chase and start using data without worrying about their type?

First of all, while JavaScript is very good at working out what data it's dealing with, there are occasions when it'll get things wrong or at least not do what you want it to do. In these situations, you need to make it explicit to JavaScript what sort of data type you intended and how it should be used. To do that, you first need to know a little bit about data types.

A second reason is that data types enable you to use data effectively in your code. The things that can be done with data and the results you'll get depend on the type of data being used, even if you don't specify explicitly what type it is. For example, although trying to multiply two numbers together makes sense, doing the same thing with text doesn't. Also, the result of adding numbers is very different from the result of adding text. With numbers you get the sum, but with text you get one big piece of text consisting of the other pieces joined together.

Let's take a brief look at some of the more commonly used data types: numerical, text, and Boolean. You will see how to use them later in the chapter.

Numerical Data

Numerical data come in two forms:

- ❑ Whole numbers, such as 145, which are also known as *integers*. These numbers can be positive or negative and can span a very wide range in JavaScript: -2^{53} to 2^{53}.

- ❑ Fractional numbers, such as 1.234, which are also known as *floating-point* numbers. Like integers, they can be positive or negative, and they also have a massive range.

In simple terms, unless you're writing specialized scientific applications, you're not going to face problems with the size of numbers available in JavaScript. Also, although you can treat integers and floating-point numbers differently when it comes to storing them, JavaScript actually treats them both as floating-point numbers. It kindly hides the detail from you so you generally don't need to worry about it. One exception is when you want an integer but you have a floating-point number, in which case you'll round the number to make it an integer. You'll take a look at rounding numbers later in this chapter.

Text Data

Another term for one or more characters of text is a *string*. You tell JavaScript that text is to be treated as text and not as code simply by enclosing it inside quote marks ("). For example, "Hello World" and "A" are examples of strings that JavaScript will recognize. You can also use the single quote marks ('), so 'Hello World' and 'A' are also examples of strings that JavaScript will recognize. However, you must end the string with the same quote mark that you started it with. Therefore, "A' is not a valid JavaScript string, and neither is 'Hello World".

What if you want a string with a single quote mark in the middle, say a string like `Peter O'Toole`? If you enclose it in double quotes, you'll be fine, so `"Peter O'Toole"` is recognized by JavaScript. However, `'Peter O'Toole'` will produce an error. This is because JavaScript thinks that your text string is `Peter O` (that is, it treats the middle single quote as marking the end of the string) and falls over wondering what the `Toole'` is.

Another way around this is to tell JavaScript that the middle `'` is part of the text and is not indicating the end of the string. You do this by using the backslash character (\), which has special meaning in JavaScript and is referred to as an *escape character*. The backslash tells the browser that the next character is not the end of the string, but part of the text. So `'Peter O\'Toole'` will work as planned.

What if you want to use a double quote inside a string enclosed in double quotes? Well, everything just said about the single quote still applies. So `'Hello "Paul"'` works, but `"Hello "Paul""` won't. However, `"Hello \"Paul\""` will also work.

JavaScript has a lot of other special characters, which can't be typed in but can be represented using the escape character in conjunction with other characters to create *escape sequences*. These work much the same as in HTML. For example, more than one space in a row is ignored in HTML, so a space is represented by the term ` `. Similarly, in JavaScript there are instances where you can't use a character directly but must use an escape sequence. The following table details some of the more useful escape sequences.

Escape Sequences	Character Represented
\b	Backspace
\f	Form feed
\n	New line
\r	Carriage return
\t	Tab
\'	Single quote
\"	Double quote
\\	Backslash
\xNN	NN is a hexadecimal number that identifies a character in the Latin-1 character set.

The least obvious of these is the last, which represents individual characters by their character number in the Latin-1 character set rather than by their normal appearance. Let's pick an example: Say you wanted to include the copyright symbol (©) in your string. What would your string need to look like? The answer is `"\xA9 Paul Wilton"`.

Similarly, you can refer to characters using their Unicode escape sequence. These are written \u*NNNN*, where *NNNN* refers to the Unicode number for that particular character. For example, to refer to the copyright symbol using this method, you use the string `\u00A9`.

Boolean Data

The use of yes or no, positive or negative, and true or false is commonplace in the physical world. The idea of true and false is also fundamental to digital computers; they don't understand maybes, only true and false. In fact, the concept of "yes or no" is so useful it has its own data type in JavaScript: the *Boolean* data type. The Boolean type has two possible values: `true` for yes and `false` for no.

The purpose of Boolean data in JavaScript is just the same as in the world outside programming: They enable you to answer questions and make decisions based on the answer. For example, if you are asked, "Is this book about JavaScript?" you would hopefully answer, "Yes it is," or you might also say, "That's true." Similarly you might say, "If it's false that the subject of the book is JavaScript, then put it down." Here you have a Boolean logic statement (named after its inventor George Boole), which asks a question and then does something based on whether the answer is true or false. In JavaScript, you can use the same sort of Boolean logic to give our programs decision-making abilities. You'll be taking a more detailed look at Boolean logic in the next chapter.

Variables — Storing Data in Memory

Data can be stored either permanently or temporarily.

You will want to keep important data, such as the details of a person's bank account, in a permanent store. For example, when Ms. Bloggs takes ten dollars or pounds or euros out of her account, you want to deduct the money from her account and keep a permanent record of the new balance. Information like this might be stored in something called a *database*.

However, there are other cases where you don't want to permanently store data, but simply want to keep a temporary note of it. Let's look at an example. Say Ms. Bloggs has a loan from BigBadBank Inc., and she wants to find out how much is still outstanding on this loan. She goes to the online banking page for loans and clicks a link to find out how much she owes. This is data that will be stored permanently somewhere. However, suppose you also provide a facility for increasing loan repayments to pay off the loan early. If Ms. Bloggs enters an increased repayment amount into the text box on the web page, you might want to show how much sooner the loan will be paid. This will involve a few possibly complex calculations, so to make it easier, you want to write code that calculates the result in several stages, storing the result at each stage as you go along, before providing a final result. After you've done the calculation and displayed the results, there's no need to permanently store the results for each stage, so rather than use a database, you need to use something called a *variable*. Why is it called a variable? Well, perhaps because a variable can be used to store temporary data that can be altered, or varied.

Another bonus of variables is that unlike permanent storage, which might be saved to disk or magnetic tape, variables are held in the computer's memory. This means that it is much, much faster to store and retrieve the data.

So what makes variables good places for temporarily storing your data? Well, variables have a limited lifetime. When your visitors close the page or move to a new one, your variables are lost, unless you take some steps to save them somewhere.

Each variable is given a name so that you can refer to it elsewhere in your code. These names must follow certain rules.

As with much of JavaScript code, you'll find that variable names are case sensitive. For example, `myVariable` is not the same as `myvariable`. You'll find that this is a very easy way for errors to slip into your code, even when you become an expert at JavaScript.

Also, you can't use certain names and characters for your variable names. Names you can't use are called *reserved* words. Reserved words are words that JavaScript keeps for its own use (for example, the word `var` or the word `with`). Certain characters are also forbidden in variable names: for example, the ampersand (`&`) and the percent sign (`%`). You are allowed to use numbers in your variable names, but the names must not begin with numbers. So `101myVariable` is not okay, but `myVariable101` is. Let's look at some more examples.

Invalid names include:

❑   with

❑   99variables

❑   my%Variable

❑   theGood&theBad

Valid names include

❑   myVariable99

❑   myPercent_Variable

❑   the_Good_and_the_Bad

You may wish to use a naming convention for your variables (for example, one that describes what sort of data you plan to hold in the variable). You can notate your variables in lots of different ways — none are right or wrong, but it's best to stick with one of them. One common method is *Hungarian notation*, where the beginning of each variable name is a three-letter identifier indicating the data type. For example, you may start integer variable names with `int`, floating-point variable names with `flt`, string variable names with `str`, and so on. However, as long as the names you use make sense and are used consistently, it really doesn't matter what convention you choose.

Creating Variables and Giving Them Values

Before you can use a variable, you should declare its existence to the computer using the `var` keyword. This warns the computer that it needs to reserve some memory for your data to be stored in later. To declare a new variable called `myFirstVariable`, write the following:

```
var myFirstVariable;
```

Note that the semicolon at the end of the line is not part of the variable name but instead is used to indicate to JavaScript the end of a statement. This line is an example of a JavaScript statement.

Once declared, a variable can be used to store any type of data. As we mentioned earlier, many other programming languages, called strongly typed languages, require you to declare not only the variable but also the type of data, such as numbers or text, that will be stored. However, JavaScript is a weakly typed language; you don't need to limit yourself to what type of data a variable can hold.

You put data into your variables, a process called *assigning values* to your variables, by using the equals sign (=). For example, if you want your variable named myFirstVariable to hold the number 101, you would write this:

```
myFirstVariable = 101;
```

The equals sign has a special name when used to assign values to a variable; it's called the *assignment operator*.

Try It Out   Declaring Variables

Let's look at an example in which a variable is declared, store some data in it, and finally access its contents. You'll also see that variables can hold any type of data, and that the type of data being held can be changed. For example, you can start by storing text and then change to storing numbers without JavaScript having any problems. Type the following code into your text editor and save it as ch2_examp1.htm:

```
<!DOCTYPE html PUBLIC "-//W3C//DTD XHTML 1.0 Transitional//EN"
"http://www.w3.org/TR/xhtml1/DTD/xhtml1-transitional.dtd">
<html xmlns="http://www.w3.org/1999/xhtml">

<head>
</head>
<body>

<script type="text/javascript">

var myFirstVariable;

myFirstVariable = "Hello";
alert(myFirstVariable);

myFirstVariable = 54321;
alert(myFirstVariable);

</script>

</body>
</html>
```

As soon as you load this into your web browser, it should show an alert box with "Hello" in it, as shown in Figure 2-1. This is the content of the variable myFirstVariable at that point in the code.

Figure 2-1

Click OK and another `alert` box appears with 54321 in it, as shown in Figure 2-2. This is the new value you assigned to the variable `myFirstVariable`.

Figure 2-2

Within the script block, you first declare your variable.

```
var myFirstVariable;
```

Currently, its value is the `undefined` value because you've declared only its existence to the computer, not any actual data. It may sound odd, but `undefined` is an actual primitive value in JavaScript, and it enables you to do comparisons. (For example, you can check to see if a variable contains an actual value or if it has not yet been given a value, that is, if it is undefined.) However, in the next line you assign `myFirstVariable` a string value, namely the value `Hello`.

```
myFirstVariable = "Hello";
```

Here you have assigned the variable a *literal* value (that is, a piece of actual data rather than data obtained by a calculation or from another variable). Almost anywhere that you can use a literal string or number, you can replace it with a variable containing number or string data. You see an example of this in the next line of code, where you use your variable `myFirstVariable` in the `alert()` function that you saw in the last chapter.

```
alert(myFirstVariable);
```

This causes the first `alert` box to appear. Next you store a new value in your variable, this time a number.

```
myFirstVariable = 54321;
```

The previous value of `myFirstVariable` is lost forever. The memory space used to store the value is freed up automatically by JavaScript in a process called *garbage collection*. Whenever JavaScript detects that the contents of a variable are no longer usable, such as when you allocate a new value, it performs the garbage collection process and makes the memory available. Without this automatic garbage collection process, more and more of the computer's memory would be consumed, until eventually the computer would run out and the system would grind to a halt. However, garbage collection is not always as efficient as it should be and may not occur until another page is loaded.

Just to prove that the new value has been stored, use the `alert()` function again to display the variable's new contents.

```
alert(myFirstVariable);
```

Assigning Variables with the Value of Other Variables

You've seen that you can assign a variable with a number or string, but can you assign a variable with the data stored inside another variable? The answer is yes, very easily, and in exactly the same way as giving a variable a literal value. For example, if you have declared the two variables myVariable and myOtherVariable and have given the variable myOtherVariable the value 22, like this:

```
var myVariable;
var myOtherVariable;
myOtherVariable = 22;
```

then you can use the following line to assign myVariable the same value as myOtherVariable (that is, 22).

```
myVariable = myOtherVariable;
```

Try It Out   **Assigning Variables the Values of Other Variables**

Let's look at another example, this time assigning variables the values of other variables.

1.   Type the following code into your text editor and save it as ch2_examp2.htm:

```
<!DOCTYPE html PUBLIC "-//W3C//DTD XHTML 1.0 Transitional//EN"
  "http://www.w3.org/TR/xhtml1/DTD/xhtml1-transitional.dtd">
<html xmlns="http://www.w3.org/1999/xhtml">
<body>

<script language="JavaScript" type="text/javascript">

var string1 = "Hello";
var string2 = "Goodbye";

alert(string1);
alert(string2);

string2 = string1;

alert(string1);
alert(string2);

string1 = "Now for something different";

alert(string1);
alert(string2);

</script>

</body>
</html>
```

2. Load the page into your browser, and you'll see a series of six `alert` boxes appear.

3. Click OK on each `alert` box to see the next alert. The first two show the values of `string1` and `string2` — `Hello` and `Goodbye`, respectively. Then you assign `string2` the value that's in `string1`. The next two `alert` boxes show the contents of `string1` and `string2`; this time both are `Hello`.

4. Finally, you change the value of `string1`. Note that the value of `string2` remains unaffected. The final two `alert` boxes show the new value of `string1` (`Now for something different`) and the unchanged value of `string2` (`Hello`).

The first thing you do in the script block is declare your two variables: `string1` and `string2`. However, notice that you have assigned them values at the same time that you have declared them. This is a shortcut, called *initializing*, that saves you typing too much code.

```
var string1 ="Hello";
var string2 = "Goodbye";
```

Note that you can use this shortcut with all data types, not just strings. The next two lines show the current value of each variable to the user using the `alert()` function.

```
alert(string1);
alert(string2);
```

Then you assign `string2` the value that's contained in `string1`. To prove that the assignment has really worked, you again show the user the contents of each variable using the `alert()` function.

```
string2 = string1;

alert(string1);
alert(string2);
```

Next, you set `string1` to a new value.

```
string1 = "Now for something different";
```

This leaves `string2` with its current value, demonstrating that `string2` has its own copy of the data assigned to it from `string1` in the previous step. You'll see in later chapters that this is not always the case. However, as a general rule, basic data types, such as text and numbers, are always copied when assigned, whereas more complex data types, like the objects you come across in Chapter 4, are actually shared and not copied. For example, if you have a variable with the string `Hello` and assign five other variables the value of this variable, you now have the original data and five independent copies of the data. However, if it was an object rather than a string and you did the same thing, you'd find you still have only one copy of the data, but that six variables share it. Changing the data using any of the six variable names would change them for all the variables.

Finally, the `alert()` function is used to show the current values of each variable.

```
alert(string1);
alert(string2);
```

Using Data — Calculations and Basic String Manipulation

Now that you've seen how to cope with errors, you can get back to the main subject of this chapter: data and how to use them. You've seen how to declare variables and how they can store information, but so far you haven't done anything really useful with this knowledge — so just why would you want to use variables at all?

What variables enable you to do is temporarily hold information that you can use for processing in mathematical calculations, in building up text messages, or in processing words that the user has entered. Variables are a little bit like the Memory Store button on the average pocket calculator. Say you were adding up your finances. You might first add up all the money you needed to spend, and then store it in temporary memory. After you had added up all your money coming in, you could deduct the amount stored in the memory to figure out how much would be left over. Variables can be used in a similar way: You can first gain the necessary user input and store it in variables, and then you can do your calculations using the values obtained.

In this section you'll see how you can put the values stored in variables to good use in both number-crunching and text-based operations.

Numerical Calculations

JavaScript has a range of basic mathematical capabilities, such as addition, subtraction, multiplication, and division. Each of the basic math functions is represented by a symbol: plus (+), minus (–), star (*), and forward slash (/), respectively. These symbols are called *operators* because they operate on the values you give them. In other words, they perform some calculation or operation and return a result to us. You can use the results of these calculations almost anywhere you'd use a number or a variable.

Imagine you were calculating the total value of items on a shopping list. You could write this calculation as follows:

Total cost of shopping = 10 + 5 + 5

Or, if you actually calculate the sum, it's

Total cost of shopping = 20

Now let's see how to do this in JavaScript. In actual fact, it is very similar except that you need to use a variable to store the final total.

```
var TotalCostOfShopping;
TotalCostOfShopping = 10 + 5 + 5;
alert(TotalCostOfShopping);
```

First, you declare a variable, `TotalCostOfShopping`, to hold the total cost.

In the second line, you have the code `10 + 5 + 5`. This piece of code is known as an *expression*. When you assign the variable `TotalCostOfShopping` the value of this expression, JavaScript automatically calculates the value of the expression (20) and stores it in the variable. Notice that the equals sign tells JavaScript to store the results of the calculation in the TotalCostOfShopping variable. This is called *assigning* the value of the calculation to the variable, which is why the single equals sign (=) is called the *assignment operator*.

Finally, you display the value of the variable in an alert box.

The operators for subtraction and multiplication work in exactly the same way. Division is a little different.

Try It Out   Calculations

Let's take a look at an example using the division operator to see how it works.

1.   Enter the following code and save it as ch2_examp3.htm:

```
<!DOCTYPE html PUBLIC "-//W3C//DTD XHTML 1.0 Transitional//EN"
"http://www.w3.org/TR/xhtml1/DTD/xhtml1-transitional.dtd">
<html xmlns="http://www.w3.org/1999/xhtml">
<body>

<script language="JavaScript" type="text/javascript">
var firstNumber = 15;
var secondNumber = 10;
var answer;
answer = 15 / 10;
alert(answer);

alert(15 / 10);

answer = firstNumber / secondNumber;
alert(answer);

</script>

</body>
</html>
```

2.   Load this into your web browser. You should see a succession of three alert boxes, each containing the value 1.5. These values are the results of three calculations.

3.   The first thing you do in the script block is declare your three variables and assign the first two of these variables values that you'll be using later.

```
var firstNumber = 15;
var secondNumber = 10;
var answer;
```

4.   Next, you set the answer variable to the results of the calculation of the expression 15/10. You show the value of this variable in an alert box.

```
answer = 15 / 10;
alert(answer);
```

This example demonstrates one way of doing the calculation, but in reality you'd almost never do it this way.

To demonstrate that you can use expressions in places you'd use numbers or variables, you show the results of the calculation of 15/10 directly by including it in the alert() function.

```
alert(15 / 10);
```

Finally, you do the same calculation, but this time using the two variables firstNumber, which was set to 15, and secondNumber, which was set to 10. You have the expression firstNumber / secondNumber, the result of which you store in our answer variable. Then, to prove it has all worked, you show the value contained in answer by using your friend the alert() function.

```
answer = firstNumber / secondNumber;
alert(answer);
```

Most calculations will be done in the third way (that is, using variables, or numbers and variables, and storing the result in another variable). The reason for this is that if the calculation used literal values (actual values, such as 15 / 10), then you might as well program in the result of the calculation, rather than force JavaScript to calculate it for you. For example, rather than writing 15 / 10, you might as well just write 1.5. After all, the more calculations you force JavaScript to do, the slower it will be, though admittedly just one calculation won't tax it too much.

Another reason for using the result rather than the calculation is that it makes code more readable. Which would you prefer to read in code: 1.5 * 45 – 56 / 67 + 2.567 or 69.231? Still better, a variable named for example PricePerKG, makes code even easier to understand for someone not familiar with it.

Increment and Decrement Operators

A number of operations using the math operators are so commonly used that they have been given their own operators. The two you'll be looking at here are the *increment* and *decrement* operators, which are represented by two plus signs (++) and two minus signs (--), respectively. Basically, all they do is increase or decrease a variable's value by one. You could use the normal + and – operators to do this, for example:

```
myVariable = myVariable + 1;
myVariable = myVariable - 1;
```

You can assign a variable a new value that is the result of an expression involving its previous value.

However, using the increment and decrement operators shortens this to

```
myVariable++;
myVariable--;
```

The result is the same — the value of myVariable is increased or decreased by one — but the code is shorter. When you are familiar with the syntax, this becomes very clear and easy to read.

Right now, you may well be thinking that these operators sound as useful as a poke in the eye. However, in Chapter 3, when you look at how you can run the same code a number of times, you'll see that these operators are very useful and widely used. In fact, the ++ operator is so widely used it has a computer language named after it: C++. The joke here is that C++ is one up from C. (Well, that's programmer humor for you!)

As well as placing the ++ or -- after the variable, you can also place it before, like so:

```
++myVariable;
--myVariable;
```

When the ++ and -- are used on their own, as they usually are, it makes no difference where they are placed, but it is possible to use the ++ and -- operators in an expression along with other operators. For example:

```
myVar = myNumber++ - 20;
```

This code takes 20 away from myNumber and then increments the variable myNumber by one before assigning the result to the variable myVar. If instead you place the ++ before and prefix it like this:

```
myVar = ++myNumber - 20;
```

First, myNumber is incremented by one, and then myNumber has 20 subtracted from it. It's a subtle difference but in some situations a very important one. Take the following code:

```
myNumber = 1;
myVar = (myNumber++ * 10 + 1);
```

What value will myVar contain? Well, because the ++ is postfixed (it's after the myNumber variable), it will be incremented afterwards. So the equation reads: Multiply myNumber by 10 plus 1 and then increment myNumber by one.

```
myVar = 1 * 10 + 1 = 11
```

Then add 1 to myNumber to get 12, but this is done after the value 11 has been assigned to myVar. Now take a look at the following code:

```
myNumber = 1;
myVar = (++myNumber * 10 + 1);
```

This time myNumber is incremented by one first, then times 10 and plus 1.

```
myVar = 2 * 10 + 1 = 21
```

As you can imagine, such subtlety can easily be overlooked and lead to bugs in code; therefore, it's usually best to avoid this syntax.

Before going on, this seems to be a good point to introduce another operator: +=. This operator can be used as a shortcut for increasing the value held by a variable by a set amount. For example,

```
myVar += 6;
```

does exactly the same thing as

```
myVar = myVar + 6;
```

You can also do the same thing for subtraction and multiplication, as shown here:

```
myVar -= 6;
myVar *= 6;
```

which is equivalent to

```
myVar = myVar - 6;
myVar = myVar * 6;
```

Operator Precedence

You've seen that symbols that perform some function — like +, which adds two numbers together, and -, which subtracts one number from another — are called operators. Unlike people, not all operators are created equal; some have a higher *precedence* — that is, they get dealt with sooner. A quick look at a simple example will help demonstrate this point.

```
var myVariable;

myVariable = 1 + 1 * 2;

alert(myVariable);
```

If you were to type this, what result would you expect the alert box to show as the value of myVariable? You might expect that since 1 + 1 = 2 and 2 * 2 = 4, the answer is 4. Actually, you'll find that the alert box shows 3 as the value stored in myVariable as a result of the calculation. So what gives? Doesn't JavaScript add up right?

Well, you probably already know the reason from your understanding of mathematics. The way JavaScript does the calculation is to first calculate 1 * 2 = 2, and then use this result in the addition, so that JavaScript finishes off with 1 + 2 = 3.

Why? Because * has a higher precedence than +. The = symbol, also an operator (called the assignment operator), has the lowest precedence — it always gets left until last.

The + and - operators have an equal precedence, so which one gets done first? Well, JavaScript works from left to right, so if operators with equal precedence exist in a calculation, they get calculated in the order in which they appear when going from left to right. The same applies to * and /, which are also of equal precedence.

Try It Out   Fahrenheit to Centigrade

Take a look at a slightly more complex example — a Fahrenheit to centigrade converter. (Centigrade is another name for the Celsius temperature scale.) Type this code and save it as ch2_examp4.htm:

```
<!DOCTYPE html PUBLIC "-//W3C//DTD XHTML 1.0 Transitional//EN"
"http://www.w3.org/TR/xhtml1/DTD/xhtml1-transitional.dtd">
<html xmlns="http://www.w3.org/1999/xhtml">
<body>
```

```
<script type="text/javascript">
// Equation is °C = 5/9 (°F - 32).
var degFahren = prompt("Enter the degrees in Fahrenheit",50);
var degCent;

degCent = 5/9 * (degFahren - 32);

alert(degCent);

</script>

</body>
</html>
```

If you load the page into your browser, you should see a prompt box, like that shown in Figure 2-3, that asks you to enter the degrees in Fahrenheit to be converted. The value 50 is already filled in by default.

Figure 2-3

If you leave it at 50 and click OK, an `alert` box with the number 10 in it appears. This represents 50 degrees Fahrenheit converted to centigrade.

Reload the page and try changing the value in the prompt box to see what results you get. For example, change the value to 32 and reload the page. This time you should see 0 appear in the box.

As it's still a fairly simple example, there's no checking of data input so it'll let you enter abc as the degrees Fahrenheit. Later, in the "Data Type Conversion" section of this chapter, you'll see how to spot invalid characters posing as numeric data.

Try It Out   **Security Issues with Internet Explorer 8**

When loading the page to Internet Explorer 8 (IE8), you may see the security warning issue shown in Figure 2-4, and the prompt window doesn't appear.

Figure 2-4

If it does you'll need change IE8's security settings and add file://*..host as a trusted site. To do this:

1. Open IE8 and select the Internet Options menu from the Tools menu bar, as shown in Figure 2-5.

Figure 2-5

2. Click the Security tab and then click the green Trusted Sites button, as shown in Figure 2-6.

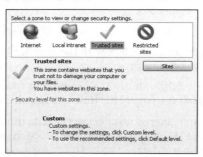

Figure 2-6

3. Click the Sites button and enter file://*..host into the Add This Website to the Zone text box, as shown in Figure 2-7.

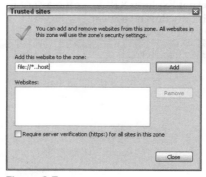

Figure 2-7

4. Make sure the Require Server Verification check box is unselected, click the Add button, and then click the Close button.

5. Click the OK button on the Internet Options dialog to return to the web page, refresh the page by pressing the F5 key, and the example will now work.

The first line of the script block is a comment, since it starts with two forward slashes (//). It contains the equation for converting Fahrenheit temperatures to centigrade and is in the example code solely for reference.

```
// Equation is °C = 5/9 (°F - 32).
```

Your task is to represent this equation in JavaScript code. You start by declaring your variables, `degFahren` and `degCent`.

```
var degFahren = prompt("Enter the degrees in Fahrenheit",50);
var degCent;
```

Instead of initializing the `degFahren` variable to a literal value, you get a value from the user using the `prompt()` function. The `prompt()` function works in a similar way to an `alert()` function, except that as well as displaying a message, it also contains a text box in which the user can enter a value. It is this value that will be stored inside the `degFahren` variable. The value returned is a text string, but this will be implicitly converted by JavaScript to a number when you use it as a number, as discussed in the section on data type conversion later in this chapter.

You pass two pieces of information to the `prompt()` function:

❑ The text to be displayed — usually a question that prompts the user for input.

❑ The default value that is contained in the input box when the prompt dialog box first appears.

These two pieces of information must be specified in the given order and separated by a comma. If you don't want a default value to be contained in the input box when the prompt box opens, use an empty string (`" "`) for the second piece of information.

As you can see in the preceding code, the text is "Enter the degrees in Fahrenheit," and the default value in the input box is 50.

Next in the script block comes the equation represented in JavaScript. You store the result of the equation in the `degCent` variable. You can see that the JavaScript looks very much like the equation you have in the comment, except you use `degFahren` instead of °F, and `degCent` rather than °C.

```
degCent = 5/9 * (degFahren - 32);
```

The calculation of the expression on the right-hand side of the equals sign raises a number of important points. First, just as in math, the JavaScript equation is read from left to right, at least for the basic math functions like +, -, and so on. Secondly, as you saw earlier, just as there is precedence in math, there is in JavaScript.

Starting from the left, first JavaScript works out 5/9 = .5556 (approximately). Then it comes to the multiplication, but wait . . . the last bit of our equation, `degFahren` – 32, is in parentheses. This raises the order of precedence and causes JavaScript to calculate the result of `degFahren` – 32 before doing the multiplication. For example, when `degFahren` is set to 50, (`degFahren` – 32) = (50 – 32) = 18. Now JavaScript does the multiplication, .5556 * 18, which is approximately 10.

What if you didn't use the parentheses? Then your code would be

```
degCent = 5/9 * degFahren - 32;
```

The calculation of 5/9 remains the same, but then JavaScript would have calculated the multiplication, 5/9 * degFahren. This is because the multiplication takes precedence over the subtraction. When degFahren is 50, this equates to 5/9 * 50 = 27.7778. Finally, JavaScript would have subtracted the 32, leaving the result as −4.2221; not the answer you want!

Finally, in your script block, you display the answer using the alert() function.

```
alert(degCent);
```

That concludes a brief look at basic calculations with JavaScript. However, in Chapter 4 you'll be looking at the Math object, which enables you to do more complex calculations.

Basic String Operations

In an earlier section, you looked at the text or string data type, as well as numerical data. Just as numerical data have associated operators, strings have operators too. This section introduces some basic string manipulation techniques using such operators. Strings are covered in more depth in Chapter 4, and advanced string handling is covered in Chapter 8.

One thing you'll find yourself doing again and again in JavaScript is joining two strings together to make one string — a process termed *concatenation*. For example, you may want to concatenate the two strings "Hello " and "Paul" to make the string "Hello Paul". So how do you concatenate? Easy! Use the + operator. Recall that when applied to numbers, the + operator adds them up, but when used in the context of two strings, it joins them together.

```
var concatString = "Hello " + "Paul";
```

The string now stored in the variable concatString is "Hello Paul". Notice that the last character of the string "Hello" is a space — if you left this out, your concatenated string would be "HelloPaul".

Try It Out   Concatenating Strings

Let's look at an example using the + operator for string concatenation.

1.   Type the following code and save it as ch2_examp5.htm:

```
<!DOCTYPE html PUBLIC "-//W3C//DTD XHTML 1.0 Transitional//EN"
"http://www.w3.org/TR/xhtml1/DTD/xhtml1-transitional.dtd">
<html xmlns="http://www.w3.org/1999/xhtml">
<body>

<script type="text/javascript">

var greetingString = "Hello";
var myName = prompt("Please enter your name", "");
var concatString;

document.write(greetingString + " " + myName + "<br>");
```

```
concatString = greetingString + " " + myName;

document.write(concatString);


</script>

</body>
</html>
```

2. If you load it into your web browser, you should see a prompt box asking for your name.

3. Enter your name and click OK. You should see a greeting and your name displayed twice on the web page.

You start the script block by declaring three variables. You set the first variable, greetingString, to a string value. The second variable, myName, is assigned to whatever is entered by the user in the prompt box. You do not initialize the third variable, concatString, here. It will be used to store the result of the concatenation that you'll do later in the code.

```
var greetingString = "Hello";
var myName = prompt("Please enter your name", "");
var concatString;
```

In the last chapter, you saw how the web page was represented by the concept of a document and that it had a number of different properties, such as bgColor. You can also use document to write text and HTML directly into the page itself. You do this by using the word document, followed by a dot, and then write(). You then use document.write() much as you do the alert() function, in that you put the text that you want displayed in the web page inside the parentheses following the word write. Don't worry too much about this here, though, because it will all be explained in detail in Chapter 4. However, you now make use of document.write() in your code to write the result of an expression to the page.

```
document.write(greetingString + " " + myName + "<br>");
```

The expression written to the page is the concatenation of the value of the greetingString variable, a space (" "), the value of the myName variable, and the HTML <br> tag, which causes a line break. For example, if you enter Paul into the prompt box, the value of this expression will be as follows:

```
Hello Paul<br>
```

In the next line of code is a similar expression. This time it is just the concatenation of the value in the variable greetingString, a space, and the value in the variable myName. You store the result of this expression in the variable concatString. Finally, you write the contents of the variable concatString to the page using document.write().

```
concatString = greetingString + " " + myName;
document.write(concatString);
```

Mixing Numbers and Strings

What if you want to mix text and numbers in an expression? A prime example of this would be in the temperature converter you saw earlier. In the example, you just display the number without telling the user what it actually means. What you really want to do is display the number with descriptive text wrapped around it, such as "The value converted to degrees centigrade is 10."

Mixing numbers and text is actually very easy. You can simply join them together using the + operator. JavaScript is intelligent enough to know that when both a string and a number are involved, you're not trying to do numerical calculations, but rather that you want to treat the number as a string and join it to the text. For example, to join the text My age is and the number 101, you could simply do the following:

```
alert("My age is " + 101);
```

This would produce an alert box with "My age is 101" inside it.

Try It Out   Making the Temperature Converter User-Friendly

You can try out this technique of concatenating strings and numbers in our temperature-converter example. You'll output some explanatory text, along with the result of the conversion calculation. The changes that you need to make are very small, so load ch2_examp4.htm into your text editor and change the following line. Then save it as ch2_examp6.htm.

```
<!DOCTYPE html PUBLIC "-//W3C//DTD XHTML 1.0 Transitional//EN"
"http://www.w3.org/TR/xhtml1/DTD/xhtml1-transitional.dtd">
<html xmlns="http://www.w3.org/1999/xhtml">
<body>

<script type="text/javascript">

var degFahren = prompt("Enter the degrees in Fahrenheit", 50);
var degCent;

degCent = 5/9 * (degFahren - 32);

alert(degFahren + "\xB0 Fahrenheit is " + degCent + "\xB0 centigrade");

</script>

</body>
</html>
```

Load the page into your web browser. Click OK in the prompt box to submit the value 50, and this time you should see the box shown in Figure 2-8.

Figure 2-8

This example is identical to ch2_examp4.htm, except for one line:

```
alert(degFahren + "\xB0 Fahrenheit is " + degCent + "\xB0 centigrade");
```

So we will just look at this line here. You can see that the alert() function contains an expression. Let's look at that expression more closely.

First is the variable degFahren, which contains numerical data. You concatenate that to the string "\xB0 Fahrenheit is ". JavaScript realizes that because you are adding a number and a string, you want to join them together into one string rather than trying to take their sum, and so automatically converts the number contained in degFahren to a string. You next concatenate this string to the variable degCent, containing numerical data. Again JavaScript converts the value of this variable to a string. Finally, you concatenate to the string "\xB0 centigrade".

Note also the escape sequence used to insert the degree character into the strings. You'll remember from earlier in the chapter that \xNN can be used to insert special characters not available to type in directly. (NN is a hexadecimal number representing a character from the Latin-1 character table). So when JavaScript spots \xB0 in a string, instead of showing those characters it does a lookup to see what character is represented by B0 and shows that instead.

Something to be aware of when using special characters is that they are not necessarily cross-platform-compatible. Although you can use \xNN for a certain character on a Windows computer, you may find you need to use a different character on a Mac or a Unix machine.

You'll look at more string manipulation techniques in Chapter 4 — you'll see how to search strings and insert characters in the middle of them, and in Chapter 8 you'll see some very sophisticated string techniques.

Data Type Conversion

As you've seen, if you add a string and a number, JavaScript makes the sensible choice and converts the number to a string, then concatenates the two. Usually, JavaScript has enough sense to make data type conversions like this whenever it needs to, but there are some situations in which you need to convert the type of a piece of data yourself. For example, you may be given a piece of string data that you want to think of as a number. This is especially likely if you are using forms to collect data from the user. Any values input by the user are treated as strings, even though they may contain numerical data, such as the user's age.

Why is changing the type of the data so important? Consider a situation in which you collect two numbers from the user using a form and want to calculate their sum. The two numbers are available to you as strings, for example "22" and "15". When you try to calculate the sum of these values using "22" + "15" you get the result "2215", because JavaScript thinks you are trying to concatenate two strings rather than trying to find the sum of two numbers. To add to the possible confusion, the order also makes a difference. So:

```
1 + 2 + 'abc'
```

results in a string containing "3abc", whereas:

```
'abc' + 1 + 2
```

would result in the string containing "abc12".

In this section you'll look at two conversion functions that convert strings to numbers: parseInt() and parseFloat().

Let's take parseInt() first. This function takes a string and converts it to an integer. The name is a little confusing at first — why parseInt() rather than convertToInt()? The main reason for the name comes from the way that the function works. It actually goes through (that is, parses) each character of the string you ask it to convert and sees if it's a valid number. If it is valid, parseInt() uses it to build up the number; if it is not valid, the command simply stops converting and returns the number it has converted so far.

For example, if your code is parseInt("123"), JavaScript will convert the string "123" to the number 123. For the code parseInt("123abc"), JavaScript will also return the number 123. When the JavaScript interpreter gets to the letter a, it assumes the number has ended and gives 123 as the integer version of the string "123abc".

The parseFloat() function works in the same way as parseInt(), except that it returns floating-point numbers — fractional numbers — and that a decimal point in the string, which it is converting, is considered to be part of the allowable number.

Try It Out   **Converting Strings to Numbers**

Let's look at an example using parseInt() and parseFloat(). Enter the following code and save it as ch2_examp7.htm:

```
<!DOCTYPE html PUBLIC "-//W3C//DTD XHTML 1.0 Transitional//EN"
"http://www.w3.org/TR/xhtml1/DTD/xhtml1-transitional.dtd">
<html xmlns="http://www.w3.org/1999/xhtml">
<body>

<script type="text/javascript">

var myString = "56.02 degrees centigrade";
var myInt;
var myFloat;

document.write("\"" + myString + "\" is " + parseInt(myString) +
    " as an integer" + "<BR>");

myInt = parseInt(myString);
document.write("\"" + myString + "\" when converted to an integer equals " +
    myInt + "<BR>");

myFloat = parseFloat(myString);
document.write("\"" + myString +
    "\" when converted to a floating point number equals " + myFloat);


</script>

</body>
</html>
```

Load it into your browser, and you'll see three lines written in the web page, as shown in Figure 2-9.

> "56.02 degrees centigrade" is 56 as an integer
> "56.02 degrees centigrade" when converted to an integer equals 56
> "56.02 degrees centigrade" when converted to a floating point number equals 56.02

Figure 2-9

Your first task in the script block is to declare some variables. The variable myString is declared and initialized to the string you want to convert. You could just as easily have used the string directly in this example rather than storing it in a variable, but in practice you'll find that you use variables more often than literal values. You also declare the variables myInt and myFloat, which will hold the converted numbers.

```
var myString = "56.02 degrees centigrade";
var myInt;
var myFloat;
```

Next, you write to the page the converted integer value of myString displayed inside a user-friendly sentence you build up using string concatenation. Notice that you use the escape sequence \" to display quotes (") around the string you are converting.

```
document.write("\"" + myString + "\" is " + parseInt(myString) +
    " as an integer" + "<BR>");
```

As you can see, you can use parseInt() and parseFloat() in the same places you would use a number itself or a variable containing a number. In fact, in this line the JavaScript interpreter is doing two conversions. First, it converts myString to an integer, because that's what you asked for by using parseInt(). Then it automatically converts that integer number back to a string, so it can be concatenated with the other strings to make up your sentence. Also note that only the 56 part of the myString variable's value is considered a valid number when you're dealing with integers. Anything after the 6 is considered invalid and is ignored.

Next, you do the same conversion of myString using parseInt(), but this time you store the result in the myInt variable. On the following line you use the result in some text you display to the user:

```
myInt = parseInt(myString);
document.write("\"" + myString + "\" when converted to an integer equals " +
    myInt + "<BR>");
```

Again, though myInt holds a number, the JavaScript interpreter knows that +, when a string and a number are involved, means you want the myInt value converted to a string and concatenated to the rest of the string so it can be displayed.

Finally, you use parseFloat() to convert the string in myString to a floating-point number, which you store in the variable myFloat. This time the decimal point is considered to be a valid part of the number, so it's anything after the 2 that is ignored. Again you use document.write() to write the result to the web page inside a user-friendly string.

```
myFloat = parseFloat(myString);
document.write("\"" + myString +
    "\" when converted to a floating point number equals " + myFloat);
```

Dealing with Strings That Won't Convert

Some strings simply are not convertible to numbers, such as strings that don't contain any numerical data. What happens if you try to convert these strings? As a little experiment, try changing the preceding example so that myString holds something that is not convertible. For example, change the line

```
var myString = "56.02 degrees centigrade";
```

to

```
var myString = "I'm a name not a number";
```

Now reload the page in your browser and you should see what's shown in Figure 2-10.

```
"I'm a name not a number" is NaN as an integer
"I'm a name not a number" when converted to an integer equals NaN
"I'm a name not a number" when converted to a floating point number equals NaN
```

Figure 2-10

You can see that in the place of the numbers you got before, you get NaN. What sort of number is that? Well, it's *Not a Number* at all!

If you use parseInt() or parseFloat() with any string that is empty or does not start with at least one valid digit, you get NaN, meaning Not a Number.

NaN is actually a special value in JavaScript. It has its own function, isNaN(), which checks whether something is NaN or not. For example,

```
myVar1 = isNaN("Hello");
```

will store the value true in the variable myVar1, since "Hello" is not a number, whereas

```
myVar2 = isNaN("34");
```

will store the value false in the variable myVar2, since 34 can be converted successfully from a string to a number by the isNaN() function.

In Chapter 3 you'll see how you can use the isNaN() function to check the validity of strings as numbers, something that proves invaluable when dealing with user input, as you'll see in Chapter 7.

Arrays

Now we're going to look at a new concept — something called an *array*. An array is similar to a normal variable, in that you can use it to hold any type of data. However, it has one important difference, which you'll see in this section.

As you have already seen, a normal variable can only hold one piece of data at a time. For example, you can set myVariable to be equal to 25 like so:

```
myVariable = 25;
```

and then go and set it to something else, say 35:

```
myVariable = 35;
```

However, when you set the variable to 35, the first value of 25 is lost. The variable myVariable now holds just the number 35.

The following table illustrates the variable:

Variable Name	Value
myVariable	35

The difference between such a normal variable and an array is that an array can hold *more than one* item of data at the same time. For example, you could use an array with the name myArray to store both the numbers 25 and 35. Each place where a piece of data can be stored in an array is called an *element*.

How do you distinguish between these two pieces of data in an array? You give each piece of data an *index* value. To refer to that piece of data you enclose its index value in square brackets after the name of the array. For example, an array called myArray containing the data 25 and 35 could be illustrated using the following table:

ElementName	Value
myArray[0]	25
myArray[1]	35

Notice that the index values start at 0 and not 1. Why is this? Surely 1 makes more sense — after all, we humans tend to say the first item of data, followed by the second item, and so on. Unfortunately, computers start from 0, and think of the first item as the zero item, the second as the first item, and so on. Confusing, but you'll soon get used to this.

Arrays can be very useful since you can store as many (within the limits of the language, which specifies a maximum of two to the power of 32 elements) or as few items of data in an array as you want. Also, you don't have to say up front how many pieces of data you want to store in an array, though you can if you wish.

So how do you create an array? This is slightly different from declaring a normal variable. To create a new array, you need to declare a variable name and tell JavaScript that you want it to be a new array using the new keyword and the Array() function. For example, the array myArray could be defined like this:

```
var myArray = new Array();
```

Note that, as with everything in JavaScript, the code is case-sensitive, so if you type `array()` rather than `Array()`, the code won't work. This way of defining an array will be explained further in Chapter 5.

As with normal variables, you can also declare your variable first, and then tell JavaScript you want it to be an array. For example:

```
var myArray;
myArray = new Array();
```

Earlier you learned that you can say up front how many elements the array will hold if you want to, although this is not necessary. You do this by putting the number of elements you want to specify between the parentheses after `Array`. For example, to create an array that will hold six elements, you write the following:

```
var myArray = new Array(6);
```

You have seen how to declare a new array, but how do you store your pieces of data inside it? You can do this when you define your array by including your data inside the parentheses, with each piece of data separated by a comma. For example:

```
var myArray = new Array("Paul",345,"John",112,"Bob",99);
```

Here the first item of data, `"Paul"`, will be put in the array with an index of 0. The next piece of data, `345`, will be put in the array with an index of 1, and so on. This means that the element with the name `myArray[0]` contains the value `"Paul"`, the element with the name `myArray[1]` contains the value `345`, and so on.

Note that you can't use this method to declare an array containing just one piece of numerical data, such as 345, because JavaScript assumes that you are declaring an array that will hold 345 elements.

This leads to another way of declaring data in an array. You could write the preceding line like this:

```
var myArray = new Array();
myArray[0] = "Paul";
myArray[1] = 345;
myArray[2] = "John";
myArray[3] = 112;
myArray[4] = "Bob";
myArray[5] = 99;
```

You use each element name as you would a variable, assigning them with values. You'll learn this method of declaring the values of array elements in the following "Try It Out" section.

Obviously, in this example the first way of defining the data items is much easier. However, there will be situations in which you want to change the data stored in a particular element in an array after they have been declared. In that case you will have to use the latter method of defining the values of the array elements.

You'll also spot from the preceding example that you can store different data types in the same array. JavaScript is very flexible as to what you can put in an array and where you can put it.

Before going on to an example, note here that if, for example, you had defined your array called `myArray` as holding three elements like this:

```
var myArray = new Array(3);
```

and then defined a value in the element with index `130` as follows:

```
myArray[130] = "Paul";
```

JavaScript would not complain and would happily assume that you had changed your mind and wanted an array that had (at least) 131 elements in it.

Try It Out   **An Array**

In the following example, you'll create an array to hold some names. You'll use the second method described in the preceding section to store these pieces of data in the array. You'll then display the data to the user. Type the code and save it as `ch2_examp8.htm`.

```
<!DOCTYPE html PUBLIC "-//W3C//DTD XHTML 1.0 Transitional//EN"
"http://www.w3.org/TR/xhtml1/DTD/xhtml1-transitional.dtd">
<html xmlns="http://www.w3.org/1999/xhtml">
<body>

<script type="text/javascript">

var myArray = new Array();
myArray[0] = "Bob";
myArray[1] = "Pete";
myArray[2] = "Paul";

document.write("myArray[0] = " + myArray[0] + "<BR>");
document.write("myArray[2] = " + myArray[2] + "<BR>");
document.write("myArray[1] = " + myArray[1] + "<BR>");

myArray[1] = "Mike";
document.write("myArray[1] changed to " + myArray[1]);

</script>

</body>
</html>
```

If you load this into your web browser, you should see a web page that looks something like the one shown in Figure 2-11.

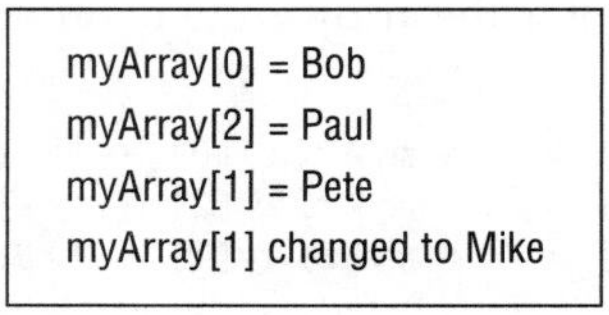

```
myArray[0] = Bob
myArray[2] = Paul
myArray[1] = Pete
myArray[1] changed to Mike
```

Figure 2-11

The first task in the script block is to declare a variable and tell the JavaScript interpreter you want it to be a new array.

```
var myArray = new Array();
```

Now that you have your array defined, you can store some data in it. Each time you store an item of data with a new index, JavaScript automatically creates a new storage space for it. Remember that the first element will be at myArray[0].

Take each addition to the array in turn and see what's happening. Before you add anything, your array is empty. Then you add an array element with the following line:

```
myArray[0] = "Bob";
```

Your array now looks like this:

Index	Data Stored
0	Bob

Then you add another element to the array, this time with an index of 1.

```
myArray[1] = "Pete";
```

Index	Data Stored
0	Bob
1	Pete

Finally, you add another element to the array with an index of 2.

```
myArray[2] = "Paul";
```

Your array now looks like this:

Index	Data Stored
0	Bob
1	Pete
2	Paul

Next, you use a series of document.write() functions to insert the values that each element of the array contains into the web page. Here the array is out of order just to demonstrate that you can access it that way.

```
document.write("myArray[0] = " + myArray[0] + "<BR>");
document.write("myArray[2] = " + myArray[2] + "<BR>");
document.write("myArray[1] = " + myArray[1] + "<BR>");
```

You can treat each particular position in an array as if it's a standard variable. So you can use it to do calculations, transfer its value to another variable or array, and so on. However, if you try to access the data inside an array position before you have defined it, you'll get undefined as a value.

Finally, you change the value of the second array position to "Mike". You could have changed it to a number because, just as with normal variables, you can store any data type at any time in each individual data position in an array.

```
myArray[1] = "Mike";
```

Now your array's contents look like this:

Index	Data Stored
0	Bob
1	Mike
2	Paul

Just to show that the change you made has worked, you use document.write() to display the second element's value.

```
document.write("myArray[1] changed to " + myArray[1]);
```

A Multi-Dimensional Array

Suppose you want to store a company's personnel information in an array. You might have data such as names, ages, addresses, and so on. One way to create such an array would be to store the information sequentially — the first name in the first element of the array, then the corresponding age in the next element, the address in the third, the next name in the fourth element, and so on. Your array could look something like this:

Index	Data Stored
0	Name1
1	Age1
2	Address1
3	Name2
4	Age2
5	Address2
6	Name3
7	Age3
8	Address3

This would work, but there is a neater solution: using a *multi-dimensional array*. Up to now you have been using single-dimension arrays. In these arrays each element is specified by just one index — that is, one dimension. So, taking the preceding example, you can see Name1 is at index 0, Age1 is at index 1, and so on.

A multi-dimensional array is one with two or more indexes for each element. For example, this is how your personnel array could look as a two-dimensional array:

Index	0	1	2
0	Name1	Name2	Name3
1	Age1	Age2	Age3
2	Address1	Address2	Address3

You'll see how to create such multi-dimensional arrays in the following "Try It Out" section.

Try It Out   A Two-Dimensional Array

The following example illustrates how you can create such a multi-dimensional array in JavaScript code and how you can access the elements of this array. Type the code and save it as ch2_examp9.htm.

```
<!DOCTYPE html PUBLIC "-//W3C//DTD XHTML 1.0 Transitional//EN"
"http://www.w3.org/TR/xhtml1/DTD/xhtml1-transitional.dtd">
<html xmlns="http://www.w3.org/1999/xhtml">
<body>

<script type="text/javascript">

var personnel = new Array();

personnel[0] = new Array();
personnel[0][0] = "Name0";
personnel[0][1] = "Age0";
personnel[0][2] = "Address0";

personnel[1] = new Array();
personnel[1][0] = "Name1";
personnel[1][1] = "Age1";
personnel[1][2] = "Address1";

personnel[2] = new Array();
personnel[2][0] = "Name2";
personnel[2][1] = "Age2";
personnel[2][2] = "Address2";

document.write("Name : " + personnel[1][0] + "<BR>");
document.write("Age : " + personnel[1][1] + "<BR>");
document.write("Address : " + personnel[1][2]);


</script>
```

```
</body>
</html>
```

If you load it into your web browser, you'll see three lines written into the page, which represent the name, age, and address of the person whose details are stored in the `personnel[1]` element of the array, as shown in Figure 2-12.

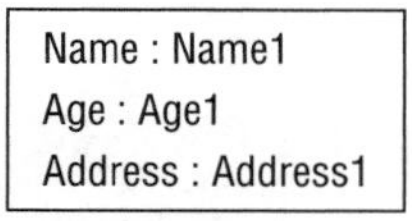

```
Name : Name1
Age : Age1
Address : Address1
```

Figure 2-12

The first thing to do in this script block is declare a variable, `personnel`, and tell JavaScript that you want it to be a new array.

```
var personnel = new Array();
```

Then you do something new; you tell JavaScript you want index 0 of the personnel array, that is, the element `personnel[0]`, to be another new array.

```
personnel[0] = new Array();
```

So what's going on? Well, the truth is that JavaScript doesn't actually support multi-dimensional arrays, only single ones. However, JavaScript enables us to fake multi-dimensional arrays by creating an array inside another array. So what the preceding line is doing is creating a new array inside the element with index 0 of our `personnel` array.

In the next three lines, you put values into the newly created `personnel[0]` array. JavaScript makes it easy to do this: You just state the name of the array, `personnel[0]`, followed by another index in square brackets. The first index (0) belongs to the `personnel` array; the second index belongs to the `personnel[0]` array.

```
personnel[0][0] = "Name0";
personnel[0][1] = "Age0";
personnel[0][2] = "Address0";
```

After these lines of code, your array looks like this:

Index	0
0	Name0
1	Age0
2	Address0

The numbers at the top, at the moment just 0, refer to the `personnel` array. The numbers going down the side, 0, 1, and 2, are actually indices for the new `personnel[0]` array inside the `personnel` array.

For the second person's details, you repeat the process, but this time you are using the `personnel` array element with index 1.

```
personnel[1] = new Array();
personnel[1][0] = "Name1";
personnel[1][1] = "Age1";
personnel[1][2] = "Address1";
```

Now your array looks like this:

Index	0	1
0	Name0	Name1
1	Age0	Age1
2	Address0	Address1

You create a third person's details in the next few lines. You are now using the element with index 2 inside the `personnel` array to create a new array.

```
personnel[2] = new Array();
personnel[2][0] = "Name2";
personnel[2][1] = "Age2";
personnel[2][2] = "Address2";
```

The array now looks like this:

Index	0	1	2
0	Name0	Name1	Name2
1	Age0	Age1	Age2
2	Address0	Address1	Address2

You have now finished creating your multi-dimensional array. You end the script block by accessing the data for the second person (Name1, Age1, Address1) and displaying it in the page by using `document .write()`. As you can see, accessing the data is very much the same as storing them. You can use the multi-dimensional array anywhere you would use a normal variable or single-dimension array.

```
document.write("Name : " + personnel[1][0] + "<BR>");
document.write("Age : " + personnel[1][1] + "<BR>");
document.write("Address : " + personnel[1][2]);
```

Try changing the `document.write()` commands so that they display the first person's details. The code would look like this:

```
document.write("Name : " + personnel[0][0] + "<BR>");
document.write("Age : " + personnel[0][1] + "<BR>");
document.write("Address : " + personnel[0][2]);
```

It's possible to create multi-dimensional arrays of three, four, or even a hundred dimensions, but things can start to get very confusing, and you'll find that you rarely, if ever, need more than two dimensions. To give you an idea, here's how to declare and access a five-dimensional array:

```
var myArray = new Array();
myArray[0] = new Array();
myArray[0][0] = new Array();
myArray[0][0][0] = new Array();
myArray[0][0][0][0] = new Array();

myArray[0][0][0][0][0] = "This is getting out of hand"

document.write(myArray[0][0][0][0][0]);
```

That's it for arrays for now, but you'll return to them in Chapter 4, where you'll find out something shocking about them. You'll also learn about some of their more advanced features.

Summary

In this chapter you have built up knowledge of the fundamentals of JavaScript's data types and variables and how to use them in operations. In particular, you saw that

❑   JavaScript supports a number of types of data, such as numbers, text, and Booleans.

❑   Text is represented by strings of characters and is surrounded by quotes. You must match the quotes surrounding strings. Escape characters enable you to include characters in your string that cannot be typed.

❑   Variables are JavaScript's means of storing data, such as numbers and text, in memory so that they can be used again and again in your code.

❑   Variable names must not include certain illegal characters, like the percent sign (%) and the ampersand (&), or be a reserved word, like `with`.

❑   Before you can give a value to a variable, you must declare its existence to the JavaScript interpreter.

❑   JavaScript has the four basic math operators, represented by the symbols plus (+), minus (–), star (*), and forward slash (/). To assign values of a calculation to a variable, you use the equals sign (=), termed the assignment operator.

❑   Operators have different levels of precedence, so multiplication and division will be calculated before addition and subtraction.

❑   Strings can be joined, or concatenated, to produce one big string by means of the + operator. When numbers and strings are concatenated with the + operator, JavaScript automatically converts the number into a string.

❑   Although JavaScript's automatic data conversion suits us most of the time, there are occasions when you need to force the conversion of data. You saw how `parseInt()` and `parseFloat()` can be used to convert strings to numbers. Attempting to convert strings that won't convert will result in `NaN` (Not a Number) being returned.

❑   Arrays are a special type of variable that can hold more than one piece of data. The data are inserted and accessed by means of a unique index number.

Exercise Questions

Suggested solutions to these questions can be found in Appendix A.

1. Write a JavaScript program to convert degrees centigrade into degrees Fahrenheit, and to write the result to the page in a descriptive sentence. The JavaScript equation for Fahrenheit to centigrade is as follows:

```
degFahren = 9 / 5 * degCent + 32
```

2. The following code uses the `prompt()` function to get two numbers from the user. It then adds those two numbers together and writes the result to the page:

```
<!DOCTYPE html PUBLIC "-//W3C//DTD XHTML 1.0 Transitional//EN"
"http://www.w3.org/TR/xhtml1/DTD/xhtml1-transitional.dtd">
<html xmlns="http://www.w3.org/1999/xhtml">
<script language="JavaScript" type="text/javascript">

var firstNumber = prompt("Enter the first number","");
var secondNumber = prompt("Enter the second number","");
var theTotal = firstNumber + secondNumber;
document.write(firstNumber + " added to " + secondNumber + " equals " +
    theTotal);

</script>
</body>
</html>
```

However, if you try the code out, you'll discover that it doesn't work. Why not? Change the code so that it does work.

Decisions, Loops, and Functions

So far, you've seen how to use JavaScript to get user input, perform calculations and tasks with that input, and write the results to a web page. However, a pocket calculator can do all this, so what is it that makes computers different? That is to say, what gives computers the appearance of having intelligence? The answer is the capability to make decisions based on information gathered.

How will decision-making help you in creating web sites? In the last chapter you wrote some code that converted temperature in degrees Fahrenheit to centigrade. You obtained the degrees Fahrenheit from the user using the prompt() function. This worked fine if the user entered a valid number, such as 50. If, however, the user entered something invalid for the Fahrenheit temperature, such as the string aaa, you would find that your code no longer works as expected. Now, if you had some decision-making capabilities in your program, you could check to see if what the user has entered is valid. If it is, you can do the calculation, and if it isn't, you can tell the user why and ask him to enter a valid number.

Validation of user input is probably one of the most common uses of decision making in JavaScript, but it's far from being the only use.

In this chapter you'll look at how decision making is implemented in JavaScript and how you can use it to make your code smarter.

Decision Making — The if and switch Statements

All programming languages enable you to make decisions — that is, they enable the program to follow a certain course of action depending on whether a particular *condition* is met. This is what gives programming languages their intelligence.

For example, in a situation in which you use JavaScript code that is compatible only with version 4 or later browsers, the condition could be that the user is using a version 4 or later browser. If you discover that this condition is not met, you could direct him to a set of pages that are compatible with earlier browsers.

Conditions are comparisons between variables and data, such as the following:

- ❑ Is *A* bigger than *B*?
- ❑ Is *X* equal to *Y*?
- ❑ Is *M* not equal to *N*?

For example, if the variable `browserVersion` held the version of the browser that the user was using, the condition would be this:

Is `browserVersion` greater than or equal to 4?

You'll notice that all of these questions have a yes or no answer — that is, they are Boolean based and can only evaluate to `true` or `false`. How do you use this to create decision-making capabilities in your code? You get the browser to test for whether the condition is `true`. If (and only if) it is `true`, you execute a particular section of code.

Look at another example. Recall from Chapter 1 the natural English instructions used to demonstrate how code flows. One of these instructions for making a cup of coffee is:

Has the kettle boiled? If so, then pour water into cup; otherwise, continue to wait.

This is an example of making a decision. The condition in this instruction is "Has the kettle boiled?" It has a `true` or `false` answer. If the answer is `true`, you pour the water into the cup. If it isn't `true`, you continue to wait.

In JavaScript, you can change the flow of the code's execution depending on whether a condition is `true` or `false`, using an `if` statement or a `switch` statement. You will look at these shortly, but first we need to introduce some new operators that are essential for the definition of conditions — *comparison operators*.

Comparison Operators

In Chapter 2 you saw how mathematical functions, such as addition and division, were represented by symbols, such as plus (+) and forward slash (/), called operators. You also saw that if you want to give a variable a value, you can assign to it a value or the result of a calculation using the equals sign (=), termed the assignment operator.

Decision making also has its own operators, which enable you to test conditions. Comparison operators, just like the mathematical operators you saw in the last chapter, have a left-hand side (LHS) and a right-hand side (RHS), and the comparison is made between the two. The technical terms for these are the *left operand* and the *right operand*. For example, the less-than operator, with the symbol <, is a comparison operator. You could write 23 < 45, which translates as "Is 23 less than 45?" Here, the answer would be `true` (see Figure 3-1).

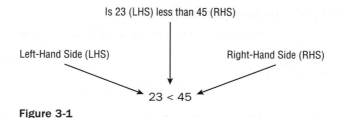

Figure 3-1

There are other comparison operators, the more useful of which are summarized in the following table:

Operator Symbol	Purpose
==	Tests if LHS is equal to RHS
<	Tests if LHS is less than RHS
>	Tests if LHS is greater than RHS
<=	Tests if LHS is less than or equal to RHS
>=	Tests if LHS is greater than or equal to RHS
!=	Tests if LHS is not equal to RHS

You'll see these comparison operators in use in the next section when you look at the if statement.

Precedence

Recall from Chapter 2 that operators have an order of precedence. This applies also to the comparison operators. The == and != comparison operators have the lowest order of precedence, and the rest of the comparison operators, <, >, <=, and >=, have an equal precedence.

All of these comparison operators have a precedence that is below operators, such as +, -, *, and /. This means that if you make a comparison such as 3 * 5 > 2 * 5, the multiplication calculations are worked out first, before their results are compared. However, in these circumstances, it's both safer and clearer if you wrap the calculations on either side inside parentheses, for example, (3 * 5) > (2 * 5). As a general rule, it's a good idea to use parentheses to ensure that the precedence is clear, or you may find yourself surprised by the outcome.

Assignment versus Comparison

One very important point to mention is the ease with which the assignment operator (=) and the comparison operator (==) can be mixed up. Remember that the = operator assigns a value to a variable and that the == operator compares the value of two variables. Even when you have this idea clear, it's amazingly easy to put one equals sign where you meant to put two.

Assigning the Results of Comparisons

You can store the results of a comparison in a variable, as shown in the following example:

```
var age = prompt("Enter age:", "");
var isOverSixty = parseInt(age) > 60;
   document.write("Older than 60: " + isOverSixty);
```

Here you obtain the user's age using the `prompt()` function. This returns, as a string, whatever value the user enters. You then convert that to a number using the `parseInt()` function you saw in the previous chapter and use the greater-than operator to see if it's greater than 60. The result (either true or false) of the comparison will be stored in the variable `isOverSixty`.

If the user enters 35, the `document.write()` on the final line will write this to the page:

```
Older than 60: false
```

If the user entered 61, this will be displayed:

```
Older than 60: true
```

The if Statement

The `if` statement is one you'll find yourself using in almost every program that is more than a couple of lines long. It works very much as it does in the English language. For example, you might say in English, "If the room temperature is more than 80 degrees Fahrenheit, then I'll turn the air conditioning on." In JavaScript, this would translate into something like this:

```
if (roomTemperature > 80)
{
    roomTemperature = roomTemperature - 10;
}
```

How does this work? See Figure 3-2.

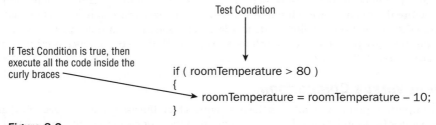

Figure 3-2

Notice that the test condition is placed in parentheses and follows the `if` keyword. Also, note that there is no semicolon at the end of this line. The code to be executed if the condition is `true` is placed in curly braces on the line after the condition, and each of these lines of code does end with a semicolon.

The curly braces, {}, have a special purpose in JavaScript: They mark out a *block* of code. Marking out lines of code as belonging to a single block means that JavaScript will treat them all as one piece of code. If the condition of an `if` statement is `true`, JavaScript executes the next line or block of code following the `if` statement. In the preceding example, the block of code has only one statement, so we could equally as well have written this:

```
if (roomTemperature > 80)
    roomTemperature = roomTemperature - 10;
```

However, if you have a number of lines of code that you want to execute, you need the braces to mark them out as a single block of code. For example, a modified version of the example with three statements of code would have to include the braces.

```
if (roomTemperature > 80)
{
    roomTemperature = roomTemperature - 10;
    alert("It's getting hot in here");
    alert("Air conditioning switched on");
}
```

A particularly easy mistake to make is to forget the braces when marking out a block of code to be executed. Instead of the code in the block being executed when the condition is true, you'll find that *only the first line* after the `if` statement is executed. However, the other lines will always be executed regardless of the outcome of the test condition. To avoid mistakes like these, it's a good idea to always use braces, even where there is only one statement. If you get into this habit, you'll be less likely to leave them out when they are actually needed.

Try It Out   The if Statement

Let's return to the temperature converter example from Chapter 2 and add some decision-making functionality.

1. Enter the following code and save it as ch3_examp1.htm:

```
<!DOCTYPE html PUBLIC "-//W3C//DTD XHTML 1.0 Transitional//EN"
"http://www.w3.org/TR/xhtml1/DTD/xhtml1-transitional.dtd">
<html xmlns="http://www.w3.org/1999/xhtml">
<body>

<script type="text/javascript">

var degFahren = Number(prompt("Enter the degrees Fahrenheit",32));
var degCent;

degCent = 5/9 * (degFahren - 32);

document.write(degFahren + "\xB0 Fahrenheit is " + degCent +
    "\xB0 centigrade<br />");

if (degCent < 0)
{
    document.write("That's below the freezing point of water");
```

```
}

if (degCent == 100)
   document.write("That's the boiling point of water");

</script>

</body>
</html>
```

2. Load the page into your browser and enter 32 into the prompt box for the Fahrenheit value to be converted. With a value of 32, neither of the if statement's conditions will be true, so the only line written in the page will be that shown in Figure 3-3.

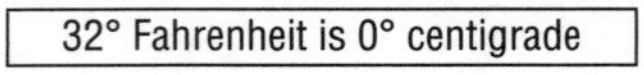

```
32° Fahrenheit is 0° centigrade
```

Figure 3-3

3. Now reload the page and enter 31 for the Fahrenheit value. This time you'll see two lines in the page, as shown in Figure 3-4.

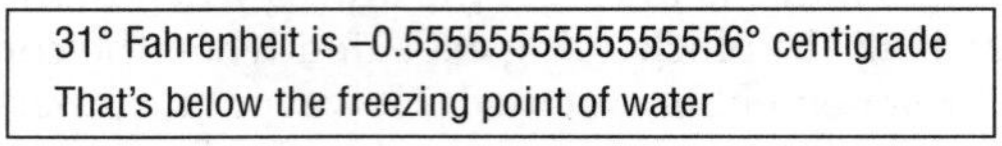

```
31° Fahrenheit is −0.5555555555555556° centigrade
That's below the freezing point of water
```

Figure 3-4

4. Finally, reload the page again, but this time, enter 212 in the prompt box. The two lines shown in Figure 3-5 will appear in the page.

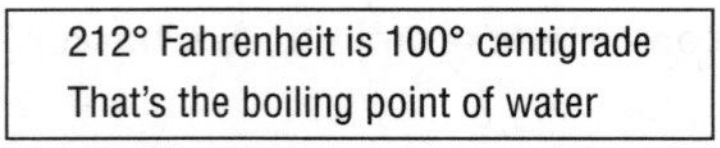

```
212° Fahrenheit is 100° centigrade
That's the boiling point of water
```

Figure 3-5

The first part of the script block in this page is taken from the example ch2_examp4.htm in Chapter 2. You declare two variables, degFahren and degCent. The variable degFahren is given an initial value obtained from the user with the prompt() function. Note the prompt() function returns a string value, which you then explicitly convert to a numeric value using the Number() function. The variable degCent is then set to the result of the calculation 5/9 * (degFahren - 32), which is the Fahrenheit-to-centigrade conversion calculation.

```
var degFahren = Number(prompt("Enter the degrees Fahrenheit",32));
var degCent;

degCent = 5/9 * (degFahren - 32);
```

Then you write the result of your calculation to the page.

```
document.write(degFahren + "\xB0 Fahrenheit is " + degCent +
   "\xB0 centigrade<br />");
```

Now comes the new code; the first of two `if` statements.

```
if (degCent < 0)
{
    document.write("That's below the freezing point of water");
}
```

This `if` statement has the condition that asks, "Is the value of the variable `degCent` less than zero?" If the answer is yes (`true`), the code inside the curly braces executes. In this case, you write a sentence to the page using `document.write()`. If the answer is no (`false`), the processing moves on to the next line after the closing brace. Also worth noting is the fact that the code inside the `if` statement's opening brace is indented. This is not necessary, but it is a good practice to get into because it makes your code much easier to read.

When trying out the example, you started by entering 32, so that `degFahren` will be initialized to 32. In this case the calculation `degCent = 5/9 * (degFahren - 32)` will set `degCent` to 0. So the answer to the question "Is `degCent` less than zero?" is `false`, because `degCent` is equal to zero, not less than zero. The code inside the curly braces will be skipped and never executed. In this case, the next line to be executed will be the second `if` statement's condition, which we'll discuss shortly.

When you entered 31 in the prompt box, `degFahren` was set to 31, so the variable `degCent` will be -0.55555555556. So how does your `if` statement look now? It evaluates to "Is -0.55555555556 less than zero?" The answer this time is `true`, and the code inside the braces, here just a `document.write()` statement, executes.

Finally, when you entered 212, how did this alter the `if` statement? The variable `degCent` is set to 100 by the calculation, so the `if` statement now asks the question, "Is 100 less than zero?" The answer is `false`, and the code inside the braces will be skipped over.

In the second `if` statement, you evaluate the condition "Is the value of variable `degCent` equal to 100?"

```
if (degCent == 100)
    document.write("That's the boiling point of water");
```

There are no braces here, so if the condition is `true`, the only code to execute is the first line below the `if` statement. When you want to execute multiple lines in the case of the condition being `true`, braces are required.

You saw that when `degFahren` is 32, `degCent` will be 0. So your `if` statement will be "Is 0 equal to 100?" The answer is clearly `false`, and the code won't execute. Again, when you set `degFahren` to 31, `degCent` will be calculated to be -0.55555555556; "Is -0.55555555556 equal to 100?" is also `false`, and the code won't execute.

Finally, when `degFahren` is set to 212, `degCent` will be 100. This time the `if` statement is "Is 100 equal to 100?" and the answer is `true`, so the `document.write()` statement executes.

As you have seen already, one of the most common errors in JavaScript, even for experts, is using one equals sign for evaluating, rather than the necessary two. Take a look at the following code extract:

```
if (degCent = 100)
    document.write("That's the boiling point of water");
```

This condition will always evaluate to `true`, and the code below the `if` statement will always execute. Worse still, your variable `degCent` will be set to 100. Why? Because a single equals sign assigns values to a variable; only a double equals sign compares values. The reason an assignment always evaluates to `true` is that the result of the assignment expression is the value of the right-hand side expression and this is the number `100`, which is then implicitly converted to a Boolean and any number besides `0` and `NaN` converts to `true`.

Logical Operators

You should have a general idea of how to use conditions in `if` statements now, but how do you use a condition such as "Is `degFahren` greater than zero but less than 100?" There are two conditions to test here. You need to test whether `degFahren` is greater than zero *and* whether `degFahren` is less than 100.

JavaScript enables you to use such multiple conditions. To do this, you need to learn about three more operators: the logical operators AND, OR, and NOT. The symbols for these are listed in the following table.

Operator	Symbol
AND	&&
OR	||
NOT	!

Notice that the AND and OR operators are *two* symbols repeated: `&&` and `||`. If you type just one symbol, `&` or `|`, strange things will happen because these are special operators called *bitwise operators* used in binary operations — for logical operations you must always use two.

After you've learned about the three logical operators, you'll take a look at how to use them in `if` statements, with plenty of practical examples. So if it seems a bit confusing on first read, don't panic. All will become clear. Let's look at how each of these works, starting with the AND operator.

AND

Recall that we talked about the left-hand side (LHS) and the right-hand side (RHS) of the operator. The same is true with the AND operator. However, now the LHS and RHS of the condition are Boolean values (usually the result of a condition).

The AND operator works very much as it does in English. For example, you might say, "If I feel cold *and* I have a coat, then I'll put my coat on." Here, the left-hand side of the "and" word is "Do I feel cold?" and this can be evaluated as `true` or `false`. The right-hand side is "Do I have a coat?" which again is evaluated to either `true` or `false`. If the left-hand side is true (I am cold) *and* the right-hand side is true (I do have a coat), then you put your coat on.

This is very similar to how the AND operator works in JavaScript. The AND operator actually produces a result, just as adding two numbers together produces a result. However, the AND operator takes two Boolean values (on its LHS and RHS) and results in another Boolean value. If the LHS and RHS conditions evaluate to `true`, the result will be `true`. In any other circumstance, the result will be `false`.

Following is a *truth table* of possible evaluations of left-hand sides and right-hand sides and the result when AND is used.

Left-Hand Side	Right-Hand Side	Result
true	true	true
false	true	false
true	false	false
false	false	false

Although the table is, strictly speaking, true, it's worth noting that JavaScript doesn't like doing unnecessary work. Well, who does! If the left-hand side is false, even if the right-hand side does evaluate to true, it won't make any difference to the final result — it'll still be false. So to avoid wasting time, if the left-hand side is false, JavaScript doesn't even bother checking the right-hand side and just returns a result of false.

OR

Just like AND, OR also works much as it does in English. For example, you might say that if it is raining *or* if it is snowing, then you'll take an umbrella. If either of the conditions "it is raining" or "it is snowing" is true, you will take an umbrella.

Again, just like AND, the OR operator acts on two Boolean values (one from its left-hand side and one from its right-hand side) and returns another Boolean value. If the left-hand side evaluates to true or the right-hand side evaluates to true, the result returned is true. Otherwise, the result is false. The following table shows the possible results.

Left-Hand Side	Right-Hand Side	Result
true	true	true
false	true	true
true	false	true
false	false	false

As with the AND operator, JavaScript likes to avoid doing things that make no difference to the final result. If the left-hand side is true, then whether the right-hand side is true or false makes no difference to the final result — it'll still be true. So, to avoid work, if the left-hand side is true, the right-hand side is not evaluated, and JavaScript simply returns true. The end result is the same — the only difference is in how JavaScript arrives at the conclusion. However, it does mean you should not rely on the right-hand side of the OR operator to be executed.

NOT

In English, we might say, "If I'm *not* hot, then I'll eat soup." The condition being evaluated is whether we're hot. The result is true or false, but in this example we act (eat soup) if the result is false.

However, JavaScript is used to executing code only if a condition is `true`. So if you want a `false` condition to cause code to execute, you need to switch that `false` value to true (and any `true` value to `false`). That way you can trick JavaScript into executing code after a `false` condition.

You do this using the NOT operator. This operator reverses the logic of a result; it takes one Boolean value and changes it to the other Boolean value. So it changes `true` to `false` and `false` to true. This is sometimes called *negation*.

To use the NOT operator, you put the condition you want reversed in parentheses and put the ! symbol in front of the parentheses. For example:

```
if (!(degCent < 100))
{
    // Some code
}
```

Any code within the braces will be executed only if the condition degCent < 100 is false.

The following table details the possible results when using NOT.

Right-Hand Side	Result
true	false
false	true

Multiple Conditions Inside an if Statement

The previous section started by asking how you could use the condition "Is degFahren greater than zero but less than 100?" One way of doing this would be to use two if statements, one nested inside another. *Nested* simply means that there is an outer if statement, and inside this an inner if statement. If the condition for the outer if statement is true, then (and only then) the nested inner if statement's condition will be tested.

Using nested if statements, your code would be:

```
if (degCent < 100)
{
    if (degCent > 0)
    {
        document.write("degCent is between 0 and 100");
    }
}
```

This would work, but it's a little verbose and can be quite confusing. JavaScript offers a better alternative — using multiple conditions inside the condition part of the if statement. The multiple conditions are strung together with the logical operators you just looked at. So the preceding code could be rewritten like this:

```
if (degCent > 0 && degCent < 100)
{
    document.write("degCent is between 0 and 100");
}
```

The if statement's condition first evaluates whether degCent is greater than zero. If that is true, the code goes on to evaluate whether degCent is less than 100. Only if both of these conditions are true will the document.write() code line execute.

Try It Out   Multiple Conditions

This example demonstrates multi-condition if statements using the AND, OR, and NOT operators. Type the following code, and save it as ch3_examp2.htm:

```
<!DOCTYPE html PUBLIC "-//W3C//DTD XHTML 1.0 Transitional//EN"
 "http://www.w3.org/TR/xhtml1/DTD/xhtml1-transitional.dtd">
<html xmlns="http://www.w3.org/1999/xhtml">
<body>

<script type="text/javascript">

var myAge = Number(prompt("Enter your age",30));

if (myAge >= 0 && myAge <= 10)
{
    document.write("myAge is between 0 and 10<br />");
}

if ( !(myAge >= 0 && myAge <= 10) )
{
    document.write("myAge is NOT between 0 and 10<br />");
}

if ( myAge >= 80 || myAge <= 10 )
{
    document.write("myAge is 80 or above OR 10 or below<br />");
}

if ( (myAge >= 30 && myAge <= 39) || (myAge >= 80 && myAge <= 89) )
{
    document.write("myAge is between 30 and 39 or myAge is between 80 and 89");
}

</script>

</body>
</html>
```

When you load it into your browser, a prompt box should appear. Enter the value 30, then press Return, and the lines shown in Figure 3-6 are written to the web page.

```
myAge is NOT between 0 and 10
myAge is between 30 and 39 or myAge is between 80 and 89
```

Figure 3-6

The script block starts by defining the variable myAge and initializing it to the value entered by the user in the prompt box and converted to a number.

```
var myAge = Number(prompt("Enter your age",30));
```

After this are four if statements, each using multiple conditions. You'll look at each in detail in turn.

The easiest way to work out what multiple conditions are doing is to split them up into smaller pieces and then evaluate the combined result. In this example you have entered the value 30, which has been stored in the variable myAge. You'll substitute this value into the conditions to see how they work.

Here's the first if statement:

```
if (myAge >= 0 && myAge <= 10)
{
    document.write("myAge is between 0 and 10<br />");
}
```

The first if statement is asking the question "Is myAge between 0 and 10?" You'll take the LHS of the condition first, substituting your particular value for myAge. The LHS asks "Is 30 greater than or equal to 0?" The answer is true. The question posed by the RHS condition is "Is 30 less than or equal to 10?" The answer is false. These two halves of the condition are joined using &&, which indicates the AND operator. Using the AND results table shown earlier, you can see that if LHS is true and RHS is false, you have an overall result of false. So the end result of the condition for the if statement is false, and the code inside the braces won't execute.

Let's move on to the second if statement.

```
if ( !(myAge >= 0 && myAge <= 10) )
{
    document.write("myAge is NOT between 0 and 10<br />");
}
```

The second if statement is posing the question "Is myAge not between 0 and 10?" Its condition is similar to that of the first if statement, but with one small difference: You have enclosed the condition inside parentheses and put the NOT operator (!) in front.

The part of the condition inside the parentheses is evaluated and, as before, produces the same result — false. However, the NOT operator reverses the result and makes it true. Because the if statement's condition is true, the code inside the braces *will* execute this time, causing a document.write() to write a response to the page.

What about the third if statement?

```
if ( myAge >= 80 || myAge <= 10 )
{
    document.write("myAge is either 80 and above OR 10 or below<br />");
}
```

The third `if` statement asks, "Is `myAge` greater than or equal to 80, or less than or equal to 10?" Taking the LHS condition first — "Is 30 greater than or equal to 80?" — the answer is `false`. The answer to the RHS condition — "Is 30 less than or equal to 10?" — is again `false`. These two halves of the condition are combined using `||`, which indicates the OR operator. Looking at the OR result table earlier in this section, you see that `false` OR `false` produces a result of `false`. So again the `if` statement's condition evaluates to `false`, and the code within the curly braces does not execute.

The final `if` statement is a little more complex.

```
if ( (myAge >= 30 && myAge <= 39) || (myAge >= 80 && myAge <= 89) )
{
    document.write("myAge is between 30 and 39 " +
                "or myAge is between 80 and 89<br />");
}
```

It asks the question, "Is `myAge` between 30 and 39 or between 80 and 89?" Let's break the condition down into its component parts. There is a left-hand-side and a right-hand-side condition, combined by means of an OR operator. However, the LHS and RHS themselves have an LHS and RHS each, which are combined using AND operators. Notice how parentheses are used to tell JavaScript which parts of the condition to evaluate first, just as you would do with numbers in a mathematical calculation.

Let's look at the LHS of the condition first, namely `(myAge >= 30 && myAge <= 39)`. By putting the condition into parentheses, you ensure that it's treated as a single condition; no matter how many conditions are inside the parentheses, it only produces a single result, either `true` or `false`. Breaking down the conditions in the parentheses, you have "Is 30 greater than or equal to 30?" with a result of `true`, and "Is 30 less than or equal to 39?" again with a result of `true`. From the AND table, you know `true` AND `true` produces a result of `true`.

Now let's look at the RHS of the condition, namely `(myAge >= 80 && myAge <= 89)`. Again breaking the condition down, you see that the LHS asks, "Is 30 greater than or equal to 80?" which gives a `false` result, and the RHS asks, "Is 30 less than or equal to 89?" which gives a `true` result. You know that `false` AND `true` gives a `false` result.

Now you can think of your `if` statement's condition as looking like `(true || false)`. Looking at the OR results table, you can see that `true` OR `false` gives a result of `true`, so the code within the braces following the `if` statement will execute, and a line will be written to the page.

However, remember that JavaScript does not evaluate conditions where they won't affect the final result, and the preceding condition is one of those situations. The LHS of the condition evaluated to `true`. After that, it does not matter if the RHS of the condition is `true` or `false` because only one of the conditions in an OR operation needs to be `true` for a result of `true`. Thus JavaScript does not actually evaluate the RHS of the condition. We did so simply for demonstration purposes.

As you have seen, the easiest way to approach understanding or creating multiple conditions is to break them down into the smallest logical chunks. You'll find that with experience, you will do this almost without thinking, unless you have a particularly tricky condition to evaluate.

Although using multiple conditions is often better than using multiple `if` statements, there are times when it makes your code harder to read and therefore harder to understand and debug. It's possible to have 10, 20, or more than 100 conditions inside your `if` statement, but can you imagine trying to read an `if` statement with even 10 conditions? If you feel that your multiple conditions are getting too complex, break them down into smaller logical chunks.

For example, imagine you want to execute some code if myAge is in the ranges 30–39, 80–89, or 100–115, using different code in each case. You could write the statement like so:

```
if ( (myAge >= 30 && myAge <= 39) || (myAge >= 80 && myAge <= 89) ||
    (myAge >= 100 && myAge <= 115) )
{
   document.write("myAge is between 30 and 39 " +
                  "or myAge is between 80 " +
                  "and 89 or myAge is between 100 and 115");
}
```

There's nothing wrong with this, but it is starting to get a little long and difficult to read. Instead, you could create another if statement for the code executed for the 100–115 range.

else and else if

Imagine a situation where you want some code to execute if a certain condition is true and some other code to execute if it is false. You can achieve this by having two if statements, as shown in the following example:

```
if (myAge >= 0 && myAge <= 10)
{
    document.write("myAge is between 0 and 10");
}

if ( !(myAge >= 0 && myAge <= 10) )
{
    document.write("myAge is NOT between 0 and 10");
}
```

The first if statement tests whether myAge is between 0 and 10, and the second for the situation where myAge is not between 0 and 10. However, JavaScript provides an easier way of achieving this: with an else statement. Again, the use of the word else is similar to its use in the English language. You might say, "If it is raining, I will take an umbrella; otherwise I will take a sun hat." In JavaScript you can say if the condition is true, then execute one block of code; else execute an alternative block. Rewriting the preceding code using this technique, you would have the following:

```
if (myAge >= 0 && myAge <= 10)
{
    document.write("myAge is between 0 and 10");
}
else
{
    document.write("myAge is NOT between 0 and 10");
}
```

Writing the code like this makes it simpler and therefore easier to read. Plus it also saves JavaScript from testing a condition to which you already know the answer.

You could also include another `if` statement with the `else` statement. For example

```
if (myAge >= 0 && myAge <= 10)
{
    document.write("myAge is between 0 and 10");
}
else if ( (myAge >= 30 && myAge <= 39) || (myAge >= 80 && myAge <= 89) )
{
    document.write("myAge is between 30 and 39 " +
                   "or myAge is between 80 and 89");
}
else
{
    document.write("myAge is NOT between 0 and 10, " +
                   "nor is it between 30 and 39, nor is it between 80 and 89");
}
```

The first `if` statement checks whether `myAge` is between 0 and 10 and executes some code if that's true. If it's `false`, an `else if` statement checks if `myAge` is between 30 and 39 or 80 and 89, and executes some other code if either of those conditions is `true`. Failing that, you have a final `else` statement, which catches the situation in which the value of `myAge` did not trigger `true` in any of the earlier `if` conditions.

When using `if` and `else if`, you need to be extra careful with your curly braces to ensure that the `if` and `else if` statements start and stop where you expect, and you don't end up with an `else` that doesn't belong to the right `if`. This is quite tricky to describe with words — it's easier to see what we mean with an example.

```
if (myAge >= 0 && myAge <= 10)
{
document.write("myAge is between 0 and 10");
if (myAge == 5)
{
document.write("You're 5 years old");
}
else
{
document.write("myAge is NOT between 0 and 10");
}
```

Notice that we haven't indented the code. Although this does not matter to JavaScript, it does make the code more difficult for humans to read and hides the missing curly brace that should be before the final `else` statement.

Correctly formatted and with the missing bracket inserted, the code looks like this:

```
if (myAge >= 0 && myAge <= 10)
{
    document.write("myAge is between 0 and 10<br />");
    if (myAge == 5)
    {
        document.write("You're 5 years old");
    }
```

```
}
else
{
    document.write("myAge is NOT between 0 and 10");
}
```

As you can see, the code is working now; it is also a lot easier to see which code is part of which `if` block.

Comparing Strings

Up to this point, you have been looking exclusively at using comparison operators with numbers. However, they work just as well with strings. All that's been said and done with numbers applies to strings, but with one important difference. You are now comparing data alphabetically rather than numerically, so there are a few traps to watch out for.

In the following code, you compare the variable `myName`, which contains the string `"Paul"`, with the string literal `"Paul"`.

```
var myName ="Paul";
if (myName == "Paul")
{
    alert("myName is Paul");
}
```

How does JavaScript deal with this? Well, it goes through each letter in turn on the LHS and checks it with the letter in the same position on the RHS to see if it's actually the same. If at any point it finds a difference, it stops, and the result is `false`. If, after having checked each letter in turn all the way to the end, it confirms that they are all the same, it returns `true`. The condition in the preceding `if` statement will return `true`, so you'll see an `alert` box.

However, string comparison in JavaScript is case sensitive. So `"P"` is not the same as `"p"`. Taking the preceding example, but changing the variable `myName` to `"paul"`, you find that the condition is `false` and the code inside the `if` statement does not execute.

```
var myName ="paul";
if (myName == "Paul")
{
    alert("myName is Paul");
}
```

The >=, >, <=, and < operators work with strings as well as with numbers, but again it is an alphabetical comparison. So `"A"` < `"B"` is `true`, because A comes before B in the alphabet. However, JavaScript's case sensitivity comes into play again. `"A"` < `"B"` is `true`, but `"a"` < `"B"` is `false`. Why? Because uppercase letters are treated as always coming *before* lowercase letters. Why is this? Each letter has a code number in the ASCII and Unicode character sets, and the code numbers for uppercase letters are lower than the code numbers for lowercase letters. This is something to watch out for when writing your own code.

The simplest way to avoid confusion with different cases is to convert both strings to either uppercase or lowercase before you compare them. You can do this easily using the `toUpperCase()` or `toLowerCase()` function, which you'll learn about in Chapter 4.

The switch Statement

You saw earlier how the if and else if statements could be used for checking various conditions; if the first condition is not valid, then another is checked, and another, and so on. However, when you want to check the value of a particular variable for a large number of possible values, there is a more efficient alternative, namely the switch statement. The structure of the switch statement is given in Figure 3-7.

The best way to think of the switch statement is "Switch to the code where the case matches." The switch statement has four important elements:

- ❑ The test expression
- ❑ The case statements
- ❑ The break statements
- ❑ The default statement

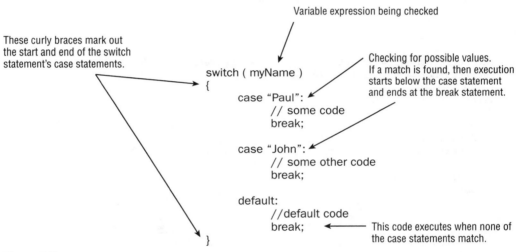

Figure 3-7

The test expression is given in the parentheses following the switch keyword. In the previous example, you are testing using the variable myName. Inside the parentheses, however, you could have any valid expression.

Next come the case statements. The case statements do the condition checking. To indicate which case statements belong to your switch statement, you must put them inside the curly braces following the test expression. Each case statement specifies a value, for example "Paul". The case statement then acts like if (myName == "Paul"). If the variable myName did contain the value "Paul", execution would commence from the code starting below the case "Paul" statement and would continue to the end of the switch statement. This example has only two case statements, but you can have as many as you like.

In most cases, you want only the block of code directly underneath the relevant case statement to execute, not *all* the code below the relevant case statement, including any other case statements.

To achieve this, you put a break statement at the end of the code that you want executed. This tells JavaScript to stop executing at that point and leave the switch statement.

Finally you have the default case, which (as the name suggests) is the code that will execute when none of the other case statements match. The default statement is optional; if you have no default code that you want to execute, you can leave it out, but remember that in this case no code will execute if no case statements match. It is a good idea to include a default case, unless you are absolutely sure that you have all your options covered.

Try It Out   **Using the switch Statement**

Let's take a look at the switch statement in action. The following example illustrates a simple guessing game. Type the code and save it as ch3_examp3.htm.

```
<!DOCTYPE html PUBLIC "-//W3C//DTD XHTML 1.0 Transitional//EN"
"http://www.w3.org/TR/xhtml1/DTD/xhtml1-transitional.dtd">
<html xmlns="http://www.w3.org/1999/xhtml">
<body>

<script type="text/javascript">

var secretNumber = prompt("Pick a number between 1 and 5:", "");
secretNumber = parseInt(secretNumber);

switch (secretNumber)
{
case 1:
   document.write("Too low!");
   break;

case 2:
   document.write("Too low!");
   break;

case 3:
   document.write("You guessed the secret number!");
   break;

case 4:
   document.write("Too high!");
   break;

case 5:
   document.write("Too high!");
   break;

default:
   document.write("You did not enter a number between 1 and 5.");
   break;
}
```

```
        document.write("<br />Execution continues here");

</script>

</body>
</html>
```

Load this into your browser and enter, for example, the value 1 in the prompt box. You should then see something like what is shown in Figure 3-8.

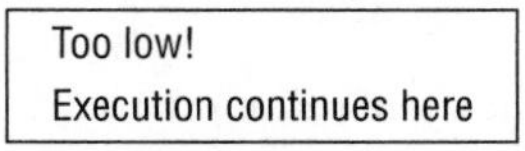

Too low!
Execution continues here

Figure 3-8

If, on the other hand, you enter the value 3, you should see a friendly message letting you know that you guessed the secret number correctly, as shown in Figure 3-9.

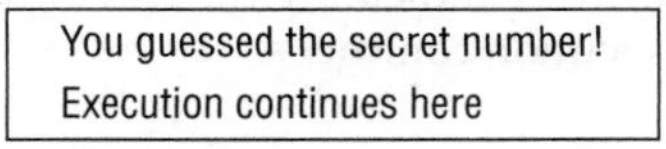

You guessed the secret number!
Execution continues here

Figure 3-9

First you declare the variable `secretNumber` and set it to the value entered by the user via the prompt box. Note that you use the `parseInt()` function to convert the string that is returned from `prompt()` to an integer value.

```
var secretNumber = prompt("Pick a number between 1 and 5:", "");
secretNumber = parseInt(secretNumber);
```

Next you create the start of the `switch` statement.

```
switch (secretNumber)
{
```

The expression in parentheses is simply the variable `secretNumber`, and it's this number that the `case` statements will be compared against.

You specify the block of code encompassing the `case` statements using curly braces. Each `case` statement checks one of the numbers between 1 and 5, because this is what you have specified to the user that she should enter. The first simply outputs a message that the number she has entered is too low.

```
case 1:
    document.write("Too low!");
    break;
```

The second `case` statement, for the value 2, has the same message, so the code is not repeated here. The third `case` statement lets the user know that she has guessed correctly.

```
case 3:
    document.write("You guessed the secret number!");
    break;
```

Finally, the fourth and fifth `case` statements output a message that the number the user has entered is too high.

```
case 4:
    document.write("Too high!");
    break;
```

You do need to add a `default` case in this example, since the user might very well (despite the instructions) enter a number that is not between 1 and 5, or even perhaps a letter. In this case, you add a message to let the user know that there is a problem.

```
default:
    document.write("You did not enter a number between 1 and 5.");
    break;
```

A `default` statement is also very useful for picking up bugs — if you have coded some of the `case` statements incorrectly, you will pick that up very quickly if you see the `default` code being run when it shouldn't be.

You finally have added the closing brace indicating the end of the `switch` statement. After this you output a line to indicate where the execution continues.

```
}
document.write("<br />Execution continues here");
```

Note that each `case` statement ends with a `break` statement. This is important to ensure that execution of the code moves to the line after the end of the `switch` statement. If you forget to include this, you could end up executing the code for each `case` following the `case` that matches.

Executing the Same Code for Different Cases

You may have spotted a problem with the `switch` statement in this example — you want to execute the same code if the user enters a 1 or a 2, and the same code for a 4 or a 5. However, in order to achieve this, you have had to repeat the code in each case. What you want is an easier way of getting JavaScript to execute the same code for different cases. Well, that's easy! Simply change the code so that it looks like this:

```
switch (secretNumber)
{
case 1:
case 2:
    document.write("Too low!");
    break;

case 3:
    document.write("You guessed the secret number!");
    break;

case 4:
case 5:
```

```
      document.write("Too high!");
      break;

   default:
      document.write("You did not enter a number between 1 and 5.");
      break;
}
```

If you load this into your browser and experiment with entering some different numbers, you should see that it behaves exactly like the previous code.

Here, you are making use of the fact that if there is no break statement underneath the code for a certain case statement, execution will continue through each following case statement until a break statement or the end of the switch is reached. Think of it as a sort of free fall through the switch statement until you hit the break statement.

If the case statement for the value 1 is matched, execution simply continues until the break statement under case 2, so effectively you can execute the same code for both cases. The same technique is used for the case statements with values 4 and 5.

Looping — The for and while Statements

Looping means repeating a block of code when a condition is true. This is achieved in JavaScript with the use of two statements, the while statement and the for statement. You'll be looking at these shortly, but why would you want to repeat blocks of code anyway?

Well, take the situation where you have a series of results, say the average temperature for each month in a year, and you want to plot these on a graph. The code needed for plotting each point will most likely be the same. So, rather than write the code 12 times (once for each point), it's much easier to execute the same code 12 times by using the next item of data in the series. This is where the for statement would come in handy, because you know how many times you want the code to execute.

In another situation, you might want to repeat the same piece of code when a certain condition is true, for example, while the user keeps clicking a Start Again button. In this situation, the while statement would be very useful.

The for Loop

The for statement enables you to repeat a block of code a certain number of times. The syntax is illustrated in Figure 3-10.

Let's look at the makeup of a for statement. You can see from Figure 3-10 that, just like the if and switch statements, the for statement also has its logic inside parentheses. However, this time that logic split into three parts, each part separated by a semicolon. For example, in Figure 3-10 you have the following:

```
(var loopCounter = 1; loopCounter <= 3; loopCounter++)
```

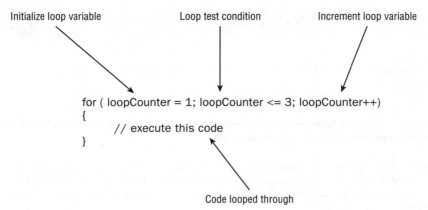

Figure 3-10

The first part of the `for` statement's logic is the *initialization* part of the `for` statement. To keep track of how many times you have looped through the code, you need a variable to keep count. It's in the initialization part that you initialize variables. In the example you have declared `loopCounter` and set it to the value of 1. This part is only executed once during the execution of the loops, unlike the other parts. You don't need to declare the variable if it was declared earlier in the code.

```
var loopCounter;
for (loopCounter = 1; loopCounter <= 3; loopCounter++)
```

Following the semicolon, you have the *test condition* part of the `for` statement. The code inside the `for` statement will keep executing for as long as this test condition evaluates to `true`. After the code is looped through each time, this condition is tested. In Figure 3-10, you execute for as long as `loopCounter` is less than or equal to 3. The number of times a loop is performed is often called the number of *iterations*.

Finally, you have the *increment* part of the `for` loop, where variables in our loop's test condition have their values incremented. Here you can see that `loopCounter` is incremented by one by means of the `++` operator you saw in Chapter 2. Again, this part of the `for` statement is repeated with every loop of the code. Although we call it the increment part, it can actually be used to decrease or *decrement* the value — for example, if you wanted to count down from the top element in an array to the first.

After the `for` statement comes the block of code that will be executed repeatedly, as long as the test condition is `true`. This block of code is contained within curly braces. If the condition is never `true`, even at the first test of the loop condition, then the code inside the `for` loop will be skipped over and never executed.

Putting all this together, how does the `for` loop work?

1. Execute initialization part of the `for` statement.

2. Check the test condition. If `true`, continue; if not, exit the `for` statement.

3. Execute code in the block after the `for` statement.

4. Execute the increment part of the `for` statement.

5. Repeat steps 2 through 4 until the test condition is `false`.

Try It Out   **Converting a Series of Fahrenheit Values**

Let's change the temperature converter so that it converts a series of values, stored in an array, from Fahrenheit to centigrade. You will be using the `for` statement to go through each element of the array. Type the code and save it as ch3_examp4.htm.

```
<!DOCTYPE html PUBLIC "-//W3C//DTD XHTML 1.0 Transitional//EN"
"http://www.w3.org/TR/xhtml1/DTD/xhtml1-transitional.dtd">
<html xmlns="http://www.w3.org/1999/xhtml">
<body>

<script type="text/javascript">

var degFahren = new Array(212, 32, -459.15);
var degCent = new Array();
var loopCounter;

for (loopCounter = 0; loopCounter <= 2; loopCounter++)
{
    degCent[loopCounter] = 5/9 * (degFahren[loopCounter] - 32);
}

for (loopCounter = 2; loopCounter >= 0; loopCounter--)
{
    document.write("Value " + loopCounter + " was " + degFahren[loopCounter] +
                " degrees Fahrenheit");
    document.write(" which is " + degCent[loopCounter] +
                " degrees centigrade<br />");
}

</script>

</body>
</html>
```

On loading this into your browser, you'll see a series of three lines in the page, containing the results of converting our array of Fahrenheit values into centigrade (as shown in Figure 3-11).

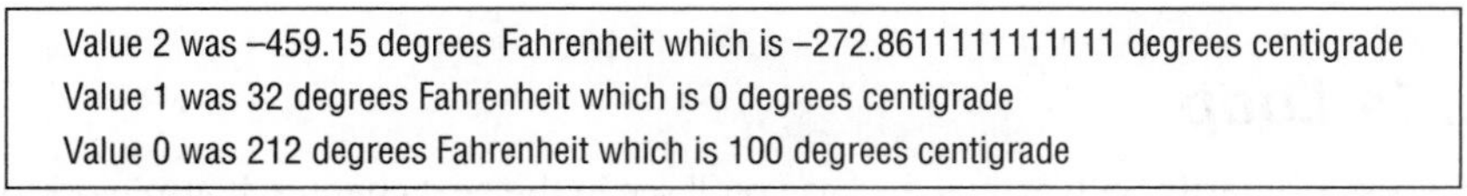

```
Value 2 was −459.15 degrees Fahrenheit which is −272.8611111111111 degrees centigrade
Value 1 was 32 degrees Fahrenheit which is 0 degrees centigrade
Value 0 was 212 degrees Fahrenheit which is 100 degrees centigrade
```

Figure 3-11

The first task is to declare the variables you are going to use. First, you declare and initialize degFahren to contain an array of three values: 212, 32, and −459.15. Next, degCent is declared as an empty array.

Finally, loopCounter is declared and will be used to keep track of which array index you are accessing during your looping.

```
var degFahren = new Array(212, 32, -459.15);
var degCent = new Array();
var loopCounter;
```

Following this comes our first for loop.

```
for (loopCounter = 0; loopCounter <= 2; loopCounter++)
{
    degCent[loopCounter] = 5/9 * (degFahren[loopCounter] - 32);
}
```

In the first line, you start by initializing the loopCounter to 0. Then the for loop's test condition, loopCounter <= 2, is checked. If this condition is true, the loop executes for the first time. After the code inside the curly braces has executed, the incrementing part of the for loop, loopCounter++, will be executed, and then the test condition will be re-evaluated. If it's still true, another execution of the loop code is performed. This continues until the for loop's test condition evaluates to false, at which point looping will end, and the first statement after the closing curly brace will be executed.

The code inside the curly braces is the equation you saw in earlier examples, only this time you are placing its result into the degCent array, with the index being the value of loopCounter.

In the second for loop, you write the results contained in the degCent array to the screen.

```
for (loopCounter = 2; loopCounter >= 0; loopCounter--)
{
    document.write("Value " + loopCounter + " was " + degFahren[loopCounter] +
                " degrees Fahrenheit");
    document.write(" which is " + degCent[loopCounter] +
                " degrees centigrade<br />");
}
```

This time you're counting *down* from 2 to 0. The variable loopCounter is initialized to 2, and the loop condition remains true until loopCounter is less than 0. This time loopCounter is actually decremented each time rather than incremented, by means of loopCounter--. Again, loopCounter is serving a dual purpose: It keeps count of how many loops you have done and also provides the index position in the array.

> *Note that in these examples, you've used whole numbers in your loops. However, there is no reason why you can't use fractional numbers, although it's much less common to do so.*

The for...in Loop

This loop works primarily with arrays, and as you'll see in the next chapter, it also works with something called objects. It enables you to loop through each element in the array without having to know how many elements the array actually contains. In plain English, what this loop says is "For each element in the array, execute some code." Rather than having to work out the index number of each element, the for...in loop does it for you and automatically moves to the next index with each iteration (loop through).

Its syntax for use with arrays is:

```
for (index in arrayName)
{
    //some code
}
```

In this code extract, `index` is a variable you declare prior to the loop, which will automatically be populated with the next index value in the array. `arrayName` is the name of the variable holding the array you want to loop through.

Let's look at an example to make things clearer. You'll define an array and initialize it with three values.

```
var myArray = new Array("Paul","Paula","Pauline");
```

To access each element using a conventional `for` loop, you'd write this:

```
var loopCounter;
for (loopCounter = 0; loopCounter < 3; loopCounter++)
{
    document.write(myArray[loopCounter]);
}
```

To do exactly the same thing with the `for...in` loop, you write this:

```
var elementIndex;
for (elementIndex in myArray)
{
    document.write(myArray[elementIndex]);
}
```

As you can see, the code in the second example is a little clearer, as well as shorter. Both methods work equally well and will iterate three times. However, if you increase the size of the array, for example, by adding the element `myArray[3] = "Philip"`, the first method will still loop only through the first three elements in the array, whereas the second method will loop through all four elements.

The while Loop

Whereas the `for` loop is used for looping a certain number of times, the `while` loop enables you to test a condition and keep on looping while it's true. The `for` loop is useful when you know how many times you need to loop, for example when you are looping through an array that you know has a certain number of elements. The `while` loop is more useful when you don't know how many times you'll need to loop. For example, if you are looping through an array of temperature values and want to continue looping when the temperature value contained in the array element is less than `100`, you will need to use the `while` statement.

Let's take a look at the structure of the `while` statement, as illustrated in Figure 3-12.

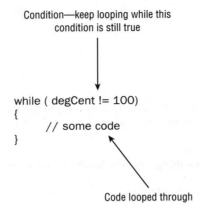

Condition—keep looping while this
condition is still true

```
while ( degCent != 100)
{
        // some code
}
```

Code looped through

Figure 3-12

You can see that the while loop has fewer parts to it than the for loop. The while loop consists of a condition which, if it evaluates to true, causes the block of code inside the curly braces to execute once; then the condition is re-evaluated. If it's still true, the code is executed again, the condition is re-evaluated, and so on until the condition evaluates to false.

One thing to watch out for is that if the condition is false to start with, the while loop never executes. For example:

```
degCent = 100;

while (degCent != 100)
{
        // some code
}
```

Here, the loop will run if degCent does not equal 100. However, since degCent is 100, the condition is false, and the code never executes.

In practice you would normally expect the loop to execute once; whether it executes again will depend on what the code inside the loop has done to variables involved in the loop condition. For example:

```
degCent = new Array();
degFahren = new Array(34, 123, 212);
var loopCounter = 0;
while (loopCounter < 3)
{
    degCent[loopCounter] = 5/9 * (degFahren[loopCounter] - 32);
    loopCounter++;
}
```

The loop will execute so long as loopCounter is less than 3. It's the code inside the loop (loopCounter++;) that increments loopCounter and will eventually cause loopCounter < 3 to be false so that the loop stops. Execution will then continue on the first line after the closing brace of the while statement.

Something to watch out for is the *infinite loop* — a loop that will never end. Suppose you forgot to include the `loopCounter++;` line in the code. Leaving this line out would mean that `loopCounter` will remain at 0, so the condition `(loopCounter < 3)` will always be `true`, and the loop will continue until the user gets bored and cross, and shuts down her browser. However, it is an easy mistake to make and one JavaScript won't warn you about.

It's not just missing lines that can cause infinite loops but also mistakes inside the loop's code. For example:

```
var testVariable = 0;
while (testVariable <= 10)
{
    alert("Test Variable is " + testVariable);
    testVariable++;
    if (testVariable = 10)
    {
        alert("The last loop");
    }
}
```

See if you can spot the deliberate mistake that leads to an infinite loop — yes, it's the `if` statement that will cause this code to go on forever. Instead of using == as the comparison operator in the condition of the `if` statement, you put =, so `testVariable` is set to 10 again in each loop, despite the line `testVariable++`. This means that at the start of each loop, the test condition always evaluates to `true`, since 10 is less than or equal to 10. Put the extra = in to make `if (testVariable == 10)`, and everything is fine.

The do...while loop

With the `while` loop, you saw that the code inside the loop only executes if the condition is `true`; if it's `false`, the code never executes, and execution instead moves to the first line after the `while` loop. However, there may be times when you want the code in the `while` loop to execute at least once, regardless of whether the condition in the `while` statement evaluates to `true`. It might even be that some code inside the `while` loop needs to be executed before you can test the `while` statement's condition. It's situations like this for which the `do...while` loop is ideal.

Look at an example in which you want to get the user's age via a prompt box. You want to show the prompt box but also make sure that what the user has entered is a number.

```
var userAge;
do
{
    userAge = prompt("Please enter your age","")
}
while (isNaN(userAge) == true);
```

The code line within the loop —

```
userAge = prompt("Please enter your age","")
```

— will be executed regardless of the `while` statement's condition. This is because the condition is not checked *until* one loop has been executed. If the condition is `true`, the code is looped through again. If it's `false`, looping stops.

Note that within the `while` statement's condition, you are using the `isNaN()` function that you saw in Chapter 2. This checks whether the `userAge` variable's value is NaN (not a number). If it is not a number, the condition returns a value of `true`; otherwise it returns `false`. As you can see from the example, it enables you to test the user input to ensure the right data has been entered. The user might lie about his age, but at least you know he entered a number!

The `do...while` loop is fairly rare; there's not much you can't do without it, so it's best avoided unless really necessary.

The break and continue Statements

You met the `break` statement earlier when you looked at the `switch` statement. Its function inside a `switch` statement is to stop code execution and move execution to the next line of code after the closing curly brace of the `switch` statement. However, the `break` statement can also be used as part of the `for` and `while` loops when you want to exit the loop prematurely. For example, suppose you're looping through an array, as you did in the temperature conversion example, and you hit an invalid value. In this situation, you might want to stop the code in its tracks, notify the user that the data is invalid, and leave the loop. This is one situation where the `break` statement comes in handy.

Let's see how you could change the example where you converted a series of Fahrenheit values (ch3_examp4.htm) so that if you hit a value that's not a number you stop the loop and let the user know about the invalid data.

```
<script language="JavaScript" type="text/javascript">
var degFahren = new Array(212, "string data", -459.67);
var degCent = new Array();
var loopCounter;

for (loopCounter = 0; loopCounter <= 2; loopCounter++)
{
    if (isNaN(degFahren[loopCounter]))
       {
           alert("Data '" + degFahren[loopCounter] + "' at array index " +
               loopCounter + " is invalid");
           break;
       }

    degCent[loopCounter] = 5/9 * (degFahren[loopCounter] - 32);
}
```

You have changed the initialization of the `degFahren` array so that it now contains some invalid data. Then, inside the `for` loop, an `if` statement is added to check whether the data in the `degFahren` array is not a number. This is done by means of the `isNaN()` function; it returns `true` if the value passed to it in the parentheses, here `degFahren[loopCounter]`, is not a number. If the value is not a number, you tell the user where in the array you have the invalid data. Then you break out of the `for` loop altogether, using the `break` statement, and code execution continues on the first line after the end of the `for` statement.

That's the `break` statement, but what about `continue`? The `continue` statement is similar to `break` in that it stops the execution of a loop at the point where it is found, but instead of leaving the loop, it starts execution at the next iteration, starting with the `for` or `while` statement's condition being re-evaluated, just as if the last line of the loop's code had been reached.

In the `break` example, it was all or nothing — if even one piece of data was invalid, you broke out of the loop. It might be better if you tried to convert all the values in `degFahren`, but if you hit an invalid item of data in the array, you notify the user and continue with the next item, rather than giving up as our `break` statement example does.

```
if (isNaN(degFahren[loopCounter]))
    {
        alert("Data '" + degFahren[loopCounter] + "' at array index " +
            loopCounter + " is invalid");
        continue;
    }
```

Just change the `break` statement to a `continue`. You will still get a message about the invalid data, but the third value will also be converted.

Functions

A function is something that performs a particular task. Take a pocket calculator as an example. It performs lots of basic calculations, such as addition and subtraction. However, many also have function keys that perform more complex operations. For example, some calculators have a button for calculating the square root of a number, and others even provide statistical functions, such as the calculation of an average. Most of these functions could be done with the basic mathematical operations of add, subtract, multiply, and divide, but that might take a lot of steps — it's much simpler for the user if she only needs to press one button. All she needs to do is provide the data — numbers in this case — and the function key does the rest.

Functions in JavaScript work a little like the function buttons on a pocket calculator: They encapsulate a block of code that performs a certain task. Over the course of the book so far, you have come across a number of handy built-in functions that perform a certain task, such as the `parseInt()` and `parseFloat()` functions, which convert strings to numbers, and the `isNaN()` function, which tells you whether a particular value can be converted to a number. Some of these functions return data, such as `parseInt()`, which returns an integer number; others simply perform an action but return no data. You'll also notice that some functions can be passed data, whereas others cannot. For example, the `isNaN()` function needs to be passed some data, which it checks to see if it is `NaN`. The data that a function requires to be passed are known as its *parameter(s)*.

As you work your way through the book, you'll be coming across many more useful built-in functions, but wouldn't it be great to be able to write your own functions? After you've worked out, written, and debugged a block of code to perform a certain task, it would be nice to be able to call it again and again when you need it. JavaScript gives us the ability to do just that, and this is what you'll be concentrating on in this section.

Creating Your Own Functions

Creating and using your own functions is very simple. Figure 3-13 shows an example of a function.

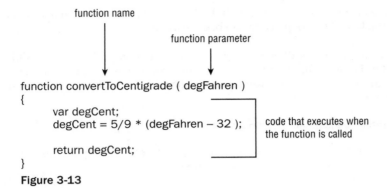

Figure 3-13

You've probably already realized what this function does and how the code works. Yes, it's the infamous Fahrenheit-to-centigrade conversion code again.

Each function you define in JavaScript must be given a unique name for that particular page. The name comes immediately after the `function` keyword. To make life easier for yourself, try using meaningful names so that when you see it being used later in your code, you'll know exactly what it does. For example, a function that takes as its parameters someone's birthday and today's date and returns the person's age could be called `getAge()`. However, the names you can use are limited, much as variable names are. For example, you can't use words reserved by JavaScript, so you can't call your function `with()` or `while()`.

The parameters for the function are given in parentheses after the function's name. A parameter is just an item of data that the function needs to be given in order to do its job. Usually, not passing the required parameters will result in an error. A function can have zero or more parameters, though even if it has no parameters, you must still put the open and close parentheses after its name. For example, the top of your function definition must look like the following:

```
function myNoParamFunction()
```

You then write the code, which the function will execute when called on to do so. All the function code must be put in a block with a pair of curly braces.

Functions also give you the ability to return a value from a function to the code that called it. You use the `return` statement to return a value. In the example function given earlier, you return the value of the variable `degCent`, which you have just calculated. You don't have to return a value if you don't want to, but you should always include a `return` statement at the end of your function, although JavaScript is a very forgiving language and won't have a problem if you don't use a `return` statement at all.

When JavaScript comes across a `return` statement in a function, it treats it a bit like a `break` statement in a `for` loop — it exits the function, returning any value specified after the `return` keyword.

You'll probably find it useful to build up a "library" of functions that you use frequently in JavaScript code, which you can cut and paste into your page whenever you need them.

Having created your functions, how do you use them? Unlike the code you've seen so far, which executes when JavaScript reaches that line, functions only execute if you ask them to, which is termed *calling* or *invoking* the function. You call a function by writing its name at the point where you want it to be called and making sure that you pass any parameters it needs, separated by commas. For example:

```
myTemp = convertToCentigrade(212);
```

This line calls the `convertToCentigrade()` function you saw earlier, passing `212` as the parameter and storing the `return` value from the function (that is, `100`) in the `myTemp` variable.

Have a go at creating your own functions now, taking a closer look at how parameters are passed. Parameter passing can be a bit confusing, so you'll first create a simple function that takes just one parameter (the user's name) and writes it to the page in a friendly welcome string. First, you need to think of a name for your function. A short but descriptive name is `writeUserWelcome()`. Now you need to define what parameters the function expects to be passed. There's only one parameter — the user name. Defining parameters is a little like defining variables — you need to stick to the same rules for naming, so that means no spaces, special characters, or reserved words. Let's call your parameter `userName`. You need to add it inside parentheses to the end of the function name (note that you don't put a semicolon at the end of the line).

```
function writeUserWelcome(userName)
```

Okay, now you have defined your function name and its parameters; all that's left is to create the function body — that is, the code that will be executed when the function is called. You mark out this part of the function by wrapping it in curly braces.

```
function writeUserWelcome(userName)
{
    document.write("Welcome to my website " + userName + "<br />");
    document.write("Hope you enjoy it!");
}
```

The code is simple enough; you write out a message to the web page using `document.write()`. You can see that `userName` is used just as you'd use any normal variable; in fact, it's best to think of parameters as normal variables. The value that the parameter has will be that specified by the JavaScript code where the function was called.

Let's see how you would call this function.

```
writeUserWelcome("Paul");
```

Simple, really — just write the name of the function you want to call, and then in parentheses add the data to be passed to each of the parameters, here just one piece. When the code in the function is executed, the variable `userName`, used in the body of the function code, will contain the text `"Paul"`.

Suppose you wanted to pass two parameters to your function — what would you need to change? Well, first you'd have to alter the function definition. Imagine that the second parameter will hold the user's age — you could call it `userAge` since that makes it pretty clear what the parameter's data represents. Here is the new code:

```
function writeUserWelcome(userName, userAge)
{
    document.write("Welcome to my website" + userName + "<br />");
```

```
        document.write("Hope you enjoy it<br />");
        document.write("Your age is " + userAge);
}
```

You've added a line to the body of the function that uses the parameter you have added. To call the function, you'd write the following:

```
writeUserWelcome("Paul",31);
```

The second parameter is a number, so there is no need for quotes around it. Here the userName parameter will be Paul, and the second parameter, userAge, will be 31.

Try It Out   **Fahrenheit to Centigrade Function**

Let's rewrite the temperature converter page using functions. You can cut and paste most of this code from ch3_examp4.htm — the parts that have changed have been highlighted. When you've finished, save it as ch3_examp5.htm.

```
<html>
<body>

<script language="JavaScript" type="text/javascript">

function convertToCentigrade(degFahren)
{
    var degCent;
    degCent = 5/9 * (degFahren - 32);

    return degCent;
}

var degFahren = new Array(212, 32, -459.15);
var degCent = new Array();
var loopCounter;

for (loopCounter = 0; loopCounter <= 2; loopCounter++)
{
    degCent[loopCounter] = convertToCentigrade(degFahren[loopCounter]);
}

for (loopCounter = 2; loopCounter >= 0; loopCounter--)
{
    document.write("Value " + loopCounter + " was " + degFahren[loopCounter] +
                " degrees Fahrenheit");
    document.write(" which is " + degCent[loopCounter] +
                " degrees centigrade<br />");
}

</script>

</body>
</html>
```

When you load this page into your browser, you should see exactly the same results that you had with ch3_examp4.htm.

At the top of the script block you declare your convertToCentigrade() function. You saw this function earlier:

```
function convertToCentigrade(degFahren)
{
    var degCent;
    degCent = 5/9 * (degFahren - 32);

    return degCent;
}
```

If you're using a number of separate script blocks in a page, it's very important that the function be defined before any script calls it. If you have a number of functions, you may want to put them all in their own script block at the top of the page — between the <head> and </head> tags is good. That way you know where to find all your functions, and you can be sure that they have been declared before they have been used.

You should be pretty familiar with how the code in the function works. You declare a variable degCent, do your calculation, store its result in degCent, and then return degCent back to the calling code. The function's parameter is degFahren, which provides the information the calculation needs.

Following the function declaration is the code that executes when the page loads. First you define the variables you need, and then you have the two loops that calculate and then output the results. This is mostly the same as before, apart from the first for loop.

```
for (loopCounter = 0; loopCounter <= 2; loopCounter++)
{
    degCent[loopCounter] = convertToCentigrade(degFahren[loopCounter]);
}
```

The code inside the first for loop puts the value returned by the function convertToCentigrade() into the degCent array.

There is a subtle point to the code in this example. Notice that you declare the variable degCent within your function convertToCentigrade(), and you also declare it as an array after the function definition.

Surely this isn't allowed?

Well, this leads neatly to the next topic of this chapter — variable scope.

Variable Scope and Lifetime

What is meant by *scope*? Well, put simply, it's the scope or extent of a variable's availability — which parts of your code can access a variable and the data it contains. Any variables declared in a web page outside of a function will be available to all script on the page, whether that script is inside a function or otherwise — we term this a *global* or *page-level scope*. However, variables declared inside a function are visible *only* inside that function — no code outside the function can access them. So, for example, you could declare a variable degCent in every function you have on a page *and* once on the page outside any function. However, you can't declare the variable *more* than once inside any one function or *more* than once on the page outside the functions. Note that reusing a variable name throughout a page in this way, although not illegal, is not standard good practice — it can make the code very confusing to read.

Function parameters are similar to variables: They can't be seen outside the function, and although you can declare a variable in a function with the same name as one of its parameters, it would cause a lot of confusion and might easily lead to subtle bugs being overlooked. It's therefore bad coding practice and best avoided, if only for the sake of your sanity when it comes to debugging!

So what happens when the code inside a function ends and execution returns to the point at which the code was called? Do the variables defined within the function retain their value when you call the function the next time?

The answer is no: Variables not only have the scope property — where they are visible — but they also have a *lifetime*. When the function finishes executing, the variables in that function die and their values are lost, unless you return one of them to the calling code. Every so often JavaScript performs garbage collection (which we talked about in Chapter 2), whereby it scans through the code and sees if any variables are no longer in use; if so, the data they hold are freed from memory to make way for the data of other variables.

Given that global variables can be used anywhere, why not make all of them global? Global variables are great when you need to keep track of data on a global basis. However, because they are available for modification anywhere in your code, it does mean that if they are changed incorrectly due to a bug, that bug could be anywhere within the code, making debugging difficult. It's best, therefore, to keep global variable use to a minimum, though sometimes they are a necessary evil — for example, when you need to share data among different functions.

Summary

In this chapter you have concluded your look at the core of the JavaScript language and its syntax. Everything from now on builds on these foundations, and with the less interesting syntax under your belt, you can move on to more interesting things in the remainder of the book.

The chapter looked at the following:

- ❑ **Decision making with the** if **and** switch **statements.** The ability to make decisions is essentially what gives the code its "intelligence." Based on whether a condition is true or false, you can decide on a course of action to follow.

- ❑ **Comparison operators.** The comparison operators compare the value on the left of the operator (left-hand side, LHS) with the value on the right of the operator (right-hand side, RHS) and return a Boolean value. Here is a list of the main comparison operators:

  - ❑ == is the LHS equal to the RHS?
  - ❑ != is the LHS not equal to the RHS?
  - ❑ <= is the LHS less than or equal to the RHS?

- ❑ >= is the LHS greater than or equal to the RHS?
- ❑ < is the LHS less than the RHS?
- ❑ > is the LHS greater than the RHS?

❑ **The** if **statement.** Using the if statement, you can choose to execute a block of code (defined by being in curly braces) when a condition is true. The if statement has a test condition, specified in parentheses. If this condition evaluates to true, the code after the if statement will execute.

❑ **The** else **statement.** If you want code to execute when the if statement is false, you can use the else statement that appears after the if statement.

❑ **Logical operators.** To combine conditions, you can use the three logical operators: AND, OR, and NOT, represented by &&, ||, and !, respectively.

- ❑ The AND operator returns true only if both sides of the expression are true.
- ❑ The OR operator returns true when either one or both sides of an expression are true.
- ❑ The NOT operator reverses the logic of an expression.

❑ The switch **statement.** This compares the result of an expression with a series of possible cases and is similar in effect to a multiple if statement.

❑ **Looping with** for, for...in, while, **and** do...while. It's often necessary to repeat a block of code a number of times, something JavaScript enables by looping.

- ❑ **The** for **loop.** Useful for looping through code a certain number of times, the for loop consists of three parts: the initialization, test condition, and increment parts. Looping continues while the test condition is true. Each loop executes the block of code and then executes the increment part of the for loop before re-evaluating the test condition to see if the results of incrementing have changed it.

- ❑ **The** for...in **loop.** This is useful when you want to loop through an array without knowing the number of elements in the array. JavaScript works this out for you so that no elements are missed.

- ❑ **The** while **loop.** This is useful for looping through some code for as long as a test condition remains true. It consists of a test condition and the block of code that's executed only if the condition is true. If the condition is never true, the code never executes.

- ❑ **The** do...while **loop.** This is similar to a while loop, except that it executes the code once and then keeps executing the code as long as the test condition remains true.

- ❑ break **and** continue **statements.** Sometimes you have a good reason to break out of a loop prematurely, in which case you need to use the break statement. On hitting a break statement, code execution stops for the block of code marked out by the curly braces and starts immediately after the closing brace. The continue statement is similar to break, except that when code execution stops at that point in the loop, the loop is not broken out of but instead continues as if the end of that reiteration had been reached.

❑ **Functions are reusable bits of code.** JavaScript has a lot of built-in functions that provide programmers services, such as converting a string to a number. However, JavaScript also enables you to define and use your own functions using the function keyword. Functions can have zero or more parameters passed to them and can return a value if you so wish.

❑   **Variable scope and lifetime.** Variables declared outside a function are available globally — that is, anywhere in the page. Any variables defined inside a function are private to that function and can't be accessed outside of it. Variables have a lifetime, the length of which depends on where the variable was declared. If it's a global variable, its lifetime is that of the page — while the page is loaded in the browser, the variable remains alive. For variables defined in a function, the lifetime is limited to the execution of that function. When the function has finished being executed, the variables die, and their values are lost. If the function is called again later in the code, the variables will be empty.

Exercise Questions

Suggested solutions to these questions can be found in Appendix A.

1.   A junior programmer comes to you with some code that appears not to work. Can you spot where he went wrong? Give him a hand and correct the mistakes.

```
var userAge = prompt("Please enter your age");

if (userAge = 0);
{
    alert("So you're a baby!");
}
else if ( userAge < 0 | userAge > 200)
    alert("I think you may be lying about your age");
else
{
    alert("That's a good age");
}
```

2.   Using `document.write()`, write code that displays the results of the 12 times table. Its output should be the results of the calculations.

```
12 * 1 = 12
12 * 2 = 24
12 * 3 = 36
...
12 * 11 = 132
12 * 12 = 144
```

3.   Change the code of Question 2 so that it's a function that takes as parameters the times table required and the values at which it should start and end. For example, you might try the four times table displayed starting with 4 * 4 and ending at 4 * 9.

4.   Modify the code of Question 3 to request the times table to be displayed from the user; the code should continue to request and display times tables until the user enters **-1**. Additionally, do a check to make sure that the user is entering a valid number; if the number is not valid, ask the user to re-enter it.

Common Mistakes, Debugging, and Error Handling

Even a JavaScript guru makes mistakes, even if they are just annoying typos. In particular, when code expands to hundreds of lines, the chance of something going wrong becomes much greater. In proportion, the difficulty in finding these mistakes, or bugs, also increases. In this chapter you will look at various techniques that will help you minimize the problems that arise from this situation.

You'll start by taking a look at the top seven JavaScript coding mistakes. After you know what they are, you'll be able to look out for them when writing code, hopefully, so that you won't make them so often!

Then you'll look at how you can cope with errors when they do happen, so that you prevent users from seeing your coding mistakes.

Finally, you'll look at the debugging tools in Microsoft's Internet Explorer (IE8), Firebug (an add-on for Firefox), Safari's and Chrome's Web Inspector, and Opera's Dragonfly. You'll see how you can use these tools to step through your code and check the contents of variables while the code is running, a process that enables us to hunt for difficult bugs. You'll also take a briefer look at the debugging tools available for Firefox.

D'oh! I Can't Believe I Just Did That: Some Common Mistakes

There are seven common mistakes made by programmers. Some of these you'll learn to avoid as you become more experienced, but others may haunt you forever!

You'll find it very useful in this chapter if your browser is set up to show errors. You did this in Chapter 2 in the section "Setting Up Your Browser for Errors." So if you don't already have error display set up, now would be a good time to do so.

Undefined Variables

JavaScript is actually very easygoing when it comes to defining your variables before assigning values to them. For example, the following will implicitly create the new global variable abc and assign it to the value 23:

```
abc = 23;
```

Although strictly speaking, you should define the variable explicitly with the var keyword like this:

```
var abc = 23;
```

Whether or not you use the var keyword to declare a variable has a consequence of what scope the variable has; so it is always best to use the var keyword. If a variable is used before it has been defined, an error will arise. For example, the following code will cause the error shown in Figure 4-1 in IE8 if the variable abc has not been previously defined (explicitly or implicitly):

```
alert(abc);
```

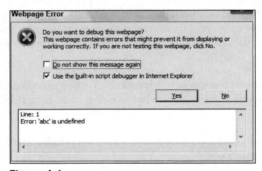

Figure 4-1

In Firefox you'll need to look in the JavaScript console, which you can view by choosing Tools ➪ Error Console.

In addition, you must remember that function definitions also have parameters, which if not declared correctly can lead to the same type of error.

Take a look at the following code:

```
function foo(parametrOne)
{
    alert(parameterOne);
}
```

If you call this function, you get an error message similar to the one shown in Figure 4-2.

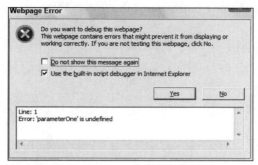

Figure 4-2

The error here is actually a simple typo in the function definition. The first parameter has the typo: it should read `parameterOne`, not `parametrOne`. What can be confusing with this type of error is that although the browser tells us the error is on one line, the source of the error is on another line.

Case Sensitivity

This is a major source of errors, particularly because it can be difficult to spot at times.

For example, spot the three case errors in the following code:

```
var myName = "Jeremy";
If (myName == "jeremy")
    alert(myName.toUppercase());
```

The first error is the `if` keyword; the code above has `If` rather than `if`. However, JavaScript won't tell us that the error is an incorrect use of case, but instead IE will tell us `Object expected` and Firefox will tell us that `If is not defined`. Although error messages give us some idea of what's gone wrong, they often do so in an oblique way. In this case IE thinks you are trying to use an object called an `If` object and Firefox thinks you are trying to use an undefined function called `If`.

Okay, with that error cleared up, you come to the next error, not one of JavaScript syntax, but a logic error. Remember that `Jeremy` does not equal `jeremy` in JavaScript, so `myName == "jeremy"` is `false`, even though it's quite likely that you didn't care whether the word is `jeremy` or `jeremy`. This type of error will result in no error message at all, just the code not executing as you'd planned.

The third fault is with the `toUpperCase()` method of the `String` object contained in `myName`. The previous code uses `toUppercase`, with the `c` in lowercase. IE will give us the message `Object doesn't support this property or method` and Firefox will report that `myName.toUppercase is not a function`. On first glance it would be easy to miss such a small mistake and start checking your JavaScript reference guide for that method. You might wonder why it's there, but your code is not working. Again, you always need to be aware of case, something that even experts get wrong from time to time.

Incorrect Number of Closing Braces

In the following code, you define a function and then call it. However, there's a deliberate mistake. See if you can spot where it is.

```
function myFunction()
{
x = 1;
y = 2;
if (x <= y)
{
if (x == y)
{
alert("x equals y");
}
}
myFunction();
```

This is why formatting your code is important — you'll have a much easier time spotting errors such as this:

```
function myFunction()
{
    x = 1;
    y = 2;
    if (x <= y)
    {
        if (x == y)
        {
            alert("x equals y");
        }
    }
    myFunction();
```

Now you can see that the ending curly brace of the function is missing. When there are a lot of if, for, or do while statements, it's easy to have too many or too few closing braces. This type of problem is much easier to spot with formatted code.

Incorrect Number of Closing Parentheses

Take a look at the following code:

```
if (myVariable + 12) / myOtherVariable < myString.length)
```

Spot the mistake? The problem is the missing parenthesis at the beginning of the condition. You want myVariable + 12 to be calculated before the division by myOtherVariable is calculated, so quite rightly you know you need to put it in parentheses.

```
(myVariable + 12) / myOtherVariable
```

However, the `if` statement's condition must also be in parentheses. Not only is the initial parenthesis missing, but there is one more closing parenthesis than opening parentheses. Like curly braces, each opening parenthesis must have a closing parenthesis. The following code is correct:

```
if ((myVariable + 12) / myOtherVariable < myString.length)
```

It's very easy to miss a parenthesis or have one too many when you have many opening and closing parentheses.

Using Equals (=) Rather than Is Equal To (==)

Consider the following code:

```
var myNumber = 99;
if (myNumber = 101)
{
    alert("myNumber is 101");
}
else
{
    alert("myNumber is " + myNumber);
}
```

You'd expect, at first glance, that the `alert()` method in the `else` part of the `if` statement would execute, telling us that the number in `myNumber` is `99`, but it won't. This code makes the classic mistake of using the assignment operator (=) instead of the equality operator (==). Hence, instead of comparing `myNumber` with `101`, this code sets `myNumber` to equal `101`. If you program in Visual Basic, or languages like it that use only one equals sign for both comparison and assignment, you'll find that every so often this mistake crops up. It's just so easy to make.

What makes things even trickier is that no error message is raised; it is just your data and logic that will suffer. Assigning a variable a value in an `if` statement may be perverse, but it's perfectly legal, so there will be no complaints from JavaScript. When embedded in a large chunk of code, a mistake like this is easily overlooked. Just remember it's worth checking for this error the next time your program's logic seems crazy.

Using a Method as a Property and Vice Versa

Another common error is where either you forget to put parentheses after a method with no parameters, or you use a property and do put parentheses after it.

When calling a method, you must always have parentheses following its name; otherwise, JavaScript thinks that it must be a pointer to the method or a property. For example, examine the following code:

```
var nowDate = new Date();
alert(nowDate.getMonth);
```

The first line creates an instance of the `Date` reference type. The second line attempts to call the `getMonth()` method of the newly created `Date` object, except the parentheses are missing. The following is the corrected code:

```
var nowDate = new Date();
alert(nowDate.getMonth());
```

Just as you should always have parentheses after a method, you should never have parentheses after a property; otherwise, JavaScript thinks you are trying to use a method of that object:

```
var myString = "Hello, World!";
alert(myString.length());
```

The second line adds parentheses after the length property, making JavaScript think it is a method. This code should have been written like the following code:

```
var myString = new String("Hello");
alert(myString.length);
```

To compound the issue, it's common for a function to be passed as a parameter to another function (or a property as you'll see in Chapter 6 when working with events). In these situations, you pass the function without the opening and closing parentheses () at the end of the function name. Take a look at the following code:

```
function foo()
{
    alert("I'm in foo()!").
}

function bar(fpToCall)
{
    alert("Calling passed function").
    fpToCall();
}

bar(foo);
```

This code defines two functions: foo() and bar(). The foo() function simply displays a message box telling the user the foo() function is currently executing. The second function, bar(), accepts one argument that is a function. It displays a message saying it's calling the passed function, and then it executes that function. The final line calls the bar() function and passes a *pointer* of the foo() function. A pointer is a reference to a location in memory (we'll discuss memory references in the next chapter).

As a rule of thumb, use parentheses at the end of the function name when you want to execute the function, and leave the parentheses off when passing the function to another function or property.

Missing Plus Signs During Concatenation

In the following code, there's a deliberate concatenation mistake:

```
var myName = "Jeremy";
var myString = "Hello";
var myOtherString = "World";
myString = myName + " said " + myString + " " myOtherString;
alert(myString);
```

There should be a + operator between " " and myOtherString in the fourth line of code.

Although easy to spot in just a few lines, this kind of mistake can be harder to spot in large chunks of code. Also, the error message this type of mistake causes can be misleading. Load this code into a browser and you'll be told `Error : Expected` by IE and `Missing ; before statement` by Firefox. It's surprising how often this error crops up.

These most common mistakes are errors caused by the programmer. There are other types of errors, called *run-time errors*, that occur when your code executes in the browser, and they aren't necessarily caused by a typo, missing curly brace, parenthesis, or other pitfalls discussed. These types of errors can still be planned for, as you'll see in the next section.

Error Handling

When writing your programs, you want to be informed of every error. However, the last thing you want the user to see are error messages when you finally deploy the code to a web server for the whole world to access. Of course, writing bug-free code would be a good start, but keep the following points in mind:

- ❑ Occasions arise when conditions beyond your control lead to errors. A good example of this is when you are relying on something, such as a Java applet, that isn't on the user's computer and that you have no way of checking for.
- ❑ Murphy's Law states that anything that can go wrong will go wrong!

Preventing Errors

The best way to handle errors is to stop them from occurring in the first place. That seems like stating the obvious, but there are a number of things you should do if you want error-free pages.

- ❑ Thoroughly check pages in as many browsers as possible. This is easier said than done on some operating systems. The alternative is for you to decide which browsers you want to support for your web page, and then verify that your code works in them. Use the browser checking code found earlier in the book to send unsupported users to a nice, safe, and probably boring web page with reduced functionality, or maybe just supply them with a message that their browser and/or platform is not supported.
- ❑ Validate your data. If users can enter dud data that will cause your program to fail, then they will. Make sure that a textbox has data entered into it if your code fails if the text box is empty. If you need a whole number, you must make sure the user entered one. Is the date the user just entered valid? Is the e-mail address `mind your own business` the user just entered likely to be valid? No, so you must check that it is in the format `something@something.something`.

Okay, so let's say you carefully checked your pages and there is not a syntax or logic error in sight. You added data validation that confirms that everything the user enters is in a valid format. Things can still go wrong, and problems may arise that you can do nothing about. Here's a real-world example of something that can still go wrong.

One of your authors, Paul, created an online message board that relies on a small Java applet to enable the transfer of data to and from the server without reloading the page. Paul checked the code and everything was fine, and it continued to work fine after launching the board, except that in about five percent of cases the Java applet initialized but then caused an error due to the user being behind a particular type of firewall (a firewall is a means of stopping hackers from getting into a local computer network). There is no way of determining whether a user is behind a certain type of firewall, so there is nothing that can be done in that sort of exceptional circumstance. Or is there?

In fact, JavaScript includes something called the try...catch statement. This enables you to try to run your code; if it fails, the error is caught by the catch clause and can be dealt with as you wish. For the message board, Paul used a try...catch clause to catch the Java applet's failure and redirected the user to a more basic page that still displayed messages, but without using the applet.

The try...catch Statements

The try...catch statements work as a pair; you can't have one without the other. You use the try statement to define a block of code that you want to try to execute, and use the catch statement to define a block of code that will execute if an exception to the normal running of the code occurs in the block of code defined by the try statement. The term *exception* is key here; it means a circumstance that is extraordinary and unpredictable. Compare that with an *error*, which is something in the code that has been written incorrectly. If no exception occurs, the code inside the catch statement is never executed. The catch statement also enables you to get the contents of the exception message that would have been shown to the user had you not caught it first.

Let's create a simple example of a try...catch clause.

```
<!DOCTYPE html PUBLIC "-//W3C//DTD XHTML 1.0 Transitional//EN"
    "http://www.w3.org/TR/xhtml1/DTD/xhtml1-transitional.dtd">

<html xmlns="http://www.w3.org/1999/xhtml">
<head>
    <title>Try/Catch</title>
</head>
<body>
<script type="text/javascript">
try
{
    alert('This is code inside the try clause');
    alert('No Errors so catch code will not execute');
}
catch(exception)
{
    alert("The error is " + exception.message);
}
</script>
</body>
</html>
```

Save this as trycatch.htm.

This code first defines the try statement; as with all other blocks of code, you mark out the try block by enclosing it in curly braces.

Next comes the `catch` statement. The code included `exception` in parentheses right after the `catch` statement. This `exception` is simply a variable name. It will store an object, of type `Error`, containing information about any exception thrown during code execution inside the `try` code block. We'll call this object the *exception object*. Although the word `exception` is used here, you can use any valid variable name. For example, `catch(exceptionObject)` would be fine and certainly more descriptive.

The exception object contains several properties that provide information about the exception that occurred. The bad news is the exception object in IE differs somewhat from the exception object in other browsers (and even Firefox, Opera, Safari, and Chrome have differing properties from each other!). The good news is there are similarities, and you don't have to worry about writing cross-browser code if you're only concerned with the exception's message and the type of exception.

All major browsers support the `name` and `message` properties. The `name` property contains the name of the error type, and the `message` property contains the error message the user would normally see. These properties are part of the ECMAScript 3 standard.

Back to the code at hand, within the curly braces after the `catch` statement is the code block that will execute if and only if an exception occurs. In this case, the code within the `try` code block is fine, and so the `alert()` method inside the `catch` block won't execute.

Insert a deliberate error.

```
try
{
    alert('This is code inside the try clause');
    ablert ('Exception will be thrown by this code');
}
catch(exception)
{
    alert("The error is " + exception.message);
}
```

Resave the document and reload the page in your browser. The first `alert()` method in the `try` block of code executes fine and the alert box will be displayed to the user. However, the second `ablert()` statement will cause an error and code execution will start at the first statement in the `catch` block.

If you're using Internet Explorer, the error description displayed will be `Object expected`. If you're using another browser, the same error is interpreted differently and reported as `ablert is not defined`.

If you change the code again, so that it has a different error, you'll see something important.

```
try
{
    alert('This is code inside the try clause');
    alert('This code won't work');
}
catch(exception)
{
    alert("The error is " + exception.message)
}
```

Loading this revised code in a browser results in a normal browser error message telling you `Expected ')'` instead of displaying the alert box in the `catch` block. This happens because this code contains a syntax error; the functions and methods are valid, but you have an invalid character. The single quote in the word `won't` has ended the string parameter being passed to the `alert()` method. At that point JavaScript's syntax rules specify that a closing parenthesis should appear, which is not the case in this code. Before executing any code, the browser's JavaScript engine goes through all the code and checks for syntax errors, or code that breaches JavaScript's rules. If the engine finds a syntax error, the browser deals with it as usual; your `try` clause never runs and therefore cannot handle syntax errors.

Throwing Errors

The `throw` statement can be used within a `try` block of code to create your own run-time errors. Why create a statement to generate errors, when a bit of bad coding will do the same?

Throwing errors can be very useful for indicating problems such as invalid user input. Rather than using lots of `if...else` statements, you can check the validity of user input, then use `throw` to stop code execution in its tracks and cause the error-catching code in the `catch` block of code to take over. In the `catch` clause, you can determine whether the error is based on user input, in which case you can notify the user what went wrong and how to correct it. Alternatively, if it's an unexpected error, you can handle it more gracefully than with lots of JavaScript errors.

To use `throw`, type `throw` and include the error message after it.

```
throw "This is my error message";
```

Remember that when you catch the exception object in the `catch` statement, you can get hold of the error message that you have thrown. Although there's a string in this example `throw` statement, you can actually throw any type of data, including numbers and objects.

Try It Out   try . . . catch and Throwing Errors

In this example you'll be creating a simple factorial calculator. The important parts of this example are the `try...catch` clause and the `throw` statements. It's a frameset page to enable you to demonstrate that things can go wrong that you can't do anything about. In this case, the page relies on a function defined within a frameset page, so if the page is loaded on its own, a problem will occur.

First let's create the page that will define the frameset and that also contains an important function.

```
<!DOCTYPE html PUBLIC "-//W3C//DTD XHTML 1.0 Frameset//EN"
    "http://www.w3.org/TR/xhtml1/DTD/xhtml1-frameset.dtd">

<html xmlns="http://www.w3.org/1999/xhtml">
<head>
<title>Example</title>
<script type="text/javascript">
function calcFactorial(factorialNumber)
{
    var factorialResult = 1;
    for (; factorialNumber > 0; factorialNumber--)
    {
        factorialResult = factorialResult * factorialNumber;
    }
```

```
        return factorialResult;
    }
</script>
</head>
<frameset cols="100%,*">
    <frame name="fraCalcFactorial" src="calcfactorial.htm" />
</frameset>
</html>
```

Save this page as `calcfactorialtopframe.htm`.

```
<!DOCTYPE html PUBLIC "-//W3C//DTD XHTML 1.0 Transitional//EN"
    "http://www.w3.org/TR/xhtml1/DTD/xhtml1-transitional.dtd">

<html xmlns="http://www.w3.org/1999/xhtml">
<head>
<title>Example</title>
<script type="text/javascript">
function butCalculate_onclick()
{
    try
    {
        if (window.top.calcFactorial == null)
            throw "This page is not loaded within the correct frameset";
        if (document.form1.txtNum1.value == "")
            throw "!Please enter a value before you calculate its factorial";
        if (isNaN(document.form1.txtNum1.value))
            throw "!Please enter a valid number";
        if (document.form1.txtNum1.value < 0)
            throw "!Please enter a positive number";

        document.form1.txtResult.value =
         window.parent.calcFactorial(document.form1.txtNum1.value);
    }
    catch(exception)
    {
        if (typeof(exception) == "string")
        {
            if (exception.charAt(0) == "!")
            {
                alert(exception.substr(1));
                document.form1.txtNum1.focus();
                document.form1.txtNum1.select();
            }
            else
            {
                alert(exception);
            }
        }
        else
        {
            alert("The following error occurred " + exception.message);
        }
    }
}
```

```
    </script>
    </head>
    <body>
    <form action="" name="form1">
        <input type="text" name="txtNum1" size="3" /> factorial is
        <input type="text" name="txtResult" size="25" /><br />
        <input type="button" value="Calculate Factorial"
            name="butCalculate" onclick="butCalculate_onclick()" />
    </form>
    </body>
    </html>
```

Save this page as `calcfactorial.htm`. Then load the first page, `calcfactorialtopframe.htm`, into your browser.

The page consists of a simple form with two text boxes and a button. Enter the number 4 into the first box and click the Calculate Factorial button. The factorial of 4, which is 24, will be calculated and put in the second text box (see Figure 4-3.)

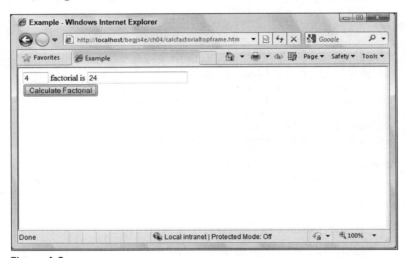

Figure 4-3

The factorial of a number is the product of all the positive integers less than or equal to that number. For example, the factorial of 4 (written 4!) is 1 * 2 * 3 * 4 = 24. Factorials are used in various branches of mathematics, including statistics. Here, you want only to create a function that does something complex enough to be worthy of a function, but not so complex as to distract you from the main purpose of this example: the `try...catch` and `throw` statements.

If you clear the first text box and click the Calculate Factorial button, you'll be told that a value needs to be entered. If you enter an invalid non-numeric value into the first text box, you'll be told to enter a valid value. If you enter a negative value, you'll be told to enter a positive value.

Also, if you try loading the page `calcfactorial.htm` into your browser and enter a value in the text box and click the Calculate Factorial button, you'll be told that the page is not loaded into the correct frameset.

As you'll see, all of these error messages are created using the `try...catch` and `throw` statements.

Because this example is all about `try...catch` and `throw`, you'll concentrate just on the `calcfactorial.htm` page, in particular the `butCalculate_onclick()` function, which is connected to the `onclick` event handler of the form's only button.

Start by looking at the `try` clause and the code inside it. The code consists of four `if` statements and another line of code that puts the calculated factorial into the second text box. Each of the `if` statements checks for a condition that, if true, would cause problems for your code.

The first `if` statement checks that the `calcFactorial()` function, in the top frameset window, actually exists. If not, it throws an error, which is caught by the `catch` block. If the user loads the `calcfactorial.htm` page rather than the frameset page `calcfactorialtopframe.htm`, then without this `throw` statement your code will fail.

```
try
{
    if (window.top.calcFactorial == null)
        throw "This page is not loaded within the correct frameset";
```

The next three `if` statements check the validity of the data entered into the text box by the user. First make sure the user entered something into the text box; then make sure the user entered a number, and then finally check that the value is not negative. Again if any of the `if` conditions is true, you throw an error, will be caught by the `catch` block. Each of the error messages you define starts with an exclamation mark, the purpose of which is to mark the error as a user input error, rather than an error such as not being in a frameset.

```
    if (document.form1.txtNum1.value == "")
        throw "!Please enter a value before you calculate its factorial";
    if (isNaN(document.form1.txtNum1.value))
        throw "!Please enter a valid number";
    if (document.form1.txtNum1.value < 0)
        throw "!Please enter a positive number";
```

If everything is fine, the `calcFactorial()` function will be executed and the results text box will be filled with the factorial of the number entered by the user.

```
    document.form1.txtResult.value =
        window.parent.calcFactorial(document.form1.txtNum1.value);
}
```

Finally, turn your attention to the `catch` part of the `try...catch` statement. First, any message thrown by the `try` code will be caught by the `exception` variable.

```
catch(exception)
{
```

The type of data contained in `exception` will depend on how the error was thrown. If it was thrown by the browser and not by your code, `exception` will be an object, the exception object. If it's thrown by your code, then in this instance you've thrown only primitive strings. So the first thing you need to do is decide what type of data `exception` contains. If it's a string, you know it was thrown by your code and can deal with it accordingly. If it's an object, and given that you know none of your code throws objects, you assume it must be the browser that has generated this exception and that `exception` is an `Exception` object.

```
if (typeof(exception) == "string")
{
```

If it was code that generated the exception using a `throw` (and so `exception` is a string), you now need to determine whether the error is a user input error, such as the text box not containing a value to calculate, or whether it was another type of error, such as the page not being loaded in your frameset. All the user input exception messages had an exclamation mark at the beginning, so you use an `if` statement to check the first character. If it is a `!`, you notify the user of the error and then return focus to your control. If it's not, you just display an error message.

```
if (exception.charAt(0) == "!")
{
    alert(exception.substr(1));
    document.form1.txtNum1.focus();
    document.form1.txtNum1.select();
}
else
{
    alert(exception);
}
}
```

If `exception` was not a string, you know you have an exception object and need to display the `message` property:

```
else
{
    alert("The following error occurred " + exception.message);
}
}
```

Nested try...catch Statements

So far you've been using just one `try...catch` statement, but it's possible to include a `try...catch` statement inside another `try` statement. Indeed, you can go further and have a `try...catch` inside the `try` statement of this inner `try...catch`, or even another inside that, the limit being what it's actually sensible to do.

So why would you use nested `try...catch` statements? Well, you can deal with certain errors inside the inner `try...catch` statement. If, however, you're dealing with a more serious error, the inner `catch` clause could pass that error to the outer `catch` clause by throwing the error to it.

Here's an example:

```
try
{
    try
    {
        ablurt("This code has an error");
```

```
        }
    catch(exception)
    {
        var eName = exception.name;

        if (eName == "TypeError" || eName == "ReferenceError")
        {
            alert("Inner try...catch can deal with this error");
        }
        else
        {
            throw exception;
        }
    }
}
catch(exception)
{
    alert("Error the inner try...catch could not handle occurred");
}
```

In this code you have two `try...catch` pairs, one nested inside the other.

The inner `try` statement contains a line of code that contains an error. The `catch` statement of the inner `try...catch` checks the value of the error's name. If the exception's name is either `TypeError` or `ReferenceError`, the inner `try...catch` deals with it by way of an alert box (see Appendix B for a full list of error types and their descriptions). Unfortunately, and unsurprisingly, the type of error thrown by the browser depends on the browser itself. In the preceding example, IE reports the error as a `TypeError` whereas the other browsers report it as a `ReferenceError`.

If the error caught by the inner `catch` statement is any other type of error, it is thrown up in the air again for the `catch` statement of the outer `try...catch` to deal with.

Let's change the `butCalculate_onclick()` function from the previous example, `calcfactorial.htm`, so that it has both an inner and an outer `try...catch`.

```
function butCalculate_onclick()
{
    try
    {
        try
        {
            if (window.top.calcFactorial == null)
                throw ("This page is not loaded within the correct frameset");
            if (document.form1.txtNum1.value == "")
                throw("!Please enter a value before you calculate its factorial");
            if (isNaN(document.form1.txtNum1.value))
                throw("!Please enter a valid number");
            if (document.form1.txtNum1.value < 0)
                throw("!Please enter a positive number");
            document.form1.txtResult.value =
                window.parent.calcFactorial(document.form1.txtNum1.value);
        }
```

```
        catch(exception)
        {
            if (typeof(exception) == "string" && exception.charAt(0) == "!")
            {
                alert(exception.substr(1));
                document.form1.txtNum1.focus();
                document.form1.txtNum1.select();
            }
            else
            {
                throw exception;
            }
        }
    }
    catch(exception)
    {
        switch (exception)
        {
            case "This page is not loaded within the correct frameset":
            alert(exception);
            break;
            default :
            alert("The following critical error has occurred \n" + exception);
        }
    }
}
```

The inner `try...catch` deals with user input errors. However, if the error is not a user input error thrown by us, it is thrown for the outer `catch` statement to deal with. The outer `catch` statement has a `switch` statement that checks the value of the error message thrown. If it's the error message thrown by us because the `calcfactorialtopframe.htm` is not loaded, the `switch` statement deals with it in the first `case` statement. Any other error is dealt with in the `default` statement. However, there may well be occasions when there are lots of different errors you want to deal with in `case` statements.

finally Clauses

The `try...catch` statement has a `finally` clause that defines a block of code that will execute whether or not an exception was thrown. The `finally` clause can't appear on its own; it must be after a `try` block, which the following code demonstrates:

```
try
{
    ablurt("An exception will occur");
}
catch(exception)
{
    alert("Exception occurred");
}
finally
{
    alert("Whatever happens this line will execute");
}
```

The `finally` part is a good place to put any cleanup code that needs to be executed regardless of any errors that occurred previously.

You've seen the top mistakes made by developers, and you've also seen how to handle errors in your code. Unfortunately, errors will still occur in your code, so let's take a look at one way to make remedying them easier by using a debugger.

Debugging

JavaScript is traditionally looked upon as a difficult language to write and debug due to the lack of decent development tools. This is not the case now, however, thanks to many tools made available to developers. Most notably are the debugging tools available for Internet Explorer, Firefox, Safari, and Opera. With these tools, you can halt the execution of your script with breakpoints and then step through code line by line to see exactly what is happening.

You can also find out what data is being held in variables and execute statements on the fly. Without debuggers, the best you can do is use the `alert()` method in your code to show the state of variables at various points.

Debugging is generally universal across all browsers, and even languages. Some debugging tools may offer more features than others, but for the most part, the following concepts can be applied to any debugger:

❑   Breakpoints tell the debugger it should break, or pause code execution, at a certain point. You can set a breakpoint anywhere in your JavaScript code, and the debugger will halt code execution when it reaches the breakpoint.

❑   Watches allow you to specify variables that you want to inspect when your code pauses at a breakpoint.

❑   The call stack is a record of what functions and methods have been executed to the breakpoint.

❑   The console allows you to execute JavaScript commands in the context of the page and within the scope of the breakpoint. In addition, it catalogs all JavaScript errors found in the page.

❑   Stepping is the most common procedure in debugging. It allows you to execute one line of code at a time. There are three ways to step through code.

   ❑   Step Into executes the next line of code. If that line is a function call, the debugger executes the function and halts at the first line of the function.

   ❑   Step Over, like Step Into, executes the next line of code. If that line is a function, Step Over executes the entire function and halts at the first line outside the function.

   ❑   Step Out returns to the calling function when you are inside a called function. Step Out resumes the execution of code until the function returns. It then breaks at the return point of the function.

Before delving into the various debuggers, let's create a page you can debug. Note the deliberate typo in line 16. Be sure to include this typo if creating the page from scratch.

```
<!DOCTYPE html PUBLIC "-//W3C//DTD XHTML 1.0 Transitional//EN"
    "http://www.w3.org/TR/xhtml1/DTD/xhtml1-transitional.dtd">
<html xmlns="http://www.w3.org/1999/xhtml">
<head>
    <title>Debug: Times Table</title>
    <script type="text/javascript">
        function writeTimesTable(timesTable)
        {
            var counter;
            var writeString;
            for (counter = 1; counter < 12; counter++)
            {
                writeString = counter + " * " + timesTable + " = ";
                writeString = writeString + (timesTable * counter);
                writeString = writeString + "<br />";
                documents.write(writeString);
            }
        }
    </script>

</head>
<body>
    <script type="text/javascript">
        writeTimesTable(2);
    </script>
</body>
</html>
```

Save this as `debug_timestable.htm`.

The next section walks you through the features and functionality of the Firebug add-on for Firefox. Because of the universal nature of debugging and debuggers, the sections for Internet Explorer, Safari, and Opera will merely familiarize you with the UI for each browser's debugger and point out any differences.

Debugging in Firefox with Firebug

For years, the only JavaScript debugger for Firefox was a Mozilla project codenamed Venkman. Its feature-set resembled that of Microsoft's Script Editor, but many developers felt Venkman wasn't user-friendly. One such developer, Joe Hewitt, decided to write his own debugger using the built-in debugging API (application programming interface) in Firefox. He christened his creation Firebug, and the rest, as they say, is history. Today, Firebug is the defacto JavaScript debugger (and much more!) for Firefox, and all other JavaScript (and web development) tools for other browsers are based, in principle, on Firebug.

Unfortunately, Firebug does not come with Firefox by default. Instead, you have to install the Firebug addon. You can download the latest version of Firebug from `http://www.getfirebug.com`, from Joe Hewitt's website at `http://www.joehewitt.com/software/firebug/`, or from Mozilla's add-on site at `https://addons.mozilla.org/en-US/firefox/addon/1843`.

To install Firebug, open Firefox and go to either of the provided URLs. Click the Install button on the web page, and follow the instructions. Be sure to restart Firefox after Firebug's installation.

You can access Firebug a couple of ways. You can click the Firebug icon in the status bar in the lower-right corner of the Firefox window. If you do not have Firefox's status bar visible, you can open Firebug by selecting Firebug ⇨ Open Firebug from the Tools menu in Firefox. By default, Firebug opens as a panel in Firefox (see Figure 4-4).

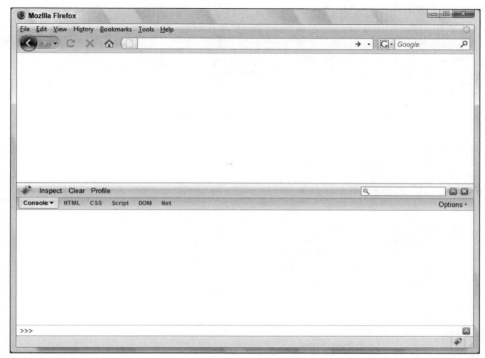

Figure 4-4

You can pop it out to its own window by clicking the up arrow next to the Close button.

Open `debug_timestable.htm` in Firefox. If the status bar is visible, you should see red text in the lower-right corner of the Firefox window stating "1 Error." Click that message (or go through the Tools menu to open Firebug), and Firebug will open to the console. The console serves multiple purposes in Firebug; it lists JavaScript errors, and it also allows you to execute JavaScript code on the fly. We'll play with the console later.

The JavaScript debugger is contained in the Script tab, and it is made up of two panels. The left panel contains the source code, and the right panel contains three different views to choose from: Breakpoints, Watch, and Stack.

- ❑ **Breakpoints:** Lists all breakpoints that you've created for the code in the current page.
- ❑ **Watch:** Lists the variables in scope and their values at the breakpoint. You can also add other variables to watch.
- ❑ **Stack:** Displays the call stack.

The source code in the left panel is read-only; if you want to change it, you have to edit the file in your text editor. Let's do so and change the offending documents in line 16 to document. Save it, and reload the web page.

Having corrected the mistake and reloaded the page, you should see the times table in your web page, as shown in Figure 4-5.

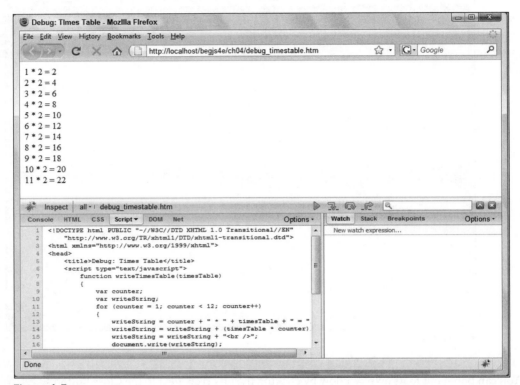

Figure 4-5

Also notice that the source code in Firebug's left panel updated to reflect your changes.

Setting Breakpoints

As mentioned earlier, breakpoints tell the debugger to pause code execution at a specific point in your code. This is handy when you want to inspect your code while it executes. Creating breakpoints in Firebug is straightforward; simply left-click in the gray area to the left of the source code's line numbers (the gutter). Breakpoints are denoted by a red circle in the gutter where you clicked.

You can also create a breakpoint when writing your code by using the debugger keyword (we'll use this a bit later).

Keeping the corrected `debug_timestable.htm` loaded in Firefox, create a breakpoint on line 14.

```
writeString = writeString + (timesTable * counter);
```

Reload the page, and notice Firebug stopped code execution at the breakpoint you just created. Firebug highlights the current line of code in light yellow and puts a yellow arrow in the gutter. This line hasn't been executed yet.

Click the Breakpoints tab in the right panel; it shows you the list of breakpoints (only one in this case). Each entry in the list consists of a checkbox to enable/disable the breakpoint, the containing function's name, the file name and line number of the source file, the source text of the breakpoint, and a Delete button.

Now click the Watch tab.

Watches

The Watch tab displays variables and their values currently in scope at the current line while code execution is paused. Figure 4-6 shows the contents of the Watch tab at this breakpoint.

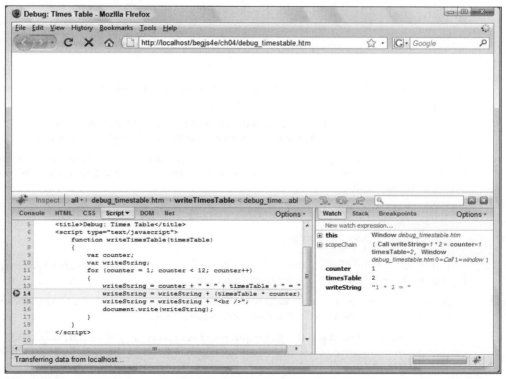

Figure 4-6

Notice that the `counter`, `timesTable`, and `writeString` variables are visible (as is `this`).

You can also add your own variables to watch, inspecting their values as you step through code. To add a watch, simply click "New watch expression...," type the variable name you want to watch, and press the Enter key. Watches that you add have a gray background, and moving your mouse over them reveals a red Delete button.

You can watch any variable you want. If the variable is in scope, the variable's value is displayed. If the variable is out of scope, a `ReferenceError` is displayed as its value.

Although this information is helpful when you want to see what exactly is going on in your code, it's not very helpful if you can't control code execution. It's impractical to set a breakpoint and reload the page multiple times just to advance to the next line, so we use a process called stepping.

Stepping Through Code

Code stepping is controlled by four buttons in the upper-right of the window, next to the source code search box (see Figure 4-7).

Figure 4-7

❑ **Continue** (shortcut key is F8): Its function is to continue code execution until either the next breakpoint or the end of all code is reached.

❑ **Step Into** (shortcut key is F11): Executes the current line of code and moves to the next statement. If the current line is a function, then it steps to the first line of the function.

❑ **Step Over** (F10): Like Step Into, this executes the current line of code and moves to the next statement. However, if the statement is a function, it executes the function and steps to the next line after the function call.

❑ **Step Out**: Returns to the calling function.

Let's do some stepping; follow these steps:

1. Step Into the code by clicking the icon or pressing F11. The debugger executes the currently highlighted line of code and moves to the next line.

2. Look in the Watch tab and at the value of `writeString`; it is `"1 * 2 = 2"`. As you can see, the values displayed in the Watch tab are updated in real time.

3. One nice feature of Firebug is the page updates, if necessary, as you step through code. Click Step Into two more times to see this in action. Figure 4-8 shows the page updated while stepping through code.

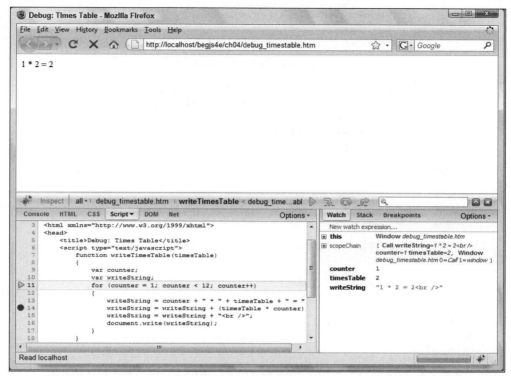

Figure 4-8

You may find that the function you stepped into is not the source of the bug and want to execute the remaining lines of code in the function to continue step by step from the point at which the function was called. Do so by clicking the Step Out icon to step out of the code. However, if you're in a loop and the breakpoint is set inside the loop, you will not step out of the function until you iterate through the loop.

There may also be times when you have some code with a bug in it that calls a number of functions. If you know that some of the functions are bug-free, then you may want to just execute those functions instead of stepping into them and seeing them executed line by line. Use Step Over in these situations to execute the code within a function but without going through it line by line.

Alter your times-table code in `debug_timestable.htm` as follows so you can use it for the three kinds of stepping:

```
<!DOCTYPE html PUBLIC "-//W3C//DTD XHTML 1.0 Transitional//EN"
    "http://www.w3.org/TR/xhtml1/DTD/xhtml1-transitional.dtd">
<html xmlns="http://www.w3.org/1999/xhtml">
<head>Av
    <title>Debug: Times Table 2</title>

    <script type="text/javascript">
```

```
             function writeTimesTable(timesTable)
             {
                 var counter;
                 var writeString;
                 for (counter = 1; counter < 12; counter++)
                 {
                     writeString = counter + " * " + timesTable + " = ";
                     writeString = writeString + (timesTable * counter);
                     writeString = writeString + "<br />";
                     document.write(writeString);
                 }
             }
         </script>

     </head>
     <body>
         <script type="text/javascript">
             var timesTable;
             for (timesTable = 1; timesTable <= 12; timesTable++)
             {
                 document.write("<p>")
                 writeTimesTable(timesTable)
                 document.write("</p>")
             }
         </script>
     </body>
     </html>
```

Save this as `debug_timestable2.htm`. Note that there are no errors in this HTML file.

The following instructions will walk you through the process of stepping through code.

1. Set a breakpoint in line 26, the `for` loop in the body of the page, and reload the page.

2. Click the Step Into icon and code execution will move to the next statement. Now the first statement inside the `for` loop, `document.write("<p>")`, is up for execution.

3. When you click the Step Into icon again, it will take you to the first calling of the `writeTimesTable()` function.

4. You want to see what's happening inside that function, so click Step Into again and you'll step into the function. Your screen should look like the one shown in Figure 4-9.

5. Click the Step Into icon a few times to get the gist of the flow of execution of the function. In fact, stepping through code line by line can get a little tedious. So let's imagine you're happy with this function and want to run the rest of it.

6. Use Step Out to run the rest of the code. The function has been fully executed, and you're back the calling line, as you can see from Figure 4-10.

7. Click the Step Into icon twice to execute `document.write()` (it won't be visible because it's a closing tag).

8. Click Step Into four more times. Execution will continue through the condition and incrementing parts of the `for` loop, ending back at the line that calls the `writeTimesTable()` function.

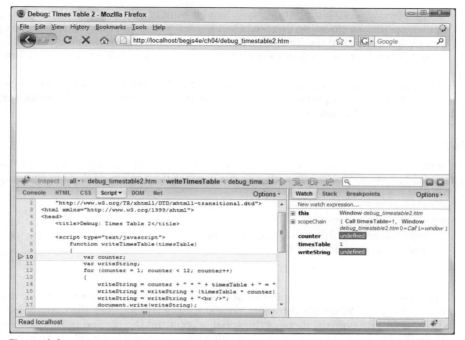

Figure 4-9

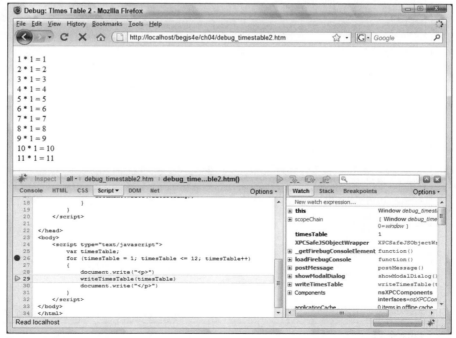

Figure 4-10

9. You've already seen this in action, so really you want to step over it and go to the next line. Well, no prizes for guessing that Step Over is what you need to do. Click the Step Over icon (or press the F10 key) and the function will be executed, but without stepping through it statement by statement. You should find yourself back at the `document.write("</p>")` line.

If you've finished debugging, you can run the rest of the code without stepping through each line by clicking the Continue icon (or pressing F8) on the toolbar. You should see a page of times tables from `1*1=1` to `11*12=132` in the browser.

The Console

While you're stepping through code and checking its flow of execution, what would be really useful is the ability to evaluate conditions and even to change things on the fly. You can do these things using the console.

Follow these steps:

1. Remove the previously set breakpoint by clicking the red circle in the source code panel and set a new breakpoint at line 17:

```
document.write(writeString);
```

2. Let's see how you can find out the value currently contained in the variable `writeString`. Reload the page. When the debugger stops at the breakpoint, click the Console tab, click in the ">>>" field, and type the name of the variable you want to examine, in this case `writeString`. Press the Enter key. This will cause the value contained in the variable to be printed below your command in the command window, as shown in Figure 4-11.

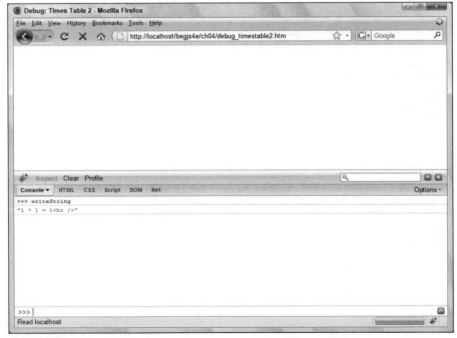

Figure 4-11

3. If you want to change a variable, you can write a line of JavaScript into the command window and press Enter. Try it with the following code:

```
writeString = "Changed on the Fly<br />"
```

4. Click the Script tab, and remove the breakpoint by clicking the red circle and then clicking the Continue icon. You see the results of your actions: where the 1*1 times table result should be, the text you changed on the fly has been inserted.

This alteration does not change your actual HTML source file, just the page currently loaded in the browser.

The console can also evaluate conditions. Recreate the breakpoint on line 26 and reload the page. Leave execution stopped at the breakpoint, and Step Into the `for` loop's condition.

Type the following into the command window and press Enter:

```
timesTable <= 12
```

Because this is the first time the loop has been run, as shown in Figure 4-12, `timesTable` is equal to 1 so the condition `timesTable <= 12` evaluates to `true`.

Figure 4-12

You can also use the console to access properties of the Browser Object Model (something we'll cover in Chapter 6). For example, if you type `window.location.href` into the command window and press Enter, it will tell you the web page's URL.

The console isn't limited to single lines of JavaScript. Click the up arrow on the right side of the screen and you can enter multiple statements to execute.

Call Stack Window

When you are single-stepping through the code, the call stack window keeps a running list of which functions have been called to get to the current point of execution in the code.

Let's create an example web page that demonstrates the call stack very nicely.

1. Enter this code:

```
<!DOCTYPE html PUBLIC "-//W3C//DTD XHTML 1.0 Transitional//EN"
    "http://www.w3.org/TR/xhtml1/DTD/xhtml1-transitional.dtd">
<html xmlns="http://www.w3.org/1999/xhtml">
<head>
    <title>Debugging: Callstack</title>
    <script type="text/javascript">
        function firstCall()
        {
            secondCall();
        }

        function secondCall()
        {
            thirdCall();
        }

        function thirdCall()
        {
            //
        }

        function button1_onclick()
        {
            debugger
            firstCall();
        }
    </script>
</head>
<body>
    <input type="button" value="Button" name="button1"
        onclick="return button1_onclick()" />
</body>
</html>
```

2. Save this page as debug_callstack.htm, and load it into Firefox. All you'll see is a blank web page with a button.

3. Click the button and the debugger will open at the debugger statement in the button1_onclick() function, which is connected to the button's onclick event handler.

4. Click the Call Stack tab in the right panel. Your debugger now looks like what is shown in Figure 4-13.

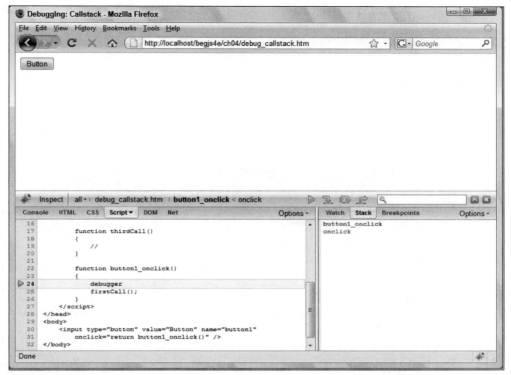

Figure 4-13

Firebug adds the function to the top of the call stack for every function call. You can already see that the first function called was actually the code attached to the `onclick` event handler of your button. Next, added to the call stack is the function called by the `onclick` event handler, which is the function `button1_onclick()` shown at the top of the call stack.

5. If you want to see where each function was first entered, just click the function name in the call stack window. Click `onclick` and the calling code (that is, the code connected to the `onclick` attribute of the `<input/>` element) will be shown. Now click the top line, `button1_onclick`, and that will take you back to the current execution point.

6. Now Step Into twice. The first step is to the line that calls the `firstCall()` function. The second step takes you into that function itself. The function is immediately added to the call stack, as shown in Figure 4-14.

7. Step Into again to enter the second function, `secondCall()`. Again this is added to the call stack. One more step takes you into the third function, `thirdCall()`, again with its name being added to the top of the call stack.

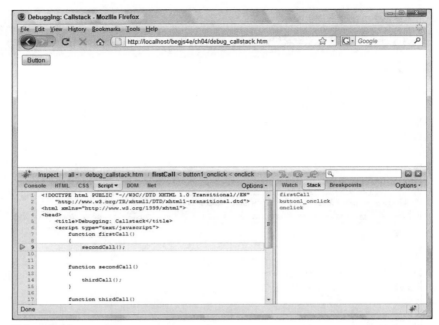

Figure 4-14

8. Step Into again, and as you leave the function `thirdCall()` you will see that its name is removed from the top of the call stack. Yet another step takes you out of the second function `secondCall()`, whose name is also now removed from the stack. Each additional click takes you out of a function, and removes its name from the call stack, until eventually all the code has been executed and you're back to the browser again.

This demo page was very simple to follow, but with complex pages, especially multi-frame pages, the call stack can prove very useful for tracking where you are, where you have been, and how you got there.

As mentioned earlier, most other developer tools for other browsers are based upon Firebug, and you'll soon see this with IE8's built-in tools.

Debugging in Internet Explorer

Before version 8, developers had to download and install the Microsoft Script Debugger for any type of script debugging. Thankfully, Microsoft built a debugger into IE8, but it is turned off by default. To enable it, follow these steps:

1. Click Tools ⇨ Internet Options.
2. Click the Advanced tab, and uncheck the box next to "Disable script debugging (Internet Explorer)" under the Browsing section (see Figure 4-15).
3. Click OK to save the settings and exit the Internet Options dialog box.

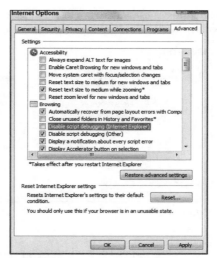

Figure 4-15

You can access the debugger in a couple of ways now that it is enabled:

❑ You can bring up the debugger by clicking Tools ➪ Developer Tools. The Developer Tools contains a variety of tools you might find useful (like Firebug, it's much more than a JavaScript debugger). For easy access, consider modifying the command bar to include the Developer Tools button. Once the Developer Tools window appears, click the Script tab as shown in Figure 4-16.

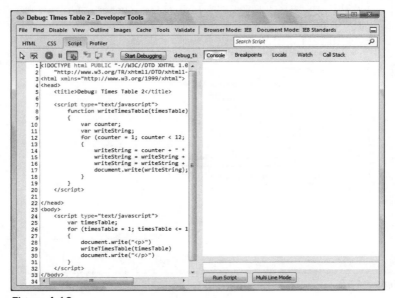

Figure 4-16

❑   This method is probably the easiest way to begin debugging. Simply navigate to the desired page. If any errors occur, a dialog box appears asking if you want to debug (see Figure 4-17).

Figure 4-17

Click the Yes button, and the Developer Tools window appears with the Script tab already selected. The debugger stops on the line where the error is and highlights it in yellow, although this may not be obvious from the black-and-white screenshot in Figure 4-18. Go ahead and load the original version of debug_timestable.htm in IE8 (the one with the error) to see this in action. Click Yes to start debugging.

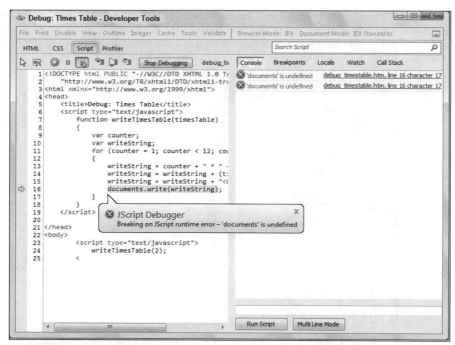

Figure 4-18

One of the primary differences in IE8's debugger is it must be in debugging mode if you want to debug. This may seem obvious, but if you recall, Firebug didn't have a debugging mode.

As you can see in Figure 4-18, the debugger is made up of two panels. The left displays the source code of the file that contains the error. If multiple files contain JavaScript, you can select those files by using the pull-down menu next to the Stop Debugging button.

The right panel contains five tabs:

- ❑ **Console**: Consists of an upper and lower panel. The lower panel allows you to enter and run JavaScript code. It has a single-line mode and a multi-line mode for larger blocks of code. The upper panel is a log of commands you entered along with their results.

- ❑ **Breakpoints**: Lists all breakpoints that you've created for the code in the current page.

- ❑ **Locals**: Lists the variables and their values in scope of the breakpoint.

- ❑ **Watches**: Lists the variables and their values you specify to watch at the breakpoint.

- ❑ **Call Stack**: Displays the call stack.

Another difference in IE8's Developer Tools is the additional Locals tab. Microsoft took Firebug's Watch tab and broke it into the Locals and Watches tabs.

The source code in the left panel is read-only, so changing it requires editing the file in your text editor. Do so, and change the offending `documents` in line 16 to `document`. Save it and try to reload the web page. Notice you cannot do so. This is because the debugger is currently running and stopped at an error. In order to reload the page, you must click the Stop Debugging button. With the debugger now stopped, you can reload the page.

Having corrected the mistake and reloaded the page, you should see the times table in your web page.

Setting Breakpoints

Creating a breakpoint in IE8 is as simple and straightforward as it is in Firebug; simply click in the gutter on the line you want the debugger to break at. After creating a breakpoint, you'll notice a red circle next to the line number.

Upon creating a breakpoint, an entry is added in the list of breakpoints found by clicking the Breakpoints tab. Each entry consists of a checkbox to enable/disable the breakpoint, the file name of the source file, and the line number the breakpoint is on. Figure 4-19 shows a breakpoint on line 17 of `debug_timestable2.htm`.

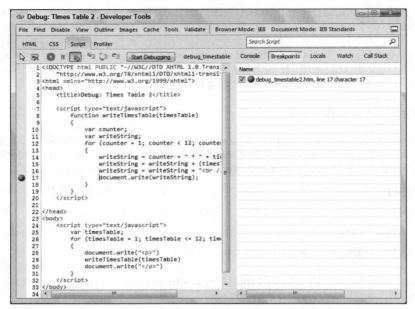

Figure 4-19

IE8's JavaScript debugger also supports the `debugger` keyword. However, you must be in debugging mode in order for IE8's debugger to pause on that line. Otherwise, you'll be greeted with the old selection screen. If you use the `debugger` keyword in your code and see Figure 4-20, then you need to turn on debugging mode.

Figure 4-20

Adding Watches

The Watch tab's sole purpose is to list the variables you want to watch and display their values and type. Adding a watch is slightly different in IE8 than it is in Firebug: You must be in debugging mode and stopped at a breakpoint to add a watch.

If you are in debugging mode and stopped at a breakpoint, simply click "Click to Add...," type the variable you want to watch, and press the Enter key (see Figure 4-21).

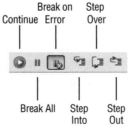

Figure 4-21

Stepping Through Code

At the top of the debugger window, and to the left of the Debugging button, are six buttons that control code execution (see Figure 4-22).

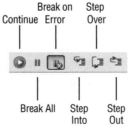

Figure 4-22

The Continue option (shortcut key F5) continues code execution until either the next breakpoint or the end of all code. The second option, Break All, ensures that the debugger breaks before the execution of the next statement. Break on Error tells the debugger to break whenever an error occurs. Step Into (F11), Step Over (F10), and Step Out (Shift+11) behave as they do in Firebug.

IE8's debugger denotes the current line by highlighting the line in yellow and adds a yellow arrow in the gutter.

Unlike Firefox and Firebug, stepping through code does not update the web page. The JavaScript executes, but you will not see the results until all code is executed.

The Console

Unlike Firebug's console, IE8's Developer Tools console is located with the rest of the JavaScript tools and is accessed via the Console tab, but that's where the primary differences end.

The console logs JavaScript errors and allows you to execute code within the context of the line the debugger is stopped at. Figure 4-23 shows the "Changed on the Fly" example from the Firebug section recreated in IE8.

By default, the console accepts only single lines of JavaScript code. You can change this by clicking the Multi Line Mode button.

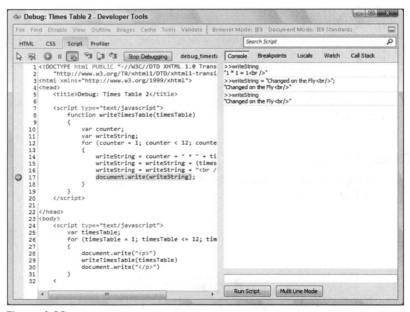

Figure 4-23

Debugging in Safari

Safari's debugging tool's story is similar to that of IE's. Safari's rendering engine is called Webkit, and the folks that write and maintain Webkit built a separate tool, codenamed Drosera, that contained the tools similar to Firebug and IE8's Developer Tools. It was a separate download, and it required you to attach it to a specific Safari/Webkit window.

Safari 3 includes a tool called Web Inspector, but it does not have any JavaScript debugging capability. Starting with Safari 4, the Web Inspector has a built-in JavaScript debugger, which we'll cover in this section.

Chrome also uses Webkit, but only version 3 beta includes the script debugger at the time of this writing.

Like IE8, the Web Inspector is disabled by default. To enable it, follow these steps:

1. Click the Settings menu button and choose the Preferences option (see Figure 4-24).

Figure 4-24

2. In the Preferences window, click the Advanced tab and select the Show Develop Menu in Menu Bar option (see Figure 4-25). Close the Preferences window.

Figure 4-25

3. Click the Settings menu button and select the Show Menu Bar option. This will display the traditional menus at the top of the window.

4. To open the debugger, select Develop ➪ Start Debugging JavaScript from the menu bar.

When the window opens, you'll see some code that definitely isn't yours. That's OK — you can change that in a bit. First, let's look at the window and identify the separate parts. Figure 4-26 shows the JavaScript debugger when it was first opened on the debug_timestable2.htm file. The code displayed may vary on your computer.

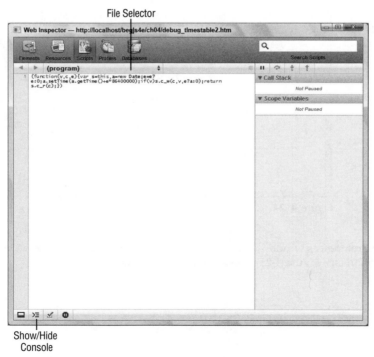

Figure 4-26

Unlike the tools you looked at previously, Safari's Web Inspector doesn't use tabs to partition the various features. Instead, it organizes everything within the window so you have easy access to all features. You can see the Call Stack and Scope Variables are not tabs, but rather individual sections you can view at the same time as you debug. Click the Console button, and you'll see that it adds a panel to the bottom of the window (see Figure 4-27).

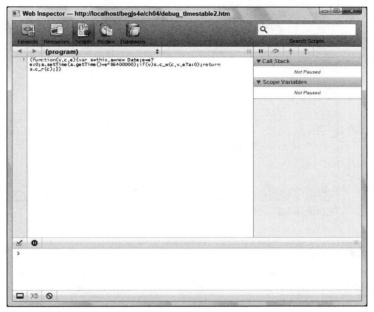

Figure 4-27

Everything is here, readily available and visible to you; so load debug_timestable2.htm in Safari and go back to the Web Inspector window. Click the file selection drop-down menu and choose the HTML file to display the source code of the file. Like the previous tools, the source code is read-only, but you can set breakpoints.

Setting Breakpoints

Creating a breakpoint follows the same procedure in Web Inspector as the other tools: click in the gutter on the line you want the debugger to break at. Breakpoints in Web Inspector are denoted by a blue tag (see Figure 4-28). Create one on line 17.

Unlike Firebug and IE's Developer Tools, Web Inspector does not list the breakpoints you set in a separate area, so remember where your breakpoints are if you use Safari and Web Inspector as your browser and debugger of choice.

Reload the page so the debugger can break and we can walk through the features.

Web Inspector supports the debugger *keyword.*

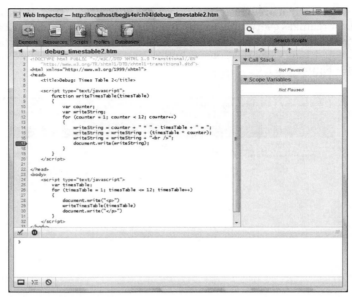

Figure 4-28

No Watches for You!

Web Inspector does not allow you to add your own variables to watch, but the Scope Variables section displays all variables in scope. Figure 4-29 shows how the variables are divided into local and global variables.

Figure 4-29

Stepping Through Code

The code-stepping buttons are at the top of the right panel and underneath the search box (see Figure 4-30).

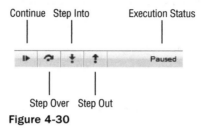

Figure 4-30

These buttons perform the same functions as in Firebug and IE; however, they are in a slightly different order. The first button continues code execution until either the next breakpoint or the end of all code. The second button is Step Over, the third is Step Into, and the fourth is Step Out.

Like Firefox and Firebug, Safari and Web Inspector update the page as you step through code. So you can see the results as each line executes.

The Console

The console serves the same purpose as it does in the previous tools. You can check the value of a variable by typing the variable and pressing the Enter key. You can also execute code in the context of the current line of code. Try the "Changed on the Fly" example from the Firebug section to see it in action.

Unlike the previous tools, the Web Inspector console does not allow for multi-line input.

Although the Web Inspector's UI is sleek and tab-less (and some would say cluttered), it's time to venture back into the world of tabs with Opera's Dragonfly.

Using Dragonfly: Opera's Development Tools

Opera's Dragonfly is a latecomer to the realm of browser-based development tools. At the time of this writing, it is currently pre-beta software, but it comes included with Opera as of version 9.5.

There are two ways to open Dragonfly:

❑   Through the Tools menu: Tools ⇨ Advanced ⇨ Developer Tools.

❑   Through the Debug menu, which can be installed by opening the following URL in Opera: `http://dragonfly.opera.com/app/debugmenu/DebugMenu.ini`.

Figure 4-31 shows Dragonfly open with `debug_timestable2.htm` loaded in Opera.

127

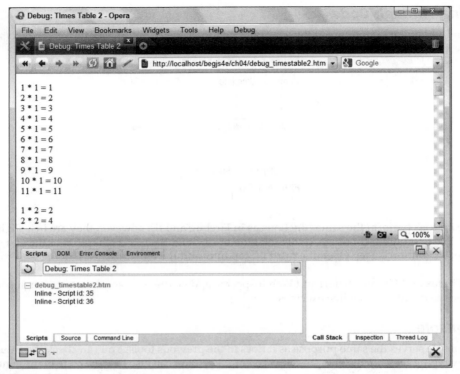

Figure 4-31

Dragonfly follows the popular two-panel layout. The left panel contains a few tabs at the top that control the several different tools offered by Dragonfly. The debugging tools are located under the Scripts tab, and it's the default tab when you open Dragonfly.

At the bottom of the left panel are more tabs: Scripts, Source, and Command Line. The Source and Command Line tabs provide the same functionality found in the other debuggers:

❑ **Scripts:** Displays the HTML files currently loaded into the browser and the JavaScript code they contain or reference. Figure 4-31 shows two inline scripts, meaning they are not contained in external files.

❑ **Source:** Displays source code. Unlike other tools, it displays only the code you select from the Script tab.

Go to the Scripts tab and click the first inline script. Doing so opens the Source tab and displays the contents of the `<script />` element in the HTML file's head (see Figure 4-32).

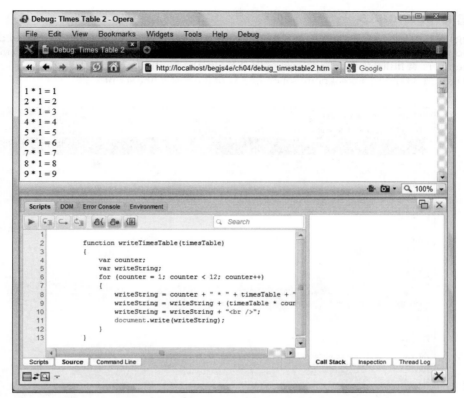

Figure 4-32

Go back to the Scripts tab (at the bottom of the window), and you'll see a pair of square brackets ([]) surrounding the inline script you clicked. This denotes the script that is currently displayed in the Source tab. Click the second inline script to view the contents of the <script /> element in the HTML document's body.

❑ **Command Line:** This is Dragonfly's console. Like the consoles of Firebug, IE8's Developer Tools, and Safari's Web Inspector, this console allows you to check variables' values and execute JavaScript commands within the context of the currently paused line.

The right panel contains the Call Stack, Inspection, and Thread Log tabs:

❑ **Call Stack:** Displays the call stack.

❑ **Inspection:** Displays the variables and their values in scope at the paused line.

❑ **Thread Log:** This is an advanced debugging tool that provides the information on the processing and execution of JavaScript code. This section will not cover the Thread Log tab.

Setting Breakpoints

Setting breakpoints in Dragonfly is as straightforward as in the other tools we've discussed thus far. Click one of the inline scripts in the Scripts tab to load it into the Source panel, and click to the left of the line numbers. A little black dot appears on the line number, indicating that a breakpoint is set for that line. Figure 4-33 shows a breakpoint set on line 11 of the first inline script.

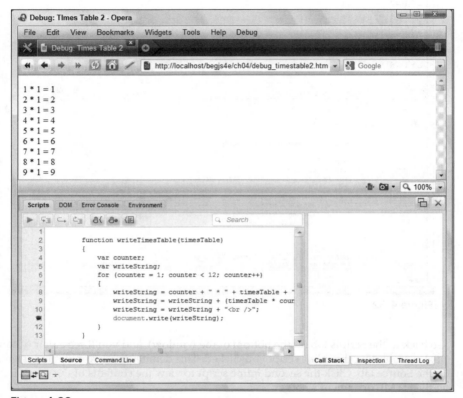

Figure 4-33

Stepping Through Code

Code stepping is controlled by a row of icons above the source code (see Figure 4-34).

Figure 4-34

These icons perform the same functions as in Firebug, IE's Developer Tools, and Web Inspector. They are, in order:

❑ Continue (F8)

❑ Step Into (F11)

❑ Step Over (F10)

❑ Step Out (Shift + F11).

Like Firefox and Firebug as well as Safari and Web Inspector, Opera and Dragonfly update the page as you step through code, allowing you to see the results of each line of code as it executes.

Summary

In this chapter you looked at the less exciting part of coding, namely bugs. In an ideal world you'd get things right the first time, every time, but in reality any code more than a few lines long is likely to suffer from bugs.

❑ You first looked at some of the more common errors, those made not just by JavaScript beginners, but also by experts with lots of experience.

❑ Some errors are not necessarily bugs in your code, but in fact exceptions to the normal circumstances that cause your code to fail. (For example, a Java applet might fail because a user is behind a firewall.) You saw that the `try...catch` statements are good for dealing with this sort of error, and that you can use the `catch` clause with the `throw` statement to deal with likely errors, such as those caused by user input. Finally, you saw that if you want a block of code to execute regardless of any error, you can use the `finally` clause.

❑ You looked at Firebug for Firefox, IE8's Developer Tools, the Web Inspector for Safari, and Opera's Dragonfly. With these tools you can analyze code as it's being run, which enables you to see its flow step by step, and to check variables and conditions. Although these debuggers have different interfaces, their principles and feature sets are pretty much the same.

Exercise Questions

Suggested solutions to these questions can be found in Appendix A.

1. The example `debug_timestable2.htm` has a deliberate bug. For each times table it creates only multipliers with values from 1 to 11.

Use the script debugger to work out why this is happening, and then correct the bug.

2. The following code contains a number of common errors. See if you can spot them:

```
<!DOCTYPE html PUBLIC "-//W3C//DTD XHTML 1.0 Transitional//EN"
    "http://www.w3.org/TR/xhtml1/DTD/xhtml1-transitional.dtd">

<html xmlns="http://www.w3.org/1999/xhtml">
<head>
```

```
    <title>Chapter 4, Question 2</title>
</head>
<body>
<script type="text/javascript">
function checkForm(theForm)
{
    var formValid = true;
    var elementCount  = 0;
    while(elementCount =<= theForm.length)
    {
        if (theForm.elements[elementcount].type == "text")
        {
            if (theForm.elements[elementCount].value() = "")
                alert("Please complete all form elements")
            theForm.elements[elementCount].focus;
            formValid = false;
            break;
        }
    }
    return formValid;
}
</script>
<form name="form1" onsubmit="return checkForm(document.form1)" action="">
    <input type="text" id="text1" name="text1" />
    <br />
    CheckBox 1<input type="checkbox" id="checkbox2" name="checkbox2" />
    <br />
    CheckBox 1<input type="checkbox" id="checkbox1" name="checkbox1" />
    <br />
    <input type="text" id="text2" name="text2" />
    <p>
        <input type="submit" value="Submit" id="submit1" name="submit1" />
    </p>
</form>
</body>
</html>
```

JavaScript — An Object-Based Language

In this chapter, you look at a concept that is central to JavaScript, namely *objects*. But what are objects, and why are they useful?

First, we have to break it to you: You have been using objects throughout this book (for example, an array is an object). JavaScript is an object-based language, and therefore most of what you do involves manipulating objects. You'll see that when you make full use of these objects, the range of things you can do with JavaScript expands immensely.

We'll start this chapter by taking a look at the idea of what objects are and why they are important. We'll move on to what kinds of objects are used in JavaScript, how to create them and use them, and how they simplify many programming tasks for you. Finally, you'll see in more detail some of the most useful objects that JavaScript provides and how to use these in practical situations.

Not only does the JavaScript language consist of a number of these things called objects (which are also called *native JavaScript objects*), but also the browser itself is modeled as a collection of objects available for your use. You'll learn about these objects in particular in the next chapter.

Object-Based Programming

Object-based programming is a slightly scarier way of saying "programming using objects." But what are these objects that you will be programming with? Where are they and how and why would you want to program with them? In this section, you'll look at the answers to these questions, both in general programming terms and more specifically within JavaScript.

What Are Objects?

To start the introduction to objects, let's think about what is meant by an object in the "real world" outside computing. The world is composed of things, or objects, such as tables, chairs, and cars (to name just a few!). Let's take a car as an example, to explore what an object really is.

How would you define the car? You might say it's a blue car with four-wheel drive. You might specify the speed at which it's traveling. When you do this, you are specifying *properties* of the object. For example, the car has a color property, which in this instance has the value blue.

How do you use the car? You turn the ignition key, press the gas pedal, beep the horn, change the gear (that is, choose between 1, 2, 3, 4, and reverse on a manual car, or drive and reverse on an automatic), and so on. When you do this, you are using *methods* of the object.

You can think of methods as being a bit like functions. Sometimes, you may need to use some information with the method, or pass it a parameter, to get it to work. For example, when you use the changing-gears method, you need to say which gear you want to change to. Other methods may pass information back to the owner. For example, the dipstick method will tell the owner how much oil is left in the car.

Sometimes using one or more of the methods may change one or more of the object's properties. For example, using the accelerator method will probably change the car's speed property. Other properties can't be changed: for example, the body-shape property of the car (unless you hit a brick wall with the speed property at 100 miles per hour!).

You could say that the car is defined by its collection of methods and properties. In object-based programming, the idea is to model real-world situations by objects, which are defined by their methods and properties.

Objects in JavaScript

You should now have a basic idea of what an object is — a "thing" with methods and properties. But how do you use this concept in JavaScript?

In the previous chapters you have (for the most part) been dealing with *primitive* data (that is, you've been working with actual data). This type of data is not too complex and is fairly easy to deal with. However, not all information is as simple as primitive data. Let's look at an example to clarify things a little.

Suppose you had written a web application that displayed timetable information for buses or trains. Once the user has selected a journey, you might want to let him know how long that journey will take. To do that, you need to subtract the arrival time from the departure time.

However, that's not quite as simple as it may appear at first glance. For example, consider a departure time of 14:53 (for 2:53 p.m.) and an arrival time of 15:10 (for 3:10 p.m.). If you tell JavaScript to evaluate the expression 15.10–14.53, you get the result 0.57, which is 57 minutes. However, you know that the real difference in time is 17 minutes. Using the normal mathematical operators on times doesn't work!

What would you need to do to calculate the difference between these two times? You would first need to separate the hours from the minutes in each time. Then, to get the difference in minutes between the two times, you would need to check whether the minutes of the arrival time were greater than the minutes of the departure. If so, you can simply subtract the departure time minutes from the arrival time minutes. If not, you need to add 60 to the arrival time minutes and subtract one from the arrival time hours to compensate, before taking the departure time minutes from the arrival time minutes. You then need to subtract the departure time hours from the arrival time hours, before putting the minutes and hours that you have arrived at back together.

This would work okay so long as the two times were in the same day. It wouldn't work, for example, with the times 23:45 and 04:32.

This way of working out the time difference obviously has its problems, but it also seems very complex. Is there an easier way to deal with more complex data such as times and dates?

This is where objects come in. You can define your departure and arrival times as Date objects. Because they are Date objects, they come with a variety of properties and methods that you can use when you need to manipulate or calculate times. For example, you can use the getTime() method to get the number of milliseconds between the time in the Date object and January 1, 1970, 00:00:00. Once you have these millisecond values for the arrival and departure times, you can simply subtract one from the other and store the result in another Date object. To retrieve the hours and minutes of this time, you simply use the getHours() and getMinutes() methods of the Date object. You'll see more examples of this later in the chapter.

The Date object is not the only type of object that JavaScript has to offer. Another object type was introduced in Chapter 2, but to keep things simple, we didn't tell you what it was at the time: the Array object. Recall that an array is a way of holding a number of pieces of data at the same time.

Array objects have a property called length that tells you how many pieces of data, or rather how many elements, the array holds. You actually used this property in the trivia quiz in Chapter 3 to work out how many times you needed to loop through the array.

Array objects also have a number of methods. One example is the sort() method, which can be used to sort the elements within the array into alphabetical order.

You should now have an idea why objects are useful in JavaScript. You have seen the Date and Array objects, but there are many other types of objects that JavaScript makes available so that you can achieve more with your code. These include the Math and String objects, which we will talk more about later in the chapter.

Using JavaScript Objects

Now that you have seen the *why* of JavaScript objects, you need to look at the *what* and the *how*.

Each of JavaScript's objects has a collection of related properties and methods that can be used to manipulate a certain kind of data. For example, the Array object consists of methods to manipulate arrays and properties to find out information from them. In most cases, to make use of these methods and properties, you need to define your data as one of these objects. In other words, you need to create an object.

In this section, you'll look at how to go about creating an object and, having done that, how you use its properties and methods.

Creating an Object

You have already seen an example of an `Array` object being created. To create an `Array` object, you used the following JavaScript statement:

```
var myArray = new Array();
```

So how is this statement made up?

The first half of the statement is familiar to you. You use the `var` keyword to define a variable called `myArray`. This variable is initialized, using the equals sign assignment operator (=), to the right-hand side of the statement.

The right-hand side of the statement consists of two parts. First you have the operator `new`. This tells JavaScript that you want to create a new object. Next you have `Array()`. This is the *constructor* for an `Array` object. It tells JavaScript what type of object you want to create. Most objects have constructors like this. For example, the `Date` object has the `Date()` constructor. The only exception you see in this book is the `Math` object, and this will be explained in a later part of the chapter.

You also saw in Chapter 2 that you can pass parameters to the constructor `Array()` to add data to your object. For example, the following code creates an `Array` object that has three elements containing the data `"Paul"`, `"Jeremy"`, and `"Nick"`:

```
var myArray = new Array("Paul", "Jeremy", "Nick");
```

Let's see some more examples, this time creating a `Date` object. The simplest way to do so is like this:

```
var myDate = new Date();
```

This will create a `Date` object containing the date and time when it was created. However, the following line creates a `Date` object containing the date 1 January 2010:

```
var myDate = new Date("1 Jan 2010");
```

How object data are stored in variables differs from how primitive data, such as text and numbers, are stored. (Primitive data are the most basic data possible in JavaScript.) With primitive data, the variable holds the data's actual value. For example:

```
var myNumber = 23;
```

This code means that the variable `myNumber` holds the data 23. However, variables assigned to objects don't hold the actual data, but rather a *reference* to the memory address where the data can be found. This doesn't mean you can get hold of the memory address — this is something only JavaScript has details of and keeps to itself in the background. All you need to remember is that when you say that a variable references an object, you mean it references a memory address. This is shown in the following example:

```
var myArrayRef = new Array(0, 1, 2);
var mySecondArrayRef = myArrayRef;
myArrayRef[0] = 100;
alert(mySecondArrayRef[0]);
```

First you set variable myArrayRef reference to the new array object, and then you set mySecondArrayRef to the same reference — for example, now mySecondArrayRef is set to reference the same array object. So when you set the first element of the array to 100, as shown here:

```
myArrayRef [0] = 100;
```

and display the contents of the first element of the array referenced in mySecondArrayRef as follows:

```
alert(mySecondArrayRef[0]);
```

you'll see it has also magically changed to 100! However, as you now know, it's not magic; it's because both variables reference the same array object, because when it comes to objects, it's a reference to the object and not the object itself that is stored in a variable. When you did the assignment, it didn't make a copy of the array object, it simply copied the reference. Contrast that with the following:

```
var myVariable = "ABC";
var mySecondVariable = myVariable;
myVariable = "DEF";
alert(mySecondVariable);
```

In this case you're dealing with a string, which is primitive data type, as are numbers. This time the actual values are stored in the variable, so when you do this:

```
var mySecondVariable = myVariable;
```

mySecondVariable gets its own separate copy of the data in myVariable. So the alert at the end will still show mySecondVariable as holding "ABC".

To summarize this section, you create JavaScript objects using the following basic syntax:

```
var myVariable = new ConstructorName(optional parameters);
```

Using an Object's Properties

Accessing the values contained in an object's properties is very simple. You write the name of the variable containing (or referencing) your object, followed by a dot, and then the name of the object's property.

For example, if you defined an Array object contained in the variable myArray, you could access its length property like this:

```
myArray.length
```

But what can you do with this property now that you have it? You can use it as you would any other piece of data and store it in a variable:

```
var myVariable = myArray.length;
```

Or you can show it to the user:

```
alert(myArray.length);
```

137

In some cases, you can even change the value of the property, like this:

```
myArray.length = 12;
```

However, unlike variables, some properties are read-only — you can get information from them, but you can't *change* information inside them.

Calling an Object's Methods

Methods are very much like functions in that they can be used to perform useful tasks, such as getting the hours from a particular date or generating a random number. Again like functions, some methods return a value, such as a `Date` object's `getHours()` method, while others perform a task, but return no data, such as an `Array` object's `sort()` method.

Using the methods of an object is very similar to using properties, in that you put the object's variable name first, then a dot, and then the name of the method. For example, to sort the elements of an `Array` in the variable `myArray`, you may use the following code:

```
myArray.sort();
```

Just as with functions, you can pass parameters to some methods by placing the parameters between the parentheses following the method's name. However, whether or not a method takes parameters, you must still put parentheses after the method's name, just as you did with functions. As a general rule, anywhere you can use a function, you can use a method of an object.

Primitives and Objects

You should now have a good idea about the difference between primitive data, such as numbers and strings, and object data, such as `Dates` and `Arrays`. However, as was mentioned earlier, there is also a `String` object. Where does this fit in?

In fact there are `String`, `Number`, and `Boolean` objects corresponding to the string, number, and Boolean primitive data types. For example, to create a `String` object containing the text `"I'm a String object"` you can use the following code:

```
var myString = new String("I'm a String object");
```

`String` objects have the `length` property just as `Array` objects do. This returns the number of characters in the `String` object. For example,

```
var lengthOfString = myString.length;
```

would store the value `19` in the variable `lengthOfString` (remember that spaces are referred to as characters too).

But what if you had declared a primitive string called `mySecondString` holding the text `"I'm a primitive string"` like this:

```
var mySecondString = "I'm a primitive string";
```

and wanted to know how many characters could be found in this primitive string?

This is where JavaScript helps you out. Recall from previous chapters that JavaScript can handle the conversion of one data type to another automatically. For example, if you tried to add a string primitive to a number primitive, like this:

```
theResult = "23" + 23;
```

JavaScript would assume that you want to treat the number as a string and concatenate the two together, the number being converted to text automatically. The variable `theResult` would contain "2323" — the concatenation of 23 and 23, and not the sum of 23 and 23, which would be 46.

The same applies to objects. If you declare a primitive string and then treat it as an object, such as by trying to access one of its methods or properties, JavaScript will know that the operation you're trying to do won't work. The operation will only work with an object; for example, it would be valid with a `String` object. In this case, JavaScript converts the plain-text string into a temporary `String` object, just for that operation, and destroys the object when it's finished the operation.

So, for your primitive string `mySecondString`, you can use the `length` property of the `String` object to find out the number of characters it contains. For example:

```
var lengthOfSecondString = mySecondString.length;
```

This would store the data 22 in the variable `lengthOfSecondString`.

The same ideas expressed here are also true for number and Boolean primitives and their corresponding `Number` and `Boolean` objects. However, these objects are not used very often, so we will not be discussing them further in this book.

JavaScript's Native Object Types

So far, you have just been looking at what objects are, how to create them, and how to use them. Now take a look at some of the more useful objects that are native to JavaScript — that is, those that are built-in to the JavaScript language.

You won't be looking at all of the native JavaScript objects, just some of the more commonly used ones, namely the `String` object, the `Math` object, the `Array` object, and the `Date` object. Later in the book, a whole chapter is devoted to each of the more complex objects, such as the `String` object (Chapter 9) and the `Date` object (Chapter 10).

String Objects

Like most objects, `String` objects need to be created before they can be used. To create a `String` object, you can write this:

```
var string1 = new String("Hello");
var string2 = new String(123);
var string3 = new String(123.456);
```

However, as you have seen, you can also declare a string primitive and use it as if it were a `String` object, letting JavaScript do the conversion to an object for you behind the scenes. For example:

```
var string1 = "Hello";
```

Using this technique is preferable so long as it's clear to JavaScript what object you expect to have created in the background. If the primitive data type is a string, this won't be a problem and JavaScript will work it out. The advantages to doing it this way are that there is no need to create a `String` object itself and you avoid the troubles with comparing string objects. When you try to compare string objects with primitive string values, the actual values are compared, but with `String` objects, the object references are compared.

The `String` object has a vast number of methods and properties. In this section, you'll be looking only at some of the less complex and more commonly used methods. However, in Chapter 9 you'll look at some of the trickier but very powerful methods associated with strings and the regular expression object (`RegExp`). Regular expressions provide a very powerful means of searching strings for patterns of characters. For example, if you want to find `"Paul"` where it exists as a whole word in the string `"Pauline, Paul, Paula"`, you need to use regular expressions. However, they can be a little tricky to use, so we won't discuss them further in this chapter — we want to save some fun for later!

With most of the `String` object's methods, it helps to remember that a string is just a series of individual characters and that, as with arrays, each character has a position, or index. Also as with arrays, the first position, or index, is labeled 0 and not 1. So, for example, the string `"Hello World"` has the character positions shown in the following table:

Character Index	0	1	2	3	4	5	6	7	8	9	10
Character	H	e	l	l	o		W	o	r	l	d

The length Property

The `length` property simply returns the number of characters in the string. For example,

```
var myName = new String("Jeremy");
document.write(myName.length);
```

will write the length of the string `"Jeremy"` (that is, 6) to the page.

Finding a String Inside Another String — The indexOf() and lastIndexOf() Methods

The methods `indexOf()` and `lastIndexOf()` are used for searching for the occurrence of one string inside another. A string contained inside another is usually termed a *substring*. They are useful when you have a string of information but only want a small part of it. For example, in the trivia quiz, when someone enters a text answer, you want to check if certain keywords are present within the string.

Both `indexOf()` and `lastIndexOf()` take two parameters:

❑   The string you want to find

❑   The character position you want to start searching from (optional)

Character positions start at 0. If you don't include the second parameter, searching starts from the beginning of the string.

The return value of `indexOf()` and `lastIndexOf()` is the character position in the string at which the substring was found. Again, it's zero-based, so if the substring is found at the start of the string, then 0 is returned. If there is no match, the value –1 is returned.

For example, to search for the substring `"Jeremy"` in the string `"Hello jeremy. How are you Jeremy"`, you may use the following code:

```
<script type="text/javascript">
var myString = "Hello jeremy. How are you Jeremy";
var foundAtPosition;

foundAtPosition = myString.indexOf("Jeremy");
alert(foundAtPosition);
</script>
```

This code should result in a message box containing the number 26, which is the character position of `"Jeremy"`. You might be wondering why it's 26, which clearly refers to the second `"Jeremy"` in the string, rather than 6 for the first `"jeremy"`. Well, this is due to case sensitivity again. It's laboring the point a bit, but JavaScript takes case sensitivity very seriously, both in its syntax and when making comparisons. If you type `IndexOf()` instead of `indexOf()`, JavaScript will complain. Similarly, `"jeremy"` is not the same as `"Jeremy"`. Remember that mistakes with case are very common and so easy to make, even for experts, that it's best to be very aware of case when programming.

You've seen `indexOf()` in action, but how does `lastIndexOf()` differ? Well, whereas `indexOf()` starts searching from the beginning of the string, or the position you specified in the second parameter, and works towards the end, `lastIndexOf()` starts at the end of the string, or the position you specified, and works towards the beginning of the string.

> In the current example, you first search using `indexOf()`, which finds the first `"Jeremy"` (changed to the correct case from the last example). The alert box displays this result, which is character position 6. Then you search using `lastIndexOf()`. This starts searching at the end of the string, and so the first `"Jeremy"` it comes to is the last one in the string at character position 26. Therefore, the second alert box displays the result 26.

```
<script type="text/javascript">
var myString = "Hello Jeremy. How are you Jeremy";
var foundAtPosition;

foundAtPosition = myString.indexOf("Jeremy");
alert(foundAtPosition);

foundAtPosition = myString.lastIndexOf("Jeremy");
alert(foundAtPosition);
</script>
```

Try It Out   **Counting Occurrences of Substrings**

In this example, you look at how to use the "start character position" parameter of indexOf(). Here
you will count how many times the word Wrox appears in the string.

```
<!DOCTYPE html PUBLIC "-//W3C//DTD XHTML 1.0 Transitional//EN"
    "http://www.w3.org/TR/xhtml1/DTD/xhtml1-transitional.dtd">

<html xmlns="http://www.w3.org/1999/xhtml">
<head>
    <title>Chapter 5: Example 1</title>
</head>
<body>
<script type="text/javascript">
var myString = "Welcome to Wrox books. ";
myString = myString + "The Wrox website is www.wrox.com. ";
myString = myString + "Visit the Wrox website today. Thanks for buying Wrox";

var foundAtPosition = 0;
var wroxCount = 0;

while (foundAtPosition != -1)
{
    foundAtPosition = myString.indexOf("Wrox",foundAtPosition);
    if (foundAtPosition != -1)
    {
        wroxCount++;
        foundAtPosition++;
    }
}

document.write("There are " + wroxCount + " occurrences of the word Wrox");

</script>
</body>
</html>
```

Save this example as ch5_examp1.htm. When you load the page into your browser, you should see the
following sentence: There are 4 occurrences of the word Wrox.

At the top of the script block, you built up a string inside the variable myString, which you then want
to search for the occurrence of the word Wrox. You also define two variables: wroxCount will contain
the number of times Wrox is found in the string, and foundAtPosition will contain the position in the
string of the current occurrence of the substring Wrox.

You then used a while loop, which continues looping all the while you are finding the word Wrox in
the string — that is, while the variable foundAtPosition is not equal to –1. Inside the while loop, you
have this line:

```
foundAtPosition = myString.indexOf("Wrox",foundAtPosition);
```

Here you search for the next occurrence of the substring Wrox in the string myString. How do you make
sure that you get the next occurrence? You use the variable foundAtPosition to give you the starting
position of your search, because this contains the index after the index position of the last occurrence
of the substring Wrox. You assign the variable foundAtPosition to the result of your search, the index
position of the next occurrence of the substring Wrox.

Each time `Wrox` is found (that is, each time `foundAtPosition` is not -1) you increase the variable `wroxCount`, which counts how many times you have found the substring, and you increase `foundAtPosition` so that you continue the search at the next position in the string.

```
if (foundAtPosition != -1)
{
    wroxCount++;
    foundAtPosition++;
}
```

Finally, you `document.write()` the value of the variable `wroxCount` to the page.

Chapter 3 talked about the danger of infinite loops, and you can see that there is a danger of one here. If `foundAtPosition++` were removed, you'd keep searching from the same starting point and never move to find the next occurrence of the word `Wrox`.

The `indexOf()` and `lastIndexOf()` methods are more useful when coupled with the `substr()` and `substring()` methods, which you'll be looking at in the next section. Using a combination of these methods enables you to cut substrings out of a string.

Copying Part of a String — The substr() and substring() Methods

If you wanted to cut out part of a string and assign that cut-out part to another variable or use it in an expression, you would use the `substr()` and `substring()` methods. Both methods provide the same end result — that is, a part of a string — but they differ in the parameters they require.

The method `substring()` accepts two parameters: the character start position and the character after the last character desired in the substring. The second parameter is optional; if you don't include it, all characters from the start position to the end of the string are included.

For example, if your string is `"JavaScript"` and you want just the text `"Java"`, you could call the method like so:

```
var myString = "JavaScript";
var mySubString = myString.substring(0,4);
alert(mySubString);
```

Character Position	0	1	2	3	4	5	6	7	8	9
Character	J	a	v	a	S	c	r	i	p	t

Like `substring()`, the method `substr()` again takes two parameters, the first being the start position of the first character you want included in your substring. However, this time the second parameter specifies the length of the string of characters that you want to cut out of the longer string. For example, you could rewrite the preceding code like this:

```
var myString = "JavaScript";
var mySubString = myString.substr(0,4);
alert(mySubString);
```

As with the `substring()` method, the second parameter is optional. If you don't include it, all the characters from the start position onward will be included.

> *The* `substring()` *method is supported by pre-version 4 browsers, and the* `substr()` *method is supported by version 4 (and later) browsers. Most of the time, you will use the* `substr()` *method.*

Let's look at the use of the `substr()` and `lastIndexOf()` methods together. In the next chapter, you'll see how you can retrieve the file path and name of the currently loaded web page. However, there is no way of retrieving the file name alone. So if, for example, your file is `http://mywebsite/temp/myfile.htm`, you may need to extract the `myfile.htm` part. This is where `substr()` and `lastIndexOf()` are useful.

```
var fileName = window.location.href;
fileName = fileName.substr(fileName.lastIndexOf("/") + 1);
document.write("The file name of this page is " + fileName);
```

The first line sets the variable `fileName` to the current file path and name, such as `/mywebsite/temp/myfile.htm`. Don't worry about understanding this line; you'll be looking at it in the next chapter.

The second line is where the interesting action is. You can see that this code uses the return value of the `lastIndexOf()` method as a parameter for another method, something that's perfectly correct and very useful. The goal in using `fileName.lastIndexOf("/")` is to find the position of the final forward slash (/), which will be the last character before the name of the file. You add one to this value, because you don't want to include that character, and then pass this new value to the `substr()` method. There's no second parameter here (the length), because you don't know it. As a result, `substr()` will return all the characters right to the end of the string, which is what you want.

> *This example retrieves the name of the page on the local machine, because you're not accessing the page from a web server. However, don't let this mislead you into thinking that accessing files on a local hard drive from a web page is something you'll be able to do with JavaScript alone. To protect users from malicious hackers, JavaScript's access to the user's system, such as access to files, is very limited. You'll learn more about this later in the book.*

Converting Case — The toLowerCase() and toUpperCase() Methods

If you want to change the case of a string (for example, to remove case sensitivity when comparing strings), you need the `toLowerCase()` and `toUpperCase()` methods. It's not hard to guess what these two methods do. Both of them return a string that is the value of the string in the `String` object, but with its case converted to either upper or lower depending on the method invoked. Any non-alphabetical characters remain unchanged by these functions.

In the following example, you can see that by changing the case of both strings you can compare them without case sensitivity being an issue.

```
var myString = "I Don't Care About Case"

if (myString.toLowerCase() == "i don't care about case")
{
    alert("Who cares about case?");
}
```

Even though `toLowerCase()` and `toUpperCase()` don't take any parameters, you must remember to put the two empty parentheses — that is, `()` — at the end, if you want to call a method.

Selecting a Single Character from a String — The charAt() and charCodeAt() Methods

If you want to find out information about a single character within a string, you need the `charAt()` and `charCodeAt()` methods. These methods can be very useful for checking the validity of user input, something you'll see more of in Chapter 7 when you look at HTML forms.

The `charAt()` method accepts one parameter: the index position of the character you want in the string. It then returns that character. `charAt()` treats the positions of the string characters as starting at 0, so the first character is at index 0, the second at index 1, and so on.

For example, to find the last character in a string, you could use this code:

```
var myString = prompt("Enter some text","Hello World!");
var theLastChar = myString.charAt(myString.length - 1);
document.write("The last character is " + theLastChar);
```

In the first line, you prompt the user for a string, with the default of `"Hello World!"`, and store this string in the variable `myString`.

In the next line, you use the `charAt()` method to retrieve the last character in the string. You use the index position of `(myString.length - 1)`. Why? Let's take the string `"Hello World!"` as an example. The `length` of this string is 12, but the last character position is 11 because the indexing starts at 0. Therefore, you need to subtract one from the length of the string to get the last character's position.

In the final line, you write the last character in the string to the page.

The `charCodeAt()` method is similar in use to the `charAt()` method, but instead of returning the character itself, it returns a number that represents the decimal character code for that character in the Unicode character set. Recall that computers only understand numbers — to the computer, all your strings are just numeric data. When you request text rather than numbers, the computer does a conversion based on its internal understanding of each number and provides the respective character.

For example, to find the character code of the first character in a string, you could write this:

```
var myString = prompt("Enter some text","Hello World!");
var theFirstCharCode = myString.charCodeAt(0);
document.write("The first character code is " + theFirstCharCode);
```

This will get the character code for the character at index position 0 in the string given by the user, and write it out to the page.

Character codes go in order, so, for example, the letter A has the code 65, B 66, and so on. Lowercase letters start at 97 (a is 97, b is 98, and so on). Digits go from 48 (for the number 0) to 57 (for the number 9). You can use this information for various purposes, as you'll see in the next example.

Checking a Character's Case

The following is an example that detects the type of the character at the start of a given string — that is, whether the character is uppercase, lowercase, numeric, or other.

```
<!DOCTYPE html PUBLIC "-//W3C//DTD XHTML 1.0 Transitional//EN"
    "http://www.w3.org/TR/xhtml1/DTD/xhtml1-transitional.dtd">

<html xmlns="http://www.w3.org/1999/xhtml">
<head>
    <title>Chapter 5: Example 2</title>
    <script type="text/javascript">
    function checkCharType(charToCheck)
    {
        var returnValue = "O";
        var charCode = charToCheck.charCodeAt(0);

        if (charCode >= "A".charCodeAt(0) && charCode <= "Z".charCodeAt(0))
        {
            returnValue = "U";
        }
        else if (charCode >= "a".charCodeAt(0) && charCode <= "z".charCodeAt(0))
        {
            returnValue = "L";
        }
        else if (charCode >= "0".charCodeAt(0) && charCode <= "9".charCodeAt(0))
        {
            returnValue = "N";
        }

        return returnValue;
    }
    </script>
</head>

<body>
<script type="text/javascript">

var myString = prompt("Enter some text","Hello World!");
switch (checkCharType(myString))
{
    case "U":
        document.write("First character was upper case");
        break;
    case "L":
        document.write("First character was lower case");
        break;
    case "N":
        document.write("First character was a number");
        break;
    default:
        document.write("First character was not a character or a number");
}
</script>
```

```
</body>
</html>
```

Type the code and save it as ch5_examp2.htm.

When you load the page into your browser, you will be prompted for a string. A message will then be written to the page informing you of the type of the first character that you entered — whether it is uppercase, lowercase, a number, or something else, such as a punctuation mark.

To start with, you define a function checkCharType(), which is used in the body of the page. You start this function by declaring the variable returnValue and initializing it to the character "O" to indicate it's some other character than a lowercase letter, uppercase letter, or numerical character.

```
function checkCharType(charToCheck)
{
    var returnValue = "O";
```

You use this variable as the value to be returned at the end of the function, indicating the type of character. It will take the values U for uppercase, L for lowercase, N for number, and O for other.

The next line in the function uses the charCodeAt() method to get the character code of the first character in the string stored in charToCheck, which is the function's only parameter. The character code is stored in the variable charCode.

```
    var charCode = charToCheck.charCodeAt(0);
```

In the following lines, you have a series of if statements, which check within what range of values the character code falls. You know that if it falls between the character codes for A and Z, it's uppercase, and so you assign the variable returnValue the value U. If the character code falls between the character codes for a and z, it's lowercase, and so you assign the value L to the variable returnValue. If the character code falls between the character codes for 0 and 9, it's a number, and you assign the value N to the variable returnValue. If the value falls into none of these ranges, then the variable retains its initialization value of O for other, and you don't have to do anything.

```
    if (charCode >= "A".charCodeAt(0) && charCode <= "Z".charCodeAt(0))
    {
        returnValue = "U";
    }
    else if (charCode >= "a".charCodeAt(0) && charCode <= "z".charCodeAt(0))
    {
        returnValue = "L";
    }
    else if (charCode >= "0".charCodeAt(0) && charCode <= "9".charCodeAt(0))
    {
        returnValue = "N";
    }
```

This probably seems a bit weird at first, so let's see what JavaScript is doing with your code. When you write

```
    "A".charCodeAt(0)
```

it appears that you are trying to use a method of the String object on a string literal, which is the same as a primitive string in that it's just characters and not an object. However, JavaScript realizes what you are doing and does the necessary conversion of literal character "A" into a temporary String object containing "A". Then, and only then, does JavaScript perform the charCodeAt() method on the String object it has created in the background. When it has finished, the String object is disposed of. Basically, this is a shorthand way of writing the following:

```
var myChar = new String("A");
myChar.charCodeAt(0);
```

In either case, the first (and, in this string, the only) character's code is returned to you. For example, "A".charCodeAt(0) will return the number 65.

Finally you come to the end of the function and return the returnValue variable to where the function was called.

```
        return returnValue;
}
```

You might wonder why you bother using the variable returnValue at all, instead of just returning its value. For example, you could write the code as follows:

```
    if (charCode >= "A".charCodeAt(0) && charCode <= "Z".charCodeAt(0))
    {
        return "U";
    }
    else if (charCode >= "a".charCodeAt(0) && charCode <= "z".charCodeAt(0))
    {
        return "L";
    }
    else if (charCode >= "0".charCodeAt(0) && charCode <= "9".charCodeAt(0))
    {
        return "N";
    }
    return "O";
```

This would work fine, so why not do it this way? The disadvantage of this way is that it's difficult to follow the flow of execution of the function, which is not that bad in a small function like this, but can get tricky in bigger functions. With the original code you always know exactly where the function execution stops: It stops at the end with the only return statement. The version of the function just shown finishes when any of the return statements is reached, so there are four possible places where the function might end.

In the body of your page, you have some test code to check that the function works. You first use the variable myString, initialized to "Hello World!" or whatever the user enters into the prompt box, as your test string.

```
var myString = prompt("Enter some text","Hello World!");
```

Next, the switch statement uses the checkCharType() function that you defined earlier in its comparison expression. Depending on what is returned by the function, one of the case statements will execute and let the user know what the character type was.

```
switch (checkCharType(myString))
{
    case "U":
        document.write("First character was upper case");
        break;
    case "L":
        document.write("First character was lower case");
```

```
        break;
    case "N":
        document.write("First character was a number");
        break;
    default:
        document.write("First character was not a character or a number");
}
```

That completes the example, but before moving on, it's worth noting that this example is just that — an example of using charCodeAt(). In practice, it would be much easier to just write

```
if (char >= "A" && char <= "Z")
```

rather than

```
if (charCode >= "A".charCodeAt(0) && charCode <= "Z".charCodeAt(0))
```

which you have used here.

Converting Character Codes to a String — The fromCharCode() Method

The method fromCharCode() can be thought of as the opposite of charCodeAt(), in that you pass it a series of comma-separated numbers representing character codes, and it converts them to a single string.

However, the fromCharCode() method is unusual in that it's a *static* method — you don't need to have created a String object to use it with, it's always available to you.

For example, the following lines put the string "ABC" into the variable myString:

```
var myString;
myString = String.fromCharCode(65,66,67);
```

The fromCharCode() method can be very useful when used with variables. For example, to build up a string consisting of all the uppercase letters of the alphabet, you could use the following code:

```
var myString = "";
var charCode;

for (charCode = 65; charCode <= 90; charCode++)
{
    myString = myString + String.fromCharCode(charCode);
}

document.write(myString);
```

You use the for loop to select each character from A to Z in turn and concatenate this to myString. Note that while this is fine as an example, it is more efficient and less memory-hungry to simply write this instead:

```
var myString = "ABCDEFGHIJKLMNOPQRSTUVWXYZ";
```

Array Objects

You saw how to create and use arrays in Chapter 2, and this chapter mentioned earlier that they are actually objects.

In addition to storing data, `Array` objects provide a number of useful properties and methods you can use to manipulate the data in the array and find out information such as the size of the array.

Again, this is not an exhaustive look at every property and method of `Array` objects but rather just some of the more useful ones.

This book uses constructor syntax when creating arrays: `var myArray = new Array()`. *But it's possible to create arrays with much shorter syntax:* `var myArray = []`. *Simply use the opening and closing square brackets instead of* `new Array()`. *Your authors will continue to use the constructor, for clarity's sake, throughout the book.*

Finding Out How Many Elements Are in an Array — The length Property

The `length` property gives you the number of elements within an array, which you have already seen in the trivia quiz in Chapter 3. Sometimes you know exactly how long the array is, but there are situations where you may have been adding new elements to an array with no easy way of keeping track of how many have been added.

The `length` property can be used to find the index of the last element in the array. This is illustrated in the following example:

```
var names = new Array();

names[0] = "Paul";
names[1] = "Jeremy";
names[11] = "Nick";

document.write("The last name is " + names[names.length - 1]);
```

Note that you have inserted data in the elements with index positions 0, 1, *and* 11. *The array index starts at* 0, *so the last element is at index* `length - 1`, *which is* 11, *rather than the value of the* `length` *property, which is* 12.

Another situation in which the `length` property proves useful is where a JavaScript method returns an array it has built itself. For example, in Chapter 9, on advanced string handling, you'll see that the `String` object has the `split()` method, which splits text into pieces and passes back the result as an `Array` object. Because JavaScript created the array, there is no way for you to know, without the `length` property, what the index is of the last element in the array.

Joining Arrays — The concat() Method

If you want to take two separate arrays and join them together into one big array, you can use the `Array` object's `concat()` method. The `concat()` method returns a new array, which is the combination of the two arrays: the elements of the first array, then the elements of the second array. To do this, you use the method on your first array and pass the name of the second array as its parameter.

For example, say you have two arrays, names and ages, and separately they look like the following tables:

names array			
Element Index	0	1	2
Value	Paul	Jeremy	Nick

ages array			
Element Index	0	1	2
Value	31	30	31

If you combine them using names.concat(ages), you will get an array like the one in the following table:

Element Index	0	1	2	3	4	5
Value	Paul	Jeremy	Nick	31	30	31

In the following code, this is exactly what you are doing:

```
var names = new Array("Paul","Jeremy","Nick");
var ages = new Array(31,30,31);

var concatArray = names.concat(ages);
```

It's also possible to combine two arrays into one but assign the new array to the name of the existing first array, using names = names.concat(ages).

If you were to use ages.concat(names), what would be the difference? Well, as you can see in the following table, the difference is that now the ages array elements are first, and the elements from the names array are concatenated on the end.

Element Index	0	1	2	3	4	5
Value	31	30	31	Paul	Jeremy	N

Copying Part of an Array — The slice() Method

When you just want to copy a portion of an array, you can use the slice() met'
method, you can slice out a portion of the array and assign it to a new variab'
method has two parameters:

- ❑ The index of the first element you want copied
- ❑ The index of the element marking the end of the portion you are

Just as with string copying with `substring()`, the start point is included in the copy, but the end point is not. Again, if you don't include the second parameter, all elements from the start index onward are copied.

Suppose you have the array `names` shown in the following table:

Index	0	1	2	3	4
Value	Paul	Sarah	Jeremy	Adam	Bob

If you want to create a new array with elements 1, `Sarah`, and 2, `Jeremy`, you would specify a start index of 1 and an end index of 3. The code would look something like this:

```
var names = new Array("Paul","Sarah","Jeremy","Adam","Bob");
var slicedArray = names.slice(1,3);
```

When JavaScript copies the array, it copies the new elements to an array in which they have indexes 0 and 1, not their old indexes of 1 and 2.

After slicing, the `slicedArray` looks the following table:

Index	0	1
Value	Sarah	Jeremy

The first array, `names`, is unaffected by the slicing.

Converting an Array into a Single String — The join() Method

The `join()` method concatenates all the elements in an array and returns them as a string. It also enables you to specify any characters you want to insert *between* elements as they are joined together. The method has only one parameter, and that's the string you want between elements.

An example will help explain things. Imagine that you have your weekly shopping list stored in an array, which looks something like this:

Index	0	1	2	3	4
Value	Eggs	Milk	Potatoes	Cereal	Banana

Now you want to write out your shopping list to the page using `document.write()`. You want each n to be on a different line, so this means you need to use the `<br />` tag between each element. First, need to declare your array.

```
r myShopping = new Array("Eggs","Milk","Potatoes","Cereal","Banana");
```

vert the array into one string with the `join()` method.

```
ShoppingList = myShopping.join("<br />");
```

Now the variable `myShoppingList` will hold the following text:

```
"Eggs<br />Milk<br />Potatoes<br />Cereal<br />Banana"
```

which you can write out to the page with `document.write()`.

```
document.write(myShoppingList);
```

The shopping list will appear in the page with each item on a new line, as shown in Figure 5-1.

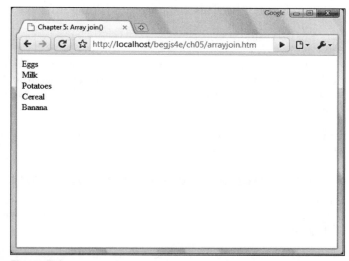

Figure 5-1

Putting Your Array in Order — The sort() Method

If you have an array that contains similar data, such as a list of names or a list of ages, you may want to put them in alphabetical or numerical order. This is something that the `sort()` method makes very easy. In the following code, you define your array and then put it in ascending alphabetical order using `names.sort()`. Finally, you output it so that you can see that it's in order.

```
var names = new Array("Paul","Sarah","Jeremy","Adam","Bob");
var elementIndex;

names.sort();
document.write("Now the names again in order" + "<br />");

for (elementIndex = 0; elementIndex < names.length; elementIndex++)
{
    document.write(names[elementIndex] + "<br />");
}
```

Don't forget that the sorting is case sensitive, so `Paul` will come before `p` stores letters encoded in their equivalent Unicode number, and that sortin numbers rather than actual letters. It just happens that Unicode numbers match the order in the alphabet. However, lowercase letters are given a different sequence of numbers, which come after the uppercase letters. So the array with elements Adam, adam, Zoë, zoë, will be sorted to the order Adam, Zoë, adam, zoë.

Note that in your for statement you've used the Array object's length property in the condition statement, rather than inserting the length of the array (5), like this:

```
for (elementIndex = 0; elementIndex < 5; elementIndex++)
```

Why do this? After all, you know in advance that there are five elements in the array. Well, what would happen if you altered the number of elements in the array by adding two more names?

```
var names = new Array("Paul","Sarah","Jeremy","Adam","Bob","Karen","Steve");
```

If you had inserted 5 rather than names.length, your loop code wouldn't work as you want it to. It wouldn't display the last two elements unless you changed the condition part of the for loop to 7. By using the length property, you've made life easier, because now there is no need to change code elsewhere if you add array elements.

Okay, you've put things in ascending order, but what if you wanted descending order? That is where the reverse() method comes in.

Putting Your Array into Reverse Order — The reverse() Method

The final method you'll look at for the Array object is the reverse() method, which, no prizes for guessing, reverses the order of the array so that the elements at the back are moved to the front. Let's take the shopping list again as an example.

Index	0	1	2	3	4
Value	Eggs	Milk	Potatoes	Cereal	Banana

If you use the reverse() method

```
var myShopping = new Array("Eggs","Milk","Potatoes","Cereal","Banana");
myShopping.reverse();
```

you end up with the array elements in this order:

Index	0	1	2	3	4
Value	Banana	Cereal	Potatoes	Milk	Eggs

ᒉ prove this, you could write it to the page with the join() method you saw earlier.

```
var myShoppingList = myShopping.join("<br />")
ᒉocument.write(myShoppingList);
```

Try It Out   Sorting an Array

When used in conjunction with the sort() method, the reverse() method can be used to sort an array so that its elements appear in reverse alphabetical or numerical order. This is shown in the following example:

```
<!DOCTYPE html PUBLIC "-//W3C//DTD XHTML 1.0 Transitional//EN"
    "http://www.w3.org/TR/xhtml1/DTD/xhtml1-transitional.dtd">

<html xmlns="http://www.w3.org/1999/xhtml">
<head>
    <title>Chapter 5: Example 3</title>
</head>
<body>
<script type="text/javascript">

var myShopping = new Array("Eggs","Milk","Potatoes","Cereal","Banana");

var ord = prompt("Enter 1 for alphabetical order, and -1 for reverse order", 1);

if (ord == 1)
{
    myShopping.sort();
    document.write(myShopping.join("<br />"));
}
else if (ord == -1)
{
    myShopping.sort();
    myShopping.reverse();
    document.write(myShopping.join("<br />"));
}
else
{
    document.write("That is not a valid input");
}
</script>
</body>
</html>
```

Save the example as ch5_examp3.htm. When you load this into your browser, you will be asked to enter some input depending on whether you want the array to be ordered in forward or backward order. If you enter 1, the array will be displayed in forward order. If you enter –1, the array will be displayed in reverse order. If you enter neither of these values, you will be told that your input was invalid.

At the top of the script block, you define the array containing your shopping list. Next you define the variable ord to be the value entered by the user in a prompt box.

```
var ord = prompt("Enter 1 for alphabetical order, and -1 for reverse order",
```

This value is used in the conditions of the if statements that follow. The first if check⌐ value of ord is 1 — that is, whether the user wants the array in alphabetical order. `⌐` code is executed:

```
myShopping.sort();
document.write(myShopping.join("<br>"));
```

The array is sorted and then displayed to the user on separate lines using the `join()` method. Next, in the `else if` statement, you check whether the value of `ord` is `-1` — that is, whether the user wants the array in reverse alphabetical order. If so, the following code is executed:

```
myShopping.sort();
myShopping.reverse();
document.write(myShopping.join("<br />"));
```

Here, you sort the array before reversing its order. Again the array is displayed to the user by means of the `join()` method.

Finally, if `ord` has neither the value 1 nor the value -1, you tell the user that his input was invalid.

```
document.write("That is not a valid input");
```

New Array Methods

In 2005, Mozilla updated the JavaScript engine in Firefox. In doing so, they added seven new methods to the `Array` object. These seven methods can be divided into two categories: location methods and iterative methods.

The following seven methods do not work Internet Explorer. They do, however, work in Firefox, Safari, Opera, and Chrome.

Finding Array Elements — The indexOf() and lastIndexOf() Methods

As you can probably guess by their names, these two methods resemble the functionality of the `String` object's `indexOf()` and `lastIndexOf()` methods — they return the index of an item's first and last occurrence in an array. Consider the following code:

```
var colors = new Array("red", "blue", "green", "blue");
alert(colors.indexOf("red"));
alert(colors.lastIndexOf("blue"));
```

The first line of code creates an array called `colors`. It has four elements (two of which are `blue`). The second line alerts 0 to the user, as `red` is the first element of the array.

Remember the `String` object's `lastIndexOf()` method searches the array backwards and returns the index of the first matching character. The `lastIndexOf()` method of the `Array` object behaves similarly, so the third line shows the user the value of 3.

Also similar to the `String` object's methods of the same name, these two methods return a value of -1 if the element could not be found in the array.

‍rating Through an Array Without Loops

‍he remaining five methods are called iterative methods because they iterate, or loop, through the array. ‍addition, these methods execute a function you define on every element while they iterate through the array. The function these methods use must follow one rule. The function must accept three arguments like the following code.

```
function functionName(value, index, array) {
    // do something here
}
```

When this function is executed, JavaScript passes three arguments to your function. The first is the value of the element, next is the index of the element, and finally is the array itself. With these parameters, you should be able to perform any operation or comparison you need.

Testing Each Element — The every(), some(), and filter() Methods

Let's look at the every() and some() methods first. These are testing methods. The every() method tests whether all elements in the array pass the test in your function. Consider the following code:

```
var numbers = new Array(1, 2, 3, 4, 5);

function isLessThan3(value, index, array)
{
    var returnValue = false;

    if (value < 3)
    {
        returnValue = true;
    }

    return returnValue;
}

alert(numbers.every(isLessThan3));
```

The first line shows the creation of an array called numbers; its elements hold the values 1 through 5. The next line defines the isLessThan3() function. It accepts the three mandatory arguments and determines if the value of each element is less than 3. The last line alerts the outcome of the every() test. Because not every value in the array is less than 3, the result of the every() test is false.

Contrast this with the some() method. Unlike every(), the some() test only cares if some of the elements pass the test in your function. Using the same numbers array and isLessThan3() function, consider this line of code:

```
alert(numbers.some(isLessThan3));
```

The result is true because some of the elements in the array are less than 3. It's easy to keep these tw~ methods straight. Just remember the every() method returns true if, and only if, all elements in '~ array pass the test in your function; the some() method returns true if, and only if, some of th~ ments in the array pass your function's test.

Let's assume you want to retrieve the elements that have a value less than 3. You a¹ elements meet this criterion, but how do you identify those elements and retri~ the filter() method becomes useful.

The `filter()` method executes your function on every element in the array, and if your function returns `true` for a particular element, that element is added to another array the `filter()` method returns. Keeping that in mind, look at the following code:

```
var numbers = new Array(1, 2, 3, 4, 5);

function isLessThan3(value, index, array)
{
    var returnValue = false;

    if (value < 3)
    {
        returnValue = true;
    }

    return returnValue;
}

if (numbers.some(isLessThan3))
{
    var result = numbers.filter(isLessThan3);
    alert("These numbers are less than 3: " + result);
}
```

This code defines the `numbers` array and the `isLessThan3` function used previously. The new code determines if any elements in the `numbers` array contain a value less than 3. If so, the `filter()` method is called and returns those elements in a new array. The result of this code can be seen in Figure 5-2.

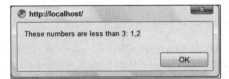

Figure 5-2

As you can see, the `filter()` method in combination with the `some()` method can be quite useful!

Before moving on, let's revisit the `isLessThan3()` function. As you have seen, the function works as is without any modification. However, the function's body can be simplified and made more efficient. The following code shows you this simplified version:

```
function isLessThan3(value, index, array)
{
    return (value < 3);
}
```

Isn't that much easier? JavaScript, like most other languages, returns conditional statements as `true` or `false`, and you can assign the returned value to a variable. In this case, the value returned from the conditional statement is simply returned to the calling code.

For clarity's sake, your authors opt to use longer, but easier to follow, approaches to code as opposed to their shorthand equivalents.

Operating on Elements — The forEach() and map() Methods

The final two methods are the `forEach()` and `map()` methods. Unlike the previous iterative methods, these two methods do not test each element in the array with your function; instead, the function you write should perform some kind of operation that uses the element in some way. Look at the following code:

```
var numbers = new Array(1, 2, 3, 4, 5);

for (var i = 0; i < numbers.length; i++ )
{
    var result = numbers[i] * 2;
    alert(result);
}
```

As a programmer, you'll often see and use this type of code. It defines an array of numbers and loops through it to perform some kind of operation on each element. In this case, the value of each element is doubled, and the result is shown in an alert box to the user. Wouldn't it be great if you could do this without writing a loop?

With the `forEach()` method, you can. All you need to do is write a function to double a given value and output the result in an alert box, like this:

```
var numbers = new Array(1, 2, 3, 4, 5);

function doubleAndAlert(value, index, array)
{
    var result = value * 2;
    alert(result);
}

numbers.forEach(doubleAndAlert);
```

Notice that the `doubleAndAlert()` function doesn't return a value like the testing methods. It cannot return any value; its only purpose is to perform an operation on every element in the array. While this is useful in some cases, it's almost useless when you want the results of the operation. That's where the `map()` method comes in.

The premise of the `map()` method is similar to that of `forEach()`, except that the results of every operation are stored in another array that the `map()` method returns.

Let's modify the previous example. The `doubleAndAlert()` function still needs to double the array element's value, but it now needs to return the result of that operation in order to be stored in `map`' returning array.

```
var numbers = new Array(1, 2, 3, 4, 5);

function doubleAndAlert(value, index, array)
{
    var result = value * 2;
```

```
        return result;
    }

    var doubledNumbers = numbers.map(doubleAndAlert);
    alert("The doubled numbers are: " + doubledNumbers);
```

Figure 5-3 shows the results of this code. You can see that there is very little difference between this code and the code for the `forEach()` method. The `doubleAndAlert()` function now returns the product of the element's value and 2 (instead of outputting it in an alert box), and you show the user the full result set after calling the `map()` method.

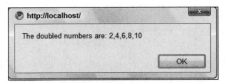

Figure 5-3

As you can see, these seven methods can come in handy when you need to find elements in an array, or you want to perform the same operation on all elements.

The only downside to these methods is that they are not supported in Internet Explorer, and Microsoft has not yet indicated if or when they will be added. One thing is for sure, though: Our jobs as developers will become much easier the day Microsoft does add support for them.

The Math Object

The `Math` object provides a number of useful mathematical functions and number manipulation methods. You'll be taking a look at some of them here, but you'll find the rest described in detail at the W3C site: www.w3schools.com/jsref/default.asp.

The `Math` object is a little unusual in that JavaScript automatically creates it for you. There's no need to declare a variable as a `Math` object or define a new `Math` object before being able to use it, making it a little bit easier to use.

The properties of the `Math` object include some useful math constants, such as the `PI` property (giving the value 3.14159 and so on). You access these properties, as usual, by placing a dot after the object name (`Math`) and then writing the property name. For example, to calculate the area of a circle, you may use the following code:

```
    var radius = prompt("Give the radius of the circle", "");
    var area = Math.PI * radius * radius;
    document.write("The area is " + area);
```

The methods of the `Math` object include some operations that are impossible, or complex, to perform using the standard mathematical operators (+, –, *, and /). For example, the `cos()` method returns the cosine of the value passed as a parameter. You'll look at a few of these methods now.

The abs() Method

The `abs()` method returns the absolute value of the number passed as its parameter. Essentially, this means that it returns the positive value of the number. So –1 is returned as 1, –4 as 4, and so on. However, 1 would be returned as 1 because it's already positive.

For example, the following code writes the number 101 to the page.

```
var myNumber = -101;
document.write(Math.abs(myNumber));
```

Finding the Largest and Smallest Numbers: the min() and max() Methods

Let's say you have two numbers, and you want to find either the largest or smallest of the two. To aid you in this task, the Math object provides the `min()` and `max()` methods. These methods both accept at least two arguments, all of which must obviously be numbers. Look at this example code:

```
var max = Math.max(21,22); // result is 22
var min = Math.min(30.1, 30.2); // result is 30.1
```

The `min()` method returns the number with the lowest value, and `max()` returns the number with the highest value. The numbers you pass to these two methods can be whole or floating point numbers.

The `max()` *and* `min()` *methods can accept many numbers; you're not limited to two.*

Rounding Numbers

The Math object provides a few methods to round numbers, each with its own specific purpose.

The ceil() Method

The `ceil()` method always rounds a number up to the next largest whole number or integer. So 10.01 becomes 11, and –9.99 becomes –9 (because –9 is greater than –10). The `ceil()` method has just one parameter, namely the number you want rounded up.

Using `ceil()` is different from using the `parseInt()` function you saw in Chapter 2, because `parseInt()` simply chops off any numbers after the decimal point to leave a whole number, whereas `ceil()` rounds the number up.

For example, the following code writes two lines in the page, the first containing the number 102 and the second containing the number 101:

```
var myNumber = 101.01;
document.write(Math.ceil(myNumber) + "<br />");
document.write(parseInt(myNumber));
```

The floor() Method

Like the `ceil()` method, the `floor()` method removes any numbers after the decimal point, and returns a whole number or integer. The difference is that `floor()` always rounds the number down. So if you pass 10.01 you will be returned 10, and if you pass –9.99 you will see –10 returned.

The round() Method

The `round()` method is very similar to `ceil()` and `floor()`, except that instead of always rounding up or always rounding down, it rounds up only if the decimal part is `.5` or greater, and rounds down otherwise.

For example:

```
var myNumber = 44.5;
document.write(Math.round(myNumber) + "<br />");

myNumber = 44.49;
document.write(Math.round(myNumber));
```

This code would write the numbers 45 and 44 to the page.

Summary of Rounding Methods

As you have seen, the `ceil()`, `floor()`, and `round()` methods all remove the numbers after a decimal point and return just a whole number. However, which whole number they return depends on the method used: `floor()` returns the lowest, `ceil()` the highest, and `round()` the nearest equivalent integer. This can be a little confusing, so the following is a table of values and what whole number would be returned if these values were passed to the `parseInt()` function, and `ceil()`, `floor()`, and `round()` methods.

Parameter	parseInt() returns	ceil() returns	floor() returns	round() returns
10.25	10	11	10	10
10.75	10	11	10	11
10.5	10	11	10	11
−10.25	−10	−10	−11	−10
−10.75	−10	−10	−11	−11
−10.5	−10	−10	−11	−10

Remember that `parseInt()` *is a native JavaScript function, not a method of the* `Math` *object, like the other methods presented in this table.*

Try It Out   **Rounding Methods Results Calculator**

If you're still not sure about rounding numbers, the following example should help. Here, you'll look at a calculator that gets a number from the user, and then writes out what the result would be when you pass that number to `parseInt()`, `ceil()`, `floor()`, and `round()`.

```
<!DOCTYPE html PUBLIC "-//W3C//DTD XHTML 1.0 Transitional//EN"
    "http://www.w3.org/TR/xhtml1/DTD/xhtml1-transitional.dtd">

<html xmlns="http://www.w3.org/1999/xhtml">
```

```
<head>
    <title>Chapter 5: Example 4</title>
</head>
<body>
<script type="text/javascript">

var myNumber = prompt("Enter the number to be rounded","");

document.write("<h3>The number you entered was " + myNumber + "</h3><br />");
document.write("<p>The rounding results for this number are</p>");
document.write("<table width='150' border='1'>");
document.write("<tr><th>Method</th><th>Result</th></tr>");
document.write("<tr><td>parseInt()</td><td>"+ parseInt(myNumber) +"</td></tr>");
document.write("<tr><td>ceil()</td><td>" + Math.ceil(myNumber) + "</td></tr>");
document.write("<tr><td>floor()</td><td>"+ Math.floor(myNumber) + "</td></tr>");
document.write("<tr><td>round()</td><td>" + Math.round(myNumber) +"</td></tr>");
document.write("</table>")

</script>
</body>
</html>
```

Save this as ch5_examp4.htm and load it into a web browser. In the prompt box, enter a number, for example 12.354, and click OK. The results of this number being passed to parseInt(), ceil(), floor(), and round() will be displayed in the page formatted inside a table, as shown in Figure 5-4.

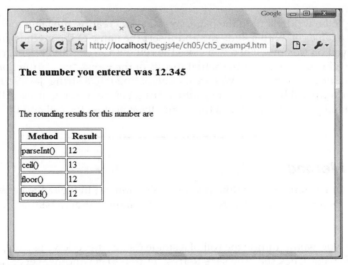

Figure 5-4

The first task is to get the number to be rounded from the user.

```
var myNumber = prompt("Enter the number to be rounded","");
```

Then you write out the number and some descriptive text.

```
document.write("<h3>The number you entered was " + myNumber + "</h3><br />");
document.write("<p>The rounding results for this number are</p>");
```

Notice how this time some HTML tags for formatting have been included — the main header being in <h3> tags, and the description of what the table means being inside a paragraph <p> tag.

Next you create the table of results.

```
document.write("<table width=150 border=1>");
document.write("<tr><th>Method</th><th>Result</th></tr>");
document.write("<tr><td>parseInt()</td><td>"+ parseInt(myNumber) +"</td></tr>");
document.write("<tr><td>ceil()</td><td>" + Math.ceil(myNumber) + "</td></tr>");
document.write("<tr><td>floor()</td><td>"+ Math.floor(myNumber) + "</td></tr>");
document.write("<tr><td>round()</td><td>" + Math.round(myNumber) +"</td></tr>");
document.write("</table>")
```

You create the table header first before actually displaying the results of each rounding function on a separate row. You can see how easy it is to dynamically create HTML inside the web page using just JavaScript. The principles are the same as with HTML in a page: You must make sure your tag's syntax is valid or otherwise things will appear strange or not appear at all.

Each row follows the same principle but uses a different rounding function. Let's look at the first row, which displays the results of parseInt().

```
document.write("<tr><td>parseInt()</td><td>"+ parseInt(myNumber) +"</td></tr>");
```

Inside the string to be written out to the page, you start by creating the table row with the <tr> tag. Then you create a table cell with a <td> tag and insert the name of the method from which the results are being displayed on this row. Then you close the cell with </td> and open a new one with <td>. Inside this next cell you are placing the actual results of the parseInt() function. Although a number is returned by parseInt(), because you are concatenating it to a string, JavaScript automatically converts the number returned by parseInt() into a string before concatenating. All this happens in the background without you needing to do a thing. Finally, you close the cell and the row with </td></tr>.

The random() Method

The random() method returns a random floating-point number in the range between 0 and 1, where 0 is included and 1 is not. This can be very useful for displaying random banner images or for writing a JavaScript game.

Let's look at how you would mimic the roll of a single die. In the following page, 10 random numbers are written to the page. Click the browser's Refresh button to get another set of random numbers.

```
<html>
<body>
<script type="text/javascript">
var throwCount;
var diceThrow;
for (throwCount = 0; throwCount < 10; throwCount++)
{
```

```
        diceThrow = (Math.floor(Math.random() * 6) + 1);
        document.write(diceThrow + "<br>");
    }

</script>
</body>
</html>
```

You want `diceThrow` to be between 1 and 6. The `random()` function returns a floating-point number between 0 and just under 1. By multiplying this number by 6, you get a number between 0 and just under 6. Then by adding 1, you get a number between 1 and just under 7. By using `floor()` to always round it down to the next lowest whole number, you can ensure that you'll end up with a number between 1 and 6.

If you wanted a random number between 1 and 100, you would just change the code so that `Math.random()` is multiplied by 100 rather than 6.

The pow() Method

The `pow()` method raises a number to a specified power. It takes two parameters, the first being the number you want raised to a power, and the second being the power itself. For example, to raise 2 to the power of 8 (that is, to calculate 2 * 2 * 2 * 2 * 2 * 2 * 2 * 2), you would write `Math.pow(2,8)` — the result being 256. Unlike some of the other mathematical methods, like `sin()`, `cos()`, and `acos()`, which are not commonly used in web programming unless it's a scientific application you're writing, the `pow()` method can often prove very useful.

Try It Out   Using pow()

In the following example, you write a function using `pow()`, which fixes the number of decimal places in a number — a function that's missing from earlier versions of JavaScript, though it has now been added to JScript 5.5 and JavaScript 1.5, as you'll see later in this chapter. This helps demonstrate that even when a function is missing from JavaScript, you can usually use existing functions to create what you want.

```
<!DOCTYPE html PUBLIC "-//W3C//DTD XHTML 1.0 Transitional//EN"
    "http://www.w3.org/TR/xhtml1/DTD/xhtml1-transitional.dtd">

<html xmlns="http://www.w3.org/1999/xhtml">
<head>
    <title>Chapter 5: Example 5</title>
</head>
<head>
<script type="text/javascript">

function fix(fixNumber, decimalPlaces)
{
    var div = Math.pow(10,decimalPlaces);
    fixNumber = Math.round(fixNumber * div) / div;
    return fixNumber;
}
</script>
</head>
<body>
```

```
<script type="text/javascript">

var number1 = prompt("Enter the number with decimal places you want to fix","");
var number2 = prompt("How many decimal places do you want?","");

document.write(number1 + " fixed to " + number2 + " decimal places is: ");
document.write(fix(number1,number2));

</script>
</body>
</html>
```

Save the page as ch5_examp5.htm. When you load the page into your browser, you will be presented with two prompt boxes. In the first, enter the number for which you want to fix the number of decimal places, for example 2.2345. In the second, enter the number of decimal places you want fixed, for example 2. Then the result of fixing the number you have entered to the number of decimal places you have chosen will be written to the page, as shown in Figure 5-5. For the example numbers, this will be 2.23.

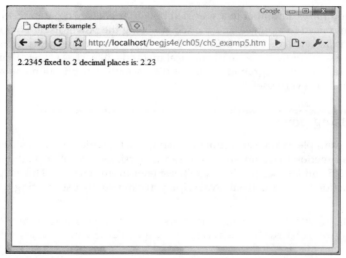

Figure 5-5

In the head of the page, you define the function fix(). This function will fix its fixNumber parameter to a maximum of its decimalPlaces parameter's number of digits after the decimal place. For example, fixing 34.76459 to a maximum of three decimal places will return 34.765.

The first line of code in the function sets the variable div to the number 10 raised to the power of the number of decimal places you want.

```
function fix(fixNumber, decimalPlaces)
{
    var div = Math.pow(10,decimalPlaces);
```

Then, in the next line, you calculate the new number.

```
    fixNumber = Math.round(fixNumber * div) / div;
```

What the code `Math.round(fixNumber * div)` does is move the decimal point in the number that you are converting to after the point in the number that you want to keep. So for `2.2345`, if you want to keep two decimal places, you convert it to `223.45`. The `Math.round()` method rounds this number to the nearest integer (in this case `223`) and so removes any undesired decimal part.

You then convert this number back into the fraction it should be, but of course only the fractional part you want is left. You do this by dividing by the same number (`div`) that you multiplied by. In this example, you divide `223` by `100`, which leaves `2.23`. This is `2.2345` fixed to two decimal places. This value is returned to the calling code in the line

```
        return fixNumber;
    }
```

In the body of the page, you use two prompt boxes to get numbers from the user. You then display the results of using these numbers in your `fix()` function to the user using `document.write()`.

Number Object

As with the `String` object, `Number` objects need to be created before they can be used. To create a `Number` object, you can write the following:

```
    var firstNumber = new Number(123);
    var secondNumber = new Number('123');
```

However, as you have seen, you can also declare a number as primitive and use it as if it were a `Number` object, letting JavaScript do the conversion to an object for you behind the scenes. For example:

```
    var myNumber = 123.765;
```

As with the `String` object, this technique is preferable so long as it's clear to JavaScript what object you expect to have created in the background. So, for example,

```
    var myNumber = "123.567";
```

will lead JavaScript to assume, quite rightly, that it's a string, and any attempts to use the `Number` object's methods will fail.

You'll look at just the `toFixed()` method of the `Number` object because that's the most useful method for everyday use.

The toFixed() Method

The `toFixed()` method cuts a number off after a certain point. Let's say you want to display a price after sales tax. If your price is $9.99 and sales tax is 7.5 percent, that means the after-tax cost will be $10.73925. Well, this is rather an odd amount for a money transaction — what you really want to do is fix the number to no more than two decimal places. Let's create an example.

```
    var itemCost = 9.99;
    var itemCostAfterTax = 9.99 * 1.075;
    document.write("Item cost is $" + itemCostAfterTax + "<br />");
```

```
itemCostAfterTax = itemCostAfterTax.toFixed(2);
document.write("Item cost fixed to 2 decimal places is $" + itemCostAfterTax);
```

The first `document.write()` outputs the following to the page:

```
Item cost is $10.73925
```

However, this is not the format you want; instead you want two decimal places, so on the next line, enter this:

```
itemCostAfterTax = itemCostAfterTax.toFixed(2);
```

You use the `toFixed()` method of the `Number` object to fix the number variable that `itemCostAfterTax` holds to two decimal places. The method's only parameter is the number of decimal places you want your number fixed to. This line means that the next `document.write` displays this:

```
Item cost fixed to 2 decimal places is $10.74
```

The first thing you might wonder is why `10.74` and not `10.73`? Well, the `toFixed()` method doesn't just chop off the digits not required; it also rounds up or down. In this case, the number was `10.739`, which rounds up to `10.74`. If it'd been `10.732`, it would have been rounded down to `10.73`.

Note that you can only fix a number from 0 to 20 decimal places.

Date Objects

The `Date` object handles everything to do with date and time in JavaScript. Using it, you can find out the current date and time, store your own dates and times, do calculations with these dates, and convert the dates into strings.

The `Date` object has a lot of methods and can be a little tricky to use, which is why Chapter 10 is dedicated to the date, time, and timers in JavaScript. You'll also see in Chapter 12 how you can use dates to determine if there's been anything new added to the web site since the user last visited it. However, in this section you'll focus on how to create a `Date` object and some of its more commonly used methods.

Creating a Date Object

You can declare and initialize a `Date` object in four ways. In the first method, you simply declare a new `Date` object without initializing its value. In this case, the date and time value will be set to the current date and time on the PC on which the script is run.

```
var theDate1 = new Date();
```

Secondly, you can define a `Date` object by passing the number of milliseconds since January 1, 1970, at 00:00:00 GMT. In the following example, the date is 31 January 2000 00:20:00 GMT (that is, 20 minutes past midnight).

```
var theDate2 = new Date(949278000000);
```

It's unlikely that you'll be using this way of defining a `Date` object very often, but this is how JavaScript actually stores the dates. The other formats for giving a date are simply for convenience.

Next, you can pass a string representing a date, or a date and time. In the following example, you have `"31 January 2010"`.

```
var theDate3 = new Date("31 January 2010");
```

However, you could have written `31 Jan 2010`, `Jan 31 2010`, or any of a number of valid variations you'd commonly expect when writing down a date normally — if in doubt, try it out. Note that Firefox doesn't support the string `"01-31-2010"` as a valid date format.

If you are writing your web pages for an international audience outside the United States, you need to be aware of the different ways of specifying dates. In the United Kingdom and many other places, the standard is day, month, year, whereas in the United States the standard is month, day, year. This can cause problems if you specify only numbers — JavaScript may think you're referring to a day when you mean a month. The easiest way to avoid such headaches is to, where possible, always use the name of the month. That way there can be no confusion.

In the fourth and final way of defining a `Date` object, you initialize it by passing the following parameters separated by commas: year, month, day, hours, minutes, seconds, and milliseconds. For example:

```
var theDate4 = new Date(2010,0,31,15,35,20,20);
```

This date is actually 31 January 2010 at 15:35:20 and 20 milliseconds. You can specify just the date part if you wish and ignore the time.

Something to be aware of is that in this instance January is month 0, not month 1, as you'd expect, and December is month 11. It's very easy to make a mistake when specifying a month.

Getting Date Values

It's all very nice having stored a date, but how do you get the information out again? Well, you just use the `get` methods. These are summarized in the following table.

Method	Returns
`getDate()`	The day of the month
`getDay()`	The day of the week as an integer, with Sunday as 0, Monday as 1, and so on
`getMonth()`	The month as an integer, with January as 0, February as 1, and so on
`getFullYear()`	The year as a four-digit number
`toDateString()`	Returns the full date based on the current time zone as a human-readable string. For example, "Wed 31 Dec 2003".

For example, if you want to get the month in `ourDateObj`, you can simply write the following:

```
theMonth = myDateObject.getMonth();
```

All the methods work in a very similar way, and all values returned are based on local time, meaning time local to the machine the code is running on. It's also possible to use Universal Time, previously known as GMT, which we'll discuss in Chapter 9.

Try It Out   **Using the Date Object to Retrieve the Current Date**

In this example, you use the get date type methods you have been looking at to write the current day, month, and year to a web page.

```
<!DOCTYPE html PUBLIC "-//W3C//DTD XHTML 1.0 Transitional//EN"
    "http://www.w3.org/TR/xhtml1/DTD/xhtml1-transitional.dtd">

<html xmlns="http://www.w3.org/1999/xhtml">
<head>
    <title>Chapter 5: Example 6</title>
</head>
<body>

<script type="text/javascript">

var months = new Array("January","February","March","April","May","June","July",
                       "August", "September", "October", "November", "December");

var dateNow = new Date();
var yearNow = dateNow.getFullYear();
var monthNow = months[dateNow.getMonth()];
var dayNow = dateNow.getDate();
var daySuffix;

switch (dayNow)
{
    case 1:
    case 21:
    case 31:
        daySuffix = "st";
        break;
    case 2:
    case 22:
        daySuffix = "nd";
        break;
    case 3:
    case 23:
        daySuffix = "rd";
        break;
    default:
        daySuffix = "th";
        break;
}

document.write("It is the " + dayNow + daySuffix + " day ");
document.write("in the month of " + monthNow);
document.write(" in the year " + yearNow);

</script>
```

```
</body>
</html>
```

Save the code as ch5_examp6.htm. If you load up the page, you should see a correctly formatted sentence telling you what the current date is.

The first thing you do in the code is declare an array and populate it with the months of a year. Why do this? Well, there is no method of the Date object that'll give you the month by name instead of as a number. However, this poses no problem; you just declare an array of months and use the month number as the array index to select the correct month name.

```
var months = new Array("January","February","March","April","May","June","July",
                    "August","September","October","November","December");
```

Next you create a new Date object, and by not initializing it with your own value, you allow it to initialize itself to the current date and time.

```
var dateNow = new Date();
```

Following this you set the yearNow variable to the current year, as returned by the getFullYear() method.

```
var yearNow = dateNow.getFullYear();
```

You then populate your monthNow variable with the value contained in the array element with an index of the number returned by getMonth(). Remember that getMonth() returns the month as an integer value, starting with 0 for January — this is a bonus because arrays also start at 0, so no adjustment is needed to find the correct array element.

```
var monthNow = months[dateNow.getMonth()];
```

Finally, the current day of the month is put into variable dayNow.

```
var dayNow = dateNow.getDate();
```

Next you use a switch statement, which you learned about in the Chapter 3. This is a useful technique for adding the correct suffix to the date that you already have. After all, your application will look more professional if you can say "it is the 1st day", rather than "it is the 1 day". This is a little tricky, however, because the suffix you want to add depends on the number that precedes it. So, for the first, twenty-first, and thirty-first days of the month, you have this:

```
switch (dayNow)
{
    case 1:
    case 21:
    case 31:
        daySuffix = "st";
        break;
```

For the second and twenty-second days, you have this:

```
    case 2:
    case 22:
        daySuffix = "nd";
        break;
```

and for the third and twenty-third days, you have this:

```
case 3:
case 23:
    daySuffix = "rd";
    break;
```

Finally, you need the `default` case for everything else. As you will have guessed by now, this is simply `"th"`.

```
    default:
        daySuffix = "th";
        break;
}
```

In the final lines you simply write the information to the HTML page, using `document.write()`.

Setting Date Values

To change part of the date in a `Date` object, you have a group of `set` functions, which pretty much replicate the `get` functions described earlier, except that you are setting, not getting, the values. These functions are summarized in the following table.

Method	Description
setDate()	The date of the month is passed in as the parameter to set the date
setMonth()	The month of the year is passed in as an integer parameter, where 0 is January, 1 is February, and so on
setFullYear()	This sets the year to the four-digit integer number passed in as a parameter

Note that for security reasons, there is no way for web-based JavaScript to change the current date and time on a user's computer.

So, to change the year to 2009, the code would be as follows:

```
myDateObject.setFullYear(2009);
```

Setting the date and month to the twenty-seventh of February looks like this:

```
myDateObject.setDate(27);
myDateObject.setMonth(1);
```

One minor point to note here is that there is no direct equivalent of the `getDay()` method. After the year, date, and month have been defined, the day is automatically set for you.

Calculations and Dates

Take a look at the following code:

```
var myDate = new Date("1 Jan 2010");
myDate.setDate(32);
document.write(myDate);
```

Surely there is some error — since when has January had 32 days? The answer is that of course it doesn't, and JavaScript knows that. Instead JavaScript sets the date to 32 days from the first of January — that is, it sets it to the first of February.

The same also applies to the setMonth() method. If you set it to a value greater than 11, the date automatically rolls over to the next year. So if you use setMonth(12), that will set the date to January of the next year, and similarly setMonth(13) is February of the next year.

How can you use this feature of setDate() and setMonth() to your advantage? Well, let's say you want to find out what date it will be 28 days from now. Given that different months have different numbers of days and that you could roll over to a different year, it's not as simple a task as it might first seem. Or at least that would be the case if it were not for setDate(). The code to achieve this task is as follows:

```
var nowDate = new Date();
var currentDay = nowDate.getDate();
nowDate.setDate(currentDay + 28);
```

First you get the current system date by setting the nowDate variable to a new Date object with no initialization value. In the next line, you put the current day of the month into a variable called currentDay. Why? Well, when you use setDate() and pass it a value outside of the maximum number of days for that month, it starts from the first of the month and counts that many days forward. So, if today's date is the January 15 and you use setDate(28), it's not 28 days from the fifteenth of January, but 28 days from the first of January. What you want is 28 days from the current date, so you need to add the current date to the number of days ahead you want. So you want setDate(15 + 28). In the third line, you set the date to the current date, plus 28 days. You stored the current day of the month in currentDay, so now you just add 28 to that to move 28 days ahead.

If you want the date 28 days prior to the current date, you just pass the current date minus 28. Note that this will most often be a negative number. You need to change only one line, and that's the third one, which you change to the following:

```
nowDate.setDate(currentDay - 28);
```

You can use exactly the same principles for setMonth() as you have used for setDate().

Getting Time Values

The methods you use to retrieve the individual pieces of time data work much like the get methods for date values. The methods you use here are:

- ❑   getHours()
- ❑   getMinutes()

- ❑ getSeconds()
- ❑ getMilliseconds()
- ❑ toTimeString()

These methods return respectively the hours, minutes, seconds, milliseconds, and full time of the specified Date object, where the time is based on the 24-hour clock: 0 for midnight and 23 for 11 p.m. The last method is similar to the toDateString() method in that it returns an easily readable string, except that in this case it contains the time (for example, "13:03:51 UTC").

Try It Out   Writing the Current Time into a Web Page

Let's look at an example that writes out the current time to the page.

```
<!DOCTYPE html PUBLIC "-//W3C//DTD XHTML 1.0 Transitional//EN"
    "http://www.w3.org/TR/xhtml1/DTD/xhtml1-transitional.dtd">

<html xmlns="http://www.w3.org/1999/xhtml">
<head>
    <title>Chapter 5: Example 7</title>
</head>
<body>
<script type="text/javascript">

var greeting;

var nowDate = new Date();
var nowHour = nowDate.getHours();
var nowMinute = nowDate.getMinutes();
var nowSecond = nowDate.getSeconds();

if (nowMinute < 10)
{
    nowMinute = "0" + nowMinute;
}

if (nowSecond < 10)
{
    nowSecond = "0" + nowSecond;
}

if (nowHour < 12)
{
    greeting = "Good Morning";
}
else if (nowHour < 17)
{
    greeting = "Good Afternoon";
}
else
{
    greeting = "Good Evening";
}
```

```
document.write("<h4>" + greeting + " and welcome to my website</h4>")
document.write("According to your clock the time is ");
document.write(nowHour + ":" + nowMinute + ":" + nowSecond);

</script>
</body>
</html>
```

Save this page as `ch5_examp7.htm`. When you load it into a web browser, it writes a greeting based on the time of day as well as the current time, as shown in Figure 5-6.

Figure 5-6

The first two lines of code declare two variables — `greeting` and `nowDate`.

```
var greeting;
var nowDate = new Date();
```

The `greeting` variable will be used shortly to store the welcome message on the web site, whether this is `"Good Morning"`, `"Good Afternoon"`, or `"Good Evening"`. The `nowDate` variable is initialized to a new `Date` object. Note that the constructor for the `Date` object is empty, so JavaScript will store the current date and time in it.

Next, you get the information on the current time from `nowDate` and store it in various variables. You can see that getting time data is very similar to getting date data, just using different methods.

```
var nowHour = nowDate.getHours();
var nowMinute = nowDate.getMinutes();
var nowSecond = nowDate.getSeconds();
```

You may wonder why the following lines are included in the example:

```
if (nowMinute < 10)
{
    nowMinute = "0" + nowMinute;
```

```
    }

    if (nowSecond < 10)
    {
        nowSecond = "0" + nowSecond;
    }
```

These lines are there just for formatting reasons. If the time is nine minutes past 10, then you expect to see something like 10:09. You don't expect 10:9, which is what you would get if you used the getMinutes() method without adding the extra zero. The same goes for seconds. If you're just using the data in calculations, you don't need to worry about formatting issues — you do here because you're inserting the time the code executed into the web page.

Next, in a series of if statements, you decide (based on the time of day) which greeting to create for displaying to the user.

```
    if (nowHour < 12)
    {
        greeting = "Good Morning";
    }
    else if (nowHour < 17)
    {
        greeting = "Good Afternoon";
    }
    else
    {
        greeting = "Good Evening";
    }
```

Finally, you write out the greeting and the current time to the page.

```
    document.write("<h4>" + greeting + " and welcome to my website</h4>");
    document.write("According to your clock the time is ");
    document.write(nowHour + ":" + nowMinute + ":" + nowSecond);
```

In Chapter 10 you'll see how you can write a continuously updating time to the web page, making it look like a clock.

Setting Time Values

When you want to set the time in your Date objects, you have a series of methods similar to those used for getting the time:

❑ setHours()

❑ setMinutes()

❑ setSeconds()

❑ setMilliseconds()

These work much like the methods you use to set the date, in that if you set any of the time parameters to an illegal value, JavaScript assumes you mean the next or previous time boundary. If it's 9:57 and you set minutes to 64, the time will be set to 10:04 — that is, 64 minutes from 9:00.

This is demonstrated in the following code:

```
var nowDate = new Date();
nowDate.setHours(9);
nowDate.setMinutes(57);
alert(nowDate);

nowDate.setMinutes(64);
alert(nowDate);
```

First you declare the `nowDate` variable and assign it to a new `Date` object, which will contain the current date and time. In the following two lines, you set the hours to 9 and the minutes to 57. You show the date and time using an `alert` box, which should show a time of 9:57. The minutes are then set to 64 and again an alert box is used to show the date and time to the user. Now the minutes have rolled over the hour so the time shown should be 10:04.

If the hours were set to 23 instead of 9, setting the minutes to 64 would not just move the time to another hour but also cause the day to change to the next date.

Creating New Types of Objects (Reference Types)

This section's focus is on some advanced stuff. It's not essential stuff, so you may want to move on and come back to it later.

You've seen that JavaScript provides a number of objects built into the language and ready for us to use. It's a bit like a house that's built already and you can just move on in. However, what if you want to create your own house, to design it for your own specific needs? In that case you'll use an architect to create technical drawings and plans that provide the template for the new house — the builders use the plans to tell them how to create the house.

So what does any of this have to do with JavaScript and objects? Well, JavaScript enables you to be an architect and create the templates for your own objects to your own specification, to fit your specific needs. Let's say, for example, you were creating a cinema booking system. JavaScript doesn't come with any built-in cinema booking objects, so you'd have to design your own. What you need to do is create objects modeled around the real world. So for a simple cinema booking system, you might have an object representing customers' booking details and an object for the cinema where the bookings have been made. As well as being able to store information, you can create your own methods for an object. So for a booking system, you might want an "add new booking" method or a method that gets the details of all the bookings currently made.

Where you have no need to store data but simply want functionality, such as the `fix()` function you saw before, it's generally easier just to have a code library rather than to create a special object.

Just as a builder of a house needs an architect's plans to know what to build and how it should be laid out, you need to provide blueprints telling JavaScript how your object should look. For example, you need to define its methods and provide the code for those methods. The key to this is JavaScript's support for the definition of *reference types*. Reference types are essentially templates for an object, as the architect's drawings are the template used to build a house. Before you can use your new object type, you need to define it along with its methods and properties. The important distinction is that when you define your reference type, no object based on that type is created. It's only when you create an instance of your reference type using the new keyword that an object of that type, based on your blueprint or prototype, is created.

Before you start, an important distinction must be made. Many developers refer to reference types as classes and use the two terms interchangeably. While this is correct for many object-oriented languages such as Java, C#, and C++, it is not correct for JavaScript. JavaScript has no formal class construct, even though the logical equivalent, reference types, are fully supported by the language.

It's also important to point out that the built-in objects discussed thus far in this chapter are also reference types. String, Array, Number, Date, and even Object are all reference types, and the objects you created are instances of these types.

A reference type consists of three things:

- ❑   A constructor
- ❑   Method definitions
- ❑   Properties

A constructor is a method that is called every time one of your objects based on this reference type is created. It's useful when you want to initialize properties or the object in some way. You need to create a constructor even if you don't pass any parameters to it or it contains no code. (In that case it'd just be an empty definition.) As with functions, a constructor can have zero or more parameters.

You used methods when you used JavaScript's built-in reference types; now you get the chance to build your own type to define your own methods performing specific tasks. Your reference type will specify what methods you have and the code that they execute. Again, you have used properties of built-in objects before and now get to define your own. You don't need to declare your type's properties. You can simply go ahead and use properties without letting JavaScript know in advance.

Let's create a simple reference type based on the real-world example of a cinema booking system.

Defining a Reference Type

Let's start by creating a type for a customer's booking. It will be called CustomerBooking. The first thing you need to do is create the constructor, which is shown here:

```
function CustomerBooking (bookingId, customerName, film, showDate)
{
    this.customerName = customerName;
    this.bookingId = bookingId;
    this.showDate = showDate;
    this.film = film;
}
```

Your first thought might be that what you have here is simply a function, and you'd be right. It's not until you start defining the properties and methods that it becomes something more than a function. This is in contrast to some programming languages, which have a more formal way of defining types.

Typically, a reference type is defined with an uppercase letter. Doing so makes it easy to differentiate a function from a reference type easily and quickly.

When you look at the code, the important thing to note is that the constructor function's name must match that of the type you are defining — in this case CustomerBooking. That way, when a new instance of your type as an object (termed an *object instance*) is created, this function will be called automatically. Note this constructor function has four parameters, and that these are used inside the definition itself. However, note that you use the this keyword. For example:

```
this.customerName = customerName;
```

Inside a constructor function or within a method, the this keyword refers to that object instance of your reference type. This code refers to the customerName property of this instance object, and you set it to equal the customerName parameter. If you have used other object-oriented programming languages, you might wonder where you defined this customerName property. The answer is that you didn't; simply by assigning a property a value, JavaScript creates it for you. There is no check that the property exists; JavaScript creates it as it needs to. The same is true if you use the object with a property never mentioned in your type definition. All this free property creation might sound great, but it has drawbacks, the main one being that JavaScript won't tell you if you accidentally misspell a property name; it'll just create a new property with the misspelled name, something that can make it difficult to track bugs. One way around this problem is to create methods that get a property's value and enable you to set a property's value. Now this may sound like hard work, but it can reduce bugs or at least make them easier to spot. Let's create a few property get/set methods for the CustomerBooking reference type.

```javascript
CustomerBooking.prototype.getCustomerName = function()
{
    return this.customerName;
}

CustomerBooking.prototype.setCustomerName = function(customerName)
{
    this.customerName = customerName;
}

CustomerBooking.prototype.getShowDate = function()
{
    return this.showDate;
}

CustomerBooking.prototype.setShowDate = function(showDate)
{
    this.showDate = showDate;
}

CustomerBooking.prototype.getFilm = function()
{
    return this.film;
}

CustomerBooking.prototype.setFilm = function(film)
{
    this.film = film;
```

```
}

CustomerBooking.prototype.getBookingId = function()
{
    return this.bookingId;
}

CustomerBooking.prototype.setBookingId = function(bookingId)
{
    this.bookingId = bookingId;
}
```

Now you have defined a set and get method for each of your four properties: bookingId, film, customerName, and showDate. Let's look at how you created one of the methods: getCustomerName().

```
CustomerBooking.prototype.getCustomerName = function()
{
    return this.customerName;
}
```

The first thing you notice is that this is a very odd way of defining a function. On the left you set the type's prototype property's getCustomerName to equal a function, which you then define immediately afterwards. In fact, JavaScript supplies most reference types with a prototype property, which allows new properties and methods to be created. So whenever you want to create a method for your type, you simply write the following:

```
typeName.prototype.methodName = function(method parameter list)
{
    // method code
}
```

You've created your type, but how do you now create new objects based on it?

Creating and Using Reference Type Instances

You create instances of your reference type in the same way you created instances of JavaScript's built-in types: using the new keyword. So to create a new instance of CustomerBooking, you'd write this:

```
var firstBooking = new
    CustomerBooking(1234, "Robert Smith","Raging Bull", "25 July 2004 18:20");

var secondBooking = new
    CustomerBooking(1244, "Arnold Palmer","Toy Story", "27 July 2004 20:15");
```

Here, as with a String object, you have created two new objects and stored them in variables, firstBooking and secondBooking, but this time it's a new object based on the CustomerBooking type.

The use of the new keyword is very important when creating an object with a constructor. The browser does not throw an error if you do not use the new keyword, but your script will not work correctly. Instead of creating a new object, you actually add properties to the global window object. The problems caused by not using the new keyword can be hard to diagnose, so make sure you specify the new keyword when creating objects with a constructor.

Let's call the `getCustomerName()` method of each of the two objects and write the results to the page.

```
document.write("1st booking person's name is " +
               firstBooking.getCustomerName() + "<br />");
document.write("2nd booking person's name is " +
               secondBooking.getCustomerName());
```

And you'll see the following written into the page from information contained in these objects:

```
1st booking person's name is Robert Smith
2nd booking person's name is Arnold Palmer
```

Now let's put this together in a page.

```
<html>
<body>

<script type="text/javascript">

// CustomerBooking type

function CustomerBooking(bookingId, customerName, film, showDate)
{

    this.customerName = customerName;
    this.bookingId = bookingId;
    this.showDate = showDate;
    this.film = film;
}

CustomerBooking.prototype.getCustomerName = function()
{
    return this.customerName;
}

CustomerBooking.prototype.setCustomerName = function(customerName)
{
    this.customerName = customerName;
}

CustomerBooking.prototype.getShowDate = function()
{
    return this.showDate;
}

CustomerBooking.prototype.setShowDate = function(showDate)
{
    this.showDate = showDate;
}

CustomerBooking.prototype.getFilm = function()
{
    return this.film;
}
```

```
CustomerBooking.prototype.setFilm = function(film)
{
    this.film = film;
}

CustomerBooking.prototype.getBookingId = function()
{
    return this.bookingId;
}

CustomerBooking.prototype.setBookingId = function(bookingId)
{
    this.bookingId = bookingId;
}


var firstBooking = new CustomerBooking(1234,
                        "Robert Smith","Raging Bull", "25 July 2004 18:20");
var secondBooking = new CustomerBooking(1244,
                        "Arnold Palmer","Toy Story", "27 July 2004 20:15");
document.write("1st booking persons name is " +
                firstBooking.getCustomerName() + "<br />");
document.write("2nd booking persons name is " +
                secondBooking.getCustomerName());

</script>

</body>
</html>
```

At the top of the page is the `<script />` element, inside of which is the code that defines your reference type. You must include type definition code in every page that uses your type to create objects. For convenience, you may therefore decide to put your definitions in a separate file and import that file into each page that uses the reference type. You can do this using the `<script />` element, but instead of putting the code inside the open and close tags, you'll use the script element's `src` attribute to point to the file containing the JavaScript. For example, if you create a file called `MyCinemaBookingTypes.js` and put your type code in there, you can import it into a page as shown here:

```
<script src="MyCinemaBookingTypes.js"></script>
```

The `src` attribute points to the URL of your JavaScript file containing your type definition, which in this case assumes the `.js` file is in the same directory as your page.

An Array of Items

So far you have a reference type for items that you can put a single booking into, but no type representing all the bookings taken by a cinema. So how can you create a cinema type that supports the storage of zero or more items? The answer is using an array, which we discussed earlier in this chapter and in Chapter 3.

Let's start by defining this new type, called `Cinema`, and add to the script block with the `CustomerBooking` definition.

```
// Cinema type

function Cinema()
{
    this.bookings = new Array();
}
```

This code defines the constructor. Inside the constructor, you initialize the `bookings` property that holds all the `CustomerBooking` instance objects.

Next you need to add a way of making bookings for the cinema; for this you create the `addBooking()` method.

```
cinema.prototype.addBooking = function(bookingId, customerName, film, showDate)
{
    this.bookings[bookingId] = new CustomerBooking(bookingId,
                                        customerName, film, showDate);
}
```

The method accepts four parameters, the details needed to create a new booking. Then, inside the method, you create a new object of type `CustomerBooking`. A reference to this object is stored inside the `bookings` array, using the unique `bookingId` to associate the place in which the new object is stored.

Let's look at how you can access the items in the array. In the following method, called `getBookingsTable()`, you go through each booking in the cinema and create the HTML necessary to display all the bookings in a table.

```
Cinema.prototype.getBookingsTable = function()
{
    var booking;
    var bookingsTableHTML = "<table border=1>";

    for (booking in this.bookings)
    {
        bookingsTableHTML += "<tr><td>";
        bookingsTableHTML += this.bookings[booking].getBookingId();
        bookingsTableHTML += "</td>";

        bookingsTableHTML += "<td>";
        bookingsTableHTML += this.bookings[booking].getCustomerName();
        bookingsTableHTML += "</td>";

        bookingsTableHTML += "<td>";
        bookingsTableHTML += this.bookings[booking].getFilm();
        bookingsTableHTML += "</td>";


        bookingsTableHTML += "<td>";
        bookingsTableHTML += this.bookings[booking].getShowDate();
        bookingsTableHTML += "</td>";
        bookingsTableHTML += "</tr>";
```

```
        }

    bookingsTableHTML += "</table>";
    return bookingsTableHTML;
}
```

You can access each booking by its unique `bookingId`, but what you want to do is simply loop through all the bookings for the cinema, so you use a `for...in` loop, which loops through each item in the `items` array. Each time the loop executes, `booking` will be set by JavaScript to contain the `bookingId` of the next booking; it doesn't contain the item itself but its associated keyword.

Since you have the associated keyword, you can access the item objects in the array like this:

```
this.bookings[booking]
```

Remember that `this` refers to the object instance of your reference type. You then use the `CustomerBooking` object's `get` methods to obtain the details for each booking. Finally, on the last line, you return the HTML — with your summary of all the bookings — to the calling code.

Let's put this all together in a page and save the page as `ch5_examp8.htm`.

```
<!DOCTYPE html PUBLIC "-//W3C//DTD XHTML 1.0 Transitional//EN"
    "http://www.w3.org/TR/xhtml1/DTD/xhtml1-transitional.dtd">

<html xmlns="http://www.w3.org/1999/xhtml">
<head>
    <title>Chapter 5: Example 8</title>
</head>
<body>

<h2>Summary of bookings</h2>

<script type="text/javascript">

// CustomerBooking type

function CustomerBooking(bookingId, customerName, film, showDate)
{
    this.customerName = customerName;
    this.bookingId = bookingId;
    this.showDate = showDate;
    this.film = film;
}

CustomerBooking.prototype.getCustomerName = function()
{
    return this.customerName;
}

CustomerBooking.prototype.setCustomerName = function(customerName)
{
    this.customerName = customerName;
}

CustomerBooking.prototype.getShowDate = function()
```

```
{
    return this.showDate;
}

CustomerBooking.prototype.setShowDate = function(showDate)
{
    this.showDate = showDate;
}

CustomerBooking.prototype.getFilm = function()
{
    return this.film;
}

CustomerBooking.prototype.setFilm = function(film)
{
    this.film = film;
}

CustomerBooking.prototype.getBookingId = function()
{
    return this.bookingId;
}

CustomerBooking.prototype.setBookingId = function(bookingId)
{
    this.bookingId = bookingId;
}

// Cinema type

function Cinema()
{
    this.bookings = new Array();
}

Cinema.prototype.addBooking = function(bookingId, customerName, film, showDate)
{
    this.bookings[bookingId] = new CustomerBooking(bookingId,
                                        customerName, film, showDate);
}

Cinema.prototype.getBookingsTable = function()
{
    var booking;
    var bookingsTableHTML = "<table border=1>";

    for (booking in this.bookings)
    {
        bookingsTableHTML += "<tr><td>";
        bookingsTableHTML += this.bookings[booking].getBookingId();
        bookingsTableHTML += "</td>";

        bookingsTableHTML += "<td>";
```

```
            bookingsTableHTML += this.bookings[booking].getCustomerName();
            bookingsTableHTML += "</td>";

            bookingsTableHTML += "<td>";
            bookingsTableHTML += this.bookings[booking].getFilm();
            bookingsTableHTML += "</td>";

            bookingsTableHTML += "<td>";
            bookingsTableHTML += this.bookings[booking].getShowDate();
            bookingsTableHTML += "</td>";
            bookingsTableHTML += "</tr>";
        }

    bookingsTableHTML += "</table>";
    return bookingsTableHTML;
}

var londonOdeon = new Cinema();
londonOdeon.addBooking(342, "Arnold Palmer","Toy Story", "15 July 2009 20:15");
londonOdeon.addBooking(335, "Louise Anderson",
                    "The Shawshank Redemption", "27 July 2009 11:25");
londonOdeon.addBooking(566, "Catherine Hughes",
                    "Never Say Never", "27 July 2009 17:55");
londonOdeon.addBooking(324, "Beci Smith","Shrek", "29 July 2009 20:15");


document.write(londonOdeon.getBookingsTable());
</script>

</body>
</html>
```

Your new code is

```
var londonOdeon = new cinema();
londonOdeon.addBooking(342, "Arnold Palmer","Toy Story", "15 July 2009 20:15");
londonOdeon.addBooking(335, "Louise Anderson",
                    "The Shawshank Redemption", "27 July 2009 11:25");
londonOdeon.addBooking(566, "Catherine Hughes",
                    "Never Say Never", "27 July 2009 17:55");
londonOdeon.addBooking(324, "Beci Smith","Shrek", "29 July 2009 20:15");


document.write(londonOdeon.getBookingsTable());
```

These create a new cinema object and store a reference to it in the variable londonOdeon. You then create four new bookings using the Cinema type's addBooking() method. On the final line, you write the HTML returned by the getBookingsTable() method to the page.

Your page should now look like that shown in Figure 5-7.

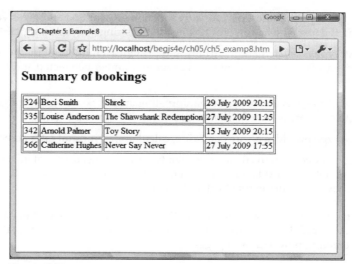

Figure 5-7

The cinema booking system you have created is very basic to say the least! However, it gives you an idea of how creating your own reference types can be used to help make code more maintainable and be used to model real-world problems and situations.

Summary

In this chapter you've taken a look at the concept of objects and seen how vital they are to an understanding of JavaScript, which represents virtually everything with objects. You also looked at some of the various native reference types that the JavaScript language provides to add to its functionality.

You saw that:

❑ JavaScript is object-based — it represents things, such as strings, dates, and arrays, using the concept of objects.

❑ Objects have properties and methods. For example, an `Array` object has the `length` property and the `sort()` method.

❑ To create a new object, you simply write `new ObjectType()`. You can choose to initialize an object when you create it.

❑ To set an object's property's value or get that value, you simply write `ObjectName.ObjectProperty`.

❑ Calling the methods of an object is similar to calling functions. Parameters may be passed, and return values may be passed back. Accessing the methods of an object is identical to accessing a property, except that you must remember to add parentheses at the end, even when there are no parameters. For example, you would write `ObjectName.ObjectMethod()`.

❑   The String type provides lots of handy functionality for text and gives you ways of finding out how long the text is, searching for text inside the string, and selecting parts of the text.

❑   The Math type is created automatically and provides a number of mathematical properties and methods. For example, to obtain a raｊndom number between 0 and 1, you use the method Math.random().

❑   The Array type provides ways of manipulating arrays. Some of the things you can do are find the length of an array, sort its elements, and join two arrays together.

❑   The Date type provides a way of storing, calculating with, and later accessing dates and times.

❑   JavaScript enables you to create your own types of objects using reference types. These can be used to model real-world situations and for making code easier to create and more maintainable, though they do require extra effort at the start.

In the next chapter, you'll turn your attention to the web browser itself and, particularly, the various objects that it makes available for your JavaScript programming. You'll see that the use of browser objects is key to creating powerful web pages.

Exercise Questions

Suggested solutions to these questions can be found in Appendix A.

1.   Using the Date type, calculate the date 12 months from now and write this into a web page.

2.   Obtain a list of names from the user, storing each name entered in an array. Keep getting another name until the user enters nothing. Sort the names in ascending order and then write them out to the page, with each name on its own line.

3.   In this chapter, you learned about how you can use the pow() method inventively to fix a number to a certain number of decimal places. However, there is a flaw in the function you created. A proper fix() function should return 2.1 fixed to three decimal places like this:

```
2.100
```

However, your fix() function instead returns it like this:

```
2.1
```

Change the fix() function so that the additional zeros are added where necessary.

Programming the Browser

Over the past few chapters, you've examined the core JavaScript language. You've seen how to work with variables and data, perform operations on those data, make decisions in your code, loop repeatedly over the same section of code, and even how to write your own functions. In the preceding chapter you moved on to learn how JavaScript is an object-based language, and you saw how to work with the native JavaScript objects. However, you are not interested only in the language itself; you want to find out how to write script for the web browser. Using this ability, you can start to create more impressive web pages.

Not only is JavaScript object-based, but the browser is also made up of objects. When JavaScript is running in the browser, you can access the browser's objects in exactly the same way that you used JavaScript's native objects in the last chapter. But what kinds of objects does the browser provide?

The browser makes available a remarkable number of objects. For example, there is a window object corresponding to the window of the browser. You have already been using two methods of this object, namely the alert() and prompt() methods. For simplicity, we previously referred to these as functions, but they are in fact methods of the browser's window object.

Another object made available by the browser is the page itself, represented by the document object. Again, you have already used methods and properties of this object. Recall from Chapter 1 that you used the document object's bgColor property to change the background color of the page. You have also been using the write() method of the document object to write information to the page.

A variety of other objects exist, representative of the HTML you write in the page. For example, there is an img object for each <img /> element that you use to insert an image into your document.

The collection of objects that the browser makes available to you for use with JavaScript is generally called the *Browser Object Model (BOM)*.

You will often see this termed the Document Object Model (DOM); it is incorrect to do so. Throughout this book, we'll use the term DOM to refer to the W3C's standard Document Object Model, which is discussed in Chapter 12.

All this added functionality of JavaScript comes with a potential downside: there is no standard BOM implementation. Which collections of objects are made available to you is highly dependent on the brand and version of the browser that you are using. Some objects are made available in some browsers and not in others, whereas other objects have different properties and methods in different browsers. The good news is that browser makers typically do not change much of their browser's BOM, as doing so would create a rift in interoperability. This means if you stick to the core functionality of the BOM (the common objects in all browsers), your code is more likely to work between the different browsers and versions. This chapter's focus is the BOM core functionality. You can achieve a lot in JavaScript by just sticking to the core. You can find more information on the core objects online at http://www.w3schools.com/dhtml/dhtml_domreference.asp and http://msdn.microsoft.com/en-us/library/ms952605.aspx.

Introduction to the Browser's Objects

In this section, we introduce the objects of the BOM that are common to all browsers.

In Chapter 5, you saw that JavaScript has a number of native objects that you have access to and can make use of. Most of the objects are those that you need to create yourself, such as the `String` and `Date` objects. Others, such as the `Math` object, exist without you needing to create them and are ready for use immediately when the page starts loading.

When JavaScript is running in a web page, it has access to a large number of other objects made available by the web browser. Rather like the `Math` object, these are created for you rather than your needing to create them explicitly. As mentioned, the objects, their methods, properties, and events are all mapped out in the BOM.

The BOM is very large and potentially overwhelming at first. However, you'll find that initially you won't be using more than 10 percent of the available objects, methods, and properties in the BOM. You'll start in this chapter by looking at the more commonly used parts of the BOM, shown in Figure 6-1. These parts of the BOM are, to a certain extent, common across all browsers. Later chapters will build on this so that by the end of the book you'll be able to really make the BOM work for you.

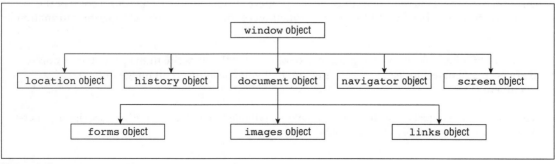

Figure 6-1

The BOM has a hierarchy. At the very top of this hierarchy is the `window` object. You can think of this as representing the frame of the browser and everything associated with it, such as the scrollbars, navigator bar icons, and so on.

Contained inside the window frame is the page. The page is represented in the BOM by the `document` object. You can see these two objects represented in Figure 6-2.

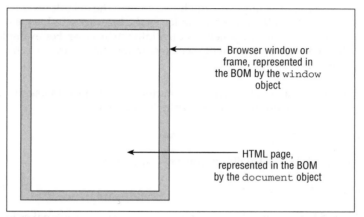

Figure 6-2

Now let's look at each of these objects in more detail.

The window Object

The `window` object represents the browser's frame or window, in which your web page is contained. To some extent, it also represents the browser itself and includes a number of properties that are there simply because they don't fit anywhere else. For example, via the properties of the `window` object, you can find out what browser is running, the pages the user has visited, the size of the browser window, the size of the user's screen, and much more. You can also use the `window` object to access and change the text in the browser's status bar, change the page that is loaded, and even open new windows.

The `window` object is a *global object*, which means you don't need to use its name to access its properties and methods. In fact, the global functions and variables (the ones accessible to script anywhere in a page) are all created as properties of the global object. For example, the `alert()` function you have been using since the beginning of the book is, in fact, the `alert()` method of the `window` object. Although you have been using this simply as this:

```
alert("Hello!");
```

You could write this with the same, exact results:

```
window.alert("Hello!");
```

However, since the `window` object is the global object, it is perfectly correct to use the first version.

Some of the properties of the `window` object are themselves objects. Those common to all browsers include the `document`, `navigator`, `history`, `screen`, and `location` objects. The `document` object represents your page, the `history` object contains the history of pages visited by the user, the `navigator` object holds information about the browser, the `screen` object contains information about the display capabilities of the client, and the `location` object contains details on the current page's location. You'll look at these important objects individually later in the chapter.

Let's start with a nice, simple example in which you change the default text shown in the browser's status bar. The status bar (usually in the bottom left of the browser window) is usually used by the browser to show the status of any document loading into the browser. For example, on IE and Firefox, after a document has loaded, you'll normally see Done in the status bar. Let's change that so it says "Hello and Welcome."

To change the default message in the window's status bar, you need to use the `window` object's `defaultStatus` property. To do this, you can write the following:

```
window.defaultStatus = "Hello and Welcome";
```

Or, because the `window` is the global object, you can just write this:

```
defaultStatus = "Hello and Welcome";
```

Either way works, and both are valid; however, writing `window` in front makes it clear exactly where the `defaultStatus` property came from. Otherwise it might appear that `defaultStatus` is a variable name. This is particularly true for less common properties and methods, such as `defaultStatus`. You'll find yourself becoming so familiar with more common ones, such as `document` and `alert()`, that you don't need to put `window` in front to remind you of their context.

Let's put the code in a page.

```
<!DOCTYPE html PUBLIC "-//W3C//DTD XHTML 1.0 Strict//EN"
    "http://www.w3.org/TR/xhtml1/DTD/xhtml1-strict.dtd">

<html xmlns="http://www.w3.org/1999/xhtml">
<head>
    <title>Chapter 6: Example 1</title>
    <script type="text/javaScript">
        window.defaultStatus = "Hello and Welcome";
    </script>
</head>
<body>
</body>
</html>
```

Save the page as `ch6_examp1.htm` and load it into your browser. You should see the specified message in the status bar.

At this point, it's worth highlighting the point that within a web page you shouldn't use names for your functions or variables that conflict with names of BOM objects or their properties and methods. If you do, you may not get an error, but instead get unexpected results. For example, the following code declares a variable named defaultStatus, and tries to set the defaultStatus property of the window object to "Welcome to my website". However, this won't change the default message in the status bar; instead the value in the defaultStatus variable will change.

```
var defaultStatus;
defaultStatus = "Welcome to my website";
```

In this situation you need to use a different variable name. This happens because any function or variable you define within the global scope actually gets appended to the window object. Look at this code as an example:

```
var myVariable = "Hello, World!";
alert(window.myVariable);
```

If you were to execute this code in a browser, the alert window will display the message "Hello, World."

As with all the BOM objects, you can look at lots of properties and methods for the window object. However, in this chapter you'll concentrate on the history, location, navigator, screen, and document properties. All five of these properties contain objects (the history, location, navigator, screen, and document objects), each with its own properties and methods. In the next few pages, you'll look at each of these objects in turn and find out how they can help you make full use of the BOM.

The history Object

The history object keeps track of each page that the user visits. This list of pages is commonly called the *history stack* for the browser. It enables the user to click the browser's Back and Forward buttons to revisit pages. You have access to this object via the window object's history property.

Like the native JavaScript Array type, the history object has a length property. You can use this to find out how many pages are in the history stack.

As you might expect, the history object has the back() and forward() methods. When they are called, the location of the page currently loaded in the browser is changed to the previous or next page that the user has visited.

The history object also has the go() method. This takes one parameter that specifies how far forward or backward in the history stack you want to go. For example, if you wanted to return the user to the page before the previous page, you'd write this:

```
history.go(-2);
```

To go forward three pages, you'd write this:

```
history.go(3);.
```

Note that go(-1) and back() are equivalent, as are go(1) and forward().

The location Object

The location object contains lots of potentially useful information about the current page's location. Not only does it contain the Uniform Resource Locator (URL) for the page, but also the server hosting the page, the port number of the server connection, and the protocol used. This information is made available through the location object's href, hostname, port, and protocol properties. However, many of these values are only really relevant when you are loading the page from a server and not, as you are doing in the present examples, loading the page directly from a local hard drive.

In addition to retrieving the current page's location, you can use the methods of the location object to change the location and refresh the current page.

You can navigate to another page in two ways. You can either set the location object's href property to point to another page, or you can use the location object's replace() method. The effect of the two is the same; the page changes location. However, they differ in that the replace() method removes the current page from the history stack and replaces it with the new page you are moving to, whereas using the href property simply adds the new page to the top of the history stack. This means that if the replace() method has been used and the user clicks the Back button in the browser, the user can't go back to the original page loaded. If the href property has been used, the user can use the Back button as normal.

For example, to replace the current page with a new page called myPage.htm, you'd use the replace() method and write the following:

```
window.location.replace("myPage.htm");
```

This will load myPage.htm and replace any occurrence of the current page in the history stack with myPage.htm.

To load the same page and to add it to the history of pages navigated to, you use the href property:

```
window.location.href = "myPage.htm";
```

and the page currently loaded is added to the history. In both of the preceding cases, window is in front of the expression, but as the window object is global throughout the page, you could have written one of the following:

```
location.replace("myPage.htm");
location.href = "myPage.htm";
```

The navigator Object

The navigator object is another object that is a property of window and is available in all browsers. Its name is more historical than descriptive. Perhaps a better name would be the "browser object," because the navigator object contains lots of information about the browser and the operating system in which it's running.

Probably the most common use of the navigator object is for handling browser differences. Using its properties, you can find out which browser, version, and operating system the user has. You can then act on that information and make sure users are directed to pages that will work with their browsers. The last section in this chapter is dedicated to this important subject, so we will not discuss it further here.

The screen Object

The `screen` object property of the `window` object contains a lot of information about the display capabilities of the client machine. Its properties include the `height` and `width` properties, which indicate the vertical and horizontal range of the screen, respectively, in pixels.

Another property of the `screen` object, which you will be using in an example later, is the `colorDepth` property. This tells you the number of bits used for colors on the client's screen.

The document Object

Along with the `window` object, the `document` object is probably one of the most important and commonly used objects in the BOM. Via this object you can gain access to the HTML elements, their properties and methods inside your page.

Unfortunately, it's here, at the `document` object, that browsers can differ greatly. This chapter concentrates on the properties and methods that are common to all browsers. More advanced manipulation of the `document` object will appear in Chapter 12.

The `document` object has a number of properties associated with it, which are also array-like structures called *collections*. The main collections are the `forms`, `images`, and `links` collections. IE supports a number of other collection properties, such as the `all` collection property, which is an array of all the elements represented by objects in the page. However, you'll be concentrating on using objects that have cross-browser support, so that you are not limiting your web pages to just one browser.

You'll be looking at the `images` and `links` collections shortly. A third collection, the `forms` collection, will be one of the topics of the next chapter when you look at forms in web browsers. First, though, you'll look at a nice, simple example of how to use the `document` object's methods and properties.

Using the document Object

You've already come across some of the `document` object's properties and methods, for example the `write()` method and the `bgColor` property.

Try It Out   **Setting Colors According to the User's Screen Color Depth**

In this example, you set the background color of the page according to how many colors the user's screen supports. This is termed *screen color depth*. If the user has a display that supports just two colors (black and white), there's no point in you setting the background color to bright red. You accommodate different depths by using JavaScript to set a color the user can actually see.

```
<!DOCTYPE html PUBLIC "-//W3C//DTD XHTML 1.0 Strict//EN"
    "http://www.w3.org/TR/xhtml1/DTD/xhtml1-strict.dtd">

<html xmlns="http://www.w3.org/1999/xhtml">
```

```
<head>
    <title>Chapter 6: Example 2</title>
</head>
<body>
<script type="text/javaScript">
switch (window.screen.colorDepth)
{
    case 1:
    case 4:
        document.bgColor = "white";
        break;
    case 8:
    case 15:
    case 16:
        document.bgColor = "blue";
        break;
    case 24:
    case 32:
        document.bgColor = "skyblue";
        break;
    default:
        document.bgColor = "white";
}

document.write("Your screen supports " + window.screen.colorDepth +
                "bit color");
</script>
</body>
</html>
```

Save the page as ch6_examp2.htm. When you load it into your browser, the background color of the page will be determined by your current screen color depth. Also, a message in the page will tell you what the color depth currently is.

You can test that the code is working properly by changing the colors supported by your screen. On Windows XP, you can do this by right-clicking on the desktop and choosing the Properties option. Under the Settings tab, there is a section called "Color quality" in which you can change the number of colors supported. By refreshing the browser, you can see what difference this makes to the color of the page.

In Firefox, Safari, and Chrome browsers, it's necessary to shut down and restart the browser to observe any effect.

As you saw earlier, the window object has the screen object property. One of the properties of this object is the colorDepth property, which returns a value of 1, 4, 8, 15, 16, 24, or 32. This represents the number of bits assigned to each pixel on your screen. (A pixel is just one of the many dots that your screen is made up of.) To work out how many colors you have, you just calculate the value of 2 to the power of the colorDepth property. For example, a colorDepth of 1 means that there are two colors available, a colorDepth of 8 means that there are 256 colors available, and so on. Currently, most people have a screen color depth of at least 8, but usually 24 or 32.

The first task of the script block is to set the color of the background of the page based on the number of colors the user can actually see. You do this in a big switch statement. The condition that is checked for in the switch statement is the value of window.screen.colorDepth.

```
switch (window.screen.colorDepth)
```

You don't need to set a different color for each `colorDepth` possible, because many of them are similar when it comes to general web use. Instead, you set the same background color for different, but similar, `colorDepth` values. For a `colorDepth` of 1 or 4, you set the background to white. You do this by declaring the `case 1:` statement, but you don't give it any code. If the `colorDepth` matches this `case` statement, it will fall through to the `case 4:` statement below, where you do set the background color to white. You then call a `break` statement, so that the case matching will not fall any further through the `switch` statement.

```
{
    case 1:
    case 4:
        document.bgColor = "white";
        break;
```

You do the same with `colorDepth` values of 8, 15, and 16, setting the background color to blue as follows:

```
    case 8:
    case 15:
    case 16:
        document.bgColor = "blue";
        break;
```

Finally, you do the same for `colorDepth` values of 24 and 32, setting the background color to sky blue.

```
    case 24:
    case 32:
        document.bgColor = "skyblue";
        break;
```

You end the `switch` statement with a `default` case, just in case the other `case` statements did not match. In this `default` case, you again set the background color to white.

```
    default:
        document.bgColor = "white";
}
```

In the next bit of script, you use the `document` object's `write()` method, something you've been using in these examples for a while now. You use it to write to the document — that is, the page — the number of bits the color depth is currently set at, as follows:

```
document.write("Your screen supports " + window.screen.colorDepth +
                "bit color")
```

You've already been using the `document` object in the examples throughout the book so far. You used its `bgColor` property in Chapter 1 to change the background color of the page, and you've also made good use of its `write()` method in the examples to write HTML and text out to the page.

Now let's look at some of the slightly more complex properties of the `document` object. These properties have in common the fact that they all contain collections. The first one you look at is a collection containing an object for each image in the page.

The images Collection

As you know, you can insert an image into an HTML page using the following tag:

```
<img alt="USA" name="myImage" src="usa.gif" />
```

The browser makes this image available for you to manipulate with JavaScript by creating an `img` object for it with the name `myImage`. In fact, each image on your page has an `img` object created for it.

Each of the `img` objects in a page is stored in the `images` collection, which is a property of the `document` object. You use this, and other collections, as you would an array. The first image on the page is found in the element `document.images[0]`, the second in `document.images[1]`, and so on.

If you want to, you can assign a variable to reference an `img` object in the `images` collection. It can make code easier to read. For example, the following code assigns a reference to the `img` object at index position 1 to the `myImage2` variable:

```
var myImage2 = document.images[1];
```

Now you can write `myImage2` instead of `document.images[1]` in your code, with exactly the same effect.

You can also access `img` objects in the `images` collection by name. For example, the `img` object created by the `<img/>` element, which has the name `myImage`, can be accessed in the `document` object's `images` collection property like this:

```
document.images["myImage"]
```

Because the `document.images` property is a collection, it has the properties similar to the native JavaScript `Array` type, such as the `length` property. For example, if you want to know how many images there are on the page, the code `document.images.length` will tell you.

Image Selection

The `img` object itself has a number of useful properties. The most important of these is its `src` property. By changing this, you can change the image that's loaded. The next example demonstrates this.

```
<!DOCTYPE html PUBLIC "-//W3C//DTD XHTML 1.0 Strict//EN"
    "http://www.w3.org/TR/xhtml1/DTD/xhtml1-strict.dtd">

<html xmlns="http://www.w3.org/1999/xhtml">
<head>
    <title>Chapter 6: Example 3</title>
</head>
<body>
<img name="img1" src="" border="0" width="200" height="150" />
<script type="text/javaScript">
    var myImages = new Array("usa.gif","canada.gif","jamaica.gif","mexico.gif");
    var imgIndex = prompt("Enter a number from 0 to 3","");
    document.images["img1"].src = myImages[imgIndex];
</script>
</body>
</html>
```

Save this as `ch6_examp3.htm`. You will also need four image files, called `usa.gif`, `canada.gif`, `jamaica.gif`, and `mexico.gif`. You can create these images yourself or obtain the ones provided with the code download for the book.

A prompt box asks you to enter a number from 0 to 3 when this page loads into the browser. A different image will be displayed depending on the number you enter.

At the top of the page you have your HTML `<img/>` element. Notice that the `src` attribute is left empty and is given the `name` value img1.

```
<img name="img1" src="" border="0" width="200" height="150">
```

Next you come to the script block where the image to be displayed is decided. On the first line, you define an array containing a list of image sources. In this example, the images are in the same directory as the HTML file, so a path is not specified. If yours are not, make sure you enter the full path (for example, `C:\myImages\mexico.gif`).

Then you ask the user for a number from 0 to 3, which will be used as the array index to access the image source in the `myImages` array.

```
var imgIndex = prompt("Enter a number from 0 to 3","");
```

Finally, you set the `src` property of the `img` object to the source text inside the `myImages` array element with the index number provided by the user.

```
document.images["img1"].src = myImages[imgIndex];
```

Don't forget that when you write `document.images["img1"]`, you are accessing the `img` object stored in the `images` collection. You've used the image's name, as defined in the `name` attribute of the `<img/>` element, but you could have used `document.images[0]`. It's an index position of 0, because it's the first (and only) image on this page.

The links Collection

For each hyperlink element `<a/>` defined with an `href` attribute, the browser creates an a object. The most important property of the a object is the `href` property, corresponding to the `href` attribute of the tag. Using this, you can find out where the link points to, and you can change this even after the page has loaded.

The collection of all a objects in a page is contained within the `links` collection, much as the `img` objects are contained in the `images` collection, as you saw earlier.

Responding to the User's Actions with Events

There's no doubt that JavaScript is a useful tool in web programming. As you've seen thus far, it's capable of limited data processing. In most web applications, however, data processing is typically relegated to the server, as it is better suited for that task. The user uses the web application through the browser, and as such, the browser is responsive to the user's actions. Wouldn't it be great if you could execute code for a specific user action? Well, you can with events.

What Are Events?

Events occur when something in particular happens. For example, the user clicking on the page, clicking on a hyperlink, or moving the mouse pointer over some text all cause events to occur. Another example, which is used quite frequently, is the `load` event for the page: the window raises (or fires) a notification when the page is completely loaded in the browser.

Why should you be interested in events?

Take as an example the situation in which you want to make a menu pop up when the user clicks anywhere in your web page. Assuming that you can write a function that will make the pop-up menu appear, how do you know *when* to make it appear, or in other words, *when* to call the function? You somehow need to intercept the event of the user clicking in the document, and make sure your function is called when that event occurs.

To do this, you need to use something called an *event handler* or listener. You associate this with the code that you want to execute when the event occurs. This provides you with a way of intercepting events and making your code execute when they have occurred. You will find that adding an event handler to your code is often known as "connecting your code to the event." It's a bit like setting an alarm clock — you set the clock to make a ringing noise when a certain event happens. With alarm clocks, the event is when a certain time is reached.

Connecting Code to Events

Chapter 5 introduced objects defined by their methods and properties. However, objects also have events associated with them. This was not mentioned before, because native JavaScript objects do not have these events, but the objects of the BOM (and Document Object Model, or DOM, which you'll see in Chapter 12) do.

Event handlers are made up of the word `on` and the event that they will handle. For example, the click event has the `onclick` event handler, and the load event has the `onload` event handler.

A number of ways exist to connect your code to an event using event handlers. In this chapter you'll look at two of the easiest ways to add events, ways that have been around a very long time and are supported even by older browsers, as well as by current ones. In Chapter 12 you're going to look at newer and standards-friendly ways of adding events.

Handling Events via HTML Attributes

The first and most common method is to add the event handler's name and the code you want to execute to the HTML element's attributes.

Let's create a simple HTML page with a single hyperlink, given by the element `<a/>`. Associated to this element is the a object. One of the events the a object has is the `click` event. The click event fires, not surprisingly, when the user clicks the hyperlink.

```
<!DOCTYPE html PUBLIC "-//W3C//DTD XHTML 1.0 Strict//EN"
    "http://www.w3.org/TR/xhtml1/DTD/xhtml1-strict.dtd">

<html xmlns="http://www.w3.org/1999/xhtml">
```

```
<head>
    <title>Connecting Events Using HTML Attributes</title>
</head>
<body>
<a href="somepage.htm" name="linkSomePage">
    Click Me
</a>
</body>
</html>
```

As it stands, this page does nothing a normal hyperlink doesn't do. You click it, and it navigates the window to another page, called somepage.htm, which would need to be created. There's been no event handler added to the link — yet!

As mentioned earlier, one very common and easy way of connecting the event to your code is to add it directly to the opening tag of the element object whose event you are capturing. In this case, it's the click event of the a object, as defined by the <a/> element. On clicking the link, you want to capture the event and connect it to your code. You need to add the event handler, in this case onclick, as an attribute to the opening <a> tag. You set the value of the attribute to the code you want to have executed when the event occurs.

Let's rewrite the opening <a> tag to do this as follows:

```
<a href="somepage.htm" name="linkSomePage" onclick="alert('You Clicked?')">
    Click Me
</a>
```

This code adds onclick="alert('You Clicked?')" to the definition of the opening <a> tag. Now, when the link is clicked, you see an alert box. After this, the hyperlink does its usual stuff and takes you to the page defined in the href attribute.

This is fine if you have only one line of code to connect to the event handler, but what if you want a number of lines to execute when the link is clicked?

Well, all you need to do is define the function you want to execute and call it in the onclick code. Let's do that now.

```
<!DOCTYPE html PUBLIC "-//W3C//DTD XHTML 1.0 Strict//EN"
    "http://www.w3.org/TR/xhtml1/DTD/xhtml1-strict.dtd">

<html xmlns="http://www.w3.org/1999/xhtml">
<head>
    <title>Connecting Events using HTML Attributes</title>
</head>
<body>
<script type="text/javascript">
function linkSomePage_onclick()
{
    alert('You Clicked?');
    return true;
}
</script>
```

```
<a href="somepage.htm" name="linkSomePage"
 onclick="return linkSomePage_onclick()">
       Click Me
</a>
</body>
</html>
```

Within the script block, you have created a standard function, and given it a descriptive name to help you when reading the code. Here we're using ObjectName_event() as the function name. That way you can instantly see what object on the page this relates to and which event is being connected to. So, in the preceding example, the function is called linkSomePage_onclick(), because you are referring to the onclick event handler for the a object with name linkSomePage. Note that this naming convention is simply something created by your authors; it's not compulsory, and you can use whatever convention you prefer as long as you are consistent.

The onclick attribute is now connected to some code that calls the function linkSomePage_onclick(). Therefore, when the user clicks the hyperlink, this function will be executed.

You'll also see that the function returns a value, true in this case. Also, where you define your onclick attribute, you return the return value of the function by using the return statement before the function name. Why do this?

The value returned by onclick="return linkSomePage_onclick()" is used by JavaScript to decide whether the normal action of the link — that is, going to a new page — should occur. If you return true, the action continues, and you go to somepage.htm. If you return false, the normal chain of events (that is, going to somepage.htm) does not happen. You say that the action associated with the event is canceled. Try changing the function to this:

```
function linkSomePage_onclick()
{
    alert("This link is going nowhere");
    return false;
}
```

Now you'll find that you just get a message, and no attempt is made to go to somepage.htm.

Not all objects and their events make use of the return value, so sometimes it's redundant. Also, it's not always the case that returning false cancels the action. For reasons of browser history rather than logic, it's sometimes true that cancels the action. Generally speaking, it's best to return true and deal with the exceptions as you find them.

Some events are not directly linked with the user's actions as such. For example, the window object has the load event, which fires when a page is loaded, and the unload event, which fires when the page is unloaded (that is, when the user either closes the browser or moves to another page).

Event handlers for the window object actually go inside the opening <body> tag. For example, to add an event handler for the load and unload events, you'd write the following:

```
<body onload="myOnLoadfunction()"
 onunload="myOnUnloadFunction()">
```

Handling Events via Object Properties

Now let's look at the second way to connect to events.

With this method, you first need to define the function that will be executed when the event occurs. Then you need to set that object's event handler property to the function you defined.

This is illustrated in the following example:

```
<!DOCTYPE html PUBLIC "-//W3C//DTD XHTML 1.0 Strict//EN"
    "http://www.w3.org/TR/xhtml1/DTD/xhtml1-strict.dtd">

<html xmlns="http://www.w3.org/1999/xhtml">
<head>
    <title>Chapter 6: Example 4</title>
</head>
<body>
<script type="text/javascript">
function linkSomePage_onclick()
{
    alert('This link is going nowhere');
    return false;
}
</script>
<a href="somepage.htm" name="linkSomePage">
    Click Me
</a>
<script type="text/javaScript">
 window.document.links[0].onclick = linkSomePage_onclick;
</script>
</body>
</html>
```

Save this as ch6_examp4.htm.

You define the function linkSomePage_onclick(), much as you did previously. As before, you can return a value indicating whether you want the normal action of that object to happen.

Next you have the <a/> element, whose object's event you are connecting to. You'll notice there is no mention of the event handler or the function within the attributes of the tag.

The connection is made between the object's event and the function on the final lines of script, as shown in the following code:

```
<script type="text/javaScript">
    document.links[0].onclick = linkSomePage_onclick;
</script>
```

As you saw before, document.links[0] returns the a object corresponding to the first link in your web page, which is your linkSomePage hyperlink. You set this object's onclick property to reference your function — this makes the connection between the object's event handler and your function. Note that no parentheses are added after the function name. Now whenever you click the link, your function gets executed.

The first method of connecting code to events is easier, so why would you ever want to use the second?

Perhaps the most common situation in which you would want to do this is one in which you want to capture an event for which there is no HTML element to write your event handler as an attribute. It is also useful if you want the code attached to an event handler to be changed dynamically.

Try It Out   Displaying a Random Image when the Page Loads

Let's look at another example in which you connect to a hyperlink's click event to randomly change the image loaded in a page.

```
<!DOCTYPE html PUBLIC "-//W3C//DTD XHTML 1.0 Strict//EN"
"http://www.w3.org/TR/xhtml1/DTD/xhtml1-strict.dtd">

<html xmlns="http://www.w3.org/1999/xhtml">
<head>
    <title>Chapter 6: Example 5</title>
    <script type="text/javascript">
    var myImages = new Array("usa.gif","canada.gif","jamaica.gif","mexico.gif");

    function changeImg(that)
    {
        var newImgNumber = Math.round(Math.random() * 3);

        while (that.src.indexOf(myImages[newImgNumber]) != -1)
        {
            newImgNumber = Math.round(Math.random() * 3);
        }

        that.src = myImages[newImgNumber];

        return false;
    }
    </script>
</head>
<body>
    <img name="img0" src="usa.gif" border="0"
        onclick="return changeImg(this)" />

    <img name="img1" src="mexico.gif" border="0"
        onclick="return changeImg(this)" />
</body>
</html>
```

Save the page as ch6_examp5.htm. Again, you will need four image files for the example, which you can create or retrieve from the code download available with this book.

Load the page into your browser. You should see a page like that shown in Figure 6-3.

If you click an image, you'll see it change to a different image, which is selected randomly.

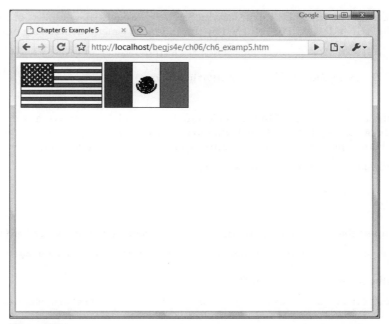

Figure 6-3

The first line in the script block at the top of the page defines a variable with page-level scope. This is an array that contains your list of image sources.

```
var myImages = new Array("usa.gif","canada.gif","jamaica.gif","mexico.gif");
```

Next you have the changeImg() function, which will be connected to the onclick event handler of the <img/> elements defined in the page. You are using the same function for both images' onclick event handlers and indeed can connect one function to as many event handlers as you like. This function accepts one parameter called that. It is called that because you pass the this keyword to the function which gives you immediate access to the img object you click. You can actually name the parameter whatever you want, but most developers use the word "that" when it references this.

In the first line of the function, you set the newImgNumber variable to a random integer between 0 and 3:

```
function changeImg(that)
{
    var newImgNumber = Math.round(Math.random() * 3);
```

The Math.random() method provides a random number between 0 and 1, and you multiply that by three to get a number between 0 and 3. This number is rounded to the nearest whole number (0, 1, 2, or 3) by means of Math.round(). This integer will provide the index for the image src that you will select from the myImages array.

The next lines are a while loop, the purpose of which is to ensure that you don't select the same image as the current one. If the string contained in myImages[newImgNumber] is found inside the src property of the current image, you know it's the same and that you need to get another random number. You keep looping until you get a new image, at which point `myImages[newImgNumber]` will not be found in the existing `src` and -1 will be returned by the `indexOf()` method, breaking out of the loop.

```
while (imgClicked.src.indexOf(myImages[newImgNumber]) != -1)
{
    newImgNumber = Math.round(Math.random() * 3);
}
```

Next, you set the `src` property of the `img` object to the new value contained in your `myImages` array. You return `false` to stop the link from trying to navigate to another page; remember that the HTML link is only there to provide a means of capturing an `onclick` event handler.

```
that.src = myImages[newImgNumber];

return false;
}
```

Now you connect the `onclick` event of the first `<img/>` element to the `changeImg()` function:

```
<img name=img0 src="usa.gif" border="0" onclick="return changeImg(this)">
```

And now to the second `<img/>` element:

```
<img name="img1" src="mexico.gif" border="0" onclick="return changeImg(this)">
```

Passing `this` in the `changeImg()` function gives the function direct access to this `<img/>` element's corresponding object. When you pass `this` to an HTML element's attribute event handler, the corresponding object of that element is passed to the function. It's a nice, clean way of accessing the element's object in your JavaScript code.

Events are an important matter for web developers — your authors wager that a good bulk of your code will handle events. Chapter 12 covers events again, but let's switch gears to another topic: the user's browser.

Determining the User's Browser

Many browsers, versions of those browsers, and operating systems are out there on the Internet, each with its own version of the BOM and its own particular quirks. It's therefore important that you make sure your pages will work correctly on all browsers, or at least *degrade gracefully*, such as by displaying a message suggesting that the user upgrade their browser.

Although you can go a long way with cross-browser-compatible code, there may come a time when you want to add extra features that only one browser supports. The solution is to write script that determines the user's browser and executes script that is compatible with the browser.

You can check for browser details in two main ways. The first is to see if the object and property you use in your code are actually available in the user's browser. Let's say for example that your code relies on the `all` collection of the `document` object in Internet Explorer (IE). If you write

```
if (window.all)
{
```

```
    // our code using the document.all collection
}
```

the `if` statement's condition will evaluate to `true` if the property returns a valid value. If the property is not supported, its value will be `undefined`, and the `if` statement will evaluate to `false`.

To check whether a particular method is supported, you can do the following:

```
if (document.getElementById)
{
    // code using document.getElementById()
}
else
{
    // code for browsers that do not have that method
}
```

You've "tested" the existence of the method as you did with properties. Just remember not to include the opening or closing parentheses after the method even if it normally has a number of parameters. The `getElementById` method, for example, has one parameter, and you'll look at it in Chapter 12.

Functions (and methods) are actually objects in the JavaScript language. While this advanced topic isn't covered in this book, Professional JavaScript for Web Developers *by Nicholas Zakas (published by Wrox) provides an in-depth discussion on the topic.*

The next example shows how to use object checking to ensure that you execute the right code for the right browser; this technique is not foolproof but can be very useful.

Try It Out   Checking for Supported Browser Properties

```
<!DOCTYPE html PUBLIC "-//W3C//DTD XHTML 1.0 Strict//EN"
    "http://www.w3.org/TR/xhtml1/DTD/xhtml1-strict.dtd">

<html xmlns="http://www.w3.org/1999/xhtml">
<head>
    <title>Chapter 6: Example 6</title>
</head>
<body>

<script type="text/javascript">
var browser = "Unknown";
var version = "0";

if (window.opera)
{
    browser = "Opera";
    version = "5+";

    if (window.opera.setPreference)
    {
        version = "9";
    }
}
```

```
    else if (document.all)
    {
        browser = "Internet Explorer";
        version = "6-";+

        if (window.XMLHttpRequest)
        {
            version = "7+";
        }
    }
    else if (window.sidebar)
    {
        browser = "Firefox";
        version = "1+";
    }

    document.write(browser + " " + version);
    </script>

    </body>
    </html>
```

Save this example as ch6_examp6.htm.

The page looks at which BOM and JavaScript properties the browser supports and, based on that, makes a rough guess as to the browser type. So the first lines checks to see if the browser's window object has the opera property.

```
    if (window.opera)
    {
        browser = "Opera";
        version = "5+";

        if (window.opera.setPreference)
        {
            version = "9";
        }
    }
```

Because only Opera supports the opera property, it is safe to assume this is at least Opera version 5. The inner if statement looks to see if the window.opera object supports the setPreference method; this method is only supported by Opera version 9.

Next you have a test for the document object's all property, a property supported by IE 4+ and Opera 7+.

```
    else if (document.all)
    {
        browser = "Internet Explorer";
        version = "6-";

        if (window.XMLHttpRequest)
        {
            version = "7+";
        }
    }
```

Since you've already tested for Opera, you don't have to worry about false results from this script. To see if the browser is an IE 7+ browser, check the window object's XMLHttpRequest property. The only

Microsoft browsers to support the XMLHttpRequest property are IE versions 7 and above (IE6 and below support the functionality of XMLHttpRequest, but not the window.XMLHttpRequest property).

The final bit of checking is for the sidebar property supported by Firefox, which deals with the sidebar tool.

```
// Firefox
else if (window.sidebar)
{
    browser = "Firefox";
    version = "1+";
}
```

The last line writes out the results of the browser object checking.

```
document.write(browser + " " + version);
```

Hopefully, this example demonstrates how to use object checking to see if a particular feature is supported by a browser. In the example, you haven't actually used the various features; it's simply a way of demonstrating how to check for browser-specific objects. When writing your own code, be sure to double-check whether a particular feature you're using is supported by all the browsers you expect to visit your web site. If some of the browsers you expect to visit don't support a particular feature, then test for the feature and write alternative code for the browsers that don't support it.

You'll be seeing much more advanced object checking in Chapter 12.

No Script at All

Sometimes people switch off JavaScript in their browsers, or use a browser that doesn't support JavaScript, though that's quite rare these days. To cover this situation, you can use the <noscript/> element. Any HTML inside opening and closing tags will be displayed only to browsers that don't support JavaScript or on which JavaScript has been disabled:

```
<!DOCTYPE html PUBLIC "-//W3C//DTD XHTML 1.0 Strict//EN"
    "http://www.w3.org/TR/xhtml1/DTD/xhtml1-strict.dtd">

<html xmlns="http://www.w3.org/1999/xhtml">
<head>
    <title>No Script</title>
</head>
<body>
<noscript>
    This website requires JavaScript to be enabled.
</noscript>
</body>
<html>
```

Browser Checking Using the Navigator Object

The second method of checking browser details is using the navigator object property of the window object. In particular, you use the appName and userAgent properties of the navigator object. The main problem with this method is that a less common browser may well declare itself to be a particular version of one of the major browsers but not actually support all the JavaScript or BOM objects, properties, or methods of that browser. Therefore this method of "browser sniffing" has fallen out of favor and is not the recommended way of checking for compatibility. It's really a last resort when all other methods have failed, such as when two different browsers support the same object and property but implement them so that they work in two different ways. Object checking wouldn't help you in that circumstance, so you'd have to fall back on using the navigator object.

The appName property returns the model of the browser, such as "Microsoft Internet Explorer" for IE, "Opera" for Opera, or "Netscape" for Firefox, Safari, and Chrome.

The userAgent property returns a string containing various bits of information, such as the browser version, operating system, and browser model. However, the value returned by this property varies from browser to browser, so you have to be very, very careful when using it. For example, the browser's version is embedded in different locations of the string.

Try It Out   Checking for and Dealing with Different Browsers

In this example, you create a page that uses the aforementioned properties to discover the client's browser and browser version. The page can then take action based upon the client's specifications.

```
<!DOCTYPE html PUBLIC "-//W3C//DTD XHTML 1.0 Strict//EN"
    "http://www.w3.org/TR/xhtml1/DTD/xhtml1-strict.dtd">

<html xmlns="http://www.w3.org/1999/xhtml">
<head>
    <title>Chapter 6: Example 7</title>
    <script type="text/javaScript">

    function getBrowserName()
    {
        var lsBrowser = navigator.userAgent;
        if (lsBrowser.indexOf("MSIE") >= 0)
        {
            lsBrowser = "MSIE";
        }
        else if (lsBrowser.indexOf("Firefox") >= 0)
        {
            lsBrowser = "Firefox";
        }
        else if (lsBrowser.indexOf("Chrome") >= 0)
        {
            lsBrowser = "Chrome";
        }
        else if (lsBrowser.indexOf("Safari") >= 0)
        {
            lsBrowser = "Safari";
        }
        else if (lsBrowser.indexOf("Opera") >= 0)
        {
            lsBrowser = "Opera";
        }
        else
        {
```

```
                lsBrowser = "UNKNOWN";
            }
            return lsBrowser;
        }

        function getBrowserVersion()
        {
            var findIndex;
            var browserVersion = 0;
            var browser = getBrowserName();

            browserVersion = navigator.userAgent;
            findIndex = browserVersion.indexOf(browser) + browser.length + 1;
            browserVersion = parseFloat(browserVersion.substring(findIndex,
                    findIndex + 3));

            return browserVersion;
        }
    </script>
</head>
<body>
<script type="text/javaScript">

var browserName = getBrowserName();
var browserVersion = getBrowserVersion();

if (browserName == "MSIE")
{
    if (browserVersion < 7)
    {
        document.write("Your version of Internet Explorer is too old");
    }
    else
    {
        document.write("Your version of Internet Explorer is fully supported");
    }

}
else if (browserName == "Firefox")
{
    document.write("Firefox is fully supported");
}
else if (browserName == "Safari")
{
    document.write("Safari is fully supported");
}
else if (browserName == "Chrome")
{
    document.write("Chrome is fully supported");
}
else if (browserName == "Opera")
{
    document.write("Opera is fully supported");
}
```

```
else
{
    document.write("<h2>Sorry this browser version is not supported</h2>");
}
</script>
<noscript>
    <h2>This website requires a browser supporting scripting</h2>
</noscript>
</body>
</html>
```

Save this script as `ch6_examp7.htm`.

If the browser is Firefox, IE7+, Safari, Chrome, or Opera, a message appears telling the user that the browser is supported. If it's an earlier version of IE, the user sees a message telling them the version of that browser is not supported.

If it's not one of those browsers, the user sees a message saying the browser is unsupported. This is not particularly friendly, so in practice you could have available a plain and simple version of the page without scripting — something with as much functionality as possible without JavaScript.

If the browser doesn't support JavaScript or the user has turned off support, the user will see a message that the web site needs JavaScript to work.

The script block in the head of the page defines two important functions. The `getBrowserName()` function finds out the name of the browser and the `getBrowserVersion()` function finds out the browser version.

The key to the browser checking code is the value returned by the `navigator.userAgent` property. Here are a few example user agent strings from current browsers:

1. Mozilla/4.0 (compatible; MSIE 8.0; Windows NT 5.1; Trident/4.0; .NET CLR 1.1.4322; .NET CLR 2.0.50727; .NET CLR 1.0.3705; .NET CLR 3.0.04506.648; .NET CLR 3.5.21022; .NET CLR 3.0.4506.2152; .NET CLR 3.5.30729)

2. Mozilla/5.0 (Windows; U; Windows NT 5.1; en-US; rv:1.9.0.10) Gecko/2009042316 Firefox/3.0.10 (.NET CLR 3.5.30729)

3. Mozilla/5.0 (Windows; U; Windows NT 5.1; en-US) AppleWebKit/530.17 (KHTML, like Gecko) Version/4.0 Safari/530.17

4. Mozilla/5.0 (Windows; U; Windows NT 5.1; en-US) AppleWebKit/531.0 (KHTML, like Gecko) Chrome/3.0.183.1 Safari/531.0

5. Opera/9.63 (Windows NT 5.1; U; en) Presto/2.1.1

Here each line of the `userAgent` string has been numbered. Looking closely at each line it's not hard to guess which browser each agent string relates to. In order:

1. Microsoft IE8

2. Firefox 3.0.10

3. Safari 4.0

4. Chrome 3.0.183.1

5. Opera 9.63

Using this information, let's start on the first function, getBrowserName(). First you get the name of the browser, as found in navigator.userAgent, and store it in the variable lsBrowser. This will also be used as the variable to store the return value for the function.

```
function getBrowserName()
{
    var lsBrowser = navigator.userAgent;
```

The string returned by this property tends to be quite long and does vary slightly sometimes. However, by checking for the existence of certain keywords, such as MSIE or Firefox, you can determine the browser name. Start with the following lines:

```
if (lsBrowser.indexOf("MSIE") >= 0)
{
    lsBrowser = "MSIE";
}
```

These lines search the lsBrowser string for MSIE. If the indexOf value of this substring is 0 or greater, you know you have found it, and so you set the return value to MSIE.

The following else if statement does the same, except that it is modified for Firefox.

```
else if (lsBrowser.indexOf("Firefox") >= 0)
{
    lsBrowser = "Firefox";
}
```

This principle carries on for another three if statements, in which you also check for Chrome, Safari, and Opera. If you have a browser you want to check for, this is the place to add its if statement. Just view the string it returns in navigator.userAgent and look for its name or something that uniquely identifies it.

If none of the if statements match, you return UNKNOWN as the browser name.

```
else
{
    lsBrowser = "UNKNOWN";
}
```

The value of lsBrowser is then returned to the calling code.

```
    return lsBrowser;
}
```

Now turn to the final function, getBrowserVersion().

The browser version details often appear in the userAgent string right after the name of the browser. For these reasons, your first task in the function is to find out which browser you are dealing with. You declare and initialize the browser variable to the name of the browser, using the getBrowserName() function you just wrote.

```
function getBrowserVersion()
{
    var findIndex;
    var browserVersion = 0;
    var browser = getBrowserName();
```

If the browser is MSIE (Internet Explorer), you need to use the userAgent property again. Under IE, the userAgent property always contains MSIE followed by the browser version. So what you need to do is search for MSIE, then get the number following that.

You set findIndex to the character position of the browser name plus the length of the name, plus one. Doing this ensures you to get the character after the name and after the following space or / character that follows the name and is just before the version number. browserVersion is set to the floating-point value of that number, which you obtain using the substring() method. This selects the character starting at findIndex, your number, and whose end is one before findIndex, plus three. This ensures that you just select three characters for the version number.

```
browserVersion = navigator.userAgent;
findIndex = browserVersion.indexOf(browser) + browser.length + 1;
browserVersion = parseFloat(browserVersion.substring(findIndex,findIndex + 3));
```

If you look back to the userAgent strings, you see that IE8's is similar to this:

```
Mozilla/4.0 (compatible; MSIE 8.0; Windows NT 5.1; .NET CLR 2.0.40607)
```

So findIndex will be set to the character index of the number 8 following the browser name. browserVersion will be set to three characters from and including the 8, giving the version number as 8.0.

At the end of the function, you return browserVersion to the calling code, as shown here:

```
    return browserVersion;
}
```

You've seen the supporting functions, but how do you make use of them? Well, in the following code, which executes as the page is loaded, you obtain two bits of information — browser name and version — and use these to filter which browser the user is running.

```
var browserName = getBrowserName();
var browserVersion = getBrowserVersion();

if (browserName == "MSIE")
{
    if (browserVersion < 7)
    {
        document.write("Your version of Internet Explorer is too old");
    }
    else
    {
        document.write("Your version of Internet Explorer is fully supported");
    }
}
```

The first of the if statements is shown in the preceding code and checks to see if the user has IE. If true, it then checks to see if the version is lower than 7. If it is, the user sees the message stating their browser is too old. If it is 7+, the message tells the user their browser is fully supported.

You do this again for Firefox, Chrome, Safari, and Opera. The versions of these browsers aren't checked in this example, but you can do so if you want to:

```
else if (browserName == "Firefox")
{
```

```
        document.write("Firefox is fully supported");
    }
    else if (browserName == "Safari")
    {
        document.write("Safari is fully supported");
    }
    else if (browserName == "Chrome")
    {
        document.write("Chrome is fully supported");
    }
    else if (browserName == "Opera")
    {
        document.write("Opera is fully supported");
    }
    else
    {
        document.write("<h2>Sorry this browser version is not supported</h2>");
    }
```

On the final part of the `if` statements is the `else` statement that covers all other browsers and tells the user the browser is not supported.

Finally, there is an `<noscript/>` element for early browsers and for users who have chosen to disable JavaScript. This displays a message informing the user their browser isn't JavaScript-enabled.

```
<noscript>
    <h2>This website requires a browser supporting scripting</h2>
</noscript>
```

As mentioned earlier, although this script works fine at the moment, it's possible that browsers will change their `userAgent` strings and you'll need to update the function to keep track of this. Also, some browsers pretend to be other browsers even if they don't function 100 percent the same, which can leave your code showing errors.

For these reasons, stick to the object checking method detailed earlier in the chapter.

Summary

You've covered a lot in this chapter, but now you have all the grounding you need to move on to more useful things such as forms and user input and later to more advanced areas of text and date manipulation.

❑ You turned your attention to the browser, the environment in which JavaScript exists. Just as JavaScript has native objects, so do web browsers. The objects within the web browser, and the hierarchy they are organized in, are described by something called the Browser Object Model (BOM). This is essentially a map of a browser's objects. Using it, you can navigate your way around each of the objects made available by the browser, together with their properties, methods, and events.

❑ The first of the main objects you looked at was the `window` object. This sits at the very top of the BOM's hierarchy. The `window` object contains a number of important sub-objects, including the `location` object, the `navigator` object, the `history` object, the `screen` object, and the `document` object.

❑ The `location` object contains information about the current page's location, such as its file name, the server hosting the page, and the protocol used. Each of these is a property of the `location` object. Some properties are read-only, but others, such as the `href` property, not only enable us to find the location of the page but can be changed so that we can navigate the page to a new location.

❑ The `history` object is a record of all the pages the user has visited since opening his or her browser. Sometimes pages are not noted (for example, when the `location` object's `replace()` method is used for navigation). You can move the browser forward and backward in the history stack and discover what pages the user has visited.

❑ The `navigator` object represents the browser itself and contains useful details of what type of browser, version, and operating system the user has. These details enable you to write pages dealing with various types of browsers, even where they may be incompatible.

❑ The `screen` object contains information about the display capabilities of the user's computer.

❑ The `document` object is one of the most important objects. It's an object representation of your page and contains all the elements, also represented by objects, within that page. The differences between the various browsers are particularly prominent here, but there are similarities between the browsers that enable you to write cross-browser code.

❑ The `document` object contains three properties that are actually collections. These are the `links`, `images`, and `forms` collections. Each contains all the objects created by the `<a/>`, `<img/>`, and `<form/>` elements on the page, and it's a way of accessing those elements.

❑ The `images` collection contains an `img` object for each `<img/>` element on the page. You found that even after the page has loaded, you can change the properties of images. For example, you can make the image change when clicked. The same principles for using the `images` collection apply to the `links` collection.

❑ You next saw that BOM objects have events as well as methods and properties. You handle these events in JavaScript by using event handlers, which you connect to code that you want to have executed when the event occurs. The events available for use depend on the object you are dealing with.

❑ Connecting a function that you have written to an event handler is simply a matter of adding an attribute to the element corresponding to the particular object you are interested in. The attribute has the name of the event handler you want to capture and the value of the function you want to connect to it.

❑ In some instances, such as for the `document` object, a second way of connecting event handlers to code is necessary. Setting the object's property with the name of the event handler to your function produces the same effect as if you did it using the event handler as an attribute.

❑ In some instances, returning values from event functions enables you to cancel the action associated with the event. For example, to stop a clicked link from navigating to a page, you return `false` from the event handler's code.

❑ Finally, you looked at how you can check what type of browser the users have so that you can make sure the users see only those pages or parts of a page that their browser is compatible with. The `navigator` object provides you with the details you need, in particular the `appName` and `userAgent` properties. You can also check specific BOM properties to see if they are supported before using them. If a browser doesn't support a specific property needed for your code to work, you can either write alternative code or let users know to upgrade their browsers.

That's it for this chapter. In the next chapter, you move on to more exciting form scripting, where you can add various controls to your page to help you gather information from the user.

Exercise Questions

Suggested solutions to these questions can be found in Appendix A. Exercise 1 Question

1. Create a page with a number of links. Then write code that fires on the window load event, displaying the href of each of the links on the page. (Hint: Remember that event handlers begin with on.)

2. Create two pages, one called `ieonly.htm` and the other called `notieonly.htm`. Each page should have a heading telling you what page is loaded. For example:

```
<H2>Welcome to the Internet Explorer only page</H2>
```

Using the functions for checking browser type, connect to the `window` object's `onload` event handler and detect what browser the user has. Then, if it's the wrong page for that browser, redirect to the other page.

3. Insert an image in the page with the `<img/>` element. When the mouse pointer rolls over the image, it should switch to a different image. When the mouse pointer rolls out (leaves the image), it should swap back again. (Hint: These events are `mouseover` and `mouseout`.)

HTML Forms: Interacting with the User

Web pages would be very boring if you could not interact with or obtain information from the user, such as text, numbers, or dates. Luckily, with JavaScript this is possible. You can use this information within the web page, or it can be posted to the web server where you can manipulate it and store it in a database if you wish. This chapter concentrates on using the information within the web browser, which is called *client-side processing*.

You're quite accustomed to various user interface elements. For example, the Windows operating system has a number of standard elements, such as buttons you can click; lists, drop-down list boxes, and radio buttons you can select from; and boxes you can check. The same applies with any graphical user interface (GUI) operating system, whether it's a Mac, Unix, or Linux system. These elements are the means by which you now interface with applications. The good news is that you can include many of these types of elements in your web page — and even better, it's very easy to do so. When you have such an element — say, a button — inside your page, you can then tie code to its events. For example, when the button is clicked, you can fire off a JavaScript function you created.

It's important to note at this point that the elements discussed in this chapter are the common elements made available by HTML, and not ActiveX elements, Java Applets, or plug-ins. You'll look at some of these in Chapter 13.

All of the HTML elements used for interaction should be placed inside an HTML form. Let's start by taking a look at HTML forms and how you interact with them in JavaScript.

HTML Forms

Forms provide you with a way of grouping together HTML interaction elements with a common purpose. For example, a form may contain elements that enable the input of a user's data for registering on a web site. Another form may contain elements that enable the user to ask for a car insurance quote. It's possible to have a number of separate forms in a single page. You don't need to worry about pages containing multiple forms until you have to submit information to a web server — then you need to be aware that the information from only one of the forms on a page can be submitted to the server at one time.

To create a form, use the `<form>` and `</form>` tags to declare where it starts and where it ends. The `<form/>` element has a number of attributes, such as the` action attribute, which determines where the form is submitted to; the method attribute, which determines how the information is submitted; and the target attribute, which determines the frame to which the response to the form is loaded.

Generally speaking, for client-side scripting where you have no intention of submitting information to a server, these attributes are not necessary. They will come into play in a later chapter when you look at programming server pages. For now the only attribute you need to set in the `<form/>` element is the name attribute, so that you can reference the form.

So, to create a blank form, the tags required would look something like this:

```
<form name="myForm">
</form>
```

You won't be surprised to hear that these tags create a Form object, which you can use to access the form. You can access this object in two ways.

First, you can access the object directly using its name — in this case document.myForm. Alternatively, you can access the object through the document object's forms collection property. Remember that the last chapter included a discussion of the document object's images collection and how you can manipulate it like any other array. The same applies to the forms collection, except that instead of each element in the collection holding an IMG object, it now holds a Form object. For example, if it's the first Form in the page, you reference it using document.forms[0].

Many of the attributes of the `<form/>` element can be accessed as properties of the Form object. In particular, the name property of the Form object mirrors the name attribute of the `<form/>` element.

Try It Out   The forms Collection

Let's have a look at an example that uses the forms collection. Here you have a page with three forms on it. Using the forms collection, you access each Form object in turn and show the value of its name property in a message box.

```
<!DOCTYPE html PUBLIC "-//W3C//DTD XHTML 1.0 Transitional//EN"
    "http://www.w3.org/TR/xhtml1/DTD/xhtml1-transitional.dtd">
<html xmlns="http://www.w3.org/1999/xhtml">
<head>
    <title>Chapter 7: Example 1</title>
    <script type="text/javascript">
    function window_onload()
    {
        var numberForms = document.forms.length;
        var formIndex;
        for (formIndex = 0; formIndex < numberForms; formIndex++)
        {
            alert(document.forms[formIndex].name);
        }
```

```
        }
    </script>
</head>
<body onload="window_onload()">
    <form action="" name="form1">
        <p>
            This is inside form1.
        </p>
    </form>
    <form action="" name="form2">
        <p>
            This is inside form2
        </p>
    </form>
    <form action="" name="form3">
        <p>
            This is inside form3
        </p>
    </form>
</body>
</html>
```

Save this as ch7_examp1.htm. When you load it into your browser, you should see three alert boxes, each of which shows the name of a form.

Within the body of the page you define three forms. Each form is given a name and contains a paragraph of text.

Within the definition of the <body/> element, the window_onload() function is connected to the window object's onload event handler.

```
<body onload="window_onload()">
```

This means that when the page is loaded, your window_onload() function will be called.

The window_onload() function is defined in a script block in the head of the page. Within this function you loop through the forms collection. Just like any other JavaScript array, the forms collection has a length property, which you can use to determine how many times you need to loop. Actually, because you know how many forms there are, you can just write the number in. However, this example uses the length property, since that makes it easier to add to the collection without having to change the function. Generalizing your code like this is a good practice to get into.

The function starts by getting the number of Form objects within the forms array and storing that number in the variable numberForms.

```
function window_onload()
{
    var numberForms = document.forms.length;
```

Next you define a variable, formIndex, to be used in the for loop.

```
    var formIndex;
    for (formIndex = 0; formIndex < numberForms; formIndex++)
    {
        alert(document.forms[formIndex].name);
    }
}
```

Remember that because the indexes for arrays start at 0, your loop needs to go from an index of 0 to an index of numberForms – 1. You enable this by initializing the formIndex variable to 0, and setting the condition of the for loop to formIndex < numberForms.

Within the for loop's code, you pass the index of the form you want (that is, formIndex) to document.forms[], which gives you the Form object at that index in the forms collection. To access the Form object's name property, you put a dot at the end of the name of the property, name.

Other Form Object Properties and Methods

The HTML form controls commonly found in forms, which you will look at in more detail shortly, also have corresponding objects. One way to access these is through the elements property of the Form object, another collection. The elements collection contains all the objects corresponding to the HTML interaction elements within the form, with the exception of the little-used <input type="image" /> element. As you'll see later, this property is very useful for looping through each of the elements in a form. For example, you can loop through each element to check that it contains valid data prior to submitting a form.

Being a collection, the elements property of the Form object has the length property, which tells you how many elements are in the form. The Form object also has the length property, which also gives you the number of elements in the form. Which of these you use is up to you because both do the same job, although writing document.myForm.length is shorter, and therefore quicker to type and less lengthy to look at in code, than document.myForm.elements.length.

When you submit data from a form to a server, you normally use the Submit button, which you will come to shortly. However, the Form object also has the submit() method, which does nearly the same thing.

> *The* submit() *method submits the form, but it does not fire the* submit *event of the* Form *object; thus, the* onsubmit *event handler is not called when submitting the form with* submit().

Recall that in Chapter 6 you saw how return values passed back from an event handler's code can affect whether the normal course of events continues or is canceled. You saw, for example, that returning false from a hyperlink's onclick event handler causes the link's navigation to be canceled. Well, the same principle applies to the Form object's onsubmit event handler, which fires when the user submits the form. If you return true to this event handler, the form submission goes ahead; if you return false, the submission is canceled. This makes the onsubmit event handler's code a great place to do form validation — that is, to check that what the user has entered into the form is valid. For example, if you ask for the users' ages and they enter mind your own business, you can spot that this is text rather than a valid number and stop them from continuing.

In addition to there being a Reset button, which is discussed later in the chapter, the Form object has the reset() method, which clears the form, or restores default values if these exist.

Creating blank forms is not exactly exciting or useful, so now let's turn our attention to the HTML elements that provide interaction functionality inside forms.

HTML Elements in Forms

About 10 elements are commonly found within <form/> elements. The most useful are shown in Figures 7-1, 7-2, 7-3, and 7-4, ordered into general types. Each type name is given and, in parentheses, the HTML needed to create it, though note this is not the full HTML but only a portion.

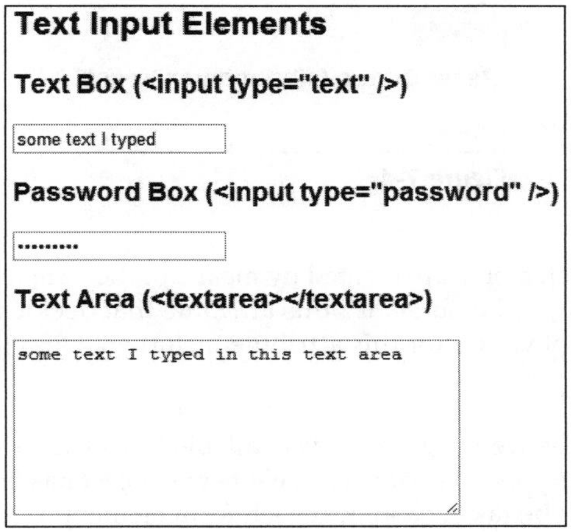

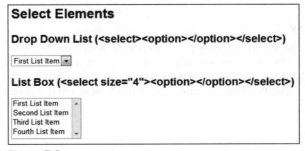

Text Input Elements

Text Box (<input type="text" />)

some text I typed

Password Box (<input type="password" />)

·········

Text Area (<textarea></textarea>)

some text I typed in this text area

Figure 7-1

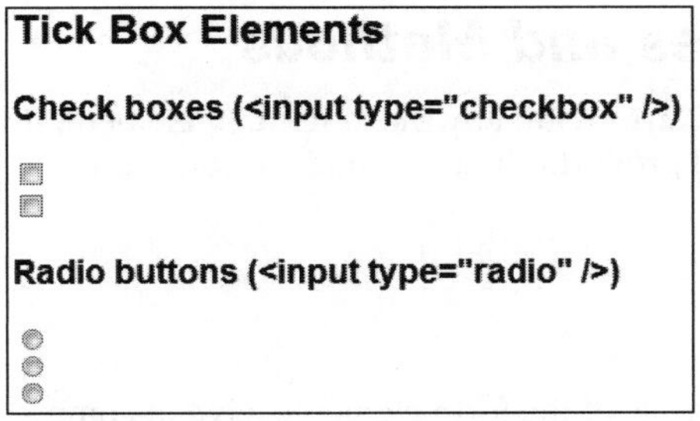

Tick Box Elements

Check boxes (<input type="checkbox" />)

Radio buttons (<input type="radio" />)

Figure 7-2

Select Elements

Drop Down List (<select><option></option></select>)

First List Item ▾

List Box (<select size="4"><option></option></select>)

First List Item
Second List Item
Third List Item
Fourth List Item

Figure 7-3

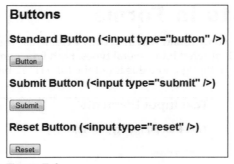

Figure 7-4

As you can see, most form elements are created by means of the `<input/>` element. One of the `<input/>` element's attributes is the `type` attribute. It's this attribute that decides which of the form elements this element will be. Examples of values for this attribute include `button` (to create a button) and `text` (to create a text box).

Each form element inside the web page is made available to you as — yes, you guessed it — an object. As with all the other objects you have seen, each element's object has its own set of distinctive properties, methods, and events. You'll be taking a look at each form element in turn and how to use its particular properties, methods, and events, but before you do that, let's look at properties and methods that the objects of the form elements have in common.

Common Properties and Methods

Because most form elements are created by the `<input/>` element, it would be correct to guess that all form elements share several properties and methods in common.

Here are a few.

The name Property

One property that all the objects of the form elements have in common is the `name` property. You can use the value of this property to reference that particular element in your script. Also, if you are sending the information in the form to a server, the element's `name` property is sent along with any value of the form element, so that the server knows what the value relates to.

The value Property

Most form element objects also have the `value` property, which returns the value of the element. For example, for a text box, the `value` property returns the text that the user entered in the text box. Also, setting the value of the `value` property enables you to put text inside the text box. However, the use of the `value` property is specific to each element, so you'll look at what it means as you look at each individual element.

The form Property

All form element objects also have the `form` property, which returns the `Form` object in which the element is contained. This can be useful in cases where you have a generic routine that checks the validity of data in a form. For example, when the user clicks a Submit button, you can pass the Form object referenced by the form property of the Submit button to your data checker, which can use it to loop through each element on the form in turn, checking that the data in the element are valid. This is handy if you have more than one form defined on the page or where you have a generic data checker that you cut and paste to different pages — this way you don't need to know the form's name in advance.

The type Property

Sometimes it's useful to know what type of element you're dealing with, particularly where you're looping through the elements in a form using the elements collection property. This information can be retrieved by means of the type property, which each element's object has. This property returns the type of the element (for example, button or text).

The focus() and blur() Methods

All form element objects also have the focus() and blur() methods. *Focus* is a concept you might not have come across yet. If an element is the center of the focus, any key presses made by the user will be passed directly to that element. For example, if a text box has focus, pressing keys will enter values into the text box. Also, if a button has the focus, pressing the Enter key will cause the button's onclick event handler code to fire, just as if a user had clicked the button with his mouse.

The user can set which element currently has the focus by clicking it or by using the Tab key to select it. However, you as the programmer can also decide which element has the focus by using the form element's object's focus() method. For example, if you have a text box for the user to enter his age and he enters an invalid value, such as a letter rather than a number, you can tell him that his input is invalid and send him back to that text box to correct his mistake.

Blur, which perhaps could be better called "lost focus," is the opposite of focus. If you want to remove a form element from being the focus of the user's attention, you can use the blur() method. When used with a form element, the blur() method usually results in the focus shifting to the page containing the form.

In addition to the focus() and blur() methods, all the form element's objects have the onfocus and onblur event handlers. These are fired, as you'd expect, when an element gets or loses the focus, respectively, due to user action or the focus() and blur() methods. The onblur event handler can be a good place to check the validity of data in the element that has just lost the focus. If the data are invalid, you can set the focus back to the element and let the user know why the data he entered are wrong.

> *Remember that the* submit() *method behaves differently than* focus() *and* blur() *in that it does not fire the* submit *event and* onsubmit *event handler.*

One thing to be careful of is using the focus() and blur() methods in the onfocus or onblur event handler code. There is the danger of an infinite loop occurring. For example, consider two elements, each of whose onfocus events passes the focus to the other element. Then, if one element gets the focus, its onfocus event will pass the focus to the second element, whose onfocus event will pass the focus back to the first element, and so on until the only way out is to close the browser down. This is not likely to please your users!

Also be very wary of using the focus() and blur() methods to put focus back in a problem field if that field or others depend on some of the user's input. For example, say you have two text boxes: one in which you want users to enter their city and the other in which you want them to enter their state. Also say that the input into the state text box is checked to make sure that the specified city is in that state. If the state does not contain the city, you put the focus back on the state text box so that the user can change the name of the state. However, if the user actually input the wrong city name and the right state name, she may not be able to go back to the city text box to rectify the problem.

Button Elements

We're starting our look at form elements with the standard button element because it's probably the most commonly used and is fairly simple. The HTML element to create a button is <input/>. For example, to create a button called myButton, which has the words "Click Me" on its face, the <input/> element would need to be as follows:

```
<input type="button" name="myButton" value="Click Me" />
```

The type attribute is set to button, and the value attribute is set to the text you want to appear on the face of the button. You can leave the value attribute off, but you'll end up with a blank button, which will leave your users guessing as to its purpose.

This element creates an associated Button object; in this example it is called myButton. This object has all the common properties and methods described earlier, including the value property. This property enables you to change the text on the button face using JavaScript, though this is probably not something you'll need to do very often. What the button is really all about is the click event.

You connect to the button's onclick event handler just as you did with the onclick events of other HTML elements such as the <a/>. All you need to do is define a function that you want to have executed when the button is clicked (say, button_onclick()) and then add the onclick event handler as an attribute of the <input/> element as follows:

```
<input type="button" onclick="button_onclick()" />
```

Try It Out   Counting Button Clicks

In the following example, you use the methods described previously to record how often a button has been clicked.

```
<!DOCTYPE html PUBLIC "-//W3C//DTD XHTML 1.0 Transitional//EN"
    "http://www.w3.org/TR/xhtml1/DTD/xhtml1-transitional.dtd">
<html xmlns="http://www.w3.org/1999/xhtml">
<head>
    <title>Chapter 7: Example 2</title>
    <script type="text/javascript">
    var numberOfClicks = 0;
    function myButton_onclick()
    {
        numberOfClicks++;
        document.form1.myButton.value = "Button clicked " +
            numberOfClicks + " times";
    }
    </script>
</head>
<body>
```

```
        <form action="" name="form1">
            <input type="button" name="myButton" value="Button clicked 0 times"
                onclick="myButton_onclick()" />
        </form>
    </body>
</html>
```

Save this page as ch7_examp2.htm. If you load this page into your browser, you will see a button with "Button clicked 0 times" on it. If you repeatedly press this button, you will see the number of button clicks recorded on the text of the button.

You start the script block in the head of the page by defining a global variable, accessible anywhere inside your page, called numberOfClicks. You record the number of times the button has been clicked in this variable and use this information to update the button's text.

The other piece of code in the script block is the definition of the function myButton_onclick(). This function is connected to the onclick event handler in the <input/> element in the body of the page. This element is for a button element called myButton and is contained within a form called form1.

```
    <form action="" name="form1">
        <input type="button" name="myButton" value="Button clicked 0 times"
            onclick="myButton_onclick()" />
    </form>
```

Let's look at the myButton_onclick() function a little more closely. First, the function increments the value of the variable numberOfClicks by one.

```
    function myButton_onclick()
    {
        numberOfClicks++;
```

Next, you update the text on the button face using the Button object's value property.

```
        document.form1.myButton.value = "Button clicked " +
            numberOfClicks + " times";
    }
```

The function in this example is specific to this form and button, rather than a generic function you'll use in other situations. Therefore, the code in this example refers to the form and button directly using document.form1.myButton. Remember the document object holds all the elements in a page, including the <form/> element, and that the button is embedded inside your form.

Try It Out   **onmouseup and onmousedown**

Two less commonly used events supported by the Button object are the mousedown and mouseup events. You can see these two events in action in the next example.

```
<!DOCTYPE html PUBLIC "-//W3C//DTD XHTML 1.0 Transitional//EN"
    "http://www.w3.org/TR/xhtml1/DTD/xhtml1-transitional.dtd">
<html xmlns="http://www.w3.org/1999/xhtml">
<head>
    <title>Chapter 7: Example 3</title>
    <script type="text/javascript">
```

```
        function myButton_onmouseup()
        {
            document.form1.myButton.value = "Mouse Goes Up"
        }
        function myButton_onmousedown()
        {
            document.form1.myButton.value = "Mouse Goes Down"
        }
    </script>
</head>
<body>
    <form action="" name="form1">
        <input type="button" name="myButton" value="Mouse Goes Up"
            onmouseup="myButton_onmouseup()"
            onmousedown="myButton_onmousedown()" />
    </form>
</body>
</html>
```

Save this page as `ch7_examp3.htm` and load it into your browser. If you click the button with your left mouse button and keep it held down, you'll see the text on the button change to "Mouse Goes Down." As soon as you release the button, the text changes to "Mouse Goes Up."

In the body of the page, you define a button called `myButton` within a form called `form1`; you attach the function `myButton_onmouseup()` to the `onmouseup` event handler, and the function `myButton_onmousedown()` to the `onmousedown` event handler.

```
<form action="" name="form1">
    <input type="button" name="myButton" value="Mouse Goes Up"
        onmouseup="myButton_onmouseup()"
        onmousedown="myButton_onmousedown()" />
</form>
```

The `myButton_onmouseup()` and `myButton_onmousedown()` functions are defined in a script block in the head of the page. Each function consists of just a single line of code, in which you use the `value` property of the `Button` object to change the text that is displayed on the button's face.

An important point to note is that events like `mouseup` and `mousedown` are triggered only when the mouse pointer is actually over the element in question. For example, if you click and hold down the mouse button over your button, then move the mouse away from the button before releasing the mouse button, you'll find that the `mouseup` event does not fire and the text on the button's face does not change. In this instance it would be the `document` object's `onmouseup` event handler code that would fire, if you'd connected any code to it.

Don't forget that, like all form element objects, the `Button` object also has the `onfocus` and `onblur` events, though they are rarely used in the context of buttons.

Two additional button types are the Submit and Reset buttons. You define these buttons just as you do a standard button, except that the `type` attribute of the `<input>` tag is set to `submit` or `reset` rather than to `button`. For example, the Submit and Reset buttons in Figure 7-4 were created using the following code:

```
<input type="submit" value="Submit" name="submit1" />
<input type="reset" value="Reset" name="reset1" />
```

These buttons have special purposes, which are not related to script.

When the Submit button is clicked, the form data from the form that the button is inside gets sent to the server automatically, without the need for any script.

When the Reset button is clicked, all the elements in a form are cleared and returned to their default values (the values they had when the page was first loaded).

The Submit and Reset buttons have corresponding objects called Submit and Reset, which have exactly the same properties, methods, and events as a standard Button object.

Text Elements

The standard text element enables users to enter a single line of text. This information can then be used in JavaScript code or submitted to a server for server-side processing.

The Text Box

A text box is created by means of the <input/> element, much as the button is, but with the type attribute set to text. Again, you can choose not to include the value attribute, but if you do include it this value will appear inside the text box when the page is loaded.

In the following example the <input/> element has two additional attributes, size and maxlength. The size attribute determines how many characters wide the text box is, and maxlength determines the maximum number of characters the user can enter in the box. Both attributes are optional and use defaults determined by the browser.

For example, to create a text box 10 characters wide, with a maximum character length of 15, and initially containing the words Hello World, your <input/> element would be as follows:

```
<input type="text" name="myTextBox" size="10" maxlength="15" value="Hello World" />
```

The Text object that this element creates has a value property, which you can use in your scripts to set or read the text contained inside the text box. In addition to the common properties and methods we discussed earlier, the Text object also has the select() method, which selects or highlights all the text inside the text box. This may be used if the user has entered an invalid value, and you can set the focus to the text box and select the text inside it. This then puts the user's cursor in the right place to correct the data and makes it very clear to the user where the invalid data is. The value property of Text objects always returns a string data type, even if number characters are being entered. If you use the value as a number, JavaScript normally does a conversion from a string data type to a number data type for you, but this is not always the case. For example, JavaScript won't do the conversion if the operation you're performing is valid for a string. If you have a form with two text boxes and you add the values returned from these, JavaScript concatenates rather than adds the two values, so 1 plus 1 will be 11 and not 2. To fix this, you need to convert all the values involved to a numerical data type, for example by using parseInt() or parseFloat() or Number(). However, if you subtract the two values, an operation only valid for numbers, JavaScript says "Aha, this can only be done with numbers, so I'll convert the values to a number data type." Therefore, 1 minus 1 will be returned as 0 without your having to use parseInt() or parseFloat(). This is a tricky bug to spot, so it's best to get into the habit of converting explicitly to avoid problems later.

In addition to the common event handlers, such as `onfocus` and `onblur`, the `Text` object has the `onchange`, `onselect`, `onkeydown`, `onkeypress`, and `onkeyup` event handlers.

The `onselect` event fires when the user selects some text in the text box.

More useful is the `onchange` event, which fires when the element loses focus if (and only if) the value inside the text box is different from the value it had when it got the focus. This enables you to do things like validity checks that occur only if something has changed.

You can use the `readonly` attribute of the `<input/>` element or the `readOnly` property of the `Text` object to prevent the contents from being changed.

```
<input type="text" name="txtReadonly" value="Look but don't change"
    onfocus="document.form1.txtReadonly.blur()"
    readonly="readonly">
```

The `onkeypress`, `onkeydown`, and `onkeyup` events fire, as their names suggest, when the user presses a key, when the user presses a key down, and when a key that is pressed down is let back up, respectively.

Try It Out   A Simple Form with Validation

Let's put all the information on text boxes and buttons together into an example. In this example, you have a simple form consisting of two text boxes and a button. The top text box is for the users' name, and the second is for their age. You do various validity checks. You check the validity of the age text box when it loses focus. However, the name and age text boxes are only checked to see if they are empty when the button is clicked.

```
<!DOCTYPE html PUBLIC "-//W3C//DTD XHTML 1.0 Transitional//EN"
    "http://www.w3.org/TR/xhtml1/DTD/xhtml1-transitional.dtd">
<html xmlns="http://www.w3.org/1999/xhtml">
<head>
    <title>Chapter 7: Example 4</title>
    <script type="text/javascript">
    function btnCheckForm_onclick()
    {
        var myForm = document.form1;
        if (myForm.txtAge.value == "" || myForm.txtName.value == "")
        {
            alert("Please complete all the form");
            if (myForm.txtName.value == "")
            {
                myForm.txtName.focus();
            }
            else
            {
                myForm.txtAge.focus();
            }
        }
        else
        {
            alert("Thanks for completing the form " + myForm.txtName.value);
        }
```

```
        }

        function txtAge_onblur()
        {
            var txtAge = document.form1.txtAge;
            if (isNaN(txtAge.value) == true)
            {
                alert("Please enter a valid age");
                txtAge.focus();
                txtAge.select();
            }
        }

        function txtName_onchange()
        {
            window.status = "Hi " + document.form1.txtName.value;
        }
        </script>
    </head>
    <body>
        <form action="" name="form1">
            Please enter the following details:
            <p>
                Name:
                <br />
                <input type="text" name="txtName" onchange="txtName_onchange()" />
            </p>
            <p>
                Age:
                <br />
                <input type="text" name="txtAge" onblur="txtAge_onblur()"
                    size="3" maxlength="3" />
            </p>
            <p>
                <input type="button" value="Check Details"
                    name="btnCheckForm" onclick="btnCheckForm_onclick()">
            </p>
        </form>
    </body>
</html>
```

After you've entered the text, save the file as ch7_examp4.htm and load it into your web browser.

In the text box shown in Figure 7-5, type your name. When you leave the text box, you'll see Hi yourname appear in the status bar at the bottom of the window.

Enter an invalid value into the age text box, such as aaaa, and when you try to leave the box, it'll tell you of the error and send you back to correct it.

Finally, click the Check Details button and both text boxes will be checked to see that you have completed them. If either is empty, you'll get a message telling you to complete the whole form, and it'll send you back to the box that's empty.

If everything is filled in correctly, you'll get a message thanking you, as shown in Figure 7-5.

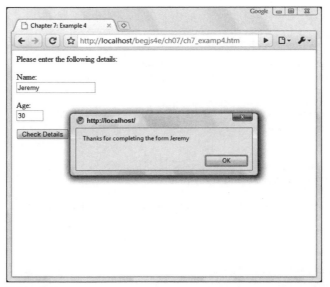

Figure 7-5

This example does not work properly on Firefox; we'll discuss this shortly.

Within the body of the page, you create the HTML elements that define your form. Inside your form, which is called form1, you create three form elements with the names txtName, txtAge, and btnCheckForm.

```
<form action="" name="form1">
    Please enter the following details:
    <p>
        Name:
        <br />
            <input type="text" name="txtName" onchange="txtName_onchange()" />
    </p>
    <p>
        Age:
        <br />
        <input type="text" name="txtAge" onblur="txtAge_onblur()"
            size="3" maxlength="3" />
    </p>
    <p>
        <input type="button" value="Check Details"
            name="btnCheckForm" onclick="btnCheckForm_onclick()">
    </p>
</form>
```

You'll see that for the second text box (the txtAge text box), you have included the size and maxlength attributes inside the <input /> element. Setting the size attribute to 3 gives the user an idea of how much text you are expecting, and setting the maxlength attribute to 3 helps ensure that you don't get overly large numbers entered for the age value.

The first text box's onchange event handler is connected to the function txtName_onchange(), the second text box's onblur event handler is connected to the function txtAge_onblur(), and the button's onclick event handler is connected to the function btnCheckForm_onclick(). These functions are defined in a script block in the head of the page. You will look at each of them in turn, starting with btnCheckForm_onclick().

The first thing you do is define a variable, myForm, and set it to reference the Form object created by the <form/> element later in the page.

```
function btnCheckForm_onclick()
{
    var myForm = document.form1;
```

Doing this reduces the size of your code each time you want to use the form1 object. Instead of document.form1, you can just type myForm. It makes your code a bit more readable and therefore easier to debug, and it saves typing. When you set a variable to be equal to an existing object, you don't (in this case) actually create a new form1 object; instead you just point your variable to the existing form1 object. So when you type myForm.name, JavaScript checks your variable, finds it's actually storing the location in memory of the object form1, and uses that object instead. All this goes on behind the scenes so you don't need to worry about it and can just use myForm as if it were document.form1.

After getting the reference to the Form object, you then use it in an if statement to check whether the value in the text box named txtAge or the text box named txtName actually contains any text.

```
    if (myForm.txtAge.value == "" || myForm.txtName.value == "")
    {
        alert("Please complete all the form");
        if (myForm.txtName.value == "")
        {
            myForm.txtName.focus();
        }
        else
        {
            myForm.txtAge.focus();
        }
    }
```

If you do find an incomplete form, you alert the user. Then in an inner if statement, you check which text box was not filled in. You set the focus to the offending text box, so that the user can start filling it in straightaway without having to move the focus to it herself. It also lets the user know which text box your program requires her to fill in. To avoid annoying your users, make sure that text in the page tells them which fields are required.

If the original outer if statement finds that the form is complete, it lets the user know with a thank-you message.

```
    else
    {
        alert("Thanks for completing the form " + myForm.txtName.value);
    }
}
```

In this sort of situation, it's probably more likely to submit the form to the server than to let the user know with a thank-you message. You can do this using the Form object's submit() method or using a normal Submit button.

The next of the three functions is `txtAge_onblur()`, which connects to the `onblur` event of the `txtAge` text box. This function's purpose is to check that the string value the user entered into the age box actually consists of number characters.

```
function txtAge_onblur()
{
    var txtAge = document.form1.txtAge;
```

Again at the start of the function, you declare a variable and set it to reference an object; this time it's the `Text` object created for the `txtAge` text box that you define further down the page. Now, instead of having to type `document.form1.txtAge` every time, you just type `txtAge`, and it does the same thing. It certainly helps save those typing fingers, especially since it's a function with multiple use of the `txtAge` object.

The following `if` statement checks to see whether what has been entered in the `txtAge` text box can be converted to a number. You use the `isNaN()` function to do this for you. If the value in the `txtAge` text box is not a number, it tells the user and sets the focus back to the text box by calling the `focus()` method. Additionally, this time you highlight the text by using the `Text` object's `select()` method. This makes it even clearer to the user what they need to fix. It also allows them to rectify the problem without needing to delete text first.

```
    if (isNaN(txtAge.value) == true)
    {
        alert("Please enter a valid age");
        txtAge.focus();
        txtAge.select();
    }
}
```

You could go further and check that the number inside the text box is actually a valid age — for example, `191` is not a valid age, nor is `255` likely to be. You just need to add another `if` statement to check for these possibilities.

This function is connected to the `onblur` event handler of the `txtAge` text box, but why didn't you use the `onchange` event handler, with its advantage that it only rechecks the value when the value has actually been changed? The `onchange` event would not fire if the box was empty both before focus was passed to it and after focus was passed away from it. However, leaving the checking of the form completion until just before the form is submitted is probably best because some users prefer to fill in information out of order and come back to some form elements later.

The final function is for the `txtName` text box's `onchange` event. Its use here is a little flippant and intended primarily as an example of the `onchange` event.

```
function txtName_onchange()
{
    window.status = "Hi " + document.form1.txtName.value;
}
```

When the `onchange` event fires (when focus is passed away from the name text box and its contents have changed), you take the value of the `txtName` box and put it into the window's status bar at the bottom of the window. It simply says `Hi yourname`. You access the status bar using the `window` object's `status` property, although you could just enter the following:

```
status = "Hi " + document.form1.txtName.value;
```

Here `window` is in front just to make it clear what you are actually accessing. It would be very easy when reading the code to mistake `status` for a variable, so in this situation, although it isn't strictly necessary, putting `window` in front does make the code easier to read, understand, and therefore debug.

Problems with Firefox and the blur Event

The previous example will fail with Firefox if you enter a name in the name text box and then an invalid age into the age box (for example, if you enter `abc` and then click the Check Form button). With Internet Explorer (IE) the blur event fires and displays an alert box if the age is invalid, but the button's click event doesn't fire. However, in Firefox, both events fire with the result that the invalid age alert is hidden by the "form completed successfully" alert box.

In addition, if you enter an invalid age for both IE and Firefox browsers and then switch to a different program altogether, the "invalid age" alert box appears, which is annoying for the user. It could be that the user was opening up another program to check the details.

Although this is a fine example, it is not great for the real world. A better option would be to check the form when it's finally submitted and not while the user is entering data. Or, alternatively, you can check the data as they are entered but not use an alert box to display errors. Instead you could write out a warning in red next to the erroneous input control, informing the user of the invalid data, and then also get your code to check the form when it's submitted. In Chapter 12 you'll see how to write to the page after it's been loaded.

The Password Text Box

The only real purpose of the password box is to enable users to type in a password on a page and to have the password characters hidden, so that no one can look over the user's shoulder and discover his or her password. However, this protection is visual only. When sent to the server, the text in the password is sent as plain text — there is no encryption or any attempt at hiding the text (unless the page is served over a secure connection from the server).

Defining a password box is identical to defining a text box, except that the `type` attribute is `password`.

```
<input name="password1" type="password" />
```

This form element creates an associated `Password` object, which is identical to the `Text` object in its properties, methods, and events.

The Hidden Text Box

The hidden text box can hold text and numbers just like a normal text box, with the difference being that it's not visible to the user. A hidden element? It may sound as useful as an invisible painting, but in fact it proves to be very useful.

To define a hidden text box, you use the following HTML:

```
<input type="hidden" name="myHiddenElement" />
```

The hidden text box creates a `Hidden` object. This is available in the `elements` array property of the `Form` object and can be manipulated in JavaScript like any other object, although you can actually set its value only through its HTML definition or through JavaScript. As with a normal text box, its value is submitted to the server when the user submits the form.

So why are hidden text boxes useful? Imagine you have a lot of information that you need to obtain from the user, but to avoid having a page stuffed full of elements and looking like the control panel of the space shuttle, you decide to obtain the information over more than one page. The problem is, how do you keep a record of what was entered in previous pages? Easy — you use hidden text boxes and put the values in there. Then, in the final page, all the information is submitted to the server — it's just that some of it is hidden.

The textarea Element

The `<textarea/>` element allows multi-line input of text. Other than this, it acts very much like the text box element.

However, unlike the text box, the `textarea` element has its own tag, the `<textarea>` tag. It also has two additional attributes: `cols` and `rows`. The `cols` attribute defines how many characters wide the text area will be, and the `rows` attribute defines how many character rows there will be. You set the text inside the element by putting it between the start and closing tags, rather than by using the `value` attribute. So if you want a `<textarea/>` element 40 characters wide by 20 rows deep with initial text `Hello World` on the first line and `Line 2` on the second line, you define it as follows:

```
<textarea name="myTextArea" cols="40" rows="20">Hello World
Line 2
</textarea>
```

Another attribute of the `<textarea/>` element is the `wrap` attribute, which determines what happens when the user types to the end of a line. The default value for this is `soft`, so the user does not have to press Return at the end of a line, though this can vary from browser to browser. To turn wrapping on, you can use one of two values: `soft` and `hard`. As far as client-side processing goes, both do the same thing: they switch wrapping on. However, when you come to server-side processing, they do make a difference in terms of which information is sent to the server when the form is posted.

If you set the `wrap` attribute on by setting it to `soft`, wrapping will occur on the client side, but the carriage returns won't be posted to the server, just the text. If the `wrap` attribute is set to `hard`, any carriage returns caused by wrapping will be converted to hard returns — it will be as if the user had pressed the Enter key, and these returns will be sent to the server. Also, you need to be aware that the carriage-return character is determined by the operating system that the browser is running on — for example, in Windows a carriage return is `\r\n`, whereas on a Macintosh the carriage return is `\r` and on Unix a carriage return is `\n`. To turn off wrapping client-side, set `wrap` to `off`.

The `Textarea` object created by the `<textarea/>` element has the same properties, methods, and events as the `Text` object you saw previously, except that the text area doesn't have the `maxlength` attribute. Note that there is a `value` property even though the `<textarea/>` element does not have a `value` attribute. The `value` property simply returns the text between the `<textarea>` and `</textarea>` tags. The events supported by the `Textarea` object include the `onkeydown`, `onkeypress`, `onkeyup`, and `onchange` event handlers.

Event Watching

To help demonstrate how the keydown, keypress, keyup, and change events work (in particular, the order in which they fire), you'll create an example that tells you what events are firing.

```
<!DOCTYPE html PUBLIC "-//W3C//DTD XHTML 1.0 Transitional//EN"
    "http://www.w3.org/TR/xhtml1/DTD/xhtml1-transitional.dtd">
<html xmlns="http://www.w3.org/1999/xhtml">
<head>
    <title>Chapter 7: Example 5</title>
    <script type="text/javascript">

    function DisplayEvent(eventName)
    {
        var myMessage = window.document.form1.textarea2.value;
        myMessage = myMessage + eventName;
        document.form1.textarea2.value = myMessage;
    }
    </script>
</head>
<body>
    <form action="" name="form1">
        <textarea rows="15" cols="40" name="textarea1"
            onchange="DisplayEvent('onchange\n');"
            onkeydown="DisplayEvent('onkeydown\n');"
            onkeypress="DisplayEvent('onkeypress\n');"
            onkeyup="DisplayEvent('onkeyup\n\n');"></textarea>

        <textarea rows="15" cols="40" name="textarea2"></textarea>
        <br />
        <br />
        <input type="button" value="Clear Event TextArea" name="button1"
            onclick="document.form1.textarea2.value=''" />
    </form>
</body>
</html>
```

Save this page as ch7_examp5.htm. Load the page into your browser and see what happens when you type any letter into the first text area box. You should see the events being fired listed in the second text area box (onkeydown, onkeypress, and onkeyup), as shown in Figure 7-6. When you click outside the first text area box, you'll see the onchange event fire.

Experiment with the example to see what events fire and when.

Within a form called form1 in the body of the page, you define two text areas and a button. The first text area is the one whose events you are going to monitor. You attach code that calls the displayEvent() function to each of the onchange, onkeydown, onkeypress, and onkeyup event handlers. The value passed to the function reflects the name of the event firing.

```
<textarea rows="15" cols="40" name="textarea1"
    onchange="DisplayEvent('onchange\n');"
    onkeydown="DisplayEvent('onkeydown\n');"
    onkeypress="DisplayEvent('onkeypress\n');"
    onkeyup="DisplayEvent('onkeyup\n\n');"></textarea>
```

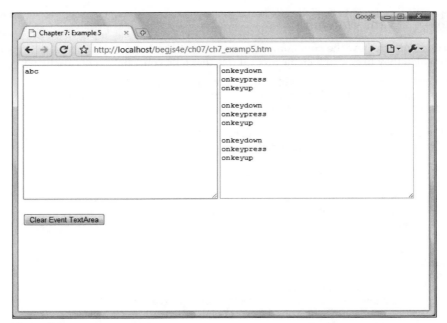

Figure 7-6

Next, you have an empty text area the same size as the first.

```
<textarea rows="15" cols="40" name="textarea2"></textarea>
```

Finally, you have your button element.

```
<input type="button" value="Clear Event TextArea" name="button1"
    onclick="document.form1.textarea2.value=''" />
```

Notice that the onclick event handler for the button is not calling a function, but just executing a line of JavaScript code. Although you normally call functions, it's not compulsory; if you have just one line of code to execute, it's easier just to insert it rather than create a function and call it. In this case, the onclick event handler is connected to some code that clears the contents of the second text area by setting its value property to an empty string (' ').

Now let's look at the displayEvent() function. This is defined in a script block in the head of the page. It adds the name of the event handler that has been passed as a parameter to the text already contained in the second text area.

```
function displayEvent(eventName)
{
    var myMessage = document.form1.textarea2.value;
    myMessage = myMessage + eventName;
    document.form1.textarea2.value = myMessage;
}
```

Check Boxes and Radio Buttons

The discussions of check boxes and radio buttons are together because their objects have identical properties, methods, and events. A check box enables the user to check and uncheck it. It is similar to the paper surveys you may get where you are asked to "check the boxes that apply to you." Radio buttons are basically a group of check boxes where only one can be checked at a time. Of course, they also look different, and their group nature means that they are treated differently.

Creating check boxes and radio buttons requires our old friend the <input/> element. Its type attribute is set to "checkbox" or "radio" to determine which box or button is created. To set a check box or a radio button to be checked when the page is loaded, you simply insert the attribute checked into the <input> tag and assign its value as checked. This is handy if you want to set a default option like, for example, those "Check this box if you want our junk mail" forms you often see on the Net, which are usually checked by default, forcing you to uncheck them. So to create a check box that is already checked, your <input> tag will be the following:

```
<input type="checkbox" name="chkDVD" checked="checked" value="DVD" />
```

To create a checked radio button, the <input> tag would be as follows:

```
<input type="radio" name="radCPUSpeed" checked="checked" value="1 GHz" />
```

As previously mentioned, radio buttons are group elements. In fact, there is little point in putting just one on a page, because the user won't be able to choose between any alternative boxes.

To create a group of radio buttons, you simply give each radio button the same name. This creates an array of radio buttons going by that name that you can access, as you would with any array, using its index.

For example, to create a group of three radio buttons, your HTML would be as follows:

```
<input type="radio" name="radCPUSpeed" checked="checked" value="800 MHz" />
<input type="radio" name="radCPUSpeed" value="1 GHz" />
<input type="radio" name="radCPUSpeed" value="1.5 GHz" />
```

You can put as many groups of radio buttons in a form as you want, by just giving each group its own unique name. Note that you have only used one checked attribute, since only one of the radio buttons in the group can be checked. If you had used the checked attribute in more than one of the radio buttons, only the last of these would have actually been checked.

Using the value attribute of the check box and radio button elements is not the same as with previous elements you've looked at. It tells you nothing about the user's interaction with an element because it's predefined in your HTML or by your JavaScript. Whether a check box or radio button is checked or not, it still returns the same value.

Each check box has an associated Checkbox object, and each radio button in a group has a separate Radio object. As mentioned earlier, with radio buttons of the same name you can access each Radio object in a group by treating the group of radio buttons as an array, with the name of the array being the name of the radio buttons in the group. As with any array, you have the length property, which will tell you how many radio buttons are in the group.

For determining whether a user has actually checked or unchecked a check box, you need to use the `checked` property of the `Checkbox` object. This property returns `true` if the check box is currently checked and `false` if not.

Radio buttons are slightly different. Because radio buttons with the same name are grouped together, you need to test each `Radio` object in the group in turn to see if it has been checked. Only one of the radio buttons in a group can be checked, so if you check another one in the group, the previously checked one will become unchecked, and the new one will be checked in its place.

Both `Checkbox` and `Radio` have the event handlers `onclick`, `onfocus`, and `onblur`, and these operate as you saw for the other elements, although they can also be used to cancel the default action, such as clicking the check box or radio button.

Try It Out   Check Boxes and Radio Buttons

Let's look at an example that makes use of all the properties, methods, and events we have just discussed. The example is a simple form that enables a user to build a computer system. Perhaps it could be used in an e-commerce situation, to sell computers with the exact specifications determined by the customer.

```
<!DOCTYPE html PUBLIC "-//W3C//DTD XHTML 1.0 Transitional//EN"
    "http://www.w3.org/TR/xhtml1/DTD/xhtml1-transitional.dtd">
<html xmlns="http://www.w3.org/1999/xhtml">
<head>
    <title>Chapter 7: Example 6</title>
    <script type="text/javascript">

var radCpuSpeedIndex = 0;

function radCPUSpeed_onclick(radIndex)
{
    var returnValue = true;
    if (radIndex == 1)
    {
        returnValue = false;
        alert("Sorry that processor speed is currently unavailable");
        // Next line works around a bug in IE that doesn't cancel the
        // Default action properly
        document.form1.radCPUSpeed[radCpuSpeedIndex].checked = true;
    }
    else
    {
        radCpuSpeedIndex = radIndex;
    }
    return returnValue;
}

function btnCheck_onclick()
{
    var controlIndex;
    var element;
    var numberOfControls = document.form1.length;
    var compSpec = "Your chosen processor speed is ";
```

```
        compSpec = compSpec + document.form1.radCPUSpeed[radCpuSpeedIndex].value;
        compSpec = compSpec + "\nWith the following additional components\n";
        for (controlIndex = 0; controlIndex < numberOfControls; controlIndex++)
        {
            element = document.form1[controlIndex];
            if (element.type == "checkbox")
            {
                if (element.checked == true)
                {
                    compSpec = compSpec + element.value + "\n";
                }
            }
        }
        alert(compSpec);
    }
    </script>
</head>
<body>
    <form action="" name="form1">
        <p>
            Tick all of the components you want included on your computer
        </p>
        <table>
            <tr>
                <td>
                    DVD-ROM
                </td>
                <td>
                    <input type="checkbox" name="chkDVD" value="DVD-ROM" />
                </td>
            </tr>
            <tr>
                <td>
                    CD-ROM
                </td>
                <td>
                    <input type="checkbox" name="chkCD" value="CD-ROM" />
                </td>
            </tr>
            <tr>
                <td>
                    Zip Drive
                </td>
                <td>
                    <input type="checkbox" name="chkZip" value="ZIP Drive" />
                </td>
            </tr>
        </table>
        <p>
            Select the processor speed you require
        </p>
        <table>
            <tr>
                <td>
                    <input type="radio" name="radCPUSpeed" checked="checked"
                        value="3.8 GHz" onclick="return radCPUSpeed_onclick(0)" />
```

```
                            </td>
                            <td>
                                3.8 GHz
                            </td>
                            <td>
                                <input type="radio" name="radCPUSpeed" value="4.8 GHz"
                                    onclick="return radCPUSpeed_onclick(1)" />
                            </td>
                            <td>
                                4.8 GHz
                            </td>
                            <td>
                                <input type="radio" name="radCPUSpeed" value="6 Ghz"
                                    onclick="return radCPUSpeed_onclick(2)"  />
                            </td>
                            <td>
                                6 GHz
                            </td>
                        </tr>
                </table>
                <input type="button" value="Check Form" name="btnCheck"
                    onclick="return btnCheck_onclick()" />
            </form>
        </body>
    </html>
```

Save the page as ch7_examp6.htm and load it into your web browser. You should see a form like the one shown in Figure 7-7.

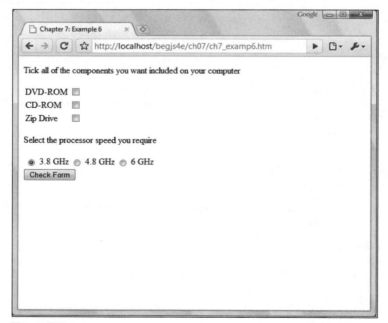

Figure 7-7

Check some of the check boxes, change the processor speed, and click the Check Form button. A message box appears and lists the components and processor speed you selected. For example, if you select a DVD-ROM and a Zip drive and a 6 GHz processor speed, you will see something like what is shown in Figure 7-8.

Figure 7-8

Note that the 4.8 GHz processor is out of stock, so if you choose that, a message box tells you it's out of stock, and the 4.8 GHz processor speed radio button won't be selected. The previous setting will be restored when the user dismisses the message box.

Let's first look at the body of the page, where you define the check boxes and radio buttons and a standard button inside a form called `form1`. You start with the check boxes. They are put into a table simply for formatting purposes. No functions are called, and no events are connected to.

```
<table>
    <tr>
        <td>
            DVD-ROM
        </td>
        <td>
            <input type="checkbox" name="chkDVD" value="DVD-ROM" />
        </td>
    </tr>
    <tr>
        <td>
            CD-ROM
        </td>
        <td>
                <input type="checkbox" name="chkCD" value="CD-ROM" />
        </td>
    </tr>
    <tr>
        <td>
            Zip Drive
        </td>
        <td>
            <input type="checkbox" name="chkZip" value="ZIP Drive" />
        </td>
    </tr>
</table>
```

Next come the radio buttons for selecting the required CPU speed, and these are a little more complex. Again they are put into a table for formatting purposes.

```
<table>
    <tr>
        <td>
            <input type="radio" name="radCPUSpeed" checked="checked"
                value="3.8 GHz" onclick="return radCPUSpeed_onclick(0)" />
        </td>
        <td>
            3.8 GHz
        </td>
        <td>
            <input type="radio" name="radCPUSpeed" value="4.8 GHz"
                onclick="return radCPUSpeed_onclick(1)" />
        </td>
        <td>
            4.8 GHz
        </td>
        <td>
            <input type="radio" name="radCPUSpeed" value="6 Ghz"
                onclick="return radCPUSpeed_onclick(2)"  />
        </td>
        <td>
            6 GHz
        </td>
    </tr>
</table>
```

The radio button group name is radCPUSpeed. Here, the first one is set to be checked by default by the inclusion of the word checked inside the <input /> element's definition. It's a good idea to ensure that you have one radio button checked by default, because if you do not and the user doesn't select a button, the form will be submitted with no value for that radio group.

You make use of the onclick event of each Radio object, and each button connects to the same function, radCPUSpeed_onclick(). But for each radio button, you pass a value — the index of that particular button in the radCPUSpeed radio button group collection. This makes it easy to determine which radio button was selected. You'll look at this function a little later, but first let's look at the standard button that completes your form.

```
<input type="button" value="Check Form" name="btnCheck"
    onclick="return btnCheck_onclick()" />
```

This button's onclick event handler is connected to the btnCheck_onclick() function and is for the user to click when they complete the form.

So you have two functions: radCPUSpeed_onclick() and btnCheck_onclick(). These are both defined in the script block in the head of the page. Let's look at this script block now. It starts by declaring a variable radCpuSpeedIndex. This will be used to store the currently selected index of the radCPUSpeed radio button group.

```
var radCpuSpeedIndex = 0;
```

Next you have the radCPUSpeed_onclick() function, which is called by the onclick event handler in each radio button. Your function has one parameter, namely the index position in the radCPUSpeed collection of the radio object selected.

```
function radCPUSpeed_onclick(radIndex)
{
    var returnValue = true;
```

The first thing you do in the function is declare the returnValue variable and set it to true. You'll be returning this as your return value from the function. In this case the return value is important because it decides whether the radio button remains checked as a result of the user clicking it. If you return false, that cancels the user's action, and the radio button remains unchecked. In fact no radio button becomes checked, which is why you keep track of the index of the checked radio button so you can track which button was the previously checked one. To allow the user's action to proceed, you return true.

As an example of this in action, you have an if statement on the next line. If the radio button's index value passed is 1 (that is, if the user checked the box for a 4.8 GHz processor), you tell the user that it's out of stock and cancel the clicking action by setting returnValue to false.

```
if (radIndex == 1)
{
    returnValue = false;
    alert("Sorry that processor speed is currently unavailable");
    // Next line works around a bug in IE that doesn't cancel the
    // Default action properly
    document.form1.radCPUSpeed[radCpuSpeedIndex].checked = true;
}
```

As previously mentioned, canceling the clicking action results in no radio buttons being checked. To rectify this, you set the previously checked box to be checked again in the following line:

```
document.form1.radCPUSpeed[radCpuSpeedIndex].checked = true;
```

What you are doing here is using the collection for the radCpuSpeed radio group. Each element in the collection actually contains an object, namely each of your three Radio objects. You use the radCpuSpeedIndex variable as the index of the Radio object that was last checked, since this is what it holds.

Finally, in the else statement, you set radCpuSpeedIndex to the new checked radio button's index value.

```
else

{
    radCpuSpeedIndex = radIndex;
}
```

In the last line of the function, the value of returnValue is returned to where the function was called and will either cancel or allow the clicking action.

```
    return returnValue;
}
```

The second function, btnCheck_onclick(), is connected to the button's onclick event. In a real e-commerce situation, this button would be the place where you'd check your form and then submit it to the server for processing. Here you use the form to show a message box confirming which boxes you have checked (as if you didn't already know)!

At the top you declare four local variables to use in the function. The variable numberOfControls is set to the form's length property, which is the number of elements on the form. The variable compSpec is used to build the string that you'll display in a message box.

```
function btnCheck_onclick()
{
    var controlIndex;
    var element;
    var numberOfControls = document.form1.length;
    var var compSpec = "Your chosen processor speed is ";
    compSpec = compSpec + document.form1.radCPUSpeed[radCpuSpeedIndex].value;
    compSpec = compSpec + "\nWith the following additional components\n";
```

In the following line, you add the value of the radio button the user has selected to your message string:

```
compSpec = compSpec + document.form1.radCPUSpeed[radCpuSpeedIndex].value;
```

The global variable radCpuSpeedIndex, which was set by the radio button group's onclick event, contains the index of the selected radio button.

An alternative way of finding out which radio button was clicked would be to loop through the radio button group's collection and test each radio button in turn to see if it was checked. The code would look something like this:

```
var radIndex;
for (radIndex = 0; radIndex < document.form1.radCPUSpeed.length; radIndex++)
{
    if (document.form1.radCPUSpeed[radIndex].checked == true)
    {
        radCpuSpeedIndex = radIndex;
        break;
    }
}
```

But to get back to the actual code, you'll notice a few new-line (\n) characters thrown into the message string for formatting reasons.

Next, you loop through the form's elements.

```
for (controlIndex = 0; controlIndex < numberOfControls; controlIndex++)
{
    element = document.form1[controlIndex];
    if (element.type == "checkbox")
    {
        if (element.checked == true)
        {
            compSpec = compSpec + element.value + "\n";
        }
    }

    alert(compSpec);
}
```

It's here that you loop through each element on the form using `document.form1[controlIndex]`, which returns a reference to the element object stored at the `controlIndex` index position.

You'll see that in this example the `element` variable is set to reference the object stored in the `form1` collection at the index position stored in variable `controlIndex`. Again, this is for convenient short-hand purposes; now to use that particular object's properties or methods, you just type `element`, a period, and then the method or property name, making your code easier to read and debug, which also saves on typing.

You only want to see which check boxes have been checked, so you use the `type` property, which every HTML form element object has, to see what element type you are dealing with. If the `type` is `checkbox`, you go ahead and see if it's a checked check box. If so, you append its value to the message string in `compSpec`. If it is not a check box, it can be safely ignored.

Finally, you use the `alert()` method to display the contents of your message string.

Selection Boxes

Although they look quite different, the drop-down list and the list boxes are actually both elements created with the `<select>` tag, and strictly speaking they are both select elements. The select element has one or more options in a list that you can select from; each of these options is defined by means of one or more `<option/>` elements inside the opening and closing `<select>` tags.

The `size` attribute of the `<select/>` element is used to specify how many of the options are visible to the user.

For example, to create a list box five rows deep and populate it with seven options, your HTML would look like this:

```
<select name="theDay" size="5">
    <option value="0" selected="selected">Monday</option>
    <option value="1">Tuesday</option>
    <option value="2">Wednesday</option>
    <option value="3">Thursday</option>
    <option value="4">Friday</option>
    <option value="5">Saturday</option>
    <option value="6">Sunday</option>
</select>
```

Notice that the `<option/>` element for Monday also contains the attribute `selected`; this will make this option selected by default when the page is loaded. The values of the options have been defined as numbers, but text would be equally valid.

If you want this to be a drop-down list, you just need to change the `size` attribute in the `<select/>` element to `1`, and presto, it's a drop-down list.

If you want to let the user choose more than one item from a list at once, you simply need to add the `multiple` attribute to the `<select/>` definition.

The `<select/>` element creates a `Select` object. This object has an `options` collection property, which is made up of `Option` objects, one for each `<option/>` element inside the `<select/>` element associated with the `Select` object. For instance, in the preceding example, if the `<select/>` element was contained in a form called `theForm` with the following:

```
document.theForm.theDay.options[0]
```

you would access the option created for Monday.

How can you tell which option has been selected by the user? Easy: You use the `Select` object's `selectedIndex` property. You can use the index value returned by this property to access the selected option using the `options` collection.

The `Option` object also has `index`, `text`, and `value` properties. The `index` property returns the index position of that option in the `options` collection. The `text` property is what's displayed in the list, and the `value` property is the value defined for the option, which would be posted to the server if the form were submitted.

If you want to find out how many options there are in a select element, you can use the `length` property of either the `Select` object itself or of its `options` collection property.

Let's see how you could loop through the `options` for the preceding select box:

```
var theDayElement = window.document.form1.theDay;
document.write("There are " + theDayElement.length + "options<br />");
var optionCounter;
for (optionCounter = 0; optionCounter < theDayElement.length; optionCounter++)
{
    document.write("Option text is " +
        theDayElement.options[optionCounter].text)
    document.write(" and its value is ");
    document.write(theDayElement.options[optionCounter].value);
    document.write("<br />")
}
```

First, you set the variable `theDayElement` to reference the `Select` object. Then you write the number of options to the page, in this case 7.

Next you use a `for` loop to loop through the `options` collection, displaying the text of each option, such as `Monday`, `Tuesday`, and so on, and its value, such as 0, 1, and so on. If you create a page based on this code, it must be placed after the `<select/>` element's definition.

It's also possible to add options to a select element after the page has finished loading. You'll look at how this is done next.

Adding and Removing Options

To add a new option to a select element, you simply create a new `Option` object using the `new` operator and then insert it into the `options` collection of the `Select` object at an empty index position.

When you create a new `Option` object, there are two parameters to pass: The first is the text you want to appear in the list, and the second the value to be assigned to the option.

```
var myNewOption = new Option("TheText","TheValue");
```

You then simply assign this Option object to an empty array element, for example:

```
document.theForm.theSelectObject.options[0] = myNewOption;
```

If you want to remove an option, you simply set that part of the options collection to null. For example, to remove the element you just inserted, you need the following:

```
document.theForm.theSelectObject.options[0] = null;
```

When you remove an Option object from the options collection, the collection is reordered so that the array index value of each of the options above the removed one has its index value decremented by one.

When you insert a new option at a certain index position, be aware that it will overwrite any Option object that is already there.

Try It Out   Adding and Removing List Options

Use the list-of-days example you saw previously to demonstrate adding and removing list options.

```
<!DOCTYPE html PUBLIC "-//W3C//DTD XHTML 1.0 Transitional//EN"
    "http://www.w3.org/TR/xhtml1/DTD/xhtml1-transitional.dtd">
<html xmlns="http://www.w3.org/1999/xhtml">
<head>
    <title>Chapter 7: Example 7</title>
    <script type="text/javascript">
function btnRemoveWed_onclick()
{
    if (document.form1.theDay.options[2].text == "Wednesday")
    {
        document.form1.theDay.options[2] = null;
    }
    else
    {
        alert('There is no Wednesday here!');
    }
}

function btnAddWed_onclick()
{
    if (document.form1.theDay.options[2].text != "Wednesday")
    {
        var indexCounter;
        var days = document.form1.theDay;
        var lastoption = new Option();
        days.options[days.options.length] = lastoption;
        for (indexCounter = days.options.length - 1;
             indexCounter > 2; indexCounter--)
        {
            days.options[indexCounter].text =
                days.options[indexCounter - 1].text;
            days.options[indexCounter].value =
                days.options[indexCounter - 1].value;
        }
        var option = new Option("Wednesday", 2);
        days.options[2] = option;
```

```
        }
        else
        {
            alert("Do you want to have TWO Wednesdays?????");
        }
    }
    </script>
</head>
<body>
    <form action="" name="form1">
        <select name="theDay" size="5">
            <option value="0" selected="selected">Monday</option>
            <option value="1">Tuesday</option>
            <option value="2">Wednesday</option>
            <option value="3">Thursday</option>
            <option value="4">Friday</option>
            <option value="5">Saturday</option>
            <option value="6">Sunday</option>
        </select>
        <br />
        <input type="button" value="Remove Wednesday" name="btnRemoveWed"
            onclick="btnRemoveWed_onclick()" />
        <input type="button" value="Add Wednesday" name="btnAddWed"
            onclick="btnAddWed_onclick()" />
        <br />
    </form>
</body>
</html>
```

Save this as ch7_examp7.htm. If you type the page in and load it into your browser, you should see the form shown in Figure 7-9. Click the Remove Wednesday button, and you'll see Wednesday disappear from the list. Add it back by clicking the Add Wednesday button. If you try to add a second Wednesday or remove a nonexistent Wednesday, you'll get a polite warning telling you that you can't do that.

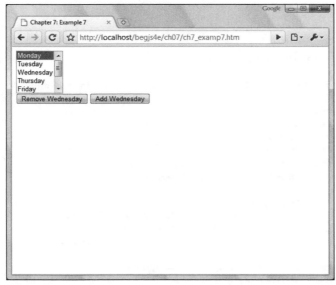

Figure 7-9

Within the body of the page, you define a form with the name `form1`. This contains the select element, which includes day-of-the-week options that you have seen previously. The form also contains two buttons, as shown here:

```
<input type="button" value="Remove Wednesday" name="btnRemoveWed"
    onclick="btnRemoveWed_onclick()" />
<input type="button" value="Add Wednesday" name="btnAddWed"
    onclick="btnAddWed_onclick()" />
```

Each of these buttons has its `onclick` event handler connected to some code that calls one of two functions: `btnRemoveWed_onclick()` and `btnAddWedc`_onclick()`. These functions are defined in a script block in the head of the page. You'll take a look at each of them in turn.

At the top of the page you have the first function, `btnRemoveWed_onclick()`, which removes the Wednesday option.

```
function btnRemoveWed_onclick()
{
    if (document.form1.theDay.options[2].text == "Wednesday")
    {
        document.form1.theDay.options[2] = null;
    }
    else
    {
        alert('There is no Wednesday here!');
    }
}
```

The first thing you do in the function is a sanity check: You must try to remove the Wednesday option only if it's there in the first place! You make sure of this by seeing if the third option in the collection (with index 2 because arrays start at index 0) has the text `"Wednesday"`. If it does, you can remove the Wednesday option by setting that particular option to `null`. If the third option in the array is not Wednesday, you alert the user to the fact that there is no Wednesday to remove. Although this code uses the `text` property in the `if` statement's condition, you could just as easily have used the `value` property; it makes no difference.

Next you come to the `btnAddWed_onclick()` function, which, as the name suggests, adds the Wednesday option. This is slightly more complex than the code required to remove an option. First, you use an `if` statement to check that there is not already a Wednesday option.

```
function btnAddWed_onclick()
{
    if (document.form1.theDay.options[2].text != "Wednesday")
    {
        var indexCounter;
        var days = document.form1.theDay;
        var lastoption = new Option();
        days.options[days.options.length] = lastoption;
        for (indexCounter = days.options.length - 1;
            indexCounter > 2; indexCounter--)
        {
            days.options[indexCounter].text =
                days.options[indexCounter - 1].text;
            days.options[indexCounter].value =
                days.options[indexCounter - 1].value;
        }
```

251

If there is no Wednesday option, you then need to make space for the new Wednesday option to be inserted.

Before you do this, you define two variables: indexCounter and days (which refers to theDay select element and is a shorthand reference for your convenience). At this point, there are six options (the last element is as index 5), so next you create a new option with the variable name lastoption and assign it to the element at the end of the collection. This new element is assigned at index position 6 by using the length property of the options collection, which previously had no contents. You next assign the text and value properties of each of the Option objects from Thursday to Sunday to the Option at an index value higher by one in the options array, leaving a space in the options array at position 2 to put Wednesday in. This is the task for the for loop within the if statement.

Next, you create a new Option object by passing the text "Wednesday" and the value 2 to the Option constructor. The Option object is then inserted into the options collection at position 2, and presto, it appears in your select box.

```
        var option = new Option("Wednesday", 2);
        days.options[2] = option;
    }
```

You end the function by alerting the user to the fact that there is already a Wednesday option in the list, if the condition in the if statement is false.

```
    else
    {
        alert("Do you want to have TWO Wednesdays?????");
    }
}
```

This example works in every browser; however, all modern browsers provide additional methods to make adding and removing options easier.

Adding New Options with Standard Methods

In particular, the Select object you are interested in has additional add() and remove() methods, which add and remove options. These make life a little simpler.

Before you add an option, you need to create it. You do this just as before, using the new operator.

The Select object's add() method enables you to insert an Option object that you have created and accepts two parameters. The first parameter is the Option object you want to add. The second parameter, unfortunately, varies depending on the browser. In Firefox, Safari, Chrome, Opera, and IE8 Standards mode, the second parameter is the Option object you want to place the new Option object before. In IE7 (or IE8 non-standards mode), the second parameter is the index position you want to add the option in. In all browsers, you can pass null as the second parameter, and the added Option object will be added at the end of the options collection.

The add() method won't overwrite any Option object already at that position, but instead will simply move the Option objects up in the collection to make space. This is basically the same as what you had to code into the btnAddWed_onclick() function using your for loop.

Using the add() method, you can rewrite the btnAddWed_onclick() function in your ch7.examp7.htm example to look like this:

```
function btnAddWed_onclick()
{
    var days = document.form1.theDay;

    if (days.options[2].text != "Wednesday")
    {
        var option = new Option("Wednesday", 2);
        var thursdayOption = theDay.options[2];

        try
        {
            days.add(option, thursdayOption);
        }
        catch (error)
        {
            days.add(option, 2);
        }
    }
    else
    {
        alert("Do you want to have TWO Wednesdays?????");
    }
}
```

In IE7 (or IE8 in non-standards mode), the browser will throw an error if you pass an Option object as the second parameter. So use a try...catch statement to catch the error and pass a number to the second argument, as this code shows.

The Select object's remove() method accepts just one parameter, namely the index of the option you want removed. When an option is removed, the options at higher index positions are moved down in the collection to fill the gap.

Using the remove() method, you can rewrite the btnRemoveWed_onclick() function in your ch7_examp7.htm example to look like this:

```
function btnRemoveWed_onclick()
{
    var days = document.form1.theDay;

    if (days.options[2].text == "Wednesday")
    {
        days.remove(2);
    }
    else
    {
        alert("There is no Wednesday here!");
    }
}
```

Modify the previous example and save it as ch7_examp8.htm before loading it into your browser. You'll see that it works just as the previous version did.

Select Element Events

Select elements have three event handlers, `onblur`, `onfocus`, and `onchange`. You've seen all these events before. You saw the `change` event with the text box element, where it fired when focus was moved away from the text box *and* the value in the text box had changed. Here it fires when the user changes which option in the list is selected.

Try It Out   **Using the Select Element for Date Difference Calculations**

Let's take a look at an example that uses the `change` event and makes good use of the select element in its drop-down list form. Its purpose is to calculate the difference, in days, between two dates set by the user via drop-down list boxes.

```
<!DOCTYPE html PUBLIC "-//W3C//DTD XHTML 1.0 Transitional//EN"
    "http://www.w3.org/TR/xhtml1/DTD/xhtml1-transitional.dtd">
<html xmlns="http://www.w3.org/1999/xhtml">
<head>
    <title>Chapter 7: Example 8</title>
    <script type="text/javascript">
    function writeOptions(startNumber, endNumber)
    {
        var optionCounter;
        for (optionCounter = startNumber;
            optionCounter <= endNumber; optionCounter++)
        {
            document.write("<option value=" + optionCounter + ">" +
                optionCounter);
        }
    }


    function writeMonthOptions()
    {
        var theMonth;
        var monthCounter;
        var theDate = new Date(1);
        for (monthCounter = 0; monthCounter < 12; monthCounter++)
        {
            theDate.setMonth(monthCounter);
            theMonth = theDate.toString();
            theMonth = theMonth.substr(4, 3);
            document.write("<option value=" + theMonth + ">" + theMonth);
        }
    }


    function recalcDateDiff()
    {
        var myForm = document.form1;
        var firstDay =
            myForm.firstDay.options[myForm.firstDay.selectedIndex].value;
        var secondDay =
            myForm.secondDay.options[myForm.secondDay.selectedIndex].value;
        var firstMonth =
            myForm.firstMonth.options[myForm.firstMonth.selectedIndex].value;
        var secondMonth =
            myForm.secondMonth.options[myForm.secondMonth.selectedIndex].value;
```

```
            var firstYear =
                myForm.firstYear.options[myForm.firstYear.selectedIndex].value;
            var secondYear =
                myForm.secondYear.options[myForm.secondYear.selectedIndex].value;
            var firstDate = new Date(firstDay + " " + firstMonth + " " + firstYear);
            var secondDate = new Date(secondDay + " " + secondMonth + " " +
                secondYear);
            var daysDiff = (secondDate.valueOf() - firstDate.valueOf());

            daysDiff = Math.floor(Math.abs((((daysDiff / 1000) / 60) / 60) / 24));
            myForm.txtDays.value = daysDiff;
        }

    function window_onload()
    {
        var theForm = document.form1;
        var nowDate = new Date();
        theForm.firstDay.options[nowDate.getDate() - 1].selected = true;
        theForm.secondDay.options[nowDate.getDate() - 1].selected = true;
        theForm.firstMonth.options[nowDate.getMonth()].selected = true;
        theForm.secondMonth.options[nowDate.getMonth()].selected = true;
        theForm.firstYear.options[nowDate.getFullYear() - 1970].selected = true;
        theForm.secondYear.options[nowDate.getFullYear() - 1970].selected = true;
    }
    </script>
</head>
<body onload="window_onload()">
    <form action="" name="form1">
        <p>
            First Date<br />
            <select name="firstDay" onchange="recalcDateDiff()">
                <script type="text/javascript">
                writeOptions(1, 31);
                </script>
            </select>
            <select name="firstMonth" onchange="recalcDateDiff()">
                <script type="text/javascript">
                writeMonthOptions();
                </script>
            </select>
            <select name="firstYear" onchange="recalcDateDiff()">
                <script type="text/javascript">
                writeOptions(1970, 2020);
                </script>
            </select>
        </p>
        <p>
            Second Date<br />
            <select name="secondDay" onchange="recalcDateDiff()">
                <script type="text/javascript">
                writeOptions(1, 31);
                </script>
            </select>
            <select name="secondMonth" onchange="recalcDateDiff()">
                <script type="text/javascript">
                writeMonthOptions();
                </script>
            </select>
```

```
    <select name="secondYear" onchange="recalcDateDiff()">
        <script type="text/javascript">
        writeOptions(1970, 2020);
        </script>
    </select>
</p>
<p>
    Total difference in days:
    <input type="text" name="txtDays" value="0" readonly="readonly" />
</p>
    </form>
</body>
</html>
```

Call the example ch7_examp9.htm and load it into your web browser. You should see the form shown in Figure 7-10, but with both date boxes set to the current date.

If you change any of the select boxes, the difference between the days will be recalculated and shown in the text box.

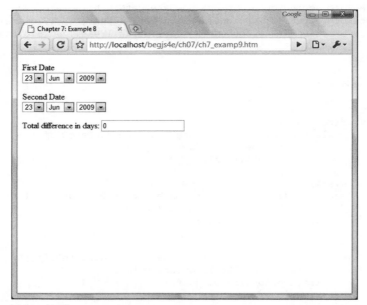

Figure 7-10

In the body of the page, the form in is built up with six drop-down list boxes and one text box. Let's look at an example of one of these select elements: Take the first <select/> element, the one that allows the user to choose the day part of the first date.

```
<select name="firstDay" onchange="recalcDateDiff()">
    <script type="text/javascript">
    writeOptions(1, 31);
    </script>
</select>
```

This select box renders as a drop-down list box in the browser; by default, a `<select/>` element's `size` attribute is set to 1. The `onchange` event handler connects to the `recalcDateDiff()` function that you'll be looking at shortly.

However, no `<option/>` elements are defined within the `<select/>` element. The drop-down list boxes need to be populated with too many options for you to enter them manually. Instead you populate the options using the functions, which make use of the `document.write()` method.

The date and year options are populated using the `writeOptions()` function declared in the head of the page. The function is passed two values: the start number and the end number of the options that you want the select element to be populated with. Let's look at the `writeOptions()` function.

```
function writeOptions(startNumber, endNumber)
{
    var optionCounter;
    for (optionCounter = startNumber;
        optionCounter <= endNumber; optionCounter++)
    {
        document.write("<option value=" + optionCounter + ">" +
            optionCounter);
    }
}
```

The function is actually quite simple, consisting of a `for` loop that loops from the first number (`startNumber`) through to the last (`endNumber`) using the variable `optionCounter` and writes out the HTML necessary for each `<option/>` element. The text for the option and the `value` attribute of the `<option/>` element are specified to be the value of the variable `optionCounter`. It's certainly a lot quicker than typing out the 31 `<option/>` elements necessary for the dates in a month.

For the year select box, the same function can be reused. You just pass 1970 and 2020 as parameters to the `writeOptions()` function to populate the year select box.

```
<select name="firstYear" onchange="recalcDateDiff()">
    <script type="text/javascript">
    writeOptions(1970, 2020);
    </script>
</select>
```

To populate the month select box with the names of each month, you will need a different function. However, the principle behind populating the `<select/>` element remains the same: You do it using `document.write()`. The function in this case is `writeMonthOptions()`, as you can see from the following month select element:

```
<select name="firstMonth" onchange="recalcDateDiff()">
    <script type="text/javascript">
    writeMonthOptions();
    </script>
</select>
```

The new function, `writeMonthOptions()`, is defined in the head of the page. Let's take a look at it now. You start the function by defining three variables and initializing the variable, `theDate`, to the current date.

```
function writeMonthOptions()
{
```

```
var theMonth;
var monthCounter;
var theDate = new Date();
```

You use the `Date` object contained in the `theDate` variable to get the months as text (Jan, Feb...Dec). You get these months by setting the month in the `theDate` variable from 0 up to 11 using the `setMonth()` method in a `for` loop. Although the `Date` object does not provide a method for returning the date as anything other than a number, it does have the `toString()` method, which returns the value, as a string, of the date stored in the variable. It returns the date in the format of day of the week, month, day of the month, time, and finally year; for example, `Wed Jul 15 2009 16:11:10 GMT-0500`. This string varies from browser to browser, but they all start the month at the fifth character. With this information, you can easily use the `String` object's `substr()` method to extract the month.

```
for (monthCounter = 0; monthCounter < 12; monthCounter++)
{
    theDate.setMonth(monthCounter);
    theMonth = theDate.toString();
    theMonth = theMonth.substr(4, 3);
    document.write("<option value=" + theMonth + ">" + theMonth);
}
}
```

Now that you have your month as a string of three characters, you can create the `<option/>` element and populate its text and value with the month.

For user convenience, it would be nice during the loading of the page to set both of the dates in the select elements to today's date. This is what you do in the `window_onload()` function, which handles the window's `load` event by means of the opening `<body>` tag.

```
<body onload="window_onload()">
```

The `window_onload()` function, defined in the head of the page, starts by setting the `theForm` variable to reference your `Form` object, because it shortens the reference needed in your code. Next, you create a variable to hold a `Date` object to store today's date.

```
function window_onload()
{
    var theForm = document.form1;
    var nowDate = new Date();
```

Setting each of the `<select/>` box's initial values is easy; the value returned by the `Date` object `nowDate` can be modified to provide the required index of the `options` collection. For the day, the correct index is simply the day of the month minus one — remember that arrays start at 0, so day 1 is actually at index 0. The `selected` property is set to `true` to make that day the currently selected option in the list.

```
theForm.firstDay.options[nowDate.getDate() - 1].selected = true;
theForm.secondDay.options[nowDate.getDate() - 1].selected = true;
```

The month is even easier because the `getMonth()` function returns a value from 0 to 11 for the month, which exactly matches the necessary index value for the `options` collection.

```
theForm.firstMonth.options[nowDate.getMonth()].selected = true;
theForm.secondMonth.options[nowDate.getMonth()].selected = true;
```

For the year, because you are starting with 1970 as your first year, you need to take 1970 from the current year to get the correct index value.

```
theForm.firstYear.options[nowDate.getFullYear() - 1970].selected = true;
theForm.secondYear.options[nowDate.getFullYear() - 1970].selected = true;
}
```

The final part of your code that you need to look at is the function connected to the change event of each select element, namely the recalcDateDiff() function. Your first task with this function is to build up the two dates the user has selected using the drop-down lists.

```
function recalcDateDiff()
{
    var myForm = document.form1;
    var firstDay = myForm.firstDay.options[myForm.firstDay.selectedIndex].value;
    var secondDay =
        myForm.secondDay.options[myForm.secondDay.selectedIndex].value;
    var firstMonth =
        myForm.firstMonth.options[myForm.firstMonth.selectedIndex].value;
    var secondMonth =
        myForm.secondMonth.options[myForm.secondMonth.selectedIndex].value;
    var firstYear =
        myForm.firstYear.options[myForm.firstYear.selectedIndex].value;
    var secondYear =
        myForm.secondYear.options[myForm.secondYear.selectedIndex].value;
```

You go through each select element and retrieve the value of the selected Option object. The selectedIndex property of the Select object provides the index you need to reference the selected Option object in the options collection. For example, in the following line, the index is provided by myForm.firstDay.selectedIndex:

```
var firstDay = myForm.firstDay.options[myForm.firstDay.selectedIndex].value;
```

You then use that value inside the square brackets as the index value for the options collection of the firstDay select element. This provides the reference to the selected Option object, whose value property you store in the variable firstDay.

You use this technique for all the remaining select elements.

You can then create new Date objects based on the values obtained from the select elements and store them in the variables firstDate and secondDate.

```
var firstDate = new Date(firstDay + " " + firstMonth + " " + firstYear);
var secondDate = new Date(secondDay + " " + secondMonth + " " + secondYear);
```

Finally, you need to calculate the difference in days between the two dates.

```
var daysDiff = (secondDate.valueOf() - firstDate.valueOf());
daysDiff = Math.floor(Math.abs((((daysDiff / 1000) / 60) / 60) / 24));
```

The Date object has a method, valueOf(), which returns the number of milliseconds from the first of January, 1970, to the date stored in the Date object. You subtract the value of the valueOf property of firstDate from the value of the valueOf property of secondDate and store this in the variable daysDiff. At this point, it holds the difference between the two dates in milliseconds, so you convert this value to days in the following line. By dividing by 1,000 you make the value seconds, dividing the resulting number by 60 makes it minutes, by 60 again makes it hours, and finally you divide by 24 to convert to your final figure of difference in days. The Math object's abs() method makes negative numbers positive. The user may have set the first date to a later date than the second, and since you want to find only the difference between the two, not which is earlier, you make any negative results positive. The Math.floor() method removes the fractional part of any result and returns just the integer part rounded down to the nearest whole number.

Finally, you write the difference in days to the txtDays text box in the page.

```
myForm.txtDays.value = daysDiff;
```

Summary

In this chapter, you looked at how to add a user interface onto your JavaScript so that you can interact with your users and acquire information from them. Let's look at some of the things we discussed in this chapter.

❑ The HTML form is where you place elements making up the interface in a page.

❑ Each HTML form groups together a set of HTML elements. When a form is submitted to a server for processing, all the data in that form are sent to the server. You can have multiple forms on a page, but only the information in one form can be sent to the server.

❑ A form is created with the opening tag <form> and ends with the close tag </form>. All the elements you want included in that form are placed in between the open and close <form> tags. The <form/> element has various attributes — for client-side scripting, the name attribute is the important one. You can access forms with either their name attribute or their ID attribute.

❑ Each <form> element creates a Form object, which is contained within the document object. To access a form named myForm, you write document.myForm. The document object also has a forms property, which is a collection containing every form inside the document. The first form in the page is document.forms[0], the second is document.forms[1], and so on. The length property of the forms property (document.forms.length) tells you how many forms are on the page.

❑ Having discussed forms, we then went on to look at the different types of HTML elements that can be placed inside forms, how to create them, and how they are used in JavaScript.

❑ The objects associated with the form elements have a number of properties, methods, and events that are common to them all. They all have the name property, which you can use to reference them in your JavaScript. They also all have the form property, which provides a reference to the Form object in which that element is contained. The type property returns a text string telling you what type of element this is; types include text, button, and radio.

❑ You also saw that the methods focus() and blur(), and the events focus and blur, are available to every form element object. Such an element is said to receive the focus when it becomes the active element in the form, either because the user has selected that element or because you used the focus() method. However an element got the focus, its focus event will fire. When another element is set as the currently active element, the previous element is said to lose its focus, or to blur. Again, loss of focus can be the result of the user selecting another element or the use of the blur() method; either way, when it happens the blur event fires. You saw that the firing of focus and blur can, if used carefully, be a good place to check things like the validity of data entered by a user into an element.

❑   All elements return a value, which is the string data assigned to that element. The meaning of the value depends on the element; for a text box, it is the value inside the text box, and for a button, it's the text displayed on its face.

❑   Having discussed the common features of elements, we then looked at each of the more commonly used elements in turn, starting with the button element.

❑   The button element's purpose in life is to be clicked by the user, where that clicking fires some script you have written. You can capture the clicking by connecting to the button's click event. A button is created by means of the <input/> element with the type attribute set to button. The value attribute determines what text appears on the button's face. Two variations on a button are the submit and reset buttons. In addition to acting as buttons, they also provide a special service not linked to code. The submit button will automatically submit the form to the server; the reset button clears the form back to its default state when loaded in the page.

❑   The text element allows the user to enter a single line of plain text. A text box is created by means of the <input/> element with the type attribute set to text. You can set how many characters the user can enter and how wide the text box is with the maxlength and size attributes, respectively, of the <input/> element. The text box has an associated object called Text, which has the additional events select and change. The select event fires when the user selects text in the box, and the more useful change event fires when the element loses focus and its contents have changed since the element gained the focus. The firing of the change event is a good place to do validation of what users has just entered. If they entered illegal values, such as letters when you wanted numbers, you can let the user know and send her back to correct her mistake. A variation on the text box is the password box, which is almost identical to the text box except that the values typed into it are hidden and shown as an asterisk. Additionally, the text box also has the keydown, keypress, and keyup events.

❑   The next element you looked at was the text area, which is similar to the text box except that it allows multiple lines of text to be entered. This element is created with the open tag <textarea> and closed with the </textarea> tag, the width and height in characters of the text box being determined by the cols and rows attributes respectively. The wrap attribute determines whether the text area wraps text that reaches the end of a line and whether that wrapping is sent when the contents are posted to the server. If this attribute is left out, or set to off, no wrapping occurs; if set to soft, it causes wrapping client-side, but is not sent to the server when the form is sent; if set to hard, it causes wrapping client-side and is sent to the server. The associated Textarea object has virtually the same properties, methods, and events as a Text object.

❑   You then looked at the check box and radio button elements together. Essentially they are the same type of element, except that the radio button is a grouped element, meaning that only one in a group can be checked at once. Checking another one causes the previously checked button to be unchecked. Both elements are created with the <input/> element, the type attribute being checkbox or radio. If checked is put inside the <input> tag, that element will be checked when the page is loaded. Creating radio buttons with the same name creates a radio button group. The name of a radio button actually refers to an array, and each element within that array is a radio button defined on the form to be within that group. These elements have associated objects called Checkbox and Radio. Using the checked property of these objects, you can find out whether a check box or radio button is currently checked. Both objects also have the click event in addition to the common events focus and blur.

❑   Next in your look at elements were the drop-down list and list boxes. Both, in fact, are the same select element, with the `size` attribute determining whether it's a drop-down or list box. The `<select>` tag creates these elements, the `size` attribute determining how many list items are visible at once. If a `size` of 1 is given, a drop-down box rather than a list box is created. Each item in a select element is defined by the `<option/>` element, or added to later by means of the `Select` object's `options` collection property, which is an array-like structure containing each `Option` object for that element. However, adding options after the page is loaded differs slightly between IE7 and other browsers. The `Select` object's `selectedIndex` property tells you which option is selected; you can then use that value to access the appropriate option in the `options` collection and use the `Option` object's `value` property. The `Option` object also has the `text` and `index` properties, `text` being the displayed text in the list and `index` being its position in the `Select` object's `options` collection property. You can loop through the `options` collection, finding out its length from the `Select` object's `length` property. The `Select` object has the `change` event, which fires when the user selects another item from the list.

In the next chapter, you'll look at how, once you have created a frameset in a page, you can access code and variables between frames. You'll also look at how to open new windows using JavaScript, and methods of manipulating them when they are open. You'll see the trivia quiz become a frame-based application.

Exercise Questions

Suggested solutions to these questions can be found in Appendix A.

1.   Using the code from the temperature converter example you saw in Chapter 2, create a user interface for it and connect it to the existing code so that the user can enter a value in degrees Fahrenheit and convert it to centigrade.

2.   Create a user interface that allows the user to pick the computer system of their dreams, similar in principle to the e-commerce sites selling computers over the Internet. For example, they could be given a choice of processor type, speed, memory, and hard drive size, and the option to add additional components like a DVD-ROM drive, a sound card, and so on. As the user changes their selections, the price of the system should update automatically and notify them of the cost of the system as they specified it, either by using an alert box or by updating the contents of a text box.

Windows and Frames

Until now, the pages you have been looking at have just been single pages. However, many web applications use frames to split up the browser's window, much as panes of glass split up a real window. It's quite possible that you'll want to build web sites that make use of such frames. The good news is that JavaScript enables the manipulation of frames and allows functions and variables you create in one frame to be used from another frame. One advantage of this is that you can keep common variables and functions in one place but use them from many places. This chapter starts by looking at how you can script across such frames.

A number of other good reasons exist for wanting to access variables and functions in another frame. Two important reasons are to make your code *modular* and to gain the ability to maintain information between pages.

What does *modular* mean? In other programming languages, like C, C++, or Visual Basic, you can create a module — an area to hold general functions and variables — and reuse it from different places in your program. When using frames, you can put all of your general functions and variables into one area, such as the top frame, which you can think of as your code module. Then you can call the functions repeatedly from different pages and different frames.

If you put the general functions and variables in a page that defines the frames that it contains (that is, a frameset-defining page), then if you need to make changes to the pages inside the frames, any variables defined in the frameset page will retain their value. This provides a very useful means of holding information even when the user is navigating your web site. A further advantage is that any functions defined in the frameset-defining page can be called by subsequent pages and have to be loaded into the browser only once, making your page's loading faster.

The second subject of this chapter is how you can open up and manipulate new browser windows. There are plenty of good uses for new windows. For example, you may wish to open up an *external* web site in a new window from your web site, but still leave your web site open for the user. *External* here means a web site created and maintained by another person or company. Let's say you have a web site about cars — well, you may wish to have a link to external sites, such as manufacturing web sites (for example, that of Ford or General Motors). Perhaps even more useful is using small windows as dialog boxes, which you can use to obtain information from the user. Just as you can script between frames, you can do similar things between certain windows. You find out how later in the chapter, but let's start by looking at scripting between frames.

Frames and the window Object

Frames are a means of splitting up the browser window into various panes, into which you can then load different HTML documents. The frames are defined in a frameset-defining page by the `<frameset/>` and `<frame/>` elements. The `<frameset/>` element contains `<frame/>` elements and specifies how the frames should look on the page. The `<frame/>` elements are then used to specify each frame and to include the required documents in the page.

You saw in Chapter 6 that the window object represents the browser's frame on your page or document. If you have a page with no frames, there will be just one window object. However, if you have more than one frame, there will be one window object for each frame. Except for the very top-level window of a frameset, each window object is contained inside another.

The easiest way to demonstrate this is through an example in which you create three frames, a top frame with two frames inside it.

Try It Out   Multiple Frames

For this multi-frame example, you'll need to create three HTML files. The first is the frameset-defining page.

```
<!DOCTYPE html PUBLIC "-//W3C//DTD XHTML 1.0 Frameset//EN"
    "http://www.w3.org/TR/xhtml1/DTD/xhtml1-frameset.dtd">

<html xmlns="http://www.w3.org/1999/xhtml">
<head>
    <title>Chapter 8: Example 1</title>
</head>
<frameset row="50%, *" id="topWindow">
    <frame name="upperWindow" src="ch08_examp1_upper.htm" />
    <frame name="lowerWindow" src="ch08_examp1_lower.htm" />
</frameset>
</html>
```

Save this as `ch08_examp1.htm`. Note that the src attributes for the two `<frame />` elements in this page are `ch08_examp1_upper.htm` and `ch08_examp1_lower.htm`. You will create these next.

```
<!DOCTYPE html PUBLIC "-//W3C//DTD XHTML 1.0 Transitional//EN"
    "http://www.w3.org/TR/xhtml1/DTD/xhtml1-transitional.dtd">

<html xmlns="http://www.w3.org/1999/xhtml">
<head>
    <title>Chapter 8: Example 1 Upper Frame</title>
    <script type="text/javascript">
```

```
function window_onload()
{
    alert("The name of the upper frame's window object is " +
        window.name);

    alert("The location of upperWindow's parent is " +
        window.parent.location.href);
}
</script>
</head>
<body onload="window_onload()">
    <p>
        Upper Frame
    </p>
</body>
</html>
```

The preceding code block is the source page for the top frame with the name upperWindow and needs to be saved as ch08_examp1_upper.htm. The final page is very similar to it:

```
<!DOCTYPE html PUBLIC "-//W3C//DTD XHTML 1.0 Transitional//EN"
    "http://www.w3.org/TR/xhtml1/DTD/xhtml1-transitional.dtd">
<html xmlns="http://www.w3.org/1999/xhtml">
<head>
    <title>Chapter 8: Example 1 Lower Frame</title>
    <script type="text/javascript">
    function window_onload()
    {
        alert("The name of the lower frame's window object is " +
            window.name);

        alert("The location of lowerWindow's parent is " +
            window.parent.location.href);
    }
    </script>
</head>
<body onload="window_onload()">
    <p>
        Lower Frame
    </p>
</body>
</html>
```

This is the source page for the lower frame; save it as ch08_examp1_lower.htm.

These three pages fit together so that ch08_examp1_upper.htm and ch08_examp1_lower.htm are contained within the ch08_examp1.htm page.

When you load them into the browser, you have three window objects. One is the *parent* window object and contains the file ch08_examp1.htm, and two are *child* window objects, containing the files ch08_examp1_upper.htm and ch08_examp1_lower.htm. The two child window objects are contained within the parent window, as shown in Figure 8-1.

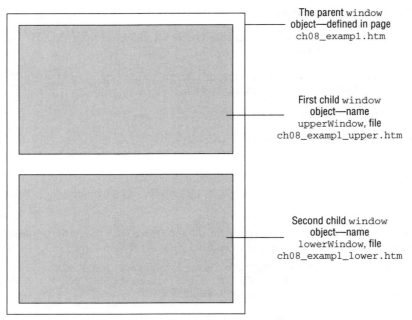

Figure 8-1

If any of the frames had frames contained inside them, these would have `window` objects that were children of the `window` object of that frame.

When you load `ch08_examp1.htm` into your browser, you'll see a series of four message boxes, as shown in Figures 8-2 through 8-5. These are making use of the `window` object's properties to gain information and demonstrate the `window` object's place in the hierarchy.

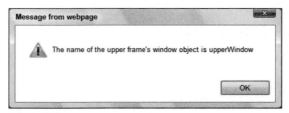

Figure 8-2

Figure 8-3

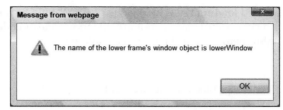

Figure 8-4

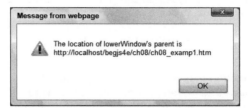

Figure 8-5

The paths in Figures 8-3 and 8-5 will vary depending upon where the files are stored on your computer.

Look at the frameset-defining page, starting with ch08_examp1.htm, as shown in the following snippet:

```
<!DOCTYPE html PUBLIC "-//W3C//DTD XHTML 1.0 Frameset//EN"
    "http://www.w3.org/TR/xhtml1/DTD/xhtml1-frameset.dtd">

<html xmlns="http://www.w3.org/1999/xhtml">
<head>
    <title>Chapter 8: Example 1</title>
</head>
<frameset rows="50%, *" id="topWindow">
    <frame name="upperWindow" src="ch08_examp1_upper.htm" />
    <frame name="lowerWindow" src="ch08_examp1_lower.htm" />
</frameset>
</html>
```

The frameset is defined with the `<frameset />` element. You use two attributes: `rows` and `id`. The `rows` attribute takes the value `"50%, *"` meaning that the first frame should take up half of the height of the window, and the second frame should take up the rest of the room. The `id` attribute is used to give a name that you can use to reference the page.

The two child windows are created using `<frame />` elements; each of which contains a `name` attribute by which the `window` objects will be known and a `src` attribute of the page that will be loaded into the newly created windows.

Let's take a look at the ch08_examp1_upper.htm file next. In the `<body />` element, you attach the `window_onload()` function to the `window` object's `onload` event handler. This event handler is called when the browser has finished loading the window, the document inside the window, and all the objects within the document. It's a very useful place to put initialization code or code that needs to change things after the page has loaded but before control passes back to the user.

```
<body onload="window_onload()">
```

This function is defined in a script block in the head of the page as follows:

```
function window_onload()
{

    alert("The name of the upper frame's window object is " + window.name);
    alert("The location of UpperWindow's parent is " +

        window.parent.location.href);
}
```

The window_onload() function makes use of two properties of the window object for the frame that the page is loaded in: its name and parent properties. The name property is self-explanatory — it's the name you defined in the frameset page. In this case, the name is upperWindow.

The second property, the parent property, is very useful. It gives you access to the window object of the frame's parent. This means you can access all of the parent window object's properties and methods. Through these, you can access the document within the parent window as well as any other frames defined by the parent. Here, you display a message box giving details of the parent frame's file name or URL by using the href property of the location object (which itself is a property of the window object).

The code for ch08_examp1_lower.htm is identical to the code for ch08_examp1_upper.htm, but with different results because you are accessing a different window object. The name of the window object this time is lowerWindow. However, it shares the same parent window as upperWindow, and so when you access the parent property of the window object, you get a reference to the same window object as in upperWindow. The message box demonstrates this by displaying the file name/URL or href property, and this matches the file name of the page displayed in the upperWindow frame.

> *The order of display of messages may vary among different types of browsers and even different operating systems. This may not be important here, but there will be times when the order in which events fire is important and affects how your code works. It's an incompatibility that's worth noting and watching out for in your own programs.*

Coding Between Frames

You've seen that each frame exists as a different window and gets its own window object. In addition, you saw that you can access the window object of a frameset-defining page from any of the frame pages it specifies, by using the window object's parent property. When you have a reference to the parent window's window object, you can access its properties and methods in the same way that you access the window object of the current page. In addition, you have access to all the JavaScript variables and functions defined in that page.

Using the Frameset Page as a Module

Let's look at a more complex example, wherein you use the top frame to keep track of pages as the user navigates the web site. You're creating five pages in this example, but don't panic; four of them are almost identical. The first page that needs to be created is the frameset-defining page.

```
<!DOCTYPE html PUBLIC "-//W3C//DTD XHTML 1.0 Frameset//EN"
    "http://www.w3.org/TR/xhtml1/DTD/xhtml1-frameset.dtd">

<html xmlns="http://www.w3.org/1999/xhtml">
<head>
    <title>Chapter 8: Example 2</title>
    <script type="text/javascript">
    var pagesVisited = new Array();
    function returnPagesVisited()
    {
        var returnValue = "So far you have visited the following pages\n";
        var pageVisitedIndex;
        var numberOfPagesVisited = pagesVisited.length;
        for (pageVisitedIndex = 0; pageVisitedIndex < numberOfPagesVisited;
            pageVisitedIndex++)
        {
            returnValue = returnValue + pagesVisited[pageVisitedIndex] + "\n";
        }
        return returnValue;
    }

    function addPage(fileName)
    {
        var fileNameStart = fileName.lastIndexOf("/") + 1;
        fileName = fileName.substr(fileNameStart);
        pagesVisited[pagesVisited.length] = fileName;

        return true;
    }
    </script>
</head>
<frameset cols="50%,*">
    <frame name="fraLeft" src="ch08_examp2_a.htm">
    <frame name="fraRight" src="ch08_examp2_b.htm">
</frameset>
</html>
```

Save this page as ch08_examp2.htm.

Notice that the two frames have the src attributes initialized as ch08_examp2_a.htm and ch08_examp2_b.htm. However, you also need to create ch08_examp2_c.htm and ch08_examp2_d.htm because you will be allowing the user to choose the page loaded into each frame from these four pages. You'll create the page_a.htm page first, as shown in the following:

```
<!DOCTYPE html PUBLIC "-//W3C//DTD XHTML 1.0 Transitional//EN"
    "http://www.w3.org/TR/xhtml1/DTD/xhtml1-transitional.dtd">
<html xmlns="http://www.w3.org/1999/xhtml">
```

```
<head>
    <title>Chapter 8: Example 2 Page A</title>
    <script type="text/javascript">
    function btnShowVisited_onclick()
    {
        document.form1.txtaPagesVisited.value =
            window.parent.returnPagesVisited();
    }
    </script>
</head>
<body onload="window.parent.addPage(window.location.href)">
    <h2>This is Page A</h2>
    <p>
        <a href="ch08_examp2_a.htm">Page A</a>
        <a href="ch08_examp2_b.htm">Page B</a>
        <a href="ch08_examp2_c.htm">Page C</a>
        <a href="ch08_examp2_d.htm">Page D</a>
    </p>
<form name="form1" action="">
        <textarea rows="10" cols="35" name="txtaPagesVisited"></textarea>
        <br />
        <input type="button" value="List Pages Visited" name="btnShowVisited"
            onclick="btnShowVisited_onclick()" />
    </form>
</body>
</html>
```

Save this page as ch08_examp2_a.htm.

The other three pages are identical to ch08_examp2_a.htm, except for the page's title and the <h2 /> element, so you can just cut and paste the text from ch08_examp2_a.htm. Change the HTML that displays the name of the page loaded to the following:

```
<h2>This is Page B</h2>
```

Then save this as ch08_examp2_b.htm.

Do the same again, to create the third page (page C):

```
<h2>This is Page C</h2>
```

Save this as ch08_examp2_c.htm.

The final page is again a copy of ch08_examp2_a.htm except for the following lines:

```
<h2>This is Page D</h2>
```

Save this as ch08_examp2_d.htm.

Load ch08_examp2.htm into your browser and navigate to various pages by clicking the links. Then click the List Pages Visited button in the left-hand frame, and you should see a screen similar to the one shown in Figure 8-6.

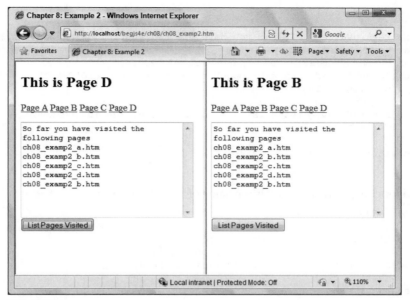

Figure 8-6

Click the links in either frame to navigate to a new location. For example, click the Page C link in the right frame, then the Page D link in the left frame. Click the left frame's List Pages Visited button and you'll see that ch08_examp2_c.htm and ch08_examp2_d.htm have been added to the list.

Normally when a new page is loaded, any variables and their values in the previous page are lost, but when using frameset pages as modules, it does not matter which page is loaded into each frame — the top frame remains loaded and its variables keep their values. What you are seeing in this example is that, regardless of which page is loaded in each frame, some global variable in the top frame is keeping track of the pages that have been viewed and the top frame's variables and functions can be accessed by any page loaded into either frame.

> *There are restrictions when the pages you load into the frames are from external sources — more on this later in the chapter.*

Let's first look at the JavaScript in ch08_examp2.htm, which is the frameset-defining page. The head of the page contains a script block. The first thing in this script block is the declaration of the pagesVisited variable, and set it to reference a new Array object. In the array, you'll be storing the file name of each page visited as the user navigates the site.

```
var pagesVisited = new Array();
```

You then have two functions. The first of the two functions, returnPagesVisited(), does what its name suggests — it returns a string containing a message and a list of each of the pages visited. It does this by looping through the pagesVisited array, building up the message string inside the returnValue variable, which is then returned to the calling function.

```
function returnPagesVisited()
{
    var returnValue = "So far you have visited the following pages\n";
    var pageVisitedIndex;
    var numberOfPagesVisited = pagesVisited.length;
    for (pageVisitedIndex = 0; pageVisitedIndex < numberOfPagesVisited;
        pageVisitedIndex++)
    {
        returnValue = returnValue + pagesVisited[pageVisitedIndex]
            + "\n";
    }
    return returnValue;
}
```

The second function, addPage(), adds the name of a page to the pagesVisited array.

```
function addPage(fileName)
{
    var fileNameStart = fileName.lastIndexOf("/") + 1;
    fileName = fileName.substr(fileNameStart);
    pagesVisited[pagesVisited.length] = fileName;

    return true;
}
```

The fileName parameter passed to this function is the full file name and path of the visited page, so you need to strip out the path to get just the file name. The format of the string will be something like file:///D:/myDirectory/ch08_examp2_b.htm, and you need just the bit after the last / character. So in the first line of code, you find the position of that character and add one to it because you want to start at the next character.

Then, using the String's substr() method in the following line, you extract everything from character position fileNameStart right up to the end of the string. Remember that the substr() method accepts two parameters, namely the starting character you want and the length of the string you want to extract, but if the second parameter is missing, all characters from the start position to the end are extracted.

You then add the file name into the array, the length property of the array providing the next free index position.

You'll now turn to look collectively at the frame pages, namely ch08_examp2_a.htm, ch08_examp2_b .htm, ch08_examp2_c.htm, and ch08_examp2_d.htm. In each of these pages, you create a form called form1.

```
<form name="form1" action="">
    <textarea rows="10" cols="35" name="txtaPagesVisited"></textarea>
    <br />
    <input type="button" value="List Pages Visited"
        name="btnShowVisited" onclick="btnShowVisited_onclick()" />
</form>
```

This contains the textarea control that displays the list of visited pages, and a button the user can click to populate the <textarea /> element.

When one of these pages is loaded, its name is put into the pagesVisited array defined in ch08_examp2.htm by the window object's onload event handler's being connected to the addPage() function that you also created in ch08_examp2.htm. You connect the code to the event handler in the <body /> element of the page as follows:

```
<body onload="window.parent.addPage(window.location.href)">
```

Recall that all the functions you declare in a page are contained, like everything else in a page, inside the window object for that page; because the window object is the global object, you don't need to prefix the name of your variables or functions with window.

However, this time the function is not in the current page, but in the ch08_examp2.htm page. The window containing this page is the parent window to the window containing the current page. You need, therefore, to refer to the parent frame's window object using the window object's parent property. The code window.parent gives you a reference to the window object of ch08_examp2.htm. With this reference, you can now access the variables and functions contained in ch08_examp2.htm. Having stated which window object you are referencing, you just add the name of the function you are calling, in this instance the addPage() function. You pass this function the location.href string, which contains the full path and file name of the page, as the value for its one parameter.

As you saw earlier, the button on the page has its onclick event handler connected to a function called btnShowVisited_onclick(). This is defined in the head of the page.

```
function btnShowVisited_onclick()
{
    document.form1.txtaPagesVisited.value =
        window.parent.returnPagesVisited();
}
```

In this function, you call the parent window object's returnPagesVisited() function, which, as you saw earlier, returns a string containing a list of pages visited. The value property of the textarea object is set to this text.

That completes your look at the code in the frame pages, and as you can see, there's not much of it because you have placed all the general functions in the frameset page. Not only does this code reuse make for less typing, but it also means that all your functions are in one place. If there is a bug in a function, fixing the bug for one page also fixes it for all other pages that use the function. Of course, it only makes sense to put general functions in one place; functions that are specific to a page and are never used again outside it are best kept in that page.

Code Access Between Frames

You've just seen how a child window can access its parent window's variables and functions, but how can frames inside a frameset access each other?

You saw a simple example earlier in this chapter, so this time let's look at a much more complex example. When created, your page will look like the one shown in Figure 8-7.

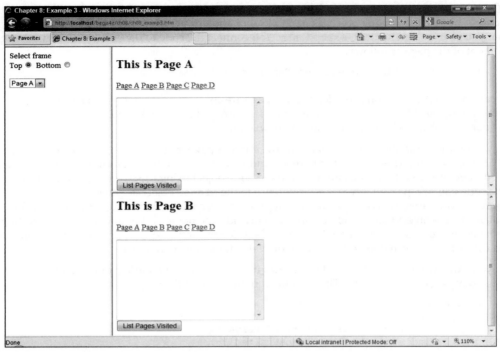

Figure 8-7

A diagram of the frame layout is shown in Figure 8-8. The text labels indicate the names that each frame has been given in the `<frameset/>` and `<frame/>` elements, with the exception of the top frame, which is simply the window at the top of the frameset hierarchy.

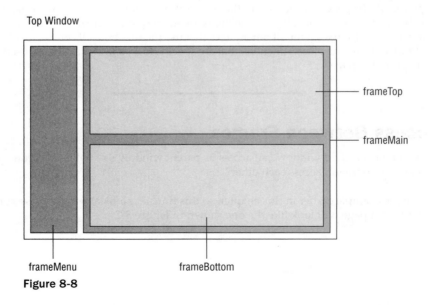

Figure 8-8

The easiest way to think of the hierarchy of such a frames-based web page is in terms of familial relationships, which can be shown in a family tree. If you represent your frameset like that, it looks something like the diagram in Figure 8-9.

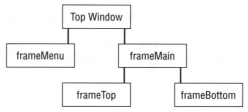

Figure 8-9

From the diagram you can see that frameBottom, the right-hand frame's bottom frame, has a parent frame called frameMain, which itself has a parent, the top window. Therefore, if you wanted to access a function in the top window from the frameBottom window, you would need to access frameBottom's parent's parent's window object. You know that the window object has the parent property, which is a reference to the parent window of that window object. So let's use that and create the code to access a function, for example, called myFunction(), in the top window.

```
window.parent.parent.myFunction();
```

Let's break this down. The following code gets you a reference to the parent window object of the window in which the code is running.

```
window.parent
```

The code is in frameBottom, so window.parent will be frameMain. However, you want the top window, which is frameMain's parent, so you add to the preceding code to make this:

```
window.parent.parent
```

Now you have a reference to the top window. Finally, you call myFunction() by adding that to the end of the expression.

```
window.parent.parent.myFunction();
```

What if you want to access the window object of frameMenu from code in frameBottom? Well, you have most of the code you need already. You saw that window.parent.parent gives you the top window, so now you want that window's child window object called frameMenu. You can get it in three ways, all with identical results.

You can use its index in the frames collection property of the window object as follows:

```
window.parent.parent.frames[0]
```

Alternatively, you can use its name in the frames collection like this:

```
window.parent.parent.frames["frameMenu"]
```

Finally, you can reference it directly by using its name as you can with any `window` object:

```
window.parent.parent.frameMenu
```

The third method is the easiest unless you don't know the name of a frame and need to access it by its index value in the `frames` collection, or are looping through each child frame in turn.

Since `window.parent.parent.frameMenu` gets you a reference to the `window` object associated with `frameMenu`, to access a function `myFunction()` or variable `myVariable`, you would just type one of these lines:

```
window.parent.parent.frameMenu.myFunction
```

or

```
window.parent.parent.frameMenu.myVariable
```

What if you want to access not a function or variable in a page within a frame, but a control on a form or even the links on that page? Well, let's imagine you want to access, from the `frameBottom` page, a control named `myControl`, on a form called `myForm` in the `frameMenu` page.

You found that `window.parent.parent.frameMenu` gives you the reference to `frameMenu`'s `window` object from `frameBottom`, but how do you reference a form there?

Basically, it's the same as how you access a form from the inside of the same page as the script, except that you need to reference not the `window` object of that page but the `window` object of `frameMenu`, the page you're interested in.

Normally you write `document.myForm.myControl.value`, with `window` being assumed since it is the global object. Strictly speaking, it's `window.document.myForm.myControl.value`.

Now that you're accessing another window, you just reference the window you want and then use the same code. So you need this code if you want to access the `value` property of `myControl` from `frameBottom`:

```
window.parent.parent.frameMenu.document.myForm.myControl.value
```

As you can see, references to other frames can get pretty long, and in this situation it's a very good idea to store the reference in a variable. For example, if you are accessing `myForm` a number of times, you could write this:

```
var myFormRef = window.parent.parent.frameMenu.document.myForm;
```

Having done that, you can now write

```
myFormRef.myControl.value;
```

rather than

```
window.parent.parent.frameMenu.document.myForm.myControl.value;
```

The top Property

Using the parent property can get a little tedious when you want to access the very top window from a frame quite low down in the hierarchy of frames and window objects. An alternative is the window object's top property. This returns a reference to the window object of the very top window in a frame hierarchy. In the current example, this is top window.

For instance, in the example you just saw, this code:

```
window.parent.parent.frameMenu.document.myForm.myControl.value;
```

could be written like this:

```
window.top.frameMenu.document.myForm.myControl.value;
```

Although, because the window is a global object, you could shorten that to just this:

```
top.frameMenu.document.myForm.myControl.value;
```

So when should you use top rather than parent, or vice versa?

Both properties have advantages and disadvantages. The parent property enables you to specify window objects relative to the current window. The window above this window is window.parent, its parent is window.parent.parent, and so on. The top property is much more generic; top is always the very top window regardless of the frameset layout being used. There will always be a top, but there's not necessarily going to always be a parent.parent. If you put all your global functions and variables that you want accessible from any page in the frameset in the very top window, window.top will always be valid regardless of changes to framesets beneath it, whereas the parent property is dependent on the frameset structure above it. However, if someone else loads your web site inside a frameset page of his own, then suddenly the top window is not yours but his, and window.top is no longer valid. You can't win, or can you?

One trick is to check to see whether the top window contains your page; if it doesn't, reload the top page again and specify that your top page is the one to be loaded. For example, check to see that the file name of the top page actually matches the name you expect. The window.top.location.href will give you the name and path — if they don't match what you want, use window.top.location.replace("myPagename.htm") to load the correct top page. However, as you'll see later, this will cause problems if someone else is loading your page into a frameset they have created — this is where something called the *same-origin policy* applies. More on this later in the chapter.

Try It Out   Scripting Frames

Let's put all you've learned about frames and scripting into an example based on the frameset you last looked at in ch08_examp2.htm. You're going to be reusing a lot of the pages and code from the previous example in this chapter.

The first page you're creating is the top window page. The highlighted lines of code show changes made to ch08_examp2.htm.

```
<!DOCTYPE html PUBLIC "-//W3C//DTD XHTML 1.0 Frameset//EN"
    "http://www.w3.org/TR/xhtml1/DTD/xhtml1-frameset.dtd">

<html xmlns="http://www.w3.org/1999/xhtml">
```

```
<head>
    <title>Chapter 8: Example 3</title>
    <script type="text/javascript">
    var pagesVisited = new Array();
    function returnPagesVisited()
    {
        var returnValue = "So far you have visited the following pages\n";
        var pageVisitedIndex;
        var numberOfPagesVisited = pagesVisited.length;
        for (pageVisitedIndex = 0; pageVisitedIndex < numberOfPagesVisited;
            pageVisitedIndex++)
        {
            returnValue = returnValue + pagesVisited[pageVisitedIndex] + "\n";
        }
        return returnValue;
    }

    function addPage(fileName)
    {
        var fileNameStart = fileName.lastIndexOf("/") + 1;
        fileName = fileName.substr(fileNameStart);
        pagesVisited[pagesVisited.length] = fileName;

        return true;
    }
    </script>
</head>
<frameset cols="200,*">
    <frame name="frameMenu" src="ch08_examp3_menu.htm">
    <frame name="frameMain" src="ch08_examp3_main.htm">
</frameset>
</html>
```

As you can see, you've reused a lot of the code from ch08_examp2.htm, so you can cut and paste the script block from there. Only the different code lines are highlighted. Save this page as ch08_examp3.htm.

Next, create the page that will be loaded into frameMenu, namely ch08_examp3_menu.htm.

```
<!DOCTYPE html PUBLIC "-//W3C//DTD XHTML 1.0 Transitional//EN"
    "http://www.w3.org/TR/xhtml1/DTD/xhtml1-transitional.dtd">
<html xmlns="http://www.w3.org/1999/xhtml">
<head>
    <title>Chapter 8: Example 3 Menu</title>
    <script type="text/javascript">
    function choosePage_onchange()
    {
        var choosePage = document.form1.choosePage;
        var windowobject;
        if (document.form1.radFrame[0].checked == true)
        {
            windowobject = window.parent.frameMain.frameTop;
        }
        else
        {
            windowobject = window.parent.frameMain.frameBottom;
```

```
            }
            windowobject.location.href =
                choosePage.options[choosePage.selectedIndex].value;
            return true;
        }
        </script>
</head>
<body>
    <form name="form1" action="">
        Select frame
        <br />
        Top
        <input name="radFrame" checked="checked" type="radio" />
        Bottom
        <input name="radFrame" type="radio" />
        <br />
        <br />
        <select name="choosePage" onchange="choosePage_onchange()">
            <option value="ch08_examp3_a.htm">Page A</option>
            <option value="ch08_examp3_b.htm">Page B</option>
            <option value="ch08_examp3_c.htm">Page C</option>
            <option value="ch08_examp3_d.htm">Page D</option>
        </select>
    </form>
</body>
</html>
```

Save this as `ch08_examp3_menu.htm`.

The `frameMain` frame contains a page that is simply a frameset for the `frameTop` and `frameBottom` pages.

```
<!DOCTYPE html PUBLIC "-//W3C//DTD XHTML 1.0 Frameset//EN"
    "http://www.w3.org/TR/xhtml1/DTD/xhtml1-frameset.dtd">

<html xmlns="http://www.w3.org/1999/xhtml">
<head>
    <title>Chapter 8: Example 3 Main</title>
</head>
<frameset rows="50%,*">
    <frame name="frameTop" src="ch08_examp3_a.htm">
    <frame name="frameBottom" src="ch08_examp3_b.htm">
</frameset>
</html>
```

Save this as `ch08_examp3_main.htm`.

The next four pages are mainly copies of the four pages — ch08_examp2_a.htm, ch08_examp2_b.htm, ch08_examp2_c.htm, and ch08_examp2_d.htm — from example two. You'll need to make a few changes, as highlighted in the following code. (Again, all the pages are identical except for the text shown in the page, so only modifications to ch08_examp2_a.htm are shown. Amend the rest in a similar way.)

```
<!DOCTYPE html PUBLIC "-//W3C//DTD XHTML 1.0 Transitional//EN"
    "http://www.w3.org/TR/xhtml1/DTD/xhtml1-transitional.dtd">

<html xmlns="http://www.w3.org/1999/xhtml">
```

```
<head>
    <title>Chapter 8: Example 3 Page A</title>
    <script type="text/javascript">
    function btnShowVisited_onclick()
    {
        document.form1.txtaPagesVisited.value =
            window.top.returnPagesVisited();
    }

    function setFrameAndPageControls(linkIndex)
    {
        var formobject = window.parent.parent.frameMenu.document.form1;
        formobject.choosePage.selectedIndex = linkIndex;

        if (window.parent.frameTop == window.self)
        {
            formobject.radFrame[0].checked = true;
        }
        else
        {
            formobject.radFrame[1].checked = true;
        }

        return true;
    }
    </script>
</head>
<body onload="window.top.addPage(window.location.href)">
    <h2>This is Page A</h2>
    <p>
        <a href="ch08_examp3_a.htm" name="pageALink"
            onclick="return setFrameAndPageControls(0)">Page A</a>
        <a href="ch08_examp3_b.htm" name="pageBLink"
            onclick="return setFrameAndPageControls(1)">Page B</a>
        <a href="ch08_examp3_c.htm" name="pageCLink"
            onclick="return setFrameAndPageControls(2)">Page C</a>
        <a href="ch08_examp3_d.htm" name="pageDLink"
            onclick="return setFrameAndPageControls(3)">Page D</a>
    </p>
    <form name="form1" action="">
        <textarea rows="10" cols="35" name="txtaPagesVisited"></textarea>
        <br />
        <input type="button" value="List Pages Visited" name="btnShowVisited"
            onclick="btnShowVisited_onclick()" />
    </form>
</body>

</html>
```

Save the pages as ch08_examp3_a.htm, ch08_examp3_b.htm, ch08_examp3_c.htm, and ch08_examp3_d.htm.

Load ch08_examp3.htm into your browser, and you'll see a screen similar to the one shown in Figure 8-7.

The radio buttons allow the user to determine which frame he wants to navigate to a new page. When he changes the currently selected page in the drop-down list, that page is loaded into the frame selected by the radio buttons.

If you navigate using the links in the pages inside the frameTop and frameBottom frames, you'll notice that the selected frame radio buttons and the drop-down list in frameMenu on the left will be automatically updated to the page and frame just navigated to. Note that as the example stands, if the user loads ch08_examp3_a.htm into a frame the select list doesn't allow it to load the same page in the other frame. You could improve on this example by adding a button that loads the currently selected page into the chosen frame.

The List Pages Visited buttons display a list of visited pages, as they did in the previous example.

You've already seen how the code defining the top window in ch08_examp3.htm works, as it is very similar to the previous example. However, look quickly at the <frameset/> element, where, as you can see, the names of the windows are defined in the names of the <frame/> elements.

```
<frameset cols="200,*">
    <frame name="frameMenu" src="ch08_examp3_menu.htm">
    <frame name="frameMain" src="ch08_examp3_main.htm">
</frameset>
```

Notice also that the cols attribute of the <frameset/> element is set to "200,*". This means that the first frame will occupy a column 200 pixels wide, and the other frame will occupy a column taking up the remaining space.

Let's look in more detail at the frameMenu frame containing ch08_examp3_menu.htm. At the top of the page, you have your main script block. This contains the function choosePage_onchange(), which is connected to the onchange event handler of the select box lower down on the page. The select box has options containing the various page URLs.

The function starts by defining two variables. One of these, choosePage, is a shortcut reference to the choosePage Select object further down the page.

```
function choosePage_onchange()
{
    var choosePage = document.form1.choosePage;
    var windowobject;
```

The if...else statement then sets your variable windowobject to reference the window object of whichever frame the user has chosen in the radFrame radio button group.

```
    if (document.form1.radFrame[0].checked == true)
    {
        windowobject = window.parent.frameMain.fraTop;
    }
    else
    {
        windowobject = window.parent.frameMain.fraBottom;
    }
```

As you saw earlier, it's just a matter of following through the references, so window.parent gets you a reference to the parent window object. In this case, window.top would have done the same thing. Then window.parent.frameMain gets you a reference to the window object of the frameMain frame. Finally, depending on which frame you want to navigate in, you reference the frameTop or frameBottom window

objects contained within `frameMain`, using `window.parent.frameMain.frameTop` or `window.parent`
`.frameMain.frameBottom`.

Now that you have a reference to the `window` object of the frame in which you want to navigate, you can go ahead and change its `location.href` property to the value of the selected drop-down list item, causing the frame to load that page.

```
windowobject.location.href =

    choosePage.options[choosePage.selectedIndex].value;
return true;
}
```

As you saw before, `ch08_examp3_main.htm` is simply a frameset-defining page for `frameTop` and `frameBottom`. Let's now look at the pages you're actually loading into `frameTop` and `frameBottom`. Because they are all the same, you'll look only at `ch08_examp3_a.htm`.

Let's start by looking at the top script block. This contains two functions, `btnShowVisited_onclick()` and `setFrameAndPageControls()`. You saw the function `btnShowVisited_onclick()` in the previous example.

```
function btnShowVisited_onclick()
{
    document.form1.txtaPagesVisited.value = window.top.returnPagesVisited();
}
```

However, because the frameset layout has changed, you do need to change the code. Whereas previously the `returnPagesVisited()` function was in the parent window, it's now moved to the top window. As you can see, all you need to do is change the reference from `window.parent.returnPagesVisited();` to `window.top.returnPagesVisited();`.

As it happens, in the previous example the `parent` window was also the `top` window, so if you had written your code in this way in the first place, there would have been no need for changes here. It's often quite a good idea to keep all your general functions in the top frameset page. That way all your references can be `window.top`, even if the frameset layout is later changed.

The new function in this page is `setFrameAndPageControls()`, which is connected to the `onclick` event handler of the links defined lower down on the page. This function's purpose is to make sure that if the user navigates to a different page using the links rather than the controls in the `frameMenu` window, those controls will be updated to reflect what the user has done.

The first thing you do is set the `formobject` variable to reference the `form1` in the `frameMenu` page, as follows:

```
function setFrameAndPageControls(linkIndex)
{
    var formobject = window.parent.parent.frameMenu.document.form1;
```

Let's break this down.

```
window.parent
```

gets you a reference to the `frameMain` window object. Moving up the hierarchy, you use the following code to get a reference to the `window` object of the top window:

```
window.parent.parent
```

Yes, you're right. You could have used `window.top` instead, and this would have been a better way to do it. We're doing it the long way here just to demonstrate how the hierarchy works.

Now you move down the hierarchy, but on the other side of your tree diagram, to reference the frameMenu's window object.

```
window.parent.parent.frameMenu
```

Finally, you are interested only in the form and its controls, so you reference that object like this:

```
window.parent.parent.frameMenu.document.form1
```

Now that you have a reference to the form, you can use it just as you would if this were code in frameMenu itself.

The function's parameter `linkIndex` tells you which of the four links was clicked, and you use this value in the next line of the function's code to set which of the options is selected in the drop-down list box on frameMenu's form.

```
formobject.choosePage.selectedIndex = linkIndex;
```

The `if...else` statement is where you set the frameMenu's radio button group `radFrame` to the frame the user just clicked on, but how can you tell which frame this is?

```
if (window.parent.frameTop == window.self)

{
    formobject.radFrame[0].checked = true
}
else
{
    formobject.radFrame[1].checked = true
}
```

You check to see whether the current window object is the same as the window object for frameTop. You do this using the self property of the window object, which returns a reference to the current window object, and window.parent.frameTop, which returns a reference to frameTop's window object. If one is equal to the other, you know that they are the same thing and that the current window is frameTop. If that's the case, the radFrame radio group in the frameMenu frame has its first radio button checked. Otherwise, you check the other radio button for frameBottom.

The last thing you do in the function is return `true`. Remember that this function is connected to an A object, so returning `false` cancels the link's action, and `true` allows it to continue, which is what you want.

```
    return true;
}
```

Scripting IFrames

Inline frames (iframes), introduced by Microsoft in Internet Explorer (IE) 3, became a part of the HTML standard in HTML 4. They're a unique element in that you can add a frame to a web page without using a frameset, and they're much simpler to add to the page because of it. For example:

```
<iframe name="myIFrame" src="child_frame.htm" />
```

This HTML adds a frame with the name `myIFrame` to the page, which loads the `child_frame.htm` file. As you may guess, this simplicity carries over to your JavaScript. Accessing the iframe's `document` object of the page loaded in it is straightforward. For example:

```
window.myIFrame.document.bgColor = "red";
```

As you can see, it's very similar to conventional frames within a frameset (you can also use the `frames` collection like `window.frames["myIFrame"]`). Accessing the parent `window` from within the iframe is also familiar; use the `parent` property. For example:

```
window.parent.document.bgColor = "yellow";
```

Opening New Windows

So far in this chapter, you have been looking at frames and scripting between them. In this section, you'll change direction slightly and look at how you can open up additional browser windows.

Why would you want to bother opening up new windows? Well, they can be useful in all sorts of different situations, such as the following:

❑   You might want a page of links to web sites, in which clicking a link opens up a new window with that web site in it.

❑   Additional windows can be useful for displaying information. For example, if you had a page with products on it, the user could click a product image to bring up a new small window listing the details of that product. This can be less intrusive than navigating the existing window to a new page with product details, and then requiring the user to click Back to return to the list of products. You'll be creating an example demonstrating this later in this chapter.

❑   Dialog windows can be very useful for obtaining information from users, although overuse may annoy them.

The latest versions of all modern browsers include a pop-up blocking feature. By default, new windows created automatically when a page loads are usually blocked. However, windows that open only when the user must perform an action, for example clicking a link or button, are not normally blocked by default, but the user may change the browser settings to block them.

Opening a New Browser Window

The `window` object has an `open()` method, which opens up a new window. It accepts three parameters, although the third is optional, and it returns a reference to the `window` object of the new browser window.

The first parameter of the `open()` method is the URL of the page that you want to open in the new window. However, you can pass an empty string for this parameter and get a blank page and then use the `document.write()` method to insert HTML into the new window dynamically. You'll see an example of this later in the chapter.

The second parameter is the name you want to allocate to the new window. This is not the name you use for scripting, but instead is used for the `target` attribute of things such as hyperlinks and forms. For example, if you set this parameter to `myWindow` and set the `target` attribute of a hyperlink on the original page to the same value (like in the following code example), clicking that hyperlink will cause the hyperlink to act on the new window opened.

```
<a href="test3.htm" target="myWindow">Test3.htm</a>
```

This means that `test3.htm` loads into the new window and not the current window when the user clicks the link. The same applies to the `<form />` element's `target` attribute. In this case, if a form is submitted from the original window, the response from the server can be made to appear in the new window.

When a new window is opened, it is opened (by default) with a certain set of properties, such as `width` and `height`, and with the normal browser-window features. Browser-window features include things such as a location entry field and a menu bar with navigation buttons.

The third parameter of the `open()` method can be used to specify values for the `height` and `width` properties. Also, because by default most of the browser window's features are switched off, you can switch them back on using the third parameter of the `open()` method. You'll look at browser features in more detail shortly.

Let's first look at an example of the code you need to open a basic window. You'll name this window `myWindow` and give it a `width` and `height` of 250 pixels. You want the new window to open with the `test2.htm` page inside.

```
var newWindow = window.open("test2.htm","myWindow","width=250,height=250");
```

You can see that `test2.htm` has been passed as the first parameter; that is the URL of the page you want to open. The window is named `myWindow` in the second parameter. In the third parameter, you've set the `width` and `height` properties to `250`.

Also notice that you've set the variable `newWindow` to the return value returned by the `open()` method, which is a reference to the `window` object of the newly opened window. You can now use `newWindow` to manipulate the new window and gain access to the `document` contained inside it using the `newWindow.document` property. You can do everything with this reference that you did when dealing with frames and their `window` objects. For example, if you wanted to change the background color of the `document` contained inside the new window, you would type this:

```
newWindow.document.bgColor = "red";
```

How would you close the window you just opened? Easy, just use the `window` object's `close()` method like this:

```
newWindow.close();
```

Opening New Windows

Let's look at the example mentioned earlier of a products page in which clicking a product brings up a window listing the details of that product. In a shameless plug, you'll be using a couple of Wrox books as examples — though with just two products on your page, it's not exactly the world's most extensive online catalog.

```html
<!DOCTYPE html PUBLIC "-//W3C//DTD XHTML 1.0 Transitional//EN"
     "http://www.w3.org/TR/xhtml1/DTD/xhtml1-transitional.dtd">

<html xmlns="http://www.w3.org/1999/xhtml">
<head>
     <title>Chapter 8: Example 4</title>
     <script type="text/javascript">
var detailsWindow;
function showDetails(bookURL)
{
     detailsWindow = window.open(bookURL, "bookDetails",
          "width=400,height=350");
     detailsWindow.focus();
}
     </script>
</head>
<body>
     <h2>Online Book Buyer</h2>
     <p>
          Click any of the images below for more details
     </p>
     <h4>Professional Ajax</h4>
     <p>
          <img src="pro_ajax.jpg" alt="Professional Ajax, 2nd Edition" border="0"
               onclick="showDetails('pro_ajax_details.htm')" />
     </p>
     <h4>Professional JavaScript for Web Developers</h4>
     <p>
          <img src="pro_js.jpg" alt="Professional JavaScript, 2nd Edition"
               border="0" onclick="showDetails('pro_js_details.htm')" />
     </p>
</body>
</html>
```

Save this page as ch08_examp4.htm. You'll also need to create two images and name them pro_ajax.jpg and pro_js.jpg. Alternatively, you can find these files in the code download.

Note that the window will not open if the user disabled JavaScript — effectively breaking your web page. You can, however, get around this by surrounding the <img/> element with an <a/> element, assigning the href attribute to the book details page, and using the <a/> element's onclick event handler to return false after launching the new window as follows:

```html
<a href="pro_ajax_details.htm"
 onclick="showDetails(this.href); return false;">
     <img src="pro_ajax.jpg" alt="Professional Ajax" />
</a>
```

In a JavaScript-enabled browser, clicking the link results in a new window containing the pro_ajax_ details.htm page, and because the onclick handler returns false, the browser does not navigate the main window to the page defined in the link's href attribute. However, in browsers that have JavaScript disabled, the browser ignores and does not execute the code within the link's onclick event handler, thus navigating the user's browser to the book details page because it is defined in the href attribute.

You now need to create the two details pages, both plain HTML.

```html
<!DOCTYPE html PUBLIC "-//W3C//DTD XHTML 1.0 Transitional//EN"
    "http://www.w3.org/TR/xhtml1/DTD/xhtml1-transitional.dtd">
<html xmlns="http://www.w3.org/1999/xhtml">
<head>
    <title>Professional ASP.NET 2.0</title>
</head>
<body>
    <h3>Professional Ajax, 2nd Edition</h3>
    <strong>Subjects</strong><br />
    Ajax<br />
    Internet<br />
    JavaScript<br />
    ASP.NET<br />
    PHP<br />
    XML<br />
    <hr color="#cc3333" />
    <h3>Book overview</h3>
    <p>
        A comprehensive look at the technologies and techniques used in Ajax,
        complete with real world examples and case studies. A must have for
        any Web professional looking to build interactive Web sites.
    </p>
</body>
</html>
```

Save this as pro_ajax_details.htm.

```html
<!DOCTYPE html PUBLIC "-//W3C//DTD XHTML 1.0 Transitional//EN"
    "http://www.w3.org/TR/xhtml1/DTD/xhtml1-transitional.dtd">
<html xmlns="http://www.w3.org/1999/xhtml">
<head>
    <title>Professional JavaScript</title>
</head>
<body>
    <h3>Professional JavaScript, 2nd Edition</h3>
    <strong>Subjects</strong><br />
    ECMAScript<br />
    Internet<br />
    JavaScript
    <br />
    XML and Scripting<br />
    <hr color="#cc3333" />
    <p>
        This book takes a comprehensive look at the JavaScript language
        and prepares the reader in-depth knowledge of the languages.
    </p>
```

```
<p>
    It includes a guide to the language - when where and how to get
    the most out of JavaScript - together with practical case studies
    demonstrating JavaScript in action. Coverage is bang up-to-date,
    with discussion of compatability issues and version differences,
    and the book concludes with a comprehensive reference section.
</p>
</body>
</html>
```

Save the final page as `pro_js_details.htm`.

Load `ch08_examp4.htm` into your browser and click either of the two images. A new window containing the book's details should appear above the existing browser window. Click the other book image, and the window will be replaced by one containing the details of that book.

The files `pro_ajax_details.htm` and `pro_js_details.htm` are both plain HTML files, so you won't look at them. However, in `ch08_examp4.htm` you find some scripting action, which you *will* look at here.

In the script block at the top of the page, you first define the variable `detailsWindow`.

```
var detailsWindow;
```

You then have the function that actually opens the new windows.

```
function showDetails(bookURL)
{
    detailsWindow = window.open(bookURL,"bookDetails","width=400,height=350");
    detailsWindow.focus();

}
```

This function is connected to the `onclick` event handlers of book images that appear later in the page. The parameter `bookURL` is passed by the code in the `onclick` event handler and will be either `pro_ajax_details.htm` or `pro_js_details.htm`.

You create the new window with the `window.open()` method. You pass the `bookURL` parameter as the URL to be opened. You pass `bookDetails` as the name you want applied to the new window. If the window already exists, another new window won't be opened, and the existing one will be navigated to the URL that you pass. This only occurs because you are using the same name (`bookDetails`) when opening the window for each book. If you had used a different name, a new window would be opened.

By storing the reference to the `window` object just created in the variable `detailsWindow`, you can access its methods and properties. On the next line, you'll see that you use the `window` object, referenced by `detailsWindow`, to set the focus to the new window — otherwise it will appear behind the existing window if you click the same image in the main window more than once.

Although you are using the same function for each of the image's `onclick` event handlers, you pass a different parameter for each, namely the URL of the details page for the book in question.

```
<h4>Professional Ajax</h4>
<p>
    <img src="pro_ajax.jpg" alt="Professional Ajax, 2nd Edition" border="0"
        onclick="showDetails('pro_ajax_details.htm')" />
```

```
</p>
<h4>Professional JavaScript for Web Developers</h4>
<p>
    <img src="pro_js.jpg" alt="Professional JavaScript, 2nd Edition" border="0"
        onclick="showDetails('pro_js_details.htm')" />
</p>
```

Adding HTML to a New Window

You learned earlier that you can pass an empty string as the first parameter of the window object's open() method and then write to the page using HTML. Let's see how you would do that.

First, you need to open a blank window by passing an empty value to the first parameter that specifies the file name to load.

```
var newWindow = window.open("","myNewWindow","width=150,height=150");
```

Now you can open the window's document to receive your HTML.

```
newWindow.document.open();
```

This is not essential when a new window is opened, because the page is blank; but with a document that already contains HTML, it has the effect of clearing out all existing HTML and blanking the page, making it ready for writing.

Now you can write out any valid HTML using the document.write() method.

```
newWindow.document.write("<h4>Hello</h4>");
newWindow.document.write("<p>Welcome to my new little window</p>");
```

Each time you use the write() method, the text is added to what's already there until you use the document.close() method.

```
newWindow.document.close();
```

If you then use the document.write() method again, the text passed will replace existing HTML rather than adding to it.

Adding Features to Your Windows

As you have seen, the window.open() method takes three parameters, and it's the third of these parameters that you'll be looking at in this section. Using this third parameter, you can control things such as the size of the new window created, its start position on the screen, whether the user can resize it, whether it has a toolbar, and so on.

Features such as menu bar, status bar, and toolbar can be switched on or off with yes or 1 for on and no or 0 for off. You can also switch these features on by including their names without specifying a value.

The list of possible options shown in the following table is not complete, and not all of them work with both IE and Firefox browsers.

Window Feature	Possible Values	Description
copyHistory	yes, no	Copy the history of the window doing the opening to the new window
directories	yes, no	Show directory buttons
height	integer	Height of new window in pixels
left	integer	Window's offset from left of screen.
location	yes, no	Show location text field
menubar	yes, no	Show menu bar
resizable	yes, no	Enable the user to resize the window after it has been opened
scrollbars	yes, no	Show scrollbars if the page is too large to fit in the window
status	yes, no	Show status bar
toolbar	yes, no	Show toolbar
top	integer	Window's offset from top of screen.
width	integer	Width of new window in pixels

As mentioned earlier, this third parameter is optional. If you don't include it, then all of the window features default to yes, except the window's size and position properties, which default to preset values. For example, if you try the following code, you'll see a window something like the one shown in Figure 8-10:

```
<!DOCTYPE html PUBLIC "-//W3C//DTD XHTML 1.0 Transitional//EN"
    "http://www.w3.org/TR/xhtml1/DTD/xhtml1-transitional.dtd">

<html xmlns="http://www.w3.org/1999/xhtml">
<head>
    <script type="text/javascript">
    var newWindow;
    newWindow = window.open("","myWindow");
    </script>
</head>
<body>
</body>
</html>
```

Location

Status

Figure 8-10

Figure 8-10 is of IE8. The default UI hides the menu and toolbars; so as long as the default settings are in effect, opened windows will not show the menu and toolbars.

However, if you specify even one of the features, all the others (except size and position properties) are set to no by default. For example, although you have defined its size, the following code produces a window with no features, as shown in Figure 8-11:

```
var newWindow = window.open("","myWindow","width=200,height=120")
```

The larger window is the original page, and the smaller one on top (shown in Figure 8-11) is the pop-up window.

Figure 8-11

Let's see another example. The following creates a resizable 250-by-250-pixel window, with a location field and menu bar:

```
var newWindow = window.open("","myWindow",
                     "width=250,height=250,location,menubar,resizable");
```

A word of warning, however: Never include spaces inside the features string; otherwise some browsers will consider the string invalid and ignore your settings.

Scripting Between Windows

You've taken a brief look at how you can manipulate the new window's properties and methods, and access its document object using the return value from the window.open() method. Now you're going to look at how the newly opened window can access the window that opened it and, just as with frames, how it can use functions there.

The key to accessing the window object of the window that opened the new window is the window object's opener property. This returns a reference to the window object of the window that opened the new window. So the following code will change the background color of the opener window to red:

```
window.opener.document.bgColor = "red";
```

You can use the reference pretty much as you used the window.parent and window.top properties when using frames.

Try It Out   Inter-Window Scripting

Let's look at an example wherein you open a new window and access a form on the opener window from the new window.

```
<!DOCTYPE html PUBLIC "-//W3C//DTD XHTML 1.0 Transitional//EN"
    "http://www.w3.org/TR/xhtml1/DTD/xhtml1-transitional.dtd">

<html xmlns="http://www.w3.org/1999/xhtml">
<head>
    <title>Chapter 8: Example 5</title>
    <script type="text/javascript">
    var newWindow;
    function btnOpenWin_onclick()
    {
        var winTop = (screen.height / 2) - 125;
        var winLeft = (screen.width / 2) - 125;
        var windowFeatures = "width=250,height=250,";
        windowFeatures = windowFeatures + "left=" + winLeft + ",";
        windowFeatures = windowFeatures + "top=" + winTop;
        newWindow = window.open("ch08_examp5_popup.htm", "myWindow",
            windowFeatures);
    }
    function btnGetText_onclick()
    {
```

```
        if (typeof (newWindow) == "undefined" || newWindow.closed == true)
        {
            alert("No window is open");
        }
        else
        {
            document.form1.text1.value = newWindow.document.form1.text1.value;
        }
    }

    function window_onunload()
    {
        if (typeof (newWindow) != "undefined" && newWindow.closed == false)
        {
            newWindow.close();
        }
    }
    </script>
</head>
<body onunload="window_onunload()">
    <form name="form1" action="">
        <input type="button" value="Open newWindow" name="btnOpenWin"
            onclick="btnOpenWin_onclick()" />
        <p>
            newWindow's Text:<br />
            <input type="text" name="text1" />
            <input type="button" value="Get Text" name="btnGetText"
                onclick="btnGetText_onclick()" />
        </p>
    </form>
</body>
</html>
```

This is the code for your original window. Save it as ch08_examp5.htm. Now you'll look at the page that will be loaded by the opener window.

```
<!DOCTYPE html PUBLIC "-//W3C//DTD XHTML 1.0 Transitional//EN"
    "http://www.w3.org/TR/xhtml1/DTD/xhtml1-transitional.dtd">
<html xmlns="http://www.w3.org/1999/xhtml">
<head>
    <title>Chapter 8: Example 5 Popup</title>
    <script type="text/javascript">
    function btnGetText_onclick()
    {
        document.form1.text1.value = window.opener.document.form1.text1.value;
    }
    </script>
</head>
<body>
    <form name="form1" action="">
        Opener window's text<br />
        <input type="text" name="text1" />
```

```
                <input type="button" value="Get Text" name="btnGetText"
                       onclick="btnGetText_onclick()" />
        </form>
    </body>
</html>
```

Save this as ch08_examp5_popup.htm.

Open ch08_examp5.htm in your browser, and you'll see a page with the simple form shown in Figure 8-12.

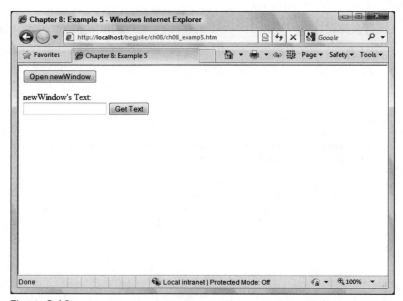

Figure 8-12

Click the Open newWindow button, and you'll see the window shown in Figure 8-13 open above the original page.

Figure 8-13

Type something into the text box of the new window. Then return to the original opener window, click the Get Text button, and you'll see what you just typed into newWindow appear in the text box on the opener window's form.

Change the text in the opener window's text box and then return to the newWindow and click the Get Text button. The text you typed into the opener window's text box will appear in newWindow's text box.

Let's look at the opener window first. In the head of the page is a script block in which a variable and three functions are defined. At the top you have declared a new variable, newWindow, which will hold the window object reference returned by the window.open() method you'll use later. Being outside any function gives this variable a global scope, so you can access it from any function on the page.

```
var newWindow;
```

Then you have the first of the three functions in this page, btnOpenWin_onclick(), which is connected further down the page to the Open newWindow button's onclick event handler. Its purpose is simply to open the new window.

Rather than have the new window open up anywhere on the page, you use the built-in screen object, which is a property of the window object, to find out the resolution of the user's display and place the window in the middle of the screen. The screen object has a number of read-only properties, but you're interested here in the width and height properties. You initialize the winTop variable to the vertical position onscreen at which you want the top edge of the popup window to appear. The winLeft variable is set to the horizontal position onscreen at which you want the left edge of the pop-up window to appear. In this case, you want the position to be in the middle of the screen both horizontally and vertically.

```
function btnOpenWin_onclick()
{
    var winTop = (screen.height / 2) - 125;
    var winLeft = (screen.width / 2) - 125;
```

You build up a string for the window features and store it in the windowFeatures variable. You set the width and height to 250 and then use the winLeft and winTop variables you just populated to create the initial start positions of the window.

```
var windowFeatures = "width=250,height=250,";
windowFeatures = windowFeatures + "left=" + winLeft + ",";
windowFeatures = windowFeatures + "top=" + winTop;
```

Finally, you open the new window, making sure you put the return value from window.open() into global variable newWindow so you can manipulate it later.

```
newWindow = window.open("newWindow.htm","myWindow",windowFeatures);
}
```

The next function is used to obtain the text from the text box on the form in newWindow.

In this function you use an if statement to check two things. First, you check that newWindow is defined and second, that the window is actually open. You check because you don't want to try to access a non-existent window, for example if no window has been opened or a window has been closed by the user. The typeof operator returns the type of information held in a variable, for example number, string, Boolean, object, and undefined. It returns undefined if the variable has never been given a value, as newWindow won't have been if no new window has been opened.

Having confirmed that a window has been opened at some point, you now need to check whether it's still open, and the `window` object's `closed` property does just that. If it returns `true`, the window is closed, and if it returns `false`, it's still open. (Do not confuse this `closed` property with the `close()` method you saw previously.)

In the `if` statement, you'll see that checking if `newWindow` is defined comes first, and this is no accident. If `newWindow` really were undefined, `newWindow.closed` would cause an error, because there are no data inside `newWindow`. However, you are taking advantage of the fact that if an `if` statement's condition will be `true` or `false` at a certain point regardless of the remainder of the condition, the remainder of the condition is not checked.

```
function butGetText_onclick()
{
    if (typeof(newWindow) == "undefined" || newWindow.closed == true)
    {
        alert("No window is open");
    }
```

If `newWindow` exists and is open, the `else` statement's code will execute. Remember that `newWindow` will contain a reference to the `window` object of the window opened. This means you can access the form in `newWindow`, just as you'd access a form on the page the script's running in, by using the document object inside the `newWindow` window object.

```
    else
    {
        document.form1.text1.value = newWindow.document.form1.text1.value;
    }
}
```

The last of the three functions is `window_onunload()`, which is connected to the `onunload` event of this page and fires when either the browser window is closed or the user navigates to another page. In the `window_onunload()` function, you check to see if `newWindow` is valid and open in much the same way that you just did. You must check to see if the `newWindow` variable is defined first. With the `&&` operator, JavaScript checks the second part of the operation only if the first part evaluates to `true`. If `newWindow` is defined, and does therefore hold a `window` object (even though it's possibly a closed window), you can check the `closed` property of the window. However, if `newWindow` is undefined, the check for its `closed` property won't happen, and no errors will occur. If you check the `closed` property first and `newWindow` is undefined, an error will occur, because an undefined variable has no `closed` property.

```
function window_onunload()
{
    if (typeof(newWindow) != "undefined" && newWindow.closed == false)
    {
        newWindow.close();
    }
}
```

If `newWindow` is defined and open, you close it. This prevents the `newWindow`'s Get Text button from being clicked when there is no opener window in existence to get text from (since this function fires when the opener window is closed).

Let's now look at the code for the page that will be loaded in the newWindow: ch08_examp5_popup.htm. This page contains one function, btnGetText_onclick(), which is connected to the onclick event handler of the Get Text button in the page. It retrieves the text from the opener window's text box.

```
function btnGetText_onclick()
{
    document.form1.text1.value = window.opener.document.form1.text1.value;
}
```

In this function, you use the window.opener property to get a reference to the window object of the window that opened this one, and then use that reference to get the value out of the text box in the form in that window. This value is placed inside the text box in the current page.

Moving and Resizing Windows

In addition to opening and closing windows, it's also possible to move and resize windows.

After opening a window, you can change its onscreen position and its size using the window object's resizeTo() and moveTo() methods, both of which take two arguments in pixels.

Consider the following code that opens a new window:

```
var newWindow = window.open(myURL, "myWindow", "width=125,height=150,resizable");
```

You want to make it 350 pixels wide by 200 pixels high and move it to a position 100 pixels from the left of the screen and 400 pixels from the top. What code would you need?

```
newWindow.resizeTo(350,200);
newWindow.moveTo(100,400);
```

You can see that you can resize your window to 350 pixels wide by 200 pixels high using resizeTo(). Then you move it so it's 100 pixels from the left of the screen and 400 pixels from the top of the screen using moveTo().

The window object also has resizeBy() and moveBy() methods. Both of these methods accept two parameters, in pixels. For example:

```
newWindow.resizeBy(100,200);
```

This code will increase the size of newWindow by 100 pixels horizontally and 200 pixels vertically. Similarly, the following code moves the newWindow by 20 pixels horizontally and 50 pixels vertically:

```
newWindow.moveBy(20,50);
```

When using these methods, you must bear in mind that users can manually resize these windows if they so wish. In addition, the size of the client's screen in pixels will vary between users.

Security

Browsers put certain restrictions on what information scripts can access between frames and windows.

If all the pages in these frames and windows are served from the same server, or on the same computer when you're loading them into the browser locally, as you are in these examples, you have a reasonably free rein over what your scripts can access and do. However, some restrictions do exist. For example, if you try to use the `window.close()` method in a script page loaded into a browser window that the user opened, as opposed to a window opened by your script, a message box will appear giving the user the option of canceling your `close()` method and keeping the window open.

When a page in one window or frame hosted on one server tries to access the properties of a window or frame that contains a page from a different server, the same-origin policy comes into play, and you'll find yourself very restricted as to what your scripts can do.

Imagine you have a page hosted on a web server whose URL is `http://www.myserver.com`. Inside the page is the following script:

```
var myWindow =
    window.open("http://www.anotherserver.com/anotherpage.htm","myWindow");
```

Now you have two windows, one that is hosted at `www.myserver.com` and another that is hosted on a different server, `www.anotherserver.com`. Although this code does work, the same-origin policy prevents any access to the `document` object of one page from another. For example, the following code in the opener page will cause a security problem and will be prevented by the browser:

```
var myVariable = myWindow.document.form1.text1.value;
```

Although you do have access to the `window` object of the page on the other server, you have access to a limited subset of its properties and methods.

The same-origin restriction applies to frames (conventional and iframes) and windows equally. The idea behind it is very sound: It is there to prevent hackers from putting your pages inside their own and extracting information by using code inside their pages. However, the restrictions are fairly severe, perhaps too severe, and mean that you should avoid scripting across frames or windows if the pages are hosted on different servers.

Summary

For various reasons, having a frame-based web site can prove very useful. Therefore, you need to be able to create JavaScript that can interact with frames and with the documents and code within those frames.

- ❑ You saw that an advantage of frames is that, by putting all of your general functions in a single frame, you can create a JavaScript code module that all of your web site can use.

- ❑ You saw that the key to coding with frames is getting a reference to the `window` objects of other frames. You saw two ways of accessing frames higher in the hierarchy, using the `window` object's `parent` property and its `top` property.

❑ The `parent` property returns the `window` object that contains the current `window` object, which will be the page containing the frameset that created the window. The `top` property returns the `window` object of the window containing all the other frames.

❑ Each frame in a frameset can be accessed through three methods. One is to use the name of the frame. The second is to use the `frames` collection and specify the index of the frame. The third way is to access the frame by its name in the frames collection — for example, `parent.frames.frameName`. This the safest way, because it avoids any collision with global variables.

❑ If the frame you want to access is defined in another window, you need the `parent` or `top` property to get a reference to the `window` object defining that frame, and then you must specify the name or position in the `frames` collection.

You then looked at how you can open new, additional browser windows using script.

❑ Using the `window` object's `open()` method, you can open new windows. The URL of the page you want to open is passed as the first parameter; the name of the new window is passed as the second parameter; the optional third parameter enables you to define what features the new window will have.

❑ The `window.open()` method returns a value, which is a reference to the `window` object of the new window. Using this reference, you can access the document, script, and methods of that window, much as you do with frames. You need to make sure that the reference is stored inside a variable if you want to do this.

❑ To close a window, you simply use the `window.close()` method. To check if a window is closed, you use the `closed` property of the `window` object, which returns `true` if it's closed and `false` if it's still open.

❑ For a newly opened `window` object to access the window that opened it, you need to use the `window.opener` property. Like `window.parent` for frames, this gives a reference to the `window` object that opened the new one and enables you to access the `window` object and its properties for that window.

❑ After a window is opened, you can resize it using `resizeTo(x,y)` and `resizeBy(x,y)`, and move it using `moveTo(x,y)` and `moveBy(x,y)`.

You also looked briefly at security restrictions for windows and frames that are not of the same origin. By "not of the same origin," you're referring to a situation in which the document in one frame is hosted on one server and the document in the other is hosted on a different server. In this situation, very severe restrictions apply, which limit the extent of scripting between frames or windows.

In the next chapter, you look at advanced string manipulation.

Exercise Questions

Suggested solutions to these questions can be found in Appendix A.

1. In the previous chapter's exercise questions, you created a form that allowed the user to pick a computer system. They could view the details of their system and its total cost by clicking a button that wrote the details to a `textarea`. Change the example so it's a frames-based web page; instead of writing to a text area, the application should write the details to another frame. Hint: use about:blank as the src of the frame you write to. Hint: use the document object's close() and open() methods to clear the details frame from previously written data.

2. The fourth example (ch08.examp4.htm) was a page with images of books, in which clicking on a book's image brought up information about that book in a pop-up window. Amend this so that the pop-up window also has a button or link that, when clicked, adds the item to a shopping basket. Also, on the main page, give the user some way of opening up a shopping basket window with details of all the items they have purchased so far, and give them a way of deleting items from this basket.

String Manipulation

In Chapter 4 you looked at the String object, which is one of the native objects that JavaScript makes available to you. You saw a number of its properties and methods, including the following:

- ❑ length — The length of the string in characters

- ❑ charAt() and charCodeAt() — The methods for returning the character or character code at a certain position in the string

- ❑ indexOf() and lastIndexOf() — The methods that allow you to search a string for the existence of another string and that return the character position of the string if found

- ❑ substr() and substring() — The methods that return just a portion of a string

- ❑ toUpperCase() and toLowerCase() — The methods that return a string converted to upper- or lowercase

In this chapter you'll look at four new methods of the String object, namely split(), match(), replace(), and search(). The last three, in particular, give you some very powerful text-manipulation functionality. However, to make full use of this functionality, you need to learn about a slightly more complex subject.

The methods split(), match(), replace(), and search() can all make use of *regular expressions*, something JavaScript wraps up in an object called the RegExp object. Regular expressions enable you to define a pattern of characters, which can be used for text searching or replacement. Say, for example, that you have a string in which you want to replace all single quotes enclosing text with double quotes. This may seem easy — just search the string for ' and replace it with " — but what if the string is Bob O'Hara said "Hello"? You would not want to replace the single-quote character in O'Hara. You can perform this text replacement without regular expressions, but it would take more than the two lines of code needed if you do use regular expressions.

Although split(), match(), replace(), and search() are at their most powerful with regular expressions, they can also be used with just plain text. You'll take a look at how they work in this simpler context first, to become familiar with the methods.

Additional String Methods

In this section you will take a look at the split(), replace(), search(), and match() methods, and see how they work without regular expressions.

The split() Method

The String object's split() method splits a single string into an array of substrings. Where the string is split is determined by the separation parameter that you pass to the method. This parameter is simply a character or text string.

For example, to split the string "A,B,C" so that you have an array populated with the letters between the commas, the code would be as follows:

```
var myString = "A,B,C";
var myTextArray = myString.split(',');
```

JavaScript creates an array with three elements. In the first element it puts everything from the start of the string myString up to the first comma. In the second element it puts everything from after the first comma to before the second comma. Finally, in the third element it puts everything from after the second comma to the end of the string. So, your array myTextArray will look like this:

A	B	C

If, however, your string were "A,B,C," JavaScript would split it into four elements, the last element containing everything from the last comma to the end of the string; in other words, the last string would be an empty string.

A	B	C	

This is something that can catch you off guard if you're not aware of it.

Try It Out   **Reversing the Order of Text**

Let's create a short example using the split() method, in which you reverse the lines written in a `<textarea>` element.

```
<!DOCTYPE html PUBLIC "-//W3C//DTD XHTML 1.0 Transitional//EN"
"http://www.w3.org/TR/xhtml1/DTD/xhtml1-transitional.dtd">
<html xmlns="http://www.w3.org/1999/xhtml">

<head>
<meta http-equiv="Content-Type" content="text/html; charset=utf-8" />
<title>Example 1</title>
<script language="JavaScript" type="text/JavaScript">
function splitAndReverseText(textAreaControl)
{
```

```
    var textToSplit = textAreaControl.value;
    var textArray = textToSplit.split('\n');
    var numberOfParts = 0;
    numberOfParts = textArray.length;
    var reversedString = "";
    var indexCount;
    for (indexCount = numberOfParts - 1; indexCount >= 0; indexCount--)
    {
        reversedString = reversedString + textArray[indexCount];
        if (indexCount > 0)
        {
            reversedString = reversedString + "\n";
        }
    }

    textAreaControl.value = reversedString;
}
</script>
</head>
<body>
<form name="form1">
<textarea rows="20" cols="40" name="textarea1" wrap="soft">Line 1
Line 2
Line 3
Line 4</textarea>
<br />
<input type="button" value="Reverse Line Order" name="buttonSplit"
    onclick="splitAndReverseText(document.form1.textarea1)">
</form>
</body>
</html>
```

Save this as ch9_examp1.htm and load it into your browser. You should see the screen shown in Figure 9-1.

Figure 9-1

Clicking the Reverse Line Order button reverses the order of the lines, as shown in Figure 9-2.

Figure 9-2

Try changing the lines within the text area to test it further.

> *Although this example works on Internet Explorer (IE) as it is, an extra line gets inserted. If this troubles you, you can fix it by replacing each instance of* \n *with* \r\n *for IE.*

The key to how this code works is the function `splitAndReverseText()`. This function is defined in the script block in the head of the page and is connected to the `onclick` event handler of the button further down the page.

```
<input type="button" value="Reverse Line Order" name=buttonSplit
    onclick="splitAndReverseText(document.form1.textarea1)">
```

As you can see, you pass a reference of the text area that you want to reverse as a parameter to the function. By doing it this way, rather than just using a reference to the element itself inside the function, you make the function more generic, so you can use it with any `textarea` element.

Now, on with the function. You start by assigning the value of the text inside the `textarea` element to the `textToSplit` variable. You then split that string into an array of lines of text using the `split()` method of the `String` object and put the resulting array inside the `textArray` variable.

```
function splitAndReverseText(textAreaControl)
{
    var textToSplit = textAreaControl.value;
    var textArray = textToSplit.split('\n');
```

So what do you use as the separator to pass as a parameter for the `split()` method? Recall from Chapter 2 that the escape character \n is used for a new line. Another point to add to the confusion is that IE seems to need \r\n rather than \n.

You next define and initialize three more variables.

```
        var numberOfParts = 0;
        numberOfParts = textArray.length;
        var reversedString = "";
        var indexCount;
```

Now that you have your array of strings, you next want to reverse them. You do this by building up a new string, adding each string from the array, starting with the last and working toward the first. You do this in the `for` loop, where instead of starting at 0 and working up as you usually do, you start at a number greater than 0 and decrement until you reach 0, at which point you stop looping.

```
for (indexCount = numberOfParts - 1; indexCount >= 0; indexCount--)
{
    reversedString = reversedString + textArray[indexCount];
    if (indexCount > 0)
    {
        reversedString = reversedString + "\n";
    }
}
```

Finally, you assign the text in the `textarea` element to the new string you've built.

```
    textAreaControl.value = reversedString;
}
```

After you've looked at regular expressions, you'll revisit the `split()` method.

The replace() Method

The `replace()` method searches a string for occurrences of a substring. Where it finds a match for this substring, it replaces the substring with a third string that you specify.

Let's look at an example. Say you have a string with the word May in it, as shown in the following:

```
var myString = "The event will be in May, the 21st of June";
```

Now, say you want to replace May with June. You can use the `replace()` method like so:

```
myCleanedUpString = myString.replace("May","June");
```

The value of `myString` will not be changed. Instead, the `replace()` method returns the value of `myString` but with May replaced with June. You assign this returned string to the variable `myCleanedUpString`, which will contain the corrected text.

```
"The event will be in June, the 21st of June"
```

The search() Method

The `search()` method enables you to search a string for a particular piece of text. If the text is found, the character position at which it was found is returned; otherwise −1 is returned. The method takes only one parameter, namely the text you want to search for.

When used with plain text, the `search()` method provides no real benefit over methods like `indexOf()`, which you've already seen. However, you'll see later that it's when you use regular expressions that the power of this method becomes apparent.

In the following example, you want to find out if the word Java is contained within the string called `myString`.

```
var myString = "Beginning JavaScript, Beginning Java, Professional JavaScript";
alert(myString.search("Java"));
```

The alert box that occurs will show the value 10, which is the character position of the J in the first occurrence of Java, as part of the word JavaScript.

The match() Method

The `match()` method is very similar to the `search()` method, except that instead of returning the position at which a match was found, it returns an array. Each element of the array contains the text of each match that is found.

Although you can use plain text with the `match()` method, it would be completely pointless to do so. For example, take a look at the following:

```
var myString = "1997, 1998, 1999, 2000, 2000, 2001, 2002";
myMatchArray = myString.match("2000");
alert(myMatchArray.length);
```

This code results in `myMatchArray` holding an element containing the value 2000. Given that you already know your search string is 2000, you can see it's been a pretty pointless exercise.

However, the `match()` method makes a lot more sense when you use it with regular expressions. Then you might search for all years in the twenty-first century — that is, those beginning with 2. In this case, your array would contain the values 2000, 2000, 2001, and 2002, which is much more useful information!

Regular Expressions

Before you look at the `split()`, `match()`, `search()`, and `replace()` methods of the `String` object again, you need to look at regular expressions and the `RegExp` object. Regular expressions provide a means of defining a pattern of characters, which you can then use to split, search for, or replace characters in a string when they fit the defined pattern.

JavaScript's regular expression syntax borrows heavily from the regular expression syntax of Perl, another scripting language. The latest versions of languages, such as VBScript, have also incorporated regular expressions, as do lots of applications, such as Microsoft Word, in which the Find facility allows regular expressions to be used. The same is true for Dreamweaver. You'll find that your regular expression knowledge will prove useful even outside JavaScript.

Regular expressions in JavaScript are used through the `RegExp` object, which is a native JavaScript object, as are `String`, `Array`, and so on. There are two ways of creating a new `RegExp` object. The easier is with a regular expression literal, such as the following:

```
var myRegExp = /\b'|'\b/;
```

The forward slashes (/) mark the start and end of the regular expression. This is a special syntax that tells JavaScript that the code is a regular expression, much as quote marks define a string's start and end. Don't worry about the actual expression's syntax yet (the \b'|'\b) — that will be explained in detail shortly.

Alternatively, you could use the RegExp object's constructor function RegExp() and type the following:

```
var myRegExp = new RegExp("\\b'|'\\b");
```

Either way of specifying a regular expression is fine, though the former method is a shorter, more efficient one for JavaScript to use and therefore is generally preferred. For much of the remainder of the chapter, you'll use the first method. The main reason for using the second method is that it allows the regular expression to be determined at runtime (as the code is executing and not when you are writing the code). This is useful if, for example, you want to base the regular expression on user input.

Once you get familiar with regular expressions, you will come back to the second way of defining them, using the RegExp() constructor. As you can see, the syntax of regular expressions is slightly different with the second method, so we'll return to this subject later.

Although you'll be concentrating on the use of the RegExp object as a parameter for the String object's split(), replace(), match(), and search() methods, the RegExp object does have its own methods and properties. For example, the test() method enables you to test to see if the string passed to it as a parameter contains a pattern matching the one defined in the RegExp object. You'll see the test() method in use in an example shortly.

Simple Regular Expressions

Defining patterns of characters using regular expression syntax can get fairly complex. In this section you'll explore just the basics of regular expression patterns. The best way to do this is through examples.

Let's start by looking at an example in which you want to do a simple text replacement using the replace() method and a regular expression. Imagine you have the following string:

```
var myString = "Paul, Paula, Pauline, paul, Paul";
```

and you want to replace any occurrence of the name "Paul" with "Ringo."

Well, the pattern of text you need to look for is simply Paul. Representing this as a regular expression, you just have this:

```
var myRegExp = /Paul/;
```

As you saw earlier, the forward-slash characters mark the start and end of the regular expression. Now let's use this expression with the replace() method.

```
myString = myString.replace(myRegExp, "Ringo");
```

You can see that the replace() method takes two parameters: the RegExp object that defines the pattern to be searched and replaced, and the replacement text.

If you put this all together in an example, you have the following:

```
<!DOCTYPE html PUBLIC "-//W3C//DTD XHTML 1.0 Transitional//EN"
"http://www.w3.org/TR/xhtml1/DTD/xhtml1-transitional.dtd">
<html xmlns="http://www.w3.org/1999/xhtml">
<body>
<script language="JavaScript" type="text/JavaScript">
  var myString = "Paul, Paula, Pauline, paul, Paul";
  var myRegExp = /Paul/;
  myString = myString.replace(myRegExp, "Ringo");
  alert(myString);
</script>
</body>
</html>
```

If you load this code into a browser, you will see the screen shown in Figure 9-3.

Figure 9-3

You can see that this has replaced the first occurrence of `Paul` in your string. But what if you wanted all the occurrences of `Paul` in the string to be replaced? The two at the far end of the string are still there, so what happened?

By default, the `RegExp` object looks only for the first matching pattern, in this case the first `Paul`, and then stops. This is a common and important behavior for `RegExp` objects. Regular expressions tend to start at one end of a string and look through the characters until the first complete match is found, then stop.

What you want is a global match, which is a search for all possible matches to be made and replaced. To help you out, the `RegExp` object has three attributes you can define. You can see these listed in the following table.

Attribute Character	Description
G	Global match. This looks for all matches of the pattern rather than stopping after the first match is found.
I	Pattern is case-insensitive. For example, `Paul` and `paul` are considered the same pattern of characters.
M	Multi-line flag. Only available in IE 5.5+ and NN 6+, this specifies that the special characters ^ and $ can match the beginning and the end of lines as well as the beginning and end of the string. You'll learn about these characters later in the chapter.

If you change the `RegExp` object in the code to the following, a global case-insensitive match will be made.

```
var myRegExp = /Paul/gi;
```

Running the code now produces the result shown in Figure 9-4.

Figure 9-4

This looks as if it has all gone horribly wrong. The regular expression has matched the `Paul` substrings at the start and the end of the string, and the penultimate `paul`, just as you wanted. However, the `Paul` substrings inside `Pauline` and `Paula` have also been replaced.

The `RegExp` object has done its job correctly. You asked for all patterns of the characters `Paul` to be replaced and that's what you got. What you actually meant was for all occurrences of `Paul`, when it's a single word and not part of another word, such as `Paula`, to be replaced. The key to making regular expressions work is to define exactly the pattern of characters you mean, so that only that pattern can match and no other. So let's do that.

1. You want `paul` or `Paul` to be replaced.

2. You don't want it replaced when it's actually part of another word, as in `Pauline`.

How do you specify this second condition? How do you know when the word is joined to other characters, rather than just joined to spaces or punctuation or the start or end of the string?

To see how you can achieve the desired result with regular expressions, you need to enlist the help of regular expression special characters. You'll look at these in the next section, by the end of which you should be able to solve the problem.

Try It Out   Regular Expression Tester

Getting your regular expression syntax correct can take some thought and time, so in this exercise you'll create a simple regular expression tester to make life easier.

Type the following code in to your text editor and save it as `ch9_examp2.htm`:

```
<!DOCTYPE html PUBLIC "-//W3C//DTD XHTML 1.0 Transitional//EN"
"http://www.w3.org/TR/xhtml1/DTD/xhtml1-transitional.dtd">
<html xmlns="http://www.w3.org/1999/xhtml">
<head>
<meta http-equiv="Content-Type" content="text/html; charset=utf-8" />
<title>Regular Expression Tester</title>
<style type="text/css">

body,td,th {
        font-family: Arial, Helvetica, sans-serif;
```

```
        }

</style>

<script type="text/javascript">

function getRegExpFlags()
{
        var regExpFlags = '';
        if ( document.form1.chkGlobal.checked )
        {
                regExpFlags = 'g';
        }

        if ( document.form1.chkCaseInsensitive.checked )
        {
                regExpFlags += 'i';
        }

        if ( document.form1.chkMultiLine.checked )
        {
                regExpFlags += 'm';
        }

        return regExpFlags;

}

function doTest()
{
        var testRegExp = new RegExp(document.form1.txtRegularExpression.value,
 getRegExpFlags());
        if ( testRegExp.test(document.form1.txtTestString.value) )
        {
                document.form1.txtTestResult.value = "Match Found!";
        }
        else
        {
                document.form1.txtTestResult.value = "Match NOT Found!";
        }
}

function findMatches()
{
        var testRegExp = new RegExp(document.form1.txtRegularExpression.value,
getRegExpFlags());
        var myTestString = new String(document.form1.txtTestString.value)
        var matchArray = myTestString.match(testRegExp);

        document.form1.txtTestResult.value = matchArray.join('\n');

}

</script>

</head>
```

```
<body>

<form id="form1" name="form1" method="post" action="">
  <p>
    Regular Expression:<br />
<label>
    <input name="txtRegularExpression" type="text" id="txtRegularExpression"
size="100" value=""/>
    <br />
    Global
    <input name="chkGlobal" type="checkbox" id="chkGlobal" value="true" />
</label>

  Case Insensitive
  <label>
    <input name="chkCaseInsensitive" type="checkbox" id="chkCaseInsensitive"
value="true" />
  </label>

  Multi Line
  <label>
    <input name="chkMultiLine" type="checkbox" id="chkMultiLine" value="true" />
  </label>
  </p>
  <p>
    <label>
      Test Text:<br />
      <textarea name="txtTestString" id="txtTestString" cols="100"
rows="8"></textarea>
    </label>
  </p>
  <p>Result:<br />
    <textarea name="txtTestResult" id="txtTestResult" cols="100"
rows="8"></textarea>
  </p>
  <p>
    <label>
      <input type="button" name="cmdTest" id="cmdTest" value="TEST"
onclick="doTest();"/>
    </label>
    <label>
      <input type="button" name="cmdMatch" id="cmdMatch" value="MATCH"
onclick="findMatches();" />
    </label>
    <label>
      <input type="reset" name="cmdClearForm" id="cmdClearForm" value="Reset Form"
 />
    </label>
  </p>
  <p> </p>
</form>
</body>
</html>
```

Load the page into your browser, and you'll see the screen shown in Figure 9-5.

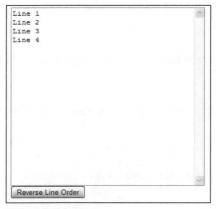

Figure 9-5

In the top box, you enter your regular expression. You can set the attributes such as global and case sensitivity by ticking the tick boxes. The text to test the regular expression against goes in the Test Text box, and the result is displayed in the Result box.

As a test, enter the regular expression \d{3}, which as you'll discover shortly, will match three digits. Also tick the Global box so all the matches will be found. Finally, your test text is ABC123DEF456GHI789.

If you click the Test button, the code will test to see if there are any matches (that is, if the test text contains three numbers). The result, as you can see in Figure 9-6, is that a match is found.

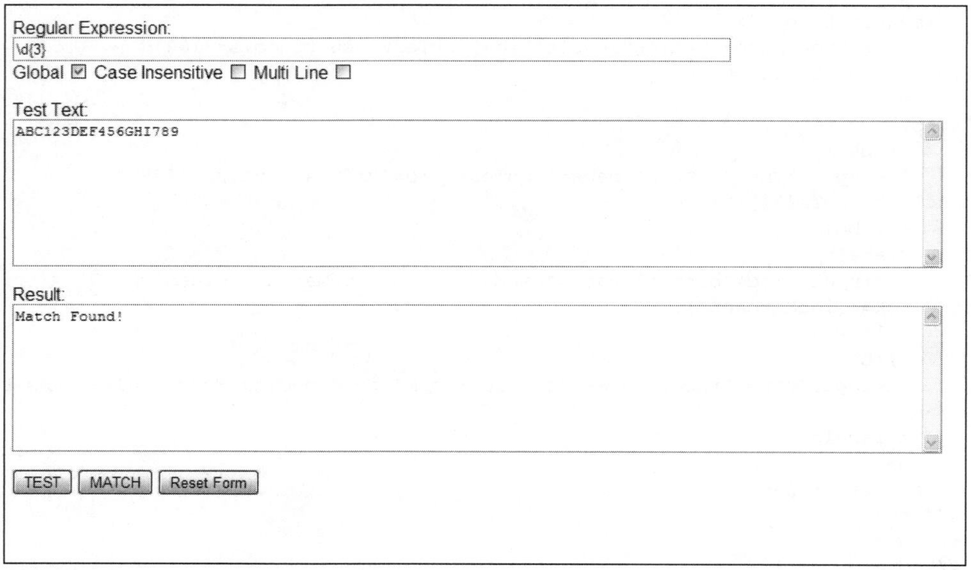

Regular Expression:
\d{3}
Global ☑ Case Insensitive ☐ Multi Line ☐

Test Text:
ABC123DEF456GHI789

Result:
Match Found!

[TEST] [MATCH] [Reset Form]

Figure 9-6

Now to find all the matches, click the Match button, and this results in the screen shown in Figure 9-7.

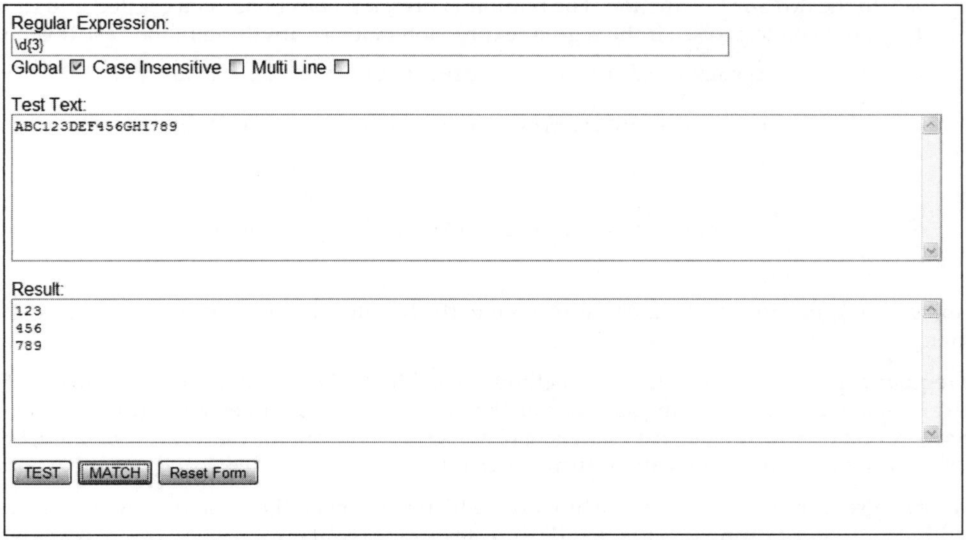

```
Regular Expression:
\d{3}
Global ☑  Case Insensitive ☐  Multi Line ☐

Test Text:
ABC123DEF456GHI789




Result:
123
456
789




[ TEST ]  [ MATCH ]  [ Reset Form ]
```

Figure 9-7

Each match of your regular expressions found in Test Text box is put on a separate line in the Results box.

The buttons cmdTest and cmdMatch have their click events linked to the `doTest()` and `findMatches()` functions. Let's start by looking at what happens in the `doTest()` function.

First, the regular expression object is created.

```
var testRegExp = new RegExp(document.form1.txtRegularExpression.value,
                            getRegExpFlags());
```

The first parameter of the object constructor is your regular expression as contained in the `txtRegularExpression` text box. This is easy enough to access, but the second parameter contains the regular expression flags, and these are generated via the tick boxes in the form. To convert the tick boxes to the correct flags, the function `getRegExpFlags()` has been created, and the return value from this function provides the flags value for the regular expressions constructor. The function `getRegExpFlags()` is used by both the `doTest()` and `getMatches()` functions. The `getRegExpFlags()` function is fairly simple. It starts by declaring `regExpFlags` and setting it to an empty string.

```
var regExpFlags = '';
```

Then for each of the tick boxes, it checks to see if the tick box is ticked. If it is, the appropriate flag is added to `regExpFlags` as shown here for the global flag:

```
if ( document.form1.chkGlobal.checked )
{
        regExpFlags = 'g';
}
```

The same principle is used for the case-insensitive and multi-line flags.

Okay, back to the doTest() function. The regular expression object has been created and its flags have been set, so now you test to see if the regular expression matches anything in the Test Text box.

```
if ( testRegExp.test(document.form1.txtTestString.value) )
{
        document.form1.txtTestResult.value = "Match Found!";
}
else
{
        document.form1.txtTestResult.value = "Match NOT Found!";
}
```

If a match is found, "Match Found!" is written to the Results box; otherwise "Match NOT Found!" is written.

The regular expression object's test() method is used to do the actual testing for a match of the regular expression with the test string supplied as the method's only parameter. It returns true when a match is found or false when it's not. The global flag is irrelevant for the test() method, because it simply looks for the first match and returns true if found.

Now let's look at the findMatches() function, which runs when the cmdMatches button is clicked. As with the doTest() function, the first line creates a new regular expression object with the regular expression entered in the Regular Expression text box in the form and the flags being set via the getRegExpFlags() function.

```
var testRegExp = new RegExp(document.form1.txtRegularExpression.value,
                    getRegExpFlags());
```

Next, a new String object is created, and you then use the String object's match() method to find the matches.

```
var myTestString = new String(document.form1.txtTestString.value)
var matchArray = myTestString.match(testRegExp);
```

The match() method returns an array with all the matches found in each element of the array. The variable matchArray is used to store the array.

Finally, the match results are displayed in the Results box on the form:

```
document.form1.txtTestResult.value = matchArray.join('\n');
```

The String object's join() method joins all the elements in an array and returns them as a single string. Each element is separated by the value you pass as the join() method's only parameter. Here \n or the newline character has been passed, which means when the string is displayed in the Results box, each match is on its own individual line.

Regular Expressions: Special Characters

You will be looking at three types of special characters in this section.

Text, Numbers, and Punctuation

The first group of special characters you'll look at contains the character class's special characters. *Character class* means digits, letters, and whitespace characters. The special characters are displayed in the following table.

Character Class	Characters It Matches	Example
\d	Any digit from 0 to 9	\d\d matches 72, but not aa or 7a
\D	Any character that is not a digit	\D\D\D matches abc, but not 123 or 8ef
\w	Any word character; that is, A–Z, a–z, 0–9, and the underscore character (_)	\w\w\w\w matches Ab_2, but not £$%* or Ab_@
\W	Any non-word character	\W matches @, but not a
\s	Any whitespace character	\s matches tab, return, formfeed, and vertical tab
\S	Any non-whitespace character	\S matches A, but not the tab character
.	Any single character other than the newline character (\n)	. matches a or 4 or @
[...]	Any one of the characters between the brackets [a-z] will match any character in the range a to z	[abc] will match a or b or c, but nothing else
[^...]	Any one character, but not one of those inside the brackets	[^abc] will match any character except a or b or c [^a-z] will match any character that is not in the range a to z

Note that uppercase and lowercase characters mean very different things, so you need to be extra careful with case when using regular expressions.

Let's look at an example. To match a telephone number in the format 1-800-888-5474, the regular expression would be as follows:

```
\d-\d\d\d-\d\d\d-\d\d\d\d
```

You can see that there's a lot of repetition of characters here, which makes the expression quite unwieldy. To make this simpler, regular expressions have a way of defining repetition. You'll see this a little later in the chapter, but first let's look at another example.

Try It Out **Checking a Passphrase for Alphanumeric Characters**

You'll use what you've learned so far about regular expressions in a full example in which you check that a passphrase contains only letters and numbers — that is, alphanumeric characters, not punctuation or symbols like @, %, and so on.

```
<!DOCTYPE html PUBLIC "-//W3C//DTD XHTML 1.0 Transitional//EN"
"http://www.w3.org/TR/xhtml1/DTD/xhtml1-transitional.dtd">
<html xmlns="http://www.w3.org/1999/xhtml">
<head>
<meta http-equiv="Content-Type" content="text/html; charset=utf-8" />
<title>Example 3</title>

<script type="text/JavaScript">
function regExpIs_valid(text)
{
    var myRegExp = /[^a-z\d ]/i;
    return !(myRegExp.test(text));
}
function butCheckValid_onclick()
{
    if (regExpIs_valid(document.form1.txtPhrase.value) == true)
    {
        alert("Your passphrase contains only valid characters");
    }
    else
    {
        alert("Your passphrase contains one or more invalid characters");
    }
}
</script>

</head>
<body>

<form name="form1">
Enter your passphrase:
<br />
<input type="text" name="txtPhrase">
<br />
<input type="button" value="Check Character Validity" name="butCheckValid"
    onclick="butCheckValid_onclick()">
</form>

</body>
</html>
```

Save the page as ch9_examp3.htm, and then load it into your browser. Type just letters, numbers, and spaces into the text box; click the Check Character Validity button, and you'll be told that the phrase contains valid characters. Try putting punctuation or special characters like @, ^, $, and so on into the text box, and you'll be informed that your passphrase is invalid.

Let's start by looking at the `regExpIs_valid()` function defined at the top of the script block in the head of the page. That does the validity checking of the passphrase using regular expressions.

```
function regExpIs_valid(text)
{
    var myRegExp = /[^a-z\d ]/i;
    return !(myRegExp.test(text));
}
```

The function takes just one parameter: the text you want to check for validity. You then declare a variable, `myRegExp`, and set it to a new regular expression, which implicitly creates a new `RegExp` object.

The regular expression itself is fairly simple, but first think about what pattern you are looking for. What you want to find out is whether your passphrase string contains any characters that are not letters between A and Z or between a and z, numbers between 0 and 9, or spaces. Let's see how this translates into a regular expression:

1. You use square brackets with the ^ symbol.

```
[^]
```

This means you want to match any character that is not one of the characters specified inside the square brackets.

2. You add `a-z`, which specifies any character in the range a through z.

```
[^a-z]
```

So far, your regular expression matches any character that is not between a and z. Note that, because you added the `i` to the end of the expression definition, you've made the pattern case-insensitive. So your regular expression actually matches any character not between A and Z or a and z.

3. Add `\d` to indicate any digit character, or any character between 0 and 9.

```
[^a-z\d]
```

4. Your expression matches any character that is not between a and z, A and Z, or 0 and 9. You decide that a space is valid, so you add that inside the square brackets.

```
[^a-z\d ]
```

Putting this all together, you have a regular expression that will match any character that is not a letter, a digit, or a space.

5. On the second and final line of the function, you use the `RegExp` object's `test()` method to return a value.

```
return !(myRegExp.test(text));
```

The `test()` method of the `RegExp` object checks the string passed as its parameter to see if the characters specified by the regular expression syntax match anything inside the string. If they do, `true` is returned; if not, `false` is returned. Your regular expression will match the first invalid character found, so if you get a result of `true`, you have an invalid passphrase. However, it's a bit illogical for an `is_valid` function to return `true` when it's invalid, so you reverse the result returned by adding the NOT operator (`!`).

Previously you saw the two-line validity checker function using regular expressions. Just to show how much more coding is required to do the same thing without regular expressions, here is a second function that does the same thing as regExpIs_valid() but without regular expressions.

```
function is_valid(text)
{
    var isValid = true;
    var validChars = "abcdefghijklmnopqrstuvwxyz1234567890 ";
    var charIndex;
    for (charIndex = 0; charIndex < text.length;charIndex++)
    {
        if ( validChars.indexOf(text.charAt(charIndex).toLowerCase()) < 0)
        {
            isValid = false;
            break;
        }
    }
    return isValid;
}
```

This is probably as small as the non-regular expression version can be, and yet it's still 15 lines long. That's six times the amount of code for the regular expression version.

The principle of this function is similar to that of the regular expression version. You have a variable, validChars, which contains all the characters you consider to be valid. You then use the charAt() method in a for loop to get each character in the passphrase string and check whether it exists in your validChars string. If it doesn't, you know you have an invalid character.

In this example, the non-regular expression version of the function is 15 lines, but with a more complex problem you could find it takes 20 or 30 lines to do the same thing a regular expression can do in just a few.

Back to your actual code: The other function defined in the head of the page is butCheckValid_onclick(). As the name suggests, this is called when the butCheckValid button defined in the body of the page is clicked.

This function calls your regExpis_valid() function in an if statement to check whether the passphrase entered by the user in the txtPhrase text box is valid. If it is, an alert box is used to inform the user.

```
function butCheckValid_onclick()
{
    if (regExpIs_valid(document.form1.txtPhrase.value) == true)
    {
        alert("Your passphrase contains valid characters");
    }
```

If it isn't, another alert box is used to let users know that their text was invalid.

```
    else
    {
        alert("Your passphrase contains one or more invalid characters");
    }
}
```

Repetition Characters

Regular expressions include something called repetition characters, which are a means of specifying how many of the last item or character you want to match. This proves very useful, for example, if you want to specify a phone number that repeats a character a specific number of times. The following table lists some of the most common repetition characters and what they do.

Special Character	Meaning	Example
{n}	Match n of the previous item	x{2} matches xx
{n, }	Match n or more of the previous item	x{2, } matches xx, xxx, xxxx, xxxxx, and so on
{n,m}	Match at least n and at most m of the previous item	x{2,4} matches xx, xxx, and xxxx
?	Match the previous item zero or one time	x? matches nothing or x
+	Match the previous item one or more times	x+ matches x, xx, xxx, xxxx, xxxxx, and so on
*	Match the previous item zero or more times	x* matches nothing, or x, xx, xxx, xxxx, and so on

You saw earlier that to match a telephone number in the format 1-800-888-5474, the regular expression would be \d-\d\d\d-\d\d\d-\d\d\d\d. Let's see how this would be simplified with the use of the repetition characters.

The pattern you're looking for starts with one digit followed by a dash, so you need the following:

```
\d-
```

Next are three digits followed by a dash. This time you can use the repetition special characters — \d{3} will match exactly three \d, which is the any-digit character.

```
\d-\d{3}-
```

Next, there are three digits followed by a dash again, so now your regular expression looks like this:

```
\d-\d{3}-\d{3}-
```

Finally, the last part of the expression is four digits, which is \d{4}.

```
\d-\d{3}-\d{3}-\d{4}
```

You'd declare this regular expression like this:

```
var myRegExp = /\d-\d{3}-\d{3}-\d{4}/
```

Remember that the first / and last / tell JavaScript that what is in between those characters is a regular expression. JavaScript creates a `RegExp` object based on this regular expression.

As another example, what if you have the string `Paul Paula Pauline`, and you want to replace `Paul` and `Paula` with `George`? To do this, you would need a regular expression that matches both `Paul` and `Paula`.

Let's break this down. You know you want the characters `Paul`, so your regular expression starts as

```
Paul
```

Now you also want to match `Paula`, but if you make your expression `Paula`, this will exclude a match on `Paul`. This is where the special character `?` comes in. It enables you to specify that the previous character is optional — it must appear zero (not at all) or one time. So, the solution is

```
Paula?
```

which you'd declare as

```
var myRegExp = /Paula?/
```

Position Characters

The third group of special characters you'll look at are those that enable you to specify either where the match should start or end or what will be on either side of the character pattern. For example, you might want your pattern to exist at the start or end of a string or line, or you might want it to be between two words. The following table lists some of the most common position characters and what they do.

Position Character	Description
^	The pattern must be at the start of the string, or if it's a multi-line string, then at the beginning of a line. For multi-line text (a string that contains carriage returns), you need to set the multi-line flag when defining the regular expression using /myreg ex/m. Note that this is only applicable to IE 5.5 and later and NN 6 and later.
$	The pattern must be at the end of the string, or if it's a multi-line string, then at the end of a line. For multi-line text (a string that contains carriage returns), you need to set the multi-line flag when defining the regular expression using /myreg ex/m. Note that this is only applicable to IE 5.5 and later and NN 6 and later.
\b	This matches a word boundary, which is essentially the point between a word character and a non-word character.
\B	This matches a position that's not a word boundary.

For example, if you wanted to make sure your pattern was at the start of a line, you would type the following:

```
^myPattern
```

This would match an occurrence of myPattern if it was at the beginning of a line.

To match the same pattern, but at the end of a line, you would type the following:

```
myPattern$
```

The word-boundary special characters \b and \B can cause confusion, because they do not match characters but the positions between characters.

Imagine you had the string "Hello world!, let's look at boundaries said 007." defined in the code as follows:

```
var myString = "Hello world!, let's look at boundaries said 007.";
```

To make the word boundaries (that is, the boundaries between the words) of this string stand out, let's convert them to the | character.

```
var myRegExp = /\b/g;
myString = myString.replace(myRegExp, "|");
alert(myString);
```

You've replaced all the word boundaries, \b, with a |, and your message box looks like the one in Figure 9-8.

Figure 9-8

You can see that the position between any word character (letters, numbers, or the underscore character) and any non-word character is a word boundary. You'll also notice that the boundary between the start or end of the string and a word character is considered to be a word boundary. The end of this string is a full stop. So the boundary between the full stop and the end of the string is a non-word boundary, and therefore no | has been inserted.

If you change the regular expression in the example, so that it replaces non-word boundaries as follows:

```
var myRegExp = /\B/g;
```

you get the result shown in Figure 9-9.

Figure 9-9

Now the position between a letter, number, or underscore and another letter, number, or underscore is considered a non-word boundary and is replaced by an | in the example. However, what is slightly confusing is that the boundary between two non-word characters, such as an exclamation mark and a comma, is also considered a non-word boundary. If you think about it, it actually does make sense, but it's easy to forget when creating regular expressions.

You'll remember this example from when you started looking at regular expressions:

```
<!DOCTYPE html PUBLIC "-//W3C//DTD XHTML 1.0 Transitional//EN"
"http://www.w3.org/TR/xhtml1/DTD/xhtml1-transitional.dtd">
<html xmlns="http://www.w3.org/1999/xhtml">
<body>
<script language="JavaScript" type="text/JavaScript">

    var myString = "Paul, Paula, Pauline, paul, Paul";
    var myRegExp = /Paul/gi;
    myString = myString.replace(myRegExp, "Ringo");
    alert(myString);


</script>
</body>
</html>
```

You used this code to convert all instances of `Paul` or `paul` to `Ringo`.

However, you found that this code actually converts all instances of `Paul` to `Ringo`, even when the word `Paul` is inside another word.

One way to solve this problem would be to replace the string `Paul` only where it is followed by a non-word character. The special character for non-word characters is \W, so you need to alter the regular expression to the following:

```
var myRegExp = /Paul\W/gi;
```

This gives the result shown in Figure 9-10.

Figure 9-10

It's getting better, but it's still not what you want. Notice that the commas after the second and third `Paul` substrings have also been replaced because they matched the `\W` character. Also, you're still not replacing `Paul` at the very end of the string. That's because there is no character after the letter `l` in the last `Paul`. What is after the `l` in the last `Paul`? Nothing, just the boundary between a word character and a non-word character, and therein lies the answer. What you want as your regular expression is `Paul` followed by a word boundary. Let's alter the regular expression to cope with that by entering the following:

```
var myRegExp = /Paul\b/gi;
```

Now you get the result you want, as shown in Figure 9-11.

Figure 9-11

At last you've got it right, and this example is finished.

Covering All Eventualities

Perhaps the trickiest thing about a regular expression is making sure it covers all eventualities. In the previous example your regular expression works with the string as defined, but does it work with the following?

```
var myString = "Paul, Paula, Pauline, paul, Paul, JeanPaul";
```

Here the `Paul` substring in `JeanPaul` will be changed to `Ringo`. You really only want to convert the substring `Paul` where it is on its own, with a word boundary on either side. If you change your regular expression code to

```
var myRegExp = /\bPaul\b/gi;
```

you have your final answer and can be sure only `Paul` or `paul` will ever be matched.

Grouping Regular Expressions

The final topic under regular expressions, before you look at examples using the `match()`, `replace()`, and `search()` methods, is how you can group expressions. In fact, it's quite easy. If you want a number of expressions to be treated as a single group, you just enclose them in parentheses, for example, `/(\d\d)/`. Parentheses in regular expressions are special characters that group together character patterns and are not themselves part of the characters to be matched.

Why would you want to do this? Well, by grouping characters into patterns, you can use the special repetition characters to apply to the whole group of characters, rather than just one.

Let's take the following string defined in `myString` as an example:

```
var myString = "JavaScript, VBScript and Perl";
```

How could you match both `JavaScript` and `VBScript` using the same regular expression? The only thing they have in common is that they are whole words and they both end in `Script`. Well, an easy way would be to use parentheses to group the patterns `Java` and `VB`. Then you can use the `?` special character to apply to each of these groups of characters to make the pattern match any word having zero or one instances of the characters `Java` or `VB`, and ending in `Script`.

```
var myRegExp = /\b(VB)?(Java)?Script\b/gi;
```

Breaking this expression down, you can see the pattern it requires is as follows:

1. A word boundary: `\b`

2. Zero or one instance of VB: `(VB)?`

3. Zero or one instance of Java: `(Java)?`

4. The characters `Script`: `Script`

5. A word boundary: `\b`

Putting these together, you get this:

```
var myString = "JavaScript, VBScript and Perl";
var myRegExp = /\b(VB)?(Java)?Script\b/gi;
myString = myString.replace(myRegExp, "xxxx");
alert(myString);
```

The output of this code is shown in Figure 9-12.

Figure 9-12

If you look back at the special repetition characters table, you'll see that they apply to the item preceding them. This can be a character, or, where they have been grouped by means of parentheses, the previous group of characters.

However, there is a potential problem with the regular expression you just defined. As well as matching VBScript and JavaScript, it also matches VBJavaScript. This is clearly not exactly what you meant.

To get around this you need to make use of both grouping and the special character `|`, which is the alternation character. It has an or-like meaning, similar to `||` in `if` statements, and will match the characters on either side of itself.

Let's think about the problem again. You want the pattern to match VBScript or JavaScript. Clearly they have the Script part in common. So what you want is a new word starting with Java or starting with VB; either way, it must end in Script.

First, you know that the word must start with a word boundary.

```
\b
```

Next you know that you want either VB or Java to be at the start of the word. You've just seen that in regular expressions | provides the "or" you need, so in regular expression syntax you want the following:

```
\b(VB|Java)
```

This matches the pattern VB or Java. Now you can just add the Script part.

```
\b(VB|Java)Script\b
```

Your final code looks like this:

```
var myString = "JavaScript, VBScript and Perl";
var myRegExp = /\b(VB|Java)Script\b/gi;
myString = myString.replace(myRegExp, "xxxx");
alert(myString);
```

Reusing Groups of Characters

You can reuse the pattern specified by a group of characters later on in the regular expression. To refer to a previous group of characters, you just type \ and a number indicating the order of the group. For example, the first group can be referred to as \1, the second as \2, and so on.

Let's look at an example. Say you have a list of numbers in a string, with each number separated by a comma. For whatever reason, you are not allowed to have two instances of the same number in a row, so although

```
009,007,001,002,004,003
```

would be okay, the following:

```
007,007,001,002,002,003
```

would not be valid, because you have 007 and 002 repeated after themselves.

How can you find instances of repeated digits and replace them with the word ERROR? You need to use the ability to refer to groups in regular expressions.

First, let's define the string as follows:

```
var myString  = "007,007,001,002,002,003,002,004";
```

325

Now you know you need to search for a series of one or more number characters. In regular expressions the \d specifies any digit character, and + means one or more of the previous character. So far, that gives you this regular expression:

```
\d+
```

You want to match a series of digits followed by a comma, so you just add the comma.

```
\d+,
```

This will match any series of digits followed by a comma, but how do you search for any series of digits followed by a comma, then followed again by the same series of digits? As the digits could be any digits, you can't add them directly into the expression like so:

```
\d+,007
```

This would not work with the 002 repeat. What you need to do is put the first series of digits in a group; then you can specify that you want to match that group of digits again. This can be done with \1, which says, "Match the characters found in the first group defined using parentheses." Put all this together, and you have the following:

```
(\d+),\1
```

This defines a group whose pattern of characters is one or more digit characters. This group must be followed by a comma and then by the same pattern of characters as in the first group. Put this into some JavaScript, and you have the following:

```
var myString  = "007,007,001,002,002,003,002,004";
var myRegExp = /(\d+),\1/g;
myString = myString.replace(myRegExp,"ERROR");
alert(myString);
```

The alert box will show this message:

```
ERROR,1,ERROR,003,002,004
```

That completes your brief look at regular expression syntax. Because regular expressions can get a little complex, it's often a good idea to start simple and build them up slowly, as was done in the previous example. In fact, most regular expressions are just too hard to get right in one step — at least for us mere mortals without a brain the size of a planet.

If it's still looking a bit strange and confusing, don't panic. In the next sections, you'll be looking at the String object's split(), replace(), search(), and match() methods with plenty more examples of regular expression syntax.

The String Object — split(), replace(), search(), and match() Methods

The main functions making use of regular expressions are the String object's split(), replace(), search(), and match() methods. You've already seen their syntax, so you'll concentrate on their use with regular expressions and at the same time learn more about regular expression syntax and usage.

The split() Method

You've seen that the split() method enables us to split a string into various pieces, with the split being made at the character or characters specified as a parameter. The result of this method is an array with each element containing one of the split pieces. For example, the following string:

```
var myListString = "apple, banana, peach, orange"
```

could be split into an array in which each element contains a different fruit, like this:

```
var myFruitArray = myListString.split(", ");
```

How about if your string is this instead?

```
var myListString = "apple, 0.99, banana, 0.50, peach, 0.25, orange, 0.75";
```

The string could, for example, contain both the names and prices of the fruit. How could you split the string, but retrieve only the names of the fruit and not the prices? You could do it without regular expressions, but it would take many lines of code. With regular expressions you can use the same code and just amend the split() method's parameter.

Try It Out   Splitting the Fruit String

Let's create an example that solves the problem just described — it must split your string, but include only the fruit names, not the prices.

```
<!DOCTYPE html PUBLIC "-//W3C//DTD XHTML 1.0 Transitional//EN"
"http://www.w3.org/TR/xhtml1/DTD/xhtml1-transitional.dtd">
<html xmlns="http://www.w3.org/1999/xhtml">
<body>

<script type="text/JavaScript">
var myListString = "apple, 0.99, banana, 0.50, peach, 0.25, orange, 0.75";
var theRegExp = /[^a-z]+/i;
var myFruitArray = myListString.split(theRegExp);
document.write(myFruitArray.join("<br />"));

</script>
</body>
</html>
```

Save the file as ch9_examp4.htm and load it in your browser. You should see the four fruits from your string written out to the page, with each fruit on a separate line.

Within the script block, first you have your string with fruit names and prices.

```
var myListString = "apple, 0.99, banana, 0.50, peach, 0.25, orange, 0.75";
```

How do you split it in such a way that only the fruit names are included? Your first thought might be to use the comma as the split() method's parameter, but of course that means you end up with the prices. What you have to ask is, "What is it that's between the items I want?" Or in other words, what is between the fruit names that you can use to define your split? The answer is that various characters are between the names of the fruit, such as a comma, a space, numbers, a full stop, more numbers, and finally another comma. What is it that these things have in common and makes them different from the fruit names that you want? What they have in common is that none of them are letters from a through z. If you say "Split the string at the point where there is a group of characters that are not between a and z," then you get the result you want. Now you know what you need to create your regular expression.

You know that what you want is not the letters a through z, so you start with this:

```
[^a-z]
```

The ^ says "Match any character that does not match those specified inside the square brackets." In this case you've specified a range of characters not to be matched — all the characters between a and z. As specified, this expression will match only one character, whereas you want to split wherever there is a single group of one or more characters that are not between a and z. To do this you need to add the + special repetition character, which says "Match one or more of the preceding character or group specified."

```
[^a-z]+
```

The final result is this:

```
var theRegExp = /[^a-z]+/i
```

The / and / characters mark the start and end of the regular expression whose RegExp object is stored as a reference in the variable theRegExp. You add the i on the end to make the match case-insensitive.

Don't panic if creating regular expressions seems like a frustrating and less-than-obvious process. At first, it takes a lot of trial and error to get it right, but as you get more experienced, you'll find creating them becomes much easier and will enable you to do things that without regular expressions would be either very awkward or virtually impossible.

In the next line of script you pass the RegExp object to the split() method, which uses it to decide where to split the string.

```
var myFruitArray = myListString.split(theRegExp);
```

After the split, the variable myFruitArray will contain an Array with each element containing the fruit name, as shown here:

Array Element Index	0	1	2	3
Element value	apple	banana	peach	orange

You then join the string together again using the Array object's join() methods, which you saw in Chapter 4.

```
document.write(myFruitArray.join("<BR>"))
```

The replace() Method

You've already looked at the syntax and usage of the `replace()` method. However, something unique to the `replace()` method is its ability to replace text based on the groups matched in the regular expression. You do this using the `$` sign and the group's number. Each group in a regular expression is given a number from 1 to 99; any groups greater than 99 are not accessible. Note that in earlier browsers, groups could only go from 1 to 9 (for example, in IE 5 or earlier or Netscape 4 and earlier). To refer to a group, you write `$` followed by the group's position. For example, if you had the following:

```
var myRegExp = /(\d)(\W)/g;
```

then `$1` refers to the group `(\d)`, and `$2` refers to the group `(\W)`. You've also set the global flag `g` to ensure that all matching patterns are replaced — not just the first one.

You can see this more clearly in the next example. Say you have the following string:

```
var myString = "1999, 2000, 2001";
```

If you wanted to change this to `"the year 1999, the year 2000, the year 2001"`, how could you do it with regular expressions?

First, you need to work out the pattern as a regular expression, in this case four digits.

```
var myRegExp = /\d{4}/g;
```

But given that the year is different every time, how can you substitute the year value into the replaced string?

Well, you change your regular expression so that it's inside a group, as follows:

```
var myRegExp = /(\d{4})/g;
```

Now you can use the group, which has group number 1, inside the replacement string like this:

```
myString = myString.replace(myRegExp, "the year $1");
```

The variable `myString` now contains the required string `"the year 1999, the year 2000, the year 2001"`.

Let's look at another example in which you want to convert single quotes in text to double quotes. Your test string is this:

```
'Hello World' said Mr. O'Connerly.
He then said 'My Name is O'Connerly, yes that's right, O'Connerly'.
```

One problem that the test string makes clear is that you want to replace the single-quote mark with a double only where it is used in pairs around speech, not when it is acting as an apostrophe, such as in the word `that's`, or when it's part of someone's name, such as in `O'Connerly`.

Let's start by defining the regular expression. First you know that it must include a single quote, as shown in the following code:

```
var myRegExp = /'/;
```

However, as it is this would replace every single quote, which is not what you want.

Looking at the text, you should also notice that quotes are always at the start or end of a word — that is, at a boundary. On first glance it might be easy to assume that it would be a word boundary. However, don't forget that the ' is a non-word character, so the boundary will be between it and another non-word character, such as a space. So the boundary will be a non-word boundary or, in other words, \B.

Therefore, the character pattern you are looking for is either a non-word boundary followed by a single quote or a single quote followed by a non-word boundary. The key is the "or," for which you use | in regular expressions. This leaves your regular expression as the following:

```
var myRegExp = /\B'|'\B/g;
```

This will match the pattern on the left of the | or the character pattern on the right. You want to replace all the single quotes with double quotes, so the g has been added at the end, indicating that a global match should take place.

Try It Out   Replacing Single Quotes with Double Quotes

Let's look at an example using the regular expression just defined.

```
<!DOCTYPE html PUBLIC "-//W3C//DTD XHTML 1.0 Transitional//EN"
"http://www.w3.org/TR/xhtml1/DTD/xhtml1-transitional.dtd">
<html xmlns="http://www.w3.org/1999/xhtml">
<head>
<title>example</title>
<script type="text/JavaScript">
function replaceQuote(textAreaControl)
{
    var myText = textAreaControl.value;
    var myRegExp = /\B'|'\B/g;
    myText = myText.replace(myRegExp,'"');
    textAreaControl.value = myText;
}
</script>
</head>
<body>
<form name="form1">
<textarea rows="20" cols="40" name="textarea1">
'Hello World' said Mr O'Connerly.
He then said 'My Name is O'Connerly, yes that's right, O'Connerly'.
</textarea>
<br>
<input type="button" VALUE="Replace Single Quotes" name="buttonSplit"
    onclick="replaceQuote(document.form1.textarea1)">
</form>

</body>
</html>
```

Save the page as `ch9_examp5.htm`. Load the page into your browser and you should see what is shown in Figure 9-13.

Figure 9-13

Click the Replace Single Quotes button to see the single quotes in the text area replaced as in Figure 9-14.

Figure 9-14

Try entering your own text with single quotes into the text area and check the results.

You can see that by using regular expressions, you have completed a task in a couple of lines of simple code. Without regular expressions, it would probably take four or five times that amount.

Let's look first at the `replaceQuote()` function in the head of the page where all the action is.

```
function replaceQuote(textAreaControl)
{
    var myText = textAreaControl.value;
    var myRegExp = /\B'|'\B/g;
```

```
        myText = myText.replace(myRegExp,'"');
        textAreaControl.value = myText;
    }
```

The function's parameter is the `textarea` object defined further down the page — this is the text area in which you want to replace the single quotes. You can see how the `textarea` object was passed in the button's tag definition.

```
<input type="button" value="Replace Single Quotes" name="buttonSplit"
    onclick="replaceQuote(document.form1.textarea1)">
```

In the `onclick` event handler, you call `replaceQuote()` and pass `document.form1.textarea1` as the parameter — that is the `textarea` object.

Returning to the function, you get the value of the `textarea` on the first line and place it in the variable `myText`. Then you define your regular expression (as discussed previously), which matches any non-word boundary followed by a single quote or any single quote followed by a non-word boundary. For example, `'H` will match, as will `H'`, but `O'R` won't, because the quote is between two word boundaries. Don't forget that a word boundary is the position between the start or end of a word and a non-word character, such as a space or punctuation mark.

In the function's final two lines, you first use the `replace()` method to do the character pattern search and replace, and finally you set the `textarea` object's value to the changed string.

The search() Method

The `search()` method enables you to search a string for a pattern of characters. If the pattern is found, the character position at which it was found is returned, otherwise `-1` is returned. The method takes only one parameter, the `RegExp` object you have created.

Although for basic searches the `indexOf()` method is fine, if you want more complex searches, such as a search for a pattern of any digits or one in which a word must be in between a certain boundary, then `search()` provides a much more powerful and flexible, but sometimes more complex, approach.

In the following example, you want to find out if the word `Java` is contained within the string. However, you want to look just for `Java` as a whole word, not part of another word such as `JavaScript`.

```
var myString = "Beginning JavaScript, Beginning Java 2, Professional JavaScript";
var myRegExp = /\bJava\b/i;
alert(myString.search(myRegExp));
```

First, you have defined your string, and then you've created your regular expression. You want to find the character pattern `Java` when it's on its own between two word boundaries. You've made your search case-insensitive by adding the `i` after the regular expression. Note that with the `search()` method, the `g` for global is not relevant, and its use has no effect.

On the final line, you output the position at which the search has located the pattern, in this case `32`.

The match() Method

The match() method is very similar to the search() method, except that instead of returning the position at which a match was found, it returns an array. Each element of the array contains the text of a match made.

For example, if you had the string

```
var myString = "The years were 1999, 2000 and 2001";
```

and wanted to extract the years from this string, you could do so using the match() method. To match each year, you are looking for four digits in between word boundaries. This requirement translates to the following regular expression:

```
var myRegExp = /\b\d{4}\b/g;
```

You want to match all the years so the g has been added to the end for a global search.

To do the match and store the results, you use the match() method and store the Array object it returns in a variable.

```
var resultsArray = myString.match(myRegExp);
```

To prove it has worked, let's use some code to output each item in the array. You've added an if statement to double-check that the results array actually contains an array. If no matches were made, the results array will contain null — doing if (resultsArray) will return true if the variable has a value and not null.

```
if (resultsArray)
{
  var indexCounter;
  for (indexCounter = 0; indexCounter < resultsArray.length; indexCounter++)
  {
     alert(resultsArray[indexCounter]);
  }
}
```

This would result in three alert boxes containing the numbers 1999, 2000, and 2001.

Try It Out   **Splitting HTML**

In the next example, you want to take a string of HTML and split it into its component parts. For example, you want the HTML <P>Hello</P> to become an array, with the elements having the following contents:

<P>	Hello	</P>

```
<!DOCTYPE html PUBLIC "-//W3C//DTD XHTML 1.0 Transitional//EN" "http://www.w3.org/
TR/xhtml1/DTD/xhtml1-transitional.dtd">
<html xmlns="http://www.w3.org/1999/xhtml">
```

```
<head>
<title>example 6</title>
<meta http-equiv="Content-Type" content="text/html; charset=utf-8" />
<script type="text/JavaScript">
function button1_onclick()
{
    var myString = "<table align=center><tr><td>";
    myString = myString + "Hello World</td></tr></table>";
    myString = myString +"<br><h2>Heading</h2>";
    var myRegExp = /<[^>\r\n]+>|[^<>\r\n]+/g;
    var resultsArray = myString.match(myRegExp);
    document.form1.textarea1.value = "";
    document.form1.textarea1.value = resultsArray.join ("\r\n");
}
</script>
</head>
<body>
<form name="form1">
    <textarea rows="20" cols="40" name="textarea1"></textarea>
    <input type="button" value="Split HTML" name="button1"
        onclick="return button1_onclick();">
</form>

</body>
</html>
```

Save this file as ch9_examp6.htm. When you load the page into your browser and click the Split HTML button, a string of HTML is split, and each tag is placed on a separate line in the text area, as shown in Figure 9-15.

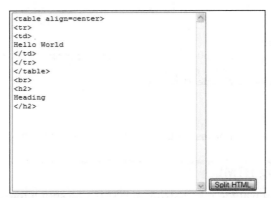

Figure 9-15

The function button1_onclick() defined at the top of the page fires when the Split HTML button is clicked. At the top, the following lines define the string of HTML that you want to split:

```
function button1_onclick()
{
    var myString = "<table align=center><tr><td>";
```

```
myString = myString + "Hello World</td></tr></table>";
myString = myString +"<br><h2>Heading</h2>";
```

Next you create your `RegExp` object and initialize it to your regular expression.

```
var myRegExp = /<[^>\r\n]+>|[^<>\r\n]+/g;
```

Let's break it down to see what pattern you're trying to match. First, note that the pattern is broken up by an alternation symbol: |. This means that you want the pattern on the left or the right of this symbol. You'll look at these patterns separately. On the left, you have the following:

❑   The pattern must start with a <.

❑   In `[^>\r\n]+`, you specify that you want one or more of any character except the > or a \r (carriage return) or a \n (linefeed).

❑   > specifies that the pattern must end with a >.

On the right, you have only the following:

❑   `[^<>\r\n]+` specifies that the pattern is one or more of any character, so long as that character is not a <, >, \r, or \n. This will match plain text.

After the regular expression definition you have a g, which specifies that this is a global match.

So the `<[^>\r\n]+>` regular expression will match any start or close tags, such as <p> or </p>. The alternative pattern is `[^<>\r\n]+`, which will match any character pattern that is not an opening or closing tag.

In the following line, you assign the `resultsArray` variable to the `Array` object returned by the `match()` method:

```
var resultsArray = myString.match(myRegExp);
```

The remainder of the code deals with populating the text area with the split HTML. You use the `Array` object's `join()` method to join all the array's elements into one string with each element separated by a \r\n character, so that each tag or piece of text goes on a separate line, as shown in the following:

```
document.form1.textarea1.value = "";
document.form1.textarea1.value = resultsArray.join("\r\n");
}
```

Using the RegExp Object's Constructor

So far you've been creating `RegExp` objects using the / and / characters to define the start and end of the regular expression, as shown in the following example:

```
var myRegExp = /[a-z]/;
```

Although this is the generally preferred method, it was briefly mentioned that a `RegExp` object can also be created by means of the `RegExp()` constructor. You might use the first way most of the time. However, there are occasions, as you'll see in the trivia quiz shortly, when the second way of creating a `RegExp` object is necessary (for example, when a regular expression is to be constructed from user input).

As an example, the preceding regular expression could equally well be defined as

```
var myRegExp = new RegExp("[a-z]");
```

Here you pass the regular expression as a string parameter to the `RegExp()` constructor function.

A very important difference when you are using this method is in how you use special regular expression characters, such as \b, that have a backward slash in front of them. The problem is that the backward slash indicates an escape character in JavaScript strings — for example, you may use \b, which means a backspace. To differentiate between \b meaning a backspace in a string and the \b special character in a regular expression, you have to put another backward slash in front of the regular expression special character. So \b becomes \\b when you mean the regular expression \b that matches a word boundary, rather than a backspace character.

For example, say you have defined your `RegExp` object using the following:

```
var myRegExp = /\b/;
```

To declare it using the `RegExp()` constructor, you would need to write this:

```
var myRegExp = new RegExp("\\b");
```

and not this:

```
var myRegExp = new RegExp("\b");
```

All special regular expression characters, such as \w, \b, \d, and so on, must have an extra \ in front when you create them using `RegExp()`.

When you defined regular expressions with the / and / method, you could add after the final / the special flags m, g, and i to indicate that the pattern matching should be multi-line, global, or case-insensitive, respectively. When using the `RegExp()` constructor, how can you do the same thing?

Easy. The optional second parameter of the `RegExp()` constructor takes the flags that specify a global or case-insensitive match. For example, this will do a global case-insensitive pattern match:

```
var myRegExp = new RegExp("hello\\b","gi");
```

You can specify just one of the flags if you wish — such as the following:

```
var myRegExp = new RegExp("hello\\b","i");
```

or

```
var myRegExp = new RegExp("hello\\b","g");
```

Try It Out   **Form Validation Module**

In this Try It Out, you'll create a set of useful JavaScript functions that use regular expressions to validate the following:

❑   Telephone numbers

❑   Postal codes

❑   E-mail addresses

The validation only checks the format. So, for example, it can't check that the telephone number actually exists, only that it would be valid if it did.

First is the `.js` code file with the input validation code. Please note that the lines of code in the following block are too wide for the book — make sure each regular expression is contained on one line.

```
function isValidTelephoneNumber( telephoneNumber )
{
            var telRegExp = /^(\+\d{1,3} ?)?(\(\d{1,5}\)|\d{1,5}) ?\d{3}
 ?\d{0,7}( (x|xtn|ext|extn|pax|pbx|extension)?\.? ?\d{2-5})?$/i
            return telRegExp.test( telephoneNumber );
}

function isValidPostalCode( postalCode )
{
        var pcodeRegExp = /^(\d{5}(-\d{4})?|([a-z][a-z]?\d\d?|[a-z{2}\d[a-z])
    ?\d[a-z][a-z])$/i
        return pcodeRegExp.test( postalCode );
}

function isValidEmail( emailAddress )
{
        var emailRegExp = /^(([^<>()\[\]\\.,;:@"\x00-\x20\x7F]|\\.)+|("""
([^\x0A\x0D"\\]|\\\\)+"""))@(([a-z]|#\d+?)([a-z0-9-]|#\d+?)*
([a-z0-9]|#\d+?)\.)+([a-z]{2,4})$/i
        return emailRegExp.test( emailAddress );
}
```

Save this as `ch9_examp7_module.js`.

To test the code, you need a simple page with a text box and three buttons that validate the telephone number, postal code, or e-mail address.

```
<!DOCTYPE html PUBLIC "-//W3C//DTD XHTML 1.0 Transitional//EN"
"http://www.w3.org/TR/xhtml1/DTD/xhtml1-transitional.dtd">
<html xmlns="http://www.w3.org/1999/xhtml">
<head>
<title>example 7</title>
<meta http-equiv="Content-Type" content="text/html; charset=utf-8" />
<script type="text/javascript" src="ch9_examp7_module.js"></script>
</head>
<body>
<form name="form1">
  <p>
    <label>
```

```
      <input type="text" name="txtString" id="txtString" />
    </label>
  </p>
  <p>
    <label>
      <input type="button" name="cmdIsValidTelephoneNumber"
    id="cmdIsValidTelephoneNumber"
    value="Is Valid Telephone Number?"
onclick="alert('Is valid is ' +
                  isValidTelephoneNumber( document.form1.txtString.value ))"
    />

      <input type="button" name="cmdIsValidPostalCode"
            id="cmdIsValidPostalCode"
            value="Is Valid Postal Code?"
            onclick="alert('Is valid is '
+ isValidPostalCode( document.form1.txtString.value ))" />
      <input type="button" name="cmdIsEmailValid" id="cmdIsEmailValid"
value="Is Valid Email?"
onclick="alert('Is valid is '
+ isValidEmail( document.form1.txtString.value ))" />
    </label>
  </p>
</form>

</body>
</html>
```

Save this as ch9_examp7.htm and load it into your browser, and you'll see a page with a text box and three buttons. Enter a valid telephone number (the example uses +1 (123) 123 4567), click the Is Valid Telephone Number button, and the screen shown in Figure 9-16 is displayed.

Figure 9-16

If you enter an invalid phone number, the result would be Is Valid is false. This is pretty basic but it's sufficient for testing your code.

The actual code is very simple, but the regular expressions are tricky to create, so let's look at those in depth starting with telephone number validation.

Telephone Number Validation

Telephone numbers are more of a challenge to validate. The problems are:

❑ Phone numbers differ from country to country.

❑ There are different ways of entering a valid number (for example, adding the national or international code or not).

For this regular expression, you need to specify more than just the valid characters; you also need to specify the format of the data. For example, all of the following are valid:

+1 (123) 123 4567

+1123123 456

+44 (123) 123 4567

+44 (123) 123 4567 ext 123

+44 20 7893 4567

The variations that our regular expression needs to deal with (optionally separated by spaces) are shown in the following table:

The international number	"+" followed by one to three digits (optional)
The local area code	Two to five digits, sometimes in parentheses (compulsory)
The actual subscriber number	Three to 10 digits, sometimes with spaces (compulsory)
An extension number	Two to five digits, preceded by `x`, `xtn`, `extn`, `pax`, `pbx`, or `extension`, and sometimes in parentheses

Obviously, there will be countries where this won't work, which is something you'd need to deal with based on where your customers and partners would be. The following regular expression is rather complex, its length meant it had to be split across two lines; make sure you type it in on one line.

```
^(\+\d{1,3} ?)?(\(\(\d{1,5}\)\)|\d{1,5}) ?\d{3} ?\d{0,7}
( (x|xtn|ext|extn|pax|pbx|extension)?\.? ?\d{2-5})?$
```

You will need to set the case-insensitive flag with this, as well as the explicit capture option. Although this seems complex, if broken down, it's quite straightforward.

Let's start with the pattern that matches an international dialing code:

```
(\+\d{1,3} ?)?
```

So far, you've matching a plus sign (\+) followed by one to three digits (\d{1,3}) and an optional space (?). Remember that since the + character is a special character, you add a \ character in front of it to specify that you mean an actual + character. The characters are wrapped inside parentheses to specify a group of characters. You allow an optional space and match this entire group of characters zero or one times, as indicated by the ? character after the closing parenthesis of the group.

Next is the pattern to match an area code:

```
(\(\d{1,5}\)|\d{1,5})
```

This pattern is contained in parentheses, which designate it as a group of characters, and matches either one to five digits in parentheses ((\d{1,5})) or just one to five digits (\d{1,5}). Again, since the parenthesis characters are special characters in regular expression syntax and you want to match actual parentheses, you need the \ character in front of them. Also note the use of the pipe symbol (|), which means "OR" or "match either of these two patterns."

Next, let's match the subscriber number:

```
 ?\d{3,4} ?\d{0,7}
```

Note that there is a space before the first ? symbol: this space and question mark mean "match zero or one space." This is followed by three or four digits (\d{3,4}) — although there are always three digits in the U.S., there are often four in the UK. Then there's another "zero or one space," and finally between zero and seven digits (\d{0,7}).

Finally, add the part to cope with an optional extension number:

```
( (x|xtn|ext|extn|extension)?\.? ?\d{2-5})?
```

This group is optional, since its parentheses are followed by a question mark. The group itself checks for a space, optionally followed by x, ext, xtn, extn, or extension, followed by zero or one periods (note the \ character, since . is a special character in regular expression syntax), followed by zero or one space, followed by between two and five digits. Putting these four patterns together, you can construct the entire regular expression, apart from the surrounding syntax. The regular expression starts with ^ and ends with $. The ^ character specifies that the pattern must be matched at the beginning of the string, and the $ character specifies that the pattern must be matched at the end of the string. This means that the string must match the pattern completely; it cannot contain any other characters before or after the pattern that is matched.

Therefore, with the regular expression explained, you can now add it to your JavaScript module ch9_examp7_module.js as follows:

```javascript
function isValidTelephoneNumber( telephoneNumber )
{
            var telRegExp = /^(\+\d{1,3} ?)?
            (\(\d{1,5}\)|\d{1,5}) ?\d{3} ?\d{0,7}
            ( (x|xtn|ext|extn|pax|pbx|extension)?
            \.? ?\d{2-5})?$/i
            return telRegExp.test( telephoneNumber );
}
```

Note in this case that it is important to set the case-insensitive flag by adding an i on the end of the expression definition; otherwise, the regular expression could fail to match the ext parts. Please also note that the regular expression itself must be on one line in your code — it's shown in four lines here due to the page-width restrictions of this book.

Validating a Postal Code

We just about managed to check worldwide telephone numbers, but doing the same for postal codes would be something of a major challenge. Instead, you'll create a function that only checks for U.S. zip codes and UK postcodes. If you needed to check for other countries, the code would need modifying. You may find that checking more than one or two postal codes in one regular expression begins to get unmanageable, and it may well be easier to have an individual regular expression for each country's postal code you need to check. For this purpose though, let's combine the regular expression for the UK and the U.S.:

```
^(\d{5}(-\d{4})?|[a-z][a-z]?\d\d? ?\d[a-z][a-z])$
```

This is actually in two parts: The first part checks for zip codes, and the second part checks UK postcodes. Start by looking at the zip code part.

Zip codes can be represented in one of two formats: as five digits (12345), or five digits followed by a dash and four digits (12345-1234). The zip code regular expression to match these is as follows:

```
\d{5}(-\d{4})?
```

This matches five digits, followed by an optional non-capturing group that matches a dash, followed by four digits.

For a regular expression that covers UK postcodes, let's consider their various formats. UK postcode formats are one or two letters followed by either one or two digits, followed by an optional space, followed by a digit, and then two letters. Additionally, some central London postcodes look like this: SE2V 3ER, with a letter at the end of the first part. Currently, it is only some of those postcodes starting with SE, WC, and W, but that may change. Valid examples of UK postcode include: CH3 9DR, PR29 1XX, M27 1AE, WC1V 2ER, and C27 3AH.

Based on this, the required pattern is as follows:

```
([a-z][a-z]?\d\d?|[a-z]{2}\d[a-z]) ?\d[a-z][a-z]
```

These two patterns are combined using the | character to "match one or the other" and grouped using parentheses. You then add the ^ character at the start and the $ character at the end of the pattern to be sure that the only information in the string is the postal code. Although postal codes should be uppercase, it is still valid for them to be lowercase, so you also set the case-insensitive option as follows when you use the regular expression:

```
^(\d{5}(-\d{4})?|([a-z][a-z]?\d\d?|[a-z{2}\d[a-z]) ?\d[a-z][a-z])$
```

The following function needed for your validation module is much the same as it was with the previous example:

```
function isValidPostalCode( postalCode )
{
```

```
        var pcodeRegExp = /^(\d{5}(-\d{4})?|
([a-z][a-z]?\d\d?|[a-z{2}\d[a-z]) ?\d[a-z][a-z])$/i
        return pcodeRegExp.test( postalCode );
}
```

Again please remember that the regular expression must be on one line in your code.

Validating an E-mail Address

Before working on a regular expression to match e-mail addresses, you need to look at the types of valid e-mail addresses you can have. For example:

- ❑   someone@mailserver.com
- ❑   someone@mailserver.info
- ❑   someone.something@mailserver.com
- ❑   someone.something@subdomain.mailserver.com
- ❑   someone@mailserver.co.uk
- ❑   someone@subdomain.mailserver.co.uk
- ❑   someone.something@mailserver.co.uk
- ❑   someone@mailserver.org.uk
- ❑   some.one@subdomain.mailserver.org.uk

Also, if you examine the SMTP RFC (http://www.ietf.org/rfc/rfc0821.txt), you can have the following:

- ❑   someone@123.113.209.32
- ❑   """Paul Wilton"""@somedomain.com

That's quite a list and contains many variations to cope with. It's best to start by breaking it down. First, there are a couple of things to note about the two immediately above. The latter two versions are exceptionally rate and not provided for in the regular expression you'll create.

You need to break up the e-mail address into separate parts, and you will look at the part after the @ symbol, first.

Validating a Domain Name

Everything has become more complicated since Unicode domain names have been allowed. However, the e-mail RFC still doesn't allow these, so let's stick with the traditional definition of how a domain can be described using ASCII. A domain name consists of a dot-separated list of words, with the last word being between two and four characters long. It was often the case that if a two-letter country word was used, there would be at least two parts to the domain name before it: a grouping domain (.co, .ac, and so on) and a specific domain name. However, with the advent of the .tv names, this is no longer the case. You could make this very specific and provide for the allowed top-level domains (TLDs), but that would make the regular expression very large, and it would be more productive to perform a DNS lookup instead.

Each part of a domain name has certain rules it must follow. It can contain any letter or number or a hyphen, but it must start with a letter. The exception is that, at any point in the domain name, you can use a #, followed by a number, which represents the ASCII code for that letter, or in Unicode, the 16-bit Unicode value. Knowing this, let's begin to build up the regular expression, first with the name part, assuming that the case-insensitive flag will be set later in the code.

```
([a-z]|#\d+)([a-z0-9-]|#\d+)*([a-z0-9]|#\d+)
```

This breaks the domain into three parts. The RFC doesn't specify how many digits can be contained here, so neither will we. The first part must only contain an ASCII letter; the second must contain zero or more of a letter, number, or hyphen; and the third must contain either a letter or number. The top-level domain has more restrictions, as shown here:

```
[a-z]{2,4}
```

This restricts you to a two, three, or four letter top-level domain. So, putting it all together, with the periods you end up with this:

```
^(([a-z]|#\d+?)([a-z0-9-]|#\d+?)*([a-z0-9]|#\d+?)\.)+([a-z]{2,4})$
```

Again, the domain name is anchored at the beginning and end of the string. The first thing is to add an extra group to allow one or more name. portions and then anchor a two-to-four-letter domain name at the end in its own group. We have also made most of the wildcards lazy. Because much of the pattern is similar, it makes sense to do this; otherwise, it would require too much backtracking. However, you have left the second group with a "greedy" wildcard: It will match as much as it can, up until it reaches a character that does not match. Then it will only backtrack one position to attempt the third group match. This is more resource-efficient than a lazy match is in this case, because it could be constantly going forward to attempt the match. One backtrack per name is an acceptable amount of extra processing.

Validating a Person's Address

You can now attempt to validate the part before the @ sign. The RFC specifies that it can contain any ASCII character with a code in the range from 33 to 126. You are assuming that you are matching against ASCII only, so you can assume that there are only 128 characters that the engine will match against. This being the case, it is simpler to just exclude the required values as follows:

```
[^<>()\[\],;:@"\x00-\x20\x7F]+
```

Using this, you're saying that you allow any number of characters, as long as none of them are those contained within the square brackets. The [,], and \ characters have to be escaped. However, the RFC allows for other kinds of matches.

Validating the Complete Address

Now that you have seen all the previous sections, you can build up a regular expression for the entire e-mail address. First, here's everything up to and including the @ sign:

```
^([^<>()\[\],;:@"\x00-\x20\x7F]|\\.)+@
```

That was straightforward. Now for the domain name part.

```
^([^<>()\[\],;:@"\x00-\x20\x7F]|\\.)+@(([a-z]|#\d+?)([a-z0-9-]
|#\d+?)*([a-z0-9]|#\d+?)\.)+([a-z]{2,4})$
```

We've had to put it on two lines to fit this book's page width, but in your code this must all be on one line.

Finally, let's create the function for the JavaScript module.

```
function isValidEmail( emailAddress )
{
        var emailRegExp = /^([^<>()\[\],;:@"\x00-\x20\x7F]|\\.)+
@(([a-z]|#\d+?)([a-z0-9-]|
#\d+?)*([a-z0-9]|#\d+?)\.)+([a-z]{2,4})$/i
        return emailRegExp.test( emailAddress );
}
```

Please note the regular expression must all be on one line in your code.

With the module completed, let's take a look at the code to test the module.

First, the module is linked to the test page like this:

```
<script type="text/javascript" src="ch9_examp7_module.js"></script>
```

Then each of the three test buttons has its click events linked to the validation functions in the module as follows:

```
<input type="button" name="cmdIsValidTelephoneNumber"
        id="cmdIsValidTelephoneNumber"
 value="Is Valid Telephone Number?"
onclick="alert('Is valid is ' +
isValidTelephoneNumber( document.form1.txtString.value ))" />
    <input type="button" name="cmdIsValidPostalCode" id="cmdIsValidPostalCode"
 value="Is Valid Postal Code?"
onclick="alert('Is valid is ' +
isValidPostalCode( document.form1.txtString.value ))" />
    <input type="button" name="cmdIsEmailValid" id="cmdIsEmailValid"
value="Is Valid Email?"
onclick="alert('Is valid is ' + isValidEmail( document.form1.txtString.value ))" />
```

So taking telephone validation test button, an `onclick` event handler is added.

```
onclick="alert('Is valid is ' +
isValidTelephoneNumber( document.form1.txtString.value ))"
```

This shows an alert box returning the true or false value from the `isValidTelephoneNumber()` function in your validation module. In a non-test situation, you'd want a more user-friendly message. The other two test buttons work in the same way but just call different validation functions.

Summary

In this chapter you've looked at some more advanced methods of the `String` object and how you can optimize their use with regular expressions.

To recap, the chapter covered the following points:

❑ The `split()` method splits a single string into an array of strings. You pass a string or a regular expression to the method that determines where the split occurs.

❑ The `replace()` method enables you to replace a pattern of characters with another pattern that you specify as a second parameter.

❑ The `search()` method returns the character position of the first pattern matching the one given as a parameter.

❑ The `match()` method matches patterns, returning the text of the matches in an array.

❑ Regular expressions enable you to define a pattern of characters that you want to match. Using this pattern, you can perform splits, searches, text replacement, and matches on strings.

❑ In JavaScript the regular expressions are in the form of a `RegExp` object. You can create a `RegExp` object using either `myRegExp = /myRegularExpression/` or `myRegExp = new RegExp("myRegularExpression")`. The second form requires that certain special characters that normally have a single \ in front now have two.

❑ The `g` and `i` characters at the end of a regular expression (as in, for example, `myRegExp = /Pattern/gi;`) ensure that a global and case-insensitive match is made.

❑ As well as specifying actual characters, regular expressions have certain groups of special characters, which allow any of certain groups of characters, such as digits, words, or non-word characters, to be matched.

❑ Special characters can also be used to specify pattern or character repetition. Additionally, you can specify what the pattern boundaries must be, for example at the beginning or end of the string, or next to a word or non-word boundary.

❑ Finally, you can define groups of characters that can be used later in the regular expression or in the results of using the expression with the `replace()` method.

In the next chapter, you'll take a look at using and manipulating dates and times using JavaScript, and time conversion between different world time zones. Also covered is how to create a timer that executes code at regular intervals after the page is loaded.

Exercise Questions

Suggested solutions to these questions can be found in Appendix A.

1. What problem does the following code solve?

```
var myString = "This sentence has has a fault and and we need to fix it."
var myRegExp = /(\b\w+\b) \1/g;
myString = myString.replace(myRegExp,"$1");
```

Now imagine that you change that code, so that you create the RegExp object like this:

```
var myRegExp = new RegExp("(\b\w+\b) \1");
```

Why would this not work, and how could you rectify the problem?

2. Write a regular expression that finds all of the occurrences of the word "a" in the following sentence and replaces them with "the":

    "a dog walked in off a street and ordered a finest beer"

    The sentence should become:

    "the dog walked in off the street and ordered the finest beer"

3. Imagine you have a web site with a message board. Write a regular expression that would remove barred words. (You can make up your own words!)

Date, Time, and Timers

Chapter 5 discussed that the concepts of date and time are embodied in JavaScript through the Date object. You looked at some of the properties and methods of the Date object, including the following:

❑   The methods getDate(), getDay(), getMonth(), and getFullYear() enable you to retrieve date values from inside a Date object.

❑   The setDate(), setMonth(), and setFullYear() methods enable you to set the date values of an existing Date object.

❑   The getHours(), getMinutes(), getSeconds(), and getMilliseconds() methods retrieve the time values in a Date object.

❑   The setHours(), setMinutes(), setSeconds(), and setMilliseconds() methods enable you to set the time values of an existing Date object.

One thing not covered in that chapter is the idea that the time depends on your location around the world. In this chapter you'll be correcting that omission by looking at date and time in relation to *world time*.

For example, imagine you have a chat room on your web site and want to organize a chat for a certain date and time. Simply stating 15:30 is not good enough if your web site attracts international visitors. The time 15:30 could be Eastern Standard Time, Pacific Standard Time, the time in the United Kingdom, or even the time in Kuala Lumpur. You could of course say 15:30 EST and let your visitors work out what that means, but even that isn't foolproof. There is an EST in Australia as well as in the United States. Wouldn't it be great if you could automatically convert the time to the user's time zone? In this chapter you'll see how.

In addition to looking at world time, you'll also be looking at how to create a *timer* in a web page. You'll see that by using the timer you can trigger code, either at regular intervals or just once (for example, five seconds after the page has loaded). You'll see how you can use timers to add a real-time clock to a web page and how to create scrolling text in the status bar. Timers can also be useful for creating animations or special effects in your web applications. Finally, you'll be using the timer to enable the users of your trivia quiz to give themselves a time limit for answering the questions.

World Time

The concept of *now* means the same point in time everywhere in the world. However, when that point in time is represented by numbers, those numbers differ depending on where you are. What is needed is a standard number to represent that moment in time. This is achieved through Coordinated Universal Time (UTC), which is an international basis of civil and scientific time and was implemented in 1964. It was previously known as GMT (Greenwich Mean Time), and, indeed, at 0:00 UTC it is midnight in Greenwich, London.

The following table shows local times around the world at 0:00 UTC time.

San ÅtFrancisco	New York (EST)	Greenwich, London	Berlin, Germany	Tokyo, Japan
4:00 pm	7:00 pm	0:00 (midnight)	1:00 am	9:00 am

Note that the times given are winter times — no daylight savings hours are taken into account.

The support for UTC in JavaScript comes from a number of methods of the Date object that are similar to those you have already seen. For each of the set-date- and get-date–type methods you've seen so far, there is a UTC equivalent. For example, whereas setHours() sets the local hour in a Date object, setUTCHours() does the same thing for UTC time. You'll be looking at these methods in more detail in the next section.

In addition, three more methods of the Date object involve world time.

You have the methods toUTCString() and toLocaleString(), which return the date and time stored in the Date object as a string based on either UTC or local time. Most modern browsers also have these additional methods: toLocaleTimeString(), toTimeString(), toLocaleDateString(), and toDateString().

If you simply want to find out the difference in minutes between the current locale's time and UTC, you can use the getTimezoneOffset() method. If the time zone is behind UTC, such as in the United States, it will return a positive number. If the time zone is ahead, such as in Australia or Japan, it will return a negative number.

Try It Out   The World Time Method of the Date Object

In the following code you use the toLocaleString(), toUTCString(), getTimezoneOffset(), toLocaleTimeString(), toTimeString(), toLocaleDateString(), and toDateString() methods and write their values out to the page.

```
<!DOCTYPE html PUBLIC "-//W3C//DTD XHTML 1.0 Transitional//EN"
"http://www.w3.org/TR/xhtml1/DTD/xhtml1-transitional.dtd">
<html xmlns="http://www.w3.org/1999/xhtml">

<head>
<title>example 1</title>

</head>
```

```
<body>
<div id="DisplayResultsDiv"></div>

<script type="text/javascript">
  var localTime = new Date();
  var resultsHTML = '<p>UTC Time is ' + localTime.toUTCString() + '</p>';
  resultsHTML += 'Local Time is ' + localTime.toLocaleString() + '</p>';

  resultsHTML += '<p>Time Zone Offset is ' + localTime.getTimezoneOffset() +
    '</p>';
  resultsHTML += '<p>Using toLocalTimeString() gives: '
                    + localTime.toLocaleTimeString() + '</p>';
  resultsHTML += '<p>Using toTimeString() gives: '
                    + localTime.toTimeString() + '</p>';
  resultsHTML += '<p>Using toLocaleDateString() gives: '
                    + localTime.toLocaleDateString() + '</p>';
  resultsHTML += '<p>Using toDateString() gives: : '
      + localTime.toDateString() + '</p>';
  document.getElementById('DisplayResultsDiv').innerHTML = resultsHTML;

</script>

</body>
</html>
```

Save this as `timetest.htm` and load it into your browser. What you see, of course, depends on which time zone your computer is set to, but your browser should show something similar to Figure 10-1.

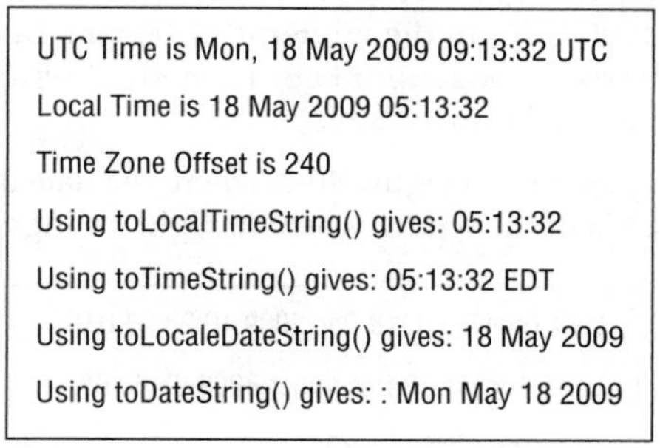

UTC Time is Mon, 18 May 2009 09:13:32 UTC

Local Time is 18 May 2009 05:13:32

Time Zone Offset is 240

Using toLocalTimeString() gives: 05:13:32

Using toTimeString() gives: 05:13:32 EDT

Using toLocaleDateString() gives: 18 May 2009

Using toDateString() gives: : Mon May 18 2009

Figure 10-1

Here the computer's time is set to 05:13:32 a.m. on May 18, 2009, in America's Eastern Standard Time (for example, New York).

So how does this work? At the top of the page's script block, you have just:

```
var localTime = new Date();
```

This creates a new Date object and initializes it to the current date and time based on the client computer's clock. (Note that the Date object simply stores the number of milliseconds between the date and time on your computer's clock and midnight UTC on January 1, 1970.)

Within the rest of the script block, you obtain the results from various time and date functions. The results are stored in variable resultsHTML, and this is then displayed in the page using the last line and the innerHTML property.

In the following line, you store the string returned by the toUTCString() method in the resultsHTML variable:

```
var resultsHTML = '<p>UTC Time is ' + localTime.toUTCString() + '</p>';
```

This converts the date and time stored inside the localTime Date object to the equivalent UTC date and time.

Then the following line stores a string with the local date and time value:

```
resultsHTML += 'Local Time is ' + localTime.toLocaleString() + '</p>';
```

Since this time is just based on the user's computer's clock, the string returned by this method also adjusts for Daylight Savings Time (as long as the clock adjusts for it).

Next, this code stores a string with the difference, in minutes, between the local time zone's time and that of UTC.

```
resultsHTML += '<p>Time Zone Offset is ' + localTime.getTimezoneOffset() +
    '</p>';
```

You may notice in Figure 10-1 that the difference between New York time and UTC time is written to be 240 minutes, or 4 hours. Yet in the previous table, you saw that New York time is 5 hours behind UTC. So what is happening?

Well, in New York on May 18, daylight savings hours are in use. While in the summer it's 8:00 p.m. in New York when it's 0:00 UTC, in the winter it's 7:00 p.m. in New York when it's 0:00 UTC. Therefore, in the summer the getTimezoneOffset() method returns 240, whereas in the winter the getTimezoneOffset() method returns 300.

To illustrate this, compare Figure 10-1 to Figure 10-2, where the date on the computer's clock has been advanced to December, which is in the winter when daylight savings is not in effect:

```
UTC Time is Fri, 18 Dec 2009 10:23:08 UTC

Local Time is 18 December 2009 05:23:08

Time Zone Offset is 300

Using toLocalTimeString() gives: 05:23:08

Using toTimeString() gives: 05:23:08 EST

Using toLocaleDateString() gives: 18 December 2009

Using toDateString() gives: : Fri Dec 18 2009
```

Figure 10-2

The next two methods are toLocaleTimeString() and toTimeString(), as follows:

```
resultsHTML += '<p>Using toLocaleTimeString() gives: ' +
                localTime.toLocaleTimeString() + '</p>';
resultsHTML += '<p>Using toTimeString() gives: ' +
                localTime.toTimeString() + '</p>';
```

These methods display just the time part of the date and time held in the `Date` object. The `toLocaleTimeString()` method displays the time as specified by the user on his computer. The second method displays the time but also gives an indication of the time zone (in the example, EST for Eastern Standard Time in America).

The final two methods display the date part of the date and time. The `toLocaleDateString()` displays the date in the format the user has specified on his computer. On Windows operating systems, this is set in the regional settings of the PC's Control Panel. However, because it relies on the user's PC setup, the look of the date varies from computer to computer. The `toDateString()` method displays the current date contained in the PC date in a standard format.

Of course, this example relies on the fact that the user's computer's clock is set correctly, not something you can be 100 percent sure of — it's amazing how many users have their local time zone settings set completely wrong.

Setting and Getting a Date Object's UTC Date and Time

When you create a new `Date` object, you can either initialize it with a value or let JavaScript set it to the current date and time. Either way, JavaScript assumes you are setting the *local* time values. If you want to specify UTC time, you need to use the `setUTC` type methods, such as `setUTCHours()`.

The following are the seven methods for setting UTC date and time:

- ❑ setUTCDate()
- ❑ setUTCFullYear()
- ❑ setUTCHours()
- ❑ setUTCMilliseconds()
- ❑ setUTCMinutes()
- ❑ setUTCMonth()
- ❑ setUTCSeconds()

The names pretty much give away exactly what each of the methods does, so let's launch straight into a simple example, which sets the UTC time.

```
<!DOCTYPE html PUBLIC "-//W3C//DTD XHTML 1.0 Transitional//EN"
"http://www.w3.org/TR/xhtml1/DTD/xhtml1-transitional.dtd">
<html xmlns="http://www.w3.org/1999/xhtml">

<head>
<title>example 2</title>

</head>
<body>
<div id="DisplayResultsDiv"></div>

<script type="text/javascript">
```

```
    var myDate = new Date();
    myDate.setUTCHours(12);
    myDate.setUTCMinutes(0);
    myDate.setUTCSeconds(0);
    var resultsHTML = '<p>' + myDate.toUTCString() + '</p>';
    resultsHTML += '<p>' + myDate.toLocaleString() + '</p>';

    document.getElementById('DisplayResultsDiv').innerHTML = resultsHTML;

</script>

</body>
</html>
```

Save this as `settimetest.htm`. When you load it in your browser, you should see something like that shown in Figure 10-3 in your web page, although the actual date will depend on the current date and where you are in the world.

Mon, 18 May 2009 12:00:00 UTC
18 May 2009 08:00:00

Figure 10-3

You might want to change your computer's time zone and time of year to see how it varies in different regions and with daylight savings changes. For example, although I'm in the United Kingdom, I have changed the settings on my computer for this example to Eastern Standard Time in the U.S. In Windows you can make the changes by opening the Control Panel and then double-clicking the Date/Time icon.

So how does this example work? You declare a variable, `myDate`, and set it to a new `Date` object. Because you haven't initialized the `Date` object to any value, it contains the local current date and time.

Then, using the `setUTC` methods, you set the hours, minutes, and seconds so that the time is 12:00:00 UTC (midday, not midnight).

Now, when you write out the value of `myDate` as a UTC string, you get 12:00:00 and today's date. When you write out the value of the `Date` object as a local string, you get today's date and a time that is the UTC time 12:00:00 converted to the equivalent local time. The local values you'll see, of course, depend on your time zone. For example, New Yorkers will see 08:00:00 during the summer and 07:00:00 during the winter because of daylight savings. In the United Kingdom, in the winter you'll see 12:00:00, but in the summer you'll see 13:00:00.

For getting UTC dates and times, you have the same functions you would use for setting UTC dates and times, except that this time, for example, it's `getUTCHours()`, not `setUTCHours()`.

❑   `getUTCDate()`

❑   `getUTCDay()`

- ❑   getUTCFullYear()

- ❑   getUTCHours()

- ❑   getUTCMilliseconds()

- ❑   getUTCMinutes()

- ❑   getUTCMonth()

- ❑   getUTCSeconds()

Notice that this time there is an additional method, getUTCDay(). This works in the same way as the getDay() method and returns the day of the week as a number, from 0 for Sunday to 6 for Saturday. Because the day of the week is decided by the day of the month, the month, and the year, there is no setUTCDay() method.

Before moving on to look at timers, let's use your newly gained knowledge of the Date object and world time to create a world time converter. Later in this chapter, when you've learned how to use timers, you'll update the example to produce a world time clock.

Try It Out   **World Time Converter (Part I)**

The World Time Converter lets you calculate the time in different countries:

```
<!DOCTYPE html PUBLIC "-//W3C//DTD XHTML 1.0 Transitional//EN"
"http://www.w3.org/TR/xhtml1/DTD/xhtml1-transitional.dtd">
<html xmlns="http://www.w3.org/1999/xhtml">

<head>
<title>example 3</title>

<script type="text/javascript">
var timeDiff;
var selectedCity;
var daylightSavingAdjust = 0;
function updateTimeZone()
{
   var lstCity = document.form1.lstCity;
   timeDiff = lstCity.options[lstCity.selectedIndex].value;
   selectedCity = lstCity.options[lstCity.selectedIndex].text;
   updateTime();
}
function getTimeString(dateObject)
{
   var timeString;
   var hours = dateObject.getHours();
   if (hours < 10)
      hours = "0" + hours;
   var minutes = dateObject.getMinutes();
   if (minutes < 10)
      minutes = "0" + minutes;
   var seconds = dateObject.getSeconds()
   if (seconds < 10)
      seconds = "0" + seconds;
   timeString = hours + ":" + minutes + ":" + seconds;
   return timeString;
```

```
}
function updateTime()
{
   var nowTime = new Date();
   var resultsText = '<p>Local Time is ' + getTimeString(nowTime) + '</p>';

   nowTime.setMinutes(nowTime.getMinutes() + nowTime.getTimezoneOffset() +
       parseInt(timeDiff) + daylightSavingAdjust);

   resultsText += '<p>' + selectedCity + ' time is ' +
                   getTimeString(nowTime) + '</p>';

   document.getElementById('ConversionResultsDIV').innerHTML = resultsText;

}
function chkDaylightSaving_onclick()
{
   if (document.form1.chkDaylightSaving.checked)
   {
      daylightSavingAdjust = 60;
   }
   else
   {
      daylightSavingAdjust = 0;
   }
   updateTime();
}
</script>
</head>
<body onload="updateTimeZone()">

<div id="ConversionResultsDIV"></div>

<form name="form1">
<select size="5" name="lstCity" onchange="updateTimeZone();">
<option value="60" selected>Berlin
<option value="330">Bombay
<option value="0">London
<option value="180">Moscow
<option value="-300">New York (EST)
<option value="60">Paris
<option value="-480">San Francisco (PST)
<option value="600">Sydney
</select>
<p>
It's summertime in the selected city
and its country adjusts for summertime daylight saving
<input type="checkbox" name="chkDaylightSaving"
   onclick="return chkDaylightSaving_onclick()">
</p>
</form>


</body>
</html>
```

Save this page as `WorldTimeConverter.htm` and then load the page into your browser.

The form layout looks something like the one shown in Figure 10-4. Whenever the user clicks a city in the list, her local time and the equivalent time in the selected city are shown. In the example shown in Figure 10-4, the local region is set to Eastern Standard Time in the U.S. (for a city such as New York), and the selected city is Berlin, with the daylight savings box checked.

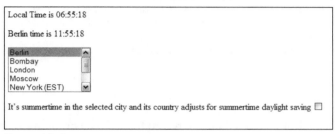

Figure 10-4

It's worth pointing out that this is just an example and not a totally foolproof one, because of the problems presented by daylight savings. Some countries don't have it, others do at fixed times of year, and yet others do but at varying times of the year. This makes it difficult to predict accurately when a country will have its daylight savings period. You have tried to solve this problem by adding a check box for the user to click if the city she chooses from the list is using daylight savings hours (which you assume will put the time in the city forward by one hour).

In addition, don't forget that some users may not even have their regional settings set correctly — there's no easy way around this problem.

In the body of the World Time Converter page is a form in which you've defined a list box using a `<select>` element.

```
<select size="5" name="lstCity" onchange="updateTimeZone();">
<option value="60" selected>Berlin
<option value="330">Bombay
<option value="0">London
<option value="180">Moscow
<option value="-300">New York (EST)
<option value="60">Paris
<option value="-480">San Francisco (PST)
<option value="600">Sydney
</select>
```

Each of the options displays the city's name in the list box and has its value set to the difference in minutes between that city's time zone (in winter) and UTC. So London, which uses UTC, has a value of 0. Paris, which is an hour ahead of UTC, has a value of 60 (that is, 60 minutes). New York, which is five hours behind UTC, has a value of -300.

You'll see that you have captured the `change` event of the `<select>` element and connected it to the function `updateTimeZone()` defined in a script block in the head of the page. This function involves three global variables defined at the top of the script block.

```
var timeDiff;
var selectedCity;
var daylightSavingAdjust = 0;
```

355

The function `updateTimeZone()` updates two of these, setting the variable `timeDiff` to the value of the list's selected option (that is, the time difference between the selected city and UTC time) and the variable `selectedCity` to the text shown for the selected option (that is, the selected city).

```
function updateTimeZone()
{
    var lstCity = document.form1.lstCity;
    timeDiff = lstCity.options[lstCity.selectedIndex].value;
    selectedCity = lstCity.options[lstCity.selectedIndex].text;
```

In the final part of the function `updateTimeZone()`, the function `updateTime()` is called, as shown in the following:

```
    updateTime();
}
```

Before you go on to look at this function, you return to the final part of the form on the page. This is a check box, which the user clicks if the city she has chosen from the select list is in the summertime of a country that uses daylight savings hours.

```
<input type="checkbox" name="chkDaylightSaving"
    onclick="return chkDaylightSaving_onclick()">
```

As you can see, this check box's `click` event is connected to another function, `chkDaylightSaving_onclick()`.

```
function chkDaylightSaving_onclick()
{
    if (document.form1.chkDaylightSaving.checked)
    {
        daylightSavingAdjust = 60;
    }
    else
    {
        daylightSavingAdjust = 0;
    }
```

Inside the `if` statement, the code accesses the check box's `checked` property, which returns `true` if it is checked and `false` otherwise. If it has been checked, you set the global variable `daylightSavingAdjust` to 60 for summertime daylight savings; otherwise it's set to 0.

```
    updateTime();
}
```

At the end of this function (as at the end of the function `updateTimeZone()` you saw earlier), the `updateTime()` function is called. You'll look at that next.

In the function `updateTime()`, you write the current local time and the equivalent time in the selected city to the results DIV with ID `ConversionResultsDIV`, which you defined in the frameset page.

You start at the top of the function by creating a new `Date` object, which is stored in the variable `nowTime`. The `Date` object will be initialized to the current local time.

```
function updateTime()
{
    var nowTime = new Date();
```

Next, to make your code more compact and easier to understand, you define a variable, resultsText, which will store the conversion results prior to them being written to the /ConversionResultsDIV DIV object contained in the page.

The first thing you store in variable resultsText is the local time based on the new Date object you just created. However, you want the time to be nicely formatted as *hours:minutes:seconds*, so you've written another function, getTimeString(), which does this for you. You'll look at that shortly.

```
var resultsText = '<p>Local Time is ' + getTimeString(nowTime) + '</p>';
```

Having stored the current time to your resultsText variable, you now need to calculate what the time would be in the selected city before also storing that to the resultsText variable.

You saw in Chapter 5 that if you set the value of a Date object's individual parts (such as hours, minutes, and seconds) to a value beyond their normal range, JavaScript assumes you want to adjust the date, hours, or minutes to take this into account. For example, if you set the hours to 36, JavaScript simply changes the hours to 12 and adds one day to the date stored inside the Date object. You use this to your benefit in the following line:

```
nowTime.setMinutes(nowTime.getMinutes() + nowTime.getTimezoneOffset() +
    parseInt(timeDiff) + daylightSavingAdjust);
```

Let's break this line down to see how it works. Suppose that you're in New York, with the local summer time of 5:11, and you want to know what time it is in Berlin. How does your line of code calculate this?

First, you get the minutes of the current local time; it's 5:11, so nowTime.getMinutes() returns 11.

Then you get the difference, in minutes, between the user's local time and UTC using nowTime .getTimezoneOffset(). If you are in New York, which is different from UTC by 4 hours during the summer, this is 240 minutes.

Then you get the integer value of the time difference between the standard winter time in the selected city and UTC time, which is stored in the variable timeDiff. You've used parseInt() here because it's one of the few situations where JavaScript gets confused and assumes you want to join two strings together rather than treat the values as numbers and add them together. Remember that you got timeDiff from an HTML element's value, and that an HTML element's values are strings, even when they hold characters that are digits. Since you want the time in Berlin, which is 60 minutes different from UTC time, this value will be 60.

Finally, you add the value of daylightSavingsAdjust. This variable is set in the function chkdaylightsaving_onclick(), which was discussed earlier. Since it's summer where you are and Berlin uses daylight savings hours, this value is 60.

So you have the following:

```
11 + 240 + 60 + 60 = 371
```

Therefore nowTime.setMinutes() is setting the minutes to 371. Clearly, there's no such thing as 371 minutes past the hour, so instead JavaScript assumes you mean 6 hours and 11 minutes after 5:00, that being 11:11 — the time in Berlin that you wanted.

Finally, the updateTime() function updates the resultsText variable and then writes the results to the ConversionResultsDIV.

```
resultsText += '<p>' + selectedCity + ' time is ' +
                    getTimeString(nowTime) + '</p>';

document.getElementById('ConversionResultsDIV').innerHTML = resultsText;
}
```

In the `updateTime()` function, you saw that it uses the function `getTimeString()` to format the time string. Let's look at that function now. This function is passed a `Date` object as a parameter and uses it to create a string with the format *hours:minutes:seconds*.

```
function getTimeString(dateObject)
{
    var timeString;
    var hours = dateObject.getHours();
    if (hours < 10)
        hours = "0" + hours;
    var minutes = dateObject.getMinutes();
    if (minutes < 10)
        minutes = "0" + minutes;
    var seconds = dateObject.getSeconds()
    if (seconds < 10)
        seconds = "0" + seconds;
    timeString = hours + ":" + minutes + ":" + seconds;
    return timeString;
}
```

Why do you need this function? Well, you can't just use this:

```
getHours() + ":" + getMinutes() + ":" + getSeconds()
```

That won't take care of those times when any of the three results of these functions is less than 10. For example, 1 minute past noon would look like 12:1:00 rather than 12:01:00.

The function therefore gets the values for hours, minutes, and seconds and checks each to see if it is below 10. If it is, a zero is added to the front of the string. When all the values have been retrieved, they are concatenated in the variable `timeString` before being returned to the calling function.

In the next section, you're going to look at how, by adding a timer, you can make the displayed time update every second like a clock.

Timers in a Web Page

You can create two types of timers: one-shot timers and continually firing timers. The *one-shot timer* triggers just once after a certain period of time, and the second type of timer continually triggers at set intervals. You will investigate each of these types of timers in the next two sections.

Within reasonable limits, you can have as many timers as you want and can set them going at any point in your code, such as at the window `onload` event or at the click of a button. Common uses for timers include advertisement banner pictures that change at regular intervals or display the changing time in a web page. Also all sorts of animations done with DHTML need `setTimeout()` or `setInterval()` — you'll be looking at DHTML later on in the book.

One-Shot Timer

Setting a one-shot timer is very easy: you just use the window object's setTimeout() method.

```
window.setTimeout("your JavaScript code", milliseconds_delay)
```

The method setTimeout() takes two parameters. The first is the JavaScript code you want executed, and the second is the delay, in milliseconds (thousandths of a second), until the code is executed.

The method returns a value (an integer), which is the timer's unique ID. If you decide later that you want to stop the timer firing, you use this ID to tell JavaScript which timer you are referring to.

For example, to set a timer that fires three seconds after the page has loaded, you could use the following code:

```
<!DOCTYPE html PUBLIC "-//W3C//DTD XHTML 1.0 Transitional//EN"
"http://www.w3.org/TR/xhtml1/DTD/xhtml1-transitional.dtd">
<html xmlns="http://www.w3.org/1999/xhtml">

<head>
<script type="text/javascript">
var timerID;
function window_onload()
{
    timerID = setTimeout("alert('Times Up!')",3000);
    alert('Timer Set');
}
</script>
</head>
<body onload="window_onload()">
</body>
</html>
```

Save this file as timertest.htm, and load it into your browser. In this page a message box appears 3,000 milliseconds (that is, 3 seconds) after the onload event of the window has fired.

The setTimeout() method can also take a direct reference to a function instead of a JavaScript string. For example if you have a function called myFunction then you call setTimeout() like this:

```
window.setTimeout(myFunction, milliseconds_delay)
```

Although setTimeout() is a method of the window object, you'll remember that because the window object is at the top of the hierarchy, you don't need to use its name when referring to its properties and methods. Hence, you can use setTimeout() instead of window.setTimeout().

It's important to note that setting a timer does not stop the script from continuing to execute. The timer runs in the background and fires when its time is up. In the meantime the page runs as usual, and any script after you start the timer's countdown will run immediately. So, in this example, the alert box telling you that the timer has been set appears immediately after the code setting the timer has been executed.

What if you decided that you wanted to stop the timer before it fired?

To clear a timer you use the `window` object's `clearTimeout()` method. This takes just one parameter, the unique timer ID that the `setTimeout()` method returns.

Let's alter the preceding example and provide a button that you can click to stop the timer.

```
<!DOCTYPE html PUBLIC "-//W3C//DTD XHTML 1.0 Transitional//EN"
"http://www.w3.org/TR/xhtml1/DTD/xhtml1-transitional.dtd">
<html xmlns="http://www.w3.org/1999/xhtml">

<head>
<script type="text/javascript">
var timerID;
function window_onload()
{
    timerID = setTimeout("alert('Times Up!')",3000);
    alert('Timer Set');
}

function butStopTimer_onclick()
{
    clearTimeout(timerID);
    alert("Timer has been cleared");
}

</script>
</head>
<body onload="window_onload()">

<form name="form1">
<input type="button" value="Stop Timer" name="butStopTimer"
    onclick="return butStopTimer_onclick()" />
</form>


</body>
</html>
```

Save this as `timertest2.htm` and load it into your browser. Now if you click the Stop Timer button before the three seconds are up, the timer will be cleared. This is because the button is connected to the `butStopTimer_onclick()` function, which uses the timer's ID `timerID` with the `clearTimeout()` method of the `window` object.

Try It Out   Updating a Banner Advertisement

You'll now look at a bigger example using the `setTimeout()` method. The following example creates a web page with an image banner advertisement that changes every few seconds.

```
<!DOCTYPE html PUBLIC "-//W3C//DTD XHTML 1.0 Transitional//EN"
"http://www.w3.org/TR/xhtml1/DTD/xhtml1-transitional.dtd">
<html xmlns="http://www.w3.org/1999/xhtml">

<head>
<script language=JavaScript type="text/javascript">
var currentImgNumber = 1;
var numberOfImages = 3;
```

```
function window_onload()
{
    setTimeout("switchImage()",3000);
}
function switchImage()
{
    currentImgNumber++;
    document.imgAdvert.src = 'AdvertImage' + currentImgNumber + '.jpg';
    if (currentImgNumber < numberOfImages)
    {
        setTimeout("switchImage()",3000);    }
    }
</script>
</head>
<body onload="window_onload()">
<img src="AdvertImage1.jpg" name="imgAdvert" />


</body>
</html>
```

After you've typed in the code, save the page as adverts.htm. You'll also need to create three images named AdvertImage1.jpg, AdvertImage2.jpg, and AdvertImage3.jpg (alternatively, the three images are supplied with the downloadable code for the book).

When the page is loaded, you start with a view of AdvertImage1.jpg, as shown in Figure 10-5.

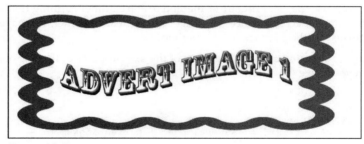

Figure 10-5

In three seconds, this changes to the second image, shown in Figure 10-6.

Figure 10-6

Finally, three seconds later, a third and final image loads, shown in Figure 10-7.

Figure 10-7

When the page loads, the `<img>` tag has its `src` attribute set to the first image.

```
<img src="AdvertImage1.jpg" name="imgAdvert" />
```

Within the `<body>` tag, you connect the `window` object's `onload` event handler to the function `window_onload()`.

```
function window_onload()
{
    setTimeout("switchImage()",3000)
}
```

In this function, you use the `setTimeout()` method to start a timer running that will call the function `switchImage()` in three seconds. Since you don't have to clear the timer, you haven't bothered to save the timer ID returned by the `setTimeout()` method.

The `switchImage()` function changes the value of the `src` property of the `img` object corresponding to the `<img>` tag in your page.

```
function switchImage()
{
    currentImgNumber++;
    document.imgAdvert.src = 'AdvertImage' + currentImgNumber + '.jpg';
```

Your advertisement images are numbered from one to three: `AdvertImage1.jpg`, `AdvertImage2.jpg`, and `AdvertImage3.jpg`. You keep track of the number of the advertisement image currently loaded in the page in the global variable `currentImgNumber`, which you defined at the top of the script block and initialized to 1. To get the next image you simply increment that variable by one, and then update the image loaded by setting the `src` property of the `img` object, using the variable `currentImgNumber` to build up its full name.

```
    if (currentImgNumber < numberOfImages)
    {
        setTimeout('switchImage()',3000);
    }
}
```

You have three advertisement images you want to show. In the `if` statement you check to see whether `currentImgNumber`, which is the number of the current image, is less than three. If it is, it means there are more images to show, and so you set another timer going, identical to the one you set in the `window` object's `onload` event handler. This timer will call this function again in three seconds.

In earlier browsers, this was the only method of creating a timer that fired continually at regular intervals. However, in most current browsers such as IE6+ and Firefox, you'll see next that there's an easier way.

Setting a Timer that Fires at Regular Intervals

Modern browsers saw new methods added to the `window` object for setting timers, namely the `setInterval()` and `clearInterval()` methods. These work in a very similar way to `setTimeout()` and `clearTimeout()`, except that the timer fires continually at regular intervals rather than just once.

The method `setInterval()` takes the same parameters as `setTimeout()`, except that the second parameter now specifies the interval, in milliseconds, between each firing of the timer, rather than just the length of time before the timer fires.

For example, to set a timer that fires the function `myFunction()` every five seconds, the code would be as follows:

```
var myTimerID = setInterval("myFunction()",5000);
```

As with `setTimeout()`, the `setInterval()` method returns a unique timer ID that you'll need if you want to clear the timer with `clearInterval()`, which works identically to `clearTimeout()`. So to stop the timer started in the preceding code, you would use the following:

```
clearInterval(myTimerID);
```

Try It Out   World Time Converter (Part 2)

Let's change the world time example that you saw earlier, so that it displays a local time and selected city time as a continually updating clock.

You'll be making changes to the `WorldTimeConverter.htm` file, so open that in your text editor. Add the following function before the functions that are already defined:

```
var daylightSavingAdjust = 0;
function window_onload()
{
    updateTimeZone();
    window.setInterval("updateTime()",1000);
}
function updateTimeZone()
{
```

Next edit the `<body>` tag so it looks like this:

```
<body onload="return window_onload()">
```

Resave the file, and then load `WorldTimeConverter.htm` into your browser. The page should look the same as the previous version of the time converter, except that the time is updated every second.

The changes you made were short and simple. In the function `window_onload()`, you have added a timer that will call the `updateTime()` function every 1,000 milliseconds — that is, every second. It'll keep doing this until you leave the page. Previously your `updateTime()` function was called only when the user clicked either a different city in the list box or the summertime check box.

The `window_onload()` function is connected to the `window` object's `onload` event in the `<body>` tag, so after the page has loaded your clock starts running.

That completes your look at this example and also your introduction to timers.

Summary

You started the chapter by looking at Coordinated Universal Time (UTC), which is an international standard time. You then looked at how to create timers in web pages.

The particular points covered were the following:

❑   The `Date` object enables you to set and get UTC time in a way similar to setting a `Date` object's local time by using methods (such as `setUTCHours()` and `getUTCHours()`) for setting and getting UTC hours with similar methods for months, years, minutes, seconds, and so on.

❑   A useful tool in international time conversion is the `getTimezoneOffset()` method, which returns the difference, in minutes, between the user's local time and UTC. One pitfall of this is that you are assuming the user has correctly set his time zone on his computer. If not, `getTimezoneOffset()` is rendered useless, as will be any local date and time methods if the user's clock is incorrectly set.

❑   Using the `setTimeout()` method, you found you could start a timer going that would fire just once after a certain number of milliseconds. `setTimeout()` takes two parameters: the first is the code you want executed, and the second is the delay before that code is executed. It returns a value, the unique timer ID that you can use if you later want to reference the timer; for example, to stop it before it fires, you use the `clearTimeout()` method.

❑   To create a timer that fires at regular intervals, you used the `setInterval()` method, which works in the same way as `setTimeout()`, except that it keeps firing unless the user leaves the page or you call the `clearInterval()` method.

In the next chapter, you'll be looking at a way of storing information on the user's computer using something called a cookie. Although they may not be powerful enough to hold a user's life history, they are certainly enough for us to keep track of a user's visits to the website and what pages they view when they visit. With that information, you can provide a more customized experience for the user.

Exercise Questions

Suggested solutions to these questions can be found in Appendix A.

1. Create a web page with an advertisement image at the top. When the page loads, select a random image for that advertisement. Every four seconds, make the image change to a different one and ensure a different advertisement is selected until all the advertisement images have been seen.

2. Create a form that gets the user's date of birth. Then, using that information, tell them on what day of the week they were born.

Storing Information: Cookies

Our goal as web site programmers should be to make the web site experience as easy and pleasant for the user as possible. Clearly, well-designed pages with easily navigable layouts are central to this, but they're not the whole story. You can go one step further by learning about your users and using information gained about them to personalize the web site.

For example, imagine a user, whose name you asked on the first visit, returns to your web site. You could welcome her back to the web site by greeting her by name. Another good example is given by a web site, such as Amazon's, that incorporates the one-click purchasing system. By already knowing the user's purchasing details, such as credit-card number and delivery address, you can allow the user to go from viewing a book to buying it in just one click, making the likelihood of the user purchasing it that much greater. Also, based on information, such as the previous purchases and browsing patterns of the user, it's possible to make book suggestions.

Such personalization requires that information about users be stored somewhere in between their visits to the web site. Previous chapters have mentioned that accessing the user's local file system from a web application is pretty much off limits because of security restrictions included in browsers. However, you, as a web site developer, can store small amounts of information in a special place on the user's local disk, using what is called a *cookie*. There may be a logical reason why they are named cookies, but it also provides authors with the opportunity to make a lot of second-rate, food-related jokes!

Baking Your First Cookie

The key to cookies is the `document` object's `cookie` property. Using this property, you can create and retrieve cookie data from within your JavaScript code.

You can set a cookie by setting `document.cookie` to a *cookie string*. You'll be looking in detail at how this cookie string is made up later in the chapter, but let's first create a simple example of a cookie and see where the information is stored on the user's computer.

A Fresh-Baked Cookie

The following code will set a cookie with the UserName set as Paul and an expiration date of 28 December, 2020.

```
<!DOCTYPE html PUBLIC "-//W3C//DTD XHTML 1.0 Transitional//EN"
"http://www.w3.org/TR/xhtml1/DTD/xhtml1-transitional.dtd">
<html xmlns="http://www.w3.org/1999/xhtml">

<head>
<script language="JavaScript" type="text/javascript">
    document.cookie = 'UserName=Paul;expires=Tue, 28 Dec 2020 00:00:00;';
</script>
</head>
<body>
<p>This page just created a cookie</p>
</body>

</html>
```

Save the page as FreshBakedCookie.htm. You'll see how the code works as you learn the parts of a cookie string, but first let's see what happens when a cookie is created.

How you view cookies without using code varies with the browser you are using. You'll see how to do it first in IE and then in Firefox (FF).

Viewing Cookies in IE

In this section, you'll see how to look at the cookies that are already stored by IE on your computer. You'll then load the cookie-creating page you just created with the preceding code to see what effect this has.

1. First, you need to open IE. The examples in this chapter use IE 8, so if you're using an earlier version of IE you may find the screenshots and menus in slightly different places.

2. Before you view the cookies, you'll first clear the temporary Internet file folder for the browser, because this will make it easier to view the cookies that your browser has stored. In IE, select Tools ➪ Internet Options, which is shown in Figure 11-1.

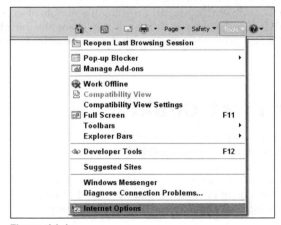

Figure 11-1

Having selected this option, you'll be presented with the Internet Options dialog box shown in Figure 11-2.

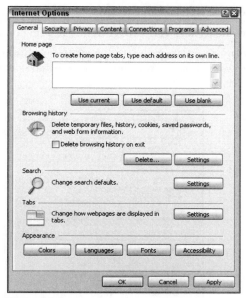

Figure 11-2

3. Click the Delete button under Browsing history. Another dialog box appears, as shown in Figure 11-3.

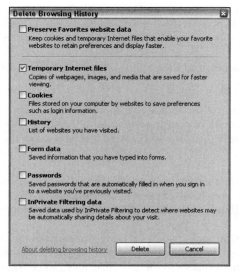

Figure 11-3

4. Make sure to just the select the tick box next to Temporary Internet Files and then click the Delete button. You now have a nice clean cache, which makes it easy to see when you create a cookie.

5. You can now close the dialog box and return to the main Internet Options dialog box.

Let's have a look at the cookies you have currently residing on your machine.

6. From the Internet Options dialog box, click the Settings button next to the Delete button grouped under Browsing history. You should see the dialog box shown in Figure 11-4.

Figure 11-4

7. Now click the View files button, and a list of all the temporary pages and cookie files on your computer will be displayed. If you followed the previous instructions and deleted all temporary Internet files, there should be nothing listed, as shown in Figure 11-5.

The actual cookies, their names, and their values, may look slightly different depending on your computer's operating system.

You can examine the contents of the cookies by double-clicking them. Note that you may get a warning about the potential security risk of opening a text file, although you are fairly safe with cookies because they are simply text files. In Figure 11-6 you can see the contents of the cookie file named `google` set by the search engine Google.

As you can see, a cookie is just a plain old text file. Each web site, or *domain name*, has its own text file where all the cookies for that web site are stored. In this case, there's just one cookie currently stored for `google.co.uk`. Domains like `amazon.com` will almost certainly have many cookies set.

In Figure 11-6, you can see the cookie's details. Here, the name of the cookie is `PREF`; its value is a series of characters, which although indecipherable to you make sense to the Google web site. It was set by the domain `google.co.uk`, and it relates to the root directory `/`. The contents probably look like a mess of characters, but don't worry: When you learn how to program cookies, you'll see that you don't need to worry about setting the details in this format.

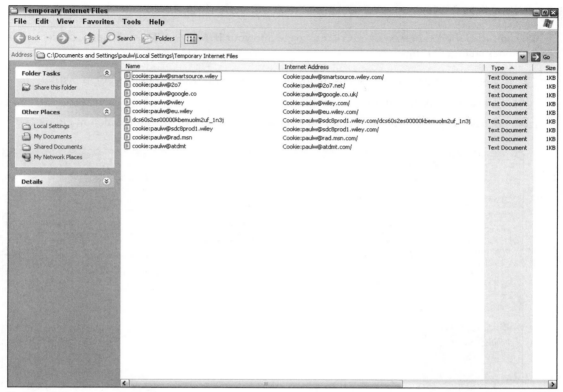

Figure 11-5

Figure 11-6

After you have finished, close the cookie and click OK on the dialog boxes to return to the browser.

Now let's load the `FreshBakedCookie.htm` page into your IE browser. This will set a cookie. Let's see how it has changed things:

1. Return to the Internet Options dialog box (by choosing Tools ➪ Internet Options).

2. Click the Settings button.

3. Click View Files. Your computer now shows something like the information in Figure 11-7.

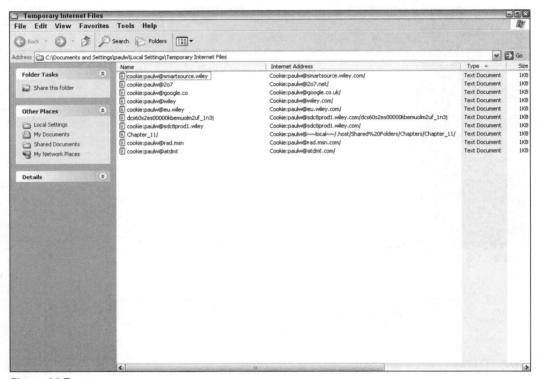

Figure 11-7

Because you are creating a cookie from a web page stored on the local hard drive rather than a server, its domain name has been set to the name of the directory the web page is stored in. Obviously, this is a little artificial. In reality, people will be loading your web pages from your web site on the Internet and not off your local hard drive. The Internet address is based on the directory the `FreshBakedCookie.htm` file was in. You can also see that it expires on December 28, 2020, as you specified when you created the cookie. Double-click the cookie to view its contents, which look like those in Figure 11-8.

You can see the name you gave to the cookie at the left, `UserName`, its value, `Paul`, and also the directory it's applicable to. The expiration date is there as well; it's just not in an easily recognizable form. Note that you may sometimes need to close the browser and reopen it before you see the cookie file.

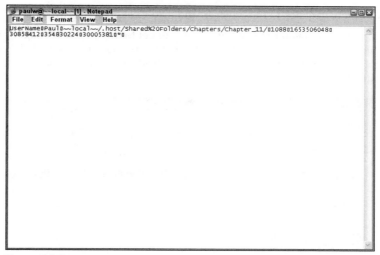

Figure 11-8

Viewing Cookies in Firefox

There is no sharing of cookies between browsers, so the cookies stored when you visited web sites using an IE browser won't be available to Firefox and vice versa.

FF keeps its cookies in a totally different place from IE, and the contents are viewed by a different means. To view cookies in Firefox:

1. Choose Tools ➪ Internet Options.
2. Select the Privacy option.
3. Click the Show Cookies button and you should see the dialog box shown in Figure 11-9.

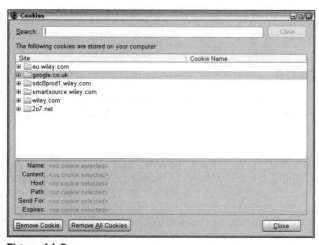

Figure 11-9

4. Click Close to get back to the browser, and load `FreshBakedCookie.htm`.

5. Repeat the process you followed previously to get to the Cookie Manager, and you should find that the `UserName` cookie has been added to the box. Because it's loaded from a file on your PC and not the Internet, the cookie has a blank web address. The expanded cookie details are shown in Figure 11-10.

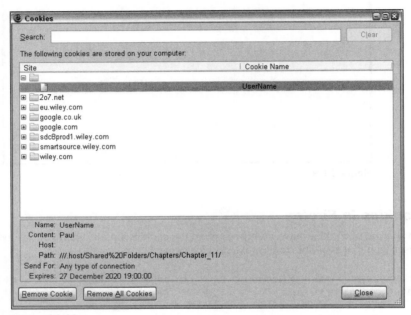

Figure 11-10

Note that buttons are provided at the bottom of the Cookie Manager to remove the cookie selected or all of the cookies that are stored.

Now that you've seen how to view cookies manually, let's look at how you create them and read them using code. You'll start by looking at each of the parts making up a cookie string.

The Cookie String

When you are creating a cookie there are six parts you can set: name, value, expires, path, domain, and secure, although the latter four of these are optional. You'll now look at each of these in turn.

name and value

The first part of the cookie string consists of the name and value of the cookie. The name is used so that you can reference the cookie later, and the value is the information part of the cookie.

This name/value part of the cookie string is compulsory; it sort of defeats the point of the cookie if you don't store a name or value, because storing information is what cookies are all about. You should make sure that this part comes first in the cookie string.

The value for the cookie is a primitive string, although the string can hold number characters if it is numerical data that you want to store. If you are storing text, certain characters, such as semicolons, cannot be used inside the value, unless you use a special encoding, which you'll see later. In the case of semicolons, this is because they are used to separate the different parts of the cookie within the cookie string.

In the following line of code, you set a cookie with the name UserName and the value Paul.

```
document.cookie = "UserName=Paul;";
```

This cookie has a very limited *lifespan*, which is the length of time the information will continue to exist. If you don't set an expiration date, a cookie will expire when the user closes the browser. The next time the user opens the browser the cookie will be gone. This is fine if you just want to store information for the life of a user *session*, which is a single visit by the user to your web site. However, if you want to ensure that your cookie is available for longer, you must set its expiration date, which you'll look at next.

expires

If you want a cookie to exist for longer than just a single user session, you need to set an expiration date using the second part of the cookie string, expires, as follows:

```
document.cookie = "UserName=Paul;expires=Tue, 28 Dec 2020 00:00:00 GMT; ";
```

The cookie set by the previous line of code will remain available for future use right up until December 28, 2020.

> *Note that the format of the expiration date is very important, especially for IE browsers. It should be the same format the cookie is given by the* toGMTString() *method. This method is similar to the* toUTCString() *method that you saw in Chapter 10.*

In practice, you'll probably use the Date object to get the current date, and then set a cookie to expire three or six months after this date. Otherwise, you're going to need to rewrite your pages on December 28, 2020.

For example, you could write the following:

```
var expireDate = new Date();
expireDate.setMonth(expireDate.getMonth() + 6);
document.cookie = "UserName=Paul;expires=" + expireDate.toGMTString() + ";";
```

This will create a new cookie called UserName with the value of Paul, which will expire six months from the current date. Note that other factors can cause a cookie to expire before its expiration date, such as the user deleting the cookie or the upper cookie limit being reached.

path

You'll find that 99 percent of the time you will only need to set the name, value, and expires parts of a cookie. However, at times the other three parts, such as the path part that you are looking at in this section, need to be set. The final two parts, domain and secure, are for advanced use beyond the scope of a beginners' book, but you'll look at them briefly just for completeness.

You're probably used to the idea of there being directories on your hard drive. Rather than storing everything on your computer in one place on the hard drive, you divide it into these directories. For example, you might keep your word-processing files in My Documents, your image files in My Images, and so on. You probably also subdivide your directories, so under My Images you might have subdirectories called My Family and My Holiday.

Well, web servers use the same principle. Rather than putting the whole web site into one web directory, it's common and indeed sensible to divide it into various different directories. For example, if you visit the Wrox web site at www.wrox.com and then click one of the book categories, you'll find that the path to the page navigated to is now www.wrox.com/Books/.

This is all very interesting, but why is it relevant to cookies?

The problem is that cookies are specific not only to a particular web domain, such as www.wrox.com, but also to a particular path on that domain. For example, if a page in www.wrox.com/Books/ sets a cookie, then only pages in that directory or its subdirectories will be able to read and change the cookie. If a page in www.wrox.com/academic/ tried to read the cookie, it would fail. Why are cookies restricted like this?

Take the common example of free web space. A lot of companies on the Web enable you to sign up for free web space. Usually everyone who signs up for this web space has a site at the same domain. For example, Bob's web site might be at www.freespace.com/members/bob/. Belinda might have hers at www.freespace.com/members/belinda. If cookies could be retrieved and changed regardless of the path, then any cookies set on Bob's web site could be viewed by Belinda and vice versa. This is clearly something neither of them would be happy about. Not only is there a security problem, but if, unknown to each other, they both have a cookie named MyHotCookie, there would be problems with each of them setting and retrieving the same cookie. When you think how many users a free web space provider often has, you can see that there is potential for chaos.

Okay, so now you know that cookies are specific to a certain path, but what if you want to view your cookies from two different paths on your server? Say, for example, you have an online store at www.mywebsite.com/mystore/ but you subdivide the store into subdirectories, such as /Books and /Games. Now let's imagine that your checkout is in the directory www.mywebsite.com/mystore/ Checkout. Any cookies set in the /Books and /Games directories won't be visible to each other or pages in the /Checkout directory. To get around this you can either set cookies only in the /mystore directory, since these can be read by that directory and any of its subdirectories, or you can use the path part of the cookie string to specify that the path of the cookie is /mystore even if it's being set in the /Games or /Books or /Checkout subdirectories.

For example, you could do this like so:

```
document.cookie = "UserName=Paul;expires=Tue, 28 Dec 2020 00:00:00" +
";path=/mystore;";
```

Now, even if the cookie is set by a page in the directory /Books, it will still be accessible to files in the /mystore directory and its subdirectories, such as /Checkout and /Games.

If you want to specify that the cookie is available to all subdirectories of the domain it is set in, you can specify a `path` of the root directory using the / character.

```
document.cookie = "UserName=Paul;expires=Tue, 28 Dec 2020 00:00:00;path=/;";
```

Now, the cookie will be available to all directories on the domain it is set from. If the web site is just one of many at that domain, it's best not to do this because everyone else will also have access to your cookie information.

It's important to note that although Windows computers don't have case-sensitive directory names, many other operating systems do. For example, if your web site is on a Unix- or Linux-based server, the `path` property will be case-sensitive.

domain

The fourth part of the cookie string is the `domain`. An example of a domain is `wrox.com` or `pawilton.com`. Like the `path` part of the cookie string, the `domain` part is optional and it's unlikely that you'll find yourself using it very often.

By default, cookies are available only to pages in the domain they were set in. For example, if you have your first web site running on a server with the domain `MyPersonalWebSite.MyDomain.Com` and you have a second web site running under `MyBusinessWebSite.MyDomain.Com`, a cookie set in one web site will not be available to pages accessed under the other domain name, and vice versa. Most of the time, this is exactly what you want, but if it is not, you can use the `domain` part of the cookie string to specify that a cookie is available to all subdomains of the specified domain. For example, the following sets a cookie that can be shared across both subdomains:

```
document.cookie = "UserName=Paul;expires=Tue, 28 Dec 2020 00:00:00;path=/" +
";domain=MyDomain.Com;";
```

Note that the domain must be the same: You can't share `www.SomeoneElsesDomain.com` with `www.MyDomain.com`.

secure

The final part of the cookie string is the `secure` part. This is simply a Boolean value; if it's set to `true` the cookie will be sent only to a web server that tries to retrieve it using a secure channel. The default value, which is `false`, means the cookie will always be sent, regardless of the security. This is only applicable where you have set up a server with SSL (Secure Sockets Layer).

Creating a Cookie

To make life easier for yourself, you'll write a function that enables you to create a new cookie and set certain of its attributes with more ease. This is the first of a number of useful functions you'll create and add to a separate .js file so you can easily re-use the code in your future projects. You'll look at the code first and create an example using it shortly. First create a file called `CookieFunctions.js` and add the following to it:

```
function setCookie(cookieName, cookieValue, cookiePath, cookieExpires)
{
```

```
        cookieValue = escape(cookieValue);
        if (cookieExpires == "")
        {
            var nowDate = new Date();
            nowDate.setMonth(nowDate.getMonth() + 6);
            cookieExpires = nowDate.toGMTString();
        }
        if (cookiePath != "")
        {
            cookiePath = ";Path=" + cookiePath;
        }
        document.cookie = cookieName + "=" + cookieValue +
            ";expires=" + cookieExpires + cookiePath;
    }
```

The secure and domain parts of the cookie string are unlikely to be needed, so you allow just the name, value, expires, and path parts of a cookie to be set by the function. If you don't want to set a path or expiration date, you just pass empty strings for those parameters. If no path is specified, the current directory and its subdirectories will be the path. If no expiration date is set, you just assume a date six months from now.

The first line of the function introduces the escape() function, which you've not seen before.

```
        cookieValue = escape(cookieValue);
```

When we talked about setting the value of a cookie, we mentioned that certain characters cannot be used directly, such as a semicolon. (This also applies to the name of the cookie.) To get around this problem, you can use the built-in escape() and unescape() functions. The escape() function converts characters that are not text or numbers into the hexadecimal equivalent of their character in the Latin-1 character set, preceded by a % character.

For example, a space has the hexadecimal value 20, and the semicolon the value 3B. So the following code produces the output shown in Figure 11-11:

```
        alert(escape("2001 a space odyssey;"));
```

Figure 11-11

You can see that each space has been converted to %20, the % indicating that it represents an escape or special character rather than an actual character, and that 20 is the ASCII value of the actual character. The semicolon has been converted to %3B, as you'd expect.

As you'll see later, when retrieving cookie values you can use the unescape() function to convert from the encoded version to plain text.

Back to your function; next you have an if statement.

```
if (cookieExpires == "")
{
    var nowDate = new Date();
    nowDate.setMonth(nowDate.getMonth() + 6);
    cookieExpires = nowDate.toGMTString();
}
```

This deals with the situation in which an empty string (" ") has been passed for the cookieExpires parameter of the function. Because most of the time you want a cookie to last longer than the session it's created in, you set a default value for expires that is six months after the current date.

Next, if a value other than an empty string (" ") has been passed to the function for the cookiePath parameter, you need to add that value when you create the cookie. You simply put "path=" in front of any value that has been passed in the cookiePath parameter.

```
if (cookiePath != "")
{
    cookiePath = ";Path=" + cookiePath;
}
```

Finally, on the last line you actually create the cookie, putting together the cookieName, cookieValue, cookieExpires, and cookiePath parts of the string.

```
document.cookie = cookieName + "=" + cookieValue +
    ";expires=" + cookieExpires + cookiePath;
```

You'll be using the setCookie() function whenever you want to create a new cookie because it makes setting a cookie slightly easier than having to remember all the parts you want to set. More important, it can be used to set the expiration date to a date six months ahead of the current date.

For example, to use the function and set a cookie with default values for expires and path, you just type the following:

```
setCookie("cookieName","cookieValue","","")
```

Try It Out   **Using setCookie()**

You'll now put all this together in a simple example in which you use your setCookie() function to set three cookies named Name, Age, and FirstVisit. You then display what is in the document.cookie property to see how it has been affected.

```
<!DOCTYPE HTML PUBLIC "-//W3C//DTD HTML 4.01 Transitional//EN"
"http://www.w3.org/TR/html4/loose.dtd">
<html>
<head>
<script language="JavaScript" type="text/JavaScript">
```

```
function setCookie (cookieName, cookieValue, cookiePath, cookieExpires)
{
    cookieValue = escape(cookieValue);
    if (cookieExpires == "")
    {
        var nowDate = new Date();
        nowDate.setMonth(nowDate.getMonth() + 6);
        cookieExpires = nowDate.toGMTString();
    }
    if (cookiePath != "")
    {
        cookiePath = ";Path=" + cookiePath;
    }
    document.cookie = cookieName + "=" + cookieValue +
        ";expires=" + cookieExpires + cookiePath;
}
setCookie("Name","Bob","","");
setCookie("Age","101","","");
setCookie("FirstVisit","10 May 2007","","");
alert(document.cookie);
</script>
</head>
<body>
</body>
</html>
```

Save the example as `CreateCookie.htm` and load it into a web browser.

You'll see the alert box shown in Figure 11-12. Note that all three cookies are displayed as name/value pairs separated from the others by semicolons, and also that the expiration date is not displayed. If you had set the path parameter, this also would not have been displayed. The `UserName` cookie from a previous example is also displayed.

Figure 11-12

You've already seen how the `setCookie()` function works, so let's look at the three lines that use the function to create three new cookies.

```
setCookie("Name","Bob","","");
setCookie("Age","101","","");
setCookie("FirstVisit","10 May 2007","","");
```

It is all fairly simple. The first parameter is the name that you'll give the cookie. (You'll see shortly how you can retrieve a value of a cookie based on the name you gave it.) It's important that the names you use be only alphanumeric characters, with no spaces, punctuation, or special characters. Although you can use cookie names with these characters, doing so is more complex and best avoided. Next you have the value you want to give the cookie. The third parameter is the path, and the fourth parameter is the date you want the cookie to expire on.

For example, take the first line where you use the `setCookie()` function. Here you are setting a cookie that will be named `Name` and have the value `Bob`. You don't want to set the `path` or `expires` parts, so you just pass an empty string (`" "`). Note that you must pass the empty string. You can't pass nothing at all.

The remaining two lines in the previous code snippet set the cookies named `Age` and `FirstVisit` and set their values to `101` and `10 May 2007`, respectively.

If you did want to set the path and the expiration date, how might you change your code?

Well, imagine that you want the path to be `/MyStore` and the expiration date to be one year in the future. Then you can use the `setCookie()` function in the following way:

```
var expireDate = new Date();
expireDate.setMonth(expireDate.getMonth() + 12);
setCookie("Name","Bob","/MyStore",expireDate.toGMTString());
```

First, you create a new `Date` object, and by passing no parameter to its constructor, you let it initialize itself to the current date. In the next line, you add 12 months to that date. When setting the cookie using `setCookie()` you pass `"/MyStore"` as the path and `expireDate.toGMTString()` as the expires parameter.

What about the situation in which you've created your cookie, say, one named `Name` with a value of `Bob`, and you want to change its value? To do this, you can simply set the same cookie again, but with the new value. To change the cookie named `Name` from a value of `Bob` to a value of `Bobby` you'd need the following code:

```
setCookie("Name","Bobby","","");
```

What if you want to delete an existing cookie? Well, that's easy. Just make it expire by changing its value and setting its expiration date to a date in the past, as in the following example:

```
setCookie("Name","","","Mon, 1 Jan 1990 00:00:00");
```

Getting a Cookie's Value

In the preceding example, you used `document.cookie` to retrieve a string containing information about the cookies that have been set. However, this string has two limitations.

❑ The cookies are retrieved in name/value pairs, with each individual cookie separated by a semicolon. The `expires`, `path`, `domain`, and `secure` parts of the cookie are not available to you and cannot be retrieved.

❑ The `cookie` property enables you to retrieve only *all* the cookies set for a particular path and, when they are hosted on a web server, that web server. So, for example, there's no simple way of just getting the value of a cookie with the name `Age`. To do this you'll have to use the string manipulation techniques you learned in previous chapters to cut the information you want out of the returned string.

A lot of different ways exist to get the value of an individual cookie, but the way you'll use has the advantage of working with all cookie-enabled browsers. You use the following function, which needs to be added to your `CookieFunctions.js` file:

```
function getCookieValue(cookieName)
{
    var cookieValue = document.cookie;
    var cookieStartsAt = cookieValue.indexOf(" " + cookieName + "=");
    if (cookieStartsAt == -1)
    {
        cookieStartsAt = cookieValue.indexOf(cookieName + "=");
    }
    if (cookieStartsAt == -1)
    {
        cookieValue = null;
    }
    else
    {
        cookieStartsAt = cookieValue.indexOf("=", cookieStartsAt) + 1;
        var cookieEndsAt = cookieValue.indexOf(";", cookieStartsAt);
        if (cookieEndsAt == -1)
        {
            cookieEndsAt = cookieValue.length;
        }
        cookieValue = unescape(cookieValue.substring(cookieStartsAt,
            cookieEndsAt));
    }
    return cookieValue;
}
```

The first task of the function is to get the `document.cookie` string and store it in the variable `cookieValue`.

```
var cookieValue = document.cookie;
```

Next, you need to find out where the cookie with the name passed as a parameter to the function is within the `cookieValue` string. You use the `indexOf()` method of the `String` object to find this information, as shown in the following line:

```
var cookieStartsAt = cookieValue.indexOf(" " + cookieName + "=");
```

The method will return either the character position where the individual cookie is found or –1 if no such name, and therefore no such cookie, exists. You search on `" " + cookieName + "="` so that you don't inadvertently find cookie names or values containing the name that you require. For example, if you have `xFoo`, `Foo`, and `yFoo` as cookie names, a search for `Foo` without a space in front would match `xFoo` first, which is not what you want!

If `cookieStartsAt` is –1, the cookie either does not exist or it's at the very beginning of the cookie string so there is no space in front of its name. To see which of these is true, you do another search, this time with no space.

```
if (cookieStartsAt == -1)
{
```

```
        cookieStartsAt = cookieValue.indexOf(cookieName + "=");
}
```

In the next `if` statement, you check to see whether the cookie has been found. If it hasn't, you set the `cookieValue` variable to `null`.

```
    if (cookieStartsAt == -1)
    {
        cookieValue = null;
    }
```

If the cookie has been found, you get the value of the cookie you want from the `document.cookie` string in an `else` statement. You do this by finding the start and the end of the value part of that cookie. The start will be immediately after the equals sign following the name. So in the following line, you find the equals sign following the name of the cookie in the string by starting the `indexOf()` search for an `equals` sign from the character at which the cookie name/value pair starts.

```
    else
    {
        cookieStartsAt = cookieValue.indexOf("=", cookieStartsAt) + 1;
```

You then add one to this value to move past the equals sign.

The end of the cookie value will either be at the next semicolon or at the end of the string, whichever comes first. You do a search for a semicolon, starting from the `cookieStartsAt` index, in the next line.

```
        var cookieEndsAt = cookieValue.indexOf(";", cookieStartsAt);
```

If the cookie you are after is the last one in the string, there will be no semicolon and the `cookieEndsAt` variable will be –1 for no match. In this case you know the end of the cookie value must be the end of the string, so you set the variable `cookieEndsAt` to the length of the string.

```
        if (cookieEndsAt == -1)
        {
            cookieEndsAt = cookieValue.length;
        }
```

You then get the cookie's value using the `substring()` method to cut the value that you want out of the main string. Because you have encoded the string with the `escape()` function, you need to unescape it to get the real value, hence the use of the `unescape()` function.

```
        cookieValue = unescape(cookieValue.substring(cookieStartsAt,
            cookieEndsAt));
    }
```

Finally you return the value of the cookie to the calling function.

```
        return cookieValue;
```

What's New?

Now you know how to create and retrieve cookies. Let's use this knowledge in an example in which you check to see if any changes have been made to a web site since the user last visited it.

You'll be creating two pages for this example. The first is the main page for a web site; the second is the page with details of new additions and changes to the web site. A link to the second page will appear on the first page only if the user has visited the page before (that is, if a cookie exists) but has not visited since the page was last updated.

Let's create the first page.

```
<!DOCTYPE html PUBLIC "-//W3C//DTD XHTML 1.0 Transitional//EN"
"http://www.w3.org/TR/xhtml1/DTD/xhtml1-transitional.dtd">
<html xmlns="http://www.w3.org/1999/xhtml">
<head>
<title>Cookie Example</title>
<script language="JavaScript" type="text/JavaScript"
src="CookieFunctions.js"></script>
<script language="JavaScript" type="text/javascript">
var lastUpdated = new Date("Tue, 28 Dec 2020");

</script>
</head>
<body>
<h1 align=center>Welcome to my website</h1>

<div align="center" id="WhatsNewDiv"></div>
<script>
var lastVisit = getCookieValue("LastVisit");
if (lastVisit != null)
{
    lastVisit = new Date(lastVisit);
    if (lastVisit < lastUpdated)
    {
                document.getElementById('WhatsNewDiv').innerHTML = '<a
href="WhatsNew.htm"><img src="WhatsNew.jpg" border=0></a>'
    }
}
var nowDate = new Date();
setCookie("LastVisit", nowDate.toGMTString(),"","")
</script>


<body>
</body>
</html>
```

This page needs to be saved as `MainPage.htm`. Note that it contains the two functions, `setCookie()` and `getCookieValue()`, that you created earlier. Also note that the image `WhatsNew.jpg` is referenced by this page; either create such an image, or retrieve the image from the code download.

Next, you'll just create a simple page to link to for the What's New details.

```
<!DOCTYPE html PUBLIC "-//W3C//DTD XHTML 1.0 Transitional//EN"
"http://www.w3.org/TR/xhtml1/DTD/xhtml1-transitional.dtd">
```

```
<html xmlns="http://www.w3.org/1999/xhtml">
<head>
<meta http-equiv="Content-Type" content="text/html; charset=utf-8" />
<title>Untitled Document</title>
</head>
<body>
<h2 align=center>Here's what's new on this website</h2>
</body>
</html>
```

Save this page as WhatsNew.htm.

Load MainPage.htm into a browser. The first time you go to the main page, there will be nothing but a heading saying "Welcome to my website." Obviously, if this were a real web site, it would have a bit more than that, but it suffices for this example. However, refresh the page and suddenly you'll see the page shown in Figure 11-13.

Welcome to my website

Click To Find Out What's New

Figure 11-13

If you click the image you're taken to the WhatsNew.htm page detailing all the things added to the web site since you last visited. Obviously nothing has actually changed in your example web site between you loading the page and then refreshing it. You got around this for testing purposes by setting the date when the web site last changed, stored in variable lastUpdated, to a date in the future (here, December 28, 2020).

The WhatsNew.htm page is just a simple HTML page with no script, so you will confine your attention to MainPage.htm. In the head of the page in the first script block, you declare the variable lastUpdated.

```
var lastUpdated = new Date("Tue, 28 Dec 2020");
```

Whenever you make a change to the web site, this variable needs to be changed. It's currently set to Tue, 28 Dec 2020, just to make sure you see a What's New image when you refresh the page. A better alternative for live pages would be the document.lastModified property, which returns the date on which the page was last changed.

The rest of the first script block contains the two functions getCookieValue() and setCookie() that you looked at earlier. These haven't changed, so they're not discussed in detail here.

The interesting material is in the second script block within the body of the page. First you get the date of the user's last visit from the LastVisit cookie using the getCookieValue() function.

```
var lastVisit = getCookieValue("LastVisit");
```

If it's null, the user has either never been here before, or it has been six or more months since the last visit and the cookie has expired. Either way, you won't put a What's New image up because everything is new if the user is a first-time visitor, and a lot has probably changed in the last six months — more than what your What's New page will detail.

If lastVisit is not null, you need to check whether the user visited the site before it was last updated, and if so to direct the user to a page that shows what is new. You do this within the if statement.

```
if (lastVisit != null)
{
   lastVisit = new Date(lastVisit);
   if (lastVisit < lastUpdated)
   {
                document.getElementById('WhatsNewDiv').innerHTML = '<a
href="WhatsNew.htm">' +
'<img src="WhatsNew.jpg" border=0></a>'
   }
}
```

You first create a new Date object based on the value of lastVisit and store that back into the lastVisit variable. Then, in the condition of the inner if statement, you compare the date of the user's last visit with the date on which you last updated the web site. If things have changed since the user's last visit, you write the What's New image to the page, so the user can click it and find out what's new. Finally, at the end of the script block, you reset the LastVisit cookie to today's date and time using the setCookie() function.

```
var nowDate = new Date();
setCookie("LastVisit", nowDate.toGMTString(),"","")
```

Cookie Limitations

You should be aware of a number of limitations when using cookies.

A User May Disable Cookies

The first limitation is that although all modern browsers support cookies, the user may have disabled them. In Firefox you can do this by selecting the Options menu, followed by the privacy tab and the cookies tab. In IE you select Internet Options on the Tools menu. Select the Privacy tab and you can change the level with the scroll control. Most users have session cookies enabled by default. Session cookies are cookies that last for as long as the user is browsing your web site. After he's closed the browser the cookie will be cleared. More permanent cookies are also normally enabled by default. However, third-party cookies, those from a third-party site, are usually disabled. These are the cookies used for tracking people from site to site and hence the ones that raise the most privacy concerns.

Both the functions that you've made for creating and getting cookies will cause no errors when cookies are disabled, but of course the value of any cookie set will be `null` and you need to make sure your code can cope with this.

You could set a default action for when cookies are disabled. In the previous example, if cookies are disabled, the What's New image will never appear.

Alternatively, you can let the user know that your web site needs cookies to function by putting a message to that effect in the web page.

Another tactic is to actively check to see whether cookies are enabled and, if not, to take some action to cope with this, such as by directing the user to a page with less functionality that does not need cookies. How do you check to see if cookies are enabled?

In the following script, you set a test cookie and then read back its value. If the value is `null`, you know cookies are disabled.

```
setCookie("TestCookie","Yes","","");
if (getCookieValue("TestCookie") == null)
    {
        alert("This website requires cookies to function");
    }
```

Number and Information Limitation

A second limitation is on the number of cookies you can set on the user's computer for your web site and how much information can be stored in each. In older browsers for each domain it was common you could store only up to 20 cookies, and each *cookie pair* — that is, the name and value of the cookie combined — must not be more than 4,096 characters in size. It's also important to be aware that all browsers do set some upper limit for the number of cookies stored. When that limit is reached, older cookies, regardless of expiration date, are often deleted. Modern, for example IE7+ and Firefox browsers have a 50-cookie limit, though this may vary between browsers.

To get around the cookie limits, you can store more than one piece of information per cookie. This example uses multiple cookies:

```
setCookie("Name","Karen","","")
setCookie("Age","44","","")
setCookie("LastVisit","10 Jan 2001","","")
```

You could combine this information into one cookie, with each detail separated by a semicolon.

```
setCookie("UserDetails","Karen;44;10 Jan 2001","","")
```

Because the `setCookie()` function escapes the value of the cookie, there is no confusion between the semicolons separating pieces of data in the value of the cookie, and the semicolons separating the parts of the cookie. When you get the cookie value back using `getCookieValue()`, you just split it into its constituent parts; however, you must remember the order you stored it in.

```
var cookieValues = getCookieValue("UserDetails");
cookieValues = cookieValues.split(";");
alert("Name = " + cookieValues[0]);
alert("Age = " + cookieValues[1]);
alert("Last Visit = " + cookieValues[2]);
```

Now you have acquired three pieces of information and still have 19 cookies left in the jar.

Cookie Security and IE6+

IE6 introduced a new security policy for cookies based on the P3P an initiative set up by the World Wide Web Consortium (W3C), a web standards body that deals with not only cookies but HTML, XML, and various other browser standards. (You'll learn more about W3C in Chapter 13. Its web site is at www.w3.org and http://www.w3.org/P3P/ and contains a host of information, though it's far from being an easy read.) The general aim of P3P is to reassure users who are worried that cookies are being used to obtain personal information about their browsing habits. In IE 6+ you can select Tools ⇨ Internet Options and click the Privacy tab to see where you can set the level of privacy with regards to cookies (see Figure 11-14). You have to strike a balance between setting it so high that no web site will work and so low that your browsing habits and potentially personal data may be recorded.

Figure 11-14

Generally, by default session cookies — cookies that last for only as long as the user is browsing your web site — are allowed. As soon as the user closes the browser, the session ends. However, if you want cookies to outlast the user's visit to your web site, you need to create a privacy policy in line with the P3P recommendations. This sounds a little complex, and certainly the fine details of the policy can be. However, IBM has created software that makes creating the XML for the policy fairly easy. It's not cheap, but there is a 90-day free trial. It can be downloaded from `www.alphaworks.ibm.com/tech/p3peditor`.

Plenty of other policy creation software is available; this just happens to be quite easy to use. P3PEdit is available for much lower cost from `http://policyeditor.com/`.

Summary

In this chapter, you looked at how you can store information on the user's computer and use this information to personalize the web site. In particular you found the following:

❑   The key to cookies is the `document` object's `cookie` property.

❑   Creating a cookie simply involves setting the `document.cookie` property. Cookies have six different parts you can set. These are the name, the value, when it expires, the path it is available on, the domain it's available on, and finally whether it should be sent only over secure connections.

❑   Although setting a new cookie is fairly easy, you found that retrieving its value actually gets all the cookies for that domain and path, and that you need to split up the cookie name/value pairs to get a specific cookie using `String` object methods.

❑   Cookies have a number of limitations. First, the user can set the browser to disable cookies, and second, you are limited to 50 cookies per domain in IE7+ and Firefox and a maximum of 4,096 characters per cookie name/value pair.

Exercise Questions

Suggested solutions to these questions can be found in Appendix A.

1.   Create a page that keeps track of how many times the page has been visited by the user in the last month.

2.   Use cookies to load a different advertisement every time a user visits a web page.

Dynamic HTML and the W3C Document Object Model

JavaScript's primary role in web development is to interact with the user, to add some kind of behavior to your web page. You've seen this in previous chapters, especially Chapter 7 and Chapter 8 when you were scripting forms, frames, and windows. User interaction doesn't stop there, though. In fact, JavaScript gives you the ability to completely change all aspects of a web page after it's loaded in the browser, a technique called *Dynamic HTML (DHTML)*. What gives JavaScript this power over a web page is the *Document Object Model (DOM)*, a tree-like representation of the web page.

The DOM is one of the most misunderstood standards set forth by the World Wide Web Consortium (W3C), a body of developers who recommend standards for browser makers and web developers to follow. The DOM gives developers a way of representing everything on a web page so that it is accessible via a common set of properties and methods in JavaScript. By everything, I mean *everything*. You can literally change anything on the page: the graphics, tables, forms, and even text itself by altering a relevant DOM property with JavaScript.

The DOM should not be confused with the Browser Object Model (BOM) that was introduced in Chapter 6. You'll see the differences between the two in detail shortly. For now, though, think of the BOM as a browser-dependent representation of every feature of the browser, from the browser buttons, URL address line, and title bar to the browser window controls, as well as parts of the web page, too. The DOM, however, deals only with the contents of the browser window or web page (in other words, the HTML document). It makes the document available in such a way that any browser can use exactly the same code to access and manipulate the content of the document. To summarize, the BOM gives you access to the browser and some of the document, whereas the DOM gives you access to all of the document, but *only* the document.

The great thing about the DOM is that it is browser- and platform-independent. This means that developers can finally consider the possibility of writing a piece of JavaScript code that dynamically updates the page, and that will work on any DOM-compliant browser without any tweaking. You should not need to code for different browsers or take excessive care when coding.

The DOM achieves this independence by representing the contents of the page as a generic tree structure. Whereas in the BOM you might expect to access something by looking up a property relevant to that part of the browser and adjusting it, the DOM requires navigation through its representation of the page through nodes and properties that are not specific to the browser. You'll explore this structure a little later.

However, to use the DOM standard, ultimately developers require browsers that completely implement the standard, something that no browser does 100 percent efficiently, unfortunately. To make matters worse, no one browser implements the exact same DOM features that other browsers support, but don't be scared off yet. All modern browsers support many of the same features outlined by the DOM standard.

To provide a true perspective on how the DOM fits in, I need to take a brief look at its relationship with some of the other currently existing web standards. I should also talk about why there is more than one version of the DOM standard, and why there are different sections within the standard itself. (Microsoft, in particular, added a number of extensions to the W3C DOM.) After understanding the relationships, you can look at using JavaScript to navigate the DOM and to dynamically change content on web pages in more than one browser, in a way that used to be impossible with pure DHTML. The following items are on your agenda:

❑   The (X)HTML, ECMAScript, and XML Web standards

❑   The DOM standards

❑   Manipulating the DOM

❑   Writing cross-browser DHTML

> *Remember that the examples within this chapter are targeted only at the DOM (with very few exceptions) and will be supported only by IE 8+, Firefox 1+, Opera, Safari 3+, and Chrome.*

The Web Standards

When Tim Berners-Lee created HTML in 1991, he probably had little idea that this technology for marking up scientific papers via a set of tags for his own global hypertext project, known as the World Wide Web, would within a matter of years become a battleground between the two giants of the software business of the mid-1990s. HTML was a simple derivation from the meta-language Standard Generalized Markup Language (SGML) that had been kicking around academic institutions for decades. Its purpose was to preserve the structure of the documents created with it. HTML depends on a protocol, HyperText Transfer Protocol (HTTP), to transmit documents back and forth between the resource and the viewer (for example, the server and the client computer). These two technologies formed the foundation of the Web, and it quickly became obvious in the early 1990s that there needed to be some sort of policing of both specifications to ensure a common implementation of HTML and HTTP so that communications could be conducted worldwide.

In 1994, Tim founded the World Wide Web Consortium (W3C), a body that set out to oversee the technical evolution of the Web. It has three main aims:

❑   To provide universal access, so that anybody can use the Web

❑   To develop a software environment to allow users to make use of the Web

❑   To guide the development of the Web, taking into consideration the legal, social, and commercial issues that arise

Each new version of a specification of a web technology has to be carefully vetted by W3C before it can become a standard. The HTML and HTTP specifications are subject to this process, and each new set of updates to these specifications yields a new version of the standard. Each standard has to go through a working draft, a candidate recommendation, and a proposed recommendation stage before it can be considered a fully operational standard. At each stage of the process, members of the W3C consortium vote on which amendments to make, or even on whether to cancel the standard completely and send it back to square one.

It sounds like a very painful and laborious method of creating a standard format, and not something you'd think of as spearheading the cutting edge of technical revolution. Indeed, the software companies of the mid-1990s found the processes involved too slow, so they set the tone by implementing new innovations themselves and then submitting them to the standards body for approval. Netscape started by introducing new elements in its browser, such as the <font /> element, to add presentational content to the web pages. This proved popular, so Netscape added a whole raft of elements that enabled users to alter aspects of presentation and style on web pages. Indeed, JavaScript itself was such an innovation from Netscape.

When Microsoft entered the fray, it was playing catch up for the first two iterations of its Internet Explorer browser. However, with Internet Explorer 3 in 1996, they established a roughly equal set of features to compete with Netscape and so were able to add their own browser-specific elements. Very quickly, the Web polarized between these two browsers, and pages viewable on one browser quite often wouldn't appear on another. One problem was that Microsoft had used its much stronger position in the market to give away its browser for free, whereas Netscape still needed to sell its own browser because it couldn't afford to freely distribute its flagship product. To maintain a competitive position, Netscape needed to offer new features to make the user want to purchase its browser rather than use the free Microsoft browser.

Things came to a head with both companies' version 4 browsers, which introduced dynamic page functionality. Unfortunately, Netscape did this by the means of a <layer /> element, whereas Microsoft chose to implement it via scripting language properties and methods. The W3C needed to take a firm stand here, because one of its three principal aims had been compromised: that of universal access. How could access be universal if users needed a specific vendor's browser to view a particular set of pages? They decided on a solution that used existing standard HTML elements and Cascading Style Sheets, both of which had been adopted as part of the Microsoft solution. As a result, Microsoft gained a dominant position in the browser war. It hasn't relinquished this position; the Netscape Navigator browser never had a counter to Internet Explorer's constant updates, and its replacement, Firefox, was slow to expand its user base. Other browsers, such as Opera, Safari, and Chrome, along with Firefox continue to chip away at Microsoft's dominance in the market. However, Microsoft's Internet Explorer is still the most widely used browser today.

With a relatively stable version of the HTML standard in place with version 4.01, which boasts a set of features that will take any browser manufacturer a long time to implement completely, attention was turned to other areas of the Web. A new set of standards was introduced in the late 1990s to govern the means of presenting HTML (style sheets) and the representation of the HTML document in script (the Document Object Model or DOM). Other standards emerged, such as Extensible Markup Language (XML), which offers a common format for representing data in a way that preserves its structure.

The W3C web site (www.w3.org) has a huge number of standards in varying stages of creation. Not all of these standards concern us, and not all of the ones that concern us can be found at this web site. However, the vast majority of standards that do concern us can be found there.

You're going to take a brief look now at the technologies and standards that have an impact on JavaScript and find out a little background information about each. Some of the technologies may be unfamiliar, but you need to be aware of their existence at the very least.

HTML

The HTML standard is maintained by W3C. This standard might seem fairly straightforward, given that each version should have introduced just a few new elements, but in reality the life of the standards body was vastly complicated by the browser wars. The versions 1.0 and 2.0 of HTML were simple, small documents, but when W3C came to debate HTML version 3.0, they found that much of the new functionality it was discussing had already been superseded by new additions, such as the `<applet />` and `<style />` elements, to the version 3.0 browser's `appletstyle`. Version 3.0 was discarded, and a new version, 3.2, became the standard.

However, a lot of the features that went into HTML 3.2 had been introduced at the behest of the browser manufacturers and ran contrary to the spirit of HTML, which was intended solely to define structure. The new features, stemming from the `<font />` element, just confused the issue and added unnecessary presentational features to HTML. These features really became redundant with the introduction of style sheets. So suddenly, in the version 3 browsers, there were three distinct ways to define the style of an item of text. Which was the correct way? And if all three ways were used, which style did the text ultimately assume? Version 4.0 of the HTML standard was left with the job of unmuddling this chaotic mess and designated a lot of elements for deprecation (removal) in the next version of the standards. It was the largest version of the standard so far and included features that linked it to style sheets and the Document Object Model, and also added facilities for the visually impaired and other unfairly neglected minority interest areas. The current version of the HTML standard is 4.01.

XML

Extensible Markup Language, or XML, is a standard for creating markup languages (such as HTML). XML itself has been designed to look as much like HTML as possible, but that's where the similarities end.

HTML is actually an application of the meta-language SGML, which is also a standard for generating markup languages. SGML has been used to create many markup languages, but HTML is the only one that enjoys universal familiarity and popularity. XML, on the other hand, is a direct subset of SGML. SGML is generally considered to be too complex for people to be able to accurately represent it on a computer, so XML is a simplified subset of SGML. XML is also much easier to read than SGML.

XML's main use is for the creation of customized markup languages that are very similar in look and structure to HTML. One main use of XML is in the representation of data. Whereas a normal database can store information, databases don't allow individual stored items to contain information about their structure. XML can use the element structure of markup languages to represent any kind of data in which information contained in the structure might otherwise be lost, from mathematical and chemical notations to the entire works of Shakespeare. For instance, an XML document could be used to record that Mark Antony doesn't appear until Scene II Act I of Shakespeare's play *Julius Caesar*, whereas a relational database would struggle to do this without a lot of extra fields, as the following example shows:

```
<play>
    <act1>
```

```
        <scene1>
           ...
        </scene1>
        <scene2>
            <mark_anthony>
                Caesar, my lord?
            </mark_anthony>
        </scene2>
        <scene3>
           ...
        </scene3>
    </act1>
    <act2>
       ...
    </act2>
    <act3>
       ...
    </act3>
    <act4>
       ...
    </act4>
    <act5>
       ...
    </act5>
</play>
```

XML is also completely cross-platform, because it contains just text. This means that an application on Windows can package up the data in this format, and a completely different application on Unix should be able to unravel and read that data.

XHTML

XHTML 1.0 is where the XML and HTML standards meet. XHTML is just a respecification of the HTML 4.01 standard as an XML application. The advantages of this allow XHTML to get around some of the problems caused by a browser's particular interpretation of HTML, and more importantly to provide a specification that allows the Web to be used by clients other than browsers, such as those provided on handheld computers, mobile phones, or any software device that might be connected to the Internet (perhaps even your refrigerator!).

XHTML also offers a common method for specifying your own elements, instead of just adding them randomly. You can specify new elements via a common method using an XML Document Type Declaration and an XML name-space. (A namespace is a means of identifying one set of elements uniquely from any other set of elements.) This is particularly useful for the new markup languages, such as Wireless Markup Language (WML), which are geared toward mobile technology and require a different set of elements to be able to display on the reduced interfaces.

That said, anyone familiar with HTML should be able to look at an XHTML page and understand what's going on. There are differences, but not ones that add new elements or attributes.

The following is a list of the main differences between XHTML and HTML:

❑ XHTML recommends an XML declaration to be placed at the top of the file in the following form: `<?xml version='1.0'?>`.

❑ You also have to provide a DTD declaration at the top of the file, referencing the version of the DTD standard you are using.

❑ You have to include a reference to the XML namespace within the HTML element.

❑ You need to supply all XHTML element names in lowercase, because XML is case-sensitive.

❑ The `<head/>` and `<body/>` elements must always be included in an XHTML document.

❑ Tags must always be closed and nested correctly. When only one tag is required, such as with line breaks, the tag is closed with a slash (for example, `<br/>`).

❑ Attribute values must always be denoted by quotation marks.

This set of rules makes it possible to keep a strict hierarchical structure to the elements, which in turn makes it possible for the Document Object Model to work correctly. This also makes it possible to standardize markup languages across all device types, so that the next version of WML (the markup language of mobile devices) will also be compliant with the XHTML standard. You should now be creating your HTML documents according to the previously specified rules. If you do so, you will find it much, much easier to write JavaScript that manipulates the page via the DOM and works in the way it was intended.

ECMAScript

JavaScript itself followed a trajectory similar to that of HTML. It was first used in Netscape Navigator and then added to Internet Explorer. The Internet Explorer version of JavaScript was christened Jscript and wasn't far removed from the version of JavaScript found in Netscape Navigator. However, once again, there were differences between the two implementations and a lot of care had to be taken in writing script for both browsers.

Oddly enough, it was left to the European Computer Manufacturers Association (ECMA) to propose a standard specification for JavaScript. This didn't appear until a few versions of JavaScript had already been released. Unlike HTML, which had been developed from the start with the W3C consortium, JavaScript was a proprietary creation. This is the reason that it is governed by a different standards body. Microsoft and Netscape both agreed to use ECMA as the standards vehicle/debating forum, because of its reputation for fast-tracking standards and perhaps also because of its perceived neutrality. The name ECMAScript was chosen so as not to be biased toward either vendor's creation and also because the "Java" part of JavaScript was a trademark of Sun licensed to Netscape. The standard, named ECMA-262, laid down a specification that was roughly equivalent to the JavaScript 1.1 specification.

That said, the ECMAScript standard covers only core JavaScript features, such as the primitive data types of numbers, strings, and Booleans, native objects like the `Date`, `Array`, and `Math` objects, and the procedural statements like `for` and `while` loops, and `if` and `else` conditionals. It makes no reference to client-side objects or collections, such as `window`, `document`, `forms`, `links`, and `images`. So, although the standard helps to make core programming tasks compatible when both JavaScript and JScript comply with it, it is of no use in making the scripting of client-side objects compatible between the main browsers. Some incompatibilities remain.

All current implementations of JavaScript are expected to conform to the current ECMAScript standard, which is ECMAScript edition 3, published in December 1999. As of November 2006, ECMAScript edition 4 is under development.

Although there used to be quite a few irregularities between the Microsoft and Netscape dialects of JavaScript, they're now similar enough to be considered the same language. The Opera and Safari browsers also support and offer the same kind of support for the standard. This is a good example of how standards have provided a uniform language across browser implementations, although a feature was similar to the one that took place over HTML still rages to a lesser degree over JavaScript.

It's now time for you to consider the Document Object Model itself.

The Document Object Model

The Document Object Model (DOM) is, as previously mentioned, a way of representing the document independent of browser type. It allows a developer to access the document via a common set of objects, properties, methods, and events, and to alter the contents of the web page dynamically using scripts.

Several types of script languages, such as JavaScript and VBScript, are available. Each requires a different syntax and therefore a different approach when you're programming. Even when you're using a language common to all browsers, such as JavaScript, you should be aware that some small variations are usually added to the language by the browser vendor. So, to guarantee that you don't fall afoul of a particular implementation, the W3C has provided a generic set of objects, properties, and methods that should be available in all scripting languages, in the form of the DOM standard.

The DOM Standard

We haven't talked about the DOM standard so far, and for a particular reason: It's not the easiest standard to follow. Supporting a generic set of properties and methods has proved to be a very complex task, and the DOM standard has been broken down into separate levels and sections to deal with the different areas. The different levels of the standard are all at differing stages of completion.

Level 0

Level 0 is a bit of a misnomer, as there wasn't really a level 0 of the standard. This term in fact refers to the "old way" of doing things — the methods implemented by the browser vendors before the DOM standard. Someone mentioning level 0 properties is referring to a more linear notation of accessing properties and methods. For example, typically you'd reference items on a form with the following code:

```
document.forms[0].elements[1].value = "button1";
```

We're not going to cover such properties and methods in this chapter, because they have been superseded by newer methods.

Level 1

Level 1 is the first version of the standard. It is split into two sections: one is defined as core (objects, properties, and methods that can apply to both XML and HTML) and the other as HTML (HTML-specific objects, properties, and methods). The first section deals with how to go about navigating and manipulating the structure of the document. The objects, properties, and methods in this section are very abstract. The second section deals with HTML only and offers a set of objects corresponding to all the HTML elements. This chapter mainly deals with the second section — level 1 of the standard.

In 2000, level 1 was revamped and corrected, though it only made it to a working draft and not to a full W3C recommendation.

Level 2

Level 2 is complete and many of the properties, methods, and events have been implemented by today's browsers. It has sections that add specifications for events and style sheets to the specifications for core and HTML-specific properties and events. (It also provides sections on views and traversal ranges, neither of which will be covered in this book; you can find more information at www.w3.org/TR/2000/PR-DOM-Level-2-Views-20000927/ and www.w3.org/TR/2000/PR-DOM-Level-2-Traversal-Range-20000927/.) You will be making use of some of the features of the event and style sections of this level of the DOM later in this chapter because they have been implemented in the latest versions of both browsers.

Level 3

Level 3 achieved recommendation status in 2004. It is intended to resolve a lot of the complications that still exist in the event model in level 2 of the standard, and adds support for XML features, such as contents models and being able to save the DOM as an XML document. Only a few browsers support some features of Level 3.

Browser Compliance with the Standards

Almost no browser has 100 percent compliance with any standard, although some, such as Firefox, Opera, and Safari/Chrome, come pretty close with the DOM. Therefore, there is no guarantee that all the objects, properties, and methods of the DOM standard will be available in a given version of a browser, although a few level 1 and level 2 objects, properties, and methods have been available in all the browsers for some time.

Much of the material in the DOM standards has only recently been clarified, and a lot of DOM features and support have been added to only the latest browser versions. For this reason, examples in this chapter will be guaranteed to work on only the latest versions of IE, Firefox, Opera, Safari, and Chrome. Although cross-browser scripting is a realistic goal, backwards compatible support isn't at all.

Although the standards might still not be fully implemented, they do give you an idea as to how a particular property or method should be implemented, and provide a guideline for all browser manufacturers to agree to work toward in later versions of their browsers. The DOM doesn't introduce any new HTML elements or style sheet properties to achieve its ends. The idea of the DOM is to make use of the existing technologies, and quite often the existing properties and methods of one or other of the browsers.

Differences Between the DOM and the BOM

As mentioned earlier, there are two main differences between the Document Object Model and the Browser Object Model. However, complicating the issue is the fact that a BOM is sometimes referred to under the name DOM. Look out for this in any literature on the subject.

❑   First, the DOM covers only the document of the web page, whereas the BOM offers scripting access to all areas of the browsers, from the buttons to the title bar, including some parts of the page.

❑   Second, the BOM is unique to a particular browser. This makes sense if you think about it: You can't expect to standardize browsers, because they have to offer competitive features. Therefore, you need a different set of properties and methods and even objects to be able to manipulate them with JavaScript.

Representing the HTML Document as a Tree Structure

Because HTML is standardized so that web pages can contain only the standard features supported in the language, such as forms, tables, images, and the like, a common method of accessing these features is needed. This is where the DOM comes in. It provides a uniform representation of the HTML document, and it does this by representing the entire HTML document/web page as a *tree structure*.

In fact, it is possible to represent any HTML document (or any XML document for that matter) as a tree structure. The only precondition is that the HTML document should be well formed. Different browsers might be tolerant, to a greater or lesser extent, of quirks such as unclosed tags, or HTML form controls not being enclosed within a `<form/>` element; however, for the structure of the HTML document to be accurately depicted, you need to be able to always predict the structure of the document. Abuses of the structure, such as unclosed tags, stop you from depicting the structure as a true hierarchy, and therefore cannot be allowed. The ability to access elements via the DOM depends on the ability to represent the page as a hierarchy.

What Is a Tree Structure?

If you're not familiar with the concept of trees, don't worry. They're just a diagrammatic means of representing a hierarchical structure.

Let's consider the example of a book with several chapters. If instructed to, you could find the third line on page 543 after a little searching. If an updated edition of the book were printed with extra chapters, more likely than not you'd fail to find the same text if you followed those same instructions. However, if the instructions were changed to, say, "Find the chapter on still-life painting, the section on using watercolors, and the paragraph on positioning light sources," you'd be able to find that even in a reprinted edition with extra pages and chapters, albeit with perhaps a little more effort than the first request required.

Books aren't particularly dynamic examples, but given something like a web page, where the information could be changed daily, or even hourly, can you see why it would be of more use to give the second set of directions than the first? The same principle applies with the DOM. Navigating the DOM in a hierarchical fashion, rather than in a strictly linear way, makes much more sense. When you treat the DOM as a tree, it becomes easy to navigate the page in this fashion. Consider how you locate files on Windows using Windows Explorer, which creates a tree view of folders through which you can drill down. Instead of looking for a file alphabetically, you locate it by going into a particular folder.

The rules for creating trees are simple. You start at the top of the tree with the document and the element that contains all other elements in the page. The document is the *root node*. A *node* is just a point on the tree representing a particular element or attribute of an element, or even the text that an element contains. The root node contains all other nodes, such as the DTD declaration, the XML declaration if applicable, and the root element (the HTML or XML element that contains all other elements). The root element should always be the <html/> element in an HTML document. Underneath the root element are the HTML elements that the root element contains. Typically an HTML page will have <head/> and <body/> elements inside the <html/> element. These elements are represented as nodes underneath the root element's node, which itself is underneath the root node at the top of the tree (see Figure 12-1).

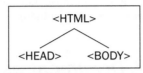

Figure 12-1

The two nodes representing the <head/> and <body/> elements are examples of *child nodes*, and the <html/> element's node above them is a *parent node*. Since the <head/> and <body/> elements are both child nodes of the <html/> element, they both go on the same level underneath the parent node <html/> element. The <head/> and <body/> elements in turn contain other child nodes/HTML elements, which will appear at a level underneath their nodes. So child nodes can also be parent nodes. Each time you encounter a set of HTML elements within another element, they each form a separate node at the same level on the tree. The easiest way of explaining this clearly is with an example.

An Example HTML Page

Let's consider a basic HTML page such as this:

```
<!DOCTYPE html PUBLIC "-//W3C//DTD XHTML 1.0 Transitional//EN"
    "http://www.w3.org/TR/xhtml1/DTD/xhtml1-transitional.dtd">

<html xmlns="http://www.w3.org/1999/xhtml">
<head>
</head>
<body>
    <h1>My Heading</h1>
    <p>This is some text in a paragraph.</p>
</body>
</html>
```

The <html/> element contains <head/> and <body/> elements. Only the <body/> element actually contains anything. It contains an <h1/> element and a <p/> element. The <h1/> element contains the text My Heading. When you reach an item, such as text, an image, or an element, that contains no others, the tree structure will terminate at that node. Such a node is termed a *leaf node*. You then continue to the <p/> node, which contains some text, which is also a node in the document. You can depict this with the tree structure shown in Figure 12-2.

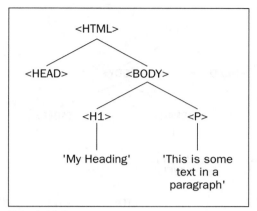

Figure 12-2

Simple, eh? This example is almost too straightforward, so let's move on to a slightly more complex one that involves a table as well.

```
<!DOCTYPE html PUBLIC "-//W3C//DTD XHTML 1.0 Transitional//EN"
    "http://www.w3.org/TR/xhtml1/DTD/xhtml1-transitional.dtd">

<html xmlns="http://www.w3.org/1999/xhtml">
<head>
    <title>This is a test page</title>
</head>
<body>
    <span>Below is a table...</span>
    <table border="1">
        <tr>
            <td>Row 1 Cell 1</td>
            <td>Row 1 Cell 2</td>
        </tr>
        <tr>
            <td>Row 2 Cell 1</td>
            <td>Row 2 Cell 2</td>
        </tr>
    </table>
</body>
</html>
```

There is nothing out of the ordinary here; the document contains a table with two rows with two cells in each row. You can once again represent the hierarchical structure of your page (for example, the fact that the <html/> element contains a <head/> and a <body/> element, and that the <head/> element contains a <title/> element, and so on) using your tree structure, as shown in Figure 12-3.

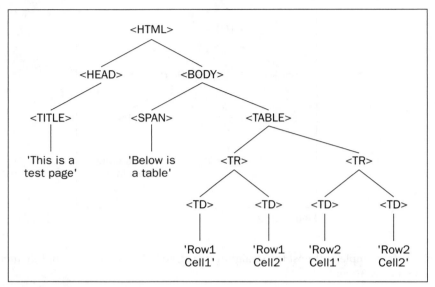

Figure 12-3

The top level of the tree is simple enough; the `<html/>` element contains `<head/>` and `<body/>` elements. The `<head/>` element in turn contains a `<title/>` element and the `<title/>` element contains some text. This text node is a child node that terminates the branch (a leaf node). You can then go back to the next node, the `<body/>` element node, and go down that branch. Here you have two elements contained within the `<body/>` element, the `<span/>` and `<table/>` elements. Although the `<span/>` element contains only text and terminates there, the `<table/>` element contains two rows (`<tr/>`), and the two `<tr/>` elements contain two table cell (`<td/>`) elements. Only then do you get to the bottom of the tree with the text contained in each table cell. Your tree is now a complete representation of your HTML code.

The Core DOM Objects

What you have seen so far has been highly theoretical, so let's get a little more practical now.

The DOM provides you with a concrete set of objects, properties, and methods that you can access through JavaScript to navigate the tree structure of the DOM. Let's start with the set of objects, within the DOM, that is used to represent the nodes (elements, attributes, or text) on your tree.

Base DOM Objects

Three objects, shown in the following table, are known as the base DOM objects.

Object	Description
Node	Each node in the document has its own Node object
NodeList	This is a list of Node objects
NamedNodeMap	This provides access by name rather than by index to all the Node objects

This is where the DOM differs from the BOM quite extensively. The BOM objects have names that relate to a specific part of the browser, such as the `window` object, or the `forms` and `images` collections. As mentioned earlier, to be able to navigate in the web page as though it were a tree, you have to do it abstractly. You can have no prior knowledge of the structure of the page; everything ultimately is just a node. To move around from HTML element to HTML element, or element to attribute, you have to go from node to node. This also means you can add, replace, or remove parts of your web page without affecting the structure as a whole, as you're just changing nodes. This is why you have three rather obscure-sounding objects that represent your tree structure.

I've already mentioned that the top of your tree structure is the root node, and that the root node contains the XML declaration, the DTD, and the root element. Therefore you need more than just these three objects to represent your document. In fact there are different objects to represent the different types of nodes on the tree.

High-Level DOM Objects

Since everything in the DOM is a node, it's no wonder that nodes come in a variety of types. Is the node an element, an attribute, or just plain text? The `Node` object has different objects to represent each possible type of node. The following is a complete list of all the different node type objects that can be accessed via the DOM. A lot of them won't concern you in this book, because they're better suited for XML documents and not HTML documents, but you should notice that your three main types of nodes, namely element, attribute, and text, are all covered.

Object	Description
Document	The root node of the document
DocumentType	The DTD or schema type of the XML document
DocumentFragment	A temporary storage space for parts of the document
EntityReference	A reference to an entity in the XML document
Element	An element in the document
Attr	An attribute of an element in the document
ProcessingInstruction	A processing instruction
Comment	A comment in an XML document or HTML document
Text	Text that must form a child node of an element
CDATASection	A CDATA section within the XML document
Entity	An unparsed entity in the DTD
Notation	A notation declared within a DTD

We won't go over most of these objects in this chapter, but if you need to navigate the DOM of an XML document, you will have to use them.

Each of these objects inherits all the properties and methods of the Node object, but also has some properties and methods of its own. You will be looking at some examples in the next section.

DOM Objects and Their Properties and Methods

If you tried to look at the properties and methods of all the objects in the DOM, it would take up half the book. Instead you're going to actively consider only three of the objects, namely the Node object, the Element object, and the Document object. This is all you'll need to be able to create, amend, and navigate your tree structure. Also, you're not going to spend ages trawling through each of the properties and methods of these objects, but rather look only at some of the most useful properties and methods and use them to achieve specific ends.

Appendix C contains a relatively complete reference to the DOM, its objects, and their properties.

The Document Object and its Methods

The Document reference type exposes various properties and methods that are very helpful to someone scripting the DOM. Its methods allow you to find individual or groups of elements and create new elements, attributes, and text nodes. Any DOM scripter should know these methods and properties, as they're used quite frequently.

The Document object's methods are probably the most important methods you'll learn. While many tools are at your disposal, the Document object's methods let you find, create, and delete elements in your page.

Finding Elements or an Element

Let's say you have an HTML web page — how do you go about getting back a particular element on the page in script? The Document reference type exposes the follow methods to perform this task:

Methods of the Document Object	Description
getElementById(idValue)	Returns a reference (a node) to an element, when supplied with the value of the id attribute of that element
getElementsByTagName(tagName)	Returns a reference (a node list) to a set of elements that have the same tag as the one supplied in the argument

The first of the two methods, getElementById(), requires you to ensure that every element you want to quickly access in the page uses an id attribute, otherwise a null value (a word indicating a missing or unknown value) will be returned by your method. Let's go back to the first example and add some id attributes to the elements.

```
<!DOCTYPE html PUBLIC "-//W3C//DTD XHTML 1.0 Transitional//EN"
    "http://www.w3.org/TR/xhtml1/DTD/xhtml1-transitional.dtd">

<html xmlns="http://www.w3.org/1999/xhtml"><head>
    <title>example</title>
</head>
```

```
<body>
    <h1 id="heading1">My Heading</h1>
    <p id="paragraph1">This is some text in a paragraph</p>
</body>
</html>
```

Now you can use the `getElementById()` method to return a reference to any of the HTML elements with `id` attributes on your page. For example, if you add the following code in the shaded section, you can find and reference the `<h1/>` element:

```
<!DOCTYPE html PUBLIC "-//W3C//DTD XHTML 1.0 Transitional//EN"
    "http://www.w3.org/TR/xhtml1/DTD/xhtml1-transitional.dtd">

<html xmlns="http://www.w3.org/1999/xhtml">
    <title>example</title>
</head>
<body>
    <h1 id="heading1">My Heading</h1>
    <p id="paragraph1">This is some text in a paragraph</p>
    <script type="text/javascript">
        alert(document.getElementById("heading1"));
    </script>
</body>
</html>
```

Figure 12-4 shows the result of this code in Firefox.

Figure 12-4

`HTMLHeadingElement` *is an object of the HTML DOM. All HTML elements have a corresponding reference type in the DOM. See Appendix C for more objects of the HTML DOM.*

You might have been expecting it to return something along the lines of `<h1/>` or `<h1 id="heading1">`, but all it's actually returning is a reference to the `<h1/>` element. This reference to the `<h1/>` element is more useful though, as you can use it to alter attributes of the element, such as by changing the color or size. You can do this via the `style` object.

```
<!DOCTYPE html PUBLIC "-//W3C//DTD XHTML 1.0 Transitional//EN"
    "http://www.w3.org/TR/xhtml1/DTD/xhtml1-transitional.dtd">

<html xmlns="http://www.w3.org/1999/xhtml">
<head>
    <title>example</title>
</head>
<body>
    <h1 id="heading1">My Heading</h1>
    <p id="paragraph1">This is some text in a paragraph</p>
    <script type="text/javascript">
        var h1Element = document.getElementById("heading1");
        h1Element.style.color = "red";
    </script>
</body>
</html>
```

If you display this in the browser, you see that you can directly influence the attributes of the `<h1/>` element in script, as you have done here by changing its text color to red.

> *The* `style` *object points to the style attribute of an element; it allows you to change the CSS style assigned to an element. The style object will be covered later in the chapter.*

The second of the two methods, `getElementsByTagName()`, works in the same way, but, as its name implies, it can return more than one element. If you were to go back to the example HTML document with the table and use this method to return the table cells (`<td/>`) in your code, you would get a node list containing a total of four table. You'd still have only one object returned, but this object would be a collection of elements. Remember that collections are array-like structures, so specify the index number for the specific element you want from the collection. You can use the square brackets if you wish; another alternative is to use the `item()` method of the `NodeList` object, like this:

```
<!DOCTYPE html PUBLIC "-//W3C//DTD XHTML 1.0 Transitional//EN"
    "http://www.w3.org/TR/xhtml1/DTD/xhtml1-transitional.dtd">

<html xmlns="http://www.w3.org/1999/xhtml">
<head>
    <title>This is a test page</title>
</head>
<body>
    <span>Below is a table...   </span>
    <table border="1">
        <tr>
            <td>Row 1 Cell 1</td>
            <td>Row 1 Cell 2</td>
        </tr>
        <tr>
            <td>Row 2 Cell 1</td>
            <td>Row 2 Cell 2</td>
        </tr>
    </table>
```

```
        <script type="text/javascript">
            var tdElement = document.getElementsByTagName("td").item(0);
            tdElement.style.color = "red";
        </script>
    </body>
</html>
```

If you ran this example, once again using the `style` object, it would alter the style of the contents of the first cell in the table. If you wanted to change the color of all the cells in this way, you could loop through the node list, like this:

```
<script type="text/javascript">
    var tdElements = document.getElementsByTagName("td");
    var length = tdElements.length;

    for (var i = 0; i < length; i++)
    {
        tdElements[i].style.color = "red";
    }
</script>
```

One thing to note about the `getElementsByTagName()` method is that it takes the element names within quotation marks and without the angle brackets <> that normally surround tags.

Creating Elements and Text

The `Document` object also boasts some methods for creating elements and text, shown in the following table.

Methods of the Document Object	Description
createElement(elementName)	Creates an element node with the specified tag name. Returns the created element.
createTextNode(text)	Creates and returns a text node with the supplied text.

The following code demonstrates the use of these methods:

```
var pElement = document.createElement("p");
var text = document.createTextNode("This is some text.");
```

This code creates a `<p/>` element and stores its reference in the `pElement` variable. It then creates a text node containing the text `This is some text.` and stores its reference in the `text` variable.

It's not enough to create nodes, however; you have to add them to the document. We'll discuss how to do this in just a bit.

Property of the Document Object: Getting the Document's Root Element

You've now got a reference to individual elements on the page, but what about the tree structure mentioned earlier? The tree structure encompasses all the elements and nodes on the page and gives them a hierarchical structure. If you want to reference that structure, you need a particular property of the `document` object that returns the outermost element of your document. In HTML, this should always be the `<html/>` element. The property that returns this element is `documentElement`, as shown in the following table.

Property of the Document Object	Description
`documentElement`	Returns a reference to the outermost element of the document (the root element, for example `<html/>`)

You can use `documentElement` as follows. If you go back to the simple HTML page, you can transfer your entire DOM into one variable like this:

```
<!DOCTYPE html PUBLIC "-//W3C//DTD XHTML 1.0 Transitional//EN"
    "http://www.w3.org/TR/xhtml1/DTD/xhtml1-transitional.dtd">

<html xmlns="http://www.w3.org/1999/xhtml">
<head>
    <title>example</title>
</head>
<body>
    <h1 id="heading1">My Heading</h1>
    <p id="paragraph1">This is some text in a paragraph</p>
    <script type="text/javascript">
        var container = document.documentElement;
    </script>
</body>
</html>
```

The variable `container` now contains the root element, which is `<html/>`. The `documentElement` property returned a reference to this element in the form of an object, an `Element` object to be precise. The `Element` object has its own set of properties and methods. If you want to use them, you can refer to them by using the variable name, followed by the method or property name.

```
container.elementObjectProperty
```

Fortunately, the `Element` object has only one property.

The Element Object

The `Element` object is quite simple, especially compared to the `Node` object (which you'll be introduced to later). It exposes only a handful of *members* (properties and methods).

Member Name	Description
`tagName`	Gets the element's tag name
`getAttribute()`	Gets the value of an attribute
`setAttribute()`	Sets an attribute with a specified value
`removeAttribute()`	Removes a specific attribute and its value from the element

Getting the Element's Tag Name: The tagName Property

The sole property of the `Element` object is a reference to the tag name of the element: the `tagName` property.

In the previous example, the variable `container` contained the `<html/>` element. Add the following highlighted line, which makes use of the `tagName` property.

```
<!DOCTYPE html PUBLIC "-//W3C//DTD XHTML 1.0 Transitional//EN"
    "http://www.w3.org/TR/xhtml1/DTD/xhtml1-transitional.dtd">

<html xmlns="http://www.w3.org/1999/xhtml">
<head>
    <title>example</title>
</head>
<body>
    <h1 id="heading1">My Heading</h1>
    <p id="paragraph1">This is some text in a paragraph</p>
    <script type="text/javascript">
        var container = document.documentElement;
        alert(container.tagName);
    </script>
</body>
</html>
```

This code will now return proof that your variable `container` holds the outermost element, and by implication all other elements within it (see Figure 12-5).

Figure 12-5

Methods of the Element Object: Getting and Setting Attributes

If you want to set any element attributes, other than the `style` attribute, you should use the DOM-specific methods of the `Element` object.

The three methods you can use to return and alter the contents of an HTML element's attributes are `getAttribute()`, `setAttribute()`, and `removeAttribute()`, as shown in the following table.

Methods of the Element Object	Description
`getAttribute(attributeName)`	Returns the value of the supplied attribute. Returns `null` or an empty string if the attribute does not exist.
`setAttribute(attributeName, value)`	Sets the value of an attribute.
`removeAttribute(attributeName)`	Removes the value of an attribute and replaces it with the default value.

Let's take a quick look at how these methods work now.

Try It Out   Playing with Attributes

Open your text editor and type the following code.

```
<!DOCTYPE html PUBLIC "-//W3C//DTD XHTML 1.0 Transitional//EN"
    "http://www.w3.org/TR/xhtml1/DTD/xhtml1-transitional.dtd">

<html xmlns="http://www.w3.org/1999/xhtml">
<head>
    <title>Chapter 12: Example 1</title>
</head>
<body>
    <p id="paragraph1">This is some text.</p>
    <script type="text/javascript">
        var pElement = document.getElementById("paragraph1");
        pElement.setAttribute("align", "center");

        alert(pElement.getAttribute("align"));

        pElement.removeAttribute("align");
    </script>
</body>
</html>
```

Save this as `ch12_examp1.htm` and open it in a browser. You'll see the text of the `<p/>` element in the center of the screen and an alert box displaying the text `center` (Figure 12-6).

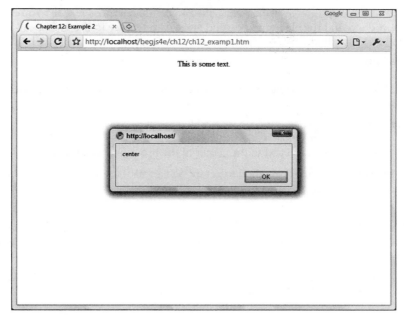

Figure 12-6

When you click the OK button, you'll see the text become left-aligned (Figure 12-7).

Figure 12-7

This HTML page contains one <p/> element with an id value of paragraph1. You use this value in the JavaScript code to find the element node and store its reference in the pElement variable with the getElementById() method.

```
var pElement = document.getElementById("paragraph1");
```

Now that you have a reference to the element, you use the setAttribute() method to set the align attribute to center.

```
pElement.setAttribute("align", "center");
```

The result of this code moves the text to the center of the browser's window.

You then use the getAttribute() method to get the align attribute's value and display it in an alert box:

```
alert(pElement.getAttribute("align"));
```

This code displays the value "center" in the alert box.

Finally, you remove the align attribute with the removeAttribute() method, effectively making the text left-aligned.

Strictly speaking, the align attribute is deprecated under HTML 4.0, but you used it because it works and because it has one of the most easily demonstrable visual effects on a web page.

The Node Object

You now have your element or elements from the web page, but what happens if you want to move through your page systematically, from element to element or from attribute to attribute? This is where you need to step back to a lower level. To move among elements, attributes, and text, you have to move among nodes in your tree structure. It doesn't matter what is contained within the node, or rather, what sort of node it is. This is why you need to go back to one of the objects of the core DOM specification. Your whole tree structure is made up of these base-level Node objects.

The Node Object: Navigating the DOM

The following table lists some common properties of the Node object that provide information about the node, whether it is an element, attribute, or text, and enable you to move from one node to another.

Properties of the Node Object	Description of Property
firstChild	Returns the first child node of an element
lastChild	Returns the last child node of an element
previousSibling	Returns the previous child node of an element at the same level as the current child node
nextSibling	Returns the next child node of an element at the same level as the current child node

Properties of the Node Object	Description of Property
ownerDocument	Returns the root node of the document that contains the node (note this is not available in IE 5 or 5.5)
parentNode	Returns the element that contains the current node in the tree structure
nodeName	Returns the name of the node
nodeType	Returns the type of the node as a number
nodeValue	Gets or sets the value of the node in plain text format

Let's take a quick look at how some of these properties work. Consider this familiar example:

```
<!DOCTYPE html PUBLIC "-//W3C//DTD XHTML 1.0 Transitional//EN"
    "http://www.w3.org/TR/xhtml1/DTD/xhtml1-transitional.dtd">

<html xmlns="http://www.w3.org/1999/xhtml">
<head>
    <title>example</title>
</head>
<body>
    <h1 id="heading1">My Heading</h1>
    <p id="paragraph1">This is some text in a paragraph</p>
    <script type="text/javascript">
        var h1Element = document.getElementById("heading1");
        h1Element.style.color = "red";
    </script>
</body>
</html>
```

You can now use h1Element to navigate your tree structure and make whatever changes you desire. The following code uses h1Element as a starting point to find the <p/> element and change its text color:

```
<!DOCTYPE html PUBLIC "-//W3C//DTD XHTML 1.0 Transitional//EN"
    "http://www.w3.org/TR/xhtml1/DTD/xhtml1-transitional.dtd">

<html xmlns="http://www.w3.org/1999/xhtml">
<head>
    <title>example</title>
</head>
<body>
    <h1 id="heading1">My Heading</h1>
    <p id="paragraph1">This is some text in a paragraph</p>
    <script type="text/javascript">
        var h1Element = document.getElementById("heading1");
        h1Element.style.color = "red";

        var pElement;
        if (h1Element.nextSibling.nodeType == 1)
        {
```

413

```
            pElement = h1Element.nextSibling;
        }
        else
        {
            pElement = h1Element.nextSibling.nextSibling;
        }
        pElement.style.color = "red";
    </script>
</body>
</html>
```

This code demonstrates a fundamental difference between IE's DOM and the DOM present in other browsers. Firefox's, Safari's, Chrome's, and Opera's DOM treat everything as a node in the DOM tree, including the whitespace between elements. On the other hand, IE strips out this unnecessary whitespace. So to locate the <p/> element in the previous example, a sibling to the <h1/> element, it is required to check the next sibling's nodeType property. An element's node type is 1 (text nodes are 3). If the nextSibling's nodeType is 1, then you assign that sibling's reference to pElement. If not, you get the next sibling (the <p/> element) of h1Element's sibling (the whitespace text node).

In effect, you are navigating through the tree structure as shown in Figure 12-8.

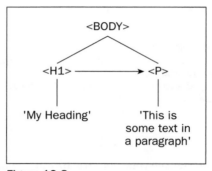

Figure 12-8

The same principles also work in reverse. You can go back and change the code to navigate from the <p/> element to the <h1/> element.

```
<!DOCTYPE html PUBLIC "-//W3C//DTD XHTML 1.0 Transitional//EN"
    "http://www.w3.org/TR/xhtml1/DTD/xhtml1-transitional.dtd">

<html xmlns="http://www.w3.org/1999/xhtml">
<head>
    <title>example</title>
</head>
<body>
    <h1 id="heading1">My Heading</h1>
    <p id="paragraph1">This is some text in a paragraph</p>
    <script type="text/javascript">
        var pElement = document.getElementById("paragraph1");
```

```
        pElement.style.color = "red";

        var h1Element;
        if (pElement.previousSibling.nodeType == 1)
        {
            h1Element = pElement.previousSibling;
        }
        else
        {
            h1Element = pElement.previousSibling.previousSibling;
        }
        h1Element.style.color = "red";
    </script>
</body>
</html>
```

What you're doing here is the exact opposite; you find the `<p/>` by passing the value of its `id` attribute to the `getElementById()` method and storing the returned element reference to the `pElement` variable. You then find the correct previous sibling so that your code works in all browsers, and you change its text color to red.

Navigating Your HTML Document Using the DOM

Up until now, you've been cheating, because you haven't truly navigated your HTML document. You've just used `document.getElementById()` to return an element and navigated to different nodes from there. Now let's use the `documentElement` property of the `document` object and do this properly. You'll start at the top of your tree and move down through the child nodes to get at those elements; then you'll navigate through your child nodes and change the properties in the same way as before.

Type the following into your text editor:

```
<!DOCTYPE html PUBLIC "-//W3C//DTD XHTML 1.0 Transitional//EN"
    "http://www.w3.org/TR/xhtml1/DTD/xhtml1-transitional.dtd">

<html xmlns="http://www.w3.org/1999/xhtml">
<head>
    <title>Chapter 12: Example 2</title>
</head>
<body>
    <h1 id="heading1">My Heading</h1>
    <p id="paragraph1">This is some text in a paragraph</p>

    <script type="text/javascript">
    var htmlElement; // htmlElement stores reference to <html>
    var headElement; // headingElement stores reference to <head>
    var bodyElement; // bodyElement stores reference to <body>
    var h1Element; // h1Element stores reference to <h1>
    var pElement; // pElement stores reference to <p>

    htmlElement = document.documentElement;
    headElement = htmlElement.firstChild;

    alert(headElement.tagName);

    if (headElement.nextSibling.nodeType == 3)
```

```
        {
            bodyElement = headElement.nextSibling.nextSibling;
        }
        else
        {
            bodyElement = headElement.nextSibling;
        }

        alert(bodyElement.tagName);

        if (bodyElement.firstChild.nodeType == 3)
        {
            h1Element = bodyElement.firstChild.nextSibling;
        }
        else
        {
            h1Element = bodyElement.firstChild;
        }

        alert(h1Element.tagName);
        h1Element.style.fontFamily = "Arial";

        if (h1Element.nextSibling.nodeType == 3)
        {
            pElement = h1Element.nextSibling.nextSibling;
        }
        else
        {
            pElement = h1Element.nextSibling;
        }

        alert(pElement.tagName);
        pElement.style.fontFamily = "Arial";

        if (pElement.previousSibling.nodeType==3)
        {
            h1Element = pElement.previousSibling.previousSibling
        }
        else
        {
            h1Element = pElement.previousSibling
        }
        h1Element.style.fontFamily = "Courier"
        </script>
    </body>
</html>
```

Save this as `ch12_examp2.htm`. Then open the page in your browser, clicking OK in each of the message boxes until you see the page shown in Figure 12-9 (unfortunately, IE does not render the style changes until all alert boxes have been opened and closed).

416

Figure 12-9

You've hopefully made this example very transparent by adding several alerts to demonstrate where you are along each section of the tree. You've also named the variables with their various elements, to give a clearer idea of what is stored in each variable. (You could just as easily have named them a, b, c, d, and e, so don't think you need to be bound by this naming convention.)

You start at the top of the script block by retrieving the whole document using the documentElement property.

```
var htmlElement = document.documentElement;
```

The root element is the <html/> element, hence the name of your first variable. Now if you refer to your tree, you'll see that the HTML element must have two child nodes: one containing the <head/> element and the other containing the <body/> element. You start by moving to the <head/> element. You get there using the firstChild property of the Node object, which contains your <html/> element. You use your first alert to demonstrate that this is true.

```
alert(headingElement.tagName);
```

Your <body/> element is your next sibling across from the <head/> element, so you navigate across by creating a variable that is the next sibling from the <head/> element.

```
if (headingElement.nextSibling.nodeType == 3)
{
    bodyElement = headingElement.nextSibling.nextSibling;
}
```

```
else
{
    bodyElement = headingElement.nextSibling;
}

alert(bodyElement.tagName);
```

Here you check to see what the nodeType of the nextSibling of headingElement is. If it returns 3, (remember that nodeType 3 is a text node), you set bodyElement to be the nextSibling of the nextSibling of headingElement; otherwise you just set it to be the nextSibling of headingElement.

You use an alert to prove that you are now at the <body/> element.

```
alert(bodyElement.tagName);
```

The <body/> element in this page also has two children, the <h1/> and <p/> elements. Using the firstChild property, you move down to the <h1/> element. Again you check whether the child node is whitespace for non-IE browsers. You use an alert again to show that you have arrived at <h1/>.

```
if (bodyElement.firstChild.nodeType == 3)
{
    h1Element = bodyElement.firstChild.nextSibling;
}
else
{
    h1Element = bodyElement.firstChild;
}

alert(h1Element.tagName);
```

After the third alert, the style will be altered on your first element, changing the font to Arial.

```
h1Element.style.fontFamily = "Arial";
```

You then navigate across to the <p/> element using the nextSibling property, again checking for whitespace.

```
if (h1Element.nextSibling.nodeType == 3)
{
    pElement = h1Element.nextSibling.nextSibling;
}
else
{
    pElement = h1Element.nextSibling;
}

alert(pElement.tagName);
```

You change the <p/> element's font to Arial also.

```
pElement.style.fontFamily = "Arial";
```

Finally, you use the previousSibling property to move back in your tree to the <h1/> element and this time change the font to Courier.

```
if (pElement.previousSibling.nodeType==3)
{
    h1Element = pElement.previousSibling.previousSibling
}
else
{
    h1Element = pElement.previousSibling
}

h1Element.style.fontFamily = "Courier";
```

This is a fairly easy example to follow because you're using the same tree structure you created with diagrams, but it does show how the DOM effectively creates this hierarchy and that you can move around within it using script.

Methods of the Node Object

While the Node object's properties enable you to navigate the DOM, its methods provide the completely different ability to add and remove nodes from the DOM, thus fundamentally altering the structure of the HTML document. The following table lists these methods.

Methods of Node Objects	Description
appendChild(newNode)	Adds a new node object to the end of the list of child nodes. This method returns the appended node.
cloneNode(cloneChildren)	Returns a duplicate of the current node. It accepts a Boolean value. If the value is true, then the method clones the current node and all child nodes. If the value is false, only the current node is cloned and child nodes are left out of the clone.
hasChildNodes()	Returns true if a node has any child nodes and false if not.
insertBefore(newNode, referenceNode)	Inserts a new node object into the list of child nodes before the node stipulated by referenceNode. Returns the inserted node.
removeChild(childNode)	Removes a child node from a list of child nodes of the node object. Returns the removed node.

Creating HTML Elements and Text with DOM Methods

You'll create a web page with just paragraph <p/> and heading <h1/> elements, but instead of HTML you'll use the DOM properties and methods to place these elements on the web page. Start up your preferred text editor and type the following:

```
<!DOCTYPE html PUBLIC "-//W3C//DTD XHTML 1.0 Transitional//EN"
    "http://www.w3.org/TR/xhtml1/DTD/xhtml1-transitional.dtd">

<html xmlns="http://www.w3.org/1999/xhtml">
<head>
    <title>Chapter 12: Example 3</title>
</head>
<body>
    <script type="text/javascript">
        var newText = document.createTextNode("My Heading");
        var newElem = document.createElement("h1");

        newElem.appendChild(newText);
        document.body.appendChild(newElem);

        newText = document.createTextNode("This is some text in a paragraph");
        newElem = document.createElement("p");

        newElem.appendChild(newText);
        document.body.appendChild(newElem);
    </script>
</body>
</html>
```

Save this page as ch12_examp3.htm and open it in a browser (Figure 12-10).

It all looks a bit dull and tedious, doesn't it? And yes, you could have done this much more simply with HTML. That isn't the point, though. The idea is that you use DOM properties and methods, accessed with JavaScript, to insert these features. The first two lines of the script block are used to define the variables in your script, which are initialized to hold the text you want to insert into the page and the HTML element you wish to insert.

```
var newText = document.createTextNode("My Heading");
var newElem = document.createElement("h1");
```

You start at the bottom of your tree first, by creating a text node with the createTextNode() method. Then use the createElement() method to create an HTML heading.

At this point, the two variables are entirely separate from each other. You have a text node, and you have an <h1/> element, but they're not connected. The next line enables you to attach the text node to your HTML element. You reference the HTML element you have created with the variable name newElem, use the appendChild() method of your node, and supply the contents of the newText variable you created earlier as a parameter.

```
newElem.appendChild(newText);
```

Figure 12-10

Let's recap. You created a text node and stored it in the newText variable. You created an <h1/> element and stored it in the newElem variable. Then you appended the text node as a child node to the <h1/> element. That still leaves you with a problem: You've created an element with a value, but the element isn't part of your document. You need to attach the entirety of what you've created so far to the document body. Again, you can do this with the appendChild() method, but this time supply it to the document.body object (which, too, is a Node).

```
document.body.appendChild(newElem);
```

This completes the first part of your code. Now all you have to do is repeat the process for the <p/> element.

```
newText = document.createTextNode("This is some text in a paragraph");
newElem = document.createElement("p");

newElem.appendChild(newText);
document.body.appendChild(newElem);
```

You create a text node first; then you create an element. You attach the text to the element, and finally you attach the element and text to the body of the document.

It's important to note that the order in which you create nodes does not matter. This example had you create the text nodes before the element nodes; if you wanted, you could have created the elements first and the text nodes second.

However, the order in which you append nodes is very important for performance reasons. Updating the DOM can be an expensive process, and performance can suffer if you make many changes to the DOM. For example, this example updated the DOM only two times by appending the completed elements to the document's body. It would require four updates if you appended the element to the document's body and then appended the text node to the element. As a rule of thumb, only append completed element nodes (that is, the element, its attributes, and any text) to the document whenever you can.

Now that you can navigate and make changes to the DOM, let's look further into manipulating DOM nodes.

Manipulating the DOM

As mentioned at the very beginning of this chapter, Dynamic HTML is the manipulation of an HTML page after it's loaded into the browser. Up to this point, you've examined the properties and methods of the basic DOM objects and learned how to traverse the DOM through JavaScript.

Throughout the previous section, you saw some examples of manipulating the DOM; more specifically, you saw that you can change the color and font family of text contained within an element. In this section, you'll expand on that knowledge.

Accessing Elements

As you saw in the previous section, the DOM holds the tools you need to find and access HTML elements; you used the getElementById() method quite frequently, and through examples you saw how easy it was to find specific elements in the page.

When scripting the DOM, chances are you have a pretty good idea of what elements you want to manipulate. The easiest way to find those elements is to use the id attribute and thus the getElementById() method. Don't be afraid to assign id attributes to your HTML elements; it is by far the easiest and most efficient way to find elements within the page.

Changing Appearances

Probably the most common DOM manipulation is to change the way an element looks. Such a change can create an interactive experience for visitors to your web site and can even be used to alert them to important information or that an action is required by them. Changing the way an element looks consists almost exclusively of changing CSS properties for an HTML element. You can do this two ways through JavaScript:

- ❑ Change each CSS property with the style property.
- ❑ Change the value of the element's class attribute.

Using the style Property

In order to change specific CSS properties, you must look to the `style` property. All modern browsers implement this object, which maps directly to the element's `style` attribute. This object contains CSS properties, and by using it you can change any CSS property that the browser supports. You've already seen the `style` property in use, but here's a quick refresher:

```
element.style.cssProperty = value;
```

The CSS property names generally match those used in a CSS style sheet; therefore, changing the text color of an element requires the use of the `color` property, like this:

```
var divAdvert = document.getElementById("divAdvert");  //Get the desired element

divAdvert.style.color = "blue";  //Change the text color to blue
```

There are some cases, however, in which the property name is a little different from the one seen in a CSS file. CSS properties that contain a hyphen (-) are a perfect example of this exception. In the case of these properties, you remove the hyphen and capitalize the first letter of the word that follows the hyphen. The following code shows the incorrect and correct ways to do this:

```
divAdvert.style.background-color = "gray";  //Wrong

divAdvert.style.backgroundColor = "gray";  //Correct
```

You can also use the `style` object to retrieve styles that have previously been declared. However, if the `style` property you try to retrieve has not been set with the `style` attribute (inline styles) or with the `style` object, you will not retrieve the property's value. Consider the following HTML containing a style sheet and `<div/>` element:

```
<style type="text/css">
#divAdvert
{
    background-color: gray;
}
</style>

<div id="divAdvert" style="color: green">I am an advertisement.</div>
```

When the browser renders this element, it will have green text on a gray background. If you had used the `style` object to retrieve the value of both the `background-color` and `color` properties, you'd get the following mixed results:

```
var divAdvert = document.getElementById("divAdvert");  // Get the desired element
alert(divAdvert.style.backgroundColor);  // Alerts an empty string
alert(divAdvert.style.color);  // Alerts green
```

You get these results because the `style` object maps directly to the `style` attribute of the element. If the style declaration is set in the `<style/>` block, you cannot retrieve that property's value with the `style` object.

Try It Out   ## Using the style Object

Let's look at a simple example of changing the appearance of some text by using the `style` object.

```
<!DOCTYPE html PUBLIC "-//W3C//DTD XHTML 1.0 Transitional//EN"
    "http://www.w3.org/TR/xhtml1/DTD/xhtml1-transitional.dtd">

<html xmlns="http://www.w3.org/1999/xhtml">
<head>
    <title>Chapter 12: Example 4</title>
    <style type="text/css">
    #divAdvert
    {
        font: 12pt arial;
    }
    </style>
    <script type="text/javascript">
    function divAdvert_onMouseOver()
    {
        var divAdvert = document.getElementById("divAdvert");
        divAdvert.style.fontStyle = "italic";
        divAdvert.style.textDecoration = "underline";
    }

    function divAdvert_onMouseOut()
    {
        var divAdvert = document.getElementById("divAdvert");
        divAdvert.style.fontStyle = "normal";
        divAdvert.style.textDecoration = "none";
    }
    </script>
</head>
<body>
    <div id="divAdvert" onmouseover="divAdvert_onMouseOver()"
        onmouseout="divAdvert_onMouseOut()">
        Here is an advertisement.
    </div>
</body>
</html>
```

Save this as `ch12_examp4.htm`. When you run this in your browser, you should see a single line of text, as shown in Figure 12-11.

Figure 12-11

Roll your mouse over the text, and you'll see it become italicized and underlined, as shown in Figure 12-12.

Figure 12-12

And when you move your mouse off of the text, it returns to normal.

In the page's body, a `<div/>` element is defined with an id of divAdvert. Hook up the mouseover and mouseout events to the divAdvert_onMouseOver() and divAdvert_onMouseOut() functions, respectively, which are defined in the `<script/>` block in the head of the page.

When the mouse pointer enters the `<div/>` element, the divAdvert_onMouseOver() function is called.

```
function divAdvert_onMouseOver()
{
    var divAdvert = document.getElementById("divAdvert");
    divAdvert.style.fontStyle = "italic";
    divAdvert.style.textDecoration = "underline";
}
```

Before you can do anything to the `<div/>` element, you must first retrieve it. You do this simply by using the getElementById() method. Now that you have the element, you manipulate its style by first italicizing the text with the fontStyle property. Next, you underline the text by using the textDecoration property and assigning its value to underline.

Naturally, you do not want to keep the text italicized and underlined; so the mouseout event allows you to change the text back to its original state. When this event fires, the divAdvert_onMouseOut() function is called.

```
function divAdvert_onMouseOut()
{
    var divAdvert = document.getElementById("divAdvert");
    divAdvert.style.fontStyle = "normal";
    divAdvert.style.textDecoration = "none";
}
```

The code for this function resembles the code for the divAdvert_onMouseOver() function. First, you retrieve the divAdvert element and then set the fontStyle property to normal, thus removing the italics. Then you set the textDecoration to none, which removes the underline from the text.

Changing the class Attribute

You can assign a CSS class to elements by using the element's class attribute. This attribute is exposed in the DOM by the className property and can be changed through JavaScript to associate a different style rule with the element.

```
element.className = sNewClassName;
```

Using the className property to change an element's style is advantageous in two ways:

❑   It reduces the amount of JavaScript you have to write, which no one is likely to complain about.

❑   It keeps style information out of the JavaScript file and puts it into the CSS file where it belongs. Making any type of changes to the style rules is easier because you do not have to have several files open in order to change them.

Using the className Property

Let's revisit the code from `ch12_examp4.htm` from the previous section and make some revisions.

```
<!DOCTYPE html PUBLIC "-//W3C//DTD XHTML 1.0 Transitional//EN"
    "http://www.w3.org/TR/xhtml1/DTD/xhtml1-transitional.dtd">

<html xmlns="http://www.w3.org/1999/xhtml">
<head>
    <title>Chapter 12: Example 5</title>
    <style type="text/css">
        .defaultStyle
        {
            font: normal 12pt arial;
            text-decoration: none;
        }
        .newStyle
        {
            font: italic 12pt arial;
            text-decoration: underline;
        }
    </style>
    <script type="text/javascript">
    function divAdvert_onMouseOver()
    {
        var divAdvert = document.getElementById("divAdvert");
        divAdvert.className = "newStyle";
    }

    function divAdvert_onMouseOut()
    {
        var divAdvert = document.getElementById("divAdvert");
        divAdvert.className = "defaultStyle";
    }
    </script>
</head>
<body>
    <div id="divAdvert" class="defaultStyle" onmouseover="divAdvert_onMouseOver()"
        onmouseout="divAdvert_onMouseOut()">
        Here is an advertisement.
    </div>
</body>
</html>
```

Save this file as `ch12_examp5.htm`. This page behaves in the exact same manner as `ch12_examp4.htm`. When you place your mouse pointer over the text, it becomes italicized and underlined; when you move your pointer off of the text, it changes back to normal.

There are a few key differences between this HTML page and the one created using the `style` object. For starters, the `#divAdvert` style rule is removed and replaced with two CSS classes:

```
.defaultStyle
{
    font: normal 12pt arial;
    text-decoration: none;
```

```
    }

    .newStyle
    {
        font: italic 12pt arial;
        text-decoration: underline;
    }
```

The first class, called `defaultStyle`, is the rule first applied to the `<div/>` element. It declares a normal 12-point Arial font with no underlining. The second class is called `newStyle`. This class contains style declarations to specify 12-point italic Arial that is underlined. With these changes, the `<div/>` element definition is changed to use the `defaultStyle` CSS class:

```
<div id="divAdvert" class="defaultStyle" onmouseover="divAdvert_onMouseOver()"
    onmouseout="divAdvert_onMouseOut()">
    Here is an advertisement.
</div>
```

Notice that the `id` attribute is the same; you still need to access the element in order to change its `className` property. The `onmouseover` and `onmouseout` event handlers remain the same, as you need the same behavior in the `style` object example.

The final change is in the JavaScript itself. When the `mouseover` event fires on the element, the `divAdvert_onMouseOver()` function is called. This function consists of two lines of code as opposed to the three lines you used for the `style` object.

```
function divAdvert_onMouseOver()
{
    var divAdvert = document.getElementById("divAdvert");
    divAdvert.className = "newStyle";
}
```

The first statement retrieves the `<div/>` element by using the `getElementById()` method. The function then changes the `className` property to the value `newStyle`. With this line, the `divAdvert` element takes on a new style rule and the browser changes the way it looks.

When you move your mouse pointer off of the text, the `mouseout` event fires and `divAdvert_onMouseOut()` executes. This function is almost identical to `divAdvert_onMouseOver()`, except that the `className` is set back to its original value:

```
function divAdvert_onMouseOut()
{
    var divAdvert = document.getElementById("divAdvert");
    divAdvert.className = "defaultStyle";
}
```

By setting `className` back to `defaultStyle`, the browser displays the `<div/>` element as it previously did, with no italics or underlining.

Although it wasn't demonstrated here, the HTML class *attribute, and thus the* className *property, can contain multiple CSS class names. You'll see more about multiple class names in Chapter 15.*

Positioning and Moving Content

Changing the appearance of an element is an important pattern in DHTML, and it finds its place in many DHTML scripts. However, there is more to DHTML than just changing the way content appears on the page; you can also change the position of an element with JavaScript.

Moving content with JavaScript is just as easy as using the `style` object. You use the `position` property to change the type of position desired, and by using the `left` and `top` properties, you can position the element.

```
var divAdvert = document.getElementById("divAdvert");

divAdvert.style.position = "absolute";
divAdvert.style.left = "100px"; //Set the left position
divAdvert.style.top = "100px";  //Set the right position
```

This code first retrieves the `divAdvert` element. Then it sets the element's position to absolute and moves the element 100 pixels from the left and top edges. Notice the addition of `px` to the value assigned to the positions. Many browsers require you to specify a unit when assigning a positional value; otherwise, the browser will not position the element.

Note that positioning elements requires the position of absolute or relative.

Try It Out   **Moving an Element Around**

Moving an element around on the page, as you've seen, is quite similar to changing other styles with the `style` object. However, the ability to move an element on the page is used quite often, and you will definitely see it later in the chapter. Therefore, you are going to build a page that enables you to specify the location of an element through form fields.

```html
<!DOCTYPE html PUBLIC "-//W3C//DTD XHTML 1.0 Transitional//EN"
    "http://www.w3.org/TR/xhtml1/DTD/xhtml1-transitional.dtd">

<html xmlns="http://www.w3.org/1999/xhtml">
<head>
    <title>Chapter 12: Example 6</title>
    <style type="text/css">
    #divBox
    {
        position: absolute;
        background-color: silver;
        width: 150px;
        height: 150px;
    }
    input
    {
        width: 100px;
    }
    </style>
    <script type="text/javascript">
    function moveBox() {
        var divBox = document.getElementById("divBox");
        var inputLeft = document.getElementById("inputLeft");
```

```
                    var inputTop = document.getElementById("inputTop");

                    divBox.style.left = parseInt(inputLeft.value) + "px";
                    divBox.style.top = parseInt(inputTop.value) + "px";
            }
        </script>
    </head>
    <body>
        <div id="divBox">
            <form id="formBoxController" onsubmit="moveBox(); return false;"
                action="">
                <p>
                    Left:
                    <input type="text" id="inputLeft" />
                </p>
                <p>
                    Top:
                    <input type="text" id="inputTop" />
                </p>
                <p>
                    <input type="submit" value="Move The Box" />
                </p>
            </form>
        </div>
    </body>
</html>
```

Save this file as ch12_examp6.htm. When you load the page into your browser, you should see a silver box in the upper-left corner of the screen. Inside this box, you'll see a form with two fields and a button, as shown in Figure 12-13.

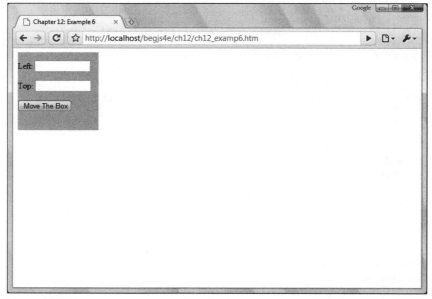

Figure 12-13

When you enter numerical values in the text fields and click the button, the box will move to the coordinates you specified. Figure 12-14 shows the box moved to 100,100.

Figure 12-14

In the body of the page, you define a `<div/>` tag with an id of `divBox`.

```
<div id="divBox"></div>
```

Inside this element is a form consisting of three `<input/>` elements. Two of these are text boxes in which you can input the `left` and `top` positions to move the `<div/>` to, and these have ids of `inputLeft` and `inputTop`, respectively. The third `<input/>` is a Submit button.

```
<div id="divBox">
    <form id="formBoxController" onsubmit="moveBox(); return false;" action="">
        <p>Left: <input type="text" value="0" id="inputLeft" /></p>
        <p>Top: <input type="text" value="0" id="inputTop" /></p>
        <p><input type="submit" value="Move The Box" /></p>
    </form>
</div>
```

When you click the Submit button, the browser fires the `submit` event for the form. When a submit button is pressed, the browser attempts to send data to the web server. This attempt at communication causes the browser to reload the page, making any change you made through DHTML reset itself. Therefore, you must force the browser to not reload the page. You do this by setting the `submit` event to return a value of `false`.

In order for the `<div/>` element to be moved around on the page, it needs to be positioned. This example positions the element absolutely, although it would be possible to position it relatively as well.

```
#divBox
{
    position: absolute;
```

```
    background-color: silver;
    width: 150px;
    height: 150px;
}
```

Aside from the position, you also specify the box to have a background color of silver, and set the height and width to be 150 pixels each, to make it a square. At this size, however, the text boxes in the form actually extend past the box's borders. In order to fix this, set a rule for the <input/> element as well.

```
input
{
    width: 100px;
}
```

By setting the <input/> elements to be 100 pixels wide, you can fit everything nicely into the box. So at this point, the HTML is primarily finished and it's styled. All that remains is to write the JavaScript to retrieve the values from the form fields and move the box to the coordinates provided by the form.

The function responsible for this is called moveBox(), and it is the only function on this page.

```
function moveBox() {
    var divBox = document.getElementById("divBox");   //Get the box
    var inputLeft = document.getElementById("inputLeft");  //Get one form field
    var inputTop = document.getElementById("inputTop");  //Get the other one
```

The function starts by retrieving the HTML elements needed to move the box. First it gets the <div/> element itself, followed by the text boxes for the left and top positions, and stores them in the inputLeft and inputTop variables, respectively. With the needed elements selected, you can now move the box.

```
    divBox.style.left = parseInt(inputLeft.value) + "px";
    divBox.style.top = parseInt(inputTop.value) + "px";
}
```

These two new lines to moveBox() do just that. In the first line, you use the value property to retrieve the value of the text box for the left position. You pass that value to the parseInt() function because you want to make sure that value is an integer. Then append px to the number, making sure that all browsers will position the box correctly. Now do the same thing for positioning the top: get the value from the inputTop text box, pass it to parseInt(), and append px to it.

As you can see, moving an element around the page is quite simple and is a building block toward another effect: animation.

Example: Animated Advertisement

Changing the appearance and position of an element are important patterns in DHTML, and they find their places in many DHTML scripts. Perhaps the most creative use of DHTML is in animating content on the page. You can perform a variety of animations with DHTML. You can fade text elements or images in and out, give them a swipe animation (making it look like as if they are wiped onto the page), and animate them to move around on the page.

Animation can give important information the flair it needs to be easily recognized by your reader, as well as adding a "that's cool" factor. Performing animation with DHTML follows the same principles of any other type of animation: You make seemingly insignificant changes one at a time in a sequential order until you reach the end of the animation. Essentially, with any animation, you have the following requisites:

1. The starting state
2. The movement towards the final goal
3. The end state; stopping the animation

Animating an absolutely positioned element, as you're going to do in this section, is no different. First, with CSS, position the element at the start location. Then perform the animation up until you reach the end point, which signals the end of the animation.

In this section, you'll learn how to animate content to bounce back and forth between two points. To do this, you need one important piece of information: the content's current location.

Are We There Yet?

The DOM in modern browsers exposes the offsetTop and offsetLeft properties of an HTML element object. These two properties return the calculated position relative to the element's parent element: offsetTop tells you the top location, and offsetLeft tells you the left position. The values returned by these properties are numerical values, so you can easily check to see where your element currently is in the animation. For example:

```
var endPointX = 394;

if (element.offsetLeft < endPointX)
{
    // Continue animation
}
```

The preceding code specifies the end point (in this case, 394) and assigns it to the endPointX variable. You can then check to see if the element's offsetLeft value is currently less than that of the end point. If it is, you can continue the animation. This example brings us to the next topic in content movement: performing the animation.

Performing the Animation

In order to perform an animation, you need to modify the top and left properties of the style object incrementally and quickly. In DHTML, you do this with periodic function execution until it's time to end the animation. To do this, use one of two methods of the window object: setTimeout() or setInterval(). This example uses the setInterval() method to periodically move an element.

Try It Out   Animating Content

The following HTML page moves an element across the page from right to left:

```
<!DOCTYPE html PUBLIC "-//W3C//DTD XHTML 1.0 Transitional//EN"
    "http://www.w3.org/TR/xhtml1/DTD/xhtml1-transitional.dtd">

<html xmlns="http://www.w3.org/1999/xhtml" >
```

```
<head>
    <title>Moving Content</title>
    <style type="text/css">
    #divAdvert
    {
        position: absolute;
        font: 12px Arial;
        top: 4px;
        left: 0px;
    }
    </style>
    <script type="text/javascript">
    var switchDirection = false;

    function doAnimation() {
        var divAdvert = document.getElementById("divAdvert");
        var currentLeft = divAdvert.offsetLeft;
        var newLocation;

        if (switchDirection == false)
        {
            newLocation = currentLeft + 2;

            if (currentLeft >= 400)
            {
                switchDirection = true;
            }
        }
        else
        {
            newLocation = currentLeft - 2;

            if (currentLeft <= 0)
            {
                switchDirection = false;
            }
        }

        divAdvert.style.left = newLocation + "px";
    }
    </script>
</head>
<body onload="setInterval(doAnimation, 10)">
    <div id="divAdvert">Here is an advertisement.</div>
</body>
</html>
```

Save this page as `ch12_examp7.htm` and load it into your browser. When you load the page into the browser, the content should start moving from left to right, starting at the left edge of the viewport. When the content reaches a left position of 400 pixels, the content switches directions and begins to move back toward the left edge. This animation is continuous, so it should bounce between the two points (0 and 400) perpetually.

Inside the body of the page is a <div/> element. This element has an id of divAdvert so that you can retrieve it with the getElementById() method, as this is the element you want to animate.

```
<div id="divAdvert">Here is an advertisement.</div>
```

There are no style attributes in this element because all the style information is inside the style sheet located in the head of the page. In the style sheet, you define a starting point for this <div/>. You want the animation to go first from left to right, and you want it to start at the left edge of the browser.

```
#divAdvert
{
    position: absolute;
    font: 12pt arial;
    top: 4px;
    left: 0px;
}
```

The first style declaration positions the element absolutely, and the second specifies the font as 12-point Arial. The next declaration positions the element four pixels from the top of the browser's viewport. Setting the top position away from the topmost edge makes the text a little easier to read. Finally, the last line positions the divAdvert element along the left edge of the viewport with the left property.

Within the script block is a global variable called switchDirection.

```
var switchDirection = false;
```

This variable keeps track of the direction in which the content is currently going. If switchDirection is false, then the content is moving from left to right, which is the default. If switchDirection is true, then the content is moving from right to left.

Next in the script block is the doAnimation() function, which performs the animation.

```
function doAnimation()
{
    var divAdvert = document.getElementById("divAdvert");  //Get the element
    var currentLeft = divAdvert.offsetLeft; //Get the current left position
    var newLocation; //Will store the new location
```

First, you retrieve the divAdvert element with the getElementById() method; you also retrieve the offsetLeft property and assign its value to the currentLeft variable. You use this variable to check the content's current position. Next, create a variable called newLocation which will contain the new left position, but before you assign its value you need to know the direction in which the content is moving.

```
        if (switchDirection == false)
        {
            newLocation = currentLeft + 2;

            if (currentLeft >= 400)
            {
                switchDirection = true;
            }
        }
```

First, check the direction by checking the switchDirection variable. Remember, if it is false, the animation is moving from left to right; so assign newLocation to contain the content's current position and add 2, thus moving the content 2 pixels to the right.

You then need to check if the content has reached the left position of 400 pixels. If it has, then you need to switch the direction of the animation, and you do this by changing switchDirection to true. So the next time doAnimation() runs, it will begin to move the content from right to left.

The code to move the element in this new direction is similar to the previous code, except for a few key differences.

```
else
{
    newLocation = currentLeft - 2;

    if (currentLeft <= 0)
    {
        switchDirection = false;
    }
}
```

The first difference is the value assigned to newLocation; instead of adding 2 to the current location, you subtract 2, thus moving the content 2 pixels to the left. Next, check if currentLeft is less than or equal to 0. If it is, you know you've reached the ending point of the right-to-left movement and need to switch directions again by assigning switchDirection to be false.

Finally, set the new position of the content:

```
    divAdvert.style.left = newLocation + "px";
}
```

This final line of the function sets the element's left property to the value stored in the newLocation variable plus the string "px".

To run the animation, use the onload event handler in the <body/> element, and use the window.setInterval() method to continuously execute doAnimation(). The following code runs doAnimation() every 10 milliseconds:

```
<body onload="setInterval(doAnimation, 10)">
```

At this speed, the content moves at a pace that is easily seen by those viewing the page. If you wanted to speed up or slow down the animation, simply change how often the setInterval() function calls doAnimation() by changing the second parameter.

What have you seen so far? Well, you've seen the DOM hierarchy and how it represents the HTML document as a tree-like structure. You navigated through the different parts of it via DOM objects (the Node objects) and their properties, and you changed the properties of objects, thus altering the content of the web page. This leaves just one area of the DOM to cover: the event model.

DOM and Events

The two major browsers in the late 1990s were Internet Explorer 4 and Netscape 4 — the first browser war. Not surprising, both browser vendors implemented vastly different DOMs and event models, fragmenting the web into two groups: websites that catered to Netscape only, and websites that catered to IE only. Very few developers chose the frustrating task of cross-browser development.

Obviously, a need for a standard grew from this fragmentation and frustration. So the W3C introduced the DOM standard, which grew into DOM level 2, which included a standard event model.

The DOM event model is a way of handling events and providing information about these events to the script. It provides a set of guidelines for a standard way of determining what generated an event, what type of event it was, and when and where the event occurred. It introduces a basic set of objects, properties, and methods, and makes some important distinctions.

Despite this attempt at standardization, developers still have to work with multiple event models. While browsers like Firefox, Chrome, Safari, and Opera implement the standard event model, Internet Explorer does not, and extra effort is required to build cross-browser event-driven applications. Don't fret, though; despite the different implementations, the DOM and IE event models share some common properties, and many non-shared properties are easily translated to other properties.

In this section, you'll learn about the two models. Later in the chapter, you'll put this information to use in writing cross-browser DHTML.

DOM Event Handling

The DOM standard describes an `Event` object, which provides information about the element that has generated an event and enables you to retrieve it in script. If you want to make it available in script, it must be passed as a parameter to the function connected to the event handler.

Internet Explorer does not implement the DOM event model. The code in this section will not work in IE because of this.

Accessing the Event Object

You learned in Chapter 6 how to handle events using HTML attributes. However, you did not learn how to access an `Event` object, something that proves very useful a majority of the time. It's very simple to do so, and all you have to do is query the event object created by the individual element that raised the event. For example, in the following code the `<p/>` element will raise a `dblclick` event:

```
<p ondblclick="handle(event)">Paragraph</p>

<script type="text/javascript">
function handle(e)
{
    alert(e.type);
}
</script>
```

Notice that `event` is passed to the `handle()` function in the `ondblclick` attribute. This `event` variable is special in that it is not defined anywhere; instead, it is an argument used only with event handlers that are connected through HTML attributes. It passes a reference to the current event object when the event fires.

If you ran the previous example, it would just tell you what kind of event raised your event-handling function. This might seem self-evident in the preceding example, but if you had included the following extra lines of code, any one of three elements could have raised the function:

```
<p ondblclick="handle(event)">Paragraph</p>
<h1 onclick="handle(event)">Heading 1</h1>
<span onmouseover="handle(event)">Special Text</span>

<script type="text/javascript">
function handle(e)
{
    alert(e.type);
}
</script>
```

This makes the code much more useful. In general, you will use relatively few event handlers to deal with any number of events, and you can use the event properties as a filter to determine what type of event happened and what HTML element triggered it, so that you can treat each event differently.

In the following example, you see that you can take different courses of action depending on what type of event is returned:

```
<p ondblclick="handle(event)">Paragraph</p>
<h1 onclick="handle(event)">Heading 1</h1>
<span onmouseover="handle(event)">Special Text</span>

<script type="text/javascript">
function handle(e)
{
    if (e.type == "mouseover")
    {
        alert("You moved over the Special Text");
    }
}
</script>
```

This code uses the type property to determine what type of event occurred. If the user moused over the <span/> element, then an alert box tells them so.

Accessing event information is relatively straightforward if you're using HTML attributes to assign event handlers. Thankfully, accessing event data when assigning event handlers using JavaScript objects' properties are even more straightforward: the browser automatically passes the event object to the handling function when the event fires. Consider the following code:

```
<p id="p">Paragraph</p>
<h1 id="h1">Heading 1</h1>
<span id="span">Special Text</span>

<script type="text/javascript">
function handle(e)
{
    if (e.type == "mouseover")
```

```
        {
            alert("You moved over the Special Text");
        }
    }

    document.getElementById("p").ondblclick = handle;
    document.getElementById("h1").onclick = handle;
    document.getElementById("span").onmouseover = handle;
    </script>
```

This code is slightly different from the last example using HTML attributes. The elements are given `id` attributes to allow easy access to their objects in the DOM with the `getElementById()` method. Each element is assigned an event handler, which calls `handle()` when their respective events fire. The result is the same as before; the user sees an alert box telling them they moved their mouse pointer over the Special Text.

Using Event Data

The standard outlines several properties of the `Event` object that offer information about that event: what element it happened at, what type of event took place, and what time it occurred? These are all pieces of data offered by the `Event` object. The following table lists the properties outlined in the specification.

Properties of the Event Object	Description
bubbles	Indicates whether an event can *bubble* — passing control from one element to another starting from the event target and bubbling up the hierarchy.
cancelable	Indicates whether an event can have its default action canceled.
currentTarget	Indicates which the event target whose event handlers are currently being processed.
eventPhase	Indicates which phase of the event flow an event is in.
target	Indicates which element caused the event; in the DOM event model, text nodes are a possible target of an event.
timestamp	Indicates at what time the event occurred.
type	Indicates the name of the event.

Secondly, the DOM event model introduces a `MouseEvent` object, which deals with events generated specifically by the mouse. This is useful because you might need more specific information about the event, such as the position in pixels of the cursor, or the element the mouse has come from.

Properties of the MouseEvent Object	Description
altKey	Indicates whether the Alt key was pressed when the event was generated.
button	Indicates which button on the mouse was pressed.

Continued

Properties of the MouseEvent Object	Description
clientX	Indicates where in the browser window, in horizontal coordinates, the mouse pointer was when the event was generated.
clientY	Indicates where in the browser window, in vertical coordinates, the mouse pointer was when the event was generated.
ctrlKey	Indicates whether the Ctrl key was pressed when the event was generated.
metaKey	Indicates whether the meta key was pressed when the event was generated.
relatedTarget	Used to identify a secondary event target. For mouseover events, this property references the element the mouse pointer exited. For mouseout events, this property references the element the mouse pointer entered.
screenX	Indicates the horizontal coordinates relative to the origin in the screen coordinates, the mouse pointer was when the event was generated.
screenY	Indicates the vertical coordinates relative to the origin in the screen coordinates, the mouse pointer was when the event was generated.
shiftKey	Indicates whether the Shift key was pressed when the event was generated.

Although any event might create an Event object, only a select set of events can generate a MouseEvent object. On the occurrence of a MouseEvent event, you'd be able to access properties from the Event object and the MouseEvent object. With a non-mouse event, none of the MouseEvent object properties in the preceding table would be available. The following mouse events can create a MouseEvent event object:

❑   click occurs when a mouse button is clicked (pressed and released) with the pointer over an element or text.

❑   mousedown occurs when a mouse button is pressed with the pointer over an element or text.

❑   mouseup occurs when a mouse button is released with the pointer over an element or text.

❑   mouseover occurs when a mouse button is moved onto an element or text.

❑   mousemove occurs when a mouse button is moved and it is already on top of an element or text.

❑   mouseout occurs when a mouse button is moved out and away from an element or text.

Take a quick look at an example that uses some properties of the MouseEvent object.

Open a text editor and type the following:

```
<!DOCTYPE html PUBLIC "-//W3C//DTD XHTML 1.0 Transitional//EN"
    "http://www.w3.org/TR/xhtml1/DTD/xhtml1-transitional.dtd">

<html xmlns="http://www.w3.org/1999/xhtml">
<head>
    <title>Chapter 12: Example 8</title>
    <style type="text/css">
    .underline
    {
        color: red;
        text-decoration: underline;
    }
    </style>
    <script type="text/javascript">
    function handleEvent(e)
    {
        if (e.target.tagName == "P")
        {
            if (e.type == "mouseover")
            {
                e.target.className = "underline";
            }

            if (e.type == "mouseout")
            {
                e.target.className = "";
            }
        }

        if (e.type == "click")
        {
            alert("You clicked the mouse button at the X:"
                + e.clientX + " and Y:" + e.clientY + " coordinates");
        }
    }

    document.onmouseover = handleEvent;
    document.onmouseout = handleEvent;
    document.onclick = handleEvent;
    </script>
</head>
<body>
<p>This is paragraph 1.</p>
<p>This is paragraph 2.</p>
<p>This is paragraph 3.</p>
</body>
</html>
```

Save this as ch12_examp8.htm and run it in your browser. When you move your mouse over one of the paragraphs, you'll notice its text changes color to red and it becomes underlined. Click anywhere in the page, and you'll see an alert box like Figure 12-15.

Figure 12-15

Now click OK, move the pointer in the browser window, and click again. A different result appears.

This example is consistent with the event-handling behavior: The browser waits for an event, and every time that event occurs it raises the corresponding function. It will continue to wait for the event until you exit the browser or that particular web page. In this example, you assign event handlers for the mouseover, mouseout, and click events on the document object.

```
document.onmouseover = handleEvent;
document.onmouseout = handleEvent;
document.onclick = handleEvent;
One function, handleEvent() handles all three of these events.
```

Whenever any of these events fire, the handleClick() function is raised and a new MouseEvent object is generated. Remember that MouseEvent objects give you access to Event object properties as well as MouseEvent object properties, and you use some of them in this example.

The function accepts the MouseEvent event object and assigns it the reference e.

```
function handleEvent(e)
{
    if (e.target.tagName == "P")
    {
```

Inside the function, the first thing you do is check if the event target (the element that caused the event) has a tagName of P. If the target is a paragraph element, then the next bit of information you need to find is what kind of event took place by using the type property.

```
        if (e.type == "mouseover")
        {
            e.target.className = "underline";
```

```
        }

        if (e.type == "mouseout")
        {
            e.target.className = "";
        }
    }
```

If the event is a mouseover, then the paragraph's CSS class is assigned the underline class defined in the page's style sheet. If the event type is mouseout, then the element's className property is cleared, which returns the text to its original style. This style-changing code runs only if the element that caused the event is a paragraph element.

Next, the function determines if the user clicked their mouse by again checking the type property.

```
if (e.type == "click")
    {
        alert("You clicked the mouse button at the X:"
            + e.clientX + " and Y:" + e.clientY + " coordinates");
    }
}
```

If the user did indeed click somewhere in the page, then you use the alert() method to display the contents of the clientX and clientY properties of the mouse event object on the screen.

The MouseEvent object supplied to this function is overwritten and re-created every time you generate an event, so the next time you click the mouse or move the pointer it creates a new MouseEvent object containing the coordinates for the x and y positions and the information on the element that caused the event to fire. One problem that precludes greater discussion of the DOM event model is the fact that not all browsers support it in any detail. Specifically, IE, the most popular browser, doesn't fully support it. Despite the lack of support for the DOM standard, you can still acquire the same useful information on a given event with IE's event model.

Event Handling in Internet Explorer

IE's event model remains relatively unchanged since the introduction of IE4 in 1997. It incorporates the use of a global event object (it is a property of the window object), and one such object exists for each open browser window. The browser updates the event object every time the user causes an event to occur, and it provides information similar to that of the standard DOM Event object.

Accessing the event Object

Because the event object is a property of window, it is very simple to access.

```
<p ondblclick="handle()">Paragraph</p>

<script type="text/javascript">
function handle()
{
    alert(window.event.type);
}
</script>
```

This code assigns the `handle()` function to handle the `<p/>` element's `dblclick` event. When the function executes, it gets the type of event that caused the `handle()` function's execution. Because the `event` object is global, there is no need to pass the object to the handling function like the DOM event model. Also note that like other properties of the `window` object, it's not required that you precede the `event` object with `window`.

The same holds true when you assign event handlers through JavaScript using object properties.

```
<p id="p">Paragraph</p>
<h1 id="h1">Heading 1</h1>
<span id="span">Special Text</span>

<script type="text/javascript">
function handle()
{
    if (event.type == "mouseover")
    {
        alert("You moved over the Special Text");
    }
}

document.getElementById("p").ondblclick = handle;
document.getElementById("h1").onclick = handle;
document.getElementById("span").onmouseover = handle;
</script>
```

Using Event Data

As you can see, IE's `event` object is straightforward and simple to use; however, it does provide different properties from the DOM standard's `Event` and `MouseEvent` objects, although they typically provide you with similar data.

The following table lists some of the properties of IE's `event` object.

Properties of the event Object	Description
altKey	Indicates whether the Alt key was pressed when the event was generated.
button	Indicates which button on the mouse was pressed.
cancelBubble	Gets or sets whether the current event should bubble up the hierarchy of event handlers.
clientX	Indicates where in the browser window, in horizontal coordinates, the mouse pointer was when the event was generated.
clientY	Indicates where in the browser window, in vertical coordinates, the mouse pointer was when the event was generated.
ctrlKey	Indicates whether the Ctrl key was pressed when the event was generated.
fromElement	Gets the element object the mouse pointer is exiting.

Properties of the event Object	Description
keyCode	Gets the Unicode keycode associated with the key that caused the event.
screenX	Indicates where in the browser window, in horizontal coordinates relative to the origin in the screen coordinates, the mouse pointer was when the event was generated.
screenY	Indicates where in the browser window, in vertical coordinates relative to the origin in the screen coordinates, the mouse pointer was when the event was generated.
shiftKey	Indicates whether the Shift key was pressed when the event was generated.
srcElement	Gets the element object that caused the event.
toElement	Gets the element object that the mouse pointer is entering.
type	Retrieves the event's name.

Let's revisit Example eight where you wrote a page to take advantage of the DOM event model and change it to work in IE.

Try it Out   Using the IE Event Model

Open your text editor and type the following. Feel free to copy and paste the elements within the body and the style sheet from Example eight.

```
<!DOCTYPE html PUBLIC "-//W3C//DTD XHTML 1.0 Transitional//EN"
    "http://www.w3.org/TR/xhtml1/DTD/xhtml1-transitional.dtd">

<html xmlns="http://www.w3.org/1999/xhtml">
<head>
    <title>Chapter 12: Example 9</title>
    <style type="text/css">
    .underline
    {
        color: red;
        text-decoration: underline;
    }
    </style>
    <script type="text/javascript">
    function handleEvent()
    {
        if (event.srcElement.tagName == "P")
        {
            if (event.type == "mouseover")
            {
                event.srcElement.className = "underline";
            }
```

445

```
                if (event.type == "mouseout")
                {
                    event.srcElement.className = "";
                }
            }

            if (event.type == "click")
            {
                alert("You clicked the mouse button at the X:"
                    + event.clientX + " and Y:" + event.clientY + " coordinates");
            }
        }

    document.onmouseover = handleEvent;
    document.onmouseout = handleEvent;
    document.onclick = handleEvent;
    </script>
</head>
<body>
<p>This is paragraph 1.</p>
<p>This is paragraph 2.</p>
<p>This is paragraph 3.</p>
</body>
</html>
```

Save this as ch12_examp9.htm, and load it into IE. It'll look and behave exactly like Example eight; the paragraph text will change to red and have an underline as you move your mouse pointer over the paragraphs. When your mouse pointer leaves a paragraph, the text returns to the original state. When you click your mouse, an alert box tells you the coordinates of where your mouse pointer was when you clicked.

You assign the handleEvent() function to handle the mouseover, mouseout, and click events on the document object.

```
document.onmouseover = handleEvent;
document.onmouseout = handleEvent;
document.onclick = handleEvent;
```

When you cause any of these events to fire, the browser updates the event object and calls the handleClick() function.

```
function handleEvent()
{
    if (event.srcElement.tagName == "P")
    {
```

First, check the source element's tagName property and see if it is P. If it is, then you check what kind of event occurred by using the type property.

```
        if (event.type == "mouseover")
        {
            event.srcElement.className = "underline";
        }

        if (event.type == "mouseout")
        {
```

```
            event.srcElement.className = "";
        }
    }
```

For `mouseover` events, you change the paragraph's CSS class to `underline`. If the event type is `mouseout`, then the element's `className` property is set to an empty string — returning the text to its original style.

The next bit of code displays the mouse pointer's location if the mouse button was clicked.

```
    if (event.type == "click")
    {
        alert("You clicked the mouse button at the X:"
            + event.clientX + " and Y:" + event.clientY + " coordinates");
    }
}
```

If you compare Example eight with Example nine, you will notice the two primary differences are how the event information is accessed, and how to retrieve the element that caused the event to occur. Most everything else is shared between the standard DOM event model and IE's event model.

In the next section, you'll learn how to handle the fundamental differences between both event models and write cross-browser DHTML code.

Writing Cross-Browser DHTML

By now you've written two versions of the same DHTML script: one for IE and one for browsers that support the standard DOM event model (Firefox, Safari, Chrome, and Opera). In the real world, creating separate versions of web sites is rarely considered best practice, and it's much, much easier to write a cross-browser version of the web page. In this section, you'll use the knowledge you've gained of the DOM, the standard DOM event model, and IE's event model to write a cross-browser DHTML script. This script will consist of a tab strip containing three tabs. Clicking any tab dynamically adds content to the web page. It is a very crude and incomplete tab strip. You'll have the opportunity to add more functionality to it for one of this chapter's questions.

Try It Out   A Crude, Cross-Browser Tab Strip

Open your text editor and type the following:

```
<!DOCTYPE html PUBLIC "-//W3C//DTD XHTML 1.0 Transitional//EN"
    "http://www.w3.org/TR/xhtml1/DTD/xhtml1-transitional.dtd">

<html xmlns="http://www.w3.org/1999/xhtml">
<head>
    <title>Chapter 12: Example 10</title>
    <style type="text/css">
    .tabStrip
    {
```

```
        background-color: #E4E2D5;
        padding: 3px;
        height: 22px;
    }

    .tabStrip div
    {
        float: left;
        font: 14px arial;
        cursor: pointer;
    }

    .tabStrip-tab
    {
        padding: 3px;
    }

    .tabStrip-tab-hover
    {
        border: 1px solid #316AC5;
        background-color: #C1D2EE;
        padding: 2px;
    }

    .tabStrip-tab-click
    {
        border: 1px solid #facc5a;
        background-color: #f9e391;
        padding: 2px;
    }
</style>
<script type="text/javascript">
function handleEvent(e)
{
    var eSrc;

    if (window.event)
    {
        e = window.event;
        eSrc = e.srcElement;
    }
    else
    {
        eSrc = e.target;
    }

    if (e.type == "mouseover")
    {
        if (eSrc.className == "tabStrip-tab")
        {
            eSrc.className = "tabStrip-tab-hover";
        }
    }
```

```
                if (e.type == "mouseout")
                {
                    if (eSrc.className == "tabStrip-tab-hover")
                    {
                        eSrc.className = "tabStrip-tab";
                    }
                }

                if (e.type == "click")
                {
                    if (eSrc.className == "tabStrip-tab-hover")
                    {
                        eSrc.className = "tabStrip-tab-click";
                        var num = eSrc.id.substr(eSrc.id.lastIndexOf("-") + 1);

                        showDescription(num);
                    }
                }
            }

            function showDescription(num)
            {
                var descContainer = document.getElementById("descContainer");

                var div = document.createElement("div");
                var text = document.createTextNode("Description for Tab " + num);

                div.appendChild(text);
                descContainer.appendChild(div);
            }

            document.onclick = handleEvent;
            document.onmouseover = handleEvent;
            document.onmouseout = handleEvent;
        </script>
    </head>
    <body>
        <div class="tabStrip">
            <div id="tabStrip-tab-1" class="tabStrip-tab">Tab 1</div>
            <div id="tabStrip-tab-2" class="tabStrip-tab">Tab 2</div>
            <div id="tabStrip-tab-3" class="tabStrip-tab">Tab 3</div>
        </div>
        <div id="descContainer"></div>
    </body>
</html>
```

Save this file as ch12_examp10.htm. Open it in multiple browsers, and you'll see that the page looks and behaves the same in all browsers. When you move your mouse pointer over a tab, its style changes to a blue background with a darker blue border. When you click a tab, its style changes yet again to make the tab's background color a light orange with a darker orange border color. Also, when you click a tab, text is added to the page. For example, clicking tab 3 results in the text "Description for Tab 3" being added to the page.

Let's look at the HTML in the body, and its style, first.

```
<div class="tabStrip">
    <div id="tabStrip-tab-1" class="tabStrip-tab">Tab 1</div>
    <div id="tabStrip-tab-2" class="tabStrip-tab">Tab 2</div>
    <div id="tabStrip-tab-3" class="tabStrip-tab">Tab 3</div>
</div>
<div id="descContainer"></div>
```

The first `<div/>` element has a CSS class of `tabStrip`. The three `<div/>` elements contained within it represent three tabs. Each tab `<div/>` element has a value assigned to its `id` attribute, and a CSS class of `tabStrip-tab`.

The tab strip `<div/>` element has a sibling `<div/>` element with an `id` value of `descContainer`. It doesn't contain any children (yet), and it doesn't have a CSS class associated with it.

In this example, the tab strip is visually set apart from the rest of the page by giving it a gray background.

```
.tabStrip
{
    background-color: #E4E2D5;
    padding: 3px;
    height: 22px;
}
```

It's given an actual height of 28 pixels (height + top padding + bottom padding). This height and padding vertically centers the tab `<div/>` elements within the tab strip.

The tabs have several CSS rules to define the way they are rendered in the browser because they have three states: normal, hover, and click. Despite these three states, they are still tabs and thus share some visual characteristics. The first rule dictates these shared properties.

```
.tabStrip div
{
    float: left;
    font: 14px arial;
    cursor: pointer;
}
```

The selector tells the browser to apply these properties to all `<div/>` elements inside the tab strip. The elements are set to float left to give them an inline appearance (`<div/>` elements are block elements, and appear on a new line by default).

The next rule, the `tabStrip-tab` class, defines the normal state.

```
.tabStrip-tab
{
    padding: 3px;
}
```

All this rule adds is a padding of three pixels on all sides of the element. Next is the hover state, as defined by the `tabStrip-tab-hover` class.

```
.tabStrip-tab-hover
{
```

```
    border: 1px solid #316AC5;
    background-color: #C1D2EE;
    padding: 2px;
}
```

This rule reduces the padding to two pixels, adds a one-pixel-wide border, and changes the background color to a shade of blue. Borders, like padding, add to the actual dimensions of an element; reducing the padding while adding a border keeps the element in a hover state the same height and width as it was in the normal state.

The final rule declares the tabStrip-tab-click class.

```
.tabStrip-tab-click
{
    border: 1px solid #facc5a;
    background-color: #f9e391;
    padding: 2px;
}
```

This class is similar to the hover class; the only difference is the dark orange border color and light orange background color.

Now let's look at the JavaScript code that performs the magic. The code consists of the handleEvent() function, which is assigned to the document object's onmouseover, onmouseout, and onclick event handlers.

```
document.onclick = handleEvent;
document.onmouseover = handleEvent;
document.onmouseout = handleEvent;
```

The function begins by declaring a variable called eSrc (short for element source; it doesn't matter what you call this variable as long as it's meaningful to you). This variable should contain the srcElement and target properties for IE and browsers that implement the DOM event model, respectively.

```
function handleEvent(e)
{
    var eSrc;

    if (window.event)
    {
        e = window.event;
        eSrc = e.srcElement;
    }
    else
    {
        eSrc = e.target;
    }
```

After the variable declaration, you check for the window.event object to determine which event model the browser implements. If window.event exists, then the browser is IE, and you assign the e variable to hold a reference to the window.event object. Remember that e is defined as a parameter to the function, and since IE doesn't pass a parameter to event handlers, it is undefined. Assigning it a reference to window.event allows you to use the properties shared between the IE event object and the DOM

451

Event and MouseEvent objects easily (as you'll see later with the type property). Next, you assign the srcElement object to the eSrc variable. If the browser isn't a version of IE, then assign the DOM Event object's target property to eSrc. Regardless of the browser used to view this page, you now have a reference to the element that caused the event to occur with the eSrc variable.

Now you need to determine what type of event took place and make the appropriate changes to the DOM. First, check for the mouseover event.

```
if (e.type == "mouseover")
{
    if (eSrc.className == "tabStrip-tab")
    {
        eSrc.className = "tabStrip-tab-hover";
    }
}
```

If the element that caused the event has a class name of tabStrip-tab, a tab in its normal state, then change the element's className property to tabStrip-tab-hover. In doing so, the tab is now in the hover state.

If a mouseout event occurred, you also need to make changes to the DOM.

```
if (e.type == "mouseout")
{
    if (eSrc.className == "tabStrip-tab-hover")
    {
        eSrc.className = "tabStrip-tab";
    }
}
```

This code changes the tab's className property to tabStrip-tab (the normal state) only when the tab the mouse pointer exited is in the hover state.

The last event you need to look for is the click event, so check for it now with the following code:

```
if (e.type == "click")
{
    if (eSrc.className == "tabStrip-tab-hover")
    {
        eSrc.className = "tabStrip-tab-click";
```

This code changes the tab element's className to tabStrip-tab-click, thus putting it into the click state. Next, you need to add the tab's description to the page, and you start this process by getting the tab's number from the <div/> element's id attribute. Remember the id values for the tab elements are in the format of tabStrip-tab-1. So all you need to retrieve is the number of the tab. Do so by using the substr() method.

```
        var num = eSrc.id.substr(eSrc.id.lastIndexOf("-") + 1);

        showDescription(num);
    }
    }
}
```

This code gets the index of the last "-" character in the id string, adds 1 to it, and passes that value to the substr() method. If you didn't add 1 to the value returned by lastIndexOf(), the result from substr() would be "-1". Now that you have the tab's number, you pass it to the showDescription() function.

```
function showDescription(num)
{
    var descContainer = document.getElementById("descContainer");
```

The tabs' descriptions are added to the <div/> element with an id of descContainer, so as this code shows, you first retrieve that element using the getElementById() method.

The descriptions are dynamically created by this function, so now you need to create the DOM nodes to add to the descCounter element. First, create a <div/> element using the createElement() method of the document object.

```
var div = document.createElement("div");
```

Now create a text node containing the description for the tab. In this example, the description is simple and includes the tab's number.

```
var text = document.createTextNode("Description for Tab " + num);
```

Finally, add the text node to the newly created <div/> element, and then append that element to descContainer. Use the Node object's appendChild() method to perform both operations.

```
    div.appendChild(text);
    descContainer.appendChild(div);
}
```

JavaScript's usefulness doesn't end with HTML; there are times when you may want or need to open an XML file and read it with JavaScript. Because of the similarities between (X)HTML and XML (namely that they are structured documents), it's not surprising that you use the DOM to load and read XML documents, too.

JavaScript and XML

The W3C developed XML for the purpose of describing data rather than to actually display information in any particular format, which is the purpose of HTML. There is nothing overly special about XML. It is just plain text with the addition of some XML tags enclosed in angle brackets. You can use any software that can handle plain text to create and edit XML.

XML is a data-centric language. It not only contains data, but it describes those data by using semantic element names. The document's structure also plays a part in the description. Unlike HTML, XML is not a formatting language; in fact, a properly structured XML document is devoid of any formatting elements. This concept is often referred to as the *separation of content and style*, and is part of XML's success, as it makes the language simple and easy to use.

For example, you can use XML as a data store like a database. In fact, XML is well suited for large and complex documents because the data are structured; you design the structure and implement it using your own elements to describe the data enclosed in the element. The ability to define the structure and elements used in an XML document is what makes XML a self-describing language. That is, the elements describe the data they contain, and the structure describes how data are related to each other.

Another method in which XML has become useful is in retrieving data from remote servers. Probably the most widely known applications of this method are the RSS and Atom formats for web syndication. These XML documents, and others like them, contain information readily available to anyone. Web sites or programs can connect to the remote server, download a copy of the XML document, and use the information however needed.

A third and extremely helpful application of XML is the ability to transfer data between incompatible systems. An XML document is a plain text document; therefore, all operating systems can read and write to XML files. The only major requirement is an application that understands the XML language and the document structure. For example, Microsoft recently released details on Microsoft Office Open XML, the file format used in Microsoft Office 2007. The files themselves are actually Zip files. However, any program written to read the XML files contained in the Zip file can display the data with no problem; it doesn't matter whether they were written under Windows, Mac OS X, any flavor of Linux, or any other operating system.

Manipulating XML with JavaScript

As previously mentioned, you use the DOM to load, read, and manipulate XML data; so you learned most of what you need to manipulate XML within the web browser from the previous sections in the chapter.

The first task is to read the XML document. This is where most cross-browser problems are located because IE, you guessed it, doesn't follow the DOM standard, whereas Firefox, Safari, Chrome, and Opera do. The good news is that once the XML document is loaded, the differences between the browsers are smaller, although Microsoft has added a lot of useful (but nonstandard) extensions to its implementation.

Retrieving an XML File in IE

Internet Explorer relies upon the `ActiveXObject()` object and the MSXML library to fetch and open XML documents. A variety of ActiveX objects are available for scripting; to create an ActiveX object, simply call the `ActiveXObject()` constructor and pass a string containing the version of the ActiveX object you wish to create.

```
var xmlDoc = new ActiveXObject("Microsoft.XMLDOM");
xmlDoc.load("myfile.xml");
```

This code creates an XML DOM object that enables you to load and manipulate XML documents by using the version string `"Microsoft.XMLDOM"`. When the XML DOM object is created, load an XML document by using the `load()` method. This code loads a fictitious file called `myfile.xml`.

There are multiple versions of the Microsoft MSXML library, with each newer version offering more features and better performance than the one before. However, the user's computer must have these versions installed before you can use them, and the version selection code can become complex. Thankfully, Microsoft recommends checking for only two versions of MSXML. Their version strings are as follows:

❑ Msxml2.DOMDocument.6.0

❑ Msxml2.DOMDocument.3.0

You want to use the latest version possible when creating an XML DOM, and the following function does this:

```
function createDocument()
{
    var xmlDoc;

    if (window.ActiveXObject)
    {
        var versions =
        [
            "Msxml2.DOMDocument.6.0",
            "Msxml2.DOMDocument.3.0"
        ];

        for (var i = 0; i < versions.length; i++)
        {
            try
            {
                xmlDoc = new ActiveXObject(versions[i]);
                return xmlDoc;
            }
            catch (error)
            {
                //do nothing here
            }
        }
    }

    return null;
}
```

This code defines the createDocument() function. Its first line creates the xmlDoc variable. This is a temporary variable used in the creation of an XML DOM. The next line of code is an if statement, and it checks to see if the browser is IE by seeing if window.ActiveXObject exists. If the condition is true, then an array called versions is created, and the two MSXML versions are added as elements to the array.

```
var versions =
[
    "Msxml2.DOMDocument.6.0",
    "Msxml2.DOMDocument.3.0"
];
```

The order in which they're added is important; you want to always check for the latest version first, so the version strings are added with the newest at index 0.

Next is a `for` loop to loop through the elements of the `versions` array. Inside the loop is a `try...catch` statement.

```
for (var i = 0; i < versions.length; i++)
{
    try
    {
        xmlDoc = new ActiveXObject(versions[i]);
        return xmlDoc;
    }
    catch (error)
    {
        //do nothing here
    }
}
```

If the `ActiveXObject` object creation fails in the `try` block, then code execution drops to the `catch` block. Nothing happens at this point: The loop iterates to the next index in `versions` and attempts to create another `ActiveXObject` object with the other MSXML version strings. If every attempt fails, then the loop exits and returns `null`. Use the `createDocument()` function like this:

```
var xmlDoc = createDocument();
```

By using this function, you can create the latest MSXML XML DOM object easily.

Before you actually attempt to manipulate the XML file, make sure it has completely loaded into the client's browser cache. Otherwise, you're rolling the dice each time the page is viewed and running the risk of a JavaScript error being thrown whenever the execution of your script precedes the complete downloading of the XML file in question. Fortunately, there are ways to detect the current download state of an XML file.

The `async` property denotes whether the browser should wait for the specified XML file to fully load before proceeding with the download of the rest of the page. This property, whose name stands for *asynchronous,* is set by default to `true`, meaning the browser will not wait on the XML file before rendering everything else that follows. Setting this property to `false` instructs the browser to load the file first and then, and only then, to load the rest of the page.

```
var xmlDoc = createDocument();
xmlDoc.async = false; //Download XML file first, then load rest of page.
xmlDoc.load("myfile.xml");
```

The simplicity of the `async` property is not without its flaws. When you set this property to `false`, IE will stall the page until it makes contact and has fully received the specified XML file. When the browser is having trouble connecting and/or downloading the file, the page is left hanging like a monkey on a branch. This is where the `onreadystatechange` event handler and `readyState` property can help (as long as the `async` property is `true`).

The `readyState` property of IE exists for XML objects and many HTML objects, and returns the current loading status of the object. The following table shows the four possible return values.

Return Values for the readyState Property	Description
1	The object is initializing, but no data are being read (loading).
2	Data are being loaded into the object and parsed (loaded).
3	Parts of the object's data have been read and parsed, so the object model is available. However, the complete object data are not yet ready (interactive).
4	The object has been loaded and its content parsed (completed).

The value you're interested in here is the last one, 4, which indicates the object has fully loaded. To use the `readyState` property, assign a function to handle the `readystatechange` event, which fires every time the `readyState` changes.

```
function xmlDoc_readyStateChange()
{
    //Check for the readyState. If it's 4, it's loaded!
    if (xmlDoc.readyState == 4)
    {
        alert("XML file loaded!");
    }
}

var xmlDoc = createDocument();
xmlDoc.onreadystatechange = xmlDoc_readyStateChange;

xmlDoc.load("myfile.xml");
```

This code first creates a function called `xmlDoc_readyStateChange()`. Use this function to handle the `readystatechange` event. Inside the function, check the `readyState` property to see if its value is equal to 4. If it is, then the XML file is completely loaded and the alert text `"XML file loaded!"` is displayed. Next, create the XML DOM object and assign the `xmlDoc_readyStateChange()` function to the `onreadystatechange` event handler. The last line of code initiates the loading of `myfile.xml`.

Retrieving an XML File in Firefox and Opera

Loading an XML document in Firefox and Opera is a little different from doing the same thing in IE, as these browsers use a more standards-centric approach. Creating an XML DOM doesn't require the use of an add-on as it does in IE; the DOM is a part of the browser and JavaScript implementation.

```
var xmlDoc = document.implementation.createDocument("","",null);
xmlDoc.load("myfile.xml");
```

Safari and Chrome do not support loading XML files into a DOM object in the way covered in this section. Instead, you must use the XMLHttpRequest *object to request the XML document from the server. This object is covered in Chapter 14.*

This code creates an empty DOM object by using the createDocument() method of the document .implementation object. After the DOM object is created, use the load() method to load an XML document; it is supported by Firefox and Opera as well.

Safari and Chrome support the createDocument() *method, but they do not support the* load() *method.*

Much like IE, Firefox and Opera support the async property, which allows the file to be loaded asynchronously or synchronously. The behavior of loading synchronously is the same in these browsers as in IE. However, things change when you want to load a file asynchronously.

Not surprising, Firefox and Opera use a different implementation from IE when it comes to checking the load status of an XML file. In fact, these browsers do not enable you to check the status with something like the readyState property. Instead, they expose an onload event handler that executes when the file is loaded and the DOM object is ready to use.

```
function xmlDoc_load()
{
    alert("XML is loaded!");
}

var xmlDoc = document.implementation.createDocument("","",null);
xmlDoc.onload = xmlDoc_load;
xmlDoc.load("myfile.xml");
```

This code loads the fictitious file myfile.xml in asynchronous mode. When the load process completes, the load event fires and calls xmlDoc_load(), which then shows the text XML is loaded! to the user.

Retrieving an XML File (Cross-Browser)

As you can see, the different ways of creating XML DOM objects require you to seek a cross-browser solution. You can easily do this with object detection to determine which browser is in use. In fact, you can easily edit the createDocument() function to include Firefox and Opera support. Look at the following code:

```
function createDocument()
{
    var xmlDoc;

    if (window.ActiveXObject)
    {
        var versions =
        [
            "Msxml2.DOMDocument.6.0",
            "Msxml2.DOMDocument.3.0"
        ];
```

```
        for (var i = 0; i < versions.length; i++)
        {
            try
            {
                xmlDoc = new ActiveXObject(versions[i]);
                return xmlDoc;
            }
            catch (error)
            {
                //do nothing here
            }
        }
    }
    else if (document.implementation && document.implementation.createDocument)
    {
        xmlDoc = document.implementation.createDocument("","",null);
        return xmlDoc;
    }
    return null;
}
```

The code highlighted in gray is the only new code added to the function. It first checks if the `implementation` object and `implementation.createDocument` method exist, and, if so, it creates an XML DOM for DOM supporting browsers with `document.implementation.createDocument()` and returns the DOM object to the caller. Using the function is exactly as you saw earlier, but now it works across IE, Firefox, and Opera.

```
var xmlDoc = createDocument();
xmlDoc.async = false;
xmlDoc.load("myfile.xml");
```

Example: Displaying a Daily Message

Now that you know how to load XML documents, let's jump right into building your first XML-enabled JavaScript application, a message-of-the-day display.

To begin, use the following simple XML file. You'll retrieve the file and then display the daily message using DHTML. Following is the XML file called `motd.xml`:

```
<?xml version="1.0"?>

<messages>
    <daily>Today is Sunday.</daily>
    <daily>Today is Monday.</daily>
    <daily>Today is Tuesday.</daily>
    <daily>Today is Wednesday.</daily>
    <daily>Today is Thursday.</daily>
    <daily>Today is Friday.</daily>
    <daily>Today is Saturday.</daily>
</messages>
```

As you can see, this basic XML file is populated with a different message for each day of the week.

Next is the HTML page, with the `createDocument()` function added in the script block.

```html
<html>
<head>
    <title>Message of the Day</title>
    <script type="text/javascript">
    function createDocument()
    {
        var xmlDoc;

        if (window.ActiveXObject)
        {
            var versions =
            [
                "Msxml2.DOMDocument.6.0",
                "Msxml2.DOMDocument.3.0"
            ];

            for (var i = 0; i < versions.length; i++)
            {
                try
                {
                    xmlDoc = new ActiveXObject(versions[i]);
                    return xmlDoc;
                }
                catch (error)
                {
                    //do nothing here
                }
            }
        }
        else if (document.implementation
                && document.implementation.createDocument)
        {
            xmlDoc = document.implementation.createDocument("","",null);
            return xmlDoc;
        }

        return null;
    }

    //More code to come
    </script>
</head>
```

Before you dig into the body of the page, there's one more function to add to the head of the page. This function is called `getDailyMessage()`, which retrieves and returns the message of the day. Add it below the `createDocument()` function definition.

```javascript
function getDailyMessage()
{
```

```
        var messages = xmlDoc.getElementsByTagName("daily");
        var dateobj = new Date();
        var today = dateobj.getDay();

        return messages[today].firstChild.nodeValue;
    }
```

First, use the `getElementsByTagName()` method to retrieve the `<daily/>` elements. As you already know, this will return a node list of all the `<daily/>` elements. The next task is to find a numerical representation of the day of the week. Do this by first creating a `Date` object and using its `getDay()` method. This gives you a digit between 0 and 6, with 0 being Sunday, 1 being Monday, and so on; the digit is assigned to the `today` variable. Finally, use that variable as an index of the `messages` node list to select the correct `<daily/>` element and retrieve its text.

You may have noticed that `xmlDoc` in `getDailyMessage()` isn't declared anywhere in the head of the HTML document. It is used in `createDocument()`, but that variable is declared within the context of the function. You actually declare the global `xmlDoc` in the body of the HTML page.

```
<body>
<div id="messageContainer"></div>

<script type="text/javascript">
    var xmlDoc = createDocument();
    xmlDoc.async = false;
    xmlDoc.load("motd.xml");

    document.getElementById("messageContainer").innerHTML = getDailyMessage();
</script>
</body>
</html>
```

The first HTML element found in the body is a `<div/>` element with an `id` of `messageContainer`. Use this `<div/>` to display the message of the day.

Following the `<div/>` is the last `<script/>` element in the page. In this code block, you create a DOM document and assign it to the global `xmlDoc` variable. Then load the `motd.xml` file synchronously and set the message container's `innerHTML` to the message of the day by calling `getDailyMessage()`.

Try It Out   Tabulating Doggie Data

In this example, you will write an application that uses an XML document containing data about one of your author's dogs. Open your text editor and type the following:

```
<html>
<head>
    <title>Chapter 12: Example 11</title>
    <script type="text/javascript">
    function createDocument()
    {
        var xmlDoc;

        if (window.ActiveXObject)
        {
            var versions =
```

```
        [
            "Msxml2.DOMDocument.6.0",
            "Msxml2.DOMDocument.3.0"
        ];

        for (var i = 0; i < versions.length; i++)
        {
            try
            {
                xmlDoc = new ActiveXObject(versions[i]);
                return xmlDoc;
            }
            catch (error)
            {
                //do nothing here
            }
        }
    }
    else if (document.implementation &&
            document.implementation.createDocument)
    {
        xmlDoc = document.implementation.createDocument("","",null);
        return xmlDoc;
    }

    return null;
}


var xmlDocument = createDocument();
xmlDocument.load("ch12_examp11.xml");

function displayDogs()
{
    var dogNodes = xmlDocument.getElementsByTagName("dog");

    var table = document.createElement("table");
    table.setAttribute("cellPadding",5); //Give the table some cell padding.
    table.setAttribute("width", "100%");
    table.setAttribute("border", "1");

    var tableHeader = document.createElement("thead");
    var tableRow = document.createElement("tr");

    for (var i = 0; i < dogNodes[0].childNodes.length; i++)
    {
        var currentNode = dogNodes[0].childNodes[i];

        if (currentNode.nodeType == 1)
        {

            var tableHeaderCell = document.createElement("th");

            var textData = document.createTextNode(currentNode.nodeName);

            tableHeaderCell.appendChild(textData);
```

```
                    tableRow.appendChild(tableHeaderCell);
                }
            }

            tableHeader.appendChild(tableRow);

            table.appendChild(tableHeader);

            var tableBody = document.createElement("tbody");

            for (var i = 0; i < dogNodes.length; i++)
            {
                var tableRow = document.createElement("tr");

                for (var j = 0; j < dogNodes[i].childNodes.length; j++)
                {
                    var currentNode = dogNodes[i].childNodes[j];
                    if (currentNode.nodeType == 1)
                    {
                        var tableDataCell = document.createElement("td");
                        var textData = document.createTextNode
                        (
                            currentNode.firstChild.nodeValue
                        );

                        tableDataCell.appendChild(textData);

                        tableRow.appendChild(tableDataCell);
                    }
                }

                tableBody.appendChild(tableRow);
            }

            table.appendChild(tableBody);

            document.body.appendChild(table);
        }
        </script>
    </head>
    <body>
        <a href="javascript: displayDogs();">Display Dogs</a>
    </body>
</html>
```

Save this as `ch12_examp11.htm`. Now type the following XML into another file and save it as `ch12_examp11.xml`.

```
<?xml version="1.0" encoding="iso-8859-1"?>

<myDogs>
    <dog>
        <name>Morgan</name>
        <breed>Labrador Retriever</breed>
```

```
        <age>4 years</age>
        <fullBlood>yes</fullBlood>
        <color>chocolate</color>
    </dog>
    <dog>
        <name>Molly</name>
        <breed>Labrador Retriever</breed>
        <age>12 years</age>
        <fullBlood>yes</fullBlood>
        <color>yellow</color>
    </dog>
    <dog>
        <name>Madison</name>
        <breed>Labrador Retriever</breed>
        <age>10 years</age>
        <fullBlood>yes</fullBlood>
        <color>chocolate</color>
    </dog>
</myDogs>
```

When you open the HTML page in your browser, you'll see a web page with only a link visible. When you click the link, you should see something like what is shown in Figure 12-16.

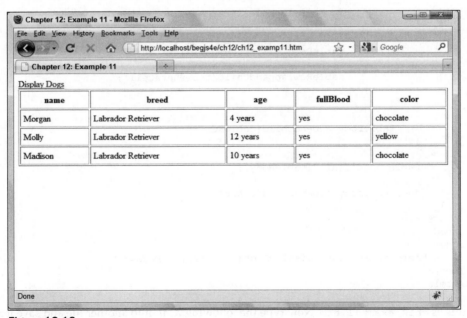

Figure 12-16

The first thing you do is create a DOM object and load an XML document into it.

```
var xmlDocument = createDocument();
```

```
xmlDocument.load("ch12_examp11.xml");
```

The workhorse of this page is the next function, `displayDogs()`. Its job is to build a table and populate it with the information from the XML file.

```
function displayDogs()
{
        var dogNodes = xmlDocument.getElementsByTagName("dog");
        var table = document.createElement("table");
        table.setAttribute("cellPadding",5); //Give the table some cell padding.
        table.setAttribute("width", "100%");
        table.setAttribute("border", "1");
```

The first thing this function does is use the `getElementsByTagName()` method to retrieve the `<dog/>` elements and assign the resulting node list to `dogNodes`. Next, create a `<table/>` element by using the `document.createElement()` method, and set its `cellPadding`, `width`, and `border` attributes using `setAttribute()`.

Next, create the table header and heading cells. For the column headers, use the element names of the `<dog/>` element's children (name, breed, age, and so on).

```
var tableHeader = document.createElement("thead");
var tableRow = document.createElement("tr");

for (var i = 0; i < dogNodes[0].childNodes.length; i++)
{
    var currentNode = dogNodes[0].childNodes[i];

    //Loop code here.
}

tableHeader.appendChild(tableRow);
table.appendChild(tableHeader);
```

The first few lines of this code create `<thead/>` and `<tr/>` elements. Then the code loops through the first `<dog/>` element's child nodes (more on this later). After the loop, append the `<tr/>` element to the table header and add the header to the table. Now let's look at the loop.

```
for (var i = 0; i < dogNodes[0].childNodes.length; i++)
{
    var currentNode = dogNodes[0].childNodes[i];
    if (currentNode.nodeType == 1)
    {
        var tableHeaderCell = document.createElement("th");
        var textData = document.createTextNode(currentNode.nodeName);

        tableHeaderCell.appendChild(textData);
        tableRow.appendChild(tableHeaderCell);
    }
}
```

The goal is to use the element names as headers for the column. However, you're looping through every child node of a `<dog/>` element, so any instance of whitespace between elements is counted as a child node in DOM supported browsers. To solve this problem, check the current node's type with the `nodeType` property. If it's equal to 1, then the child node is an element. Next, create a `<th/>` element, and a text node containing the current node's `nodeName`, which you append to the header cell. And finally, append the `<th/>` element to the row.

The second part of `displayDogs()` builds the body of the table and populates it with data. It is similar in look and function to the header-generation code.

```
var tableBody = document.createElement("tbody");

for (var i = 0; i < dogNodes.length; i++)
{
    var tableRow = document.createElement("tr");

    //Inner loop code here

    tableBody.appendChild(tableRow);
}

table.appendChild(tableBody);
```

First, create the `<tbody/>` element, and then loop through the `dogNodes` node list, cycling through the `<dog/>` elements. Inside this loop, create a `<tr/>` element and append it to the table's body. When the loop exits, append the `<tbody/>` element to the table. Now look at the inner loop, which adds data cells to the row.

```
for (var j = 0; j < dogNodes[i].childNodes.length; j++)
{
    var currentNode = dogNodes[i].childNodes[j];

    if (currentNode.nodeType == 1)
    {
        var tableDataCell = document.createElement("td");
        var textData = document.createTextNode(
            currentNode.firstChild.nodeValue
        );

        tableDataCell.appendChild(textData);

        tableRow.appendChild(tableDataCell);
    }

    tableBody.appendChild(tableRow);
}
```

This inner loop cycles through the child elements of `<dog/>`. First, assign the `currentNode` variable to reference the current node. This enables you to access this node a little more easily (much less typing!). Next, check the node's type. Again, DOM-based browsers count whitespace as child nodes, so you need to make sure the current node is an element. When it's confirmed that the current node is an element, create a `<td/>` element and a text node containing the text of `currentNode`. Append the text node to the data cell, and append the data cell to the table row created in the outer `for` loop.

At this point, the table is completed, so add it to the HTML page. You do this with the following:

```
    document.body.appendChild(table);
}
```

Now all you have to do is invoke the `displayDogs()` function. To do this, place a hyperlink in the page's body to call the function when clicked.

```
<a href="javascript: displayDogs();">Display Dogs</a>
```

Summary

This chapter has featured quite a few diversions and digressions, but these were necessary to demonstrate the position and importance of the Document Object Model in JavaScript.

This chapter covered the following points:

❑   You started by outlining four of the main standards — HTML, ECMAScript, XML, and XHTML — and examined the relationships among them. You saw that a common aim emerging from these standards was to provide guidelines for coding HTML web pages. Those guidelines in turn benefited the Document Object Model, making it possible to access and manipulate any item on the web page using script if web pages were coded according to these guidelines.

❑   You examined the Document Object Model and saw that it offered a browser- and language-independent means of accessing the items on a web page, and that it resolved some of the problems that dogged older browsers. You saw how the DOM represents the HTML document as a tree structure and how it is possible for you to navigate through the tree to different elements and use the properties and methods it exposes in order to access the different parts of the web page.

❑   Although sticking to the standards provides the best method for manipulating the contents of the web page, none of the main browsers yet implements it in its entirety. You looked at the most up-to-date examples and saw how they provided a strong basis for the creation of dynamic, interoperable web pages because of their support of the DOM.

❑   Despite leaps and bounds by browser makers, some discrepancies still exist. You learned how to cope with two different event objects by branching your code to consolidate two different APIs into one.

❑   DHTML enables you to change a page after it is loaded into the browser, and you can perform a variety of user interface tricks to add some flair to your page.

❑   You learned how to change a tag's style by using the `style` and `className` properties.

❑   You also learned the basics of animation in DHTML and made text bounce back and forth between two points.

❑   Finally, you learned how to load an XML file and then manipulate its document with JavaScript.

Exercise Questions

Suggested solutions to these questions can be found in Appendix A.

1. Here's some HTML code that creates a table. Re-create this table using only JavaScript and the core DOM objects to generate the HTML. Test your code in all browsers available to you to make sure it works in them. Hint: Comment each line as you write it to keep track of where you are in the tree structure, and create a new variable for every element on the page (for example, not just one for each of the TD cells but nine variables).

```
<table>
    <thead>
        <tr>
            <td>Car</td>
            <td>Top Speed</td>
            <td>Price</td>
        </tr>
    </thead>
    <tbody>
        <tr>
            <td>Chevrolet</td>
            <td>120mph</td>
            <td>$10,000</td>
        </tr>
        <tr>
            <td>Pontiac</td>
            <td>140mph</td>
            <td>$20,000</td>
        </tr>
    </tbody>
</table>
```

2. It was mentioned that Example 10 is an incomplete tab strip DHTML script. Make it not so incomplete by making the following changes:

❑ Only one tab should be active at a time.

❑ Only the active tab's description should be visible.

Using ActiveX and Plug-Ins with JavaScript

Today's browsers provide a lot of built-in functionality; however, there are many things they cannot do unaided, such as playing video or sound. Functionality of this sort is quite common on the Internet, and plug-ins and their ability to extend browser functionality make it possible to enjoy a richer web experience.

Plug-ins are downloaded applications and, as their name suggests, "plugged into" the browser. Many different plug-ins exist today; the more common ones include Adobe Flash Player, Microsoft's Silverlight, and Apple's QuickTime player.

Essentially, plug-ins are objects that encapsulate all the functionality they need to perform their tasks, such as playing audio files, in a way that hides the complexity from the website author. They are usually written in languages such as C++ and Java.

Plug-ins usually, but not always, have some sort of user interface. For example, the QuickTime plug-in has a user interface that displays buttons to play/pause the audio or video file, a seek bar to go to a precise point in the playback, and a volume control (see Figure 13-1).

Figure 13-1

Some plug-ins make objects with various methods and properties available to you to access with JavaScript, much as you access the methods and properties of the `window` object or the Document Object Model. For example, the QuickTime player plug-in exposes the `Play()` method that you can use to play a sound or video clip.

Plug-ins have been around for quite some time; in fact, Netscape supported them as early as version 3. You probably won't be shocked to find out that Microsoft does things differently from the other browser makers. Internet Explorer (IE) does not support plug-ins, but IE 4.0+ running on Windows does support ActiveX controls, which provide the same functionality.

Fortunately, as you'll see, using ActiveX controls is similar to using plug-ins in other browsers, and with a few tweaks can be done with almost the same code. The main difference is actually making sure that the plug-in or ActiveX control is available for use and ready to run in the user's browser in the first place. This problem is covered in more detail for Firefox and IE before going on to discuss using the plug-ins and ActiveX controls.

Checking for and Embedding Plug-ins (Non-IE Browsers)

It's nice to create a script to use a specific plug-in for the web page experience of a lifetime, but unless the visitor to your web page also has the same plug-in installed on their computer, their experience of the web page is going to be one full of bugs and error messages. It is therefore important that you not only correctly add the HTML required to use the plug-in in your page but also use JavaScript to check if the user's browser has the plug-in installed that your page makes use of. You look at both these topics in this section.

Even though this section focuses on Firefox, the same principles can be applied to Safari, Opera, and Chrome.

Adding a Plug-in to the Page

To make use of a plug-in that is installed in the user's browser, you need to use HTML to tell the browser where and when in your page you want to use it. This process is called *embedding* the plug-in.

In Firefox, the key to embedding plug-ins is the non-standard <embed/> element. This inserts the visible interface, if any, of the plug-in at that point in the page. The <embed/> element supports a number of general attributes applicable to all plug-ins, such as height, width, pluginspage, src, and type. You'll look at the last two of these attributes, src and type, in more detail here. You will also look at the pluginspage attribute in the next section.

Most plug-ins display content that is stored on a web server. For example, a plug-in for sound, such as QuickTime player, will play music from a file with a variety of extensions, notably the .mp3 and .aac extensions, and the Flash plug-in will play Flash movies (files with the .swf extension). The <embed/> element's src attribute enables you to specify the initial file for the plug-in to load and play. This will be a URL pointing to the file, usually hosted on the same web server as the HTML page. It's from this file that the browser determines what sort of plug-in is required. For example, if the src is http://www .myserver.com/myflashmovie.swf, then by checking the type of the file, the browser can see that a Flash player plug-in needs to be used.

However, not all plug-ins require data from an external source and therefore a value for the src attribute. In such situations, how can the browser tell what plug-in to load? Well, that's where the <embed/> element's type attribute comes in. The actual value for the type attribute will be specific to the plug-in. You can find out this information by typing about:plugins in the location bar. The plug-in information loads into the browser, as shown in Figure 13-2.

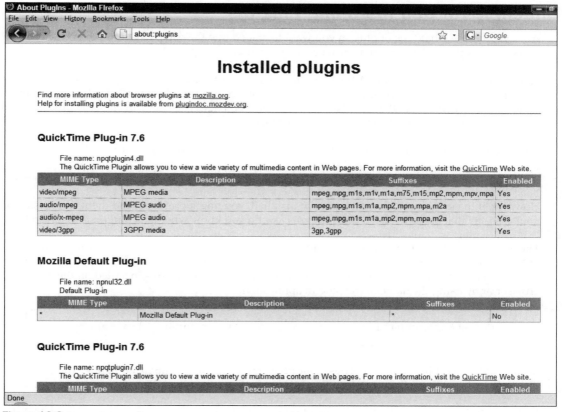

Figure 13-2

You'll see a list of all the plug-ins installed on your browser. The value required for the `type` attribute is listed as the Multipurpose Internet Mail Extensions (MIME) type, which specifies a type of content such as a web page, an image, or a Flash file. For example, the MIME type for Flash is `application/x-shockwave-flash`.

In addition to a number of attributes common to all plug-ins, you can also use the `<embed/>` element to specify properties specific to a particular plug-in. For example, the Flash plug-in supports the `quality` attribute, which determines the image quality of the Flash movie. To set this attribute in the `<embed/>` element, you just add it to the list of attributes set, as shown in the following example:

```
<embed id="FlashPlugIn1"
    src="topmenu.swf"
    border=0
    height=100
    width=500
    quality=high
    type="application/x-shockwave-flash" />
```

Although Firefox supports the `<embed/>` element, it also supports the use of the HTML standard `<object/>` element for embedding plug-ins into the page, in a similar way to IE, which you will see shortly.

Checking for and Installing Plug-ins

After you decide what type of plug-in you want to embed into the page, what happens if the browser finds that this particular plug-in does not exist on the user's computer?

To solve this problem you can set the `pluginspage` attribute of `<embed/>` to point to a URL on the plug-in creator's page. If the plug-in is not on the user's computer, a link to the URL specified in the `pluginspage` attribute will be displayed within the web page. The user can click the link and load the plug-in so that your web page will function properly.

For example, with Flash the value for the `pluginspage` attribute needed is this:

```
http://www.adobe.com/shockwave/download/index.cgi?P1_Prod_Version=ShockwaveFlash
```

However, if the user doesn't have the plug-in installed, you might prefer to send them to a version of your web site that doesn't rely on that plug-in. How do you know whether a plug-in is installed?

The `navigator` object, introduced in Chapter 6, has a property called `plugins`, which is a collection of `Plugin` objects, one for each plug-in installed on that browser. You can access a `Plugin` object in the `plugins` array either by using an index value that indexes all the plug-ins installed on the user's browser or by using the name of the plug-in application.

> **Internet Explorer has a** `navigator.plugins` **collection, but it is always empty.**

Each `Plugin` object has four properties: `description`, `filename`, `length`, and `name`. You can find these values by viewing the plug-ins information page that you saw earlier.

Let's use Flash as an example. Type **about:plugins** in the location bar and press enter. Figure 13-3 shows the Installed plug-ins page in Chrome, but this page remains largely the same for all non-IE browsers. Flash has "Shockwave Flash" as its `name` property. The `filename` and `description` properties have obvious meanings. The `length` property gives the number of MIME types supported by the plug-in.

As mentioned earlier, the `name` property can be used to reference the `Plugin` object in the `plugins` array. So, the following code will set the variable `shockWavePlugIn` to the `Plugin` object for Flash, if it's installed:

```
var shockWavePlugIn = navigator.plugins["Shockwave Flash"];
```

If it's not, `navigator.plugins["Shockwave Flash"]` will return as `undefined`.

You can use the following to redirect users on browsers that do not have installed the plug-in you need:

```
if (navigator.plugins["Shockwave Flash"])
{
    window.location.replace("my_flash_enabled_page.htm");
}
else
{
    window.location.replace("my_non_flash_page.htm");
}
```

Length   Description
Name   File Name

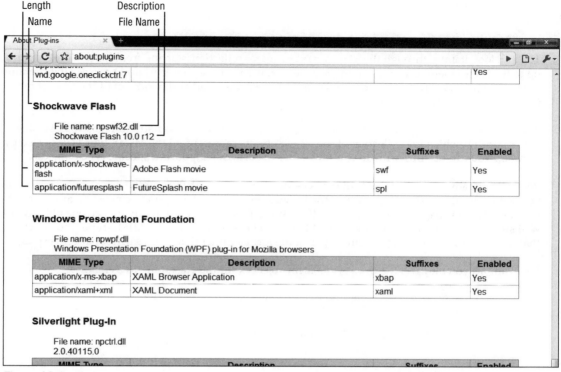

Figure 13-3

If the Flash plug-in is not installed, `navigator.plugins["Shockwave Flash"]` will be `undefined`, which JavaScript considers to be `false`, thereby causing the `else` statement to execute. If Flash is installed, `navigator.plugins["Shockwave Flash"]` will return the Flash `Plugin` object, which JavaScript treats as `true`, and the main `if` statement will execute.

The problem with this method of detection is that the name given to a plug-in may vary from operating system to operating system. For example, the name of the Windows XP version of the plug-in may vary from the name of the Mac version, which in turn may vary from the name of the Linux version. Some plug-ins, such as RealPlayer, will not work reliably at all with this detection method, because the name is not simply RealPlayer but something that contains the word "RealPlayer."

An alternative method for determining whether a plug-in is installed is to loop through the `plugins[]` array and check each `name` for certain keywords. If you find them, you can assume that the control is installed. For example, to check for QuickTime, you may use the following:

```
var pluginsLength = navigator.plugins.length;
for (var i = 0; i < pluginslength; plugInCounter++)
{
    var name = navigator.plugins[i].name.toLowerCase();
    if (name.indexOf("quicktime") > -1)
    {
        alert("QuickTime is installed");
```

```
        break;
    }
}
```

The `for` loop iterates through the `navigator.plugins` collection, starting from index 0 and continuing up to the last element. Each plug-in in the collection has its `name` property checked to see if it contains the text `quicktime`. If it does, you know QuickTime is installed and break out of the loop; if not, QuickTime is clearly not installed.

An alternative to using `navigator` object's `plugins[]` collection is using the `navigator` object's `mimeTypes[]`, which is a collection of `mimeType` objects representing the MIME types supported by the browser. You can use this array to check whether the browser supports a specific type of media.

You have already come across MIME types before — the `type` attribute of the `<embed/>` element can be used to specify a MIME type so that the browser knows which plug-in to embed. Again, using the Installed plug-ins page can give you the MIME types for a particular plug-in. In fact, one plug-in may well support more than one MIME type. When you check for a particular MIME type, you are checking that the browser supports a particular type of file format rather than necessarily a particular plug-in.

For example, you may use the `mimeTypes` array to check for the Flash plug-in as follows:

```
if (navigator.mimeTypes["application/x-shockwave-flash"] &&
    navigator.mimeTypes["application/x-shockwave-flash"].enabledPlugin)
{
    window.location.replace("my_flash_enabled_page.htm");
}
else
{
    window.location.replace("my_non_flash_page.htm");
}
```

The `if` statement's condition has two parts separated by the AND operator `&&`.

The first part checks that the specified MIME type is supported by trying to access a specific `mimeType` object in the `mimeTypes` collection. If there such object exists, then `undefined` is returned, which evaluates to `false`.

The second part of the condition checks to see if a plug-in to handle this MIME type is enabled. Although unusual, it is possible for a MIME type to be supported, or recognized, by the browser, but for no plug-in to be installed. For example, if the user has Microsoft Word installed, the MIME type `application/msword` would be valid, but that does not mean a plug-in exists to display it in the browser! The `enabledPlugin` property of the `mimeType` object actually returns a `Plugin` object unless it does not exist.

Checking for and Embedding ActiveX Controls on Internet Explorer

Although IE does support plug-ins to a certain extent, its support for ActiveX controls is more complete. The main difference between an ActiveX control and a plug-in is how they are embedded into a page and how they are installed. Once they are embedded and installed, their use, as far as scripting goes, will be very similar to that for plug-ins.

ActiveX controls are a little like mini-programs, usually created in languages like C++ or Visual Basic. Unlike normal programs, like Notepad or Microsoft Word, ActiveX controls cannot run on their own; they need to be sited in a container program. Not all programs can act as containers for ActiveX controls, only those specifically designed to do so, such as Microsoft Access and, of course, Internet Explorer. When the creators of the ActiveX control compile their code, they also assign it a unique identification string that enables programmers like you to specify exactly which control you want to embed in your IE ActiveX container.

Adding an ActiveX Control to the Page

Adding an ActiveX control to a page for an IE browser requires the use of the `<object/>` element. Two very important attributes of the `<object/>` element are common to all controls, namely `classid` and `codebase`. The `classid` attribute is the unique ID that the creator of the control gave to it when it was compiled. The `codebase` attribute gives a URL where the ActiveX control can be found — you'll look at this attribute in more detail in the next section.

How can you find out the `classid`? Well, one way to do this is by checking the documentation that came with the control or is available on the control creator's web site. If you have the control installed, another way to do this is via IE itself, which will tell you which controls are installed on the computer and available to IE. Also, IE gives you additional information such as `classid`, though it won't inform you about any controls that were installed with the operating system. For example, Flash 3 is installed with Windows 98 and therefore won't appear.

To get this information, open up IE and select Internet Options from the Tools menu, as shown in Figure 13-4.

Figure 13-4

This opens up the window shown in Figure 13-5. In the Browsing history area, click the Settings button.

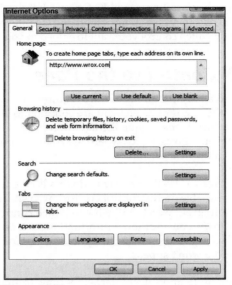

Figure 13-5

In the next window that opens, click the View objects button, shown in Figure 13-6.

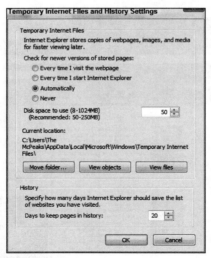

Figure 13-6

This will display a list of all the ActiveX controls IE has installed from the Internet. The list shown in Figure 13-7 will most likely be different from that on your own computer.

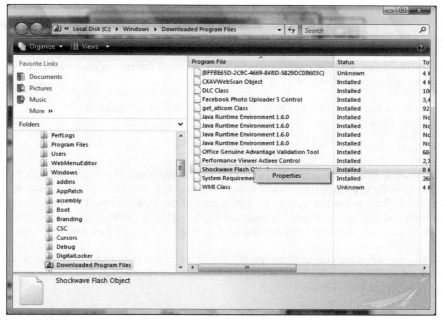

Figure 13-7

You can see lots of information about each control, such as when it was created and its version number. To find out the classid, right-click the name of the control you're interested in and select Properties from the menu that pops up.

The information shown in Figure 13-8 is displayed, though this may be slightly different on your system.

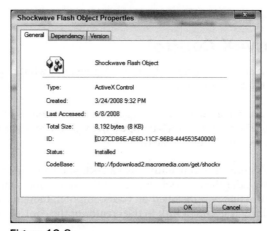

Figure 13-8

You can see that the `classid` attribute, listed as just ID, and the `codebase` attribute, listed as CodeBase, are both displayed, although for `codebase` you may need to select the line and then scroll using the arrow keys to see all the information.

From this information, you see that to insert a Flash ActiveX control in your web page you need to add the following `<object/>` element:

```
<object classid="clsid:D27CDB6E-AE6D-11cf-96B8-444553540000"
    id="flashPlayer1"
    width="500"
    height="100" />
```

You can also set attribute or parameter values for the control itself. For example, with Flash you need to set the `src` attribute to point to the `.swf` file you want loaded, and you may also want to set the `quality` attribute, which determines the quality of appearance of the Flash movie. However, to set the parameters of the ActiveX control such as these (as opposed to the attributes of the `<object/>` element), you need to insert the `<param/>` element between the start `<object>` tag and the close `</object>` tag.

In each `<param/>` element you need to specify the name of the parameter you want to set and the value you want it set to. For example, if you want to set the `src` attribute to `myFlashMovie.swf`, you need to add a `<param/>` element like this:

```
<param name="src" value="myFlashMovie.swf">
```

Let's add this to the full `<object/>` element definition and also define the `quality` attribute at the same time.

```
<object classid="clsid:D27CDB6E-AE6D-11cf-96B8-444553540000"
    id="flashPlayer1"
    width="500"
    height="100">
        <param name="src" value="myFlashMovie.swf">
        <param name="quality" value="high">
</object>
```

Installing an ActiveX Control

You've seen how to insert an ActiveX control into your page, but what happens if the user doesn't have that control installed on their computer?

This is where the `codebase` attribute of the `<object/>` element comes in. If the browser finds that the ActiveX control is not installed on the user's computer, it will try to download and install the control from the URL pointed to by the `codebase` attribute.

The creator of the ActiveX control will usually have a URL you can use as a value for the `codebase` attribute. The information under the Internet Options option of the Tools menu you saw earlier provides the `codebase` for the control that was installed on your computer, though this may not necessarily be the best URL to use, particularly if it's not a link to the creator of the control.

For Flash, the codebase is http://fpdownload.macromedia.com/get/shockwave/cabs/flash/swflash.cab, so your <object> tag will look like this:

```
<object classid="clsid:D27CDB6E-AE6D-11CF-96B8-444553540000"
codebase="http://fpdownload.macromedia.com/get/shockwave/cabs/flash/swflash.cab"
    id="flashPlayer1"
    width="500"
    height="100">
        <param name="src" value="myFlashMovie.swf">
        <param name="quality" value="high">
</object>
```

Subject to license agreements, you may be able to download the .cab file that installs the control to your own server and point the codebase attribute to that.

Unfortunately, there is no easy foolproof way of checking which ActiveX controls are installed on the user's computer. However, the Object object of the <object/> element does have the readyState property. This returns 0, 1, 2, 3, or 4, indicating the object's operational status. The possible values are as follows:

- ❑ 0 — Control is un-initialized and not ready for use
- ❑ 1 — Control is still loading
- ❑ 2 — Control has finished loading its data
- ❑ 3 — User can interact with control even though it is not fully loaded
- ❑ 4 — Control is loaded and ready for use

You need to give the control time to load before checking its readyState property, so any checking is best left until the window's onload event handler or even the document object's onreadystatechange event handler fires.

To redirect the user to another page that doesn't need the control, you need to write this:

```
function window_onload() {
    var flashPlayer1;

    // code to retrieve ActiveX plug-in

    if (flashPlayer1.readyState == 0)
    {
        window.location.replace("NoControlPage.htm");
    }
}

onload = window_onload;
```

This code checks to see if the ActiveX control's readyState is 0. Since this code executes after the browser loads the page, it's safe to assume the ActiveX control isn't installed on the computer.

Using Plug-ins and ActiveX Controls

When you have the plug-ins or ActiveX controls embedded into the page, their actual use is very uniform. To make life easier for you, most plug-in and ActiveX developers make the properties, methods, and events supported by each plug-in and ActiveX control similar. However, it's important to check the developer's documentation because it's likely that there will be some idiosyncrasies.

Inside the `<embed/>` or `<object/>` element, you give your plug-in or control a unique `id` value. You can then access the corresponding object's methods, properties, and events just as you would for any other element. The actual properties, methods, and events supported by a plug-in or control will be specific to that control, but let's look at one of the more commonly available controls, Apple's QuickTime player, which comes in both plug-in form for non-IE browsers and ActiveX control form for IE. You can find more information on this control at the following URL:

```
http://developer.apple.com/documentation/QuickTime/Conceptual/QTScripting_
JavaScript/bQTScripting_JavaScri_Document/QuickTimeandJavaScri.html
```

To run the examples in this chapter, you need the free QuickTime player from `http://www.apple.com/quicktime/`.

Note that you can buy a version with more features, but it is not necessary for this book.

First, you need to embed the control in a web page. Type the following into a text editor:

```html
<!DOCTYPE html PUBLIC "-//W3C//DTD XHTML 1.0 Transitional//EN"
    "http://www.w3.org/TR/xhtml1/DTD/xhtml1-transitional.dtd">
<html xmlns="http://www.w3.org/1999/xhtml">
<head>
    <title>Using JavaScript to Interface with Quicktime</title>
</head>
<body>
    <object classid="clsid:02BF25D5-8C17-4B23-BC80-D3488ABDDC6B"
        codebase="http://www.apple.com/qtactivex/qtplugin.cab"
        id="audioPlayer" width="0" height="0">
            <param name="src" value="sound1.mp3" />
            <embed height="0" width="0" type="audio/mpeg" src="sound1.mp3"
                pluginspage="www.apple.com/quicktime/download"
                enablejavascript="true" name="audioPlayer" />
    </object>
    <form id="form1" name="form1" action="">
        <input type="button" value="Play" id="buttonPlay" name="buttonPlay"
            onclick="buttonPlay_onclick()" />
        <input type="button" value="Stop" id="buttonStop" name="buttonStop"
            onclick="buttonStop_onclick()" />
    </form>
</body>
</html>
```

Save this code as `quicktime.htm`.

The first thing to note is the `<embed/>` element (for non-IE browsers) resides as a child of the `<object/>` element. Firefox, Opera, Safari, and Chrome ignore the `<object/>` element and display only the plug-in defined by `<embed/>`. IE ignores the `<embed/>` element within the `<object/>` element, even though the browser supports `<embed/>`. If you placed the `<embed/>` element outside of `<object/>`, IE would recognize both the <object/> and <embed/> elements and get confused — particularly over the id values, because both have the same id of audioPlayer.

Beneath the <object/> element is a form with two buttons. The first has an id and name value of buttonPlay and executes the buttonPlay_onclick() function when the user clicks it. The second button is called buttonStop, and it executes the buttonStop_onclick() function when clicked.

Determining Plug-in/ActiveX Control Availability

You want to make sure that users without QuickTime don't see error messages when they attempt to use the scripted controls. In this exercise, let's disable the buttons used to control the audio playback. Add the following <script/> element to the HTML page's head; it defines a function to do disable the buttons and attaches it to the window object's onload event handler.

```
<script type="text/javascript">
    function window_onload() {
        var plugInInstalled = false;
        if (!window.ActiveXObject) {
            var pluginsLength = navigator.plugins.length;
            for (var i = 0; i < pluginsLength; i++) {
                var pluginName = navigator.plugins[i].name.toLowerCase();
                if (pluginName.indexOf("quicktime") > -1) {
                    plugInInstalled = true;
                    break;
                }
            }
        } else {
            if (document.audioPlayer.readyState == 4) {
                plugInInstalled = true;
            }
        }

        if (!plugInInstalled) {
            document.forms[0].buttonPlay.disabled = true;
            document.forms[0].buttonStop.disabled = true;
            alert("You need Quicktime to play the audio file!");
        }
    }

    onload = window_onload;
</script>
```

In the window_onload() function, you first define a variable, plugInInstalled, and initialize it as false. Next, since checking for plug-ins or controls is browser-dependent, you check to see if this is a Microsoft browser. A simple check for the ActiveXObject property of the window object will suffice.

If the browser is a non-IE browser, use a for loop to iterate over the navigator object's plugins collection, checking each installed plug-in's name for the word quicktime (note that you're checking the lowercase version of the word; this is to provide a more accurate search). Set the variable plugInInstalled to true and break out of the for loop if this name is found.

If this is a Microsoft browser, use the `readyState` property of the `<object/>` element's `Object` object to see if the ActiveX control is loaded, initialized successfully, and now ready for action. If its value is 4, you know all systems are ready to go, so you set the variable `plugInInstalled` to `true`.

Finally, the last `if` statement in the function checks to see if `plugInInstalled` is `true` or `false`. If `false`, the buttons are disabled and an alert box tells the user they need QuickTime in order to play the audio file.

Finishing Up

The last step in creating this audio player is adding functionality to the buttons. As mentioned earlier, these buttons start and stop the audio file's playback. Add the following functions to the script element:

```
function buttonPlay_onclick() {
    document.audioPlayer.Play();
}

function buttonStop_onclick() {
    document.audioPlayer.Stop();
}
```

The QuickTime plug-in control exposes `Play()` and `Stop()` methods to play and pause playback respectively. So the play button should call `Play()` and the stop button `Stop()`.

You completed the page with this last bit of code. The HTML and JavaScript should now look like this:

```
<!DOCTYPE html PUBLIC "-//W3C//DTD XHTML 1.0 Transitional//EN"
    "http://www.w3.org/TR/xhtml1/DTD/xhtml1-transitional.dtd">
<html xmlns="http://www.w3.org/1999/xhtml">
<head>
    <title>Using JavaScript to Interface with Quicktime</title>

    <script type="text/javascript">
        function buttonPlay_onclick() {
            document.audioPlayer.Play();
        }

        function buttonStop_onclick() {
            document.audioPlayer.Stop();
        }

        function window_onload() {
            var plugInInstalled = false;
            if (!window.ActiveXObject) {
                var pluginsLength = navigator.plugins.length;
                for (var i = 0; i < pluginsLength; i++) {
                    var pluginName = navigator.plugins[i].name.toLowerCase();
                    if (pluginName.indexOf("quicktime") > -1) {
                        plugInInstalled = true;
                        break;
                    }
                }
```

```
            } else {
                if (document.audioPlayer.readyState == 4) {
                    plugInInstalled = true;
                }
            }

            if (!plugInInstalled) {
                document.forms[0].buttonPlay.disabled = true;
                document.forms[0].buttonStop.disabled = true;
                alert("You need Quicktime to play the audio file!");
            }
        }

        onload = window_onload;
    </script>
</head>
<body>
    <object classid="clsid:02BF25D5-8C17-4B23-BC80-D3488ABDDC6B"
        codebase="http://www.apple.com/qtactivex/qtplugin.cab"
        id="audioPlayer" width="0" height="0">
            <param name="src" value="sound1.mp3" />
            <embed height="0" width="0" type="audio/mpeg" src="sound1.mp3"
                pluginspage="www.apple.com/quicktime/download"
                enablejavascript="true" name="audioPlayer" />
    </object>
    <form id="form1" name="form1" action="">
        <input type="button" value="Play" id="buttonPlay" name="buttonPlay"
            onclick="buttonPlay_onclick()" />
        <input type="button" value="Stop" id="buttonStop" name="buttonStop"
            onclick="buttonStop_onclick()" />
    </form>
</body>
</html>
```

Load `quicktime.htm` into your browser. As long as your browser supports plug-ins or ActiveX controls and the QuickTime plug-in is installed, you should see something like what is shown in Figure 13-9.

Figure 13-9

When the browser loads the page, the provided .mp3 file begins to play automatically. Use the play and stop buttons to demonstrate the functionality of your audio player.

So how does this work?

The form in the body of the page contains two standard buttons that are connected to JavaScript functions via the onclick event handlers. Inside these functions, you access the QuickTime plug-in and plug-in controls that you embedded into the page by using its name prefixed with document. The play function calls the plug-in's and plug-in control's Play() method to play the sound, and the stop function calls Stop() pause the sound. This script works in all major browsers, though IE accesses the ActiveX control defined in the <object/> element, and non-IE browsers access the plug-in defined in the <embed/> element.

Testing the Disabling of the Form

It's quite likely that if you plan to use an ActiveX control or plug-in, you're going to make sure it's installed on your computer. The problem is that while that's great for testing pages to see if they work when there is a control installed, it can become difficult to test scripts for users without that control. You have the following possible options:

❑   Get a second computer with a clean install of an operating system and browser; then load your pages on that computer. This is the only sure way of checking your pages.

❑   Uninstall the plug-in. Depending on how the plug-in or control was installed, there may be an uninstall program for it. Windows users can use the Add/Remove programs option in the Control Panel.

❑   For non-IE browsers, install a different version of the browser. For example, if you have Firefox 3 installed, try installing an older version, say Firefox 2 or even a beta version if you can find it. The plug-ins currently installed are not normally available to a browser installed later, though this may not be true all the time.

❑   With IE, you can only have one version of the browser installed at once. However, IE does make it quite easy to remove ActiveX controls. In IE 5+, choose Internet Options from the Tools menu. Click the Settings button under Temporary Internet Files (Browsing History in IE7), followed by the View Objects button. From here you need to right-click the name of the control you want removed and select Remove from the pop-up menu.

Thankfully, this situation is rather easy to test. Recall the end of the window_onload() function; you tested the pluginInstalled variable to determine whether or not the form should be disabled. Simply reversing that check will allow you to see what happens when a user without QuickTime installed on their computer visits the page. So change the last bit of code of window_onload() to look like this:

```
if (plugInInstalled) {
    document.forms[0].buttonPlay.disabled = true;
    document.forms[0].buttonStop.disabled = true;
    alert("You need Quicktime to play the audio file!");
}
```

Resave the HTML document and refresh the page in your browser. Figure 13-10 shows what happens in Chrome.

Figure 13-10

Potential Problems

Plug-ins and ActiveX controls provide a great way to extend a browser's functionality, but they do so at a price — compatibility problems. Some of the problems you may face are discussed in the following sections.

Similar but Not the Same — Differences Among Browsers

Although a plug-in for non-IE browsers and the equivalent ActiveX control for IE may support many similar properties and methods, you will often find significant, and sometimes subtle, differences.

For example, both the plug-in and ActiveX control versions of RealPlayer support the SetSource() method. The following code works in IE:

```
document.real1.SetSource("D:\\MyDir\\MyFile.ra")
```

This code, however, will cause problems with the other browsers. To work with Firefox and the like, specify the protocol by which the file will be loaded. If it is a URL, specify http://, but for a file on a user's local hard drive, use file:///.

To make the code work across platforms, you must type this:

```
document.real1.SetSource("file:///D:\MyDir\MyFile.ra")
```

Differences in the Scripting of Plug-ins

When scripting the QuickTime plug-in for non-IE browsers, you embedded it like this:

```
<embed height="0" width="0" type="audio/mpeg" src="sound1.mp3"
    pluginspage="www.apple.com/quicktime/download"
    enablejavascript="true" name="audioPlayer" />
```

You then accessed it via script just by typing this:

```
document.audioPlayer.Play()
```

However, if you are scripting a Flash player, you need to add the following attribute to the `<embed/>` definition in the HTML:

```
swliveconnect="true"
```

Otherwise, any attempts to access the plug-in will result in errors.

```
<embed name="map" swLiveConnect="true" src="topmenu.swf"
width="300" height="200"
pluginspage="http://http://www.macromedia.com/go/getflashplayer">
```

It's very important to study any available documentation that comes with a plug-in to check that there are no subtle problems.

Differences Between Operating Systems

Support for ActiveX controls varies greatly between different operating systems. IE for the Mac supports it, but not as well as under Win32 operating systems, such as Windows 2000, XP, and Vista. You also need to be aware that an ActiveX control written for Win32 will not work on the Mac; you need to make sure a Mac-specific control is downloaded.

IE on the Mac supports plug-ins as well as ActiveX controls; so, for example, Flash is a plug-in on the Mac and an ActiveX control on Win32. Clearly, if you want to support both Mac and Windows users, you need to write more complex code.

It's very important to check which operating system the user is running (for example, using the scripts given at the end of Chapter 6) and deal with any problems that may arise.

Differences Between Different Versions of the Same Plug-in or ActiveX Control

Creators of plug-ins and controls will often periodically release new versions with new features. If you make use of these new features, you need to make sure not only that the user has the right plug-in or ActiveX control loaded, but also that it is the right version.

ActiveX Controls

With ActiveX controls, you can add version information in the `codebase` attribute of the `<object/>` element.

```
<object classid=clsid:AAA03-8BE4-11CF-B84B-0020AFBBCCFA
    id="myControl"
    codebase="http://myserver/mycontrol.cab#version=3,0,0,0">
</object>
```

Now, not only will the browser check that the control is installed on the user's system, but it also checks that the installed version is version 3 or greater.

What if you want to check the version and then redirect to a different page if it's a version that is earlier than your page requires?

With ActiveX controls there's no easy way of using JavaScript code to check the ActiveX control version. One way is to find a property that the new control supports but that older versions don't, and then compare that to `null`. For example, imagine you have a control whose latest version introduces the property `BgColor`. To check if the installed version is the one you want, you type the following:

```
if (document.myControl.BgColor == null)
{
    alert("This is an old version");
}
```

It's also possible that the ActiveX creator has added to his control's object a `version` property of some sort that you can check against, but this will vary from control to control.

Plug-ins

With plug-ins you need to make use of the `Plugin` objects in the `navigator` object's `plugins[]` array property. Each `Plugin` object in the array has a `name`, `filename`, and `description` property, which may provide version information. However, this will vary between plug-ins.

For example, for Flash Player 10 on Win32, the description for the following code is Shockwave Flash 10.0 r12.

```
navigator.plugins["Shockwave Flash"].description
```

Using regular expressions, which were introduced in Chapter 9, you could extract the version number from this string:

```
var myRegExp = /\d{1,}.\d{1,}/;
var flashVersion = navigator.plugins["Shockwave Flash"].description;
flashVersion = parseFloat(flashVersion.match(myRegExp)[0]);
```

The first line of code defines a regular expression that matches one or more digits, followed by a dot, and then one or more numbers. Next, you store the description of the Flash plug-in in the variable `flashVersion`. Finally you search the variable for the regular expression, returning an array of all the matches made. Then use the `parseFloat()` function on the contents of the element in the array at index `0` (in other words, the first element in the array).

Changes to Internet Explorer 6 Service Pack 1b and ActiveX Controls

For mostly legal reasons, Microsoft made changes to how ActiveX controls work in IE. Whenever a user browses to a page with an ActiveX control, she gets a warning about the control, and by default it's blocked unless she chooses to unblock it. There are two ways around this:

1. Don't access any external data or have any `<param/>` elements in the definition, as the following example demonstrates:

```
<object classid="CLSID:6BF52A52-394A-11d3-B153-00C04F79FAA6"></object>
```

2. Use the new `noexternaldata` attribute to specify that no external access of data is used.

```
<object noexternaldata="true" classid="CLSid:6BF52A52-394A-11d3-B153-00C04F79FAA6">
  <param name="URL"
  value="http://msdn.microsoft.com/workshop/samples/author/dhtml/media/drums.wav"/>
</object>
```

The URL parameter will be ignored, and no external data from the URL, in this case a `.wav` file, will be accessed.

Summary

In this chapter you looked at how you can use plug-ins and ActiveX controls to extend a browser's functionality. You saw that:

❑ Internet Explorer supports ActiveX controls, and to some extent plug-ins, on Windows operating systems. Non-IE browsers have good support for plug-ins but do not support ActiveX controls.

❑ Most creators of plug-ins also provide an ActiveX control equivalent. Internet Explorer and other browsers are incompatible as far as the installation of plug-ins and ActiveX controls goes.

❑ Plug-ins are embedded in a web page by means of the `<embed/>` element. You let non-IE browsers know which plug-in to embed by specifying either a `source` file or a `MIME` type using the `src` and `type` attributes of the `<embed/>` element. If you define a value for the `<embed/>` element's `pluginspage` attribute, users who don't have that plug-in installed will be able to click a link and install it.

❑ You can find detailed information about what plug-ins are installed on your non-IE browser, as well as their descriptions and types, by typing `about:plugins` in the location bar.

❑ To use script to check if a user has a certain plug-in, you can use the `navigator` object's `plugins` collection. For each plug-in installed, there will be a `Plugin` object defined in this collection. Each `Plugin` object has the properties `name`, `description`, `filename`, and `length`, which you can use to determine if a plug-in exists on the user's computer. You can also use the `navigator` object's `mimeTypes` collection property to check if a certain type of file is supported.

❑ Internet Explorer supports ActiveX controls as an alternative to plug-ins. These are embedded into a web page using the `<object/>` element. Specify which ActiveX control you want by using the `classid` attribute. If you want to have controls automatically install for users who don't have a particular control already installed, you need to specify the `codebase` attribute.

❑ Any parameters particular to the control are specified by means of the `<param/>` element, which is inserted between the opening and closing `<object>` tags.

❑ You can check whether a control has loaded successfully using the `readyState` property of the `Object` object, which returns a number: 0 if the control is not installed, 1 if it's still loading, 2 if it has loaded, 3 if you can interact with it, and 4 if it's installed and ready for use.

❑ Virtually every different type of plug-in and ActiveX control has its own interface, for which the control's documentation will provide the details. You looked briefly at Apple's QuickTime control.

❑ You also saw that while plug-ins and controls are great for extending functionality, they are subject to potential pitfalls. These include differences in the way plug-ins and ActiveX controls are scripted, differences in operating systems, and differences between versions of the same plug-in or control.

In Chapter 14, you change direction to cover a "new" JavaScript technique that has rekindled web application development.

Exercise Question

A suggested solution to this question can be found in Appendix A.

1. Using the Quicktime plug-in or ActiveX control, create a page with three links, so that when you click any of them a sound is played. Use an alert box to tell the users who do not have QuickTime installed that they must install it when they click a link.

The page should work in IE, Firefox, Safari, Chrome, and Opera. The method to tell QuickTime what file to play is SetURL().

Ajax

Since its inception, the Internet has used a transaction-like communication model; a browser sends a request to a server, which sends a response back to the browser, which (re)loads the page. This is typical HTTP communication, and it was designed to be this way. But this model is rather cumbersome for developers, as it requires web applications to consist of several pages. The resulting user experience becomes disjointed and interrupted due to these separate page loads.

In the early 2000s, a movement began to look for and develop new techniques to enhance the user's experience; to make Web applications behave more like conventional applications. These new techniques offered the performance and usability usually associated with conventional desktop applications. It wasn't long before developers began to refine these processes to offer richer functionality to the user.

At the heart of this movement was one language: JavaScript, and its ability to make HTTP requests transparent to the user.

What Is Ajax?

Essentially, *Ajax* allows client-side JavaScript to request and receive data from a server without refreshing the web page. This technique enables the developer to create an application that is uninterrupted, making only portions of the page reload with new data.

The term Ajax was originally coined by Jesse James Garrett in 2005. He wrote an article entitled "Ajax: A New Approach to Web Applications" (`www.adaptivepath.com/publications/essays/archives/000385.php`). In it, Garrett states that the interactivity gap between web and desktop applications is becoming smaller, and he cites applications such as Google Maps and Google Suggest as proof of this. The term originally stood for Asynchronous JavaScript + XML (XML was the format in which the browser and server communicated with each other). Today, Ajax simply refers to the pattern of using JavaScript to send and receive data from the web server without reloading the entire page.

Although the term Ajax was derived in 2005, the underlying methodology was used years before. Early Ajax techniques consisted of using hidden frames/iframes, dynamically adding <script/> elements to the document, and/or using JavaScript to send HTTP requests to the server; the latter has become quite popular in the last few years. These new techniques refresh only portions of a page, both cutting the size of data sent to the browser and making the web page feel more like a conventional application.

What Can It Do?

Ajax opened the doors for advanced web applications — ones that mimic desktop applications in form and in function. A variety of commercial web sites employ the use of Ajax. These sites look and behave more like desktop applications than web sites. The most notable Ajax-enabled web applications come from the search giant Google: Google Maps and Google Suggest.

Google Maps

Designed to compete with existing commercial mapping sites (and using images from its Google Earth), Google Maps (http://maps.google.com) uses Ajax to dynamically add map images to the web page. When you enter a location, the main page does not reload at all; the images are dynamically loaded in the map area. Google Maps also enables you to drag the map to a new location, and once again, the map images are dynamically added to the map area (see Figure 14-1).

Figure 14-1

Google Suggest

Google Suggest (http://labs.google.com/suggest/) is another Google innovation that employs the use of Ajax. Upon first glance, it appears to be a normal Google search page. When you start typing, however, a drop-down box displays suggestions for search terms that might interest you. To the right of the suggested word or phrase is the number of results the search term returns (see Figure 14-2).

Figure 14-2

Browser Support

Ajax is limited to the browser that runs the web application, and like every other advanced JavaScript concept covered in this book, Ajax capabilities differ from browser to browser. Thankfully, the most common forms of Ajax work in the following browsers:

- ❑   Internet Explorer 5+
- ❑   Firefox 1+
- ❑   Opera 9+
- ❑   Safari 2+
- ❑   Chrome 1+

When using hidden frames, a popular Ajax approach, with these browsers, you'll notice few differences in the code, as each Browser Object Model (BOM) handles frames the same way (frame-based Ajax is covered later in the chapter). However, when you start using other forms of Ajax, such as XMLHttpRequest, the differences in code become apparent.

Using the XMLHttpRequest Object

As stated before, there are a variety of ways you can create Ajax-enabled applications. However, probably the most popular Ajax technique incorporates the JavaScript XMLHttpRequest object, which is present in all major browsers.

Despite its name, you can retrieve other types of data, like plain text, with XMLHttpRequest.

The XMLHttpRequest object originated as a Microsoft component, called XmlHttp, in the MSXML library first released with IE 5. It offered developers an easy way to open HTTP connections and retrieve XML data. Microsoft improved the component with each new version of MSXML, making it faster and more efficient.

As the popularity of the Microsoft XMLHttpRequest object grew, Mozilla decided to include its own version of the object with Firefox. The Mozilla version maintained the same properties and methods used in Microsoft's ActiveX component, making cross-browser usage possible. Soon after, Opera Software and Apple copied the Mozilla implementation, thus bringing the easy-to-use object to all modern browsers.

Cross-Browser Issues

The XMLHttpRequest object is no different from other web standards supported by the browsers, and the differences can be divided into two camps: ActiveX (for IE 5 and 6) and native support (for all other browsers). Thankfully, the two browser types only differ when you need to create an XMLHttpRequest object. After the object's creation, the remainder of the code is compatible for every browser.

Using ActiveX

Because the XMLHttpRequest object originated as a part of the MSXML library, an ActiveX XML parser, instantiating an XMLHttpRequest under these browsers, requires the creation of an ActiveX object. In Chapter 12, you created ActiveX objects to traverse the XML DOM. Creating an XMLHttp object isn't much different.

```
var oHttp = new ActiveXObject("Microsoft.XMLHttp");
```

This line creates the first version of Microsoft's XMLHttpRequest. There are many other versions of Microsoft's XmlHttp, but Microsoft recommends using one of the following versions:

- ❑   MSXML2.XmlHttp.6.0
- ❑   MSXML2.XmlHttp.3.0

You want to use the latest version possible when creating an XmlHttpRequest object as it contains bug fixes and enhanced performance. The downside is that not everyone will have the same version installed on their computer. However, you can write a function to use the latest version of XmlHttp installed on the user's computer.

With the previous version information, write a function called createXmlHttpRequest() to create an XMLHttpRequest object with the latest version supported by the user's computer.

```
function createXmlHttpRequest()
{
    var versions =
    [
        "MSXML2.XmlHttp.6.0",
        "MSXML2.XmlHttp.3.0"
    ];
    //more code here
}
```

This code defines the createXmlHttpRequest() function. Inside it, an array called versions contains the different version names recommended by Microsoft. Notice that the version names are listed starting with the newest first. This is done because you always want to check for the newest version first and continue with the next newest version until you find the version installed on the computer.

To decide what version to use, use a for loop to iterate through the elements in the array and then attempt to create an XMLHttpRequest object.

```
function createXmlHttpRequest()
{
    var versions =
    [
        "MSXML2.XmlHttp.6.0",
        "MSXML2.XmlHttp.3.0"
    ];

    for (var i = 0; i < versions.length; i++)
    {
        try
        {
            var oHttp = new ActiveXObject(versions[i]);
            return oHttp;
        }
        catch (error)
        {
            //do nothing here
        }
    }
    //more code here
}
```

An error is thrown if a specific version isn't installed on the user's computer. Therefore, use a try...catch block inside the loop to catch the error; this is the only way to determine if a version is installed on the computer. Code execution drops to the catch block if a version doesn't exist. Since nothing happens in this block, the loop iterates to the next element in the array. If no version is found on the computer, then the function returns `null`, like this:

```
function createXmlHttpRequest()
{
    var versions =
    [
        "MSXML2.XmlHttp.6.0",
        "MSXML2.XmlHttp.3.0"
    ];

    for (var i = 0; i < versions.length; i++)
    {
        try
        {
            var oHttp = new ActiveXObject(versions[i]);
            return oHttp;
        }
        catch (error)
        {
          //do nothing here
        }
    }

    return null;
}
```

Now you don't have to worry about ActiveX objects to create an XMLHttp object. If you call this function, it'll do all the work for you.

```
var oHttp = createXmlHttpRequest();
```

Calling the Native Constructor: The Other Browsers

IE 7+, Firefox, Opera, Safari, and Chrome boast a native implementation of the XMLHttpRequest object; it is an object located in the window object. Creating an XMLHttpRequest object is as simple as calling its constructor.

```
var oHttp = new XMLHttpRequest();
```

This line creates an XMLHttpRequest object, which you can use to connect to, and request and receive data from, a server. Unlike the ActiveX object in the previous section, XMLHttpRequest does not have different versions. Simply calling the constructor creates a ready to use XMLHttpRequest object.

Playing Together: One Function to Create them All

Just as with all other cross-browser issues, a solution can be found to create an XMLHttpRequest object for all browsers. You already wrote the createXmlHttpRequest() function, so expand it to provide cross-browser functionality.

```
function createXmlHttpRequest()
{
    if (window.XMLHttpRequest)
```

```
        {
            var oHttp = new XMLHttpRequest();
            return oHttp;
        }
        else if (window.ActiveXObject)
        {
            var versions =
            [
                "MSXML2.XmlHttp.6.0",
                "MSXML2.XmlHttp.3.0"
            ];

            for (var i = 0; i < versions.length; i++)
            {
                try
                {
                    var oHttp = new ActiveXObject(versions[i]);
                    return oHttp;
                }
                catch (error)
                {
                  //do nothing here
                }
            }
        }
    }

    return null;
}
```

This new code first checks to see if `window.XMLHttpRequest` exists. If it does, then the function creates an `XMLHttpRequest` object with the `XMLHttpRequest` constructor. If not, the code checks for `window.ActiveXObject` for IE 5 and 6 and tries to create an object with the latest `XMLHttp` version. If no `XMLHttpRequest` object can be created any browser, then the function returns `null`.

The order in which browsers are tested is important; test for `window.XMLHttpRequest` first because IE 7+ supports both `window.XMLHttpRequest` and `window.ActiveXObject`.

Regardless of the user's browser, if it supports `XMLHttpRequest`, this revised function creates an `XMLHttpRequest` object.

Using the XMLHttpRequest Object

Once you create the `XMLHttpRequest` object, you are ready to start requesting data with it. The first step in this process is to call the `open()` method to initialize the object.

```
oHttp.open(requestType, url, async);
```

This method accepts three arguments. The first, `requestType`, is a string value consisting of the type of request to make. The values can be either GET or POST. The second argument is the URL to send the request to, and the third is a `true` or `false` value indicating whether the request should be made in asynchronous or synchronous mode. For more on synchronous and asynchronous modes, see

Chapter 12; as a refresher, requests made in synchronous mode halt all JavaScript code from executing until a response is received from the server.

Asynchronous mode is preferred for real applications.

The next step is to send the request; do this with the send() method. This method accepts one argument, which is a string that contains the request body to send along with the request. GET requests do not contain any information, so pass null as the argument.

```
var oHttp = createXmlHttpRequest();
oHttp.open("GET", "http://localhost/myTextFile.txt", false);
oHttp.send(null);
```

This code makes a GET request to retrieve a file called myTextFile.txt in synchronous mode. Calling the send() method sends the request to the server.

> The send() method requires an argument to be passed; even if it is null.

Each XMLHttpRequest object has a status property. This property contains the HTTP status code sent with the server's response. The server returns a status of 200 for a successful request, and one of 404 if it cannot find the requested file. With this in mind, consider the following example:

```
var oHttp = createXmlHttpRequest();
oHttp.open("GET", "http://localhost/myTextFile.txt", false);
oHttp.send(null);

if (oHttp.status == 200)
{
    alert("The text file was found!");
}
else if (oHttp.status == 404)
{
    alert("The text file could not be found!");
}
else
{
    alert("The server returned a status code of " + oHttp.status);
}
```

This code checks the status property to determine what message to display to the user. If successful (a status of 200), an alert box tells the user the request file exists. If the file doesn't exist (status 404), then the user sees a message stating that the server cannot find the file. Finally, an alert box tells the user the status code if it equals something other than 200 or 404.

There are many different HTTP status codes, and checking for every code is not feasible. Most of the time, you should only be concerned with whether your request is successful. Therefore, you can cut the previous code down to this:

```
var oHttp = createXmlHttpRequest();
oHttp.open("GET", "http://localhost/myTextFile.txt", false);
```

```
oHttp.send(null);

if (oHttp.status == 200)
{
    alert("The text file was found!");
}
else
{
    alert("The server returned a status code of " + oHttp.status);
}
```

This code performs the same basic function, but it only checks for a status code of 200 and alert a generic message to the user for other status codes.

Asynchronous Requests

The previous code samples demonstrate the simplicity of synchronous requests. Asynchronous requests, on the other hand, add some complexity to your code because you have to handle the readystatechange event. In asynchronous requests, the XMLHttpRequest object exposes a readyState property, which holds a numeric value; each value refers to a specific state in a request's lifespan, as follows:

- ❑   0 — The object has been created, but the open() method hasn't been called
- ❑   1 — The open() method has been called, but the request hasn't been sent
- ❑   2 — The request has been sent; headers and status are received and available
- ❑   3 — A response has been received from the server
- ❑   4 — The requested data has been fully received

The readystatechange event fires every time the readyState property changes, calling the onreadystatechange event handler. The fourth and final state is the most important; it lets you know that the request completed.

It is important to note that even if the request was successful, you may not have the information you wanted. An error may have occurred on the server's end of the request (a 404, 500, or some other error). Therefore, you still need to check the status code of the request.

Code to handle the readystatechange event could look like this:

```
var oHttp = createXmlHttpRequest();

function oHttp_readyStateChange()
{
    if (oHttp.readyState == 4)
    {
        if (oHttp.status == 200)
        {
            alert(oHttp.responseText);
        }
        else
        {
```

```
                    alert("The server returned a status code of " + oHttp.status);
            }
        }
    }

    oHttp.open("GET", "http://localhost/myTextFile.txt", true);
    oHttp.onreadystatechange = oHttp_readyStateChange;

    oHttp.send(null);
```

This code first defines the oHttp_readyStateChange() function, which handles the readystatechange event; it first checks if the request completed by comparing readyState to 4. The function then checks the request's status to make sure the server returned the requested data. Once these two criteria are met, the code alerts the value of the responseText property (the actual requested data in plain text format). Note the open() method's call; the final argument passed to the method is true. This makes the XMLHttpRequest object request data asynchronously.

The benefits of using asynchronous communication are well worth the added complexity of the readystatechange event, as the browser can continue to load the page and execute your other JavaScript code while the request object sends and receives data. Perhaps a user-defined module that wraps an XMLHttpRequest object could make asynchronous requests easier to use and manage.

An XMLHttpRequest object also has a property called responseXML, *which attempts to load the received data into an XML DOM (whereas* responseText *returns plain text). This is the only way Safari 2 can load XML data into a DOM.*

Creating a Simple Ajax Module

The concept of code reuse is important in programming; it is the reason why functions are defined to perform specific, common, and repetitive tasks. Chapter 5 introduced you to the object-oriented construct of code reuse: reference types. These constructs contain properties that contain data and/or methods that perform actions with that data.

In this section, you write your own Ajax module called HttpRequest, thereby making asynchronous requests easier to make and manage. Before getting into writing this module, let's go over the properties and methods the HttpRequest reference type exposes.

Planning the HttpRequest Module

There's only one piece of information that you need to keep track of: the underlying XMLHttpRequest object. Therefore, this module will have only one property: request, which contains the underlying XMLHttpRequest object.

The methods are equally easy to identify.

❑   createXmlHttpRequest() — Creates the XMLHttpRequest object for all supporting browsers. It is essentially a copy of the function of the same name written earlier in the chapter.

❑   send() — Sends the request to the server.

With the properties and methods identified, let's begin to write the module.

The HttpRequest Constructor

A reference type's constructor defines its properties and performs any logic needed to function properly.

```
function HttpRequest(sUrl, fpCallback)
{
    this.request = this.createXmlHttpRequest();

    //more code here
}
```

The constructor accepts two arguments. The first, sUrl, is the URL the XMLHttpRequest object will request. The second, fpCallback, is a callback function; it will be called when the server's response is received (when the request's readyState is 4 and its status is 200). The first line of the constructor initializes the request property, assigning an XMLHttpRequest object to it.

With the request property created and ready to use, it's time to prepare the request for sending.

```
function HttpRequest(sUrl, fpCallback)
{
    this.request = this.createXmlHttpRequest();
    this.request.open("GET", sUrl, true);

    function request_readystatechange()
    {
        //more code here
    }

    this.request.onreadystatechange = request_readystatechange;
}
```

The first line of the new code uses the XMLHttpRequest object's open() method to initialize the request object. Set the request type to GET, use the sUrl parameter to specify the URL you want to request, and set the request object to use asynchronous mode. The next few lines define the request_readystatechange() function. Defining a function within a function may seem weird, but it is perfectly legal to do so; it's an advanced technique called a *closure*. Closures, like the request_readystatechange() function, cannot be accessed outside their containing function (the constructor in this case), but they have access to the variables and parameters of the containing function. This function handles the request object's readystatechange event, and you bind it to do so by assigning it to the onreadystatechange event handler.

```
function HttpRequest(sUrl, fpCallback)
{
    this.request = this.createXmlHttpRequest();
    this.request.open("GET", sUrl, true);

    var tempRequest = this.request;
    function request_readystatechange()
    {
```

```
            if (tempRequest.readyState == 4)
            {
                if (tempRequest.status == 200)
                {
                    fpCallback(tempRequest.responseText);
                }
                else
                {
                    alert("An error occurred trying to contact the server.");
                }
            }
        }

        this.request.onreadystatechange = request_readystatechange;
}
```

The new lines of code may again look strange. The first new line creates the `tempRequest` variable. This variable is a pointer to the current object's `request` property, and it's used within the `request_readystatechange()` function. This is a technique to get around scoping issues. Ideally, you would use `this.request` inside the `request_readystatechange()` function. However, the `this` keyword points to the `request_readystatechange()` function instead of to the `XMLHttpRequest` object, which would cause the code to not function properly. So when you see `tempRequest`, think `this.request`.

Inside the `request_readystatechange()` function, you see the following line:

```
fpCallback(tempRequest.responseText);
```

This line calls the callback function specified by the constructor's `fpCallback` parameter, and you pass the `responseText` property to this function. This will allow the callback function to use the information received from the server.

Creating the Methods

There are two methods in this reference type: one is used inside the constructor, and the other enables you to send the request to the server.

Cross-Browser XMLHttpRequest Creation ... Again

The first method is `createXmlHttpRequest()`. The inner workings of cross-browser object creation were covered earlier in the chapter, so let's just see the method definition.

```
HttpRequest.prototype.createXmlHttpRequest = function ()
{
    if (window.XMLHttpRequest)
    {
        var oHttp = new XMLHttpRequest();
        return oHttp;
    }
    else if (window.ActiveXObject)
    {
        var versions =
        [
```

```
            "MSXML2.XmlHttp.6.0",
            "MSXML2.XmlHttp.3.0"
    ];

    for (var i = 0; i < versions.length; i++)
    {
        try
        {
            var oHttp = new ActiveXObject(versions[i]);
            return oHttp;
        }
        catch (error)
        {
          //do nothing here
        }
    }
}

    alert("Your browser doesn't support XMLHttp");
}
```

In Chapter 5, you learned that user-defined reference type methods are assigned through the `prototype` object. This code follows that rule when writing the `createXmlHttpRequest()` method and the next method.

Sending the Request

Sending a request to the server involves the `XMLHttpRequest` object's `send()` method. This `send()` is similar, with the difference being that it doesn't accept arguments.

```
HttpRequest.prototype.send = function ()
{
    this.request.send(null);
}
```

This version of `send()` is simple in that all you do is call the `XMLHttpRequest` object's `send()` method and pass it `null`.

The Full Code

Now that the code's been covered, open your text editor and type the following:

```
function HttpRequest(sUrl, fpCallback)
{
    this.request = this.createXmlHttpRequest();
    this.request.open("GET", sUrl, true);

    var tempRequest = this.request;
    function request_readystatechange()
    {
        if (tempRequest.readyState == 4)
        {
```

```
                    if (tempRequest.status == 200)
                    {
                        fpCallback(tempRequest.responseText);
                    }
                    else
                    {
                        alert("An error occurred trying to contact the server.");
                    }
                }
            }

            this.request.onreadystatechange = request_readystatechange;
        }

        HttpRequest.prototype.createXmlHttpRequest = function ()
        {
            if (window.XMLHttpRequest)
            {
                var oHttp = new XMLHttpRequest();
                return oHttp;
            }
            else if (window.ActiveXObject)
            {
                var versions =
                [
                    "MSXML2.XmlHttp.6.0",
                    "MSXML2.XmlHttp.3.0"
                ];

                for (var i = 0; i < versions.length; i++)
                {
                    try
                    {
                        var oHttp = new ActiveXObject(versions[i]);
                        return oHttp;
                    }
                    catch (error)
                    {
                      //do nothing here
                    }
                }
            }

            return null;
        }

        HttpRequest.prototype.send = function ()
        {
            this.request.send(null);
        }
```

Save this file as `httprequest.js`. You'll use it later in the chapter.

The goal of this module was to make asynchronous requests easier to use, so let's look at a brief code-only example and see if that goal was accomplished.

The first thing you need is a function to handle the data received from the request; this function gets passed to the `HttpRequest` constructor.

```
function handleData(sResponseText)
{
    alert(sResponseText);
}
```

This code defines a function called `handleData()` that accepts one argument called `sResponseText`. When executed, the function merely alerts the data passed to it. Now create an `HttpRequest` object and send the request.

```
var request = new HttpRequest("http://localhost/myTextFile.txt", handleData);
request.send();
```

Pass the text file's location and a pointer of the `handleData()` function to the constructor, and send the request with the `send()` method. The `handleData()` function is called in the event of a successful request.

This module encapsulates the code related to asynchronous `XMLHttpRequest` requests nicely. You don't have to worry about creating the request object, handling the `readyStateChange` event, or checking the request's `status`; the `HttpRequest` module does it all for you.

Validating Form Fields with Ajax

You've probably seen it many times: registering as a new user on a web site's forum or signing up for web-based e-mail, only to find that your desired user name is taken. Of course, you don't find this out until after you've filled out the entire form, submitted it, and watched the page reload with new data (not to mention that you've lost some of the data you entered). As you can attest, form validation can be a frustrating experience; thankfully, Ajax can soften this experience by sending data to the server before submitting the form — allowing the server to validate the data, and letting the user know the outcome of the validation without reloading the page!

In this section, you'll create a form that uses Ajax techniques to validate form fields. It's possible to approach building such a form in a variety of ways; the easiest of which to implement provides a link that initiates an HTTP request to the server application to check whether the user's desired information is available to use.

The form you'll build will resemble typical forms used today; it will contain the following fields:

- ❑ `Username` (validated) — The field where the user types their desired user name
- ❑ `Email` (validated) — The field where the user types their e-mail
- ❑ `Password` (not validated) — The field where the user types their password
- ❑ `Verify Password` (not validated) — The field where the user verifies their password

Note that the `Password` and `Verify Password` fields are just for show in this example. Verifying a password is certainly something the server application can do; however, it is far more efficient to let JavaScript perform that verification. Doing so adds more complexity to this example, and I want to keep this as simple as possible to help you get a grasp of using Ajax.

Next to the `Username` and `Email` fields will be a hyperlink that calls a JavaScript function to query the server with the `HttpRequest` module you built earlier in this chapter.

As mentioned earlier, Ajax is communication between the browser and server. So this example needs a simple server application to validate the form fields. PHP programming is beyond the scope of this book. However, I should discuss how to request data from the PHP application, as well as look at the response the application sends back to JavaScript.

Requesting Information

The PHP application looks for one of two arguments in the query string: `username` and `email`.

To check the availability of a user name, use the `username` argument. The URL to do this looks like the following:

```
http://localhost/formvalidator.php?username=[usernameToSearchFor]
```

When searching for a user name, replace *[usernameToSearchFor]* with the actual name.

Searching for an e-mail follows the same pattern. The e-mail URL looks like this:

```
http://localhost/formvalidator.php?email=[emailToSearchFor]
```

The Received Data

A successful request will result in one of two values:

❑   `available` — Means that the user name and/or e-mail is available for use.

❑   `not available` — Signifies that the user name and/or e-mail is in use and therefore not available.

These values are sent to the client in plain text format. A simple comparison will enable you to tell the user whether their name or e-mail is already in use.

Before You Begin

This is a live-code Ajax example; therefore, your computer must meet a few requirements if you wish to run this example.

A Web Server

First, you need a web server. If you are using Windows 2000 (Server or Professional), Windows XP Professional, Windows Server 2003, Windows Vista Business or higher, or Windows Server 2008, you have Microsoft's web server software, Internet Information Services, freely available to you. To install it on Windows XP, open Add/Remove Programs in the Control Panel and click Add/Remove Windows Components. Figure 14-3 shows the Windows Component Wizard in Windows XP Professional.

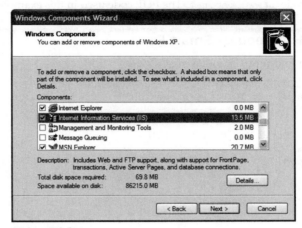

Figure 14-3

Check the box next to IIS and click Next to install. In Windows Vista, open the Programs and Features applet in the Control Panel and click the Turn Windows Features On or Off link in the side panel. Expand Internet Information Services and check the features you want to install. World Wide Web Services must be checked (Figure 14-4). You may need your operating system's installation CD to complete the installation.

Figure 14-4

If your operating system isn't in the preceding list, or you wish to use another web server application, you can install Apache HTTP Server (www.apache.org). This is an open-source web server and can run on a variety of operating systems, such as Linux, Unix, and Windows, to list only a few.

PHP

PHP is a popular open source server-side scripting language and must be installed on your computer if you wish to run PHP scripts. You can download PHP in a variety of forms (binaries, Windows installation wizards, and source code) at www.php.net. The PHP code used in this example was written in PHP 5.

Try It Out   XMLHttpRequest Smart Form

Open your text editor and type the following:

```
<!DOCTYPE HTML PUBLIC "-//W3C//DTD HTML 4.01//EN"
    "http://www.w3.org/TR/html4/strict.dtd">
<html>
<head>
    <title>Form Field Validation</title>
    <style type="text/css">
        .fieldname
        {
            text-align: right;
        }

        .submit
        {
            text-align: right;
        }
    </style>
    <script type="text/javascript" src="httprequest.js"></script>
    <script type="text/javascript">
        function checkUsername()
        {
            var userValue = document.getElementById("username").value;

            if (userValue == "")
            {
                alert("Please enter a user name to check!");
                return;
            }

            var url = "formvalidator.php?username=" + userValue;

            var request = new HttpRequest(url, checkUsername_callBack);
            request.send();
        }

        function checkUsername_callBack(sResponseText)
        {
            var userValue = document.getElementById("username").value;

            if (sResponseText == "available")
            {
                alert("The username " + userValue + " is available!");
            }
            else
            {
```

```
                    alert("We're sorry, but " + userValue + " is not available.");
                }
            }

            function checkEmail()
            {
                var emailValue = document.getElementById("email").value;

                if (emailValue == "")
                {
                    alert("Please enter an email address to check!");
                    return;
                }

                var url = "formvalidator.php?email=" + emailValue;

                var request = new HttpRequest(url, checkEmail_callBack);
                request.send();
            }

            function checkEmail_callBack(sResponseText)
            {
                var emailValue = document.getElementById("email").value;

                if (sResponseText == "available")
                {
                    alert("The email " + emailValue + " is currently not in use!");
                }
                else
                {
                    alert("I'm sorry, but " + emailValue + " is in use by another user.");
                }
            }
        </script>
    </head>
    <body>
        <form>
            <table>
                <tr>
                    <td class="fieldname">
                        Username:
                    </td>
                    <td>
                        <input type="text" id="username" />
                    </td>
                    <td>
                        <a href="javascript: checkUsername()">Check Availability</a>
                    </td>
                </tr>
                <tr>
                    <td class="fieldname">
                        Email:
                    </td>
                    <td>
```

```
                        <input type="text" id="email" />
                </td>
                <td>
                    <a href="javascript: checkEmail()">Check Availability</a>
                </td>
            </tr>
            <tr>
                <td class="fieldname">
                    Password:
                </td>
                <td>
                    <input type="text" id="password" />
                </td>
                <td />
            </tr>
            <tr>
                <td class="fieldname">
                    Verify Password:
                </td>
                <td>
                    <input type="text" id="password2" />
                </td>
                <td />
            </tr>
            <tr>
                <td colspan="2" class="submit">
                    <input type="submit" value="Submit" />
                </td>
                <td />
            </tr>
        </table>
    </form>
</body>
</html>
```

Save this file in your web server's root directory. If you're using IIS for your web server, save it as `c:\inetpub\wwwroot\validate_form.htm`. If you're using Apache, you'll want to save it inside the `htdocs` folder: `pathTohtdocs\htdocs\validate_form.htm`.

You also need to place `httprequest.js` (the `HttpRequest` module) and the `formvalidator.php` file (from the code download) into the same directory as `validate_form.htm`.

Now open your browser and navigate to `http://localhost/formvalidator.php`. If everything is working properly, you should see the text "PHP is working correctly. Congratulations!" as in Figure 14-5.

Now point your browser to `http://localhost/validate_form.htm`, and you should see something like Figure 14-6.

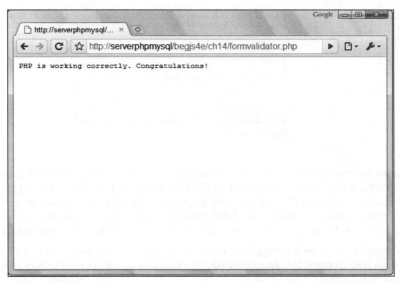

Figure 14-5

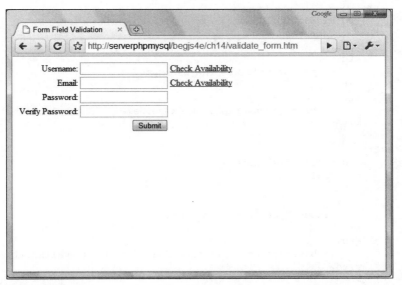

Figure 14-6

Type **jmcpeak** into the `Username` field and click the Check Availability link next to it. You'll see an alert box like the one shown in Figure 14-7.

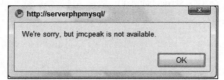

We're sorry, but jmcpeak is not available.

Figure 14-7

Now type **someone@xyz.com** in the `Email` field and click the Check Availability link next to it. Again, you'll be greeted with an alert box stating that the e-mail's already in use. Now input your own user name and e-mail into these fields and click the appropriate links. Chances are an alert box will tell you that your user name and/or e-mail is available (the user names `jmcpeak` and `pwilton` and the e-mails `someone@xyz.com` and `someone@zyx.com` are the only ones used by the application).

The body of this HTML page is a simple form whose fields are contained within a table. Each form field exists in its own row in the table. The first two rows contain the fields you're most interested in, the `Username` and `Email` fields.

```
<form>
    <table>
        <tr>
            <td class="fieldname">
                Username:
            </td>
            <td>
                <input type="text" id="username" />
            </td>
            <td>
                <a href="javascript: checkUsername()">Check Availability</a>
            </td>
        </tr>
        <tr>
            <td class="fieldname">
                Email:
            </td>
            <td>
                <input type="text" id="email" />
            </td>
            <td>
                <a href="javascript: checkEmail()">Check Availability</a>
            </td>
        </tr>
        <!-- HTML to be continued later -->
```

The first column contains text identifiers for the fields. The second column contains the `<input/>` elements themselves. Each of these tags has an `id` attribute, `username` for the `Username` field and `email` for the `Email` field. This enables you to easily find the `<input/>` elements and get the text entered into them. The third column contains an `<a/>` element. The hyperlinks use the `javascript:` protocol to call JavaScript code. In this case, the `checkUsername()` and `checkEmail()` functions are called when the user clicks the links. You'll examine these functions in a few moments.

The remaining three rows in the table contain two password fields and the Submit button (the smart form currently does not use these fields).

```html
<!-- HTML continued from earlier -->
<tr>
    <td class="fieldname">
        Password:
    </td>
    <td>
        <input type="text" id="password" />
    </td>
    <td />
</tr>
<tr>
    <td class="fieldname">
        Verify Password:
    </td>
    <td>
        <input type="text" id="password2" />
    </td>
    <td />
</tr>
<tr>
    <td colspan="2" class="submit">
        <input type="submit" value="Submit" />
    </td>
    <td />
</tr>
</table>
</form>
```

The CSS in this HTML page consists of only a couple of CSS rules.

```css
.fieldname
{
    text-align: right;
}

.submit
{
    text-align: right;
}
```

These rules align the fields to give the form a clean and unified look.

As stated earlier, the hyperlinks are key to the Ajax functionality, as they call JavaScript functions when clicked. The first function, checkUsername(), retrieves the text the user entered into the Username field and performs an HTTP request using that information.

```javascript
function checkUsername()
{
    var userValue = document.getElementById("username").value;

    if (userValue == "")
    {
```

```
        alert("Please enter a user name to check!");
        return;
    }

    var url = "formvalidator.php?username=" + userValue;

    var request = new HttpRequest(url, checkUsername_callBack);
    request.send();
}
```

Use the document.getElementById() method to find the <input/> element and use the value property to retrieve the text typed into the text box. Then check to see if the user typed any text by comparing the userValue variable to an empty string (" "). If the text box is empty, the function alerts the user to input a user name and stops the function from processing further. The application would make unnecessary requests to the server if the code didn't do this.

Next construct the URL to make the request to the PHP application and assign it to the url variable. The final steps in this function create an HttpRequest object, pass the URL and the callback function to the constructor, and send the request.

The checkUsername_callBack() function executes when the HttpRequest object receives a complete response from the server. This function uses the requested information to tell the user whether the user name is available. Remember, there are two possible values sent from the server, available and not available; therefore, you only need to check for one of these values.

```
function checkUsername_callBack(sResponseText)
{
    var userValue = document.getElementById("username").value;

    if (sResponseText == "available")
    {
        alert("The username " + userValue + " is available!");
    }
    else
    {
        alert("We're sorry, but " + userValue + " is not available.");
    }
}
```

If the server's response is available, the function tells the user that their desired user name is okay to use. If not, the alert box says that his user name is taken.

Checking the e-mail's availability follows an almost identical process. The checkEmail() function retrieves the text typed in the Email field, and passes that information to the server application.

```
function checkEmail()
{
    var emailValue = document.getElementById("email").value;

    if (emailValue == "")
    {
        alert("Please enter an email address to check!");
        return;
    }

    var url = "formvalidator.php?email=" + emailValue;
```

```
    var request = new HttpRequest(url, checkEmail_callBack);
    request.send();
}
```

The `checkEmail_callBack()` function uses the same logic as `checkUsername_callBack()`, but it is based on the `Email` field's value.

```
function checkEmail_callBack(sResponseText)
{
    var emailValue = document.getElementById("email").value;

    if (sResponseText == "available")
    {
        alert("The email " + emailValue + " is currently not in use!");
    }
    else
    {
        alert("I'm sorry, but " + emailValue + " is in use by another user.");
    }
}
```

Once again, the function checks to see if the server's response is `available`, and lets the user know that the e-mail address is currently not being used. If the address is not available, a different message tells the user his e-mail is not available.

Things to Watch Out For

Using JavaScript to communicate between server and client adds tremendous power to the language's abilities. However, this power does not come without its share of caveats. The two most important issues are security and usability.

Security Issues

Security is a hot topic in today's Internet, and as a Web developer you must consider the security restrictions placed on Ajax. Knowing the security issues surrounding Ajax can save you development and debugging time.

The Same-Origin Policy

Since the early days of Netscape Navigator 2.0, JavaScript cannot access scripts or documents from a different origin. This is a security measure that browser makers adhere to; otherwise, malicious coders could execute code wherever they wanted. The same-origin policy dictates that two pages are of the same origin only if the protocol (HTTP), port (the default is 80), and host are the same.

Consider the following two pages:

❑   Page 1 is located at `http://www.site.com/folder/mypage1.htm`

❑   Page 2 is located at `http://www.site.com/folder10/mypage2.htm`

According to the same-origin policy, these two pages are of the same origin. They share the same host (www.site.com), use the same protocol (HTTP), and are accessed on the same port (none is specified; therefore, they both use 80). Since they are of the same origin, JavaScript on one page can access the other page.

Now consider the next two pages:

❑   Page 1 is located at http://www.site.com/folder/mypage1.htm

❑   Page 2 is located at https://www.site.com/folder/mypage2.htm

These two pages are not of the same origin. The host is the same.. However, their protocols and ports are different. Page 1 uses HTTP (port 80) while Page 2 uses HTTPS (port 443). This difference, while slight, is enough to give the two pages two separate origins. Therefore, JavaScript on one of these pages cannot access the other page.

So what does this have to do with Ajax? Everything because a large part of Ajax is JavaScript. For example, because of this policy, an XMLHttpRequest object cannot retrieve any file or document from a different origin. You can easily overcome this hurdle by using the server in the page's origin as a proxy to retrieve data from servers of a different origin. This policy also affects the hidden frame/iframe technique. JavaScript cannot interact with two pages of different origins, even if they are in the same frameset.

ActiveX

One of the downsides of XMLHttpRequest is in ActiveX, and only affects Internet Explorer on Windows; however, IE currently has the highest market share of all browsers, and it seems that isn't going to change anytime soon. Over the past few years, more security concerns have been raised with ActiveX, especially since many adware and spyware companies have used the technology to install their wares onto trusting user's computers.

Because of this rise in the awareness of security concerns, Microsoft (and users) is taking steps to make the browser more secure from hijacking attempts by restricting access to ActiveX plug-ins and objects. If a user turns off ActiveX completely, or your site is flagged for a certain security zone, ActiveX objects cannot be created, rendering your XMLHttpRequest-based Ajax applications dead in the water.

Usability Concerns

Ajax breaks the mold of traditional web applications and pages. It enables developers to build applications that behave in a more conventional, non-"webbish" way. This, however, is also a drawback, as the Internet has been around for many, many years, and users are accustomed to traditional web pages.

Therefore, it is up to developers to ensure that the user can use their web pages, and use them as they expect to, without causing frustration.

The Browser's Back Button

One of the advantages of XMLHttpRequest is its ease of use. You simply create the object, send the request, and await the server's response. Unfortunately, this object does have a downside: most browsers do not log a history of requests made with the object. Therefore, XMLHttpRequest essentially breaks the browser's Back button. This might be a desired side-effect for some Ajax-enabled applications or components, but it can cause serious usability problems for the user.

At the time of this writing, IE 8 is the only browser that logs requests made with an XMLHttpRequest *object in the history. One thing you have to keep in mind is that the Internet and browsers have been around much longer than Ajax, and users have come to expect certain behavior when they click the Back and Forward buttons. Breaking that behavior causes frustration for the user, and that's something a responsible developer must take into account when designing their application.*

Creating a Back/Forward-Capable Form with an IFrame

It's possible to avoid breaking the browser's navigational buttons by using an older Ajax technique: using hidden frames/iframes to facilitate client-server communication. You must use two frames in order for this method to work properly. One must be hidden, and one must be visible.

Note that when you are using an iframe, the document that contains the iframe is the visible frame.

The hidden-frame technique consists of a four-step process.

1. The user initiates a JavaScript call to the hidden frame. This can be done by the user clicking a link in the visible frame or some other form of user interaction. This call is usually nothing more complicated that redirecting the hidden frame to a different web page. This redirection automatically triggers the second step.

2. The request is sent to the server, which processes the data.

3. The server sends its response (a web page) back to the hidden frame.

4. The browser loads the web page in the hidden frame and executes any JavaScript code to contact the visible frame.

The example in this section is based upon the form validator built earlier in the chapter, but you'll use a hidden iframe to facilitate the communication between the browser and the server instead of an XMLHttpRequest object. Before getting into the code, you should first know about the data received from the server.

> **The following example does not work in Safari 2, as it does not log the history of an iframe.**

The Server Response

You expected only a few words as the server's response when using XMLHttpRequest to get data from the server. The response in this example is different and must consist of two things:

❑ The data, which must be in HTML format

❑ A mechanism to contact the parent document when the iframe receives the HTML response

The following code is an example of the response HTML page:

```
<!DOCTYPE HTML PUBLIC "-//W3C//DTD HTML 4.01//EN"
    "http://www.w3.org/TR/html4/strict.dtd">

<html>
<head>
    <title>Returned Data</title>
</head>
<body>
    <script type="text/javascript">
        //more code here
    </script>
</body>
</html>
```

This simple HTML page contains a single <script/> element in the body of the document. The JavaScript code contained in this script block is generated by the PHP application, calling either checkUsername_callBack() or checkEmail_callBack() in the visible frame and passing available or not available as their arguments. Therefore, the following HTML document is a valid response from the PHP application:

```
<!DOCTYPE HTML PUBLIC "-//W3C//DTD HTML 4.01//EN"
    "http://www.w3.org/TR/html4/strict.dtd">

<html>
<head>
    <title>Returned Data</title>
</head>
<body>
    <script type="text/javascript">
        top.checkUsername_callBack("available", "some_username");
    </script>
</body>
</html>
```

The user name is available in this sample response. Therefore, the HTML page calls the checkUsername_callBack() function in the parent window and passes the string available. Also, the searched user name (or e-mail) is sent back to the client because the client application will display the correct user name or e-mail when the Back or Forward button is pressed. With the response in this format, you can keep a good portion of the JavaScript code the same.

Try It Out   Iframe Smart Form

The code for this revised smart form is very similar to the code used previously with the XMLHttpRequest example. There are, however, a few changes. Open up your text editor and type the following:

```
<!DOCTYPE HTML PUBLIC "-//W3C//DTD HTML 4.01//EN"
    "http://www.w3.org/TR/html4/strict.dtd">

<html>
<head>
    <title>Form Field Validation</title>
```

```
<style type="text/css">
    .fieldname
    {
        text-align: right;
    }

    .submit
    {
        text-align: right;
    }

    #hiddenFrame
    {
        display: none;
    }
</style>
<script type="text/javascript">
    function checkUsername()
    {
        var userValue = document.getElementById("username").value;

        if (userValue == "")
        {
            alert("Please enter a user name to check!");
            return;
        }

        var url = "iframe_formvalidator.php?username=" + userValue;

        frames["hiddenFrame"].location = url;
    }

    function checkUsername_callBack(data, userValue)
    {
        if (data == "available")
        {
            alert("The username " + userValue + " is available!");
        }
        else
        {
            alert("We're sorry, but " + userValue + " is not available.");
        }
    }

    function checkEmail()
    {
        var emailValue = document.getElementById("email").value;

        if (emailValue == "")
        {
            alert("Please enter an email address to check!");
            return;
        }

        var url = "iframe_formvalidator.php?email=" + emailValue;

        frames["hiddenFrame"].location = url;
```

```
            }

        function checkEmail_callBack(data, emailValue)
        {
            if (data == "available")
            {
                alert("The email " + emailValue + " is currently not in use!");
            }
            else
            {
                alert("We're sorry, but " + emailValue
                    + " is in use by another user.");
            }
        }
    </script>
</head>
<body>
    <form>
        <table>
            <tr>
                <td class="fieldname">
                    Username:
                </td>
                <td>
                    <input type="text" id="username" />
                </td>
                <td>
                    <a href="javascript: checkUsername()">Check Availability</a>
                </td>
            </tr>
            <tr>
                <td class="fieldname">
                    Email:
                </td>
                <td>
                    <input type="text" id="email" />
                </td>
                <td>
                    <a href="javascript: checkEmail()">Check Availability</a>
                </td>
            </tr>
            <tr>
                <td class="fieldname">
                    Password:
                </td>
                <td>
                    <input type="text" id="password" />
                </td>
                <td />
            </tr>
            <tr>
                <td class="fieldname">
                    Verify Password:
                </td>
```

```
            <td>
                <input type="text" id="password2" />
            </td>
            <td />
        </tr>
        <tr>
            <td colspan="2" class="submit">
                <input type="submit" value="Submit" />
            </td>
            <td />
        </tr>
      </table>
    </form>
    <iframe src="about:blank" id="hiddenFrame" name="hiddenFrame" />
  </body>
</html>
```

Save this file as `validate_iframe_form.htm`, and save it in your web server's root directory. Also locate the `iframe_formvalidator.php` file from the code download and place it in the same directory.

Open your web browser and navigate to `http://localhost/validate_iframe_form.htm`. You should see something like what is shown in Figure 14-8.

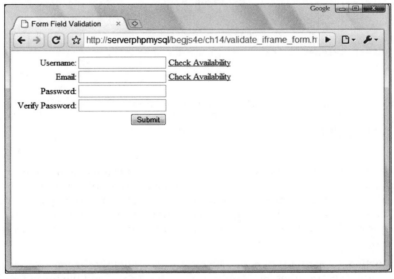

Figure 14-8

Check for three user names and e-mail addresses. After you clear the final alert box, press the browser's Back button a few times. You'll notice that it is cycling through the information you previously entered. The text in the text box will not change; however, the alert box will display the names and e-mails you entered. You can do the same thing with the Forward button.

The HTML in the body of the page remains unchanged except for the addition of the `<iframe/>` tag after the closing `<form/>` tag.

```
<iframe src="about:blank" id="hiddenFrame" name="hiddenFrame" />
```

This frame is initialized to have a blank HTML page loaded. Its `name` and `id` attributes contain the value of `hiddenFrame`. Use the value of the `name` attribute later to retrieve this frame from the `frames` collection in the BOM. Next, I set the CSS for the frame.

```
#hiddenFrame
{
    display: none;
}
```

This rule contains one style declaration to hide the iframe from view.

Hiding an iframe through CSS enables you to easily show it if you need to debug the server-side application.

Next up, the JavaScript.

```
function checkUsername()
{
    var userValue = document.getElementById("username").value;

    if (userValue == "")
    {
        alert("Please enter a user name to check!");
        return;
    }

    var url = "iframe_formvalidator.php?username=" + userValue;

    frames["hiddenFrame"].location = url;
}
```

The `checkUsername()` function has undergone a small change: It makes a request via the iframe instead of using `XMLHttpRequest`. It starts by retrieving the value of the `Username` text box. It then checks to see if the user typed anything into the box; if not, an alert box displays a message to the user telling her to enter a user name. If the value isn't an empty string, then the function continues and constructs the request URL. The final step is to load the URL into the hidden iframe by using the `frames` collection and the `location` property.

The second function, `checkUsername_callBack()`, is also slightly changed. It now accepts two arguments: the first will contain either `available` or `not available`, and the second will contain the user name sent in the request.

```
function checkUsername_callBack(data, userValue)
{
    if (data == "available")
    {
        alert("The username " + userValue + " is available!");
    }
    else
    {
```

```
        alert("We're sorry, but " + userValue + " is not available.");
    }
}
```

The function first checks to see if the user name is available. If so, an alert box tells the user that the user name is available. If not, the user sees an alert box stating that the user name is not available.

The functions for searching e-mail addresses follow the same pattern as those for searching user names.

```
function checkEmail()
{
    var emailValue = document.getElementById("email").value;

    if (emailValue == "")
    {
        alert("Please enter an email address to check!");
        return;
    }

    var url = "iframe_formvalidator.php?email=" + emailValue;

    frames["hiddenFrame"].location = url;
}

function checkEmail_callBack(data, emailValue)
{
    if (data == "available")
    {
        alert("The email " + emailValue + " is currently not in use!");
    }
    else
    {
        alert("We're sorry, but " + emailValue + " is in use by another user.");
    }
}
```

The checkEmail() function retrieves the text box's value, checks to see if the user entered data, constructs the URL, and loads the URL into the iframe.

The checkEmail_callBack() function contains changes similar to those made to checkUsername_callBack(). The function now accepts two arguments, checks to see if the e-mail is available, and displays a message accordingly.

Dealing with Delays

The web browser is just like any other conventional application in that user interface (UI) cues tell the user that something is going on. When a user clicks a link, the throbber animation runs, an hourglass appears next to the cursor (in Windows), and a status bar usually shows the browser's progress in loading the page.

This is another area in which Ajax solutions, and XMLHttpRequest specifically, miss the mark. This problem, however, is simple to overcome: Simply add UI elements to tell the user something is going on and remove them when the action is completed. Consider the following code:

```
function requestComplete(sResponseText)
{

    //do something with the data here

    document.getElementById("divLoading").style.display = "none";
}

var myRequest = new HttpRequest("http://localhost/myfile.txt", requestComplete);
document.getElementById("divLoading").style.display = "block";//show that we're
loading
myRequest.send();
```

This code uses the HttpRequest module built earlier to request a text file. Before sending the request, retrieve an HTML element in the document with an id of divLoading. This <div/> element tells the user that data is loading; hide it when the request completes, which lets the user know that the loading process is completed.

Offering this information to your users lets them know the application is performing some operation that they requested. Otherwise, they may wonder if the application is working correctly when they click something and see nothing instantly happen.

Degrade Gracefully When Ajax Fails

In a perfect world, the code you write would work every time it runs. Unfortunately, you have to face the fact that many times Ajax-enabled web pages will not use the Ajax-enabled goodness because a user turned off JavaScript in his browser.

The only real answer to this problem is to build an old-fashioned web page with old-fashioned forms, links, and other HTML elements. Then, using JavaScript, you can disable the default behavior of those HTML elements and add Ajax functionality. Consider this hyperlink as an example:

```
<a href="http://www.wrox.com" title="Wrox Publishing">Wrox Publishing</a>
```

This is a normal, run-of-the-mill hyperlink. When the user clicks it, it will take them to http://www.wrox.com. By using JavaScript, you can override this action and replace it with your own.

```
<a href="http://www.wrox.com" title="Wrox Publishing"
   onclick="return false;">Wrox Publishing</a>
```

The key to this functionality is the onclick event handler, highlighted in this code, and returning a value of false. You can execute any code you wish with the event handler; just remember to return false at the end. This tells the browser to not perform its default action when the link is clicked. If the user's JavaScript is turned off, the onclick event handler is ignored, and the link behaves as it normally should.

As a rule of thumb, build your web page first and add Ajax later.

Summary

This chapter introduced you to Ajax, and it barely scratched the surface of Ajax and its many uses.

❑ You looked at the XMLHttpRequest object, and how it differed between IE 5 & 6, and the other browsers. You learned how to make both synchronous and asynchronous requests to the server and how to use the onreadystatechange event handler.

❑ You built your own Ajax module to make asynchronous HTTP requests easier for you to code.

❑ You used our new Ajax module in a smarter form, one that checks user names and e-mails to see if they are already in use.

❑ You discussed how XMLHttpRequest breaks the browser's Back and Forward buttons, and addressed this problem by rebuilding the same form by using a hidden iframe to make requests.

❑ You looked at some of the downsides to Ajax, the security issues and the gotchas.

Exercise Questions

Suggested solutions for these questions can be found in Appendix A.

1. Extend the HttpRequest module to include synchronous requests in addition to the asynchronous requests the module already makes. You'll have to make some adjustments to your code to incorporate this functionality. (Hint: Create an async property for the module.)

2. It was mentioned earlier in the chapter that the smart forms could be modified to not use hyperlinks. Change the form that uses the HttpRequest module so that the user name and e-mail fields are checked when the user submits the form. Use the form's onsubmit event handler and cancel the submission if a user name or e-mail is taken. Also use the updated HttpRequest module from Question 1 and use synchronous requests. The only time you need to alert the user is when the user name or e-mail is taken, so make sure to return true if the user name and e-mail pass muster.

JavaScript Frameworks

As you've seen in several examples in this book, especially the latter chapters, the problem with client-side development is the many different web browsers you have to account for. Be it writing event-driven code or an Ajax application, somewhere down the line you'll run into the incompatibilities between the browsers.

Many professional developers found cross-browser development to be too time-consuming and cumbersome to deal with on a daily basis, so they set out to develop frameworks or libraries to aid in their cross-browser development. Some framework authors released their frameworks to the public, and a few of them gained quite a following, like jQuery, Prototype, and MooTools.

In this chapter, you'll take a look at three of the many JavaScript frameworks available on the Internet, and you'll learn how to use them to make your cross-browser development much easier.

Before beginning, a word of note from your authors: There is no doubt that JavaScript frameworks add benefit to your development time and process. But they are no substitute for a solid understanding of the JavaScript language and the intricacies of the different browsers you have to develop for. Frameworks and libraries come and go, but knowledge is forever.

Picking a Framework to Work With

Over the course of several years, the web has seen many JavaScript frameworks, and they can typically be categorized into two groups: general and specialty.

The aim of general frameworks is to balance the differences between browsers by creating a new, unified API to perform general tasks like DOM manipulation and Ajax functionality. Specialty frameworks, on the other hand, focus on a specific ability, such as animation. So identify what it is you want to achieve and choose a framework based on that. For example, if you wanted to perform animations and only animations, the script.aculo.us framework (`http://script.aculo.us/`) would be a good choice for you.

This chapter focuses on general frameworks, and even general frameworks differ in their goals. When deciding which framework to use, look at the framework's browser support, documentation, and community involvement. The frameworks covered in this chapter are a few years old, stable, and popular and are compatible with every major modern browser (and even some old ones like IE6). They are as follows:

- ❑ **jQuery:** A framework whose primary emphasis is the ability to use CSS selectors to select and work with DOM objects. It also provides a plug-in architecture, as well as a companion UI framework. (`http://jquery.com`)

- ❑ **Prototype:** A framework that provides a simple API to perform web tasks. While it offers ways of manipulating the DOM, Prototype's primary aim is to enhance the JavaScript language by providing class definition and inheritance. (`http://www.prototypejs.org`)

- ❑ **MooTools:** A framework whose aim is to be compact while offering a simple API to make common tasks easier. Like Prototype, MooTools also aims to enhance the JavaScript languages — not just make DOM manipulation and Ajax easier. It also includes a lightweight effects component originally called moo.fx. (`http://www.mootools.net`)

These three frameworks are just a sampling of what is available for you to use in your web pages. Other general frameworks not covered in this chapter are the following:

- ❑ **Yahoo! User Interface Framework (YUI):** A framework that ranges from basic JavaScript utilities to complete DHTML widgets. Yahoo! has a team devoted to developing YUI. (`http://developer.yahoo.com/yui/`)

- ❑ **Ext JS:** This framework started as an extension to the YUI. It offers customizable UI widgets for building rich Internet applications. (`http://www.extjs.com`)

- ❑ **Dojo:** A toolkit designed around a package system. The core functionality resembles that of any other framework (DOM manipulation, event normalization, DHTML widgets, etc.), but it provides and allows a way to add more functionality by adding more packages. (`http://www.dojotoolkit.org`)

- ❑ **MochiKit:** A framework that prides itself on its well-testedness (hundreds of tests according to the MochiKit site) and its compatibility with other JavaScript frameworks and libraries. (`http://www.mochikit.com`)

Getting Started

Once you choose the framework you want to develop with, you need to install the framework and verify its installation before you do any work with the framework.

Installing a framework is very different from installing an application on your computer; there is no setup program, and the installation doesn't change any portion of your system. Basically, all you do is download a file and reference the file in your web page. The following sections will walk you through this process.

Installing the Frameworks

First, you need to acquire the framework's JavaScript file. Most frameworks come in at least two versions: compressed and uncompressed.

❑ Compressed versions: These are *minified* (all comments and unnecessary white space are removed) in order to make their file size as small as possible; doing so makes them faster to download when someone visits your web page. Unfortunately, the minification process makes the JavaScript code difficult to read if you open it in a text editor, but that's a reasonable tradeoff in a production environment.

❑ Uncompressed versions: These are not minified; they are simply normal JavaScript code files with their white space and comments intact. It's perfectly OK to use uncompressed JavaScript files. Since they are easier to read than compressed files, you can learn much from the gurus who design and develop these frameworks. However, if you plan to roll out a web page using a framework, be sure to download and use the compressed version, as their file sizes are smaller and download faster.

Downloading the Frameworks

Unlike other downloads on the web, jQuery, Prototype, and MooTools do not use a compression algorithm (like ZIP or RAR) for their downloadable files; instead you download the JavaScript file itself. These files have an extension of `.js`.

First you need to acquire a copy of jQuery as follows:

1. Open your browser and go to `http://jquery.com`.

2. Find the Download button on the site's front page.

3. Before clicking the Download button, choose the version you want — either the production version (compressed) or the development version (uncompressed). jQuery will work the same regardless of what version you choose. At the time of this writing, jQuery project downloads are actually housed at Google code, so clicking the Download link will take you away from `jquery.com`.

4. Download the JavaScript file and save it in a location you can easily get to.

You can also see a list of all downloadable files at `http://code.google.com/p/jqueryjs/downloads/list`.

The production version of jQuery 1.3.2 is provided in the code download from Wrox.

5. Now point your browser to Prototype's download page at `http://www.prototypejs.org/download`. Here, you'll be given the choice to download a *bleeding edge* version, a version still in testing, or the latest stable version. You can download the in-testing version if you'd like, but the examples in this book will use the stable version.

The stable version of Prototype 1.6.0.3 is provided in the code download from Wrox.

Now let's download MooTools. The download URL for MooTools is `http://www.mootools.net/download`. Like jQuery, the folks at MooTools offer you compressed and uncompressed versions of their framework. Of the compressed versions, you can choose a version compressed with YUI Compressor or JSMin. The current version at the time of this writing is MooTools 1.2.3, and the smallest-sized download is the YUI Compressor version, so download it. Smaller is typically better, since it takes less time to download.

The YUI compressed version of MooTool 1.2.3 is included in the code download.

Adding the Frameworks to Your Pages

Now that you've acquired the JavaScript framework files for each framework, you need to add them to a web page before you can use them. This is as simple as adding an HTML `<script/>` element to your page.

Keep in mind that you do not want to add each framework to the same page. It would certainly be nothing but awesomeness to have every framework work together seamlessly to give you all the features of every framework at the same time. Unfortunately, frameworks are notorious for stepping on each others' toes, so create a separate HTML page for each framework.

The following HTML page, called ch15_examp1_jq.htm, shows you how easy it is to add jQuery, or any other framework, to a web page.

```
<!DOCTYPE html PUBLIC "-//W3C//DTD XHTML 1.0 Transitional//EN"
    "http://www.w3.org/TR/xhtml1/DTD/xhtml1-transitional.dtd">

<html xmlns="http://www.w3.org/1999/xhtml">
<head>
    <title>Chapter 15: Example 1 jQuery</title>
    <script type="text/javascript" src="jquery-1.3.2.min.js"></script>
</head>
<body>

</body>
</html>
```

Simply use the `<script/>` element's `src` attribute, and set its value as the path to the JavaScript file. In this example, the `jquery-1.3.2.min.js` file is in the same directory as the HTML document. It is absolutely imperative that the value of the `src` attribute is correct; otherwise, the browser will not be able to find the framework file, download it, and load it — meaning that your code will not work.

Go ahead and type this page and save it. Then create two similar pages for MooTools and Prototype, and name them ch15_examp1_mt.htm and ch15_examp1_p.htm respectively. Don't forget to change the `<script/>` element's `src` attribute to point to the appropriate JavaScript file!

Testing the Frameworks

Now that you downloaded each library and added them to their respective pages, you should run through a quick test to ensure that everything works correctly. Because each library is different, you'll have to perform a similar test for each library. Start with jQuery.

Testing Your jQuery Installation

At the heart of jQuery is the `$()` function (called the jQuery function), which returns `jQuery` objects. The jQuery function is quite powerful because it allows you to select elements by passing CSS selectors, create elements by passing HTML, and wrap jQuery functionality around DOM objects by passing the DOM objects you want to add functionality to.

To illustrate the jQuery function and the objects it returns, assume you want to run some code when the page loads. In plain JavaScript, you know you can assign a function to handle the `window`'s `load` event. The jQuery equivalent is quite different:

```
function document_ready()
{
    alert("Hello, jQuery World!");
}

// the normal way
onload = document_ready;

// the jquery way
$(document).ready(document_ready);
```

Look at the last line of this code, which calls the jQuery function and passes the `document` DOM object to it. The jQuery function returns a `jQuery` object, of which `ready()` is a method. By passing a DOM object to the jQuery function, you've actually created a new object that wraps itself around the DOM object. This might be better understood with the following code:

```
var jDocument = $(document);
jDocument.ready(document_ready);
```

This code achieves the same results as the previous code, except you have a `jQuery` object contained in the `jDocument` variable, which you can reuse.

It's important to note that `jQuery` objects cannot be used in place of DOM objects. In the previous example, the jQuery function returns a completely different object than the `document` object it was passed.

This type of reuse — assigning a variable and reusing it later — is perfectly fine to use with jQuery objects, but jQuery adds the ability to chain method calls together. If the idea of method chaining is new to you, then consider the following code:

```
$(document.body).attr("bgColor", "yellow").html("<h1>Hello, jQuery World</h1>");
```

The `jQuery` object has many methods, and nearly all of them return the current `jQuery` object. Because of this, you can call one method after another, thus enhancing readability while writing less code. This code uses the jQuery function and passes the `document.body` DOM object to it. Immediately after the function call, you call the `attr()` method to set the `bgColor` attribute to yellow. Since the jQuery function returns a `jQuery` object encapsulating a reference to the `document.body` DOM object, the `bgColor` attribute is set on the `document.body` DOM object.

After the `attr()` method call is yet another method call because `attr()` returns the same `jQuery` object encapsulating the `document.body` DOM object. The second method is the `html()` method, which accepts a string of HTML that is written to the page. The way in which `html()` writes HTML into the page is different from `document.write()`. Instead, jQuery's `html()` method uses the `innerHTML` DOM property to set the HTML inside a DOM object (in this case `document.body`).

As you can see from this example, chaining is a handy way of performing multiple tasks on one object, and jQuery is built around this concept.

Use this code to test your jQuery installation. Open `ch15_examp1_jq.htm` and add in the second `<script/>` element shown in the following code:

```
<!DOCTYPE html PUBLIC "-//W3C//DTD XHTML 1.0 Transitional//EN"
    "http://www.w3.org/TR/xhtml1/DTD/xhtml1-transitional.dtd">

<html xmlns="http://www.w3.org/1999/xhtml">
<head>
    <title>Chapter 15: Example 2 jQuery</title>
    <script type="text/javascript" src="jquery-1.3.2.min.js"></script>
    <script type="text/javascript">
    function document_ready($)
    {
        $(document.body).attr("bgColor", "yellow")
            .html("<h1>Hello, jQuery World!</h1>");
    }

    $(document).ready(document_ready);
    </script>
</head>
<body>

</body>
</html>
```

Save this as `ch15_examp2_jq.htm`, and open it in your browser. You should see something like Figure 15-1.

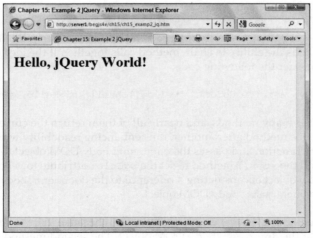

Figure 15-1

If the page's background color is not yellow and you don't see the Hello World message, then something is wrong with your installation. Make sure the jQuery .js file is in the same directory as your HTML file.

Now let's test your Prototype installation. Don't worry; you'll revisit jQuery soon enough.

Testing Your Prototype Installation

The largest portion of the Prototype library is its DOM extensions. Like jQuery, it provides you a variety of helpful utility functions to make DOM programming a bit easier; it even has its own $() function (unlike jQuery, Prototype doesn't have a special name for this function; it's simply called the dollar function).

Prototype's $() function only accepts element id attribute values or DOM element objects to select and add extra functionality to DOM objects.

Prototype does have a function that allows you to use CSS selectors to select elements, and you'll see that in a later section.

Also unlike jQuery, there is no ready() method, or an equivalent method, to take the place of window.onload. Instead, you can take advantage of one of the many extensions that Prototype adds to the browser and DOM: the Event.observe() method.

```
function window_onload()
{
    alert("Hello, Prototype World!");
}

Event.observe(window, "load", window_onload);
```

The Event.observe() method accepts three arguments; the first is the DOM or BOM object you want to add an event handler to, the second is the event you want to handle, and the third is the function to call when the event fires. Event.observe() can be used to add an event handler to any DOM or BOM object that allows you to handle events. You'll look at this method, and other ways to handle events in Prototype, later in this chapter.

Like jQuery, you can chain method calls together on wrapper objects created with the $() function, although the method names are more verbose than jQuery's.

```
function window_onload()
{
    $(document.body).writeAttribute("bgColor", "yellow").
        insert("<h1>Hello, Prototype World!</h1>");
}

Event.observe(window, "load", window_onload);
```

The new body of the window_onload() function changes the page's background color to yellow and adds HTML to the page. The writeAttribute() method sets an attribute's value and accepts two arguments: the attribute name and the attribute value. The next method call, the insert() method, inserts the provided content into the document.body element, as specified by the DOM object passed to the initial $() function.

Use this code to test your Prototype installation. Open `ch15_examp1_p.htm` and add the second `<script/>` element as shown in the following code:

```
<!DOCTYPE html PUBLIC "-//W3C//DTD XHTML 1.0 Transitional//EN"
    "http://www.w3.org/TR/xhtml1/DTD/xhtml1-transitional.dtd">

<html xmlns="http://www.w3.org/1999/xhtml">
<head>
    <title>Chapter 15: Example 2 Prototype</title>
    <script type="text/javascript" src="prototype-1.6.0.3.js"></script>
    <script type="text/javascript">
    function window_onload()
    {
        $(document.body).writeAttribute("bgColor", "yellow")
            .insert("<h1>Hello, Prototype World!</h1>");
    }

    Event.observe(window, "load", window_onload);
    </script>
</head>
<body>

</body>
</html>
```

Save this as `ch15_examp2_p.htm`, and open it in your browser. You should see something like Figure 15-2. If you do not, make sure that Prototype JavaScript file is in the same directory as the HTML file.

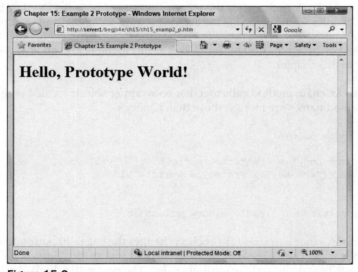

Figure 15-2

You'll dig deeper into Prototype in a moment; let's do one final test with MooTools to make sure your installation is correct.

Testing Your MooTools Installation

Testing the MooTools installation will look similar to the jQuery and Prototype tests. Like those two frameworks, MooTools defines a dollar function, and its functionality is similar to Prototype's.

```
$("myDiv")
```

Like Prototype, MooTool's dollar function accepts either a string containing an element's id or a DOM element, and returns the element or DOM object with an extended set of methods. One such method is the addEvent() method. This method accepts two arguments: the first is the event to watch for, and the second is the function to call when the event fires. The MooTools framework adds the addEvent() method to the window and document objects. So simply call the addEvent() method to add a domready event handler, like this:

```
function window_domready()
{
    alert("Hello, MooTools World!");
}

window.addEvent("domready", window_domready);
```

The domready event is also added by the MooTools framework, and it fires when the DOM is completely loaded.

Also like jQuery and Prototype, you can chain MooTools methods to perform multiple operations on an element with less code than if you didn't use a framework. Look at the following code:

```
function window_domready()
{
    $(document.body).setProperty("bgColor", "yellow")
        .set("html", "<h1>Hello, MooTools World!</h1>");
}

window.addEvent("domready", window_domready);
```

The new function body of window_domready() passes the document.body object to the dollar function. Then, by using the setProperty() method, it sets the bgColor attribute to yellow. It then calls the set() method and passes the string "html" as the first parameter to set the second parameter's value as the HTML within the page's body.

Use this code to test your MooTools installation. Open the ch15_examp1_mt.htm file and change it to look like the following code:

```
<!DOCTYPE html PUBLIC "-//W3C//DTD XHTML 1.0 Transitional//EN"
    "http://www.w3.org/TR/xhtml1/DTD/xhtml1-transitional.dtd">

<html xmlns="http://www.w3.org/1999/xhtml">
```

```
<head>
    <title>Chapter 15: Example 2 MooTools</title>
    <script type="text/javascript" src="mootools-1.2.3-core-yc.js"></script>
        <script type="text/javascript">
        function window_domready()
        {
            $(document.body).setProperty("bgColor", "yellow")
                .set("html", "<h1>Hello, MooTools World!</h1>");
        }

        window.addEvent("domready", window_domready);
    </script>
</head>
<body>

</body>
</html>
```

Save this as ch15_examp2_mt.htm. Load it into your browser, and the page should look like Figure 15-3.

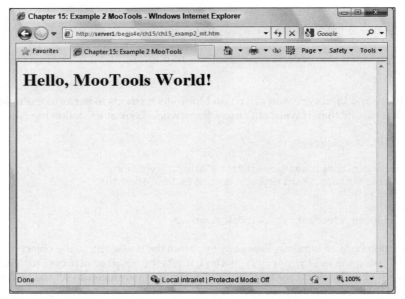

Figure 15-3

If you get the results shown in Figure 15-3, then you've set up MooTools correctly. If not, make sure the MooTools JavaScript file is located in the same directory as your HTML page.

Now that you have jQuery, Prototype, and MooTools installed and working correctly, you can begin to delve deeper into the frameworks to get a better understanding of how you can benefit by using them.

So come, young padawan, and take the crash course on jQuery, Prototype, and MooTools.

Digging Deeper Into jQuery

The code you wrote to test your jQuery installation gave you just a small taste of what the framework is capable of. You saw how easy it was to change property values and add HTML to the page; well, pretty much all operations are about as simple. Whether you're creating HTML elements and appending them to the page or making Ajax calls to the server, jQuery lets you do it in an easy fashion.

jQuery is a DOM-centered framework, and to do any DOM manipulation you first need to locate and retrieve specific elements.

Selecting Elements

The W3C DOM standard gives you the `getElementById()` and `getElementsByTagName()` methods to find and retrieve elements in the DOM. These methods work perfectly fine, but their most obvious drawback is they limit you on how you can select elements. You can either select elements by `id` attribute value or by tag name. There may be times you want to select elements based on their CSS class name or their relationship to other elements.

This is one area where jQuery truly shines; using CSS selectors, you can select elements based on their CSS class name, their relationship with other elements, their `id` attribute value, or simply their tag name. Let's start with something simple like this:

```
$("a")
```

This code selects all `<a/>` elements within the page and returns them in an array. Because it is an array, you can use the `length` property to find out how many elements were selected, like this:

```
alert($("a").length);
```

jQuery was designed to make DOM manipulation easy, and because of this design philosophy, you can make changes to several elements at the same time. For example, you built a web page with over 100 links in the document, and one day you decide you want them to open in a new window by setting the `target` attribute to _blank. That's a tall task to take on, but it is something you can easily achieve with jQuery. Because you can retrieve all `<a/>` elements in the document by calling `$("a")`, you can call the `attr()` method to set the `target` attribute. The following code does this:

```
$("a").attr("target", "_blank");
```

Calling `$("a")` results in a `jQuery` object, but this object also doubles as an array. Any method you call on this particular `jQuery` object will perform the same operation on all elements in the array. By executing this line of code, you set the `target` attribute to _blank on every `<a/>` element in the page, and you didn't even have to use a loop!

The next way you can select elements is with CSS id syntax; that is, the value of an element's id attribute prepended with the pound sign (#). You could use the DOM's `getElementById()` method to perform the same task, but using the jQuery function requires less keystrokes, and you have the benefit of returning a `jQuery` object.

```
$("#myDiv")
```

Even though you know only one element can be selected with this code, you can still use the `length` property to make sure the element was found in the page. If the element wasn't found, `length` will be 0. You can apply the same logic to select elements by their CSS class name. Simply pass the CSS selector to the jQuery function like this:

```
$(".myCssClass")
```

Because jQuery uses CSS selectors to select elements, you can easily select elements based on their hierarchy. Consider the following HTML:

```
<p>
    <div>Div 1</div>
    <div>Div 2</div>
    <span>Span 1</div>
</p>
<span>Span 2</span>
```

This HTML code defines a `<p/>` element that contains two `<div/>` elements and a `<span/>` element. Outside the `<p/>` element is another `<span/>` element. You would have to write several lines of code to identify and retrieve the `<span/>` element inside the `<p/>` element if you use traditional DOM methods and properties. With jQuery, you only need to write one:

```
$("p > span")
```

This line of code uses the `parent > child` CSS selector syntax to select all `<span/>` elements that are children to `<p/>` elements.

Internet Explorer 6 does not natively support this specific CSS selector; however, you would find it still works if you ran this code in that browser. JQuery and other frameworks support a wide array of CSS selectors — even if the selector is not supported by the browser. See the framework's web site for a complete list of supported CSS selectors.

The jQuery function also grants you the ability to use multiple selectors in one function call. Look at the following code as an example:

```
$("a, #myDiv, .myCssClass, p > span")
```

Simply delimit each selector with a comma. This code retrieves all `<a/>` elements, an element with an `id` of myDiv, elements with the CSS class myCssClass, and all `<span/>` children of `<p/>` elements. If you wanted to set the text color of these elements to red, you could simply use the following code:

```
$("a, #myDiv, .myCssClass, p > span").attr("style", "color:red;");
```

This isn't the best way to change an element's style. In fact, jQuery provides you with many methods to alter an element's style.

For a complete list of supported selectors, see `http://docs.jquery.com/Selectors`.

Changing Style

As with the DOM, you change an element's style by changing individual CSS properties or by changing an element's CSS class. To do so, you use the `css()` method. This method can accept two arguments: the property's name and its value.

```
$("#myDiv").css("color", "red");
```

This code sets the `color` property to red, thus making the text's color red. The property names you pass to the `css()` method can be in either style sheet format or in script format. That means if you wanted to change an element's background color, you can pass `background-color` or `backgroundColor` to the method, like this:

```
$("#myDiv").css("background-color", "yellow"); // CORRECT!!!
$("#myDiv").css("backgroundColor", "yellow"); // CORRECT, TOO!!!
```

Typically, though, if you want to change an element's style (that isn't animation-based), it's better to change the element's CSS class instead of the individual style properties. Doing so keeps the style content in the style sheet where it belongs.

Using Multiple CSS classes

The jQuery object exposes several methods to manipulate an element's `className` property. Before looking at them, you should know that it's legal for an element to have multiple CSS classes. Look at the following HTML:

```
<div class="myClass1 myClass2">
    My div with two CSS classes!
</div>
```

To apply two or more CSS classes to an element, simply separate the class names with spaces. In this HTML snippet, the style of two CSS classes are applied to the `<div/>` element: `myClass1` and `myClass2`. This concept is being introduced to you because jQuery's methods to manipulate class names are built around this concept.

The first method, `addClass()`, adds the specified CSS class(es) to the element.

```
$("#myDiv").addClass("myClass1")
    .addClass("myClass2");
```

This code adds the `myClass1` and `myClass2` CSS classes to the element. You can shorten this code by simply passing both class names to the `addClass()` method in one call:

```
$("#myDiv").addClass("myClass1 myClass2");
```

Just make sure you separate the class names with a space. When you want to remove a specific class or classes from the element, use the `removeClass()` method.

```
$("#myDiv").removeClass("myClass2");
```

This code removes the myClass2 CSS class from the element, leaving myClass1 as the only CSS class applied to the element. The arguments passed to the removeClass() method are optional; all CSS classes are removed from the element if you do not pass an argument to the method. The following code removes all CSS classes from the element:

```
$("#myDiv").removeClass();
```

Using the toggleClass Method

The next method is the toggleClass() method. Unlike the previous CSS class methods, this method accepts only one class name. It checks if the specified class is present, and removes it if it is. If the class isn't present, then it adds the class to the element. Look at the following example:

```
$("#myDiv").addClass("myClass1 myClass2")
    .toggleClass("myClass2")
    .toggleClass("myClass2");
```

This code first adds the myClass1 and myClass2 CSS classes to the element. The first toggleClass() call removes myClass2 from the element, and the second call adds it back. This method is handy when you need to add or remove a specific class from the element. For example, the following code is plain old JavaScript and DOM coding to add and remove a specific CSS class depending on the type of event:

```
if (e.type == "mouseover")
{
    eSrc.className = "mouseover";
}
else if (e.type == "mouseout")
{
    eSrc.className = "";
}
```

With the toggleClass() method, you can cut this code down to the following four lines:

```
if (e.type == "mouseover" || e.type == "mouseout")
{
    $(eSrc).toggleClass("mouseover");
}
```

Using the toggleClass() method can make your code more efficient and quicker to download thanks to a reduced size, which is always a noble goal to shoot for.

Using the hasClass Method

The last CSS class method is the hasClass() method, and it returns true or false value depending on if the specified CSS class is applied to the element.

```
$("#myDiv").addClass("myClass1 myClass2")
    .hasClass("myClass1");
```

Like toggleClass(), this method accepts only one class name. In this code, hasClass() returns true because the element does indeed have the myClass1 CSS class applied to it. This example isn't very practical because you know exactly what classes are assigned to the element; it was merely provided to demonstrate how it can be used.

It's important to note that since this method returns `true` *or* `false`, *you cannot chain any more methods after calling it.*

jQuery makes other types of DOM manipulation easy, as you'll see by creating, adding, and removing objects from the DOM.

Creating, Appending, and Removing Elements

Think back to Chapter 12 and how you create and append elements to the page. The following code will refresh your memory:

```
function window_onload()
{
    var a = document.createElement("a");
    a.id = "myLink";
    a.setAttribute("href", "http://jquery.com");
    a.setAttribute("title", "jQuery's Website");

    var text = document.createTextNode("Click to go to jQuery's website");

    a.appendChild(text);
    document.body.appendChild(a);
}

onload = window_onload;
```

This code defines the `window_onload()` function, which is called when the browser completely loads the page. When `window_onload()` executes, it creates an `<a/>` element, assigns it an `id`, and sets the `href` and `title` attributes. Then you create a text node and assign the object to the `text` variable. Finally, you append the text node to the `<a/>` element, and then append the `<a/>` element to the document's `<body/>` element.

Creating Elements

There's technically nothing wrong with this code; it is standard DOM element creation, population, and insertion. However, it is rather long and verbose. You can do the same thing with less typing with jQuery, and the following code shows you how:

```
function document_ready()
{
    var a = $(document.createElement("a"));
    $(document.body).append
    (
        a.attr("id", "myLink")
        .attr("href", "http://jquery.com")
        .attr("title", "jQuery's Website")
        .text("Click here to go to jQuery's website.")
    );
}

$(document).ready(document_ready);
```

Let's break the `document_ready()` function down to get a better understanding of what's taking place. First, you create the `<a/>` element with the `document.createElement()` method.

```
var a = $(document.createElement("a"));
```

Instead of simply assigning the element to a variable, you pass it to the jQuery function so you can use the jQuery methods to populate it with attributes and text. Next, you pass the `document.body` object to the jQuery function and call the `append()` method.

```
$(document.body).append
(
```

Appending Elements

The `append()` method is similar to the DOM `appendChild()` method in that it appends child nodes to the DOM object. The `append()` method accepts a DOM object, a `jQuery` object, or a string containing HTML content. Regardless of what you pass as the parameter to `append()`, it will append the content to the DOM object. In the case of this code, you pass the `jQuery` object that references the `<a/>` element you created earlier, and you assign attributes to the element.

```
a.attr("id", "myLink")
.attr("href", "http://jquery.com")
.attr("title", "jQuery's Website")
```

After you assign the `id`, `href`, and `title` attributes, you then add text to the link, and there are a couple of ways you can do this. You could use the `append()` method and pass the text to it, or you could use the `text()` method. Either method would result in the same outcome, but use `text()` in this case simply because you haven't used it yet.

```
.text("Click here to go to jQuery's website.")
);
```

Remember what makes method chaining possible in jQuery is that most methods return the `jQuery` object you called the method on. So the `text()` method returns the `jQuery` object referencing the `<a/>` element object to the `append()` method called on the `jQuery` object referencing the `document.body` object.

You could rewrite this code in a couple of other ways. First, you could do this:

```
function document_ready()
{
    var a = $(document.createElement("a"))
        .attr("id", "myLink")
        .attr("href", "http://jquery.com")
        .attr("title", "jQuery's Website")
        .text("Click here to go to jQuery's website.");

    $(document.body).append(a);
}
```

This code results in the same outcome, and it's a little bit easier to understand. However, if you wanted to save even more lines, you could do something like the following code:

```
function document_ready()
{
    $(document.body).append($(document.createElement("a"))
        .attr("id", "myLink").attr("href", "http://jquery.com")
        .attr("title", "jQuery's Website")
        .text("Click here to go to jQuery's website."));
}
```

This code certainly is smaller and more compact, and it is the type of code you'd see if you looked at lots of the jQuery-based code out on the Internet (and it's the type of code you'd see your authors write). You do lose some readability, however. The important thing is to code in a manner that you feel comfortable with. Method chaining can get a little confusing if several methods are chained together. For this purpose, the remainder of the code examples will put each method call on a separate line.

Removing Elements

Removing elements from the DOM is also much easier with jQuery than with the traditional DOM methods. Using the latter, you have to find at least two elements in the DOM tree: the element you want to remove and its parent element. With jQuery, you only need to find the element you want to remove and call the remove() method, like this:

```
$("#myLink").remove();
```

This code finds the <a/> element you created in the previous code example and removes it from the DOM. You can also remove all of a parent's child nodes by calling the empty() method.

```
$(document.body).empty();
```

This code empties the <body/> element, thus removing all content from the page.

Most DOM changes you'll make are in response to something the user did, whether it be moving their mouse over a particular element or clicking somewhere on the page. So naturally, you'll have to handle events at some point.

The jQuery Event Model and Handling Events

All jQuery objects expose a method called bind(), which you use to assign event handlers to specific events.

```
function myButton_click(event)
{
    alert("You clicked me!");
}

$("#myButton").bind("click", myButton_click);
```

543

This code assigns the myButton_click() function to handle the click event for an element with an id value of myButton element.

jQuery passes a jQuery.Event object to the function handling the event. Because of the extreme difference between the IE and W3C DOM event models, John Resig, the creator of jQuery, decided to merge both event models into his own, which is based on the W3C event model's Event and MouseEvent objects. That means you do not have to worry about checking for window.event or using any property of the IE event model; the jQuery.Event object provides you the same information as window.event, and you'll use the W3C Mouse and MouseEvent objects' properties to get at that information.

All this means is you have one unified object that works across all supported browsers, to work with events. To demonstrate, you can write something like the following code, and it'll work in every supported browser:

```
function myButton_click(event)
{
    alert(event.target.tagName + " clicked at X:" + event.pageX
        + " and Y:" + event.pageY);
}

$("#myButton").bind("click", myButton_click);
```

Figure 15-4 shows the results of this code in IE, and Figure 15-5 shows the results in Firefox.

Figure 15-4

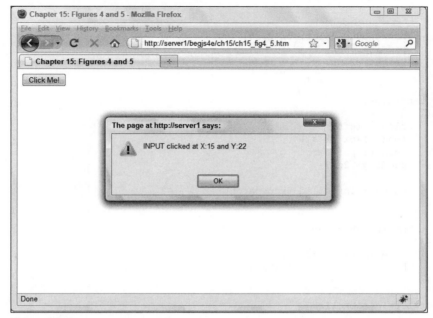

Figure 15-5

Because of the jQuery.Event object, you code using the W3C model, and it simply works in all browsers.

For a complete list of supported events, see jQuery's web site at http://docs.jquery.com/ Events.

Rewriting the DHTML Toolbar with jQuery

You have learned how to retrieve elements in the DOM, change an element's style by adding and removing classes, add and remove elements from the page, and use events with jQuery.

Now you'll put this newfound knowledge to work by refactoring the DHTML toolbar from Chapter 12 (the answer to Chapter 12's second exercise question at the end of the chapter, to be exact).

Try It Out   **Revisiting the Toolbar with jQuery**

Open your text editor and type the following code:

```
<!DOCTYPE html PUBLIC "-//W3C//DTD XHTML 1.0 Transitional//EN"
    "http://www.w3.org/TR/xhtml1/DTD/xhtml1-transitional.dtd">

<html xmlns="http://www.w3.org/1999/xhtml">
<head>
    <title>Chapter 15: Example 3 with jQuery</title>
    <style type="text/css">
```

```css
.tabStrip
{
    background-color: #E4E2D5;
    padding: 3px;
    height: 22px;
}

.tabStrip-tab
{
    float: left;
    font: 14px arial;
    cursor: pointer;
    padding: 2px;

    border: 1px solid transparent;
}

.tabStrip-tab-hover
{
    border-color: #316AC5;
    background-color: #C1D2EE;
}

.tabStrip-tab-click
{
    border-color: #facc5a;
    background-color: #f9e391;
}
</style>
<script type="text/javascript" src="jquery-1.3.2.min.js"></script>
<script type="text/javascript">
var currentNum = 0;
function handleEvent(e)
{
    var el = $(e.target);

    if (e.type == "mouseover" || e.type == "mouseout")
    {
        if (el.hasClass("tabStrip-tab") && !el.hasClass("tabStrip-tab-click"))
        {
            el.toggleClass("tabStrip-tab-hover");
        }
    }

    if (e.type == "click")
    {
        if (el.hasClass("tabStrip-tab-hover"))
        {
            var id = e.target.id;
            var num = id.substr(id.lastIndexOf("-") + 1);

            if (currentNum != num)
            {
```

```
                            deactivateTab();

                            el.toggleClass("tabStrip-tab-hover")
                                .toggleClass("tabStrip-tab-click");
                            showDescription(num);
                            currentNum = num;
                        }
                    }
                }
            }

    function showDescription(num)
    {
        var div = $(document.createElement("div"));

        $("#descContainer").append
        (
            div.attr("id", "tabStrip-desc-" + num)
                .text("Description for tab " + num)
        );
    }

    function deactivateTab()
    {
        var descEl = $("#tabStrip-desc-" + currentNum);

        if (descEl.length > 0)
        {
            descEl.remove();

            $("#tabStrip-tab-"+ currentNum).toggleClass("tabStrip-tab-click");
        }
    }

    $(document).bind("click mouseover mouseout", handleEvent);
    </script>
</head>
<body>
    <div class="tabStrip">
        <div id="tabStrip-tab-1" class="tabStrip-tab">Tab 1</div>
        <div id="tabStrip-tab-2" class="tabStrip-tab">Tab 2</div>
        <div id="tabStrip-tab-3" class="tabStrip-tab">Tab 3</div>
    </div>
    <div id="descContainer"></div>
</body>
</html>
```

Save this as ch15_examp3.htm and feel free to compare it to ch12_q2.htm. Open ch15_examp3.htm in any browser you choose, as long as it's supported by jQuery, and notice that its behavior is identical to that of ch12_q2.htm.

The first major change in this new version is the CSS because jQuery's CSS class methods are more geared to adding and removing CSS classes than simply changing the className property. This ability allows you to layer styles on top of each other; so instead of changing an element's style completely with the `className` property, you simply add or remove a layer of style. This reduces the amount of CSS you have to write.

```css
.tabStrip-tab
{
    float: left;
    font: 14px arial;
    cursor: pointer;
    padding: 2px;
    border: 1px solid transparent;
}

.tabStrip-tab-hover
{
    border-color: #316AC5;
    background-color: #C1D2EE;
}

.tabStrip-tab-click
{
    border-color: #facc5a;
    background-color: #f9e391;
}
```

The first notable change is the removal of the `.tabStrip div` selector, and its style properties were moved to the `tabStrip-tab` class. The second change is that the `tabStrip-tab` class reduces the `padding` to two pixels (down from three pixels), and adds a transparent one-pixel-width border. The final CSS changes were to the `tabStrip-tab-hover` and `tabStrip-tab-click` classes. Formerly, they added a border, changed the background color, and reduced the padding to two pixels. Because `tabStrip-tab` now applies its own border to the element, the hover and click classes only need to change the border and background colors.

Now turn your attention to the JavaScript code. This version of the DHTML toolbar still incorporates the use of the `currentNum` global variable to keep track of the active tab's number.

```javascript
var currentNum = 0;
```

Next is the `handleEvent()` function. Remember in the original version you had to code for both the IE and W3C DOM event models. You don't have to here!

```javascript
function handleEvent(e)
{
    var el = $(e.target);
```

All you need to do is create a jQuery object referencing the `jQuery.Event.target` property — the element that caused the event to occur. Next, you determine if the mouse was moved over or out of an element.

```javascript
    if (e.type == "mouseover" || e.type == "mouseout")
    {
        if (el.hasClass("tabStrip-tab") && !el.hasClass("tabStrip-tab-click"))
        {
            el.toggleClass("tabStrip-tab-hover");
        }
    }
```

This code is also different from the original version of the script. In the original version, you checked for the mouseover and mouseout events separately. You don't have to do that with this new version due to the CSS design change.

You do, however, still need to determine if the element has the tabStrip-tab CSS class as one of its classes to make sure this particular element is a tab in the tab strip. Since the handleEvent() function handles the mouseover, mouseout, and mouseclick events of the document object, these events can fire off any element in the page. You want to make sure the element that caused the event to fire is, in fact, a tab, and you can do so by seeing if the element has the tabStrip-tab CSS class applied to it.

You also want to ensure that the element doesn't have the tabStrip-tab-click CSS class, either. Otherwise, the jQuery toggleClass() method will actually add the tabStrip-tab-hover CSS class when you move your mouse out of an element with the click class applied. So by making sure the tabStrip-tab-click class isn't applied to the element, you can be sure that the tabStrip-tab-hover class will be toggled correctly; it'll be added when you move your mouse pointer over the element, and it will be removed when your pointer leaves the element.

Now look at what happens when you click your mouse on a tab.

```
if (e.type == "click")
{
    if (el.hasClass("tabStrip-tab-hover"))
    {
        var id = e.target.id;
        var num = id.substr(id.lastIndexOf("-") + 1);

        if (currentNum != num)
        {
            deactivateTab();
```

Not much new happens here. A new variable, id, is declared and assigned the event target's id. This change is primarily a convenience, as id is easier to type than e.target.id. The next lines are relatively the same:

```
        el.toggleClass("tabStrip-tab-hover")
            .toggleClass("tabStrip-tab-click");

        showDescription(num);
        currentNum = num;
        }
    }
}
```

The only thing different here is the change to use jQuery's toggleClass() method two times. The first toggleClass() call removes the tabStrip-tab-hover CSS class, and the second call adds the tabStrip-tab-click CSS class to the element.

The code in showDescription() completely changed, even though it performs the same operations of creating a <div/> element, giving it text, and appending it to the <div/> element with an id of descContainer.

```
function showDescription(num)
{
    var div = $(document.createElement("div"));

    $("#descContainer").append
    (
```

```
        div.attr("id", "tabStrip-desc-" + num)
            .text("Description for tab " + num)
    );
}
```

Using jQuery objects to perform these operations cuts down on the amount of code you have to write, which is also evident with the following deactivateTab() function:

```
function deactivateTab()
{
    var descEl = $("#tabStrip-desc-" + currentNum);

    if (descEl.length > 0)
    {
```

The first line uses the jQuery function to select the <div/> element containing the tab's description. You then use the length property to make sure jQuery found an element. Doing so ensures you won't try to remove a nonexistent object from the DOM, which would result in an error.

If an element was found, then you use jQuery's remove() method to remove the element from the DOM as follows:

```
        descEl.remove();

        $("#tabStrip-tab-"+ currentNum).toggleClass("tabStrip-tab-click");
    }
}
```

You then select the active tab's <div/> element and remove the tabStrip-tab-click CSS class with the toggleClass() method.

Finally, you assign the handleEvent() function to handle the mouseover, mouseout, and click events on the document object. The following code does this:

```
$(document).bind("click mouseover mouseout", handleEvent);
```

As you can see from this example, jQuery can make DOM manipulation much easier and requires less typing from you. In this particular example, you wrote 28 less lines of CSS and JavaScript. That's well worth the time of learning a framework, isn't it?!

DOM manipulation isn't the only area in which a framework such as jQuery can help you. In fact, it can greatly reduce the amount of work you have to do to make XMLHttpRequest objects and requests.

Using jQuery for Ajax

The previous chapter walked you through the creation of a module to enable you to create and use XMLHttpRequest objects to retrieve data from the web server. The module you created certainly made Ajax requests easier to code, but Ajax requests are even easier with jQuery.

Understanding the jQuery Function

The jQuery function ($()) is the doorway into all things jQuery, and you've used it quite a bit throughout this chapter. However, there are other uses for this function. It was mentioned only once in this book, and it was as an aside comment, but functions are objects, too. If you look back at the end of Chapter 5, you created your own objects and reference types. When you did so, you used the prototype object, which is a property of the Function object.

Just like all other objects, you access a Function object's properties and methods using the object.property or object.method() syntax. As such, jQuery's Ajax functionality is provided by methods of the $ function object. For example, to make a request to the server, you use the get() method, as the following code shows:

```
$.get("textFile.txt");
```

This code makes a request to the server to retrieve the textFile.txt text file, but it isn't useful, as you can't do anything with the data you retrieved. So like the HttpRequest module you built in the previous chapter, the $.get() method lets you assign a callback function that is called when the request successfully contacts the server and retrieves your specified data.

```
function get_callBack(data, status)
{
    alert(data);
}

$.get("textFile.txt", get_callBack);
```

This code adds a function called get_callBack(), which jQuery calls on a successful request. When jQuery executes an Ajax callback function, it passes two parameters to it. The first, data, is the data you requested from the server. The second, status, is the status of the request. Because jQuery only calls the callback function on a successful request, status is always "success".

Many developers forego using the second status *parameter, because it's only possible value at this time is* success. *You can forego it as well.*

Using jQuery's Ajax Event Handling

jQuery's Ajax event handling is quite different from what you might expect. There are local events (that is, events of a specific request object) and global Ajax events. Global events are easier to use, and you can use them to add UI cues to enhance the user's experience. You set the global events to fire on any valid DOM object. One specific global event is the ajaxError event, and you set it to call an event handler with the jQuery object's ajaxError() method, or you can use the bind() method. The following code demonstrates the use of the ajaxError() method:

```
function request_ajaxError(event, request, settings)
{
    alert("An Ajax error occurred.");
}

$(document).ajaxError(request_ajaxError);
```

Ajax event handlers are passed the following three parameters:

❑   An `event` object that has information about the event.

❑   The `XMLHttpRequest` object that is used to make the request.

❑   An object containing the settings used for the request. With the `settings` object, you can retrieve the URL of the request, its HTTP method, whether or not the request was sent in asynchronous mode, and much more.

You can build some pretty thorough error messages between the `request` and `settings` parameters.

Visit `http://docs.jquery.com/Ajax` *for a complete list of Ajax events.*

Remember the examples from the previous chapter? You created a form that checked if user names and e-mail addresses were available using Ajax, and you sent those values to the server as parameters in the URL. For example, when you wanted to test a user name, you used the `username` parameter, like this:

```
phpformvalidator.php?username=jmcpeak
```

With the `$.get()` method, you can do the same thing by passing an object containing the key/value pairs to the method.

```
var parms = new Object();
parms.username = "jmcpeak";

function get_callBack(data, status)
{
    alert(data);
}

$.get("phpformvalidator.php", parms, get_callBack);
```

In this code, you create a new object called `parms` and add the `username` property to the object, assigning it the value of `jmcpeak`. You then write the `get_callBack()` function, and afterwards, you call `$.get()` and pass the URL, the `parms` object, and the callback function.

Sending Multiple Parameters

You can send multiple parameters to the URL by simply adding more properties to the object, like this:

```
var parms = new Object();
parms.username = "jwmcpeak";
parms.email = "someone@xyz.com";
```

You can send as many parameters you want or need in a single request.

By default, the `$.get()` method sends requests in asynchronous mode, and in most cases, this is desired. However, you may find situations, like the answer to Question 2 in Chapter 14, where you want to use synchronous communication. You cannot specify what type of communication mode you want to use with

`$.get()`, but jQuery does provide the `$.ajaxSetup()` method. This method accepts an object containing a number of properties to set options that affects all Ajax requests. One such option is the `async` option.

```
var options = new Object();
options.async = false;

$.ajaxSetup(options);
```

This code sets all Ajax calls to use synchronous mode. Again, only set this option to `false` when you absolutely need it. Most (about 99.9 percent) of the time, you want to use asynchronous communication.

Let's revisit the form validator script using `XMLHttpRequest` from the previous chapter, and you'll replace the HttpRequest module code with the Ajax capabilities of jQuery.

The `$.get()` method is quite simple to use and provides basic functionality. jQuery offers much more advanced, low-level Ajax functionality, and you can find out more at `http://docs.jquery.com/Ajax`.

Try It Out   Revisiting the Form Validator

Open your text editor and type the following code:

```
<!DOCTYPE HTML PUBLIC "-//W3C//DTD HTML 4.01//EN"
    "http://www.w3.org/TR/html4/strict.dtd">
<html>
<head>
    <title>Chapter 15: Example 4 with jQuery</title>
    <style type="text/css">
        .fieldname
        {
            text-align: right;
        }

        .submit
        {
            text-align: right;
        }
    </style>
    <script type="text/javascript" src="jquery-1.3.2.min.js"></script>
    <script type="text/javascript">
    function checkUsername()
    {
        var userValue = $("#username").val();

        if (userValue == "")
        {
            alert("Please enter a user name to check!");
            return;
        }

        var parms = new Object();
```

```
        parms.username = userValue;

        $.get("formvalidator.php", parms, checkUsername_callBack);
}

function checkUsername_callBack(data, status)
{
        var userValue = $("#username").val();

        if (data == "available")
        {
                alert("The username " + userValue + " is available!");
        }
        else
        {
                alert("We're sorry, but " + userValue + " is not available.");
        }
}

function checkEmail()
{
        var emailValue = $("#email").val();

        if (emailValue == "")
        {
                alert("Please enter an email address to check!");
                return;
        }

        var parms = new Object();
        parms.email = emailValue;

        $.get("formvalidator.php", parms, checkEmail_callBack);
}

function checkEmail_callBack(data, status)
{
        var emailValue = $("#email").val();

        if (data == "available")
        {
                alert("The email " + emailValue + " is currently not in use!");
        }
        else
        {
                alert("I'm sorry, but " + emailValue + " is in use by another user.");
        }
}

function request_error(event, request, settings)
{
        alert("An error occurred with the following URL:\n"
                + settings.url +".\nStatus code: " + request.status);
}

$(document).ajaxError(request_error);
```

```html
            </script>
    </head>
    <body>
        <form>
            <table>
                <tr>
                    <td class="fieldname">
                        Username:
                    </td>
                    <td>
                        <input type="text" id="username" />
                    </td>
                    <td>
                        <a href="javascript: checkUsername()">Check Availability</a>
                    </td>
                </tr>
                <tr>
                    <td class="fieldname">
                        Email:
                    </td>
                    <td>
                        <input type="text" id="email" />
                    </td>
                    <td>
                        <a href="javascript: checkEmail()">Check Availability</a>
                    </td>
                </tr>
                <tr>
                    <td class="fieldname">
                        Password:
                    </td>
                    <td>
                        <input type="text" id="password" />
                    </td>
                    <td />
                </tr>
                <tr>
                    <td class="fieldname">
                        Verify Password:
                    </td>
                    <td>
                        <input type="text" id="password2" />
                    </td>
                    <td />
                </tr>
                <tr>
                    <td colspan="2" class="submit">
                        <input type="submit" value="Submit" />
                    </td>
                    <td />
                </tr>
            </table>
        </form>
    </body>
</html>
```

Save this as `ch15_examp4.htm` in your web server's root directory. Like the examples using `XMLHttpRequest` in the previous chapter, this file must be hosted on a web server in order to work correctly. Open your web browser to `http://yourserver/ch15_examp4.htm`. Type **jmcpeak** into the `Username` field and click the Check Availability link next to it. You'll see an alert box telling you the user name is taken.

Now type **someone@xyz.com** in the `Email` field and click the Check Availability link next to it. Again, you'll be greeted with an alert box stating that the e-mail is already in use. Now input your own user name and e-mail into these fields and click the appropriate links. Chances are an alert box will tell you that your user name and/or e-mail is available (the user names `jmcpeak` and `pwilton` and the e-mails `someone@xyz.com` and `someone@zyx.com` are the only ones used by the application).

This page works exactly like `validate_form.htm` from Chapter 14 does, and the code is the same for the most part.

The first change is the removal of `httprequest.js` and the inclusion of the jQuery JavaScript file `jquery-1.3.2.min.js`.

The second change is located in the `checkUsername()` function.

```
function checkUsername()
{
    var userValue = $("#username").val();

    if (userValue == "")
    {
        alert("Please enter a user name to check!");
        return;
    }
```

The first line retrieves the `Username` text box's value by selecting the element and calling the `val()` method. The `val()` method retrieves the `value` property `<input/>` elements. You then check to make sure the user input something into the text box and politely ask them to enter a user name if they did not.

Next, you make the following request:

```
    var parms = new Object();
    parms.username = userValue;

    $.get("formvalidator.php", parms, checkUsername_callBack);
}
```

You first create an object called `parms` and create a `username` property. You pass this object to the `$.get()` method, along with the URL and the name of the function to call back.

Upon a successful request, jQuery calls the `checkUsername_callBack()` function. The parameters to this function changed to reflect the two parameters that jQuery passes the function upon a successful request.

```
function checkUsername_callBack(data, status)
{
    var userValue = $("#username").val();

    if (data == "available")
    {
        alert("The username " + userValue + " is available!");
    }
```

```
    else
    {
        alert("We're sorry, but " + userValue + " is not available.");
    }
}
```

Other than the parameters, the only change to this function is the use of the val() method to retrieve the textbox's value. Everything else remains the same; the function compares the data returned from the server and displays a message to the user telling them the results of the user name query.

The changes to checkEmail() resemble those made to checkUsername().

```
function checkEmail()
{
    var emailValue = $("#email").val();

    if (emailValue == "")
    {
        alert("Please enter an email address to check!");
        return;
    }

    var parms = new Object();
    parms.email = emailValue;

    $.get("formvalidator.php", parms, checkEmail_callBack);
}
```

You use the jQuery function to select the Email text box and retrieve its value with the val() method. You then determine if the user entered data, and ask them to do so if they didn't. Next, you create the parms object, create and assign a value to the email property, and make the request with the $.get() method.

On a successful request, the checkEmail_callBack() function executes, and the changes to this function mirror that of checkUsername_callBack().

```
function checkEmail_callBack(data, status)
{
    var emailValue = $("#email").val();

    if (data == "available")
    {
        alert("The email " + emailValue + " is currently not in use!");
    }
    else
    {
        alert("I'm sorry, but " + emailValue + " is in use by another user.");
    }
}
```

In case an Ajax error occurs, you register an Ajax event handler for the ajaxError event. The event handler function is called ajax_error(), and it displays an error message to the user. Its definition follows:

```
function ajax_error(event, request, settings)
{
```

```
      alert("An error occurred with the following URL:\n"
          + settings.url +".\nStatus code: " + request.status);
}

$(document).ajaxError(ajax_error);
```

The message tells the user that an error occurred, what the URL of the request was, and the HTTP status code the server returned. With this information, you can begin to debug the error if one should arise.

―――――――――――

jQuery is an extensive framework, and providing in-depth coverage and information requires more than this section can provide. However, the jQuery documentation is quite good, and you can view it at http://docs.jquery.com. jQuery's web site also lists a variety of tutorials, so don't forget to check them out at http://docs.jquery.com/Tutorials. The inclusion of its effects/animation components and the optional UI library makes jQuery a very versatile framework.

Diving into Prototype

jQuery is probably the most popular framework today, but that crown used to sit upon Prototype's head. Unlike jQuery, Prototype's focus is augmenting the way you program with JavaScript by providing classes and inheritance. It does, however, also provide a robust set of tools for working with the DOM and Ajax support.

You were briefly introduced to Prototype, so let's dive a little deeper into this library and see what it can do for you with cross-browser scripting.

Retrieving Elements

When testing your Prototype installation, you were introduced to the dollar function $(). This function is different from the jQuery function in that it simply extends the element you want to retrieve by adding many new methods. If you pass an element's id value, then it retrieves that element and extends it with more methods and properties.

```
$("myDiv")
```

This code retrieves the element with an id of myDiv from the DOM and extends it. So you can use this extended object just like you would any other Element object, like this:

```
alert($("myDiv").tagName);
```

You can also pass it an Element object, which results in an extended version of that element. The following code passes the document.body object to the dollar function:

```
$(document.body)
```

By doing this, you can use both native DOM methods and properties as well as the methods provided by Prototype.

Prototype's dollar function returns null *if the specified element cannot be found. This is unlike jQuery's* $() *function because Prototype returns an extended DOM element object; even though it is extended, it is still a DOM element object.*

Selecting Elements With CSS Selectors

Another difference between Prototype's dollar function and jQuery's $() function is that it does not accept CSS selectors; it only accepts element id values and Element objects. Prototype does, however, have another function that behaves similarly to jQuery's $() function, and that is the $$() function.

You can pass several selector types to the $$() function to locate and retrieve elements that match the selector. For example, the following code retrieves all <div/> elements in the page and returns them in an array, so you can use the length property:

```
$$("div")
```

The $$() function always returns an array, so even if you use an id selector, you'll get an array with one element in it if the element is found. One downside to the double dollar function is that it returns an array of extended elements. If you want to perform an operation on every element in the array, you have to either loop through them or iterate over them with the Prototype-provided each() method.

Performing an Operation on Elements Selected With $$()

The each() method is similar to the new Array.every() method you learned about in Chapter 5. It accepts a function as a parameter and executes that function on every element in the array. The following code demonstrates this:

```
function insertText(item)
{
    item.insert("This text inserted using the each() method.");
}

$$("div").each(insertText);
```

The jQuery *object also has an* each() *method that performs the same function.*

You can use several CSS selector types to select elements with the double dollar function, and you can select elements based upon multiple selectors, although it is different from how you did it with jQuery.

```
$$("#myDiv", "p > span, .myCssClass");
```

Instead of passing one string with commas separating each selector, you pass multiple strings with each string containing one selector. Once you retrieve an element (or elements), you can then begin to manipulate them, such as changing their style.

For more information on the CSS selector supported in Prototype, see http://www.prototypejs.org/api/utility/dollar-dollar.

Manipulating Style

Prototype provides you several methods to change an element's style, and they are not unlike those found in the jQuery framework.

The `setStyle()` method lets you set individual style properties. To set style in this way, you must create an object, and create properties for this object whose names are those of CSS properties. For example, the following code sets an element's text color to red and underlines it:

```
var styles = new Object();
styles.color = "red";
styles.textDecoration = "underline";

$("myDiv").setStyle(styles);
```

As previously mentioned in the jQuery section, changing an element's style in this manner is undesirable because style should be defined in the page's style sheet. A better alternative is to manipulate an element's CSS class, and Prototype allows you to easily do that with the `addClassName()`, `removeClassName()`, `toggleClassName()`, and `hasClassName()` methods.

The first method, `addClassName()`, adds a CSS class name to the element. Simply pass the class name to the method, and it is applied to the element.

```
$("myDiv").addClassName("someClass");
```

The second method, `removeClassName()`, removes the specified class from the element. The following code adds a class name and then removes it:

```
$("myDiv").addClassName("someClass")
    .removeClassName("someClass");
```

This code isn't very practical, but it demonstrates how both methods are used. Next is the `toggleClassName()` method. This method checks if the specified class is applied to the element and removes it if so. If the class name isn't found, then it applies the class to the element.

```
$("myDiv").hasClassName("someClass");
$("myDiv").toggleClassName("someClass");
$("myDiv").hasClassName("someClass");
```

This code demonstrates the `toggleClassName()` method and the fourth method: `hasClassName()`. The first line of code checks if the `someClass` CSS class is applied to the element. Since it's not, this method returns `false`. The second line calls the `toggleClassName()` method, which adds the `someClass` CSS class to the element. The final line calls `hasClassName()` again, which now returns `true` since `someClass` was added in the previous line.

These CSS methods closely resemble those of jQuery. However, other types of DOM manipulation such as creating and inserting elements are areas where Prototype differs greatly from jQuery. However, as you'll soon see, removing DOM objects is very similar.

Creating, Inserting, and Removing Elements

Manipulating the DOM with Prototype is a simple process. The framework extends the `Element` object and allows you to create an element using a constructor, populate it with data, and remove it from the DOM.

Creating an Element

The `Element` object's constructor accepts two arguments: the tag name and an object containing attributes and their values. The following code demonstrates creating an `<a/>` element and adds it to the document's body:

```
var attributes = new Object();
attributes.id = "myLink";
attributes.href = "http://www.prototypejs.org";
attributes.target = "_blank";

var a = new Element("a", attributes);
```

The first few lines of this code create an object called `attributes`. You create the `id`, `href`, and `target` properties and assign their values. You then create an `<a/>` element by using the `Element` object's constructor. You pass the string `"a"` as the first parameter and the `attributes` object as the second.

Inserting an Element

The `update()` and `insert()` methods both add content to the `Element` object. The difference is `update()` replaces all existing content while `insert()` simply adds the content to the existing content. Both methods can accept a string value, containing simple text or HTML, or an `Element` object.

The following code creates the `<a/>` element from the previous code example, adds content to it, and inserts it into the page:

```
var attributes = new Object();
attributes.id = "myLink";
attributes.href = "http://www.prototypejs.org";
attributes.target = "_blank";

var a = new Element("a", attributes).update("Go to Prototype's Website");
$(document.body).insert(a);
```

This code calls the `update()` method, which replaces the element's existing content with the new content as specified by the data passed to it (in this example, there was no existing content). Because the `update()` method returns the `Element` object you created, you assign the object to the variable a, which you then pass to the `insert()` method of the `document.body` object.

Removing an Element

Removing elements from the DOM is even easier, and in fact is the same as in jQuery. You first find the element you want to remove from the DOM and then call the `remove()` method.

```
$("myLink").remove();
```

This code finds the element with an `id` of `myLink` and removes it from the DOM. There's no need to find the element's parent and call the `removeChild()` method.

Using Events

When you extend an `Element` object with the dollar sign function, you gain access to the `observe()` method, which registers an event handler on a DOM element. This method accepts two arguments: the name of the event to observe for and the function to call when the event fires.

```
function myDiv_click(event)
{
    // do something
}

$("myDiv").observe("click", myDiv_click);
```

This code registers the `myDiv_click()` function to handle the click event on the element with an `id` of `myDiv`. This isn't the only way to assign event handlers; you can use the `Event.observe()` method, too. The following code writes the previous code using `Event.observe()`:

```
function myDiv_click(event)
{
    // do something
}

Event.observe("myDiv", "click", myDiv_click);
```

The first argument to `Event.observe()` can be a string value containing an element's `id`, or a BOM/DOM object you want to assign an event handler to, like `window` or `document`. This method is particularly useful for objects like `window`; you cannot pass `window` to the dollar function and use the `observe()` method because the browser will throw an error. Instead, you have to use `Event.observe()`.

Unlike jQuery, Prototype doesn't emulate the W3C DOM event model. In fact, it doesn't aim to create a separate, unifying event model at all. Instead, it extends the `event` objects of both browsers and gives you a set of utility methods to obtain the information you want to acquire.

These methods are of the extended browser's `Event` object. For example, the `element()` method accepts an IE or W3C event object as a parameter and returns the value of the `srcElement` and `target` properties for IE and W3C DOM browsers, respectively.

For example, the following code gets the element that fired the event and toggles a CSS class called `someClass`:

```
function myDiv_click(event)
{
    var eSrc = event.element();
    eSrc.toggleClassName("someClass");
}

$("myDiv").observe("click", myDiv_click);
```

In order for this to work properly, the parameter your event handling function accepts needs to be called `event`. That way, IE's `window.event` object is referenced when you call the `element()` method as well as the `event` object passed to the function by W3C DOM browsers.

Rewriting the DHTML Toolbar with Prototype

You now know how to retrieve elements, change an element's style, add and remove elements from the DOM, and wire up events, and get the element that fired the event with Prototype. Let's apply that knowledge and rewrite the DHML toolbar.

Try It Out   Revisiting the Toolbar with Prototype

Open your text editor and type the following:

```
<!DOCTYPE html PUBLIC "-//W3C//DTD XHTML 1.0 Transitional//EN"
    "http://www.w3.org/TR/xhtml1/DTD/xhtml1-transitional.dtd">

<html xmlns="http://www.w3.org/1999/xhtml">
<head>
    <title>Chapter 15: Example 5 with Prototype</title>
    <style type="text/css">
    .tabStrip
    {
        background-color: #E4E2D5;
        padding: 3px;
        height: 22px;
    }

    .tabStrip-tab
    {
        float: left;
        font: 14px arial;
        cursor: pointer;
        padding: 2px;
        border: 1px solid transparent;
    }

    .tabStrip-tab-hover
    {
        border-color: #316AC5;
        background-color: #C1D2EE;
    }

    .tabStrip-tab-click
    {
        border-color: #facc5a;
        background-color: #f9e391;
    }
    </style>
    <script type="text/javascript" src="prototype-1.6.0.3.js"></script>
    <script type="text/javascript">
var currentNum = 0;
```

```
function handleEvent(event)
{
    var el = event.element();

    if (event.type == "mouseover" || event.type == "mouseout")
    {
        if (el.hasClassName("tabStrip-tab") &&
            !el.hasClassName("tabStrip-tab-click"))
        {
            el.toggleClassName("tabStrip-tab-hover");
        }
    }

    if (event.type == "click")
    {
        if (el.hasClassName("tabStrip-tab-hover"))
        {
            var id = el.id;
            var num = id.substr(id.lastIndexOf("-") + 1);

            if (currentNum != num)
            {
                deactivateTab();

                el.toggleClassName("tabStrip-tab-hover")
                    .toggleClassName("tabStrip-tab-click");
                showDescription(num);
                currentNum = num;
            }
        }
    }
}

function showDescription(num)
{
    var attributes = new Object();
    attributes.id = "tabStrip-desc-" + num;

    var div = new Element("div", attributes)
        .update("Description for tab " + num);

    $("descContainer").update(div);
}

function deactivateTab()
{
    var currentTab = $("tabStrip-tab-"+ currentNum);

    if (currentTab)
    {
        currentTab.toggleClassName("tabStrip-tab-click");
    }
```

```
        }

    $(document).observe("click", handleEvent);
    $(document).observe("mouseover", handleEvent);
    $(document).observe("mouseout", handleEvent);
    </script>
</head>
<body>
    <div class="tabStrip">
        <div id="tabStrip-tab-1" class="tabStrip-tab">Tab 1</div>
        <div id="tabStrip-tab-2" class="tabStrip-tab">Tab 2</div>
        <div id="tabStrip-tab-3" class="tabStrip-tab">Tab 3</div>
    </div>
    <div id="descContainer"></div>
</body>
</html>
```

Save this file as `ch15_examp5.htm` and load it into your browser. You'll notice it behaves the same as Chapter 12's Question 2 answer, and as the rewritten version with jQuery.

Because the CSS and markup remains unchanged from `ch15_examp3.htm` (the jQuery version), you'll focus on the JavaScript functions and how they changed, and you'll start with the `handleEvent()` function.

```
function handleEvent(event)
{
    var el = event.element();
```

The first thing to notice about this function is the parameter's name being changed to `event`. You did this for the purpose of calling the `element()` method. Had you used another name for the parameter, you would need to determine the user's browser and call the `element()` method on the `window.event` object and the W3C event object. In other words, it would require more work from you, and look like the cross-browser version in Chapter 12.

Next, you determine the type of event that took place. You first check for `mouseover` and `mouseout` events.

```
if (event.type == "mouseover" || event.type == "mouseout")
{
    if (el.hasClassName("tabStrip-tab") &&
        !el.hasClassName("tabStrip-tab-click"))
    {
```

If either of these events take place, you have to check whether or not the element that fired the event is a tab in the tab strip. To do that, you determine if the element has the `tabStrip-tab` class name with the `hasClassName()` method. You also need to make sure the element does not have the `tabStrip-tab-click` class name. Failing to do so would result in improper style changes.

If the element meets all your requirements, then toggle the `tabStrip-tab-hover` class name.

```
        el.toggleClassName("tabStrip-tab-hover");
    }
}
```

Use the `toggleClassName()` method to perform that task. Now when you move your mouse pointer over a tab element, the `tabStrip-tab-hover` class will be applied to the element. When you move your mouse pointer off the element, your code removes the hover class and returns the element to its original state.

Next, determine if the `click` event fired, and if so, determine if the element has the `tabStrip-tab-hover` class.

```
if (event.type == "click")
{
    if (el.hasClassName("tabStrip-tab-hover"))
    {
```

If so, then you know that this element should change its style to that of a clicked tab. To start this process, get the number associated with this particular tab element.

```
var id = el.id;
var num = id.substr(id.lastIndexOf("-") + 1);
```

To do this, you get the element's `id` value and use the `substr()` method to retrieve all the text after the last hyphen and assign the result of `substr()` to the `num` variable.

Next, you determine if the element clicked is a different one in the tab strip by comparing `num` to `currentNum`.

```
if (currentNum != num)
{
    deactivateTab();
```

If it is a different tab element, then you call the `deactivateTab()` function. Then you use the `toggleClassName()` method to remove the `tabStrip-tab-hover` class and add the `tabStrip-tab-click` class to the element.

```
el.toggleClassName("tabStrip-tab-hover")
    .toggleClassName("tabStrip-tab-click");
```

You then call the `showDescription()` function, passing it the value of the element's number. You then assign the `currentNum` variable the value contained within the `num` variable. Doing so tells your script that this new tab element is the currently active tab.

```
showDescription(num);
currentNum = num;
                }
            }
        }
    }
```

Now look at the `showDescription()` function, which adds the tab's description to the page. The first thing you do in this function is create the `attributes` object and then create an `id` property.

```
function showDescription(num)
{
    var attributes = new Object();
    attributes.id = "tabStrip-desc-" + num;
```

Then you create the new <div/> element by using the Element object's constructor. You specify that you want to create a <div/> element and you pass the attributes object. After the constructor call, you chain a call to the update() method, giving the element some text.

```
var div = new Element("div", attributes)
    .update("Description for tab " + num);
```

The final step of this function is to add the element to the page. Do so with the update() method.

```
$("descContainer").update(div);
}
```

Using the update() method here means you do not have to remove the currently displaying description in deactivateTab() because the update() method removes all preexisting content and replaces it with the content you pass to the method.

Because you use the update() method in showDescription(), you simplify the function body of deactivateTab().

```
function deactivateTab()
{
    var currentTab = $("tabStrip-tab-"+ currentNum);

    if (currentTab)
    {
        currentTab.toggleClassName("tabStrip-tab-click");
    }
}
```

You first attempt to retrieve the currently active tab element by its id. If it can be found in the document, then the code within the if block executes and removes the tabStrip-tab-click class from the element. If the element cannot be found in the document, then currentTab is null and the function exits without doing anything else.

Like jQuery, Prototype isn't just about DOM manipulation and language enhancement. It, too, provides you with Ajax capabilities that are easy to learn and use.

Using Ajax Support

The Ajax support in Prototype isn't as straightforward as the high-level $.get() method in jQuery. Prototype's Ajax functionality centers on its Ajax object, which contains a variety of methods you can use to make Ajax calls. This object is much like the native Math object in that you do not create an instance of the Ajax object; you simply use the methods made available by the object.

At the heart of the Ajax object is the Ajax.Request() constructor. This constructor accepts two arguments: the first being the URL to make the request to and the second an object containing a set of options that the object uses when making a request. The `options` object can contain a variety of option properties to alter the behavior of `Ajax.Request()`; the following table describes just a few of them.

Option	Description
asynchronous	Determines whether the XMLHttpRequest object makes the request in asynchronous mode or not. The default is true.
method	The HTTP method used for the request. The default is "post". "get" is another valid value.
onSuccess	A callback function invoked when the request completes successfully.
onFailure	A callback function invoked when the request completes, but results in an error status code.
parameters	Either a string containing the parameters to send with the request, or an object containing the parameters and their values.

For a complete list of options, visit the Prototype documentation at `http://www.prototypejs.org/api/ajax/options`.

All callback functions are executed and passed a parameter containing the XMLHttpRequest object used to make the request. Making a request with Prototype looks something like the following code:

```
function request_onsuccess(request)
{
    alert(request.responseText);
}

function request_onfailure(request)
{
    alert("An error occurred! HTTP status code is " + request.status);
}

var options = new Object();
options.method = "get";
options.onSuccess = request_onsuccess;
options.onFailure = request_onfailure;

new Ajax.Request("someTextFile.txt", options);
```

The first few lines of code define the `request_onsuccess()` and `request_onfailure()` functions. These functions all accept one parameter called `request`. The value of this parameter will be the XMLHttpRequest object used to make the request.

Prototype actually passes an `Ajax.Response` *object to all Ajax request callbacks. It is very similar to the* XMLHttpRequest *object and adds extra functionality. To access the* XMLHttpRequest *object directly, use the* transport *property; for example,* `request.transport`. *After the function definition, you create an* options *object The first option you set is the method option, which you set to* get. *The next option is the* onSuccess *option, and you assign the* `request_onsuccess()` *function to this option. The final option is* onFailure, *which you assign the* `request_onfailure()` *function.*

Once all preparation is made, you finally make the request for the `someTextFile.txt` file, and you pass the `options` object to the `Ajax.Request()` constructor (don't forget the `new` keyword!!).

If you need to send parameters with your request, you'll have to do a bit more preparation before calling `new Ajax.Request()`. Like jQuery, you can create an object whose property names match those of the parameter names. For example, if your URL requires you to pass two parameters named `name` and `state`, you can do something like the following code:

```
var parms = new Object();
parms.name = "Jeremy";
parms.state = "Texas";

options.parameters = parms;
```

By adding parameters and then calling `new Ajax.Request()`, the parameters are added to the URL before the request is sent to the server.

Now that you've been given a crash course in Prototype's Ajax function, alter the form validator script from Chapter 14 to use Prototype instead of the HttpRequest module.

Try It Out   **Revisiting the Form Validator with Prototype**

Open your text editor and type the following:

```
<!DOCTYPE HTML PUBLIC "-//W3C//DTD HTML 4.01//EN"
    "http://www.w3.org/TR/html4/strict.dtd">
<html>
<head>
    <title>Chapter 15: Example 6 with jQuery</title>
    <style type="text/css">
        .fieldname
        {
            text-align: right;
        }

        .submit
        {
            text-align: right;
        }
    </style>
    <script type="text/javascript" src="prototype-1.6.0.3.js"></script>
    <script type="text/javascript">
    function checkUsername()
    {
        var userValue = $F("username");

        if (userValue == "")
        {
            alert("Please enter a user name to check!");
            return;
        }

        var parms = new Object();
```

```
        parms.username = userValue;

        var options = getBasicOptions();
        options.onSuccess = checkUsername_callBack;
        options.parameters = parms;

        new Ajax.Request("formvalidator.php", options);
    }

    function checkUsername_callBack(request)
    {
        var userValue = $F("username");

        if (request.responseText == "available")
        {
            alert("The username " + userValue + " is available!");
        }
        else
        {
            alert("We're sorry, but " + userValue + " is not available.");
        }
    }

    function checkEmail()
    {
        var emailValue = $F("email");

        if (emailValue == "")
        {
            alert("Please enter an email address to check!");
            return;
        }

        var parms = new Object();
        parms.email = emailValue;

        var options = getBasicOptions();
        options.onSuccess = checkEmail_callBack;
        options.parameters = parms;

        new Ajax.Request("formvalidator.php", options);
    }

    function checkEmail_callBack(request)
    {
        var emailValue = $F("email");

        if (request.responseText == "available")
        {
            alert("The email " + emailValue + " is currently not in use!");
        }
        else
        {
```

```
                    alert("I'm sorry, but " + emailValue + " is in use by another user.");
            }
    }

    function request_onfailure(request)
    {
        alert("An error occurred. HTTP Status Code: " + request.status);
    }

    function getBasicOptions()
    {
        var options = new Object();
        options.method = "get";
        options.onFailure = request_onfailure;

        return options;
    }
    </script>
</head>
<body>
    <form>
        <table>
            <tr>
                <td class="fieldname">
                    Username:
                </td>
                <td>
                    <input type="text" id="username" />
                </td>
                <td>
                    <a href="javascript: checkUsername()">Check Availability</a>
                </td>
            </tr>
            <tr>
                <td class="fieldname">
                    Email:
                </td>
                <td>
                    <input type="text" id="email" />
                </td>
                <td>
                    <a href="javascript: checkEmail()">Check Availability</a>
                </td>
            </tr>
            <tr>
                <td class="fieldname">
                    Password:
                </td>
                <td>
                    <input type="text" id="password" />
                </td>
                <td />
            </tr>
            <tr>
```

```
                    <td class="fieldname">
                        Verify Password:
                    </td>
                    <td>
                        <input type="text" id="password2" />
                    </td>
                    <td />
                </tr>
                <tr>
                    <td colspan="2" class="submit">
                        <input type="submit" value="Submit" />
                    </td>
                    <td />
                </tr>
            </table>
        </form>
    </body>
</html>
```

Save this as ch15_examp6.htm in your web server's root directory, as this file must be hosted on a web server in order to work correctly. Point your browser to http://youserver/ch15_examp6.htm and test out the form.

This page works exactly like ch15_examp4.htm (the jQuery version) and the original validate_form .htm, but quite a few changes were made to this version. The first major change is the addition of two new functions called getBasicOptions() and request_onfailure().

The purpose of the first function is to create an object containing the basic options needed for the Ajax.Request() constructor to check the user name and e-mail the user wants to use.

```
function getBasicOptions()
{
    var options = new Object();
    options.method = "get";
    options.onFailure = request_onfailure;

    return options;
}
```

This function first creates an object called options. You then add a method property and assign it a value containing the string "get".

Next, you add another property, called onFailure, and assign a pointer to the request_onfailure() function to it. You return the options object to the caller, thus creating the basic options for the Ajax.Request() constructor. This function is primarily for convenience; instead of having to type these lines of code twice (one in checkUsername() and one in checkEmail()), you simply have to type it once here and call this function to return these options.

The second new function, request_onfailure(), is used for both the user name and e-mail check requests. If the request fails for some reason, the request_onfailure() function executes.

```
function request_onfailure(request)
{
    alert("An error occurred. HTTP Status Code: " + request.status);
}
```

This is a simple function; it lets the user know an error occurred.

Turn your attention to the checkUsername() function, as many changes were made in it.

```
function checkUsername()
{
    var userValue = $F("username");
```

The first line of code inside the function changed. It now uses Prototype's $F() function. This function is used for form elements; you pass the element's id to the function, and it retrieves the element's value. So $F("username") is the equivalent of document.getElementById("username").value. The former is definitely easier to type.

Now you determine if the user entered information into the Username field. Simply compare the userValue variable to an empty string.

```
    if (userValue == "")
    {
        alert("Please enter a user name to check!");
        return;
    }
```

If the user didn't enter data into the text box, ask them to in an alert box, and return from the function.

Now gather the information you need in preparation for making the request to the server. Create a parms object, make a username property, and assign it the value contained in userValue.

```
    var parms = new Object();
    parms.username = userValue;
```

Now create your options object to pass to the Ajax.Request() constructor.

```
    var options = getBasicOptions();
    options.onSuccess = checkUsername_callBack;
    options.parameters = parms;
```

You first call getBasicOptions() to create the basic options. Then you create the onSuccess and parameters properties; you set the former's value to a pointer to checkUsername_callback() and the latter to the parms object you previously created.

```
    new Ajax.Request("formvalidator.php", options);
}
```

As the last step in this function, you call the Ajax.Request() constructor, prepended by the new keyword, and pass the URL to formvalidator.php and the options object.

If this request fails, then request_onfailure() executes. However, checkUsername_callback() executes on a successful request, and this function saw a few changes.

The first change is the parameter name; instead of data, it is now request to better reflect that it now contains the XMLHttpRequest-like Ajax.Response object.

```
function checkUsername_callBack(request)
{
```

Next, you get the value of the Username field by using the `$F()` function and passing the string `username` to it.

```
var userValue = $F("username");
```

Next, you use the `responseText` property of the `XMLHttpRequest` object to get the server application's response and check to see if the user name is available.

```
if (request.responseText == "available")
{
    alert("The username " + userValue + " is available!");
}
else
{
    alert("We're sorry, but " + userValue + " is not available.");
}
}
```

Based upon the outcome of the `if` statement, you tell the user either their desired user name is or isn't available for them to use.

The `checkEmail()` function saw similar changes as `checkUsername()`.

```
function checkEmail()
{
    var emailValue = $F("email");

    if (emailValue == "")
    {
        alert("Please enter an email address to check!");
        return;
    }
```

This code retrieves the value from the `Email` text box and determines if the user entered any information into it. If they didn't, an alert box asks them to enter information and the function exits.

Next, go through the preparation steps for sending a request with Prototype. First create the `parms` object.

```
var parms = new Object();
parms.email = emailValue;
```

You create an `email` property and assign it the value contained within the `emailValue` variable. Now create the `options` object.

```
var options = getBasicOptions();
options.onSuccess = checkEmail_callBack;
options.parameters = parms;
```

You once again call the `getBasicOptions()` function to create the basic options for this request. Next, you create and assign values for the `onSuccess` and `parameters` option properties.

Before the function exits, you perform the request by calling the `Ajax.Request()` constructor.

```
new Ajax.Request("formvalidator.php", options);
}
```

On a successful request, the Prototype Ajax component calls `checkEmail_callBack()` and passes it the `XMLHttpRequest` object used to make the request to the server.

```
function checkEmail_callBack(request)
{
    var emailValue = $F("email");

    if (request.responseText == "available")
    {
        alert("The email " + emailValue + " is currently not in use!");
    }
    else
    {
        alert("I'm sorry, but " + emailValue + " is in use by another user.");
    }
}
```

You first get the value of the `Email` text box and store it in the `emailValue` variable. Next, you determine if the e-mail is available for the user to use by comparing the request's `responseText` property with the string `"available"`. You then display a message to the user, telling them their e-mail is or isn't available, based upon the result of the `if` statement.

Prototype is a powerful framework that provides a rich set of utilities to change the way you write JavaScript. Like jQuery, a simple section such as this is far too small to cover the framework adequately. For further information on Prototype and the utility it offers, see the API documentation at `http://www.prototypejs.org/api` and the tutorials at `http://www.prototypejs.org/learn`.

Delving into MooTools

At first glance, MooTools looks identical to Prototype, and rightly so. MooTools was first developed to work with Prototype, so it shouldn't be surprising to see some of the utility provided by MooTools is almost identical to that of Prototype.

However, MooTools is more of a cross between jQuery and Prototype as far as DOM manipulation is concerned. Like Prototype, MooTools' goal is to augment the way you write JavaScript, providing tools to write classes and inherit from them. Also like Prototype, MooTools adds in a rich set of extensions to make DOM manipulation easier, and you'll find that selecting DOM objects in MooTools is exactly the same as Prototype. But as you'll see in the following sections, the extension method names and the way in which you use them is reminiscent of jQuery.

Finding Elements

When testing your MooTools installation, you saw the dollar function used, and you learned that it was similar to Prototypes. Well, let's clear it up now; they are exactly the same. They find the element and extend it, albeit with different methods that you'll see in the following sections.

```
$("myDiv")
```

This code finds an element with an `id` of `myDiv`, extends it with MooTools' methods, and returns the extended element. You can use the methods and properties of the DOM `Element` object, as well as the methods provided to you by MooTools.

MooTools also gives you the double dollar function `$$()` and you use it, you guessed it, to retrieve elements using CSS selectors, and you can use multiple selectors by passing them as a parameter to the double dollar function.

```
$$(".myClass");
$$("div", ".myClass", "p > div")
```

One huge difference between MooTools and Prototype is you don't have to iterate over the returned array to perform operations on them.

```
$$("div", "a").setStyle("color", "red");
```

This code selects all `<div/>` and `<a/>` elements in the page and sets their text color to red. Contrast that with Prototype in the following code example:

```
function changeColor(item)
{
    var styles = new Object();
    styles.color = "red";

    item.setStyle(styles);
}

$$("div", "a").each(changeColor);
```

So the `$$()` function is kind of a cross between Prototype's `$$()` function and jQuery's `$()`.

MooTools has an `each()` method, too, if you wanted to perform an operation on every element in the array.

Altering Style

The previous MooTools code example introduced you to the `setStyle()` method. It accepts two arguments: the first is the CSS property, and the second is its value. Like jQuery, you can use the CSS property used in a style sheet or the camel-case version used in script:

```
$("myDiv").setStyle("background-color", "red");
$("myDiv").setStyle("backgroundColor", "red");
```

Both lines of this code set the element's background color to red; so you can use either property name to set individual style properties.

This is, of course, not the ideal means of changing an element's style. MooTools adds the `addClass()`, `removeClass()`, `toggleClass()`, and `hasClass()` methods to `Element` objects.

The `addClass()` and `removeClass()` methods do just what their names imply. They add and remove the specified class to the element, as in the following code:

```
$("myDiv").addClass("someClass").removeClass("someClass");
```

The `toggleClass()` method works as you would expect; if the element has the CSS class specified by the passed parameter, then `toggleClass()` removes the CSS class from the element. If the element doesn't have the CSS class, then `toggleClass()` adds it to the element.

```
$("myDiv").toggleClass("myClass").toggleClass("myClass");
```

This code first adds the `myClass` CSS class to the element because you removed it in the previous example. The second `toggleClass()` call removes it again because you just added it to the element.

The `hasClass()` method returns a `true` or `false` value depending on whether the element has the CSS class or not.

```
$("myDiv").hasClass("myClass");
```

This code returns `false`, since the CSS class `myClass` isn't applied to the element.

Changing an element's style is only part of the DOM manipulation equation, and MooTools fills in the other part with the ability to create, insert, and remove elements from the DOM.

Creating, Inserting, and Removing Elements

Creating elements with MooTools is very similar to creating them with Prototype. You simply use the `Element` object's constructor and pass it the type of element you want to create along with an object containing the attributes you want the element to have. The following code creates an `<a/>` element; assigns its `id`, `href`, and `target` attributes; and adds the element to the document.

```
var attributes = new Object();
attributes.id = "myLink";
attributes.href = "http://www.prototypejs.org";
attributes.target = "_blank";

var a = new Element("a", attributes).appendText("Go to Prototype's Website");
$(document.body).adopt(a);
```

The first four lines of this code create an `attributes` object and its `id`, `href`, and `target` properties and assign their values. Then a new `<a/>` element is created with the `Element` object constructor, and text is added to the element with the `appendText()` method. Finally, the element is appended to the `document.body` object with the `adopt()` method.

Removing `Element` objects from the DOM is quite simple and straightforward; simply call the `dispose()` method. The following code demonstrates this:

```
$("myLink").dispose();
```

This code finds the element with an `id` of `myLink` and then removes it from the DOM by calling the `dispose()` method.

Using and Handling Events

When you extend an `Element` object with the `$()` function, MooTools adds the `addEvent()` method to the element. This method attaches an event handler to the element for a specified event. The following code is an example of its use:

```
function myDiv_click(event)
{
    alert("You clicked me!");
}

$("myDiv").addEvent("click", myDiv_click);
```

The `addEvent()` method accepts two arguments: the first is the event to watch for, and the second is a function to handle the event when it fires.

The `window` *and* `document` *objects automatically have the* `addEvent()` *method added to them by MooTools.*

You can register multiple event handlers at one time with the `addEvents()` method. This method accepts an object whose property names mirror those of event types, and their values are the functions you want to handle the events with.

For example, the following code registers event handlers for the `mouseover` and `mouseout` events on an element:

```
function eventHandler(e)
{
    // do something with the event here
}

var handlers = new Object();
handlers.mouseover = eventHandler;
handlers.mouseout = eventHandler;

$("myDiv").addEvents(handlers);
```

When an event fires, and if the handler was set via the `addEvent()` or `addEvents()` method, MooTools passes its own `Event` object to the event handling function. This object has its own set of proprietary properties, some like the W3C `Event` and `MouseEvent` objects, and some unlike any property from either the IE or W3C event models even though they offer the same information. The following table lists some of the properties available with MooTools' `Event` object.

Property	Description
page.x	The horizontal position of the mouse relative to the browser window.
page.y	The vertical position of the mouse relative to the browser window.

Property	Description
client.x	The horizontal position of the mouse relative to the client area.
client.y	The vertical position of the mouse relative to the client area.
target	The event target.
relatedTarget	The element related to the event target.
type	The type of event that called the event handler.

Visit http://mootools.net/docs/core/Native/Event *for a complete list of properties of MooTools'* Event *object.*

For example, the following code registers an event handler for the click event on an element with an id of myDiv:

```
function myDiv_onclick(e)
{
    var eSrc = $(e.target).addClass("myClass");

    alert("You clicked at X:" + e.client.x + " Y:" + e.client.y);
}

$("myDiv").addEvent("click", myDiv_onclick);
```

When the event fires and executes myDiv_onclick(), a MooTools Event object is passed to the function. The first line of the function extends the event target element and calls the addClass() method, adding the myClass CSS class to the element. The addClass() method returns the extended Element object, which you store in the eSrc variable. You then use an alert box to display the mouse pointer's coordinates relative to the viewport by using the client.x and client.y properties.

Rewriting the DHTML Toolbar with MooTools

You've been introduced to MooTools DOM manipulation capabilities, so let's put them to good use and rewrite the DHTML toolbar from Chapter 12 (again!).

Try It Out   **Revisiting the Toolbar with MooTools**

Open your text editor and type the following:

```
<!DOCTYPE html PUBLIC "-//W3C//DTD XHTML 1.0 Transitional//EN"
    "http://www.w3.org/TR/xhtml1/DTD/xhtml1-transitional.dtd">

<html xmlns="http://www.w3.org/1999/xhtml">
<head>
    <title>Chapter 15: Example 7 with MooTools</title>
    <style type="text/css">
    .tabStrip
    {
```

```
    background-color: #E4E2D5;
    padding: 3px;
    height: 22px;
}

.tabStrip-tab
{
     float: left;
    font: 14px arial;
    cursor: pointer;
    padding: 2px;
    border: 1px solid transparent;
}

.tabStrip-tab-hover
{
    border-color: #316AC5;
    background-color: #C1D2EE;
}

.tabStrip-tab-click
{
    border-color: #facc5a;
    background-color: #f9e391;
}
</style>
<script src="mootools-1.2.3-core-yc.js" type="text/javascript">
</script>
<script type="text/javascript">
var currentNum = 0;
function handleEvent(e)
{
    var el = $(e.target);

    if (e.type == "mouseover" || e.type == "mouseout")
    {
        if (el.hasClass("tabStrip-tab") &&
            !el.hasClass("tabStrip-tab-click"))
        {
            el.toggleClass("tabStrip-tab-hover");
        }
    }

    if (e.type == "click")
    {
        if (el.hasClass("tabStrip-tab-hover"))
        {
            var id = el.id;
            var num = id.substr(id.lastIndexOf("-") + 1);

            if (currentNum != num)
            {
                deactivateTab();

                el.toggleClass("tabStrip-tab-hover")
                    .toggleClass("tabStrip-tab-click");
```

```
                            showDescription(num);
                            currentNum = num;
                    }
                }
            }
        }

        function showDescription(num)
        {
            var attributes = new Object();
            attributes.id = "tabStrip-desc-" + num;

            var div = new Element("div", attributes)
                .appendText("Description for tab " + num);

            $("descContainer").adopt(div);
        }

        function deactivateTab()
        {
            var descEl = $("tabStrip-desc-" + currentNum);

            if (descEl)
            {
                descEl.dispose();
                $("tabStrip-tab-" + currentNum)
                    .toggleClass("tabStrip-tab-click");
            }
        }

        var handlers = new Object();
        handlers.mouseover = handleEvent;
        handlers.mouseout = handleEvent;
        handlers.click = handleEvent;

        document.addEvents(handlers);
        </script>
    </head>
    <body>
        <div class="tabStrip">
            <div id="tabStrip-tab-1" class="tabStrip-tab">Tab 1</div>
            <div id="tabStrip-tab-2" class="tabStrip-tab">Tab 2</div>
            <div id="tabStrip-tab-3" class="tabStrip-tab">Tab 3</div>
        </div>
        <div id="descContainer"></div>
    </body>
</html>
```

Save this file as ch15_examp7.htm, and open it in any browser supported by MooTools. Notice that this page works just like all the other versions.

Let's jump right into the code, starting with the handleEvent() function.

```
function handleEvent(e)
{
    var el = $(e.target);
```

MooTools passes its `Event` object to this function. One property of this object is the `target` property. Exactly like the W3C event model's `Event` object, it contains the element that caused the event. You pass the target to the dollar method to add MooTools' extensions and save the resulting extended `Element` object to the `el` variable.

Next you check what type of event took place. In this case, you're primarily interested in `mouseover` and `mouseout` events.

```
if (e.type == "mouseover" || e.type == "mouseout")
{
    if (el.hasClass("tabStrip-tab") &&
            !el.hasClass("tabStrip-tab-click"))
    {
        el.toggleClass("tabStrip-tab-hover");
    }
}
```

In either case, you determine if the event target is a tab element by checking if it has the `tabStrip-tab` CSS class. If so, and only if the tab doesn't have the `tabStrip-tab-click` class, you toggle the `tab-Strip-tab-hover` class.

Next, you determine if a click event caused the event handler's execution, and you determine if the event target is a tab with the `tabStrip-tab-hover` CSS class applied to it.

```
if (e.type == "click")
{
    if (el.hasClass("tabStrip-tab-hover"))
    {
```

If so, you retrieve the number associated with the tab and assign it to the `num` variable, as the following code shows:

```
var id = el.id;
var num = id.substr(id.lastIndexOf("-") + 1);
```

The next step is to determine if the tab is currently the active tab. If it isn't, you deactivate the current active tab.

```
if (currentNum != num)
{
    deactivateTab();
}
```

Then you toggle the hover class off of the element while turning the click class on.

```
el.toggleClass("tabStrip-tab-hover")
    .toggleClass("tabStrip-tab-click");
```

The final steps of this function are to show the description for this newly clicked tab and store the value contained in `num` to the `currentNum` variable.

```
        showDescription(num);
        currentNum = num;
    }
    }
    }
}
```

Because of the similarities between Prototype and MooTools, the `showDescription()` function is very similar to that of the Prototype version.

```
function showDescription(num)
{
    var attributes = new Object();
    attributes.id = "tabStrip-desc-" + num;
```

You first create the `attributes` object, assigning the `id` property the value you want the new `<div/>` element to have. Next, you create the `<div/>` element by calling the `Element` constructor and chaining the `appendText()` method. You assign the returned value of `appendText()`, the `Element` object, to the `div` variable.

```
    var div = new Element("div", attributes)
        .appendText("Description for tab " + num);
```

And lastly, at least for this function, you append the new element to the `<div/>` element with an id of `descContainer` by using the `adopt()` method.

```
    $("descContainer").adopt(div);
}
```

Unlike `showDescription()`, the `deactivateTab()` function resembles more of the jQuery version than the Prototype version.

```
function deactivateTab()
{
    var descEl = $("tabStrip-desc-" + currentNum);
```

You first get the `<div/>` element containing the currently active tab's description. This element may, or may not, be in the DOM. In order to stave off errors, you need to check if the element was found or not. The dollar function returns `null` if the element cannot be found, and `null` is a false-y value, so simply use the `descEl` variable as the condition of the `if` statement.

```
    if (descEl)
    {
        descEl.dispose();
        $("tabStrip-tab-" + currentNum)
            .toggleClass("tabStrip-tab-click");
    }
}
```

If the element is found, use the `dispose()` method to remove it from the DOM. Then retrieve the currently active tab `<div/>` element and remove the `tabStrip-tab-click` class with the `toggleClass()` method.

Finally, register your event handler to handle the `mouseover`, `mouseout`, and `click` events.

```
var handlers = new Object();
handlers.mouseover = handleEvent;
handlers.mouseout = handleEvent;
handlers.click = handleEvent;

document.addEvents(handlers);
```

You create a `handlers` object, and create its properties to have the same names as the events you want to handle. Assign these properties a pointer to the `handleEvent()` function, and then pass the `handlers` object to the `addEvents()` method of the `document` object.

Ajax Support in MooTools

The Ajax utilities of MooTools are quite different from jQuery and somewhat different from Prototype. The MooTools Ajax utility revolves around the `Request` reference type. Like Prototype's `Ajax.Request`, you create an instance of `Request`, and pass it an object that contains a set of options. The following table lists some of these options.

Option	Description
async	Determines whether the XMLHttpRequest object makes the request in asynchronous mode or not. The default is true.
method	The HTTP method used for the request. The default is "post". "get" is another valid value.
onSuccess	A callback function invoked when the request completes successfully.
onFailure	A callback function invoked when the request completes, but results in an error status code.
url	The URL to send the request to.

> Visit `http://mootools.net/docs/core/Request/Request` *for a complete list of options and callback functions.*

All callback functions are executed and passed varying parameters. The `onSuccess` callback function is passed two parameters, the first being the XMLHttpRequest object's `responseText` and the second being the `responseXML`. The `onFailure` callback is simply passed the XMLHttpRequest object. Making a request using the `Request` reference type looks something like the following code:

```
function request_onsuccess(text, xml)
{
    alert(text);
}

function request_onfailure(request)
{
    alert("An error occurred! HTTP status code is " + request.status);
}

var options = new Object();
options.method = "get";
options.onSuccess = request_onsuccess;
```

```
options.onFailure = request_onfailure;
options.url = "someTextFile.txt";

var request = new Request(options).send();
```

The first few lines of code define the `request_onsuccess()` and `request_onfailure()` functions. After the function definitions, you create an `options` object. The first option you set is the `method` option, which you set to get. The next two options are the `onSuccess` and `onFailure` options, and you assign them the `request_onsuccess()` and `request_onfailure()` functions. The final option is `url`, which you assign `someTextFile.txt`.

Once you have all the options created, you call the `Request` constructor and pass the `options` object to it. You then chain the `send()` method, which sends the request.

You can send parameters by using the `send()` method. Simply pass it a string containing the parameters, as the following code shows:

```
var request = new Request(options).send("name=Jeremy");
```

Let's use MooTools' Ajax utilities to modify the form validator from the previous chapter one last time!

Try It Out   **Revisiting the Form Validator with MooTools**

Open your text editor and type the following:

```
<!DOCTYPE HTML PUBLIC "-//W3C//DTD HTML 4.01//EN"
    "http://www.w3.org/TR/html4/strict.dtd">
<html>
<head>
    <title>Chapter 15: Example 8 with MooTools</title>
    <style type="text/css">
        .fieldname
        {
            text-align: right;
        }

        .submit
        {
            text-align: right;
        }
    </style>
    <script src="mootools-1.2.3-core-yc.js" type="text/javascript"></script>
    <script type="text/javascript">
    function checkUsername()
    {
        var userValue = $("username").value;

        if (userValue == "")
        {
            alert("Please enter a user name to check!");
            return;
```

```
        }

        var options = getBasicOptions();
        options.onSuccess = checkUsername_callBack;

        new Request(options).send("username=" + userValue);
    }

    function checkUsername_callBack(text, xml)
    {
        var userValue = $("username").value;

        if (text == "available")
        {
            alert("The username " + userValue + " is available!");
        }
        else
        {
            alert("We're sorry, but " + userValue + " is not available.");
        }
    }

    function checkEmail()
    {
        var emailValue = $("email").value;

        if (emailValue == "")
        {
            alert("Please enter an email address to check!");
            return;
        }

        var options = getBasicOptions();
        options.onSuccess = checkEmail_callBack;

        new Request(options).send("email=" + emailValue);
    }

    function checkEmail_callBack(text, xml)
    {
        var emailValue = $("email").value;

        if (text == "available")
        {
            alert("The email " + emailValue + " is currently not in use!");
        }
        else
        {
            alert("I'm sorry, but " + emailValue + " is in use by another user.");
        }
    }

    function request_onfailure(request)
    {
```

```
                    alert("An error occurred. HTTP Status Code: " + request.status);
        }

        function getBasicOptions()
        {
            var options = new Object();
            options.method = "get";
            options.onFailure = request_onfailure;
            options.url = "formvalidator.php";

            return options;
        }
    </script>
</head>
<body>
    <form>
        <table>
            <tr>
                <td class="fieldname">
                    Username:
                </td>
                <td>
                    <input type="text" id="username" />
                </td>
                <td>
                    <a href="javascript: checkUsername()">Check Availability</a>
                </td>
            </tr>
            <tr>
                <td class="fieldname">
                    Email:
                </td>
                <td>
                    <input type="text" id="email" />
                </td>
                <td>
                    <a href="javascript: checkEmail()">Check Availability</a>
                </td>
            </tr>
            <tr>
                <td class="fieldname">
                    Password:
                </td>
                <td>
                    <input type="text" id="password" />
                </td>
                <td />
            </tr>
            <tr>
                <td class="fieldname">
                    Verify Password:
                </td>
                <td>
                    <input type="text" id="password2" />
                </td>
                <td />
```

```
                </tr>
                <tr>
                    <td colspan="2" class="submit">
                        <input type="submit" value="Submit" />
                    </td>
                    <td />
                </tr>
            </table>
        </form>
    </body>
</html>
```

Save this file as ch15_examp8.htm, and save it in your web server's root directory. Open and point your browser to http://yourserver/ch15_examp8.htm and test it. You'll find that it behaves just as all the previous versions did.

The usual suspects, checkUsername(), checkUsername_callback(), checkEmail(), and checkEmail_callback(), all consist of changes. You also added two new functions: request_onfailure() and getBasicOptions().

Let's examine the new functions first, starting with getBasicOptions(). Like the Prototype version of this script, you created this function to generate an options object with the settings all requests will use. This saves you time and keystrokes, as you only have to write them once and call the function whenever you need it. The function definition follows:

```
function getBasicOptions()
{
    var options = new Object();
    options.method = "get";
    options.onFailure = request_onfailure;
    options.url = "formvalidator.php";

    return options;
}
```

In this function, you create the options object and create the method, onFailure, and url properties. You assign them the following values: get, request_onfailure, and formvalidator.php. The XMLHttpRequest object will make a GET request to formvalidator.php, and the request_onfailure() function will execute only when the request object encounters an error.

The request_onfailure() function simply tells the user an error occurred, as the following code shows:

```
function request_onfailure(request)
{
    alert("An error occurred. HTTP Status Code: " + request.status);
}
```

You display the status code, as it could be helpful debugging the script if an error does indeed occur with the request.

The checkUsername() and checkUsername_callback() functions underwent the same changes as in the previous versions. So you'll only look at the lines that changed. The first change in checkUsername() is how the information entered into the Username field is retrieved.

```
var userValue = $("username").value;
```

With MooTools, you simply use the dollar function to retrieve the element and use the `value` property.

The next change is at the end of the function when you make the request. First, you use the `getBasicOptions()` function to return an `options` object with the predefined options you want to use for the request. Then you add the `onSuccess` option and assign it a pointer to the `checkUsername_callback()` function.

```
var options = getBasicOptions();
options.onSuccess = checkUsername_callBack;
```

You then make the request by creating a new `Request` object with its constructor, passing it the `options` object, and sending the request with the `username` parameter.

```
new Request(options).send("username=" + userValue);
```

On a successful request, the `checkUsername_callback()` function is called. The first change you made to this function is the parameters. MooTools passes the `XMLHttpRequest`'s `responseText` and `responseXML` properties, respectively, to the `Request` object's callback functions.

```
function checkUsername_callBack(text, xml)
```

Here they are simply called `text` and `xml`. Next, you retrieve the text in the `Username` text box again, using the dollar function and the `value` property.

```
var userValue = $("username").value;
```

The final change of this function is the condition of the `if` statement.

```
if (text == "available")
```

Compare the value of the `text` parameter with the string `"available"`, and display a message to the user either stating that the user name is or isn't available.

The `checkEmail()` and `checkEmail_callback()` functions underwent the same changes as `checkUsername()` and `checkUsername_callback()`. Again, you'll focus only on the changes made to these functions starting with `checkEmail()`.

The first change to this function is the retrieval of the `Email` text box:

```
var emailValue = $("email").value;
```

Use the dollar function, pass it the id of the `<input/>` element, and use the `value` property to retrieve the text. The next change is making the request, but before you can make the request, you must create the `options` object, populate it with the basic settings, and add the `onSuccess` option.

```
var options = getBasicOptions();
options.onSuccess = checkEmail_callBack;
```

Now that all options are set, simply call the `Request` constructor, pass it the `options` object, and send the `email` parameter and its value to the server.

```
new Request(options).send("email=" + emailValue);
```

On a successful request, the `Request` object calls `checkEmail_callback()` and passes it the `XMLHttpRequest` object's `reponseText` and `responseXML` properties.

```
function checkEmail_callBack(text, xml)
```

You again retrieve the value in the `Email` text box by selecting the element and using the `value` property.

```
var emailValue = $("email").value;
```

You then determine if the response from the server designates that the e-mail is available for the user to use.

```
if (text == "available")
```

MooTools is a popular framework because it offers you utility similar to jQuery while maintaining aspects of traditional DOM programming like Prototype. MooTools also has an animation/effects component, making it a well-rounded framework. This section can hardly do the framework justice, so make sure to visit the API documentation at `http://www.mootools.net/docs/core`.

Summary

This chapter introduced you into the rather large world of JavaScript frameworks.

- ❑ You learned that JavaScript frameworks were the answer to cross-browser development.

- ❑ You learned that there are two types of frameworks: general and specific. You were also given a short list of the popular frameworks available today.

- ❑ You learned where to obtain the files needed to use the jQuery, Prototype, and MooTools frameworks.

- ❑ You installed jQuery, Prototype, and MooTools and tested each installation with an identical test page.

- ❑ You learned how to select and retrieve elements, manipulate the DOM, and work with events with the jQuery, Prototype, and MooTools frameworks; and you rewrote the DHTML toolbar script using all three of the frameworks.

- ❑ Finally, you learned how to make basic Ajax requests using the Ajax components of jQuery, Prototype, and MooTools; you also rewrote the form validator script using the Ajax capabilities of the three frameworks.

Exercise Questions

Suggested solutions for these questions can be found in Appendix A.

1. Modify the answer to Chapter 14's Question 2 using jQuery. Also add error reporting for when an error occurs with the Ajax request.

2. Alter the answer to Chapter 14's Question 2 using Prototype. Add error reporting for when an error occurs with the Ajax request.

3. If you guessed that this question would be: "Change the answer to Chapter 14's Question 2 using MooTools, and add error reporting for when an error occurs with the Ajax request" then you won!! Your prize is… completing the exercise.

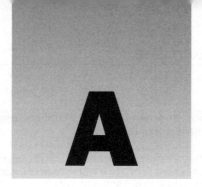

Answers to Exercises

This Appendix provides the answers to the questions you find at the end of each chapter in this book.

Chapter 2

Exercise 1 Question

Write a JavaScript program to convert degrees centigrade into degrees Fahrenheit, and to write the result to the page in a descriptive sentence. The JavaScript equation for Fahrenheit to centigrade is as follows:

```
degFahren = 9 / 5 * degCent + 32
```

Exercise 1 Solution

```
<!DOCTYPE html PUBLIC "-//W3C//DTD XHTML 1.0 Transitional//EN"
"http://www.w3.org/TR/xhtml1/DTD/xhtml1-transitional.dtd">
<html xmlns="http://www.w3.org/1999/xhtml">
<body>

<script type="text/javascript">

var degCent = prompt("Enter the degrees in centigrade",0);
var degFahren = 9 / 5 * degCent + 32;

document.write(degCent + " degrees centigrade is " + degFahren +
   " degrees Fahrenheit");

</script>

</body>
</html>
```

Save this as ch2_q1.htm.

Exercise 2 Question

The following code uses the `prompt()` function to get two numbers from the user. It then adds those two numbers together and writes the result to the page:

```
<!DOCTYPE html PUBLIC "-//W3C//DTD XHTML 1.0 Transitional//EN"
"http://www.w3.org/TR/xhtml1/DTD/xhtml1-transitional.dtd">
<html xmlns="http://www.w3.org/1999/xhtml">
<script language="JavaScript" type="text/javascript">

var firstNumber = prompt("Enter the first number","");
var secondNumber = prompt("Enter the second number","");
var theTotal = firstNumber + secondNumber;
document.write(firstNumber + " added to " + secondNumber + " equals " +
    theTotal);

</script>
</body>
</html>
```

However, if you try the code out, you'll discover that it doesn't work. Why not? Change the code so that it does work.

Exercise 2 Solution

The data that the `prompt()` actually obtains is a string. So both `firstNumber` and `secondNumber` contain text that happens to be number characters. When we use the + symbol to add the two variables together, JavaScript assumes that since it's string data, we must want to concatenate the two together and not sum them.

To make it explicit to JavaScript that we want to add the numbers together, we need to convert the data to numbers using the `parseFloat()` function.

```
var firstNumber = parseFloat(prompt("Enter the first number",""));
var secondNumber = parseFloat(prompt("Enter the second number",""));
var theTotal = firstNumber + secondNumber;
document.write(firstNumber + " added to " + secondNumber + " equals " +
    theTotal);
```

Save this as `ch2_q2.htm`.

Now the data returned by the `prompt()` function is converted to a floating-point number before being stored in the `firstNumber` and `secondNumber` variables. Then, when we do the addition that is stored in `theTotal`, JavaScript makes the correct assumption that, because both the variables are numbers, we must mean to add them up and not concatenate them.

The general rule is that where we have expressions with only numerical data, the + operator means "do addition." If there is any string data, the + will mean concatenate.

Chapter 3

Exercise 1 Question

A junior programmer comes to you with some code that appears not to work. Can you spot where he went wrong? Give him a hand and correct the mistakes.

```
var userAge = prompt("Please enter your age");

if (userAge = 0);
{
   alert("So you're a baby!");
}
else if ( userAge < 0 | userAge > 200)
   alert("I think you may be lying about your age");
else
{
   alert("That's a good age");
}
```

Exercise 1 Solution

Oh dear, our junior programmer is having a bad day! There are two mistakes on the line

```
if (userAge = 0);
```

First, he has only one equals sign instead of two in the `if`'s condition, which means `userAge` will be assigned the value of 0 rather than `userAge` being compared to 0. The second fault is the semicolon at the end of the line — statements such as `if` and loops such as `for` and `while` don't require semicolons. The general rule is that if the statement has an associated block (that is, code in curly braces) then no semicolon is needed. So the line should be

```
if (userAge == 0)
The next fault is with these lines:
else if ( userAge < 0 | userAge > 200)
   alert("I think you may be lying about your age");
else
```

The junior programmer's condition is asking if `userAge` is less than 0 OR `userAge` is greater than 200. The correct operator for a Boolean OR is | |, but the programmer has only used one |.

Exercise 2 Question

Using `document.write()`, write code that displays the results of the 12 times table. Its output should be the results of the calculations.

```
12 * 1 = 12
12 * 2 = 24
12 * 3 = 36
...
```

```
12 * 11 = 132
12 * 12 = 144
```

Exercise 2 Solution

```
<!DOCTYPE html PUBLIC "-//W3C//DTD XHTML 1.0 Transitional//EN"
"http://www.w3.org/TR/xhtml1/DTD/xhtml1-transitional.dtd">
<html xmlns="http://www.w3.org/1999/xhtml">
<body>

<script type="text/javascript">

var timesTable = 12;
var timesBy;

for (timesBy = 1; timesBy < 13; timesBy++)
{
    document.write(timesTable + " * " + timesBy + " = " + timesBy * timesTable +
        "<br />");
}


</script>

</body>
</html>
```

Save this as ch3_q2.htm.

You use a for loop to calculate from 1 * 12 up to 12 * 12. The results are written to the page with document.write(). What's important to note here is the effect of the order of precedence; the concatenation operator (the +) has a lower order of precedence than the multiplication operator, *. This means that the timesBy * timesTable is done before the concatenation, which is the result you want. If this were not the case, you'd have to put the calculation in parentheses to raise its order of precedence.

Exercise 3 Question

Change the code of Question 2 so that it's a function that takes as parameters the times table required and the values at which it should start and end. For example, you might try the four times table displayed starting with 4 * 4 and ending at 4 * 9.

Exercise 3 Solution

```
<!DOCTYPE html PUBLIC "-//W3C//DTD XHTML 1.0 Transitional//EN"
"http://www.w3.org/TR/xhtml1/DTD/xhtml1-transitional.dtd">
<html xmlns="http://www.w3.org/1999/xhtml">
<body>

<script type="text/javascript">

function writeTimesTable(timesTable, timesByStart, timesByEnd)
```

```
    {
        for (;timesByStart <= timesByEnd; timesByStart++)
        {
            document.write(timesTable + " * " + timesByStart + " = " +
                timesByStart * timesTable + "<br />");
        }
    }

    writeTimesTable(4,4,9);


    </script>

    </body>
    </html>
```

Save this as `ch3_q3.htm`.

You've declared your function, calling it `writeTimesTable()`, and given it three parameters. The first is the times table you want to write, the second is the start point, and the third is the number it should go up to.

You've modified your `for` loop. First you don't need to initialize any variables, so the initialization part is left blank — you still need to put a semicolon in, but there's no code before it. The `for` loop continues while the `timesByStart` parameter is less than or equal to the `timesByEnd` parameter. You can see that, as with a variable, you can modify parameters — in this case, `timesByStart` is incremented by one for each iteration through the loop.

The code to display the times table is much the same. For the function's code to be executed, you now actually need to call it, which you do in the line

```
    writeTimesTable(4,4,9);
```

This will write the 4 times table starting at 4 times 4 and ending at 9 times 4.

Exercise 4 Question

Modify the code of Question 3 to request the times table to be displayed from the user; the code should continue to request and display times tables until the user enters **-1**. Additionally, do a check to make sure that the user is entering a valid number; if the number is not valid, ask the user to re-enter it.

Exercise 4 Solution

```
<!DOCTYPE html PUBLIC "-//W3C//DTD XHTML 1.0 Transitional//EN"
"http://www.w3.org/TR/xhtml1/DTD/xhtml1-transitional.dtd">
<html xmlns="http://www.w3.org/1999/xhtml">
<body>

<script type="text/javascript">

function writeTimesTable(timesTable, timesByStart, timesByEnd)
```

```
    {
        for (;timesByStart <= timesByEnd; timesByStart++)
        {
            document.write(timesTable + " * " + timesByStart + " = " +
                timesByStart * timesTable + "<br />");
        }
    }

    var timesTable;

    while ( (timesTable = prompt("Enter the times table",-1)) != -1)
    {
        while (isNaN(timesTable) == true)
        {
         timesTable = prompt(timesTable + " is not a valid number, please retry",-1);
        }

        if (timesTable == -1)
        {
            break;
        }

        document.write("<br />The " + timesTable + " times table<br />");
        writeTimesTable(timesTable,1,12);

    }

    </script>

    </body>
    </html>
```

Save this as ch3_q4.htm.

The function remains the same, so let's look at the new code. The first change from Question 3 is that you declare a variable, timesTable, and then initialize it in the condition of the first while loop. This may seem like a strange thing to do at first, but it does work. The code in parentheses inside the while loop's condition

```
    (timesTable = prompt("Enter the times table",-1))
```

is executed first because its order of precedence has been raised by the parentheses. This will return a value, and it is this value that is compared to –1. If it's not –1, then the while condition is true, and the body of the loop executes. Otherwise it's skipped over, and nothing else happens in this page.

In a second while loop nested inside the first, you check to see that the value the user has entered is actually a number using the function isNaN(). If it's not, then you prompt the user to try again, and this will continue until a valid number is entered.

If the user had entered an invalid value initially, then in the second while loop, that user may have entered –1, so following the while is an if statement that checks to see if –1 has been entered. If it has, you break out of the while loop; otherwise the writeTimesTable() function is called.

Chapter 4

Exercise 1 Question

The example `debug_timestable2.htm` has a deliberate bug. For each times table it creates only multipliers with values from 1 to 11.

Use the script debugger to work out why this is happening, and then correct the bug.

Exercise 1 Solution

The problem is with the code's logic rather than its syntax. Logic errors are much harder to spot and deal with because, unlike with syntax errors, the browser won't inform you that there's such and such error at line so and so but instead just fails to work as expected. The error is with this line:

```
for (counter = 1; counter < 12; counter++)
```

You want the loop to go from 1 to 12 inclusive. Your `counter < 12` statement will be `true` up to and including 11 but will be `false` when the counter reaches 12; hence 12 gets left off. To correct this, you could change the code to the following:

```
for (counter = 1; counter <= 12; counter++)
```

Exercise 2 Question

The following code contains a number of common errors. See if you can spot them:

```
<!DOCTYPE html PUBLIC "-//W3C//DTD XHTML 1.0 Transitional//EN"
    "http://www.w3.org/TR/xhtml1/DTD/xhtml1-transitional.dtd">

<html xmlns="http://www.w3.org/1999/xhtml">
<head>
    <title>Chapter 4, Question 2</title>
</head>
<body>
<script type="text/javascript">
function checkForm(theForm)
{
    var formValid = true;
    var elementCount  = 0;
    while(elementCount =< theForm.length)
    {
        if (theForm.elements[elementcount].type == "text")
        {
            if (theForm.elements[elementCount].value() = "")
                alert("Please complete all form elements")
            theForm.elements[elementCount].focus;
            formValid = false;
            break;
        }
```

```
        }
        return formValid;
    }
</script>
<form name="form1" onsubmit="return checkForm(document.form1)" action="">
    <input type="text" id="text1" name="text1" />
    <br />
    CheckBox 1<input type="checkbox" id="checkbox2" name="checkbox2" />
    <br />
    CheckBox 1<input type="checkbox" id="checkbox1" name="checkbox1" />
    <br />
    <input type="text" id="text2" name="text2" />
    <p>
        <input type="submit" value="Submit" id="submit1" name="submit1" />
    </p>
</form>
</body>
</html>
```

Exercise 2 Solution

The bug-free version looks like this:

```
<!DOCTYPE html PUBLIC "-//W3C//DTD XHTML 1.0 Transitional//EN"
    "http://www.w3.org/TR/xhtml1/DTD/xhtml1-transitional.dtd">

<html xmlns="http://www.w3.org/1999/xhtml">
<head>
    <title>Chapter 4, Question 2: Answer</title>
</head>
<body>
<script type="text/javascript">
function checkForm(theForm)
{
    var formValid = true;
    var elementCount  = 0;

    while(elementCount < theForm.length)
    {
        if (theForm.elements[elementCount].type == "text")
        {
            if (theForm.elements[elementCount].value == "")
            {
                alert("Please complete all form elements")
                theForm.elements[elementCount].focus();
                formValid = false;
                break;
            }
        }

        elementCount++;
    }

    return formValid;
```

```
    }
</script>
<form name="form1" onsubmit="return checkForm(document.form1)" action="">
    <input type="text" id="text1" name="text1" />
    <br />
    CheckBox 1<input type="checkbox" id="checkbox2" name="checkbox2" />
    <br />
    CheckBox 1<input type="checkbox" id="checkbox1" name="checkbox1" />
    <br />
    <input type="text" id="text2" name="text2" />
    <p>
        <input type="submit" value="Submit" id="submit1" name="submit1" />
    </p>
</form>
</body>
</html>
```

Let's look at each error in turn.

The first error is a logic error.

```
while(elementCount =< theForm.length)
```

Arrays start at 0 so the first Form object is at index array 0, the second at 1, and so on. The last Form object has an index value of 4. However, theForm.length will return 5 because there are five elements in the form. So the while loop will continue until elementCount is less than or equal to 5, but as the last element has an index of 4, this is one past the limit. You should write either this:

```
while(elementCount < theForm.length)
```

or this:

```
while(elementCount <= theForm.length - 1)
```

Either is fine, though the first is shorter.

You come to your second error in the following line:

```
if (theForm.elements[elementcount].type == "text")
```

On a quick glance it looks fine, but it's JavaScript's strictness on case sensitivity that has caused the downfall. The variable name is elementCount, not elementcount with a lowercase c. So this line should read as follows:

```
if (theForm.elements[elementCount].type == "text")
```

The next line with an error is this:

```
if (theForm.elements[elementCount].value() = "")
```

This has two errors. First, `value` is a property and not a method, so there is no need for parentheses after it. Second, you have the all-time classic error of one equals sign instead of two. Remember that one equals sign means "Make it equal to," and two equals signs mean "Check if it is equal to." So with the changes, the line is:

```
if (theForm.elements[elementCount].value == "")
```

The next error is the failure to put your block of `if` code in curly braces. Even though JavaScript won't throw an error since the syntax is fine, the logic is not so fine, and you won't get the results you expect. With the braces, the `if` statement should be as follows:

```
if (theForm.elements[elementCount].value == "")
{
    alert("Please complete all form elements")
    theForm.elements[elementCount].focus;
    formValid = false;
    break;
}
```

The penultimate error is in this line:

```
theForm.elements[elementCount].focus;
```

This time you have a method but with no parentheses after it. Even methods that have no parameters must have the empty parentheses after them if you intend to execute that method. So, corrected, the line is as follows:

```
theForm.elements[elementCount].focus();
```

Now you're almost done; there is just one more error. This time it's not something wrong with what's there, but rather something very important that should be there but is missing. What is it? It's this:

```
elementCount++;
```

This line should be in your `while` loop, otherwise `elementCount` will never go above 0 and the `while` loop's condition will always be `true`, resulting in the loop continuing forever: a classic infinite loop.

Chapter 5

Exercise 1 Question

Using the `Date` type, calculate the date 12 months from now and write this into a web page.

Exercise 1 Solution

```
<!DOCTYPE html PUBLIC "-//W3C//DTD XHTML 1.0 Transitional//EN"
    "http://www.w3.org/TR/xhtml1/DTD/xhtml1-transitional.dtd">

<html xmlns="http://www.w3.org/1999/xhtml">
```

```
<head>
    <title>Chapter 5: Question 1</title>
</head>
<body>
<script type="text/javascript">

var months = new Array("Jan","Feb","Mar","Apr","May","Jun","Jul","Aug",
                       "Sep","Oct","Nov","Dec");
var nowDate = new Date();

nowDate.setMonth(nowDate.getMonth() + 12);
document.write("Date 12 months ahead is " + nowDate.getDate());
document.write(" " + months[nowDate.getMonth()]);
document.write(" " + nowDate.getFullYear());

</script>
</body>
</html>
```

Save this as ch05_q1.htm.

Because the getMonth() method returns a number between 0 and 11 for the month rather than its name, an array called months has been created that stores the name of each month. You can use getMonth() to get the array index for the correct month name.

The variable nowDate is initialized to a new Date object. Because no initial value is specified, the new Date object will contain today's date.

To add 12 months to the current date you simply use setMonth(). You get the current month value with getMonth(), and then add 12 to it.

Finally you write the result out to the page.

Exercise 2 Question

Obtain a list of names from the user, storing each name entered in an array. Keep getting another name until the user enters nothing. Sort the names in ascending order and then write them out to the page, with each name on its own line.

Exercise 2 Solution

```
<!DOCTYPE html PUBLIC "-//W3C//DTD XHTML 1.0 Transitional//EN"
    "http://www.w3.org/TR/xhtml1/DTD/xhtml1-transitional.dtd">

<html xmlns="http://www.w3.org/1999/xhtml">
<head>
    <title>Chapter 5: Question 2</title>
</head>
<body>
<script type="text/javascript">
var inputName = "";
```

```
var namesArray = new Array();

while ( (inputName = prompt("Enter a name","")) != "" )
{
    namesArray[namesArray.length] = inputName;
}

namesArray.sort();

var namesList = namesArray.join("<br/>")
document.write(namesList);
</script>
</body>
</html>
```

Save this as ch05_q2.htm.

First you declare two variables: inputName, which will hold the name entered by the user, and namesArray, which holds an Array object that stores each of the names entered.

You use a while loop to keep getting another name from the user as long as the user hasn't left the prompt box blank. Note that the use of parentheses in the while condition is essential. By placing the following code inside parentheses, you ensure that this is executed first and that a name is obtained from the user and stored in the inputName variable.

```
(inputName = prompt("Enter a name",""))
```

Then you compare the value returned inside the parentheses — whatever was entered by the user — with an empty string (denoted by ""). If they are not equal — that is, if the user did enter a value, you loop around again.

Now, to sort the array into order, you use the sort() method of the Array object.

```
namesArray.sort();
```

Finally, to create a string containing all values contained in the array elements with each being on a new line, you use the HTML <br/> element and write the following:

```
var namesList = namesArray.join("<br/>")
document.write(namesList);
```

The code namesArray.join("<br/>") creates the string of array elements with a <br/> between each. Finally, you write the string into the page with document.write().

Exercise 3 Question

In this chapter, you learned how you can use the pow() method inventively to fix a number to a certain number of decimal places. However, there is a flaw in the function you created. A proper fix() function should return 2.1 fixed to three decimal places like this:

```
2.100
```

However, your `fix()` function instead returns it like this:

```
2.1
```

Change the `fix()` function so that the additional zeros are added where necessary.

Exercise 3 Solution

```
<!DOCTYPE html PUBLIC "-//W3C//DTD XHTML 1.0 Transitional//EN"
    "http://www.w3.org/TR/xhtml1/DTD/xhtml1-transitional.dtd">

<html xmlns="http://www.w3.org/1999/xhtml">
<head>
    <title>Chapter 5: Question 3</title>
    <script type="text/javascript">
    function fix(fixNumber, decimalPlaces)
    {
        var div = Math.pow(10,decimalPlaces);
        fixNumber = new String(Math.round(fixNumber * div) / div);
        if (fixNumber.lastIndexOf(".")==-1)
        {
            fixNumber = fixNumber + ".";
        }

        var zerosRequired = decimalPlaces -
            (fixNumber.length - fixNumber.lastIndexOf(".") - 1);

        for (; zerosRequired > 0; zerosRequired--)
        {
            fixNumber = fixNumber + "0";
        }
        return fixNumber;
    }
    </script>
</head>
<body>
<script type="text/javascript">
var number1 = prompt("Enter the number with decimal " +
    "places you want to fix","");
var number2 = prompt("How many decimal places do you " +
    "want?","");

document.write(number1 + " fixed to " + number2 +
    " decimal places is: ");
document.write(fix(number1,number2));
</script>
</body>
</html>
```

Save this as ch05_q3.htm.

The function declaration and the first line remain the same as in the `fix()` function you saw earlier in the chapter. However, things change after that.

You create the fixed number as before, using `Math.round(fixNumber * div) / div`. What is new is that you pass the result of this as the parameter to the `String()` constructor that creates a new `String` object, storing it back in `fixNumber`.

Now you have your number fixed to the number of decimal places required, but it will still be in the form `2.1` rather than `2.100`, as required. Your next task is therefore to add the extra zeros required. To do this you need to subtract the number of digits after the decimal point from the number of digits required after the decimal point as specified in `decimalPlaces`. First, to find out how many digits are after the decimal point, you write this:

```
(fixNumber.length - fixNumber.lastIndexOf(".") - 1)
```

For your number of `2.1`, `fixNumber.length` will be `3`. `fixNumber.lastIndexOf(".")` will return `1`; remember that the first character is `0`, the second is `1`, and so on. So `fixNumber.length - fixNumber .lastIndexOf(".")` will be `2`. Then you subtract `1` at the end, leaving a result of `1`, which is the number of digits after the decimal place.

The full line is as follows:

```
var zerosRequired = decimalPlaces -
            (fixNumber.length - fixNumber.lastIndexOf(".") - 1);
```

You know the last bit (`fixNumber.length - fixNumber.lastIndexOf(".") - 1`) is `1` and that the `decimalPlaces` parameter passed is `3`. Three minus one leaves two zeros that must be added.

Now that you know how many extra zeros are required, let's add them.

```
for (; zerosRequired > 0; zerosRequired--)
{
    fixNumber = fixNumber + "0";
}
```

Now you just need to return the result from the function to the calling code.

```
return fixNumber;
```

Chapter 6

Exercise 1 Question

Create a page with a number of links. Then write code that fires on the window `load` event, displaying the `href` of each of the links on the page. (Hint: Remember that event handlers begin with `on`.)

Exercise 1 Solution

```
<!DOCTYPE html PUBLIC "-//W3C//DTD XHTML 1.0 Strict//EN"
    "http://www.w3.org/TR/xhtml1/DTD/xhtml1-strict.dtd">

<html xmlns="http://www.w3.org/1999/xhtml">
```

```
<head>
    <title>Chapter 6: Question 1</title>
    <script type="text/javascript">
    function displayLinks()
    {
        var linksCounter;

        for (linksCounter = 0; linksCounter < document.links.length;
linksCounter++)
        {
            alert(document.links[linksCounter].href);
        }
    }
    </script>
</head>
<body onload="displayLinks()">
<a href="link0.htm" >Link 0</a>
<a href="link1.htm">Link 2</a>
<a href="link2.htm">Link 2</a>
</body>
</html>
```

Save this as ch06_q1.htm.

You connect to the window object's onload event handler by adding an attribute to the opening <body> tag.

```
<body onload="displayLinks()">
```

On the onload event firing, this will run the script in quotes calling the displayLinks() function.

In this function you use a for loop to cycle through each a object in the document object's links collection.

```
function displayLinks()
{
    var linksCounter

    for (linksCounter = 0; linksCounter < document.links.length; linksCounter++)
    {
        alert(document.links[linksCounter].href);
    }
}
```

You used the length property of the links collection in your condition to determine how many times you need to loop. Then, using an alert box, you display each a object's href property. You can't use document.write() in the load event because it occurs when the page has finished loading.

Exercise 2 Question

Create two pages, one called `ieonly.htm` and the other called `notieonly.htm`. Each page should have a heading telling you what page is loaded. For example:

```
<H2>Welcome to the Internet Explorer only page</H2>
```

Using the functions for checking browser type, connect to the `window` object's `onload` event handler and detect what browser the user has. Then, if it's the wrong page for that browser, redirect to the other page.

Exercise 2 Solution

The `notieonly.htm` page is as follows:

```
<!DOCTYPE html PUBLIC "-//W3C//DTD XHTML 1.0 Strict//EN"
    "http://www.w3.org/TR/xhtml1/DTD/xhtml1-strict.dtd">

<html xmlns="http://www.w3.org/1999/xhtml">
<head>
    <title>Chapter 6: Example Question 2</title>
    <script type="text/javaScript">
    function getBrowserName()
    {
        var lsBrowser = navigator.userAgent;
        if (lsBrowser.indexOf("MSIE") >= 0)
        {
            lsBrowser = "MSIE";
        }
        else if (lsBrowser.indexOf("Firefox") >= 0)
        {
            lsBrowser = "Firefox";
        }
        else if (lsBrowser.indexOf("Chrome") >= 0)
        {
            lsBrowser = "Chrome";
        }
        else if (lsBrowser.indexOf("Safari") >= 0)
        {
            lsBrowser = "Safari";
        }
        else if (lsBrowser.indexOf("Opera") >= 0)
        {
            lsBrowser = "Opera";
        }
        else
        {
            lsBrowser = "UNKNOWN";
        }
        return lsBrowser;
    }

    function getBrowserVersion()
    {
```

```
        var findIndex;
        var browserVersion = 0;
        var browser = getBrowserName();

        browserVersion = navigator.userAgent;
        findIndex = browserVersion.indexOf(browser) + browser.length + 1;
        browserVersion = parseFloat(browserVersion.substring(findIndex,
                findIndex + 3));

        return browserVersion;
    }

    function checkBrowser()
    {
        if (getBrowserName() == "MSIE")
        {
          window.location.replace("ieonly.htm");
        }
    }
    </script>
</head>
<body onload="checkBrowser()">
<h2>Welcome to the Not-IE only page</h2>
</body>
</html>
```

The ieonly.htm page is very similar:

```
<!DOCTYPE html PUBLIC "-//W3C//DTD XHTML 1.0 Strict//EN"
    "http://www.w3.org/TR/xhtml1/DTD/xhtml1-strict.dtd">

<html xmlns="http://www.w3.org/1999/xhtml">
<head>
    <title>Chapter 6: Example Question 2</title>
    <script type="text/javaScript">
    function getBrowserName()
    {
        var lsBrowser = navigator.userAgent;
        if (lsBrowser.indexOf("MSIE") >= 0)
        {
            lsBrowser = "MSIE";
        }
        else if (lsBrowser.indexOf("Firefox") >= 0)
        {
            lsBrowser = "Firefox";
        }
        else if (lsBrowser.indexOf("Chrome") >= 0)
        {
            lsBrowser = "Chrome";
        }
        else if (lsBrowser.indexOf("Safari") >= 0)
        {
            lsBrowser = "Safari";
        }
```

```
                else if (lsBrowser.indexOf("Opera") >= 0)
                {
                        lsBrowser = "Opera";
                }
                else
                {
                        lsBrowser = "UNKNOWN";
                }
                return lsBrowser;
        }

        function getBrowserVersion()
        {
            var findIndex;
            var browserVersion = 0;
            var browser = getBrowserName();

            browserVersion = navigator.userAgent;
            findIndex = browserVersion.indexOf(browser) + browser.length + 1;
            browserVersion = parseFloat(browserVersion.substring(findIndex,
                    findIndex + 3));

            return browserVersion;
        }

        function checkBrowser()
        {
            if (getBrowserName() != "MSIE")
            {
               window.location.replace("notieonly.htm");
            }
        }
    </script>
</head>
<body onload="checkBrowser()">
<h2>Welcome to the Internet Explorer only page</h2>
</body>
</html>
```

Starting with the ieonly.htm page, first you add an onload event handler, connected to the checkBrowser() function, so that the function is called when the page loads.

```
    <body onload="checkBrowser()">
```

Then, in checkBrowser(), you use your getBrowserName() function to tell you which browser the user has. If it's not IE, you replace the page loaded with the notieonly.htm page. Note that you use replace() rather than href, because you don't want the user to be able to click the browser's Back button. This way it's less easy to spot that a new page is being loaded.

```
function checkBrowser()
{
    if (getBrowserName() != "MSIE")
```

```
        {
            window.location.replace("notieonly.htm");
        }
    }
```

The `notieonly.htm` page is identical, except that in your `if` statement you check if the browser is `MSIE` and redirect to `ieonly.htm` if it is.

```
function checkBrowser()
{
    if (getBrowserName() == "MSIE")
    {
        window.location.replace("ieonly.htm");
    }
}
```

Exercise 3 Question

Insert an image in the page with the `<img/>` element. When the mouse pointer rolls over the image, it should switch to a different image. When the mouse pointer rolls out (leaves the image), it should swap back again. (Hint: These events are `mouseover` and `mouseout`.)

Exercise 3 Solution

```
<!DOCTYPE html PUBLIC "-//W3C//DTD XHTML 1.0 Strict//EN"
    "http://www.w3.org/TR/xhtml1/DTD/xhtml1-strict.dtd">

<html xmlns="http://www.w3.org/1999/xhtml">
<head>
    <title>Chapter 6: Question 3</title>
    <script type="text/javascript">
    function mouseOver(that)
    {
        that.src = "Img2.jpg";
    }

    function mouseOut(that)
    {
        that.src = "Img1.jpg";
    }
    </script>
</head>
<body>
<img src="Img1.jpg" name="myImage" onmouseover="mouseOver(this)"
    onmouseout="mouseOut(this)" />
</body>
</html>
```

Save this as `ch06_q3.htm`.

At the top of the page you define your two functions to handle the mouseover and mouseout events.

```
function mouseOver(that)
{
    that.src = "Img2.jpg";
}

function mouseOut(that)
{
    that.src = "Img1.jpg";
}
```

The function names tell you what events they will be handling. You access the img object for your <img/> element by passing a reference to the img object to the function. In the mouseover event you change the src property of the image to Img2.tif, and in the mouseout event you change it back to img1.tif, the image you specified when the page was loaded.

In the page itself you have your <img/> element.

```
<img src="Img1.jpg" name="myImage" onmouseover="mouseOver(this)"
    onmouseout="mouseOut(this)" />
```

Chapter 7

Exercise 1 Question

Using the code from the temperature converter example you saw in Chapter 2, create a user interface for it and connect it to the existing code so that the user can enter a value in degrees Fahrenheit and convert it to centigrade.

Exercise 1 Solution

```
<!DOCTYPE html PUBLIC "-//W3C//DTD XHTML 1.0 Transitional//EN"
    "http://www.w3.org/TR/xhtml1/DTD/xhtml1-transitional.dtd">
<html xmlns="http://www.w3.org/1999/xhtml">
<head>
    <title>Chapter 7: Question 1</title>
    <script type="text/javascript">
function convertToCentigrade(degFahren)
{
    var degCent = 5 / 9 * (degFahren - 32);

    return degCent;
}

function btnToCent_onclick()
{
```

```
            var calcBox = document.form1.txtCalcBox;

            if (isNaN(calcBox.value) == true || calcBox.value == "")
            {
                calcBox.value = "Error Invalid Value";
            }
            else
            {
                calcBox.value = convertToCentigrade(calcBox.value);
            }
        }
    </script>
</head>
<body>
    <form action="" name="form1">
        <p>
            <input type="text" name="txtCalcBox" value="0.0" />
        </p>
        <input type="button" value="Convert to centigrade"
            name="btnToCent" onclick="btnToCent_onclick()" />
    </form>
</body>
</html>
```

Save this as ch07_q1.htm.

The interface part is simply a form containing a text box into which users enter the Fahrenheit value and a button they click to convert that value to centigrade. The button has its onclick event handler set to call a function named btnToCent_onclick().

The first line of btnToCent_onclick() declares a variable and sets it to reference the object representing the text box.

```
    var calcBox = document.form1.txtCalcBox;
```

Why do this? Well, in your code when you want to use document.form1.txtCalcBox, you can now just use the much shorter calcBox; it saves typing and keeps your code shorter and easier to read.

So

```
    alert(document.form1.txtCalcBox.value);
```

is the same as

```
    alert(calcBox.value);
```

In the remaining part of the function you do a sanity check — if what the user has entered is a number (that is, it is not NotANumber) and the text box does contain a value, you use the Fahrenheit-to-centigrade conversion function you saw in Chapter 2 to do the conversion, the results of which are used to set the text box's value.

Exercise 2 Question

Create a user interface that allows the user to pick the computer system of their dreams, similar in principle to the e-commerce sites selling computers over the Internet. For example, they could be given a choice of processor type, speed, memory, and hard drive size, and the option to add additional components like a DVD-ROM drive, a sound card, and so on. As the user changes their selections, the price of the system should update automatically and notify them of the cost of the system as they specified it, either by using an alert box or by updating the contents of a text box.

Exercise 2 Solution

```html
<!DOCTYPE html PUBLIC "-//W3C//DTD XHTML 1.0 Transitional//EN"
    "http://www.w3.org/TR/xhtml1/DTD/xhtml1-transitional.dtd">
<html xmlns="http://www.w3.org/1999/xhtml">
<head>
    <title>Chapter 7: Question 1</title>
    <script type="text/javascript">
var compItems = new Array();
compItems[100] = 1000;
compItems[101] = 1250;
compItems[102] = 1500;

compItems[200] = 35;
compItems[201] = 65;
compItems[202] = 95;

compItems[300] = 50;
compItems[301] = 75;
compItems[302] = 100;

compItems[400] = 10;
compItems[401] = 15;
compItems[402] = 25;
function updateOrderDetails()
{
    var total = 0;
    var orderDetails = "";
    var formElement;
    var theForm = document.form1;
    formElement = theForm.cboProcessor[theForm.cboProcessor.selectedIndex];
    total = parseFloat(compItems[formElement.value]);
    orderDetails = "Processor : " + formElement.text;
    orderDetails = orderDetails + " $" + compItems[formElement.value] + "\n";

    formElement = theForm.cboHardDrive[theForm.cboHardDrive.selectedIndex];
    total = total + parseFloat(compItems[formElement.value]);
    orderDetails = orderDetails + "Hard Drive : " + formElement.text;
    orderDetails = orderDetails + " $" + compItems[formElement.value] + "\n";

    formElement = theForm.chkCDROM;
    if (formElement.checked == true)
    {
        orderDetails = orderDetails + "CD-ROM : $" +
```

```
                    compItems[formElement.value] + "\n";
                total = total + parseFloat(compItems[formElement.value]);
            }

            formElement = theForm.chkDVD;
            if (formElement.checked == true)
            {
                orderDetails = orderDetails + "DVD-ROM : $" +
                    compItems[formElement.value] + "\n";
                total = total + parseFloat(compItems[formElement.value]);
            }

            formElement = theForm.chkScanner;
            if (formElement.checked == true)
            {
                orderDetails = orderDetails + "Scanner : $" +
                    compItems[formElement.value] + "\n";
                total = total + parseFloat(compItems[formElement.value]);
            }

            formElement = theForm.radCase;
            if (formElement[0].checked == true)
            {
                orderDetails = orderDetails + "Desktop Case : $" +
                    compItems[formElement[0].value];
                total = total + parseFloat(compItems[formElement[0].value]);
            }
            else if (formElement[1].checked == true)
            {
                orderDetails = orderDetails + "Mini Tower Case : $" +
                    compItems[formElement[1].value];
                total = total + parseFloat(compItems[formElement[1].value]);
            }
            else
            {
                orderDetails = orderDetails + "Full Tower Case : $" +
                    compItems[formElement[2].value];
                total = total + parseFloat(compItems[formElement[2].value]);
            }

            orderDetails = orderDetails + "\n\nTotal Order Cost is $" + total;

            theForm.txtOrder.value = orderDetails;
        }

    </script>
</head>
<body>
    <form action="" name="form1">
        <table>
            <tr>
                <td width="300">
                    Processor
                    <br />
```

```
                            <select name="cboProcessor">
                                <option value="100">MegaPro 10ghz</option>
                                <option value="101">MegaPro 12</option>
                                <option value="102">MegaPro 15ghz</option>
                            </select>
                            <br />
                            <br />
                            Hard drive
                            <br />
                            <select name="cboHardDrive">
                                <option value="200">30tb</option>
                                <option value="201">40tb</option>
                                <option value="202">60tb</option>
                            </select>
                            <br />
                            <br />
                            CD-ROM
                            <input type="checkbox" name="chkCDROM" value="300" />
                            <br />
                            DVD-ROM
                            <input type="checkbox" name="chkDVD" value="301" />
                            <br />
                            Scanner
                            <input type="checkbox" name="chkScanner" value="302" />
                            <br />
                            <br />
                            Desktop Case
                            <input type="radio" name="radCase" checked value="400" />
                            <br />
                            Mini Tower
                            <input type="radio" name="radCase" value="401" />
                            <br />
                            Full Tower
                            <input type="radio" name="radCase" value="402" />
                            <br />
                            <br />
                            <input type="button" value="Update" name="butUpdate"
                                onclick="updateOrderDetails()" />
                        </td>
                        <td>
                            <textarea rows="20" cols="35" id="txtOrder"
                                name="txtOrder"></textarea>
                        </td>
                    </tr>
                </table>
            </form>
    </body>
</html>
```

Save this as ch07_q2.htm.

This is just one of many ways to tackle this question — you may well have thought of a better way.

Here you are displaying the results of the user's selection as text in a `textarea` box, with each item and its cost displayed on separate lines and a final total at the end.

Each form element has a value set to hold a stock ID number. For example, a full tower case is stock ID 402. The actual cost of the item is held in arrays defined at the beginning of the page. Why not just store the price in the `value` attribute of each form element? Well, this way is more flexible. Currently your array just holds price details for each item, but you could modify it that so it holds more data — for example price, description, number in stock, and so on. Also, if this form is posted to a server the values passed will be stock IDs, which you could then use for a lookup in a stock database. If the values were set to prices and the form were posted, you'd have no way of telling what the customer ordered — all you'd know is how much it all cost.

This solution includes an Update button which, when clicked, updates the order details in the `textarea` box. However, you may want to add event handlers to each form element and update when anything changes.

Turning to the function that actually displays the order summary, `updateOrderDetails()`, you can see that there is a lot of code, and although it looks complex, it's actually fairly simple. A lot of it is repeated with slight modification.

To save on typing and make the code a little more readable, this solution declares two variables: `theForm` to contain the `Form` object, and `formElement`, which will be set to each element on the form in turn and used to extract the stock ID and, from that, the price. After the variable's declaration, you then find out which processor has been selected, calculate the cost, and add the details to the `textarea`.

```
formElement = theForm.cboProcessor[document.form1.cboProcessor.selectedIndex];
total = parseFloat(compItems[formElement.value]);
orderDetails = "Processor : " + formElement.text;
orderDetails = orderDetails + " $" + compItems[formElement.value] + "\n";
```

The `selectedIndex` property tells us which `Option` object inside the select control has been selected by the user, and you set the `formElement` variable to reference that.

The same principle applies when you find the hard drive size selected, so let's turn next to the check boxes for the optional extra items, looking first at the CD-ROM check box.

```
formElement = theForm.chkCDROM
if (formElement.checked == true)
{
    orderDetails = orderDetails + "CD-ROM : $" +
        compItems[formElement.value] + "\n";
    total = total + parseFloat(compItems[formElement.value]);
}
```

Again, set the `formElement` variable to now reference the `chkCDROM` check box object. Then, if the check box is checked, you add a CD-ROM to the order details and update the running total. The same principle applies for the DVD and scanner check boxes.

Finally, you have the case type. Because only one case type out of the options can be selected, you used a radio button group. Unfortunately, there is no selectedIndex for radio buttons as there is for check boxes, so you have to go through each radio button in turn and find out if it has been selected.

```
formElement = theForm.radCase
if (formElement[0].checked == true)
{
    orderDetails = orderDetails + "Desktop Case : $" +
        compItems[formElement[0].value];
    total = total + parseFloat(compItems[formElement[0].value]);
}
else if (formElement[1].checked == true)
{
    orderDetails = orderDetails + "Mini Tower Case : $" +
        compItems[formElement[1].value];
    total = total + parseFloat(compItems[formElement[1].value]);
}
else
{
    orderDetails = orderDetails + "Full Tower Case : $" +
        compItems[formElement[2].value]
    total = total + parseFloat(compItems[formElement[2].value]);
}
```

You check to see which radio button the user selected and add its details to the textarea and its price to the total. If the array of stock defined at the beginning of the code block had further details, such as description as well as price, you could have looped through the radio button array and added the details based on the compItems array.

Finally, set the textarea to the details of the system the user has selected.

```
orderDetails = orderDetails + "\n\nTotal Order Cost is " + total;
theForm.txtOrder.value = orderDetails;
```

Chapter 8

Exercise 1 Question

In the previous chapter's exercise questions, you created a form that allowed the user to pick a computer system. They could view the details of their system and its total cost by clicking a button that wrote the details to a textarea. Change the example so it's a frames-based web page; instead of writing to a text area, the application should write the details to another frame. Hint: use about:blank as the src of the frame you write to. Hint: use the document object's close() and open() methods to clear the details frame from previously written data.

Exercise 1 Solution

The solution shown here involves a frameset that divides the page into left and right frames. In the left frame displays the form that allows the user to pick their system. A summarization of the user's choices display in the right frame when the user clicks an Update button.

The first page is the frameset page, which the browser loads first.

```
<!DOCTYPE html PUBLIC "-//W3C//DTD XHTML 1.0 Frameset//EN"
    "http://www.w3.org/TR/xhtml1/DTD/xhtml1-frameset.dtd">

<html xmlns="http://www.w3.org/1999/xhtml">
<head>
<title>Chapter 8: Question 1 Answer</title>
</head>
<frameset cols="55%,*">
    <frame src="ch8_q1_picksystem.htm" name="pickSystem">
    <frame src="about:blank" name="systemSummary">
</frameset>
</html>
```

Save this as ch8_q1_frameset.htm.

Finally, you come to the page loaded into the left frame; it allows the user to choose their computer system and its components. This is very similar to the solution to Question 2 in the previous chapter, so this example shows only what changed. All the changes are within the updateOrderDetails() function, and they're highlighted in the following code:

```
function updateOrderDetails()
{
    var total = 0;
    var orderDetails = "";
    var formElement;
    var theForm = document.form1;
    formElement = theForm.cboProcessor[theForm.cboProcessor.selectedIndex];
    total = parseFloat(compItems[formElement.value]);
    orderDetails = "Processor : " + formElement.text;
    orderDetails = orderDetails + " $" + compItems[formElement.value] + "<br />";

    formElement = theForm.cboHardDrive[theForm.cboHardDrive.selectedIndex];
    total = total + parseFloat(compItems[formElement.value]);
    orderDetails = orderDetails + "Hard Drive : " + formElement.text;
    orderDetails = orderDetails + " $" + compItems[formElement.value] + "<br />";

    formElement = theForm.chkCDROM;
    if (formElement.checked == true)
    {
        orderDetails = orderDetails + "CD-ROM : $"
            + compItems[formElement.value] + "<br />";
        total = total + parseFloat(compItems[formElement.value]);
    }

    formElement = theForm.chkDVD;
    if (formElement.checked == true)
    {
        orderDetails = orderDetails + "DVD-ROM : $"
            + compItems[formElement.value] + "<br />";
        total = total + parseFloat(compItems[formElement.value]);
    }

    formElement = theForm.chkScanner;
```

```
if (formElement.checked == true)
{
    orderDetails = orderDetails + "Scanner : $"
        + compItems[formElement.value] + "<br />";
    total = total + parseFloat(compItems[formElement.value]);
}

formElement = theForm.radCase;
if (formElement[0].checked == true)
{
    orderDetails = orderDetails + "Desktop Case : $"
        + compItems[formElement[0].value] + "<br />";
    total = total + parseFloat(compItems[formElement[0].value]);
}
else if (formElement[1].checked == true)
{
    orderDetails = orderDetails + "Mini Tower Case : $"
        + compItems[formElement[1].value] + "<br />";
    total = total + parseFloat(compItems[formElement[1].value]);
}
else
{
    orderDetails = orderDetails + "Full Tower Case : $"
        + compItems[formElement[2].value] + "<br />";
    total = total + parseFloat(compItems[formElement[2].value]);
}


orderDetails = orderDetails + "<p>Total Order Cost is $" + total + "</p>";

top.systemSummary.document.close();
top.systemSummary.document.open();
top.systemSummary.document.write(orderDetails);
}
```

Remove the <textarea/> element from the page, as you no longer need it. Save the file as ch8_q1_picksystem.htm, and load ch8_q1_frameset.htm into your browser to try out the code.

The first difference between this version and the version from Question 2 in the last chapter is that when creating the text summarizing the system, you are creating HTML rather than plain text, so rather than \n for new lines you use the <br/> element.

The main change, however, is the following three lines:

```
top.systemSummary.document.close();
top.systemSummary.document.open();
top.systemSummary.document.write(orderDetails);
```

Instead of setting the value of a <textarea/> box as you did in the solution to Question 2 in the last chapter, this time you write the order summary to an HTML page, the page contained in the right-hand frame, systemSummary. First you close the document with the close() method. Otherwise, subsequent updates result in HTML being appended to the page as opposed to replacing the current contents. Then you open the document for writing with open(), and you write out the summarization string.

Exercise 2 Question

The fourth example (ch08_examp4.htm) was a page with images of books, in which clicking on a book's image brought up information about that book in a pop-up window. Amend this so that the pop-up window also has a button or link that, when clicked, adds the item to a shopping basket. Also, on the main page, give the user some way of opening up a shopping basket window with details of all the items they have purchased so far, and give them a way of deleting items from this basket.

Exercise 2 Solution

This is the most challenging exercise so far, but by the end you'll see how a more complex application can be created using JavaScript. The solution to this exercise involves four pages: two that display the book's details (very similar to the pages you created in the example), a third that displays the book's images and opens the new windows, and a fourth, totally new page, which holds the shopping basket.

Let's look at the main page to be loaded, called ch8_q2_online_books.htm.

```
<!DOCTYPE html PUBLIC "-//W3C//DTD XHTML 1.0 Transitional//EN"
    "http://www.w3.org/TR/xhtml1/DTD/xhtml1-transitional.dtd">

<html xmlns="http://www.w3.org/1999/xhtml">
<head>
    <title>Chapter 8: Question 2</title>
    <script type="text/javascript">
    var detailsWindow;
    var basketWindow;

    var stockItems = new Array();
    stockItems[0] = new StockItem("Professional Ajax, 2nd Edition", "$39.99");
    stockItems[1] = new StockItem("Professonal JavaScript, 2nd Edition", "$46.99");

    function removeItem(stockId)
    {
        stockItems[stockId].quantity = 0;
        alert("Item Removed");
        showBasket();
        return false;
    }

    function addBookToBasket(stockId)
    {
        stockItems[stockId].quantity = 1;
        alert("Item added successfully");
        detailsWindow.close();
    }

    function showDetails(bookURL)
    {
        detailsWindow = window.open(bookURL, "bookDetails",
"width=400,height=500");
        detailsWindow.focus();
        return false;
```

```
    }

    function showBasket()
    {
        basketWindow = window.open('about:blank', 'shoppingBasket',
            'width=400,height=350');
        basketWindow.document.open();
        var basketItem;
        var containsItems = false;
        basketWindow.document.write("<h4>Your shopping basket contains :</h4>");

        for (var i = 0; i < stockItems.length; i++)
        {
            var stockItem = stockItems[i];

            if (stockItem.quantity > 0)
            {
                basketWindow.document.write(stockItem.title + " at ");
                basketWindow.document.write(stockItem.price);
                basketWindow.document.write("    ");
                basketWindow.document.write("<a href='' onclick='return "
                    + "window.opener.removeItem(" + i + ")'>");
                basketWindow.document.write("Remove Item</a><br />");
                containsItems = true;
            }
        }

        if (!containsItems)
        {
            basketWindow.document.write("<h4>No items</h4>");
        }

        basketWindow.document.close();
        basketWindow.focus();
    }

    function StockItem(title, price)
    {
        this.title = title;
        this.price = price;
        this.quantity = 0;
    }
    </script>
</head>
<body>
    <h2 align="center">
        Online Book Buyer</h2>
    <form name="form1" action="">
        <input type="button" value="Show Shopping Basket" onclick="showBasket()"
name="btnShowBasket" />
    </form>
    <p>
        Click any of the images below for more details
    </p>
```

```
        <h4>Professional Ajax</h4>
        <p>
            <img src="pro_ajax.jpg" alt="Professional Ajax, 2nd Edition" border="0"
                onclick="showDetails('pro_ajax_details.htm')" />
        </p>
        <h4>Professional JavaScript for Web Developers</h4>
        <p>
            <img src="pro_js.jpg" alt="Professional JavaScript, 2nd Edition" border="0"
                onclick="showDetails('pro_js_details.htm')" />
        </p>
</body>
</html>
```

The details of the books are stored in the stockItems array, which will contain StockItem objects, a reference type you define with the StockItem() constructor function.

```
function StockItem(title, price)
{
    this.title = title;
    this.price = price;
    this.quantity = 0;
}
```

Objects created by this function have title, price, and quantity properties. The first two are assigned values from the two parameters of the same name, and the third initializes as 0.

So you populate the stockItems array first, with each element containing a StockItem object as the following code shows:

```
        var stockItems = new Array();
        stockItems[0] = new StockItem("Professional Ajax, 2nd Edition", "$39.99");
        stockItems[1] = new StockItem("Professonal JavaScript, 2nd Edition", "$46.99");
```

The first function defined in the code is removeItem().

```
        function removeItem(stockId)
        {
            stockItems[stockId].quantity = 0;
            alert("Item Removed");
            showBasket();
            return false;
        }
```

This removes a book from the shopping basket. It accepts one parameter called stockId, the array element index of that book, which you use to set the quantity property to 0.

Next, you have the function that adds a book to the shopping basket, addBookToBasket().

```
        function addBookToBasket(stockId)
        {
            stockItems[stockId].quantity = 1;
            alert("Item added successfully");
```

```
        detailsWindow.close();
    }
```

The final function displays the contents of the shopping basket in a new window.

```
function showBasket()
{
    basketWindow = window.open('about:blank','shoppingBasket',
        'width=400,height=350');
    basketWindow.document.open();
    var basketItem;
    var containsItems = false;
    basketWindow.document.write("<h4>Your shopping basket contains :</h4>");

    for (var i = 0; i < stockItems.length; i++)
    {
        var stockItem = stockItems[i];

        if (stockItem.quantity > 0)
        {
            basketWindow.document.write(stockItem.title + " at ");
            basketWindow.document.write(stockItem.price);
            basketWindow.document.write("    ");
            basketWindow.document.write("<a href='' onclick='return "
                + "window.opener.removeItem(" + i + ")'>");
            basketWindow.document.write("Remove Item</a><br />");
            containsItems = true;
        }
    }

    if (!containsItems)
    {
        basketWindow.document.write("<h4>No items</h4>");
    }

    basketWindow.document.close();
    basketWindow.focus();
}
```

First, you open a new window and store its `window` object reference in `basketWindow`. You then write a heading to the new window's `document`, and then you loop through each item in the `stockItems` array and check the `quantity` property of the `StockItem` object. If it is greater than zero, you write the book's details to the shopping list window. You also write out a link to the shopping basket that when clicked calls your `removeItem()` function.

Finally, you need to create the book description pages. First you have `pro_ajax_details.htm`. This is identical to the version you created for the example, except for the addition of the form and button inside. When clicked, the button calls the `addToBasket()` function in the window that opened this window — that is, `ch8_q2_online_books.htm`. The highlighted portion of the following code shows the changes made to this file:

```
<!DOCTYPE html PUBLIC "-//W3C//DTD XHTML 1.0 Transitional//EN"
    "http://www.w3.org/TR/xhtml1/DTD/xhtml1-transitional.dtd">
```

```
<html xmlns="http://www.w3.org/1999/xhtml">
<head>
    <title>Professional ASP.NET 2.0</title>
</head>
<body>
    <h3>Professional Ajax, 2nd Edition</h3>
    <form name="form1" action="">
        <input type="button" value="Add to basket" name="btnAddBook"
            onclick="window.opener.addBookToBasket(0)" />
    </form>
    <strong>Subjects</strong><br />
    Ajax<br />
    Internet<br />
    JavaScript<br />
    ASP.NET<br />
    PHP<br />
    XML<br />
    <hr color="#cc3333" />
    <h3>Book overview</h3>
    <p>
        A comprehensive look at the technologies and techniques used in Ajax,
        complete with real world examples and case studies. A must have for
        any Web professional looking to build interactive Web sites.
    </p>
</body>
</html>
```

Finally, you create the `pro_js_details.htm` page. Again, it is identical to the version created in the example, with a form and button to add the book to the shopping basket, as in the `pro_ajax_details.htm` page. The highlighted portion of the following code shows the changes made to this file:

```
<!DOCTYPE html PUBLIC "-//W3C//DTD XHTML 1.0 Transitional//EN"
    "http://www.w3.org/TR/xhtml1/DTD/xhtml1-transitional.dtd">
<html xmlns="http://www.w3.org/1999/xhtml">
<head>
    <title>Professional JavaScript</title>
</head>
<body>
    <h3>Professional JavaScript, 2nd Edition</h3>
    <form name="form1">
        <input type="button" value="Add to basket" name="btnAddBook"
            onclick="window.opener.addBookToBasket(1)" />
    </form>
    <strong>Subjects</strong>
    ECMAScript<br />
    Internet<br />
    JavaScript
    <br />
    XML and Scripting<br />
    <hr color="#cc3333" />
    <p>
        This book takes a comprehensive look at the JavaScript language
        and prepares the reader with in-depth knowledge of the languages.
    </p>
```

```
    <p>
        It includes a guide to the language - when where and how to get
        the most out of JavaScript - together with practical case studies
        demonstrating JavaScript in action. Coverage is bang up-to-date, with
        discussion of compatability issues and version differences, and the
        book concludes with a comprehensive reference section.
    </p>
</body>
</html>
```

Chapter 9

Exercise 1 Question

What problem does the following code solve?

```
var myString = "This sentence has has a fault and and we need to fix it."
var myRegExp = /(\b\w+\b) \1/g;
myString = myString.replace(myRegExp,"$1");
```

Now imagine that you change that code, so that you create the RegExp object like this:

```
var myRegExp = new RegExp("(\b\w+\b) \1");
```

Why would this not work, and how could you rectify the problem?

Exercise 1 Solution

The problem is that the sentence has "has has" and "and and" inside it, clearly a mistake. A lot of word processors have an autocorrect feature that fixes common mistakes like this, and what your regular expression does is mimic this feature.

So the erroneous myString

"This sentence has has a fault and and we need to fix it."

will become

"This sentence has a fault and we need to fix it."

Let's look at how the code works, starting with the regular expression.

```
/(\b\w+\b) \1/g;
```

By using parentheses, you have defined a group, so (\b\w+\b) is group 1. This group matches the pattern of a word boundary followed by one or more alphanumeric characters, that is, a–z, A–Z, 0–9, and _, followed by a word boundary. Following the group you have a space then \1. What \1 means is match exactly the same characters as were matched in pattern group 1. So, for example, if group 1 matched "has," then \1 will match "has" as well. It's important to note that \1 will match the exact previous match by group 1. So when group 1 then matches the "and," the \1 now matches "and" and not the "has" that was previously matched.

You use the group again in your replace() method; this time the group is specified using the $ symbol, so $1 matches group 1. It's this that causes the two matched "has" and "and" to be replaced by just one.

Turning to the second part of the question, how do you need to change the following code so that it works?

```
var myRegExp = new RegExp("(\b\w+\b) \1");
```

Easy; now you are using a string passed to the RegExp object's constructor, and you need to use two slashes (\\) rather than one when you mean a regular expression syntax character, like this:

```
var myRegExp = new RegExp("(\\b\\w+\\b) \\1","g");
```

Notice you've also passed a g to the second parameter to make it a global match.

Exercise 2 Question

Write a regular expression that finds all of the occurrences of the word "a" in the following sentence and replaces them with "the":

"a dog walked in off a street and ordered a finest beer"

The sentence should become:

"the dog walked in off the street and ordered the finest beer"

Exercise 2 Solution

```
<!DOCTYPE html PUBLIC "-//W3C//DTD XHTML 1.0 Transitional//EN"
"http://www.w3.org/TR/xhtml1/DTD/xhtml1-transitional.dtd">
<html xmlns="http://www.w3.org/1999/xhtml">
<body>
<script language="JavaScript" type="text/javascript">
var myString = "a dog walked in off a street and ordered a finest beer";
var myRegExp = /\ba\b/gi;
myString = myString.replace(myRegExp,"the");
alert(myString);
</script>
</body>
</html>
```

Save this as ch09_q2.htm.

With regular expressions, it's often not just what you want to match, but also what you don't want to match that is a problem. Here you want to match the letter a, so why not just write

```
var myRegExp = /a/gi;
```

Well, that would work, but it would also replace the "a" in "walked," which you don't want. You want to replace the letter "a" but only where it's a word on its own and not inside another word. So when does a letter become a word? The answer is when it's between two word boundaries. The word boundary is represented by the regular expression special character \b so the regular expression becomes

```
var myRegExp = /\ba\b/gi;
```

The gi at the end ensures a global, case-insensitive search.

Now with your regular expression created, you can use it in the replace() method's first parameter.

```
myString = myString.replace(myRegExp,"the");
```

Exercise 3 Question

Imagine you have a web site with a message board. Write a regular expression that would remove barred words. (You can make up your own words!)

Exercise 3 Solution

```
<!DOCTYPE html PUBLIC "-//W3C//DTD XHTML 1.0 Transitional//EN"
"http://www.w3.org/TR/xhtml1/DTD/xhtml1-transitional.dtd">
<html xmlns="http://www.w3.org/1999/xhtml">
<body>
<script language="JavaScript" type="text/javascript">
    var myRegExp = /(sugar )?candy|choc(olate|oholic)?/gi;
    var myString = "Mmm, I love chocolate, I'm a chocoholic. " +
        "I love candy too, sweet, sugar candy";
    myString = myString.replace(myRegExp,"salad");
    alert(myString)
</script>
</body>
</html>
```

Save this as ch09_q3.htm.

For this example, pretend you're creating script for a board on a dieting site where text relating to candy is barred and will be replaced with a much healthier option, salad.

The barred words are

❑   chocolate

❑   choc

- ❑ chocoholic
- ❑ sugar candy
- ❑ candy

Let's examine the regular expression to remove the offending words.

1. Start with the two basic words, so to match "choc" or "candy," you use

```
candy|choc
```

2. Add the matching for "sugar candy." Since the "sugar" bit is optional, you group it by placing it in parentheses and adding the "?" after it. This means match the group zero times or one time.

```
(sugar )?candy|choc
```

3. You need to add the optional "olate" and "oholic" end bits. You add these as a group after the "choc" word and again make the group optional. You can match either of the endings in the group by using the | character.

```
(sugar )?candy|choc(olate|oholic)?/gi
```

4. You, then, declare it as

```
var myRegExp = /(sugar )?candy|choc(olate|oholic)?/gi
```

The `gi` at the end means the regular expression will find and replace words on a global, case-insensitive basis.

So, to sum up

```
/(sugar )?candy|choc(olate|oholic)?/gi
```

reads as:

Either match zero or one occurrences of "sugar" followed by "candy." Or alternatively match "choc" followed by either one or zero occurrences of "olate" or match "choc" followed by zero or one occurrence of "oholic."

Finally, the following:

```
myString = myString.replace(myRegExp,"salad");
```

replaces the offending words with "salad" and sets `myString` to the new clean version:

```
"Mmm, I love salad, I'm a salad. I love salad too, sweet, salad."
```

Chapter 10

Exercise 1 Question

Create a web page with an advertisement image at the top. When the page loads, select a random image for that advertisement. Every four seconds, make the image change to a different one and ensure a different advertisement is selected until all the advertisement images have been seen.

Exercise 1 Solution

The solution below displays three images but changes them via a timer:

```
<!DOCTYPE html PUBLIC "-//W3C//DTD XHTML 1.0 Transitional//EN"
"http://www.w3.org/TR/xhtml1/DTD/xhtml1-transitional.dtd">
<html xmlns="http://www.w3.org/1999/xhtml">
<head>
<script type="text/javascript">

var imagesSelected = new Array(false,false,false);
var noOfImages = 3;
var totalImagesSelected = 0;

function window_onload()
{
    setInterval("switchImage()",4000);
}

function switchImage()
{

    var imageIndex;

    if (totalImagesSelected == noOfImages)
    {
        for (imageIndex = 0; imageIndex < noOfImages; imageIndex++)
        {
            imagesSelected[imageIndex] = false;
        }

        totalImagesSelected = 0;
    }

var selectedImage = Math.floor(Math.random() * noOfImages) + 1;
while (imagesSelected[selectedImage - 1] == true)
{
    selectedImage = Math.floor(Math.random() * noOfImages) + 1;
}
totalImagesSelected++;
imagesSelected[selectedImage - 1] = true;
```

```
        document.imgAdvert.src = "AdvertImage" + selectedImage + ".jpg";

}

</script>
</head>
<body onload="window_onload()">
<img src="AdvertImage1.jpg" name="imgAdvert" />
</body>
</html>
```

Save this as ch10_q1.htm.

This solution is based on the example in the chapter, Adverts.htm, where you displayed three images at set intervals one after the other. The first difference is that you select a random image each time, rather than the images in sequence. Second, you make sure you don't select the same image twice in one sequence by having an array, imagesSelected, with each element of that array being true or false depending on whether the image has been selected before. Once you've shown each image, you reset the array and start the sequence of selecting images randomly again.

The final difference between this solution and the example in the chapter is that you set the timer going continuously with setInterval(). So, until the user moves to another page, your random display of images will continue.

Exercise 2 Question

Create a form that gets the user's date of birth. Then, using that information, tell them on what day of the week they were born.

Exercise 2 Solution

```
<!DOCTYPE html PUBLIC "-//W3C//DTD XHTML 1.0 Transitional//EN"
 "http://www.w3.org/TR/xhtml1/DTD/xhtml1-transitional.dtd">
<html xmlns="http://www.w3.org/1999/xhtml">

<head>
<script type="text/javascript">

var days = new Array();
days[0] = "Sunday";
days[1] = "Monday";
days[2] = "Tuesday";
days[3] = "Wednesday";
days[4] = "Thursday";
days[5] = "Friday";
days[6] = "Saturday";

function dayOfWeek()
{

    var form = document.form1;
```

```
        var date = parseInt(form.txtDate.value)
        var year = parseInt(form.txtYear.value)

        if (isNaN(date) || isNaN(year))
        {
            alert("Please enter a valid whole number");
        }
        else
        {
            if (date < 1 || date > 31)
            {
                alert("Day of the month must be between 1 and 31");
            }
            else
            {
                userDate = date + " ";
                userDate = userDate +
                  form.selMonth.options[form.selMonth.selectedIndex].value;
                userDate = userDate + " " + year;
                var dateThen = new Date(userDate);
                alert(days[dateThen.getDay()]);
            }
        }
    }
}
</script>
</head>
<body>
<p>Find the day of your birth</p>
<p>
<form name="form1">
<input type="text" name="txtDate" size="2" maxlength="2">
<select name=selMonth>
    <option selected value="Jan">Jan</option>
    <option selected value="Feb">Feb</option>
    <option selected value="Mar">Mar</option>
    <option selected value="Apr">Apr</option>
    <option selected value="May">May</option>
    <option selected value="Jun">Jun</option>
    <option selected value="Jul">Jul</option>
    <option selected value="Aug">Aug</option>
    <option selected value="Sept">Sept</option>
    <option selected value="Oct">Oct</option>
    <option selected value="Nov">Nov</option>
    <option selected value="Dec">Dec</option>
</select>
<input type="text" name="txtYear" size="4" maxlength="4" />
<br>
<input type="button" value="Day of the week"
       onclick="dayOfWeek()" name="button1" />
</form>
</p>

</body>
</html>
```

Save this as ch10_q2.htm.

The solution is surprisingly simple. You create a new Date object based on the date entered by the user. Then you get the day of the week using the Date object's getDay() method. This returns a number, but by defining an array of days of the week to match this number, you can use the value of getDay() as the index to your days array.

You also do some basic sanity checking to make sure that the user has entered numbers and that in the case of the date, it's between 1 and 31. You could have defined a select element as the method of getting the date and only including numbers from 1 to 31. Of course, neither of these methods checks whether invalid dates are entered (for example, the 31st of February). You might want to try this as an additional exercise.

Hint: To get the last day of the month, get the first day of the next month, and then subtract 1.

Chapter 11

Exercise 1 Question

Create a page that keeps track of how many times the page has been visited by the user in the last month.

Exercise 1 Solution

```
<!DOCTYPE html PUBLIC "-//W3C//DTD XHTML 1.0 Transitional//EN"
"http://www.w3.org/TR/xhtml1/DTD/xhtml1-transitional.dtd">

<html xmlns="http://www.w3.org/1999/xhtml">

<head>
<script language="JavaScript"
type="text/JavaScript"
src="CookieFunctions.js"></script>
<script type="text/javascript">
var pageViewCount = getCookieValue("pageViewCount");
var pageFirstVisited = getCookieValue("pageFirstVisited");

if (pageViewCount == null)
{
    pageViewCount = 1;
    pageFirstVisited = new Date();
    pageFirstVisited.setMonth(pageFirstVisited.getMonth());
    pageFirstVisited = pageFirstVisited.toGMTString();
    setCookie("pageFirstVisited",pageFirstVisited,"","")
}
else
{
    pageViewCount = Math.floor(pageViewCount) + 1;
```

```
    }

    setCookie("pageViewCount",pageViewCount,"","")

</script>
</head>
<body>
<script>
var pageHTML = "You've visited this page " + pageViewCount;
pageHTML = pageHTML + " times since " + pageFirstVisited;
document.write(pageHTML);
</script>
</body>
</html>
```

Save this as ch11_q1.htm.

You looked at the cookie functions in Chapter 11, so let's turn straight to the new code.

The first two lines get two cookies and store them in variables. The first cookie holds the number of visits, the second the date the page was first visited.

```
var pageViewCount = getCookieValue("pageViewCount");
var pageFirstVisited = getCookieValue("pageFirstVisited");
```

If the pageViewCount cookie does not exist, it's either because the cookie expired (remember you are counting visits in the last month) or because the user has never visited the site before. Either way you need to set the pageViewCount to 1 and store the date the page was first visited plus one month in the pageFirstVisited variable. You'll need this value later when you want to set the expires value for the pageViewCount cookie you'll create because there is no way of using code to find out an existing cookie's expiration date.

```
if (pageViewCount == null)
{
    pageViewCount = 1;
    pageFirstVisited = new Date();
    pageFirstVisited.setMonth(pageFirstVisited.getMonth() + 1)
    pageFirstVisited = pageFirstVisited.toGMTString();
    setCookie("pageFirstVisited",pageFirstVisited,"","")
}
```

In the else statement, increase the value of pageViewCount.

```
else
{
    pageViewCount = Math.floor(pageViewCount) + 1;
}
```

You then set the cookie keeping track of the number of page visits by the user.

```
setCookie("pageViewCount",pageViewCount,"","")
```

Finally, later on in the page, write the number of page visits and the date since the counter was reset.

```
var pageHTML = "You've visited this page " + pageViewCount;
pageHTML = pageHTML + " times since " + pageFirstVisited;
document.write(pageHTML);
```

Exercise 2 Question

Use cookies to load a different advertisement every time a user visits a web page.

Exercise 2 Solution

```
<!DOCTYPE html PUBLIC "-//W3C//DTD XHTML 1.0 Transitional//EN"
"http://www.w3.org/TR/xhtml1/DTD/xhtml1-transitional.dtd">
<html xmlns="http://www.w3.org/1999/xhtml">

<head>
<script language="JavaScript" type="text/JavaScript" src="CookieFunctions.js"></
script>
</head>
<body>
<img src="AdvertImage1.jpg" name="imgAdvert">
<script type="text/javascript">

var imageNumber = getCookieValue("displayedImages");
var totalImages = 3;

if (imageNumber == null)
{
    imageNumber = "1";
}
else
{
    imageNumber = Math.floor(imageNumber) + 1;
}

if (totalImages == imageNumber)
{
    setCookie("displayedImages","","","Mon, 1 Jan 1970 00:00:00");
}
else
{
    setCookie("displayedImages",imageNumber,"","");
}

document.imgAdvert.src = "AdvertImage" + imageNumber + ".jpg";
</script>
</body>
</html>
```

Save this as ch11_q2.htm.

This solution is based on similar questions in previous chapters, such as Chapter 10, which displayed a randomly selected image. In this case you display a different image in the page each time the user visits it, as far as our selection of images allows.

You've seen the cookie setting and reading functions before in the chapter, so let's look at the new code.

Store the number of the previously displayed image in a cookie named `displayedImages`. The next image you display is that image number + 1. Once all of the images have been displayed, you start again at 1. If the user has never been to the web site, no cookie will exist so `null` will be returned from `getCookieValue()`, in which case you set `imageNumber` to 1.

Most of the code is fairly self-explanatory, except perhaps this line:

```
if (totalImages == imageNumber)
{
    setCookie("displayedImages","","","Mon, 1 Jan 1970 00:00:00")
}
```

What this bit of code does is delete the cookie by setting the cookie's expiration date to a date that has already passed.

Chapter 12

Exercise 1 Question

Here's some HTML code that creates a table. Re-create this table using only JavaScript and the core DOM objects to generate the HTML. Test your code in all browsers available to you to make sure it works in them. Hint: Comment each line as you write it to keep track of where you are in the tree structure, and create a new variable for every element on the page (for example, not just one for each of the TD cells but nine variables).

```
<table>
    <thead>
        <tr>
            <td>Car</td>
            <td>Top Speed</td>
            <td>Price</td>
        </tr>
    </thead>
    <tbody>
        <tr>
            <td>Chevrolet</td>
            <td>120mph</td>
            <td>$10,000</td>
        </tr>
        <tr>
            <td>Pontiac</td>
```

```
            <td>140mph</td>
            <td>$20,000</td>
        </tr>
    </tbody>
</table>
```

Exercise 2 Solution

It seems a rather daunting example, but rather than being difficult, it is just a conjunction of two areas, one building a tree structure and the other navigating the tree structure. You start by navigating to the `<body/>` element and creating a `<table/>` element. Now you can navigate to the new `<table/>` element you've created and create a new `<thead/>` element and carry on from there. It's a lengthy and repetitious process, so that's why it's a good idea to comment your code to keep track of where you are.

```
<!DOCTYPE html PUBLIC "-//W3C//DTD XHTML 1.0 Transitional//EN"
    "http://www.w3.org/TR/xhtml1/DTD/xhtml1-transitional.dtd">

<html xmlns="http://www.w3.org/1999/xhtml">
<head>
    <title>Chapter 12: Question 1 Answer</title>
</head>
<body>
<script type="text/javascript">
var tableElem = document.createElement("table")
var thElem = document.createElement("thead")
var trElem1 = document.createElement("tr")
var trElem2 = document.createElement("tr")
var trElem3 = document.createElement("tr")
var tdElem1 = document.createElement("td")
var tdElem2 = document.createElement("td")
var tdElem3 = document.createElement("td")
var tdElem4 = document.createElement("td")
var tdElem5 = document.createElement("td")
var tdElem6 = document.createElement("td")
var tdElem7 = document.createElement("td")
var tdElem8 = document.createElement("td")
var tdElem9 = document.createElement("td")
var tbodyElem = document.createElement("tbody")
var textNodeA1 = document.createTextNode("Car")
var textNodeA2 = document.createTextNode("Top Speed")
var textNodeA3 = document.createTextNode("Price")
var textNodeB1 = document.createTextNode("Chevrolet")
var textNodeB2 = document.createTextNode("120mph")
var textNodeB3 = document.createTextNode("$10,000")
var textNodeC1 = document.createTextNode("Pontiac")
var textNodeC2 = document.createTextNode("140mph")
var textNodeC3 = document.createTextNode("$14,000")

docNavigate = document.documentElement;    //Starts with HTML document
docNavigate = docNavigate.firstChild.nextSibling; //Moves to the head
                                            // then body element
docNavigate.appendChild(tableElem);        //Adds the table element
docNavigate = docNavigate.lastChild;       //Moves to the table element
```

```
docNavigate.appendChild(thElem);              //Adds the thead element
docNavigate = docNavigate.firstChild;         //Moves to the thead element
docNavigate.appendChild(trElem1);             //Adds the TR element
docNavigate = docNavigate.firstChild;         //Moves the TR element
docNavigate.appendChild(tdElem1);             //Adds the first TD element in the
                                              // heading
docNavigate.appendChild(tdElem2);             //Adds the second TD element in the
                                              // heading
docNavigate.appendChild(tdElem3);             //Adds the third TD element in the
                                              // heading
docNavigate = docNavigate.firstChild;         //Moves to the first TD element
docNavigate.appendChild(textNodeA1);          //Adds the second text node
docNavigate = docNavigate.nextSibling;        //Moves to the next TD element
docNavigate.appendChild(textNodeA2);          //Adds the second text node
docNavigate = docNavigate.nextSibling;        //Moves to the next TD element
docNavigate.appendChild(textNodeA3);          //Adds the third text node

docNavigate = docNavigate.parentNode;         //Moves back to the TR element
docNavigate = docNavigate.parentNode;         //Moves back to the thead element
docNavigate = docNavigate.parentNode;         //Moves back to the table element
docNavigate.appendChild(tbodyElem);           //Adds the tbody element
docNavigate = docNavigate.lastChild;          //Moves to the tbody element
docNavigate.appendChild(trElem2);             //Adds the second TR element
docNavigate = docNavigate.lastChild;          //Moves to the second TR element
docNavigate.appendChild(tdElem4);             //Adds the TD element
docNavigate.appendChild(tdElem5);             //Adds the TD element
docNavigate.appendChild(tdElem6);             //Adds the TD element
docNavigate = docNavigate.firstChild;         //Moves to the first TD element
docNavigate.appendChild(textNodeB1);          //Adds the first text node
docNavigate = docNavigate.nextSibling;        //Moves to the next TD element
docNavigate.appendChild(textNodeB2);          //Adds the second text node
docNavigate = docNavigate.nextSibling;        //Moves to the next TD element
docNavigate.appendChild(textNodeB3);          //Adds the third text node
docNavigate = docNavigate.parentNode;         //Moves back to the TR element
docNavigate = docNavigate.parentNode;         //Moves back to the tbody element
docNavigate.appendChild(trElem3);             //Adds the TR element
docNavigate = docNavigate.lastChild;          //Moves to the TR element
docNavigate.appendChild(tdElem7);             //Adds the TD element
docNavigate.appendChild(tdElem8);             //Adds the TD element
docNavigate.appendChild(tdElem9);             //Adds the TD element
docNavigate = docNavigate.firstChild;         //Moves to the TD element
docNavigate.appendChild(textNodeC1);          //Adds the first text node
docNavigate = docNavigate.nextSibling;        //Moves to the next TD element
docNavigate.appendChild(textNodeC2);          //Adds the second text node
docNavigate = docNavigate.nextSibling;        //Moves to the next TD element
docNavigate.appendChild(textNodeC3);          //Adds the third text node
</script>
</body>
</html>
```

Exercise 2 Question

It was mentioned that Example 10 is an incomplete tab strip DHTML script. Make it not so incomplete by making the following changes:

- ❑ Only one tab should be active at a time.
- ❑ Only the active tab's description should be visible.

Exercise 2 Solution

Example 10 is incomplete because the script doesn't keep track of which tab is active. Probably the simplest way to add state recognition to the script is to add a global variable that keeps track of the tab number that was last clicked. This particular solution uses this idea. Changed lines of code are highlighted.

```
<!DOCTYPE html PUBLIC "-//W3C//DTD XHTML 1.0 Transitional//EN"
    "http://www.w3.org/TR/xhtml1/DTD/xhtml1-transitional.dtd">

<html xmlns="http://www.w3.org/1999/xhtml">
<head>
    <title>Chapter 12: Question 2 Answer</title>
    <style type="text/css">
    .tabStrip
    {
        background-color: #E4E2D5;
        padding: 3px;
        height: 22px;
    }

    .tabStrip div
    {
        float: left;
        font: 14px arial;
        cursor: pointer;
    }

    .tabStrip-tab
    {
        padding: 3px;
    }

    .tabStrip-tab-hover
    {
        border: 1px solid #316AC5;
        background-color: #C1D2EE;
        padding: 2px;
    }

    .tabStrip-tab-click
    {
        border: 1px solid #facc5a;
```

```
        background-color: #f9e391;
        padding: 2px;
}
</style>
<script type="text/javascript">
var currentNum = 0;
function handleEvent(e)
{
    var eSrc;

    if (window.event)
    {
        e = window.event;
        eSrc = e.srcElement;
    }
    else
    {
        eSrc = e.target;
    }

    if (e.type == "mouseover")
    {
        if (eSrc.className == "tabStrip-tab")
        {
            eSrc.className = "tabStrip-tab-hover";
        }
    }

    if (e.type == "mouseout")
    {
        if (eSrc.className == "tabStrip-tab-hover")
        {
            eSrc.className = "tabStrip-tab";
        }
    }

    if (e.type == "click")
    {
        if (eSrc.className == "tabStrip-tab-hover")
        {
            var num = eSrc.id.substr(eSrc.id.lastIndexOf("-") + 1);

            if (currentNum != num)
            {
                deactivateTab();

                eSrc.className = "tabStrip-tab-click";
                showDescription(num);
                currentNum = num;
            }
        }
    }
}

function showDescription(num)
```

```
    {
        var descContainer = document.getElementById("descContainer");

        var div = document.createElement("div");
        div.id = "tabStrip-desc-" + num;
        var text = document.createTextNode("Description for tab " + num);

        div.appendChild(text);
        descContainer.appendChild(div);
    }

    function deactiveTab()
    {
        var descContainer = document.getElementById("descContainer");
        var descEl = document.getElementById("tabStrip-desc-" + currentNum);

        if (descEl)
        {
            descContainer.removeChild(descEl);

            document.getElementById("tabStrip-tab-"
                + currentNum).className = "tabStrip-tab";
        }
    }
    document.onclick = handleEvent;
    document.onmouseover = handleEvent;
    document.onmouseout = handleEvent;
    </script>
</head>
<body>
    <div class="tabStrip">
        <div id="tabStrip-tab-1" class="tabStrip-tab">Tab 1</div>
        <div id="tabStrip-tab-2" class="tabStrip-tab">Tab 2</div>
        <div id="tabStrip-tab-3" class="tabStrip-tab">Tab 3</div>
    </div>
    <div id="descContainer"></div>
</body>
</html>
```

Let's go over these new lines one at a time. First look at the new line in the showDescription() function in the following code:

```
div.id = "tabStrip-desc-" + num;
```

This line of code simply adds an id to the <div/> element that contains the tab's description. This is done so that you can easily find this element when a different tab is clicked and you need to change the description.

The next line to look at is the first new line of the script; it adds a global variable called currentNum and gives it the value of 0.

```
var currentNum = 0;
```

When you click a tab, the code that handles the `click` event checks to see if the clicked tab's number is different from the value contained in `currentNum`. If it is, then you know the clicked tab is different from the currently active tab, and you can begin to go through the process of deactivating the current tab and making the new tab the active tab.

```
var num = eSrc.id.substr(eSrc.id.lastIndexOf("-") + 1);

if (currentNum != num)
{
    deactivateTab();

    eSrc.className = "tabStrip-tab-click";
    showDescription(num);
    currentNum = num;
}
```

The first line in the `if` statement calls the `deactivateTab()` function, which deactivates the current tab (you'll look at it later). The `className` property of tab is changed to reflect that it was clicked, the description is added to the page, and the `currentNum` variable is changed to contain the value of the new active tab's number.

Now turn your attention to the `deactivateTab()` function. Its job is to remove the currently active tab's description from the page and change the active tab's style back to normal.

```
function deactiveTab()
{
    var descContainer = document.getElementById("descContainer");
    var descEl = document.getElementById("tabStrip-desc-" + currentNum);
```

The first line of his function gets the `<div/>` element with an id of `descContainer`, and the second line attempts to locate the description element by using the id value the `showDescription()` function assigned it.

The word "attempts" is key here; remember that `currentNum` was initialized with a value of 0, and there is no tab with a number of 0. Yet when you first click any tab, `deactivateTab()` is called because 0 does not equal to the clicked tab's number. So the first time you click a tab, your code attempts to find an element with an id value of `tabStrip-desc-0`, which obviously doesn't exist, and `getElementById()` returns `null` if it cannot find the element with the specified id. This is a potential problem because the browser will throw an error if you attempt to do anything with the `descEl` variable if it is `null`.

The solution to this problem is rather simple; check if the `descEl` variable has a value, and only perform operations when it does.

```
    if (descEl)
    {
        descContainer.removeChild(descEl);

        document.getElementById("tabStrip-tab-"
            + currentNum).className = "tabStrip-tab";
    }
}
```

When `descEl` contains a value, you remove it from the `descContainer` element and change the `className` property of the active tab to `tabStrip-tab`, changing its style to that of a tab in the normal state.

Chapter 13

Exercise 1 Question

Using the Quicktime plug-in or ActiveX control, create a page with three links, so that when you click any of them a sound is played. Use an alert box to tell the users who do not have QuickTime installed that they must install it when they click a link.

The page should work in IE, Firefox, Safari, Chrome, and Opera. The method to tell QuickTime what file to play is `SetURL()`.

Exercise 1 Solution

```
<!DOCTYPE html PUBLIC "-//W3C//DTD XHTML 1.0 Transitional//EN"
"http://www.w3.org/TR/xhtml1/DTD/xhtml1-transitional.dtd">
<html xmlns="http://www.w3.org/1999/xhtml">
<head>
    <title>Chapter 13: Question Answer</title>
    <script type="text/javascript">
    var plugInInstalled = false;
    function play(fileName)
    {
        if (plugInInstalled)
        {
            document.audioPlayer.SetURL(fileName);
            document.audioPlayer.Play();
        }
        else
        {
            alert("You must have QuickTime installed to play this file.");
        }

        return false;
    }

    function window_onload()
    {
        if (!window.ActiveXObject)
        {
            var pluginsLength = navigator.plugins.length;
            for (var i = 0; i < pluginsLength; i++)
            {
                var pluginName = navigator.plugins[i].name.toLowerCase();
                if (pluginName.indexOf("quicktime") > -1)
                {
                    plugInInstalled = true;
```

```
                        break;
                }
            }
        }
        else
        {
            if (document.audioPlayer.readyState == 4)
            {
                plugInInstalled = true;
            }
        }

        if (!plugInInstalled)
        {
            alert("You need Quicktime to play the audio files!");
        }
    }

    onload = window_onload;
    </script>
</head>
<body>
    <object id="audioPlayer"
    classid="clsid:02BF25D5-8C17-4B23-BC80-D3488ABDDC6B"
    codebase="http://www.apple.com/qtactivex/qtplugin.cab"
    width="320" height="260">
    <param name="src" value="sound1.mp3" />
    <param name="controller" value="false" />
    <param name="autoplay" value="false" />
    <embed name="audioPlayer"
        height="260"
        width="320"
        src="sound1.mp3"
        type="video/quicktime"
        pluginspage="www.apple.com/quicktime/download"
        controller="false"
        autoplay="false"
    />
    </object>
    <a href="#" onclick="return play('sound1.mp3')">Sound 1</a>
    <a href="#" onclick="return play('sound2.mp3')">Sound 2</a>
    <a href="#" onclick="return play('sound3.mp3')">Sound 3</a>
</body>
</html>
```

Save this as ch13_q1.htm.

This solution is based on the QuickTime example in the chapter. Note that the three sound files, sound1.mp3, sound2.mp3, and sound3.mp3, can be found in the code download for this book.

The first line of JavaScript code declares the plugInInstalled variable; this is the same variable that was declared within the window_onload() function in the original example. Verify that the user has the ability to use the QuickTime plug-in in the window's onload event handler, which calls the window_onload() function.

Because the support for plug-ins is different between IE and other browsers, the means of checking for plug-ins is also different. For Firefox, Safari, Chrome, and Opera, go through the navigator object's plugins collection and check each installed plug-in for the name quicktime; if it's found, you know the user has the QuickTime player installed.

With IE, simply use the ActiveX control's readyState property to see if it's installed and initialized correctly.

To play the sounds, a function called play() is defined whose parameter is the file name of the sound file to be played. This function checks whether or not the QuickTime plug-in or ActiveX control is installed.

```
function play(fileName)
{
    if (plugInInstalled)
    {
        document.audioPlayer.SetURL(fileName);
        document.audioPlayer.Play();
    }
    else
    {
        alert("You must have QuickTime installed to play this file.");
    }

    return false;
}
```

If it is installed, then the function makes use of the QuickTime player's SetURL() method to set the sound file to be played and the Play() method to start playing the clip. If it isn't installed, an alert box tells the user they must have QuickTime installed in order to hear the sound file.

You have used different sounds for each link by simply specifying a different file name each time as the parameter for the play() function. The onclick event handler starts playing the sound when you click the link.

```
<a href="#" onclick="return play('sound1.mp3')">Sound 1</a>
```

Chapter 14

Exercise 1 Question

Extend the HttpRequest module to include synchronous requests in addition to the asynchronous requests the module already makes. You'll have to make some adjustments to your code to incorporate this functionality. (Hint: Create an async property for the module.)

Exercise 1 Solution

```
function HttpRequest(sUrl, fpCallback)
{
    this.url = sUrl;
    this.callBack = fpCallback;
    this.async = true;
    this.request = this.createXmlHttpRequest();
}

HttpRequest.prototype.createXmlHttpRequest = function () {
    if (window.XMLHttpRequest)
    {
        var oHttp = new XMLHttpRequest();
        return oHttp;
    }
    else if (window.ActiveXObject)
    {
        var versions =
        [
            "MSXML2.XmlHttp.6.0",
            "MSXML2.XmlHttp.3.0"
        ];

        for (var i = 0; i < versions.length; i++)
        {
            try
            {
                oHttp = new ActiveXObject(versions[i]);
                return oHttp;
            }
            catch (error)
            {
                //do nothing here
            }
        }
    }
    return null;
}

HttpRequest.prototype.send = function()
{
    this.request.open("GET", this.url, this.async);

    if (this.async)
    {
        var tempRequest = this.request;
        var fpCallback = this.callBack;

        function request_readystatechange()
        {
            if (tempRequest.readyState == 4)
            {
```

```
                    if (tempRequest.status == 200)
                    {
                        fpCallback(tempRequest.responseText);
                    }
                    else
                    {
                        alert("An error occurred while attempting to " +
                            "contact the server.");
                    }
                }
            }

        this.request.onreadystatechange = request_readystatechange;
    }

    this.request.send(null);

    if (!this.async)
    {
        this.callBack(this.request.responseText);
    }
}
```

It's possible to add synchronous communication to your `HttpRequest` module in a variety of ways. The approach in this solution refactors the code to accommodate a new property called `async`, which contains either `true` or `false`. If it contains `true`, then the underlying `XMLHttpRequest` object uses asynchronous communication to retrieve the file. If `false`, the module uses synchronous communication. In short, this property resembles an XML DOM's `async` property for determining how an XML document is loaded.

The first change made to the module is in the constructor itself. The original constructor initializes and readies the `XMLHttpRequest` object to send data. This will not do for this new version, however. Instead, the constructor merely initializes all the properties.

```
function HttpRequest(sUrl, fpCallback)
{
    this.url = sUrl;
    this.callBack = fpCallback;
    this.async = true;
    this.request = this.createXmlHttpRequest();
}
```

There are three new properties here. The first, `url`, contains the URL that the `XMLHttpRequest` object should attempt to request from the server. The `callBack` property contains a reference to the callback function, and the `async` property determines the type of communication the `XMLHttpRequest` object uses. Setting `async` to true in the constructor gives the property a default value. Therefore, you can send the request in asynchronous mode without setting the property externally.

The new constructor and properties are actually desirable, as they enable you to reuse the same `HttpRequest` object for multiple requests. If you wanted to make a request to a different URL, all you would need to do is assign the `url` property a new value. The same can be said for the callback function as well.

The `createXmlHttpRequest()` method remains untouched. This is a helper method and doesn't really have anything to do with sending the request.

The majority of changes to the module are in the `send()` method. It is here that the module decides whether to use asynchronous or synchronous communication. Both types of communication have very little in common when it comes to making a request; asynchronous communication uses the `onreadystatechange` event handler, and synchronous communication allows access to the `XMLHttpRequest` object's properties when the request is complete. Therefore, code branching is required.

```
HttpRequest.prototype.send = function()
{
    this.request.open("GET", this.url, this.async);

    if (this.async)
    {
        //more code here
    }

    this.request.send(null);

    if (!this.async)
    {
        //more code here
    }
}
```

The first line of this method uses the `open()` method of the `XMLHttpRequest` object. The `async` property is used as the final parameter of the method. This determines whether or not the XHR object uses asynchronous communication. Next, an `if` statement tests to see if `this.async` is true; if it is, the asynchronous code will be placed in this `if` block. Next, the `XMLHttpRequest` object's `send()` method is called, sending the request to the server. The final `if` statement checks to see whether `this.async` is `false`. If it is, synchronous code is placed within the code block to execute.

```
HttpRequest.prototype.send = function()
{
    this.request.open("GET", this.url, this.async);

    if (this.async)
    {
        var tempRequest = this.request;
        var fpCallback = this.callBack;

        function request_readystatechange()
        {
            if (tempRequest.readyState == 4)
            {
                if (tempRequest.status == 200)
                {
```

```
                    fpCallback(tempRequest.responseText);
            }
            else
            {
                alert("An error occurred while attempting to " +
                    "contact the server.");
            }
        }
    }

    this.request.onreadystatechange = request_readystatechange;
}

this.request.send(null);

if (!this.async)
{
    this.callBack(this.request.responseText);
}
}
```

This new code finishes off the method. Starting with the first if block, a new variable called fpCallback is assigned the value of this.callBack. This is done for the same reasons as with the tempRequest variable — scoping issues — as this points to the request_readystatechange() function instead of the HttpRequest object. Other than this change, the asynchronous code remains the same. The request_readystatechange() function handles the readystatechange event and calls the callback function when the request is successful.

The second if block is much simpler. Because this code executes only if synchronous communication is desired, all you have to do is call the callback function and pass the XMLHttpRequest object's responseText property.

Using this newly refactored module is quite simple. The following code makes an asynchronous request for a fictitious text file called test.txt.

```
function request_callback(sResponseText)
{
    alert(sResponseText);
}

var oHttp = new HttpRequest("test.txt", request_callback);

oHttp.send();
```

Nothing has really changed for asynchronous requests. This is the exact same code used earlier in the chapter. If you want to use synchronous communication, simply set async to false, like this:

```
function request_callback(sResponseText)
{
    alert(sResponseText);
}

var oHttp = new HttpRequest("test.txt", request_callback);
```

```
oHttp.async = false;

oHttp.send();
```

You now have an Ajax module that requests information in both asynchronous and synchronous communication!

Exercise 2 Question

It was mentioned earlier in the chapter that the smart forms could be modified to not use hyperlinks. Change the form that uses the HttpRequest module so that the user name and e-mail fields are checked when the user submits the form. Use the form's onsubmit event handler and cancel the submission if a user name or e-mail is taken. Also use the updated HttpRequest module from Question 1 and use synchronous requests. The only time you need to alert the user is when the user name or e-mail is taken, so make sure to return true if the user name and e-mail pass muster.

Exercise 2 Solution

```
<!DOCTYPE HTML PUBLIC "-//W3C//DTD HTML 4.01//EN"
    "http://www.w3.org/TR/html4/strict.dtd">

<html>
<head>
    <title>Form Field Validation</title>
    <style type="text/css">
        .fieldname
        {
            text-align: right;
        }

        .submit
        {
            text-align: right;
        }
    </style>
    <script type="text/javascript" src="HttpRequest.js"></script>
    <script type="text/javascript">
        var isUsernameTaken;
        var isEmailTaken;

        function checkUsername_callBack(sResponseText)
        {
            if (sResponseText == "available")
            {
                isUsernameTaken = false;
            }
            else
            {
                isUsernameTaken = true;
            }
        }

        function checkEmail_callBack(sResponseText)
        {
```

```
        if (sResponseText == "available")
        {
            isEmailTaken = false;
        }
        else
        {
            isEmailTaken = true;
        }
    }

    function form_submit()
    {
        var request = new HttpRequest();
        request.async = false;

        //First check the username
        var userValue = document.getElementById("username").value;

        if (userValue == "")
        {
            alert("Please enter a user name to check!");
            return false;
        }

        request.url = "formvalidator.php?username=" + userValue;
        request.callBack = checkUsername_callBack;
        request.send();

        if (isUsernameTaken)
        {
            alert("The username " + userValue + " is not available!");
            return false;
        }

        //Now check the email
        var emailValue = document.getElementById("email").value;

        if (emailValue == "")
        {
            alert("Please enter an email address to check!");
            return false;
        }

        request.url = "formvalidator.php?email=" + emailValue;
        request.callBack = checkEmail_callBack;
        request.send();

        if (isEmailTaken)
        {
            alert("I'm sorry, but " + emailValue + " is in use by " +
                "another user.");
            return false;
        }
```

```
                //If the code's made it this far, everything's good
                return true;
            }
        </script>
</head>
<body>
    <form onsubmit="return form_submit()">
        <table>
            <tr>
                <td class="fieldname">
                    Username:
                </td>
                <td>
                    <input type="text" id="username" />
                </td>
            </tr>
            <tr>
                <td class="fieldname">
                    Email:
                </td>
                <td>
                    <input type="text" id="email" />
                </td>
            </tr>
            <tr>
                <td class="fieldname">
                    Password:
                </td>
                <td>
                    <input type="text" id="password" />
                </td>

            </tr>
            <tr>
                <td class="fieldname">
                    Verify Password:
                </td>
                <td>
                    <input type="text" id="password2" />
                </td>

            </tr>
            <tr>
                <td colspan="2" class="submit">
                    <input type="submit" value="Submit" />
                </td>
            </tr>
        </table>
    </form>
</body>
</html>
```

Beginning with the HTML: the links were removed, as well as the third column of the table. The key difference in this new HTML is the onsubmit event handler in the opening <form> tag. Ideally, the form should submit its data only when the form fields have been validated. Therefore, the onsubmit event handler is set to return form_submit(). The form_submit() function returns either true or false, making the browser submit the form's data if everything is okay and not submit if a field is not validated.

The JavaScript code holds the most changes; in this new implementation, two global variables, called isUsernameTaken and isEmailTaken, are declared. These variables hold true or false values: true if the user name or e-mail is taken, or false if it is not.

```
var isUsernameTaken;
var isEmailTaken;

function checkUsername_callBack(sResponseText)
{
    if (sResponseText == "available")
    {
        isUsernameTaken = false;
    }
    else
    {
        isUsernameTaken = true;
    }
}

function checkEmail_callBack(sResponseText)
{
    if (sResponseText == "available")
    {
        isEmailTaken = false;
    }
    else
    {
        isEmailTaken = true;
    }
}
```

The first two functions, checkUsername_callBack() and checkEmail_callBack(), are somewhat similar to their original versions. Instead of alerting information to the user, however, they simply assign the isUsernameTaken and isEmailTaken variables their values.

The function that performs most of the work is form_submit(). It is responsible for making the requests to the server and determines if the data in the form fields are ready for submission.

```
function form_submit()
{
    var request = new HttpRequest();
    request.async = false;

    //more code here
}
```

This code creates the HttpRequest object and sets it to synchronous communication. There are times when synchronous communication is appropriate to use, and during form validation is one of those times. Validating fields in a form is a sequential process, and its submission depends upon the outcome of the `onsubmit` event handler. Using synchronous communication forces the function to wait for information to be retrieved from the server before attempting to validate the field. If you used asynchronous communication, `form_submit()` would execute and return a value before the username and email could be validated. Also note that the `HttpRequest` constructor received no arguments. This is because you can explicitly set the `url` and `callBack` properties with the new version.

The first field to check is the `Username` field.

```
function form_submit()
{
    var request = new HttpRequest();
    request.async = false;

    //First check the username
    var userValue = document.getElementById("username").value;

    if (userValue == "")
    {
        alert("Please enter a user name to check!");
        return false;
    }

    request.url = "formvalidator.php?username=" + userValue;
    request.callBack = checkUsername_callBack;
    request.send();

    if (isUsernameTaken)
    {
        alert("The username " + userValue + " is not available!");
        return false;
    }

    //more code here
}
```

This code retrieves the value of the `Username` field and checks to see whether any information was entered. If none was entered, a message is alerted to the user informing them to enter data. If the user entered information in the `Username` field, then code execution continues. The `url` and `callBack` properties are assigned their values and the request is sent to the server. If it turns out that the user's desired user name is taken, an alert box tells them so. Otherwise, the code continues to execute and checks the e-mail information.

```
function form_submit()
{
    var request = new HttpRequest();
    request.async = false;

    //First check the username
    var userValue = document.getElementById("username").value;

    if (userValue == "")
```

```
    {
        alert("Please enter a user name to check!");
        return false;
    }

    request.url = "formvalidator.php?username=" + userValue;
    request.callBack = checkUsername_callBack;
    request.send();

    if (isUsernameTaken)
    {
        alert("The username " + userValue + " is not available!");
        return false;
    }

    //Now check the email
    var emailValue = document.getElementById("email").value;

    if (emailValue == "")
    {
        alert("Please enter an email address to check!");
        return false;
    }

    request.url = "formvalidator.php?email=" + emailValue;
    request.callBack = checkEmail_callBack;
    request.send();

    if (isEmailTaken)
    {
        alert("I'm sorry, but " + emailValue + " is in use by another user.");
        return false;
    }

    //If the code's made it this far, everything's good
    return true;
}
```

The e-mail-checking code goes through the same process that was used to check the user name. The value of the Email field is retrieved and checked to determine whether the user typed anything into the text box. Then that value is used to make another request to the server. Notice again that the url and callBack properties are explicitly set. If isEmailTaken is true, an alert box shows the user that another user has taken the e-mail address and the function returns false. If the address is available, the function returns true, thus making the browser submit the form.

Chapter 15

Exercise 1 Question

Modify the answer to Chapter 14's Question 2 using jQuery. Also add error reporting for when an error occurs with the Ajax request.

Exercise 1 Solution

The key to this solution is synchronous communication. Without it, the form validation fails. Make sure you set the async setting. The highlighted lines in the following code were changed to work with jQuery:

```
<!DOCTYPE HTML PUBLIC "-//W3C//DTD HTML 4.01//EN"
    "http://www.w3.org/TR/html4/strict.dtd">

<html>
<head>
    <title>Chapter 15: Question 1 Answer with jQuery</title>
    <style type="text/css">
        .fieldname
        {
            text-align: right;
        }

        .submit
        {
            text-align: right;
        }
    </style>
    <script type="text/javascript" src="jquery-1.3.2.min.js"></script>
    <script type="text/javascript">
        var isUsernameTaken;
        var isEmailTaken;

        function checkUsername_callBack(data, status)
        {
            if (data == "available")
            {
                isUsernameTaken = false;
            }
            else
            {
                isUsernameTaken = true;
            }
        }

        function checkEmail_callBack(data, status)
        {
            if (data == "available")
            {
                isEmailTaken = false;
            }
            else
            {
                isEmailTaken = true;
            }
        }

        function form_submit()
        {
            //First check the username
```

```
        var userValue = $("#username").val();

        if (userValue == "")
        {
            alert("Please enter a user name to check!");
            return false;
        }

        var userParms = new Object();
        userParms.username = userValue;

        $.get("formvalidator.php", userParms, checkUsername_callBack);

        if (isUsernameTaken)
        {
            alert("The username " + userValue + " is not available!");
            return false;
        }

        //Now check the email
        var emailValue = $("#email").val();

        if (emailValue == "")
        {
            alert("Please enter an email address to check!");
            return false;
        }

        var emailParms = new Object();
        emailParms.email = emailValue;

        $.get("formvalidator.php", emailParms, checkEmail_callBack);

        if (isEmailTaken)
        {
            alert("I'm sorry, but " + emailValue +
                " is in use by another user.");
            return false;
        }

        //If the code's made it this far, everything's good
        return true;
    }

    var ajaxOptions = new Object();
    ajaxOptions.async = false;

    $.ajaxSetup(ajaxOptions);

    function request_error(event, request, settings)
    {
        alert("An error occurred with the following URL:\n"
          + settings.url + ".\nStatus code: " + request.status);
    }
```

```
                    $(document).ajaxError(request_error);
        </script>
</head>
<body>
    <form onsubmit="return form_submit()">
        <table>
            <tr>
                <td class="fieldname">
                    Username:
                </td>
                <td>
                    <input type="text" id="username" />
                </td>
            </tr>
            <tr>
                <td class="fieldname">
                    Email:
                </td>
                <td>
                    <input type="text" id="email" />
                </td>
            </tr>
            <tr>
                <td class="fieldname">
                    Password:
                </td>
                <td>
                    <input type="text" id="password" />
                </td>

            </tr>
            <tr>
                <td class="fieldname">
                    Verify Password:
                </td>
                <td>
                    <input type="text" id="password2" />
                </td>

            </tr>
            <tr>
                <td colspan="2" class="submit">
                    <input type="submit" value="Submit" />
                </td>
            </tr>
        </table>
    </form>
</body>
</html>
```

Exercise 2 Question

Modify the answer to Chapter 14's Question 2 using Prototype. Also add error reporting for when an error occurs with the Ajax request.

Exercise 2 Solution

As with the answer to Question 1, synchronous communication is key to the script working correctly, so add it to the request options. The highlighted lines make Prototype work with this script.

```html
<!DOCTYPE HTML PUBLIC "-//W3C//DTD HTML 4.01//EN"
    "http://www.w3.org/TR/html4/strict.dtd">

<html>
<head>
    <title>Chapter 15: Question 2 Answer with Prototype</title>
    <style type="text/css">
        .fieldname
        {
            text-align: right;
        }

        .submit
        {
            text-align: right;
        }
    </style>
    <script type="text/javascript" src="prototype-1.6.0.3.js"></script>
    <script type="text/javascript">
        var isUsernameTaken;
        var isEmailTaken;

        function checkUsername_callBack(request)
        {
            if (request.responseText == "available")
            {
                isUsernameTaken = false;
            }
            else
            {
                isUsernameTaken = true;
            }
        }

        function checkEmail_callBack(request)
        {
            if (request.responseText == "available")
            {
                isEmailTaken = false;
            }
            else
            {
                isEmailTaken = true;
```

```
        }
    }

    function form_submit()
    {
        //First check the username
        var userValue = $F("username");

        if (userValue == "")
        {
            alert("Please enter a user name to check!");
            return false;
        }

        var userParms = new Object();
        userParms.username = userValue;

        var options = getBasicOptions();
        options.onSuccess = checkUsername_callBack;
        options.parameters = userParms;

        new Ajax.Request("formvalidator.php", options);

        if (isUsernameTaken)
        {
            alert("The username " + userValue + " is not available!");
            return false;
        }

        //Now check the email
        var emailValue = $F("email");

        if (emailValue == "")
        {
            alert("Please enter an email address to check!");
            return false;
        }

        var emailParms = new Object();
        emailParms.email = emailValue;

        options.onSuccess = checkEmail_callBack;
        options.parameters = emailParms;

        new Ajax.Request("formvalidator.php", options);

        if (isEmailTaken)
        {
            alert("I'm sorry, but " + emailValue +
                " is in use by another user.");
            return false;
        }

        //If the code's made it this far, everything's good
```

```
        return true;
    }

    function request_onfailure(request)
    {
        alert("An error occurred. HTTP Status Code: " + request.status);
    }

    function getBasicOptions()
    {
        var options = new Object();
        options.method = "get";
        options.onFailure = request_onfailure;
        options.asynchronous = false;

        return options;
    }
    </script>
</head>
<body>
    <form onsubmit="return form_submit()">
        <table>
            <tr>
                <td class="fieldname">
                    Username:
                </td>
                <td>
                    <input type="text" id="username" />
                </td>
            </tr>
            <tr>
                <td class="fieldname">
                    Email:
                </td>
                <td>
                    <input type="text" id="email" />
                </td>
            </tr>
            <tr>
                <td class="fieldname">
                    Password:
                </td>
                <td>
                    <input type="text" id="password" />
                </td>

            </tr>
            <tr>
                <td class="fieldname">
                    Verify Password:
                </td>
                <td>
                    <input type="text" id="password2" />
```

```
                    </td>

                </tr>
                <tr>
                    <td colspan="2" class="submit">
                        <input type="submit" value="Submit" />
                    </td>
                </tr>
            </table>
        </form>
    </body>
</html>
```

Exercise 3 Question

If you guessed that this question would be: "Change the answer to Chapter 14's Question 2 using MooTools, and add error reporting for when an error occurs with the Ajax request" then you won!! Your prize is… completing the exercise.

Exercise 3 Solution

You guessed it! Synchronous communication!

```
<!DOCTYPE HTML PUBLIC "-//W3C//DTD HTML 4.01//EN"
    "http://www.w3.org/TR/html4/strict.dtd">

<html>
<head>
    <title>Chapter 15: Question 3 Answer with MooTools</title>
    <style type="text/css">
        .fieldname
        {
            text-align: right;
        }

        .submit
        {
            text-align: right;
        }
    </style>
    <script src="mootools-1.2.3-core-yc.js" type="text/javascript"></script>
    <script type="text/javascript">
        var isUsernameTaken;
        var isEmailTaken;

        function checkUsername_callBack(text, xml)
        {
            if (text == "available")
            {
                isUsernameTaken = false;
            }
```

```
        else
        {
            isUsernameTaken = true;
        }
}

function checkEmail_callBack(text, xml)
{
    if (text == "available")
    {
        isEmailTaken = false;
    }
    else
    {
        isEmailTaken = true;
    }
}

function form_submit()
{
    //First check the username
    var userValue = $("username").value;

    if (userValue == "")
    {
        alert("Please enter a user name to check!");
        return false;
    }

    var options = getBasicOptions();
    options.onSuccess = checkUsername_callBack;

    new Request(options).send("username=" + userValue);

    if (isUsernameTaken)
    {
        alert("The username " + userValue + " is not available!");
        return false;
    }

    //Now check the email
    var emailValue = $("email").value;

    if (emailValue == "")
    {
        alert("Please enter an email address to check!");
        return false;
    }

    options.onSuccess = checkEmail_callBack;

    new Request(options).send("email=" + emailValue);

    if (isEmailTaken)
```

```
                {
                    alert("I'm sorry, but " + emailValue +
                        " is in use by another user.");
                    return false;
                }

                //If the code's made it this far, everything's good
                return true;
            }

            function request_onfailure(request)
            {
                alert("An error occurred. HTTP Status Code: " + request.status);
            }

            function getBasicOptions()
            {
                var options = new Object();
                options.method = "get";
                options.onFailure = request_onfailure;
                options.url = "formvalidator.php";
                options.async = false;

                return options;
            }
        </script>
    </head>
    <body>
        <form onsubmit="return form_submit()">
            <table>
                <tr>
                    <td class="fieldname">
                        Username:
                    </td>
                    <td>
                        <input type="text" id="username" />
                    </td>
                </tr>
                <tr>
                    <td class="fieldname">
                        Email:
                    </td>
                    <td>
                        <input type="text" id="email" />
                    </td>
                </tr>
                <tr>
                    <td class="fieldname">
                        Password:
                    </td>
                    <td>
                        <input type="text" id="password" />
                    </td>

                </tr>
```

```
        <tr>
            <td class="fieldname">
                Verify Password:
            </td>
            <td>
                <input type="text" id="password2" />
            </td>

        </tr>
        <tr>
            <td colspan="2" class="submit">
                <input type="submit" value="Submit" />
            </td>
        </tr>
    </table>
    </form>
</body>
</html>
```

JavaScript Core Reference

This appendix outlines the syntax of all the JavaScript core language functions and objects with their properties and methods. If changes have occurred between versions, they have been noted.

Browser Reference

The following table outlines which JavaScript version is in use and in which browser it is used. Note that Internet Explorer implements Jscript, Microsoft's version of JavaScript. However, Jscript's features are relatively the same as JavaScript.

JavaScript Version	Netscape Navigator	Mozilla Firefox	Internet Explorer	Safari / Chrome	Opera
1.0	2.x		3.0		
1.1	3.x				
1.2	4.0–4.05				
1.3	4.06–4.7x		4.0		
1.4	5.0				
1.5	6.x	1.0	5.5, 6, 7, 8	3.0, 3.1	6, 7, 8, 9
1.6	6.2	1.5		3.2, 4.0	1.0
1.7		2.0			
1.8		3.0			
1.8.1		3.5			

Reserved Words

Various words and symbols are reserved by JavaScript. These words cannot be used as variable names, nor can the symbols be used within them. They are listed in the following table.

abstract	boolean	break
byte	case	catch
char	class	const
continue	debugger	default
delete	do	double
else	enum	export
extends	false	final
finally	float	for
function	goto	if
implements	import	in
instanceof	int	interface
long	native	new
null	package	private
protected	public	return
short	static	super
switch	synchronized	this
throw	throws	transient
true	try	typeof
var	void	volatile
while	with	
-	!	~
%	/	*
>	<	=
&	^	|
+	?	

Other Identifiers to Avoid

It is best to avoid the use of the following identifiers as variable names.

JavaScript 1.0

abs acos anchor asin atan atan2 big blink bold ceil charAt comment cos Date E escape eval exp fixed floor fontcolor fontsize getDate getDay getHours getMinutes getMonth getSeconds getTime getTimezoneOffset getYear indexOf isNaN italics lastIndexOf link log LOG10E LOG2E LN10 LN2 Math max min Object parse parseFloat parseInt PI pow random round,,c setDate setHours setMinutes setMonth setSeconds setTime setYear sin slice small sqrt SQRT1_2 SQRT2 strike String sub substr substring sup tan toGMTString toLocaleString toLowerCase toUpperCase unescape UTC

JavaScript 1.1

caller className constructor java JavaArray JavaClass JavaObject JavaPackage join length MAX_VALUE MIN_VALUE NaN NEGATIVE_INFINITY netscape Number POSITIVE_INFINITY prototype reverse sort split sun toString valueOf

JavaScript 1.2

arity callee charCodeAt compile concat exec fromCharCode global ignoreCase index input label lastIndex lastMatch lastParen leftContext match multiline Number Packages pop push RegExp replace rightContext search shift slice splice source String test unshift unwatch watch

JavaScript 1.3

apply call getFullYear getMilliseconds getUTCDate getUTCDay getUTCFullYear getUTCHours getUTCMilliseconds getUTCMinutes getUTCMonth getUTCSeconds Infinity isFinite NaN setFullYear setMilliseconds setUTCDate setUTCFullYear setUTCHours setUTCMilliseconds setUTCMinutes setUTCMonth setUTCSeconds toSource toUTCString undefined

JavaScript Operators

The following sections list the various operators available to you in JavaScript.

Assignment Operators

Assignment operators allow you to assign a value to a variable. The following table lists the different assignment operators you can use.

Name	Introduced	Meaning
Assignment	JavaScript 1.0	Sets variable `v1` to the value of variable `v2`. `var v1 = v2;`
Shorthand addition *or* Shorthand concatenation same as `v1 = v1 + v2`	JavaScript 1.0	`v1 += v2`
Shorthand subtraction same as `v1 = v1 - v2`	JavaScript 1.0	`v1 -= v2`
Shorthand multiplication same as `v1 = v1 * v2`	JavaScript 1.0	`v1 *= v2`
Shorthand division same as `v1 = v1 / v2`	JavaScript 1.0	`v1 /= v2`
Shorthand modulus same as `v1 = v1 % v2`	JavaScript 1.0	`v1 %= v2`
Shorthand left-shift same as `v1 = v1 << v2`	JavaScript 1.0	`v1 <<= v2`
Shorthand right-shift same as `v1 = v1 >> v2`	JavaScript 1.0	`v1 >>= v2`

Name	Introduced	Meaning
Shorthand zero-fill right-shift same as `v1 = v1 >>> v2`	JavaScript 1.0	`v1 >>>= v2`
Shorthand AND same as `v1 = v1 & v2`	JavaScript 1.0	`v1 &= v2`
Shorthand XOR same as `v1 = v1 ^ v2`	JavaScript 1.0	`v1 ^= v2`
Shorthand OR same as `v1 = v1	v2`	JavaScript 1.0	`v1 |= v2`

Comparison Operators

Comparison operators allow you to compare one variable or value with another. Any comparison statement returns a Boolean value.

Name	Introduced	Meaning
Equal	JavaScript 1.0	`v1 == v2` True if two operands are strictly equal or equal once cast to the same type.
Not equal	JavaScript 1.0	`v1 != v2` True if two operands are not strictly equal or not equal once cast to the same type.
Greater than	JavaScript 1.0	`v1 > v2` True if left-hand side (LHS) operand is greater than right-hand side (RHS) operand.
Greater than or equal to	JavaScript 1.0	`v1 >= v2` True if LHS operand is greater than or equal to RHS operand.
Less than	JavaScript 1.0	`v1 < v2` True if LHS operand is less than RHS operand.

Continued

Comparison Operators *(continued)*

Name	Introduced	Meaning
Less than or equal to	JavaScript 1.0	`v1 <= v2` True if LHS operand is less than or equal to RHS operand.
Strictly equal	JavaScript 1.3	`v1 === v2` True if operands are equal and of the same type.
Not strictly equal	JavaScript 1.3	`v1 !== v2` True if operands are not strictly equal.

Arithmetic Operators

Arithmetic operators allow you to perform arithmetic operations between variables or values.

Name	Introduced	Meaning
Addition	JavaScript 1.0	`v1 + v2` Sum of `v1` and `v2`. (Concatenation of `v1` and `v2`, if either operand is a string.)
Subtraction	JavaScript 1.0	`v1 - v2` Difference between `v1` and `v2`.
Multiplication	JavaScript 1.0	`v1 * v2` Product of `v1` and `v2`.
Division	JavaScript 1.0	`v1 / v2` Quotient of `v2` into `v1`.
Modulus	JavaScript 1.0	`v1 % v2` Integer remainder of dividing `v1` by `v2`.
Prefix increment	JavaScript 1.0	`++v1 * v2` `(v1 + 1) * v2`. Note: `v1` will be left as `v1 + 1`.
Postfix increment	JavaScript 1.0	`v1++ * v2` `(v1 * v2)`; `v1` is then incremented by 1.

Name	Introduced	Meaning

Prefix decrement	JavaScript 1.0	`-- v1 * v2`
		
		`(v1 - 1) * v2.`
		Note: `v1` is left as `v1 - 1`.

Postfix decrement	JavaScript 1.0	`v1 -- * v2` `(v1 * v2);` `v1` is then decremented by `1`.

Bitwise Operators

Bitwise operators work by converting values in `v1` and `v2` to 32-bit binary numbers and then comparing the individual bits of these two binary numbers. The result is returned as a normal decimal number.

Name	Introduced	Meaning
Bitwise AND	JavaScript 1.0	`v1 & v2` The bitwise AND lines up the bits in each operand and performs an AND operation between the two bits in the same position. If both bits are `1`, the resulting bit in this position of the returned number is `1`. If either bit is `0`, the resulting bit in this position of the returned number is `0`.
Bitwise OR	JavaScript 1.0	`v1 | v2` The bitwise OR lines up the bits in each operand and performs an OR operation between the two bits in the same position. If either bit is `1`, the resulting bit in this position of the returned number is `1`. If both bits are `0`, the resulting bit in this position of the returned number is `0`.
Bitwise XOR	JavaScript 1.0	`v1 ^ v2` The bitwise XOR lines up the bits in each operand and performs an XOR operation between the two bits in the same position. The resulting bit in this position is `1` only if one bit from both operands is `1`. Otherwise, the resulting bit in this position of the returned number is `0`.
Bitwise NOT	JavaScript 1.0	`v1 ~ v2` Inverts all the bits in the number.

Bitwise Shift Operators

These work by converting values in v1 to 32-bit binary numbers and then moving the bits in the number to the left or the right by the specified number of places.

Name	Introduced	Meaning
Left-shift	JavaScript 1.0	v1 << v2 Shifts v1 to the left by v2 places, filling the new gaps in with zeros.
Sign-propagating right-shift	JavaScript 1.4	v1 >> v2 Shifts v1 to the right by v2 places, ignoring the bits shifted off the number.
Zero-fill right-shift	JavaScript 1.0	v1 >>> v2 Shifts v1 to the right by v2 places, ignoring the bits shifted off the number and adding v2 zeros to the left of the number.

Logical Operators

These should return one of the Boolean literals, true or false. However, this may not happen if v1 or v2 is neither a Boolean value nor a value that easily converts to a Boolean value, such as 0, 1, null, the empty string, or undefined.

Name	Introduced	Meaning
Logical AND	JavaScript 1.0	v1 && v2 Returns true if both v1 and v2 are true, or false otherwise. Will not evaluate v2 if v1 is false.
Logical OR	JavaScript 1.0	v1 || v2 Returns false if both v1 and v2 are false, or true if one operand is true. Will not evaluate v2 if v1 is true.
Logical NOT	JavaScript 1.0	!v1 Returns false if v1 is true, or true otherwise.

Object Operators

JavaScript provides a number of operators to work with objects. The following table lists them.

Name	Introduced	Meaning
delete	JavaScript 1.2	`delete obj` Deletes an object, one of its properties, or the element of an array at the specified index. Also deletes variables *not* declared with the `var` keyword.
in	JavaScript 1.4	`for (prop in somObj)` Returns `true` if `someObj` has the named property.
instanceof	JavaScript 1.4	`someObj instanceof ObjType` Returns `true` if `someObj` is of type `ObjType`; otherwise, returns `false`.
new	JavaScript 1.0	`new ObjType()` Creates a new instance of an object with type `ObjType`.
this	JavaScript 1.0	`this.property` Refers to the current object.

Miscellaneous Operators

The following table lists miscellaneous operators.

Name	Introduced	Meaning
Conditional operator	JavaScript 1.0	`(evalquery) ? v1 : v2;` If `evalquery` is `true`, the operator returns `v1`; otherwise it returns `v2`.
Comma operator	JavaScript 1.0	`var v3 = (v1 + 2, v2 * 2)` Evaluates both operands while treating the two as one expression. Returns the value of the second operand. In this example, `v3` holds the resulting value of `v2 * 2`.
typeof	JavaScript 1.1	`typeof v1` Returns a string holding the type of `v1`, which is not evaluated.
void	JavaScript 1.1	`void(eval)` Evaluates `eval1` but does not return a value.

Operator Precedence

Does `1 + 2 * 3 = 1 + (2 * 3) = 7` or does it equal `(1 + 2) * 3 = 9`?

Operator precedence determines the order in which operators are evaluated. For example, the multiplicative operator (*) has a higher precedence than the additive operator (+). Therefore, the correct answer to the previous question is

```
1 + (2 * 3)
```

The following table lists the operator precedence in JavaScript from highest to lowest. The third column explains whether to read `1+2+3+4` as `((1+2)+3)+4` (left to right) or `1+(2+(3+(4)))` (right to left).

Operator Type	Operators	Evaluation Order for Like Elements
Member	`.` or `[]`	Left to right
Create instance	`new`	Right to left
Function call	`()`	Left to right
Increment	`++`	N/a
Decrement	`–`	N/a
Logical not	`!`	Right to left
Bitwise not	`~`	Right to left
Unary +	`+`	Right to left
Unary -	`–`	Right to left
Type of	`typeof`	Right to left
Void	`void`	Right to left
Delete	`delete`	Right to left
Multiplication	`*`	Left to right
Division	`/`	Left to right
Modulus	`%`	Left to right
Addition	`+`	Left to right
Subtraction	`–`	Left to right
Bitwise shift	`<<, >>, >>>`	Left to right
Relational	`<, <=, >, >=`	Left to right

Operator Type	Operators	Evaluation Order for Like Elements
In	`in`	Left to right
Instance of	`instanceof`	Left to right
Equality	`==, !=, ===, !===`	Left to right
Bitwise AND	`&`	Left to right
Bitwise XOR	`^`	Left to right
Bitwise OR	`|`	Left to right
Logical AND	`&&`	Left to right
Logical OR	`||`	Left to right
Conditional	`?:`	Right to left
Assignment	`=, +=, -=, *=, /=, %=, <<=, >>=, >>>=, &=, ^=, |=`	Right to left
Comma	`,`	Left to right

JavaScript Statements

The following tables describe core JavaScript statements.

Block

JavaScript blocks start with an opening curly brace ({) and end with a closing curly brace (}). Block statements are meant to make the contained single statements execute together, such as the body of a function or a condition.

Statement	Introduced	Description
`{ }`	JavaScript 1.5	Used to group statements as delimited by the curly brackets.

Conditional

The following table lists conditional statements for JavaScript as well as the version in which they were introduced.

Statement	Introduced	Description
if	JavaScript 1.2	Executes a block of code if a specified condition is `true`.
else	JavaScript 1.2	The second half of an `if` statement. Executes a block of code if the result of the `if` statement is `false`.
switch	JavaScript 1.2	Specifies various blocks of statements to be executed depending on the value of the expression passed in as the argument.

Declarations

These keywords declare variables or functions in JavaScript code.

Statement	Introduced	Description
var	JavaScript 1.0	Used to declare a variable. Initializing it to a value is optional at the time of declaration.
function	JavaScript 1.0	Used to declare a function with the specified parameters, which can be strings, numbers, or objects. To return a value, the function must use the `return` statement.

Loop

Loops execute a block of code while a specified condition is `true`.

Statement	Introduced	Description
do...while	JavaScript 1.2	Executes the statements specified until the test condition after the `while` evaluates to `false`. The statements are executed at least once because the test condition is evaluated last.
for	JavaScript 1.0	Creates a loop controlled according to the three optional expressions enclosed in the parentheses after the `for` and separated by semicolons. The first of these three expressions is the initial-expression, the second is the test condition, and the third is the increment-expression.
for...in	JavaScript 1.0	Used to iterate over all the properties of an object using a variable. For each property the specified statements within the loop are executed.

Statement	Introduced	Description
while	JavaScript 1.0	Executes a block of statements if a test condition evaluates to `true`. The loop then repeats, testing the condition with each repeat, ceasing if the condition evaluates to `false`.
break	JavaScript 1.0	Used within a `while` or `for` loop to terminate the loop and transfer program control to the statement following the loop. Can also be used with a `label` to `break` to a particular program position outside of the loop.
label	JavaScript 1.2	An identifier that can be used with `break` or `continue` statements to indicate where the program should continue execution after the loop execution is stopped.

Execution Control Statements

Code execution is controlled in a variety of ways. In addition to the conditional and loop statements, the following statements also contribute to execution control.

Statement	Introduced	Description
continue	JavaScript 1.0	Used to stop execution of the block of statements in the current iteration of a `while` or `for` loop; execution of the loop continues with the next iteration.
return	JavaScript 1.0	Used to specify the value to be returned by a function.
with	JavaScript 1.0	Specifies the default object for a block of code.

Exception Handling Statements

Errors are a natural part of programming, and JavaScript provides you the means to catch errors and handle them gracefully.

Statement	Introduced	Description
throw	JavaScript 1.4	Throws a custom exception defined by the user.
try...catch ...finally	JavaScript 1.4	Executes the statements in the `try` block; if any exceptions occur, these are handled in the `catch` block. The `finally` block allows you to stipulate statements that will be executed after both the `try` and `catch` statements.

Other Statements

The following table lists other JavaScript statements and when they were introduced.

Statement	Introduced	Description

comment	JavaScript 1.0	Notes that are ignored by the script engine and that can be used to explain the code. There are two types of comments: single-line and multi-line.
		
		`// single line comment`
		
		`/* multi`
		`    line`
		`        comment */`

Top-Level Properties and Functions

These are core properties and functions, which are not associated with any lower-level object, although in the terminology used by ECMAScript and by Jscript, they are described as properties and methods of the global object.

The top-level properties were introduced in JavaScript 1.3, but in previous versions, Infinity and NaN existed as properties of the Number object.

Top-Level Properties

Property	Introduced	Description
Infinity	JavaScript 1.3	Returns infinity.
NaN	JavaScript 1.3	Returns a value that is not a number.
undefined	JavaScript 1.3	Indicates that a value has not been assigned to a variable.

Top-Level Functions

Function	Introduced	Description
decodeURI()	JavaScript 1.5	Used to decode a URI encoded with encodeURI().
decodeURIcomponent()	JavaScript 1.5	Used to decode a URI encoded with encodeURIComponent().
encodeURI()	JavaScript 1.5	Used to compose a new version of a complete URI, replacing each instance of certain characters. It is based on the UTF-8 encoding of the characters.

Function	Introduced	Description
encodeURIComponent()	JavaScript 1.5	Used to compose a new version of a complete URI by replacing each instance of the specified character with escape sequences. Representation is via the UTF encoding of the characters.
escape()	JavaScript 1.0	Used to encode a string in the ISO Latin-1 character set; for example, to add to a URL.
eval()	JavaScript 1.0	Returns the result of the JavaScript code, which is passed in as a string parameter.
isFinite()	JavaScript 1.3	Indicates whether the argument is a finite number.
isNaN()	JavaScript 1.1	Indicates if the argument is not a number.
Number()	JavaScript 1.2	Converts an object to a number.
parseFloat()	JavaScript 1.0	Parses a string and returns it as a floating-point number.
parseInt()	JavaScript 1.0	Parses a string and returns it as an integer. An optional second parameter specifies the base of the number to be converted.
String()	JavaScript 1.2	Converts an object to a string.
unescape()	JavaScript 1.0	Returns the ASCII string for the specified hexadecimal encoding value.

JavaScript and Jscript Core Objects

This section describes the objects available in the JavaScript and Jscript core languages and their methods and properties.

ActiveXObject

The ActiveXObject object represents an ActiveX object when accessed from within Microsoft's JScript code. Introduced in Jscript 3.0, it's not available in ECMAScript or JavaScript. It is created with the ActiveXObject constructor; for example, to create a Microsoft Word document, you would write

```
var objActiveX = new ActiveXObject("Word.Document");
```

The properties and methods of this object will be those of the ActiveX object thus created. For example, the following code opens a Word document and writes some text to it and to the HTML page:

```
var objActiveX = new ActiveXObject("Word.Document");
strText="This is being written both to the HTML page and to the Word document.";
objActiveX.application.selection.typeText(strText);
document.write(strText);
```

Array

The `Array` object represents an array of variables. It was introduced in JavaScript 1.1. An `Array` object can be created with the `Array` constructor.

```
var objArray = new Array(10)              // an array of 11 elements
var objArray = new Array("1", "2", "4")   // an array of 3 elements
```

Arrays can also be created using array literal syntax.

```
var objArray = [];
```

Literal syntax is the preferred method of creating an array.

Properties

Property	Introduced	Description
constructor	JavaScript 1.1	Used to reference the constructor function for the object.
length	JavaScript 1.1	Returns the number of elements in the array.
prototype	JavaScript 1.1	Returns the prototype for the object, which can be used to extend the object's interface.

Methods

Square brackets (`[]`) surrounding a parameter means that parameter is optional.

Method	Introduced	Description
concat(value1 [, value2,…])	JavaScript 1.2	Concatenates two arrays and returns the new array thus formed.
every(testFn(element, index, array))	JavaScript 1.6	Iterates over the array, executing `testFn()` on every element. Returns `true` if all iterations return `true`. Otherwise, it returns `false`.
filter(testFn(element, index, array))	JavaScript 1.6	Iterates over the array, executing `testFn()` on every element. Returns a new array of elements that pass `testFn()`.
foreach(fn(element, index, array))	JavaScript 1.6	Iterates over the array, executing `fn()` on every element.
indexOf(element [, startIndex])	JavaScript 1.6	Returns an index of the specified element if found, or `-1` if not found. Starts at `startIndex` if specified.

Method	Introduced	Description
`join([separator])`	JavaScript 1.1	Joins all the elements of an array into a single string delimited by separator if specified.
`lastIndexOf(element [, startIndex])`	JavaScript 1.6	Searches an array starting at last element and moves backwards. Returns an index of the specified element if found, or -1 if not found. Starts at `startIndex` if specified.
`map(fn(element, index, array))`	JavaScript 1.6	Iterates over the array, executing `fn()` on every element. Returns a new array based on the outcome of `fn()`.
`pop()`	JavaScript 1.2	Pops the last element from the end of the array and returns that element.
`push(value1 [, value2, …])`	JavaScript 1.2	Pushes one or more elements onto the end of the array and returns the new length of the array. The array's new `length` is returned.
`reverse()`	JavaScript 1.1	Reverses the order of the elements in the array, so the first element becomes the last and the last becomes the first.
`shift()`	JavaScript 1.2	Removes the first element from the beginning of the array and returns that element.
`slice(startIndex [, endIndex])`	JavaScript 1.2	Returns a slice of the array starting at the start index and ending at the element before the end index.
`some(testFn(element, index, array))`	JavaScript 1.6	Iterates over the array, executing `testFn()` on every element. Returns `true` if at least one result of `testFn()` is `true`.
`sort([sortFn(a,b)])`	JavaScript 1.1	Sorts the elements of the array. Executes `sortFn()` for sorting if it is provided.
`splice(startIndex [, length, value1, …)`	JavaScript 1.2	Removes the amount of elements denoted by `length` starting at `startIndex`. Provided values replace the deleted elements. Returns the deleted elements.
`toString()`	JavaScript 1.1	Converts the `Array` object into a string.

Continued

Methods *(continued)*

Method	Introduced	Description
unshift(value1 [, value2, …])	JavaScript 1.2	Adds elements to the beginning of the array and returns the new length.
valueOf()	JavaScript 1.1	Returns the primitive value of the array.

Boolean

The Boolean object is used as a wrapper for a Boolean value. It was introduced in JavaScript 1.1. It is created with the Boolean constructor, which takes as a parameter the initial value for the object (if this is not a Boolean value, it will be converted into one).

False-y values are null, undefined, "", and 0. All other values are considered truth-y.

Properties

Property	Introduced	Description
constructor	JavaScript 1.1	Specifies the function that creates an object's prototype.
prototype	JavaScript 1.1	Returns the prototype for the object, which can be used to extend the object's interface.

Methods

Method	Introduced	Description
toString()	JavaScript 1.1	Converts the Boolean object into a string.
valueOf()	JavaScript 1.1	Returns the primitive value of the Boolean object.

Date

The Date object is used to represent a given date-time. It was introduced in JavaScript 1.0.

Properties

Property	Introduced	Description
constructor	JavaScript 1.1	Used to reference the constructor function for the object.
prototype	JavaScript 1.1	Returns the prototype for the object, which can be used to extend the object's interface.

Methods

Method	Introduced	Description
getDate()	JavaScript 1.0	Retrieves the date in the month from the Date object.
getDay()	JavaScript 1.0	Retrieves the day of the week from the Date object.
getFullYear()	JavaScript 1.3	Retrieves the full year from the Date object.
getHours()	JavaScript 1.0	Retrieves the hour of the day from the Date object.
getMilliseconds()	JavaScript 1.3	Retrieves the number of milliseconds from the Date object.
getMinutes()	JavaScript 1.0	Retrieves the number of minutes from the Date object.
getMonth()	JavaScript 1.0	Retrieves the month from the Date object.
getSeconds()	JavaScript 1.0	Retrieves the number of seconds from the Date object.
getTime()	JavaScript 1.0	Retrieves the number of milliseconds since January 1 1970 00:00:00 from the Date object.
getTimezoneOffset()	JavaScript 1.0	Retrieves the difference in minutes between the local time zone and universal time (UTC).
getUTCDate()	JavaScript 1.3	Retrieves the date in the month from the Date object adjusted to universal time.
getUTCDay()	JavaScript 1.3	Retrieves the day of the week from the Date object adjusted to universal time.
getUTCFullYear()	JavaScript 1.3	Retrieves the year from the Date object adjusted to universal time.
getUTCHours()	JavaScript 1.3	Retrieves the hour of the day from the Date object adjusted to universal time.
getUTCMilliseconds()	JavaScript 1.3	Retrieves the number of milliseconds from the Date object adjusted to universal time.

Continued

Methods *(continued)*

Method	Introduced	Description
getUTCMinutes()	JavaScript 1.3	Retrieves the number of minutes from the Date object adjusted to universal time.
getUTCMonth()	JavaScript 1.3	Retrieves the month from the Date object adjusted to universal time.
getUTCSeconds()	JavaScript 1.3	Retrieves the number of seconds from the Date object adjusted to universal time.
getYear()	JavaScript 1.0	Retrieves the year from the Date object.
parse(dateString)	JavaScript 1.0	Retrieves the number of milliseconds in a date since January 1 1970 00:00:00, local time.
setDate(dayOfMonth)	JavaScript 1.0	Sets the date in the month for the Date object.
setFullYear(year [, month, day])	JavaScript 1.3	Sets the full year for the Date object.
setHours(hours [, minutes, seconds, milliseconds])	JavaScript 1.0	Sets the hour of the day for the Date object.
setMilliseconds(milliseconds)	JavaScript 1.3	Sets the number of milliseconds for the Date object.
setMinutes(minutes [, seconds, milliseconds])	JavaScript 1.0	Sets the number of minutes for the Date object.
setMonth(month [, day])	JavaScript 1.0	Sets the month for the Date object.
setSeconds(seconds [, milliseconds])	JavaScript 1.0	Sets the number of seconds for the Date object.
setTime(milliseconds)	JavaScript 1.0	Sets the time for the Date object according to the number of milliseconds since January 1 1970 00:00:00.
setUTCDate(dayOfMonth)	JavaScript 1.3	Sets the date in the month for the Date object according to universal time.
setUTCFullYear(year [, month, day])	JavaScript 1.3	Sets the full year for the Date object according to universal time.

Method	Introduced	Description
`setUTCHours(hours [, minutes, seconds, milliseconds])`	JavaScript 1.3	Sets the hour of the day for the `Date` object according to universal time.
`setUTCMilliseconds(milliseconds)`	JavaScript 1.3	Sets the number of milliseconds for the `Date` object according to universal time.
`setUTCMinutes(mintes [, seconds, milliseconds])`	JavaScript 1.3	Sets the number of minutes for the `Date` object according to universal time.
`setUTCMonth(month [, day])`	JavaScript 1.3	Sets the month for the `Date` object according to universal time.
`setUTCSeconds()`	JavaScript 1.3	Sets the number of seconds for the `Date` object according to universal time.
`setYear(year)`	JavaScript 1.0	Sets the year for the `Date` object. Deprecated in favor of `setFullYear()`.
`toGMTString()`	JavaScript 1.0	Converts the `Date` object to a string according to Greenwich Mean Time. Replaced by `toUTCString`.
`toLocaleString()`	JavaScript 1.0	Converts the `Date` object to a string according to the local time zone.
`toString()`	JavaScript 1.1	Converts the `Date` object into a string.
`toUTCString()`	JavaScript 1.3	Converts the `Date` object to a string according to universal time.
`UTC(year, month [, day, hours, minutes, seconds, milliseconds])`	JavaScript 1.0	Retrieves the number of milliseconds in a date since January 1 1970 00:00:00, universal time.
`valueOf()`	JavaScript 1.1	Returns the primitive value of the `Date` object.

Function

ActiveXObject functions represent a block of JavaScript code that is called on demand. Introduced in JavaScript 1.1, a `Function` object is created with the `Function` constructor.

Functions can be defined in a variety of ways. You can create a function using the following standard function statement:

```
function functionName() {
    // code here
}
```

You can also create an anonymous function and assign it to a variable. The following code demonstrates this approach:

```
var functionName = function() {
    // code here
};
```

The trailing semi-colon is not a typo because this statement is an assignment operation, and all assignment operations should end with a semi-colon.

Functions are objects, and thus they have a constructor. It's possible to create a function using the Function object's constructor as shown in the following code:

```
var functionName = new Function("arg1", "arg2", "return arg1 + arg2");
```

The first arguments to the constructor are the names of the function's parameters — you can add as many parameters as you need. The last parameter you pass to the constructor is the function's body. The previous code creates a function that accepts two arguments and returns their sum.

There are very few instances where you will use the Function constructor. It is preferred to define a function using the standard function statement or by creating an anonymous function and assigning it to a variable.

Properties

Property	Introduced	Description
arguments	JavaScript 1.1	An array containing the parameters passed into the function.
arguments.length	JavaScript 1.1	Returns the number of parameters passed into the function.
constructor	JavaScript 1.1	Used to reference the constructor function for the object.
length	JavaScript 1.1	Returns the number of parameters expected by the function. This differs from arguments.length, which returns the number of parameters actually passed into the function.
prototype	JavaScript 1.1	Returns the prototype for the object, which can be used to extend the object's interface.

Methods

Method	Introduced	Description
apply(thisObj, arguments)	JavaScript 1.3	Calls a function or method as if it belonged to thisObj and passes arguments to the function or method. arguments must be an array.
call(thisObj, arg1, …)	JavaScript 1.3	Identical to apply(), except arguments are passed individually instead of in an array.
toString()	JavaScript 1.1	Converts the Function object into a string.
valueOf()	JavaScript 1.1	Returns the primitive value of the Function object.

Math

The Math object provides methods and properties used for mathematical calculations. Introduced in JavaScript 1.0, the Math object is a top-level object, which can be accessed without a constructor.

Properties

Property	Introduced	Description
E	JavaScript 1.0	Returns Euler's constant (the base of natural logarithms; approximately 2.718).
LN10	JavaScript 1.0	Returns the natural logarithm of 10 (approximately 2.302).
LN2	JavaScript 1.0	Returns the natural logarithm of 2 (approximately 0.693).
LOG10E	JavaScript 1.0	Returns the base 10 logarithm of E (approximately 0.434).
LOG2E	JavaScript 1.0	Returns the base 2 logarithm of E (approximately 1.442).
PI	JavaScript 1.0	Returns pi, the ratio of the circumference of a circle to its diameter (approximately 3.142).
SQRT1_2	JavaScript 1.0	Returns the square root of 1/2 (approximately 0.707).
SQRT2	JavaScript 1.0	Returns the square root of 2 (approximately 1.414).

Methods

Method	Introduced	Description
abs(x)	JavaScript 1.0	Returns the absolute (positive) value of a number.
acos(x)	JavaScript 1.0	Returns the arccosine of a number (in radians).
asin(x)	JavaScript 1.0	Returns the arcsine of a number (in radians).

Continued

Methods *(continued)*

Method	Introduced	Description
atan(x)	JavaScript 1.0	Returns the arctangent of a number (in radians).
atan2(y, x)	JavaScript 1.0	Returns the angle (in radians) between the x-axis and the position represented by the y and x coordinates passed in as parameters.
ceil(x)	JavaScript 1.0	Returns the value of a number rounded up to the nearest integer.
cos(x)	JavaScript 1.0	Returns the cosine of a number.
exp(x)	JavaScript 1.0	Returns E to the power of the argument passed in.
floor(x)	JavaScript 1.0	Returns the value of a number rounded down to the nearest integer.
log(x)	JavaScript 1.0	Returns the natural logarithm (base E) of a number.
max(a, b)	JavaScript 1.0	Returns the greater of two numbers passed in as parameters.
min(a, b)	JavaScript 1.0	Returns the lesser of two numbers passed in as parameters.
pow(x, y)	JavaScript 1.0	Returns the first parameter raised to the power of the second.
random()	JavaScript 1.1	Returns a pseudo-random number between 0 and 1.
round(x)	JavaScript 1.0	Returns the value of a number rounded up or down to the nearest integer.
sin(x)	JavaScript 1.0	Returns the sine of a number.
sqrt(x)	JavaScript 1.0	Returns the square root of a number.
tan(x)	JavaScript 1.0	Returns the tangent of a number.

Number

The Number object acts as a wrapper for primitive numeric values. Introduced in JavaScript 1.1, a Number object is created using the Number constructor with the initial value for the number passed in as a parameter.

Properties

Property	Introduced	Description
constructor	JavaScript 1.1	Used to reference the constructor function for the object.
MAX_VALUE	JavaScript 1.1	Returns the largest number that can be represented in JavaScript (approximately 1.79E+308).

Property	Introduced	Description
MIN_VALUE	JavaScript 1.1	Returns the smallest number that can be represented in JavaScript (5E-324).
NaN	JavaScript 1.1	Returns a value that is "not a number."
NEGATIVE_ INFINITY	JavaScript 1.1	Returns a value representing negative infinity.
POSITIVE_ INFINITY	JavaScript 1.1	Returns a value representing (positive) infinity.
prototype	JavaScript 1.1	Returns the prototype for the object, which can be used to extend the object's interface.

Methods

Method	Introduced	Description
toExponential(fractionDigits)	JavaScript 1.5	Returns a string containing the exponent notation of a number. The parameter should be between 0 and 20 and determines the number of digits after the decimal.
toFixed([digits])	JavaScript 1.5	The format number for digits number of digits. The number is rounded up, and 0s are added after the decimal point to achieve the desired decimal length.
toPrecision([precision])	JavaScript 1.5	Returns a string representing the Number object to the specified precision.
toString()	JavaScript 1.1	Converts the Number object into a string.
valueOf()	JavaScript 1.1	Returns the primitive value of the Number object.

Object

Object is the primitive type for JavaScript objects, from which all other objects are descended (that is, all other objects inherit the methods and properties of the Object object). Introduced in JavaScript 1.0, an Object object can be created using the Object constructor as follows:

```
var obj = new Object();
```

You can also create an object using object literal notation like this:

```
var obj = {};
```

Literal notation is the preferred method of creating an object.

Properties

Property	Introduced	Description
constructor	JavaScript 1.1	Used to reference the constructor function for the object.
prototype	JavaScript 1.1	Returns the prototype for the object, which can be used to extend the object's interface.

Methods

Method	Introduced	Description
hasOwnProperty(propertyName)	JavaScript 1.5	Checks whether the specified property is inherited. Returns true if not inherited; false if inherited.
isPrototypeOf(obj)	JavaScript 1.5	Determines if the specified object is the prototype of another object.
propertyIsEnumerable(propertyName)	JavaScript 1.5	Determines if the specified property can be seen by a for in loop.
toString()	JavaScript 1.0	Converts the Object object into a string.
valueOf()	JavaScript 1.1	Returns the primitive value of the Object object.

RegExp

The RegExp object is used to find patterns within string values. RegExp objects can be created in two ways: using the RegExp constructor or a text literal. It was introduced in JavaScript 1.2.

Some of the properties in the following table have both long and short names. The short names are derived from the Perl programming language.

Properties

Property	Introduced	Description
constructor	JavaScript 1.2	Used to reference the constructor function for the object.
global	JavaScript 1.2	Indicates whether all possible matches in the string are to be made, or only the first. Corresponds to the g flag.
ignoreCase	JavaScript 1.2	Indicates whether the match is to be case-insensitive. Corresponds to the i flag.
input	JavaScript 1.2	The string against which the regular expression is matched.
lastIndex	JavaScript 1.2	The position in the string from which the next match is to be started.
multiline	JavaScript 1.2	Indicates whether strings are to be searched across multiple lines. Corresponds with the m flag.
prototype	JavaScript 1.2	Returns the prototype for the object, which can be used to extend the object's interface.
source	JavaScript 1.2	The text of the pattern for the regular expression.

Methods

Method	Introduced	Description
exec(stringToSearch)	JavaScript 1.2	Executes a search for a match in the string parameter passed in.
test(stringToMatch)	JavaScript 1.2	Tests for a match in the string parameter passed in.
toString()	JavaScript 1.2	Converts the RegExp object into a string.
valueOf()	JavaScript 1.2	Returns the primitive value of the RegExp object.

Special Characters Used in Regular Expressions

Character	Examples	Function
\	/n/ matches n; /\n/ matches a linefeed character; /^/ matches the start of a line; and /\^/ matches ^	For characters that are by default treated as normal characters, the backslash indicates that the next character is to be interpreted with a special value. For characters that are usually treated as special characters, the backslash indicates that the next character is to be interpreted as a normal character.

Continued

691

Special Characters Used in Regular Expressions *(continued)*

Character	Examples	Function
^	`/^A/` matches the first but not the second `A` in "A man called Adam"	Matches the start of a line or of the `input`.
$	`/r$/` matches only the last `r` in "horror"	Matches the end of a line or of the `input`.
*	`/ro*/` matches `r` in "right," `ro` in "wrong," and "roo" in "room"	Matches the preceding character zero or more times.
+	`/l+/` matches `l` in "life," `ll` in "still," and `lll` in "stilllife"	Matches the preceding character one or more times. For example, `/a+/` matches the `a` in "candy" and all the `a`'s in "caaaaaaandy."
?	`/Smythe?/` matches "Smyth" and "Smythe"	Matches the preceding character once or zero times.
.	`/.b/` matches the second but not the first `ob` in "blob"	Matches any character apart from the newline character.
(x)	`/(Smythe?)/` matches "Smyth" and "Smythe" in "John Smyth and Rob Smythe" and allows the substrings to be retrieved as `RegExp.$1` and `RegExp.$2` respectively.	Matches x and remembers the match. The matched substring can be retrieved from the elements of the array that results from the match, or from the `RegExp` object's properties `$1`, `$2` ... `$9`, or `lastParen`.
x|y	`/Smith|Smythe/` matches "Smith" and "Smythe"	Matches either x or y (where x and y are blocks of characters).
{n}	`/l{2}/` matches `ll` in "still" and the first two `l`s in "stilllife"	Matches exactly n instances of the preceding character (where n is a positive integer).
{n,}	`/l{2,}/` matches `ll` in "still" and `lll` in "stilllife"	Matches n or more instances of the preceding character (where n is a positive integer).
{n,m}	`/l{1,2}/` matches `l` in "life", `ll` in "still," and the first two `l`s in "stilllife"	Matches between n and m instances of the preceding character (where n and m are positive integers).
[xyz]	`[ab]` matches a and b; `[a-c]` matches a, b and c	Matches any one of the characters in the square brackets. A range of characters in the alphabet can be matched using a hyphen.

Character	Examples	Function
[^xyz]	[^aeiouy] matches s in "easy"; [^a-y] matches z in "lazy"	Matches any character except those enclosed in the square brackets. A range of characters in the alphabet can be specified using a hyphen.
[\b]		Matches a backspace.
\b	/t\b/ matches the first t in "about time"	Matches a word boundary (for example, a space or the end of a line).
\B	/t\Bi/ matches ti in "it is time"	Matches when there is no word boundary in this position.
\cX	/\cA/ matches Ctrl-A	Matches a control character.
\d	/IE\d/ matches IE4, IE5, etc.	Matches a digit character. This is identical to [0-9].
\D	/\D/ matches the decimal point in "3.142"	Matches any character that is not a digit. This is identical to [^0-9].
\f		Matches a form-feed character.
\n		Matches a line-feed character.
\r		Matches a carriage return character.
\s	/\s/ matches the space in "not now"	Matches any white space character, including space, tab, line-feed, etc. This is identical to [\f\n\r\t\v].
\S	/\S/ matches a in " a "	Matches any character other than a white space character. This is identical to [^ \f\n\r\t\v].
\t		Matches a tab character.
\v		Matches a vertical tab character.
\w	/\w/ matches 0 in "0?!" and 1 in "$1"	Matches any alphanumeric character or the underscore. This is identical to [A-Za-z0-9_].
\W	/\W/ matches $ in "$10million" and @ in "j_smith@wrox"	Matches any non-alphanumeric character (excluding the underscore). This is identical to [^A-Za-z0-9_].
()\n	/(Joh?n) and \1/ matches John and John in "John and John's friend" but does not match "John and Jon"	Matches the last substring that matched the nth match placed in parentheses and remembered (where n is a positive integer).
\octal \xhex	/\x25/ matches %	Matches the character corresponding to the specified octal or hexadecimal escape value.

String

The `String` object is used to contain a string of characters. It was introduced in JavaScript 1.0. This must be distinguished from a string literal, but the methods and properties of the `String` object can also be accessed by a string literal, since a temporary object will be created when they are called.

The HTML methods in the last table are not part of any ECMAScript standard, but they have been part of the JavaScript language since version 1.0. They can be useful because they dynamically generate HTML.

Properties

Property	Introduced	Description
constructor	JavaScript 1.1	Used to reference the constructor function for the object.
length	JavaScript 1.0	Returns the number of characters in the string.
prototype	JavaScript 1.1	Returns the prototype for the object, which can be used to extend the object's interface.

Methods

Method	Introduced	Description
charAt(index)	JavaScript 1.0	Returns the character at the specified position in the string.
charCodeAt(index)	JavaScript 1.2	Returns the Unicode value of the character at the specified position in the string.
concat(value1, value2, ...)	JavaScript 1.2	Concatenates the strings supplied as arguments and returns the string thus formed.
fromCharCode(value1, value2, ...)	JavaScript 1.2	Returns the string formed from the concatenation of the characters represented by the supplied Unicode values.
indexOf(substr [, startIndex])	JavaScript 1.0	Returns the position within the String object of the first match for the supplied substring. Returns –1 if the substring is not found. Starts the search at startIndex if specified.
lastIndexOf(substr [, startIndex])	JavaScript 1.0	Returns the position within the String object of the last match for the supplied substring. Returns –1 if the substring is not found. Starts the search at startIndex if specified.
match(regexp)	JavaScript 1.2	Searches the string for a match to the supplied pattern. Returns an array or null if not found.

Methods *(continued)*

Method	Introduced	Description
replace(regexp, newValue)	JavaScript 1.2	Used to replace a substring that matches a regular expression with a new value.
search(regexp)	JavaScript 1.2	Searches for a match between a regular expression and the string. Returns the index of the match, or -1 if not found.
slice(startIndex [, endIndex])	JavaScript 1.0	Returns a substring of the String object.
split(delimiter)	JavaScript 1.1	Splits a String object into an array of strings by separating the string into substrings.
substr(startIndex [, length])	JavaScript 1.0	Returns a substring of the characters from the given starting position and containing the specified number of characters.
substring(startIndex [, endIndex])	JavaScript 1.0	Returns a substring of the characters between two positions in the string. The character at endIndex is not included in the substring.
toLowerCase()	JavaScript 1.0	Returns the string converted to lowercase.
toUpperCase()	JavaScript 1.0	Returns the string converted to uppercase.

HTML Methods

Method	Introduced	Description
anchor(name)	JavaScript 1.0	Returns the string surrounded by <a>...</a> tags with the name attribute assigned the passed parameter.
big()	JavaScript 1.0	Encloses the string in <big>...</big> tags.
blink()	JavaScript 1.0	Encloses the string in <blink>...</blink> tags.
bold()	JavaScript 1.0	Encloses the string in ... tags.
fixed()	JavaScript 1.0	Encloses the string in <tt>...</tt> tags.
fontcolor(color)	JavaScript 1.0	Encloses the string in <font>...</font> tags with the color attribute assigned a parameter value.
fontsize(size)	JavaScript 1.0	Encloses the string in <font>...</font> tags with the size attribute assigned a parameter value.
italics()	JavaScript 1.0	Encloses the string in <i>...</i> tags.

Continued

HTML Methods *(continued)*

Method	Introduced	Description
link(url)	JavaScript 1.0	Encloses the string in <a>...</a> tags with the href attribute assigned a parameter value.
small()	JavaScript 1.0	Encloses the string in <small>...</small> tags.
strike()	JavaScript 1.0	Encloses the string in <strike>...</strike> tags.
sub()	JavaScript 1.0	Encloses the string in _{...} tags.
sup()	JavaScript 1.0	Encloses the string in ^{...} tags and causes a string to be displayed as superscript.

W3C DOM Reference

Because JavaScript is primarily used to program the browser and add behavior to web pages, it's only natural to include a reference to the W3C DOM.

The following pages lists the objects made available by the W3C DOM.

DOM Core Objects

This section describes and lists objects defined by the DOM standards — starting with the lowest level of DOM objects. All objects are in alphabetical order.

Low-Level DOM Objects

The DOM specification describes the Node, NodeList, and NamedNodeMap objects. These are the lowest-level objects in the DOM, and are the primary building blocks of higher-level objects.

Node

Defined in DOM Level 1, the Node object is the primary datatype for the entire DOM. All objects in the DOM inherit from Node. There are 12 different types of Node objects; each type has an associated integer value. The following tables list the Node object's type values, properties, and methods.

Node Types

Type Name	Integer Value	Introduced	Associated Data Type
ELEMENT_NODE	1	Level 1	Element
ATTRIBUTE_NODE	2	Level 1	Attr
TEXT_NODE	3	Level 1	Text

Continued

Node Types *(continued)*

Type Name	Integer Value	Introduced	Associated Data Type
CDATA_SECTION_NODE	4	Level 1	CDATASection
ENTITY_REFERENCE_NODE	5	Level 1	EntityReference
ENTITY_NODE	6	Level 1	Entity
PROCESSING_INSTRUCTION_NODE	7	Level 1	ProcessingInstruction
COMMENT_NODE	8	Level 1	Comment
DOCUMENT_NODE	9	Level 1	Document
DOCUMENT_TYPE_NODE	10	Level 1	DocumentType
DOCUMENT_FRAGMENT_NODE	11	Level 1	DocumentFragment
NOTATION_NODE	12	Level 1	Notation

Properties

Property Name	Description	Introduced
attributes	A NamedNodeMap containing the attributes of this node if it is an Element, or null otherwise.	Level 1
childNodes	A NodeList containing all children of this node.	Level 1
firstChild	Gets the first child of this node. Returns null if no child exists.	Level 1
lastChild	Gets the last child of this node. Returns null if no child exists.	Level 1
localName	Returns the local part of the node's qualified name (the part after the colon of the qualified name when namespaces are used). Used primarily in XML DOMs.	Level 2
namespaceURI	The namespace URI of the node, or null if not specified.	Level 2
nextSibling	Gets the node immediately following this node. Returns null if no following sibling exists.	Level 1
nodeName	Gets the name of this node.	Level 1

Property Name	Description	Introduced
nodeType	An integer representing the type of this node. See previous table.	Level 1
nodeValue	Gets the value of this node, depending on the type.	Level 1
ownerDocument	Gets the Document object this node is contained in. If this node is a Document node, it returns null.	Level 1
parentNode	Gets the parent node of this node. Returns null for nodes that are currently not in the DOM tree.	Level 1
prefix	Returns the namespace prefix of this node, or null if not specified.	Level 2
previousSibling	Gets the node immediately before this node. Returns null if no previous sibling.	Level 1

Methods

Method Name	Description	Introduced
appendChild(newChild)	Adds the newChild to the end of the list of children.	Level 1
cloneNode(deep)	Returns a duplicate of the node. The returned node has no parent. If deep is true, this clones all nodes contained within the node.	Level 1
hasAttributes()	Returns a Boolean value based on if the node has any attributes (if the node is an element).	Level 2
hasChildNodes()	Returns a Boolean value based on whether the node has any child nodes.	Level 1
insertBefore(newChild, refChild)	Inserts the newChild node before the existing child referenced by refChild. If refChild is null, newChild is added at the end of the list of children.	Level 1
removeChild(oldChild)	Removes the specified child node and returns it.	Level 1
replaceChild(newChild, oldChild)	Replaces oldChild with newChild and returns oldChild.	Level 1

NodeList

The NodeList object is an ordered collection of nodes. The items contained in the NodeList are accessible via an index starting from 0.

A `NodeList` is a live snapshot of nodes. Any change made to the nodes within the DOM are immediately reflected in every reference of the `NodeList`.

Properties

Property Name	Description	Introduced
length	The number of nodes in the list.	Level 1

Methods

Method Name	Description	Introduced
item(index)	Returns the item at the specified index. Returns `null` if the index is greater than or equal to the list's length.	Level 1

NamedNodeMap

Objects referred to as `NamedNodeMaps` represent collections of nodes that can be accessed by name. This object does not inherit from `NodeList`. An element's attribute list is an example of a `NamedNodeMap`.

Properties

Property Name	Description	Introduced
length	The number of nodes in the map.	Level 1

Methods

Method Name	Description	Introduced
getNamedItem(name)	Retrieves a node by the specified name.	Level 1
removeNamedItem(name)	Removes an item by the specified name.	Level 1
setNamedItem(node)	Adds a node to the list by using its `nodeName` property as its key.	Level 1

High-Level DOM Objects

These objects inherit `Node` and are the basis for even higher-level DOM objects as specified by the HTML DOM. These objects mirror the different node types.

The following objects are listed in alphabetical order. The `CDATASection`, `Comment`, `DocumentType`, `Entity`, `EntityReference`, `Notation`, and `ProcessingInstruction` objects are purposefully omitted from this section.

Attr

The `Attr` object represents an `Element` object's attribute. Even though `Attr` objects inherit from `Node`, they are not considered children of the element they describe, and thus are not part of the DOM tree. The `Node` properties of `parentNode`, `previousSibling`, and `nextSibling` return `null` for `Attr` objects.

Properties

Property Name	Description	Introduced
ownerElement	Returns the `Element` object the attribute is attached to.	Level 2
name	Returns the name of the attribute.	Level 1
value	Returns the value of the attribute.	Level 1

Document

The `Document` object represents the entire HTML or XML document. It is the root of the document tree. The `Document` is the container for all nodes within the document, and each `Node` object's `ownerDocument` property points to the `Document`.

Properties

Property Name	Description	Introduced
docType	The `DocType` object associated with this document. Returns `null` for HTML and XML documents without a document type declaration.	Level 1
documentElement	Returns the root element of the document. For HTML documents, the `documentElement` is the `<html/>` element.	Level 1
implementation	The `DOMImplementation` object associated with the `Document`.	Level 1

Methods

Method Name	Description	Introduced
createAttribute(name)	Returns a new `Attr` object with the specified name.	Level 1
createAttributeNS(namespaceURI, qualifiedName)	Returns an attribute with the given qualified name and namespace URI. Not for HTML DOMs.	Level 2

Continued

Methods *(continued)*

Method Name	Description	Introduced
createComment(data)	Returns a new Comment object with the specified data.	Level 1
createCDATASection(data)	Returns a new CDATASection object whose value is the specified data.	Level 1
createDocumentFragment()	Returns an empty DocumentFragment object.	Level 1
createElement(tagName)	Returns a new Element object with the specified tag name.	Level 1
createElementNS(namespaceURI, qualifiedName)	Returns an element of the specified qualified name and namespace URI. Not for HTML DOMs.	Level 2
createTextNode(text)	Returns a new Text object containing the specified text.	Level 1
getElementById(elementId)	Returns the Element with the specified ID value. Returns null if the element does not exist.	Level 2
getElementsByTagName(tagName)	Returns a NodeList of all Element objects with the specified tag name in the order in which they appear in the DOM tree.	Level 1
getElementsByTagNameNS(namespaceURI, localName)	Returns a NodeList of all elements with the specified local name and namespace URI. Elements returned are in the order they appear in the DOM.	Level 2
importNode(importedNode, deep)	Imports a node from another document. The source node is not altered or removed from its document. A copy of the source is created. If deep is true, all child nodes of the imported node are imported. If false, only the node is imported.	Level 2

DocumentFragment

The DocumentFragment object is a lightweight Document object. Its primary purpose is efficiency. Making many changes to the DOM tree, such as appending several nodes individually, is an expensive process. It is possible to append Node objects to a DocumentFragment object, which allows you to easily and efficiently insert all nodes contained within the DocumentFragment into the DOM tree.

The following code shows the use of a DocumentFragment:

```
var documentFragment = document.createDocumentFragment();

for (var i = 0; i < 1000; i++) {
    var element = document.createElement("div");
    var text = document.createTextNode("Here is test for div #" + i);

    element.setAttribute("id", i);

    documentFragment.appendChild(element);
}

document.body.appendChild(documentFragment);
```

Without the DocumentFragment object, this code would update the DOM tree 1,000 times, thus degrading performance. With the DocumentFragment object, the DOM tree is updated only once.

The DocumentFragment object inherits the Node object, and as such has Node's properties and methods. It does not have any other properties or methods.

Element

Elements are the majority of objects, other than text, that you will encounter in the DOM.

Properties

Property Name	Description	Introduced
tagName	Returns the name of the element. The same as Node.nodeName for this node type.	Level 1

Methods

Method Name	Description	Introduced
getAttribute(name)	Retrieves the attribute's value by the specified name.	Level 1
getAttributeNS(namespaceURI, localName)	Returns the Attr object by local name and namespace URI. Not for HTML DOMs.	Level 2
getAttributeNode(name)	Returns the Attr object associated with the specified name. Returns null if no attribute by that name exists.	Level 1

Continued

Methods *(continued)*

Method Name	Description	Introduced
getElementsByTagName(tagName)	Returns a NodeList of all descendant elements with the specified tagName in the order in which they appear in the tree.	Level 1
getElementsByTagNameNS(namespaceURI, localName)	Returns a NodeList of all the descendant Element objects with the specified local name and namespace URI. Not for HTML DOMs.	Level 2
hasAttribute(name)	Returns a Boolean value based on whether or not the element has an attribute with the specified name.	Level 2
hasAttributeNS(namespaceURI, localName)	Returns a Boolean value based on whether the Element has an attribute with the given local name and namespace URI. Not for HTML DOMs.	Level 2
removeAttribute(name)	Removes the attribute with the specified name.	Level 1
removeAttributeNS(namespaceURI, localName)	Removes an attribute specified by the local name and namespace URI. Not for HTML DOMs.	Level 2
removeAttributeNode(oldAttr)	Removes and returns the specified attribute.	Level 1
setAttribute(name, value)	Creates and adds a new attribute, or changes the value of an existing attribute. The value is a simple string.	Level 1
setAttributeNS(namespaceURI, qualifiedName, value)	Creates and adds a new attribute with the specified namespace URI, qualified name, and value.	Level 2
setAttributeNode(newAttr)	Adds the specified attribute to the element. Replaces the existing attribute with the same name if it exists.	Level 1
setAttributeNodeNS(newAttr)	Adds the specified attribute to the element.	Level 2

Text

The Text object represents text content of an Element or Attr object.

Methods

Method Name	Description	Introduced
splitText(indexOffset)	Breaks the Text node into two nodes at the specified offset. The new nodes stay in the DOM tree as siblings.	Level 1

HTML DOM Objects

In order to adequately interface with the DOM, the W3C extends the DOM Level 1 and 2 specifications to describe objects, properties, and methods, specific to HTML documents.

Most of the objects you'll interface with as a front-end developer are contained in this section.

Miscellaneous Objects: The HTML Collection

The HTMLCollection object is a list of nodes, much like NodeList. It does not inherit from NodeList, but HTMLCollections are considered live, like NodeLists, and are automatically updated when changes are made to the document.

Properties

Property Name	Description	Introduced
length	Returns the number of elements in the collection.	Level 1

Methods

Method Name	Description	Introduced
item(index)	Returns the element at the specified index. Returns null if index it larger than the collection's length.	Level 1
namedItem(name)	Returns the element using a name. It first searches for an element with a matching id attribute value. If none are found, it searches for elements with a matching name attribute value.	Level 1

HTML Document Objects: The HTML Document

The HTMLDocument object is the root of HTML documents and contains the entire content.

Properties

Property Name	Description	Introduced
anchors	Returns an HTMLCollection of all <a/> elements in the document that have a value assigned to their name attribute.	Level 1
applets	Returns an HTMLCollection of all <applet/> elements and <object/> elements that include applets in the document.	Level 1
body	Returns the element that contains the document's content. Returns the <body/> element, or the outermost <frameset/> element depending on the document.	Level 1
cookie	Returns the cookies associated with the document. Returns an empty string if none.	Level 1
domain	Returns the domain name of the server that served the document. Returns null if the domain name cannot be identified.	Level 1
forms	Returns an HTMLCollection of all <form/> elements in the document.	Level 1
images	Returns an HTMLCollection object containing all <img/> elements in the document.	Level 1
links	Returns an HTMLCollection of all <area/> and <a/> elements (with an href value) in the document.	Level 1
referrer	Returns the URL of the page that linked to the page. Returns an empty string if the user navigated directly to the page.	Level 1
title	The title of the document as specified by the <title/> element in the document's <head/> element.	Level 1
URL	The complete URL of the document.	Level 1

Methods

Method Name	Description	Introduced
close()	Closes a document and opened with open() forces page rendering.	Level 1
getElementById(elementId)	Returns the element with the given elementId or null if no element could be found. Removed in DOM Level 2 and added to the Document object.	Level 1

Method Name	Description	Introduced
getElementsByName(name)	Returns an HTMLCollection of elements with the specified name attribute value.	Level 1
open()	Opens a document for writing.	Level 1
write()	Writes a string of text to the document.	Level 1
writeln()	Writes a string of text to the document followed by a newline.	Level 1

HTML Element Objects

HTML element attributes are exposed as properties of the various HTML element objects. Their data type is determined by the attribute's type in the HTML 4.0 specification.

Other than HTMLElement, all HTML element objects are described here in alphabetical order. The following pages do not contain a complete list of HTML element object types. Instead, only the following element object types are listed:

- ❑ HTMLAnchorElement
- ❑ HTMLBodyElement
- ❑ HTMLButtonElement
- ❑ HTMLDivElement
- ❑ HTMLFormElement
- ❑ HTMLFrameElement
- ❑ HTMLFrameSetElement
- ❑ HTMLIFrameElement
- ❑ HTMLImageElement
- ❑ HTMLInputElement
- ❑ HTMLOptionElement
- ❑ HTMLParagraphElement
- ❑ HTMLSelectElement
- ❑ HTMLTableCellElement
- ❑ HTMLTableElement
- ❑ HTMLTableRowElement
- ❑ HTMLTableSectionElement
- ❑ HTMLTextAreaElement

HTMLElement

`HTMLElement` is the base object for all HTML elements, much like how `Node` is the base object for all DOM nodes. Therefore, all HTML elements have the following properties.

Properties

Property Name	Description	Introduced
className	Gets or sets the value of the element's `class` attribute.	Level 1
id	Gets or sets the value of the element's `id` attribute.	Level 1

HTMLAnchorElement

Represents the HTML `<a/>` element.

Properties

Property Name	Description	Introduced
accessKey	Gets or sets the value of the `accessKey` attribute	Level 1
href	Gets or sets the value of the `href` attribute.	Level 1
name	Gets or sets the value of the `name` attribute.	Level 1
target	Gets or set the value of the `target` attribute.	Level 1

Methods

Method Name	Description	Introduced
blur()	Removes the keyboard focus from the element.	Level 1
focus()	Gives keyboard focus to the element.	Level 1

HTMLBodyElement

Represents the `<body/>` element.

Properties

Property Name	Description	Introduced
aLink	Deprecated. Gets or sets the value of the `alink` attribute.	Level 1
background	Deprecated. Gets or sets the value of the `background` attribute.	Level 1

Property Name	Description	Introduced
bgColor	Deprecated. Gets or sets the value of the bgColor attribute.	Level 1
link	Deprecated. Gets or sets the value of the link attribute.	Level 1
text	Deprecated. Gets or sets the value of the text attribute.	Level 1
vLink	Deprecated. Gets or sets the value of the vlink attribute.	Level 1

HTMLButtonElement

Represents <button/> elements.

Properties

Property Name	Description	Introduced
accessKey	Gets or sets the value of the accessKey attribute.	Level 1
disabled	Gets or sets the value of the disabled attribute.	Level 1
form	Gets the HTMLFormElement object containing the button. Returns null if the button is not inside a form.	Level 1
name	Gets or sets the value of the name attribute.	Level 1
type	Gets the value of the type attribute.	Level 1
value	Gets or sets the value of the value attribute.	Level 1

HTMLDivElement

Represents the <div/> element.

Properties

Property Name	Description	Introduced
align	Deprecated. Gets or sets the value of the align attribute.	Level 1

HTMLFormElement

Represents the `<form/>` element.

Properties

Property Name	Description	Introduced
action	Gets or sets the value of the `action` attribute.	Level 1
elements	Returns an `HTMLCollection` object containing all form control elements in the form.	Level 1
enctype	Gets or sets the value of the `enctype` attribute.	Level 1
length	Returns the number of form controls within the form.	Level 1
method	Gets or sets the value of the `method` attribute.	Level 1
name	Gets or sets the value of the `name` attribute.	Level 1
target	Gets or sets the value of the `target` attribute.	Level 1

Methods

Method Name	Description	Introduced
reset()	Resets all form control elements contained within the form to their default values.	Level 1
submit()	Submits the form. Does not fire the `submit` event.	Level 1

HTMLFrameElement

Represents the `<frame/>` element.

Properties

Property Name	Description	Introduced
contentDocument	Gets the `Document` object for the frame. Returns `null` if one isn't available.	Level 2
frameBorder	Gets or sets the value of the `frameBorder` attribute.	Level 1
marginHeight	Gets or sets the value of the `marginHeight` attribute.	Level 1
marginWidth	Gets or sets the value of the `marginWidth` attribute.	Level 1
name	Gets or sets the value of the `name` attribute.	Level 1

Property Name	Description	Introduced
noResize	Gets or sets the value of the noResize attribute.	Level 1
scrolling	Gets or sets the value of the scrolling attribute.	Level 1
src	Gets or sets the value of the src attribute.	Level 1

HTMLFrameSetElement

Represents the <frameset/> element.

Properties

Property Name	Description	Introduced
cols	Gets or sets the value of the cols attribute.	Level 1
rows	Gets or sets the value of the rows attribute.	Level 1

HTMLIFrameElement

Represents the <iframe/> element.

Properties

Property Name	Description	Introduced
align	Deprecated. Gets or sets the value of the align attribute.	Level 1
contentDocument	Gets the Document object of the frame. Returns null if one doesn't exist.	Level 2
frameBorder	Gets or sets the value of the frameBorder attribute.	Level 1
height	Gets or sets the value of the height attribute.	Level 1
marginHeight	Gets or sets the value of the marginHeight attribute.	Level 1
marginWidth	Gets or sets the value of the marginWidth attribute.	Level 1
name	Gets or sets the value of the name attribute.	Level 1
noResize	Gets or sets the value of the noResize attribute.	Level 1
scrolling	Gets or sets the value of the scrolling attribute.	Level 1
src	Gets or sets the value of the src attribute.	Level 1
width	Gets or sets the value of the width attribute.	Level 1

HTMLImageElement

Represents the `<img/>` element.

Properties

Property Name	Description	Introduced
align	Deprecated. Gets or sets the value of the `align` attribute.	Level 1
alt	Gets or sets the value of the `alt` attribute.	Level 1
border	Deprecated. Gets or sets the value of the `border` attribute.	Level 1
height	Gets or sets the value of the `height` attribute.	Level 1
name	Gets or sets the value of the `name` attribute.	Level 1
src	Gets or sets the value of the `src` attribute.	Level 1
width	Gets or sets the value of the `width` attribute.	Level 1

HTMLInputElement

Represents the `<input/>` element.

Properties

Property Name	Description	Introduced
accessKey	Gets or sets the value of the `accessKey` attribute.	Level 1
align	Deprecated. Gets or sets the value of the `align` attribute.	Level 1
alt	Gets or sets the value of the `alt` attribute.	Level 1
checked	Used when `type` is `checkbox` or `radio`. Returns a Boolean value depending on whether or not the checkbox or radio button is checked.	Level 1
default-Checked	Used when `type` is `checkbox` or `radio`. Gets or sets the checked attribute. The value does not change when other checkboxes or radio buttons are checked.	Level 1
disabled	Gets or sets the value of the `disabled` attribute.	Level 1
form	Gets the `HTMLFormElement` object containing the `<input/>` element. Returns `null` if the element is not inside a form.	Level 1
maxLength	Gets or sets the value of the `maxLength` attribute.	Level 1
name	Gets or sets the value of the `name` attribute.	Level 1
readOnly	Used only if `type` is `text` or `password`. Gets or sets the value of the `readonly` attribute.	Level 1

Property Name	Description	Introduced
size	Gets or sets the value of the size attribute.	Level 1
src	If type is image, this gets or sets the value of the src attribute.	Level 1
type	Gets the value of the type attribute.	Level 1
value	Gets or sets the value of the value attribute.	Level 1

Methods

Method Name	Description	Introduced
blur()	Removes keyboard focus from the element.	Level 1
click()	Simulates a mouse click for <input/> elements with type button, checkbox, radio, reset, and submit.	Level 1
focus()	Gives keyboard focus to the element.	Level 1
select()	Selects content of <input/> elements with type text, password, and file.	Level 1

HTMLOptionElement

Represents the <option/> element.

Properties

Property Name	Description	Introduced
defaultSelected	Gets or sets the selected attribute. The value of this property does not change as other <option/> elements in the <select/> element are selected.	Level 1
disabled	Gets or sets the value of the disabled attribute.	Level 1
form	Gets the HTMLFormElement object containing the <option/> element. Returns null if the element is not inside a form.	Level 1
index	Gets the index position of the <option/> element in its containing <select/> element. Starts at 0.	Level 1
label	Gets or sets the value of the label attribute.	Level 1
selected	Returns a Boolean value depending on whether or not the <option/> element is currently selected.	Level 1

Continued

Properties *(continued)*

Property Name	Description	Introduced
text	Gets the text contained within the <option/> element.	Level 1
value	Gets or sets the value of the value attribute.	Level 1

HTMLOptionCollection

The HTMLOptionCollection object was introduced in DOM Level 2. It contains a list of <option/> elements.

Property Name	Description	Introduced
length	Gets the number of <option/> elements in the list.	Level 2

Methods

Method Name	Description	Introduced
item(index)	Retrieves the <option/> element at the specified index.	Level 2
namedItem(name)	Retrieves the <option/> element by the specified name. It first attempts to find an <option/> element with the specified id. If none can be found, it looks for <option/> elements with the specified name attribute.	Level 2

HTMLParagraphElement

Represents the <p/> element.

Properties

Property Name	Description	Introduced
align	Deprecated. Gets or sets the value of the align attribute.	Level 1

HTMLSelectElement

Represents the <select/> element.

Properties

Property Name	Description	Introduced
disabled	Gets or sets the value of the disabled attribute.	Level 1
form	Gets the HTMLFormElement object containing the <select/> element. Returns null if the element is not inside a form.	Level 1

Property Name	Description	Introduced
length	Returns the number of <option/> elements.	Level 1
multiple	Gets or sets the value of the multiple attribute.	Level 1
name	Gets or sets the value of the name attribute.	Level 1
options	Returns an HTMLOptionsCollection object containing the list of the <option/> elements.	Level 1
selectedIndex	Returns the index of the currently selected <option/> element. Returns -1 if nothing is selected and returns the first <option/> element selected if multiple items are selected.	Level 1
size	Gets or sets the value of the size attribute.	Level 1
type	Gets the value of the type attribute.	Level 1
value	Gets or sets the current form control's value.	Level 1

Methods

Method Name	Description	Introduced
add(element[, before])	Adds an <option/> element to the <select/> element. If before is null, then element is added at the end of the list.	Level 1
blur()	Removes keyboard focus from the elements.	Level 1
focus()	Gives keyboard focus to the element.	Level 1
remove(index)	Removes the <option/> element at the given index. Does nothing if index is out of range.	Level 1

HTMLTableCellElement

Represents the <td/> element.

Properties

Property Name	Description	Introduced
align	Deprecated. Gets or sets the value of the align attribute.	Level 1
bgColor	Deprecated. Gets or sets the value of the bgcolor attribute.	Level 1
cellIndex	The index of the cell in the row in DOM tree order.	Level 1
colSpan	Gets or sets the value of the colspan attribute.	Level 1
height	Deprecated. Gets or sets the value of the height attribute.	Level 1

Continued

715

Properties *(continued)*

Property Name	Description	Introduced
noWrap	Deprecated. Gets or sets the value of the nowrap attribute.	Level 1
rowSpan	Gets or sets the value of the rowSpan attribute.	Level 1
vAlign	Gets or sets the value of the valign attribute.	Level 1
width	Deprecated. Gets or sets the value of the width attribute.	Level 1

HTMLTableElement

Represents the `<table/>` element.

Properties

Property Name	Description	Introduced
align	Deprecated. Gets or sets the value of the align attribute.	Level 1
bgColor	Deprecated. Gets or sets the value of the bgcolor attribute.	Level 1
border	Gets or sets the value of the border attribute.	Level 1
cellPadding	Gets or sets the value of the cellPadding attribute.	Level 1
cellSpacing	Gets or sets the value of the cellSpacing attribute.	Level 1
rows	Returns an HTMLCollection containing all rows in the table.	Level 1
tBodies	Returns an HTMLCollection of the defined `<tbody/>` element objects in the table.	Level 1
tFoot	Returns the table's `<tfoot/>` element object (HTMLTableSectionElement), or null if one doesn't exist.	Level 1
tHead	Returns the table's `<thead/>` element object (HTMLTableSectionElement), or null if one doesn't exist.	Level 1
width	Gets or sets the value of the width attribute.	Level 1

Methods

Method Name	Description	Introduced
createTFoot()	Creates and returns a `<tfoot/>` element if one does not exist. Returns the existing `<tfoot/>` element if it exists.	Level 1
createTHead()	Creates and returns a `<thead/>` element if one does not exist. Returns the existing `<thead/>` element if it exists.	Level 1

Method Name	Description	Introduced
deleteRow(index)	Deletes the row at the specified index.	Level 1
deleteTFoot()	Deletes the table's footer if one exists.	Level 1
deleteTHead()	Deletes the table's header if one exists.	Level 1
insertRow(index)	Inserts and returns a new row at the specified index. If index is -1 or equal to the number of rows, the new row is appended to the end of the row list.	Level 1

HTMLTableRowElement

Represents the <tr/> element.

Properties

Property Name	Description	Introduced
align	Deprecated. Gets or sets the value of the align attribute.	Level 1
bgColor	Deprecated. Gets or sets the value of the bgcolor attribute.	Level 1
cells	Returns an HTMLCollection containing the cells in the row.	Level 1
rowIndex	The index of the row in the table.	Level 1
sectionRowIndex	The index of the row relative to the section it belongs to (<thead/>, <tfoot/>, or <tbody/>).	Level 1
vAlign	Gets or sets the value of the valign attribute.	Level 1

Methods

Method Name	Description	Introduced
deleteCell(index)	Deletes the cell at the specified index.	Level 1
insertCell(index)	Inserts and returns an empty <td/> element. If index is -1 or equal to the number of cells in the row, then the new cell is appended to the end of the list.	Level 1

HTMLTableSectionElement

Represents the `<thead/>`, `<tbody/>`, and `<tfoot/>` elements.

Properties

Property Name	Description	Introduced
align	Deprecated. Gets or sets the value of the `align` attribute.	Level 1
rows	Returns an `HTMLCollection` containing the rows of the section.	Level 1
vAlign	Gets or sets the value of the `valign` attribute.	Level 1

Methods

Method Name	Description	Introduced
deleteRow(index)	Deletes the row at the specified index relative to the section.	Level 1
insertRow(index)	Inserts and returns a new row into the section at the specified index (relative to the section). If `index` is `-1` or equal to the number of rows, the row is appended to the end of the list.	Level 1

HTMLTextAreaElement

Represents the `<textarea/>` element.

Properties

Property Name	Description	Introduced
accessKey	Gets or sets the value of the `accessKey` attribute.	Level 1
cols	Gets or sets the value of the `cols` attribute.	Level 1
defaultValue	Gets or sets the contents of the element. The value does not change when the content changes.	Level 1
disabled	Gets or sets the value of the `disabled` attribute.	Level 1
form	Gets the `HTMLFormElement` object containing the `<textarea/>` element. Returns `null` if the element is not inside a form.	Level 1
name	Gets or sets the value of the `name` attribute.	Level 1

Property Name	Description	Introduced
readOnly	Used only if type is text or password. Gets or sets the value of the readonly attribute.	Level 1
rows	Gets or sets the value of the rows attribute.	Level 1
type	Gets the value of the type attribute. Always set to textarea.	Level 1
value	Gets or sets the current value of the element.	Level 1

Methods

Method Name	Description	Introduced
blur()	Removes keyboard focus from the element.	Level 1
focus()	Gives keyboard focus to the element.	Level 1
select()	Selects the contents of the element.	Level 1

DOM Event Model and Objects

The DOM event model was introduced in DOM Level 2. It describes an event system where every event has an event target. When an event reaches an event target, all registered event handlers on the event target are triggered for that specific event. The following objects are described by the DOM event model.

EventTarget

The EventTarget object is inherited by all HTMLElement objects in the DOM. This object provides the means for the registration and removal of event handlers on the event target.

Methods

Method Name	Description
addEventListener(type, listener, useCapture)	Registers an event handler on an element. type is the event type to listen for, listener is the JavaScript function to call when the event is fired, and useCapture determines whether the event is captured or bubbles.
removeEventListener(type, listener, useCapture)	Removes a listener from the element.

Event

When an event fires, an Event object is passed to the event handler if one is specified. This object contains contextual information about an event.

Properties

Property Name	Description	Introduced
bubbles	Indicates whether or not the event is a bubbling event.	Level 2
cancelable	Indicates whether or not the event can have its default action prevented.	Level 2
currentTarget	Indicates the EventTarget whose listeners are currently being processed.	Level 2
target	Indicates the EventTarget object to which the event was originally fired.	Level 2
timeStamp	Specifies the time (in milliseconds) at which the event was fired.	Level 2
type	The name of the event (remember: this is the name without the on prefix).	Level 2

Methods

Method Name	Description	Introduced
preventDefault()	Cancels the event, preventing the default action from taking place, only if the event is cancelable.	Level 2
stopPropagation()	Prevents further propagation of an event.	Level 2

MouseEvent

The MouseEvent object provides specific information associated with mouse events. MouseEvent objects contain not only the following properties, but also the properties and methods of the Event object.

Valid mouse events are shown in the following table.

Event Name	Description
click	Occurs when the mouse button is clicked over an element. A click is defined as a mousedown and mouseup over the same screen location.
mousedown	Occurs when the mouse button is pressed over an element.

Event Name	Description
mouseup	Occurs when the mouse button is released over an element.
mouseover	Occurs when the mouse pointer moves onto an element.
mousemove	Occurs when the mouse pointer moves while it is over the element.
mouseout	Occurs when the mouse pointer moves away from an element.

Properties

Property Name	Description	Introduced
altKey	Returns a Boolean value indicating whether or not the Alt key was pressed during the event's firing.	Level 2
button	Indicates which mouse button was pressed, if applicable. The number 0 represents the left button, 1 indicates the middle button, and 2 indicates the right button. Left-hand-configured mice reverse the buttons (right is 0, middle is 1, and left is 2).	Level 2
clientX	The horizontal coordinate relative to the client area.	Level 2
clientY	The vertical coordinate relative to the client area.	Level 2
ctrlKey	Returns a Boolean value indicating whether or not the Ctrl key was pressed when the event fired.	Level 2
relatedTarget	Indentifies a secondary EventTarget. Currently, this property is used with the mouseover event to indicate the EventTarget that the mouse pointer exited and with the mouseout event to indicate which EventTarget the pointer entered.	Level 2
screenX	The horizontal coordinate relative to the screen.	Level 2
screenY	The vertical coordinate relative to the screen.	Level 2
shiftKey	Returns a Boolean value indicating whether or not the Shift key was pressed when the event fired.	Level 2

Miscellaneous Events

The following tables describe the events available in client-side JavaScript.

Mouse Events

Event	Description
click	Raised when the user clicks an HTML control.
dblclick	Raised when the user double-clicks an HTML control.
mousedown	Raised when the user presses a mouse button.
mousemove	Raised when the user moves the mouse pointer.
mouseout	Raised when the user moves the mouse pointer out from within an HTML control.
mouseover	Raised when the user moves the mouse pointer over an HTML control.
mouseup	Raised when the user releases the mouse button.

Keyboard Events

Event	Description
keydown	Raised when the user presses a key on the keyboard.
keypress	Raised when the user presses a key on the keyboard. This event will be raised continually until the user releases the key.
keyup	Raised when the user releases a key that had been pressed.

HTML Control Events

Event	Description
blur	Raised when an HTML control loses focus.
change	Raised when an HTML control loses focus and its value has changed.
focus	Raised when focus is set to the HTML control.
reset	Raised when the user resets a form.
select	Raised when the user selects text in an HTML control.
submit	Raised when the user submits a form.

Window Events

Event	Description
load	Raised when the window has completed loading.
resize	Raised when the user resizes the window.
unload	Executes JavaScript code when the user exits a document.

Other Events

Event	Description
abort	Raised when the user aborts loading an image.
error	Raised when an error occurs loading the page.

Latin-1 Character Set

This appendix contains the Latin-1 character set and the character codes in both decimal and hexa-decimal formats. As explained in Chapter 2, the escape sequence \xNN, where NN is a hexadecimal character code from the Latin-1 character set shown here, can be used to represent characters that can't be typed directly in JavaScript.

Decimal Character Code	Hexadecimal Character Code	Symbol
32	20	Space
33	21	!
34	22	"
35	23	#
36	24	$
37	25	%
38	26	&
39	27	'
40	28	(
41	29	)
42	2A	*
43	2B	+
44	2C	,
45	2D	-
46	2E	.

Decimal Character Code	Hexadecimal Character Code	Symbol
47	2F	/
48	30	0
49	31	1
50	32	2
51	33	3
52	34	4
53	35	5
54	36	6
55	37	7
56	38	8
57	39	9
58	3A	:
59	3B	;
60	3C	<
61	3D	=
62	3E	>
63	3F	?
64	40	@
65	41	A
66	42	B
67	43	C
68	44	D
69	45	E
70	46	F
71	47	G
72	48	H
73	49	I

Decimal Character Code	Hexadecimal Character Code	Symbol
74	4A	J
75	4B	K
76	4C	L
77	4D	M
78	4E	N
79	4F	O
80	50	P
81	51	Q
82	52	R
83	53	S
84	54	T
85	55	U
86	56	V
87	57	W
88	58	X
89	59	Y
90	5A	Z
91	5B	[
92	5C	\
93	5D	]
94	5E	^
95	5F	_
96	60	`
97	61	a
98	62	b
99	63	c
100	64	d

Decimal Character Code	Hexadecimal Character Code	Symbol
101	65	e
102	66	f
103	67	g
104	68	h
105	69	i
106	6A	j
107	6B	k
108	6C	l
109	6D	m
110	6E	n
111	6F	o
112	70	p
113	71	q
114	72	r
115	73	s
116	74	t
117	75	u
118	76	v
119	77	w
120	78	x
121	79	y
122	7A	z
123	7B	{
124	7C		
125	7D	}
126	7E	~
160	A0	Non-breaking space

Decimal Character Code	Hexadecimal Character Code	Symbol
161	A1	¡
162	A2	¢
163	A3	£
164	A4	¤
165	A5	¥
166	A6	¦
167	A7	§
168	A8	¨
169	A9	©
170	AA	ª
171	AB	«
172	AC	¬
173	AD	Soft hyphen
174	AE	®
175	AF	¯
176	B0	°
177	B1	±
178	B2	²
179	B3	³
180	B4	´
181	B5	µ
182	B6	¶
183	B7	·
184	B8	¸
185	B9	¹
186	BA	º
187	BB	»

Decimal Character Code	Hexadecimal Character Code	Symbol
188	BC	¼
189	BD	½
190	BE	¾
191	BF	¿
192	C0	À
193	C1	Á
194	C2	Â
195	C3	Ã
196	C4	Ä
197	C5	Å
198	C6	Æ
199	C7	Ç
200	C8	È
201	C9	É
202	CA	Ê
203	CB	Ë
204	CC	Ì
205	CD	Í
206	CE	Î
207	CF	Ï
208	D0	Ð
209	D1	Ñ
210	D2	Ò
211	D3	Ó
212	D4	Ô
213	D5	Õ
214	D6	Ö

Decimal Character Code	Hexadecimal Character Code	Symbol
215	D7	×
216	D8	Ø
217	D9	Ù
218	DA	Ú
219	DB	Û
220	DC	Ü
221	DD	Ý
222	DE	Þ
223	DF	ß
224	E0	à
225	E1	á
226	E2	â
227	E3	ã
228	E4	ä
229	E5	å
230	E6	æ
231	E7	ç
232	E8	è
233	E9	é
234	EA	ê
235	EB	ë
236	EC	ì
237	ED	í
238	EE	î
239	EF	ï
240	F0	ð
241	F1	ñ

Appendix D: Latin-1 Character Set

Decimal Character Code	Hexadecimal Character Code	Symbol
242	F2	ò
243	F3	ó
244	F4	ô
245	F5	õ
246	F6	ö
247	F7	÷
248	F8	ø
249	F9	ù
250	FA	ú
251	FB	û
252	FC	ü
253	FD	ý
254	FE	þ
255	FF	ÿ

Index

SYMBOLS

D